Frommer's®

W9-AWE-922

Honolulu & Oahu
day BY **day**™
1st Edition

by Jeanette Foster

WILEY

Wiley Publishing, Inc.

Contents

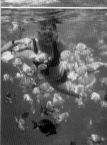

Published by:

Wiley Publishing, Inc.

111 River St.
Hoboken, NJ 07030-5774

ISBN: 978-0-470-14578-4

Editor: Christine Ryan
Production Editor: Michael Brumitt
Photo Editor: Richard Fox
Cartographer: Roberta Stockwell
Production by Wiley Indianapolis Composition Services

For information on our other products and services or to obtain technical
support, please contact our Customer Care Department within the U.S.
at 800/762-2974, outside the U.S. at 317/572-3993 or fax 317/572-4002.

Wiley also publishes its books in a variety of electronic formats. Some
content that appears in print may not be available in electronic formats.

Manufactured in China

5   4   3   2   1

A Note from the Publisher

Organizing your time. That's what this guide is all about.

Other guides give you long lists of things to see and do and then expect you to fit the pieces together. The Day by Day guides are different. They tell you the best of everything, and then show you how to see it *in the smartest, most time-efficient way*. Our authors have designed detailed itineraries for you, organized by time, neighborhood, or special interest. Each tour comes with a bulleted map that takes you from stop to stop.

Hoping to pay your respects at the Pearl Harbor memorials, snorkel through schools of rainbow-colored fish, or hike to the top of Diamond Head? Planning a leisurely walk through Chinatown, or a whirlwind tour of the very best Oahu has to offer? Whatever your interest or schedule, the Day by Days give you the smartest routes to follow. Not only do we take you to the top attractions, hotels, and restaurants, but we also help you access those special moments that locals get to experience—those "finds" that turn tourists into travelers.

The Day by Days are also your top choice if you're looking for one complete guide for all your travel needs. The best hotels and restaurants for every budget, the greatest shopping values, the wildest nightlife—it's all here.

Why should you trust our judgment? Because our authors personally visit each place they write about. They're an independent lot who say what they think and would never include places they wouldn't recommend to their best friends. They're also open to suggestions from readers. If you'd like to contact them, please send your comments my way at mspring@wiley.com, and I'll pass them on.

Enjoy your Day by Day guide—the most helpful travel companion you can buy. And have the trip of a lifetime.

Warm regards,

Michael Spring

Michael Spring, Publisher
Frommer's Travel Guides

About the Author

A resident of the Big Island, **Jeanette Foster** has skied the slopes of Mauna Kea—during a Fourth of July ski meet, no less—and gone scuba diving with manta rays off the Kona Coast. A prolific writer widely published in travel, sports, and adventure magazines, she's also a contributing editor to *Hawaii* magazine, the editor of *Zagat's Survey to Hawaii's Top Restaurants,* and the Hawaii chapter author of *1,000 Places to See in the U.S.A. and Canada Before You Die.* In addition to writing this guide, Jeanette is the author of *Frommer's Hawaii 2008; Frommer's Maui 2008; Frommer's Kauai; Frommer's Hawaii with Kids; Frommer's Honolulu, Waikiki & Oahu;* and *Frommer's Maui Day by Day.*

Acknowledgments

Special thanks to Priscilla Life, the best researcher in Hawaii.

An Additional Note

Please be advised that travel information is subject to change at any time—and this is especially true of prices. We therefore suggest that you write or call ahead for confirmation when making your travel plans. The authors, editors, and publisher cannot be held responsible for the experiences of readers while traveling. Your safety is important to us, however, so we encourage you to stay alert and be aware of your surroundings.

Star Ratings, Icons & Abbreviations

Every hotel, restaurant, and attraction listing in this guide has been ranked for quality, value, service, amenities, and special features using a **star-rating system.** Hotels, restaurants, attractions, shopping, and nightlife are rated on a scale of zero stars (recommended) to three stars (exceptional). In addition to the star-rating system, we also use a **kids icon** to point out the best bets for families. Within each tour, we recommend cafes, bars, or restaurants where you can take a break. Each of these stops appears in a shaded box marked with a coffee-cup-shaped bullet ☕ .

The following **abbreviations** are used for credit cards:

AE	American Express	DISC	Discover	V	Visa
DC	Diners Club	MC	MasterCard		

Frommers.com

Now that you have this guidebook to help you plan a great trip, visit our website at **www.frommers.com** for additional travel information on more than 3,600 destinations. We update features regularly to give you instant access to the most current trip-planning information available. At Frommers. com, you'll find scoops on the best airfares, lodging rates, and car rental bargains. You can even book your travel online through our reliable travel booking partners. Other popular features include:

- Online updates of our most popular guidebooks
- Vacation sweepstakes and contest giveaways
- Newsletters highlighting the hottest travel trends
- Online travel message boards with featured travel discussions

A Note on Prices

In the "Take a Break" and "Best Bets" sections of this book, we have used a system of dollar signs to show a range of costs for 1 night in a hotel (the price of a double-occupancy room) or the cost of an entree at a restaurant. Use the following table to decipher the dollar signs:

Cost	Hotels	Restaurants
$	under $130	under $10
$$	$130–$200	$10–$20
$$$	$200–$300	$20–$30
$$$$	$300–$395	$30–$40
$$$$$	over $395	over $40

An Invitation to the Reader

In researching this book, we discovered many wonderful places—hotels, restaurants, shops, and more. We're sure you'll find others. Please tell us about them, so we can share the information with your fellow travelers in upcoming editions. If you were disappointed with a recommendation, we'd love to know that, too. Please write to:

Frommer's Honolulu & Oahu, Day by Day, 1st Edition
Wiley Publishing, Inc. • 111 River St. • Hoboken, NJ 07030-5774

16 Favorite
Moments

16 Favorite **Moments**

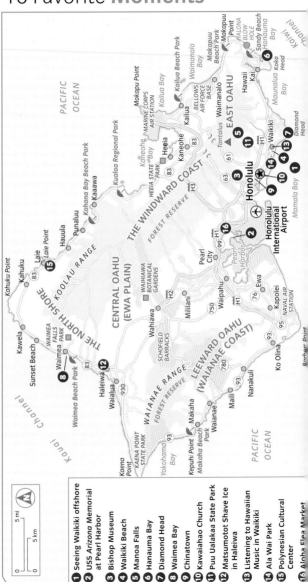

PACIFIC
OCEAN

Mokapuu
Point
HALONA
BLOW
HOLE
Makapuu Beach Park
Sandy Beach
Hanauma Bay
Kaiwi Channel

Makapuu
Point

Kailua Beach Park

Mokapu Point

Kailua Bay

MARINE CORPS
AIR STATION

BELLOWS
AIR FORCE
BASE

EAST OAHU

Kaneohe
Bay

HEEIA STATE
PARK

Heeia

Kailua

Waimanalo

Hawaii Kai

Maunalua Koko
Bay Head

Diamond
Head

Kaneohe

Tantalus

Waikiki

Honolulu

Kahana Bay Beach Park

Kualoa Regional Park

THE WINDWARD COAST

FOREST RESERVE

Mamala Bay

Honolulu
International
Airport

Kaaawa

Punaluu

Hauula

Laie

Laie Point

THE NORTH SHORE

KOOLAU RANGE

**CENTRAL OAHU
(EWA PLAIN)**

WAIHIAWA
BOTANICAL
GARDENS

Pearl
City

Pearl
Harbor

Ewa

Kahuku Point

Kahuku

Kawela

Sunset Beach

WAIMEA
FALLS
PARK

Waimea Beach Park

Haleiwa

Waialua

Waimea
Bay Park

Wahiawa

SCHOFIELD
BARRACKS

Mililani

Waipahu

Kapolei

NAVAL AIR
STATION

Ko Olina

Barber's Point

**LEEWARD OAHU
(WAIANAE COAST)**

WAIANAE RANGE

FOREST RESERVE

Kaena Point

KAENA POINT
STATE PARK

Yokohama
Bay

Kepuhi Point

Mokaha Beach
Park

Makaha

Waianae

Maili

Nanakuli

PACIFIC
OCEAN

Kauai Channel

0   5 mi

0   5 km

Previous page: Kualoa Regional Park at sunset.

Honolulu is filled with so many magic moments: the orange glow as the sun rises behind the outline of Diamond Head, the silvery reflection of the moon on the inky black waters of Waikiki at night, the intoxicating smell of plumeria flowers in the air, or the quiet whisper of bamboo dancing in the breeze. I hope this chapter will help you find a few favorite moments of your own.

1 Seeing Waikiki offshore. If you think Waikiki is beautiful, wait until you see it from a boat. I strongly urge you to either take a boat cruise during the day or, for the more romantically inclined, take a sunset cruise and watch the sun go down and the lights of Waikiki and Honolulu come up. If you are prone to sea sickness, try the *Navatek* cruise; a high-tech stabilizing device eliminates any bobbing around in the water. *See p 178.*

2 Experiencing a turning point in America's history: the bombing of Pearl Harbor. I guarantee that you will never forget your reaction when you step on the deck of the USS *Arizona* Memorial at Pearl Harbor, and look down at the dark oil oozing like dripping blood from the ship underneath. December 7, 1941, the day when the 608-foot (185m) *Arizona* sank in just 9 minutes after being

USS Arizona *memorial.*

bombed during the Japanese air raid, will no longer seem like something from a book—it will be very real. The 1,177 men on board plunged to a fiery death—and the United States went to war. My tip: Go early; you'll wait 2 to 3 hours if you visit at midday. You must wear closed-toed shoes. *See p 46.*

3 Walking back in history by exploring Bishop Museum. People always ask me: Where do I see the "real" Hawaii? I always send them to the Bishop Museum. Don't think dreary rooms with stuff crowded into cases—think living history, as in experiencing goose bumps as a deep booming voice breaks into Hawaiian chant when you enter the Hawaiian Hall, or excitement as you watch live performances of traditional hula. Created by a Hawaiian princess in 1899, not only is it the foremost repository for Hawaiian cultural artifacts, but it also has a new Science Center, where you can step into the interior of an erupting volcano. *See p 15.*

4 Getting a tan on Waikiki Beach. I've soaked up rays all over the globe, but nothing compares to the special experience of being kissed by the sun and serenaded by the sound of the tumbling surf while you lie on the soft sand of this world-famous beach. My favorite place to put my beach mat is directly in front of the big, pink Royal Hawaiian Hotel (where the angle of the beach is perfect for sunning). It's also a great spot for people-watching. I recommend

Explore Oahu's underwater world at calm, shallow Hanauma Bay.

arriving early; by midday (when the rays are at their peak), it's towel-to-towel out there. *See p 159.*

⑤ Venturing into a rainforest just 15 minutes from Waikiki. Don't miss my favorite magical experience on Oahu: immersing yourself in the misty sunbeams, where colorful birds flit among giant ferns and hanging vines, while towering tropical trees form a thick canopy that shelters all below in cool shadows. The emerald world of the Manoa Falls trail is a true Eden, and it's also a very short hike (less than a mile) to a freshwater pool and waterfall. *See p 165.*

⑥ Snorkeling among the rainbow-colored fish in the warm waters of Hanauma Bay. I love this underwater park, once a volcanic crater, because it's teeming with tropical fish and bordered by a 2,000-foot (610m) gold-sand beach. Plus, the bay's shallow water (10 ft./.9m in places) is perfect for neophyte snorkelers. Arrive early to beat the crowds—and be aware that the bay is closed on Tuesday, when the fish have the day off. *See p 175.*

⑦ Hiking to the top of Diamond Head for the perfect view of the island. See Waikiki and Honolulu from the top of Hawaii's most famous landmark. Nearly everyone can handle this 1.4-mile (2.2km) round-trip hike, which goes up to the top of the 750-foot (229m) volcanic cone, where you have a 360° view of Oahu. Allow an hour for the trip up and back, bring $1 for the entry fee, and don't forget your camera. *See p 163.*

⑧ Watching the North Shore's big waves. When monstrous waves—some 30 feet tall—steam roll into Waimea Bay (from November to March), I head out to the North Shore. Not only is it an amazing show, watching the best surfers in the world paddle out to challenge these freight trains, it's also shocking to see how small they appear in the lip of the giant waves. My favorite part is feeling those waves when they break on the shore—the ground actually shakes and everyone on the beach is covered with salt spray mist. And this unforgettable experience won't cost you a dime. *See p 136.*

⑨ Buying a lei in Chinatown. I love dipping into the cultural sights and exotic experiences to be had in Honolulu's Chinatown. Wander through this several-square-block area with its jumble of Asian shops offering herbs, Chinese groceries, and acupuncture services. Be sure to check out the lei sellers on Maunakea Street (near N. Hotel St.), where Hawaii's finest leis go for as little as $5. *See p 120.*

⑩ Attending a Hawaiian language church service. On Sunday, I head over to the historic Kawaiahao Church, built in 1842, for the service (which is in Hawaiian) and the Hawaiian music. You can practically feel the presence of the Hawaiian monarchy, many of whom were crowned in this very building. Admission is free—let your conscience be your guide as to a donation. *See p 23.*

⑪ Basking in the best sunset you'll ever see. Anyone can stand on the beach and watch the sun set, but my favorite viewing point for saying aloha-oe to Sol is driving up a 1,048-foot (320m) hill named after a sweet potato. Actually, it's more romantic than it sounds. Puu Ualakaa State Park, at the end of Round Hill Drive, translates into "rolling sweet potato hill" (the name describes how early Hawaiians harvested the crop). This majestic view of the sunset is not to be missed. *See p 21.*

⑫ Ordering a shave ice in a tropical flavor you can hardly pronounce. I think you can actually taste the islands by slurping shave

You'll find leis of every color and description for sale in Chinatown.

ice. It's not quite a snow cone, but similar: Ice is shaved and then an exotic flavor is poured over it. My favorite is *li hing mui* (lee hing moo-ee), or dried plum, with sweet Japanese adzuki beans hidden inside. This taste of tropical paradise goes for less than $1.50 at Matsumoto Shave Ice in Haleiwa. *See p 16.*

⑬ Listening to the soothing sounds of Hawaiian music. Just before sunset, I head for the huge banyan tree at the Moana Surfrider's Banyan Veranda in Waikiki, order a libation, and sway to live Hawaiian music. Another quintessential sunset oasis is the Halekulani's House Without a Key, a sophisticated oceanfront lounge with wonderful hula and steel-guitar music, a great view of Diamond Head, and the best mai tais on the island. *See p 129.*

⑭ Discovering the ancient Hawaiian sport of canoe paddling. For something you most likely will only see in Hawaii, find a comfortable spot at Ala Wai Park, next to the canal, and watch hundreds of canoe paddlers re-create this centuries-old sport of taking traditional Hawaiian canoes out to sea. Or try it yourself off Waikiki Beach. *See p 36 & p 159.*

⑮ Immersing yourself at the Polynesian Cultural Center. Even though I have traveled throughout the Pacific, I still love spending a day (yes, plan for the entire day) at the Polynesian Cultural Center, a kind of living museum of Polynesia. Here you can see firsthand the lifestyles, songs, dance, costumes, and architecture of seven Pacific islands or archipelagos—Fiji, New Zealand, Marquesas, Samoa, Tahiti, Tonga, and Hawaii—in the re-created villages scattered throughout a 42-acre (17ha) lagoon park. *See p 17.*

House Without a Key is one of my favorite places to listen to music and sip a mai tai.

16 Finding a Bargain at the Aloha Flea Market. I'm not sure whether to categorize this as shopping or entertainment, but 50¢ will get you into this all-day show at the Aloha Stadium parking lot, where more than 1,000 vendors sell everything from junk to jewels. Half the fun is talking to the vendors and listening to their stories. Serious shoppers should go early for the best deals. Open Wednesday, Saturday, and Sunday from 6am to 3pm. ●

Finding Your Way Around, Oahu Style

Mainlanders sometimes find the directions given by locals a bit confusing. Seldom will you hear the terms east, west, north, and south; instead, islanders refer to directions as either **makai** (ma-*kae*), meaning toward the sea, or **mauka** (*mow*-kah), toward the mountains. In Honolulu, people use **Diamond Head** as a direction meaning to the east (in the direction of the world-famous crater called Diamond Head), and **Ewa** as a direction meaning to the west (toward the town called Ewa, on the other side of Pearl Harbor).

So, if you ask a local for directions, this is what you're likely to hear: "Drive 2 blocks makai (toward the sea), then turn Diamond Head (east) at the stoplight. Go 1 block, and turn mauka (toward the mountains). It's on the Ewa (western) side of the street."

1 Strategies for Seeing **Oahu**

Strategies for Seeing **Oahu**

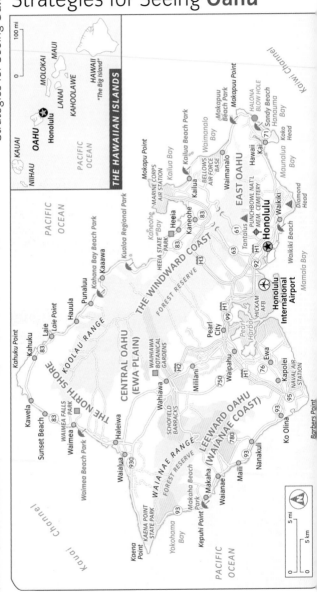

THE HAWAIIAN ISLANDS

Previous page: Waimea Canyon.

Oahu may be an island, but it's a good-sized island, and your vacation time is precious. There really is just one cardinal rule: relax. Don't run yourself ragged trying to see absolutely everything—take the time to experience the magic of the island. In this chapter I have several suggestions for making the most out of your time.

Rule #1. Go in the off season.

Not only will you save a bundle, but there will be fewer people, you'll get better service, the beaches will be less crowded, and you'll be able to get into your favorite restaurants. The "off season," September 1 to mid-December and March to June 1, is also when the weather is at its best (not too hot, not too rainy).

Rule #2. To get the best deals, do some research.

In this book, I'll give you my favorite picks of hotels, restaurants, activities, and airlines, but use that as a starting point. Go online and check out airfares, hotels, and package deals (airfare plus accommodations and sometimes car rental). Find out what prices are being offered before you book.

Stop and smell the plumeria.

Rule #3. Think about how you want to spend your vacation.

Is this a lie-on-the-beach vacation or a get-up-early-and-do-an-adventure-every-day vacation? Or a combination? If you are traveling with your sweetie, be sure you have a plan that makes both parties happy (such as plenty of golfing plus lots of shopping). If you're bringing your family, make sure that everyone gets in on the planning—it makes for a vacation that everyone can enjoy.

Rule #4. Don't over-schedule.

Don't make your days jam-packed from the time you get up until you drop off to sleep at night. This is Hawaii: Stop and smell the plumeria. Allow time to just relax. And don't

forget that you will most likely arrive jet lagged, so ease into your vacation. Exposure to sunlight can help reset your internal clock, so hit the beach on your first day (and bring your suntan lotion).

Rule #5. Allow plenty of time to get around the island.

If you glance at a map, Oahu looks deceptively small—like you could just zip from one side of the island to the other. But you have to take traffic into consideration; from 6 to 9am and 3 to 6pm the main roads will be bumper-to-bumper with rush-hour traffic. Plan accordingly: Sleep in late and get on the road after the traffic has cleared out.

I highly recommend that you rent a car, but don't just "view" the island from the car window. Plan to get out as much as possible to breathe in the tropical aroma, fill up on those views, and listen to the sounds of the tropics.

A relaxed drive along a winding coastal road may be a highlight of your trip.

Rule #6. If your visit is short, stay in one place.

Most places on Oahu are within easy driving distance of each other, and checking in and out of several hotels isn't easy. There's the schlepping of the luggage, the waiting in line to check in, the unpacking, and more . . . only to repeat the entire process a few days later. Your vacation time is too dear.

Rule #7. Pick the key activity of the day and plan accordingly.

To maximize your time, decide what you really want to do that day, then plan all other activities in the same geographical area. That way you won't have to track back and forth across the island.

Rule #8. Remember you are on the island of aloha.

Honolulu is not the U.S. mainland. The islanders' way of life is very different. Slow down. Smile and say "aloha"; it's what the local residents do. Ask them: "Howzit?" (the local expression for "how are you?"). When they ask you tell 'em "Couldn't be better—I'm in Hawaii!" Wave at everyone. Laugh a lot, even if things

aren't going as planned (hey, you're in paradise, how bad can it be?).

Rule #9. Use this book as a reference, not a concrete plan.

You will not hurt my feelings if you don't follow every single tour and do absolutely everything I suggest in the itinerary. Pick and choose according to your interests—don't feel like you have to follow all my suggestions to the letter. ●

Attending a Hula competition is a great way to experience Hawaiian culture.

The Best of Oahu in Three Days

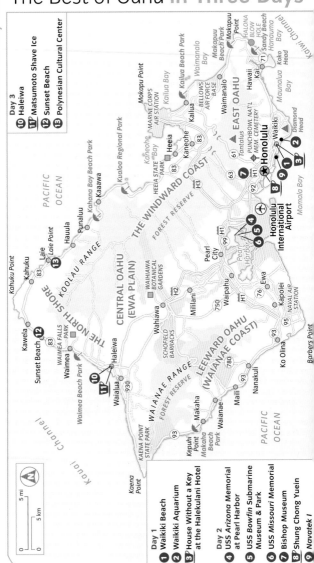

Day 3
- ⑩ Haleiwa
- ⑪ Matsumoto Shave Ice
- ⑫ Sunset Beach
- ⑬ Polynesian Cultural Center

Day 1
- ❶ Waikiki Beach
- ❷ Waikiki Aquarium
- ❸ House Without a Key at the Halekulani Hotel

Day 2
- ❹ USS Arizona Memorial at Pearl Harbor
- ❺ USS Bowfin Submarine Museum & Park
- ❻ USS Missouri Memorial
- ❼ Bishop Museum
- ❽ Shung Chong Yuein
- ❾ Navatek I

Previous page: Statues at Polynesian Cultural Center.

You could spend weeks on Oahu without running out of things to do, but it's possible to see the highlights of this romantic isle in just 3 days. Following this tour will let you see the best of Oahu, from Waikiki to the North Shore. You'll definitely need to rent a car, so remember to plan for that cost. Each day begins and ends in Waikiki, which, like most urban cities, has traffic congestion, so allow plenty of travel time, especially during rush hour. START: **Waikiki**. **Trip length: 108½-mile (175km) loop.**

Day 1

① ★★★ kids Waikiki Beach. You'll never forget your first steps onto the powdery sands of this world-famous beach. If you're just off the plane, plan to spread your towel on the beach, take in the smell of the salt air, feel the warm breeze on your skin, and relax; you're in Hawaii. *See p 159.*

Chambered nautilus.

Walk down Waikiki Beach towards Diamond Head. Bus: 20.

② ★★ kids Waikiki Aquarium. Explore Hawaii's underwater world without getting wet. This small but fabulous aquarium houses some 2,500 animals representing more than 420 species. You'll find everything from translucent jellyfish to lumbering turtles to endangered Hawaiian monk seals—and even sharks. My favorite things to see are the chambered nautilus (nature's submarine and inspiration for Jules Verne's *20,000 Leagues Under the Sea*), the Edge of the Reef exhibit (where you see reef fish up close and personal), and the Mahimahi Hatchery (where these delicious eating fish are raised from egg to adult). ⏱ 2½ hr.; get there early on weekends before the crowds come. 2777 Kalakaua Ave. (across from Kapiolani Park). ☎ 808/923-9741. www.waquarium.org. Admission $9 adults, $6 active military, seniors, and college students, $4 children 13–17, $2 for children 5–12, children 4 and under free. Daily 9am–5pm (last ticket sold at 4:30 pm).

Waikiki Beach. Spending some time in the sun is a great way to combat jet lag.

Retrace your steps down Waikiki Beach to Halekulani Hotel, or take bus no. 42.

3 ★★★ **House Without a Key at the Halekulani Hotel.** As the sun sinks towards the horizon, take a break with a libation at one of the most beautiful hotels on Waikiki Beach. You can watch the former Miss Hawaii Kanoelehua Miller dance hula to the riffs of Hawaiian steel guitar under a century-old kiawe tree. With the sunset and ocean glowing behind her, and Diamond Head visible in the distance, the scene is straight out of a storybook—romantic, evocative, nostalgic. *2199 Kalia Rd. (Diamond Head side of Lewers St.)* ☎ *808/923-2311. $$$.*

Day 2

Get an early start to beat the crowds at Pearl Harbor. Drive west on H-1 past the airport to the USS *Arizona* Memorial exit, then follow the green-and-white signs; there's ample free parking. Or take the *Arizona* Memorial Shuttle Bus VIP (☎ 808/839-0911), which picks up at Waikiki hotels 6:50am–1pm ($9/person round-trip). Bus: 20.

4 ★★★ **kids** USS *Arizona* **Memorial at Pearl Harbor.** The top attraction on Oahu is this unforgettable memorial. On December 7, 1941, the Japanese launched an air raid on Pearl Harbor that plunged the U.S. into World War II. This 608-foot battleship sank in 9 minutes without firing a shot, taking 1,177 sailors and Marines to their deaths. The deck of the *Arizona* lies 6 feet (1.8m) below the surface of the sea, with oil slowly oozing up from the engine room and staining the harbor's calm, blue water. Some say the ship still weeps for its lost crew. The excellent, 2½-hour ★★★ **Audio Tour** will make the trip even more meaningful—it's like having your own personal park ranger as a guide. The fee is $5 and worth every nickel. **Note:** Due to increased security measures visitors cannot carry purses, handbags, fanny packs, backpacks, camera bags, diaper bags, or other items that offer concealment on the boat. Storage is available for a fee. ⏱ *3 hr.; go first thing in the morning to avoid the huge crowds; waits of 1–3 hours are common. Pearl Harbor.* ☎ *808/422-0561 (recorded info), or 808/422-2771. www.nps.gov/usar. Free admission. Daily 7:30am–5pm*

Observation deck at the USS Arizona *memorial.*

(programs run 7:45am–3pm). Shirts and closed-toed shoes required; no swimsuits or flip-flops allowed. Wheelchairs gladly accommodated.

If you're a real nautical history buff, stop in at the next few museums, which are described in the "Wartime in Honolulu" tour starting on p. 46. Otherwise, head directly to the Bishop Museum.

5 ★ kids USS *Bowfin* Submarine Museum & Park. *See p 47, bullet* **2**.

6 ★ kids USS *Missouri* Memorial. *See p 47, bullet* **3**.

From Arizona Memorial Dr. turn right on Kamehameha Hwy. (Hwy. 99). Take the ramp on to H-1 East toward Honolulu. Take Exit 20A (Likelike Hwy. exit). Turn left on Kalihi St. (Hwy. 63) to Bernice St. and turn right. Bus: 40, then transfer to the B City Express.

7 ★★★ kids Bishop Museum. If you are the least bit curious about what ancient Hawaii was like, this museum is a must-see. This multi-building museum has the world's greatest collection of natural and cultural artifacts from Hawaii and the Pacific. Another highlight is the terrific new 16,500-square-foot Science Adventure Center, specializing in volcanology (one exhibit lets you walk inside an erupting volcano) and oceanography. In the Hawaiian Hall, you can venture back in history and see what Hawaiian culture was like before Westerners arrived. Don't miss my faves: the **Hula performances ★,** Monday to Friday at 11am and 2pm, and the terrific show in the planetarium, **Explorers of Polynesia,** 3:30pm daily. 🕐 *3–4 hr. 1525 Bernice St., just off Kalihi St. (aka Likelike Hwy.).* 📞 *808/847-3511. www.bishopmuseum.org. Admission $16 adults, $13 children 4–12 and seniors. Daily 9am–5pm.*

The Bishop Museum is a great rainy-day activity, but it's worth a visit even if it's not raining.

Turn right from the Bishop Museum parking lot on to Bernice St., right again on Houghtailing St., then left on Olomea St. (which becomes Vineyard Blvd.). Turn right on Maunakea St. Bus: 2.

8 ★ kids Shung Chong Yuein. Venture into Chinatown for delicious Asian pastries, such as moon cakes and almond cookies, all at very reasonable prices. The shop also has a wide selection of dried and sugared candies (ginger, pineapple, lotus root) that make great gifts for friends back home. *1027 Maunakea St. (near Hotel St.).* 📞 *808/531-1983. $.*

Continue down Maunakea St., turn left on N. King St., then right on Nuuanu Ave. Make a slight left on Nimitz Hwy. (Hwy. 92). Look for the sign for Pier 6 just after Aloha Tower, and turn right. Bus: 56.

9 ★ kids *Navatek I.* Wrap up your second day on Oahu with a sunset dinner cruise aboard a 140-foot-long (43m) SWATH (Small

Waterplane Area Twin Hull) vessel. This unique ship's superstructure—the part you ride on—rests on twin torpedo-like hulls that cut through the water so you don't bob like a cork and spill your mai tai; it also cuts down greatly on seasickness. Highlights of the cruise include gazing at the horizon as the sun sinks into the Pacific, then watching Waikiki light up as darkness descends. If you go between January and April you might be lucky enough to see a humpback whale. ⏱ *2 hr. Aloha Tower Marketplace, Pier 6.* ☎ *808/973-1311. www.navatek.us. Dinner cruises $80–$112 adults, $74–$95 children 2–12.*

This colorful sign welcomes visitors to Haleiwa.

Take a right on Ala Moana Blvd. and follow it into Waikiki. Bus: 19 or 20.

Day 3
Spend your third day on Oahu on the North Shore. Take H-1 west out of Waikiki, then take the H-2 north exit (Exit 8A) towards Mililani/Wahiwa. After 7 miles (11km) H2 becomes

Kamehameha Hwy. (Hwy. 80). Look for the turnoff to Haleiwa town. Bus: 19, then transfer to no. 52.

🔟 ★★★ kids Haleiwa. Start your day exploring this famous North Shore surfing town. *See p 136, bullet ❹.*

1️⃣1️⃣ ★ kids Matsumoto Shave Ice. For a tropical taste of the islands, stop at this nearly 50-year-old shop where Hawaii's rendition of a snow cone is served: instead of crushed ice, the ice is actually shaved and has a unique texture. My favorite of the rainbow of flavors available is the li hing mui (pronounced lee hing moo-ee), which is a preserved plum with a mixture of Chinese spices, sugar, and salt. *66-087 Kamehameha Hwy., Haleiwa.* ☎ *808/637-4827. $.*

Continue down Kamehameha Hwy. for about 6½ miles (10.5km). Bus: 52.

1️⃣2️⃣ ★★★ kids Sunset Beach. Swim in the summer or just sit and

Even die-hard landlubbers can enjoy a cruise on the stable Navatek.

Try to catch one of the performances at the Polynesian Cultural Center.

watch the big wave surfers in winter. *See p 159.*

Drive another 11½ miles (18.5km) down Kamehameha Hwy. to the town of Laie. Bus: 52 to Turtle Bay Resort, then 55.

⓭ ★★ **kids** **Polynesian Cultural Center.** This "living museum" of Polynesia features the lifestyles, songs, dance, costumes, and architecture of seven Pacific islands or archipelagos—Fiji, New Zealand, Marquesas, Samoa, Tahiti, Tonga, and

Hawaii—in the re-created villages scattered throughout the 42-acre (17ha) lagoon park. I recommend traveling through this museum via canoe on a man-made freshwater lagoon. Each village is "inhabited" by native students from Polynesia who attend Hawaii's Brigham Young University. The park, which is operated by the Mormon Church, also features a variety of stage shows celebrating the music, dance, history, and culture of Polynesia. Stay for the show, but skip the luau. ⏱ *4–6 hr., get there when the doors open to avoid the crowds. 55–370 Kamehameha Hwy., Laie.* ☎ *800/367-7060, 808/293-3333, or 808/923-2911. www.polynesia.com. Admission $55 adults, $44 children 3–11 (includes IMAX movie and show). Other packages available; see website for details. Mon–Sat 12:30–9:30pm.*

To get back to Waikiki, just continue along Kamehameha Hwy. (Hwy. 83), which follows the windward coastline for about 22 miles (35km). Look for the sign for the Likelike Hwy. (Hwy. 63). From Likelike Hwy. take the Kalihi St./H-1 exit. Take H-1 to Waikiki. Bus: 55, then transfer to no. 19 or 20.

It's Sure Not New York City

Unfortunately, Honolulu does not have convenient public transportation, which is why I strongly recommend that you rent a car. In case that's not possible, I've added information on how to get around using Honolulu's public bus system (called TheBus), which costs $2 per ride. But TheBus is set up for Hawaii residents, not tourists carrying coolers, beach toys, or suitcases (all carry-ons must fit under the bus seat). Some trips may be extremely complicated, requiring several bus transfers, or TheBus may not stop right in front of your destination, forcing you to walk several blocks. Before you set out, always call **TheBus** (☎ **808/848-5555,** or 808/296-1818 for recorded information) or check out **www.thebus.org**, to get information on your route.

The Best of Oahu in One Week

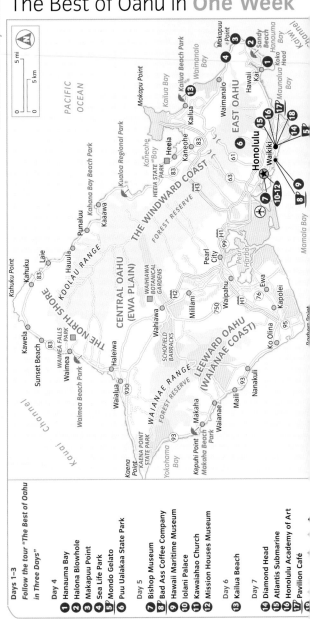

If possible, stay on Oahu for at least 1 week, so you can take in the sights at a slow, leisurely, island-style pace. You'll have time to see all the sights I recommended in the 3-day tour, plus explore the enchanting underwater world at Hanauma Bay and Sealife Park, delve into Hawaiian history and culture, visit the art world, do some shopping, and spend more time at the beach. START: **Waikiki. Trip Length: 223 miles (359km).**

Days 1–3

For your first 3 days on Oahu, follow the itinerary for "The Best of Oahu in Three Days," starting on p 12, with one exception: On day 2, instead of visiting the Bishop Museum (don't worry—you'll see it later on this tour),

Spend a relaxing morning swimming with the turtles at Hanauma Bay.

spend the afternoon exploring Chinatown (see my tour of this exotic neighborhood on p 72) before the *Navatek* dinner cruise.

Day 4

From Waikiki, take H-1 East, which becomes the Kalaniaole Hwy. Look for the Koko Head Regional Park on the left; the beach is on the right (oceanside). Avoid the crowds by going early, about 8am, on a weekday morning; once the parking lot's full, you're out of luck. The Hanauma Bay Shuttle Bus runs from Waikiki to Hanauma Bay every half-hour from 8:45am to 1pm. You can catch it at any city bus stop in Waikiki. It returns every hour from noon to 4pm.

1 ★★★ **kids** **Hanauma Bay.** Spend the morning at Oahu's best snorkeling beach. **Note:** The beach is closed on Tuesdays. *See p 175.*

Continue to drive east on Kalanianaole Hwy. Stop at mile marker 11.

2 **kids** **Halona Blowhole.** *See p 141, bullet* **3**.

Continue to drive east on Kalanianaole Hwy. Look for the Makapuu Point sign.

3 **kids** **Makapuu Point.** *See p 142, bullet* **6**.

Continue east on Kalanianaloe Hwy. Bus: 58.

4 ★ **kids** **Sea Life Park.** This 62-acre (25ha) ocean theme park, located in East Oahu, is one of the island's top attractions. You can swim with dolphins, get up close to the sea lions, or just relax and watch the marine mammal shows. My favorite stops are the stingray

The Halona Blowhole shoots water up to 30 ft. (9m) in the air.

You can swim with the dolphins at Sea Life Park.

lagoon (where you can get a good look at these normally shy creatures) and the sea turtle lagoon (which also doubles as a breeding sanctuary for the endangered Hawaiian green sea turtle). There's also a Hawaiian reef tank full of tropical fish; a "touch" pool, where you can touch a real sea cucumber (commonly found in tide pools); and a bird sanctuary, where you can see birds like the red-footed booby and the frigate bird. The chief curiosity, though, is the world's only "wholphin"—a cross between a false killer whale and an Atlantic bottle-nosed dolphin. On-site, marine biologists operate a recovery center for endangered marine life; during your visit, you may be able to see rehabilitated Hawaiian monk seals and seabirds. ⏱ *if you have kids allow 3 hours, if not, 1 hr. 41–202 Kalanianaole Hwy. (at Makapuu Point), Honolulu.* ☎ *808/259-7933. www.sealifeparkhawaii.com. Admission $29 adults, $19 children 4–12. Daily 9:30am–5pm. Parking $3. Shuttle buses from Waikiki $5. Bus: 22 or 58.*

Continue on Kalanianaole Hwy. (Hwy. 72), turn left on Pali Hwy. (Hwy. 61), then take H-1 east to Waikiki. Bus: 58.

Tour Honolulu from a Trolley Car

Hop on a 34-seat, open-air, motorized Waikiki Trolley for a fun way to get around the island. The Honolulu City Line loops around Waikiki and downtown Honolulu, stopping every 40 minutes at 12 key places (such as Iolani Palace, Chinatown, the State Capitol, the Aloha Tower, and Restaurant Row). The driver provides commentary along the way. Stops on the new 3-hour, fully narrated, Ocean Coast Line on the southeast side of Oahu include Sea Life Park, Diamond Head, and Waikiki Beach. A 1-day trolley pass—which costs $25 for adults, $18 for seniors over 62, and $12 for kids ages 4 to 11—allows you to jump on and off all day long (8:30am–11:35pm). Four-day passes cost $45 for adults, $27 for seniors, and $18 for kids 4 to 11. Call ☎ **800/824-8804** or 808/593-2822 for more information, or go online (www.waikikitrolley.com).

The Bishop Museum was founded by a Hawaiian princess, Bernice Pauahi, and her husband, Charles Reed Bishop.

5 kids **Mondo Gelato.** Cool off with a real Italian-style gelato, sorbetto, or yogurt gelato. Out of the more than 100 flavors, my fave is the papaya sorbetto. *Waikiki Beach Walk, 226 Lewers St. (at Kalia St.)* ☎ *808/926-6961. $.*

From Waikiki, take Ala Wai Blvd. to McCully St., turn right, and drive mauka (inland) beyond the H-1 on-ramps to Wilder St. Turn left and go to Makiki St. Turn right and continue onward and upward about 3 miles (4.8km).

6 ★ **Puu Ualakaa State Park.** My favorite sunset view of Honolulu is from a 1,048-foot-high hill named for sweet potatoes. The poetic Hawaiian name means "rolling sweet potato hill," which describes how early planters used gravity to harvest their crop. On a clear day (which is almost always), the majestic, sweeping views stretch from Diamond Head to the Waianae Range—almost the length of Oahu. At night, several scenic overlooks provide romantic spots for young lovers to smooch under the stars with the city lights at their feet. It's a top-of-the-world experience— the view, that is. ⏱ *15–20 min. At the end of Round Top Dr. Daily 7am–6:45pm (to 7:45pm in summer). No bus service.*

Day 5
Take Ala Wai Blvd. out of Waikiki. Turn right at Kalakaua Ave., then left on S. Beretania St. and right at Piikoi St. Make a left on to Lunalilo St., and bear left on to H-1 West. Take Exit 20B, which puts you on Haloma St. Turn right at Houghtailing St., and then left on to Bernice St. Bus: 2.

7 ★★★ kids **Bishop Museum.** This entrancing museum may be the highlight of your trip. *See p 15, bullet* **7**.

Bad Ass is a great place to stop for a cup of 100% Kona.

Iolani Palace, the only royal palace in the U.S.

Turn right out of the parking lot onto Bernice St., left at Kapalama Ave., and right again on N. School St. Make a right on Liliha St., a left on N King St., and right on River St. Turn left on Nimitz Hwy. and then right at Aloha Tower Drive. Bus: A (City Express A).

8 Bad Ass Coffee Company. Take a break at this gourmet Hawaiian coffee shop. My favorite is the delicious Kona coffee, but they also offer java from Molokai, Kauai, and Maui. *Aloha Tower MarketPlace, 1 Aloha Tower Dr.* ☎ *808/524-0888. www.badasscoffee.com. $.*

Walk towards Diamond Head along the waterfront.

9 ★★ kids Hawaii Maritime Center. Learn the story of Hawaii's rich maritime past, from the ancient journey of Polynesian voyagers to the nostalgic days of the *Lurline,* which once brought tourists from San Francisco on 4-day cruises. Inside the Hawaii Maritime Center's Kalakaua Boat House, patterned after His Majesty King David Kalakaua's own canoe house, are more than 30 exhibits, including Matson cruise ships (which brought the first tourists to Waikiki), flying boats that delivered the mail, and the skeleton of a Pacific humpback whale that beached on Kahoolawe. ⌚ *2 hr. Pier 7 (next to Aloha Tower).* ☎ *808/536-6373. Daily 8:30am–5pm.*

Walk mauka (inland) up Bishop St., right on S. King, and left on Richards St.

10 ★ kids Iolani Palace. Once the site of a *heiau* (temple), Iolani palace took 3 years and $350,000 to complete in 1882, with all the modern conveniences for its time (electric lights were installed here 4 years before they were in the White House). It was also in this palace that Queen Liliuokalani was overthrown and placed under house arrest for 9 months. The territorial and then the state government used the palace until 1968. At that point, the palace was in shambles and has since undergone a $7 million overhaul to restore it to its former glory. Admission options include the Grand Tour, a 90-minute docent-led tour that covers the state apartments, private quarters, and basement galleries; the 50-minute Audio Tour, which covers the same areas as the Grand Tour, but is self-guided; or the Galleries Tour, a self-guided tour of the basement galleries only, where you'll see the crown jewels, ancient feathered cloaks, royal china, and more. ⌚ *1–2hr. At S. King* and Richards sts. ☎ 808/522-0832. Grand Tour $20 adults, $5 children 5–12; audio tour $12 adults, $5 children, Gallery Tour $6 adults, $3 children. Children under 5 free, but only allowed in the basement galleries. Tues–Sat 9am–4:30pm (last Grand tour at 11:15am; last Audio Tour at 3pm).

Continue to walk towards Diamond Head on S. King St. to Punchbowl St.

⓫ ★ Kawaiahao Church. When the missionaries came to Hawaii, the first thing they did was build churches. Four thatched grass churches had been built on this site before Rev. Hiram Bingham began building what he considered a "real" church—a New England–style congregational structure with Gothic influences. Between 1837 and 1842, the building of the church required some 14,000 giant coral slabs (some weighing more than 1,000 lb.). Hawaiian divers raped the reefs, digging out huge chunks of coral and causing irreparable environmental damage. Kawaiahao, Hawaii's oldest church, has been the site of numerous historical events, such as a speech made by King Kamehameha III in 1843, an excerpt from which became Hawaii's state motto ("Ua mau ke ea o ka aina i ka pono," which translates as "The life of the land is preserved in righteousness"). The clock tower in the church, which was donated by King Kamehameha III and installed in 1850, continues to tick today. Don't sit in the pews in the back, marked with kahili feathers and velvet cushions; they are still reserved for the descendants of royalty. 957 Punchbowl St. (at King St.). ☎ 808/522-1333. Free admission (donations appreciated). Mon–Fri 8am–4pm; Sun services in Hawaiian 9am.

Continue in the Diamond Head direction on S. King St.

I highly recommend attending a Hawaiian-language service at Kawaiahao Church.

⓬ Mission Houses Museum. The original buildings of the Sandwich Islands Mission Headquarters still stand, and tours are often led by descendants of the original missionaries to Hawaii. The missionaries brought their own prefab houses along with them when they came around Cape Horn from Boston in 1819. The Frame House was designed for New England winters and had small windows. (It must have been stiflingly hot inside.) Finished in 1921, it is Hawaii's oldest wooden structure. The missionaries believed that the best way to spread the Lord's message to the Hawaiians was to learn their language, and then to print literature for them to read. So it was the missionaries who gave the Hawaiians a written language. ⏱ 1 hr.. 553 S. King St. (at Kawaiahao St.). ☎ 808/531-0481. www.missionhouses.org. $10 adults, $6 students (age 6–college). Tues–Sat 10am–4pm.

A trek to the top of Diamond Head is rewarded with spectacular views.

To get back to Waikiki, pick up your car at Aloha Tower Marketplace and turn right on Nimitz Hwy., which becomes Ala Moana Blvd. and leads into Waikiki. Bus: 13.

Day 6

Take H-1 west to Exit 21 B (Pali Hwy. north). The Pali Hwy. (Hwy. 61) becomes the Kalanianaole Hwy., which becomes Kailua Rd. Veer to the right on to Kuulei Rd., then turn right on Kalahelo Ave., which becomes Kawailoa Rd., and follow it to the beach. Take TheBus 8 or 19 transfer to TheBus 57.

⑬ ★★★ kids Kailua Beach. Spend the entire day on the windward side of Oahu at one of the island's most fabulous beaches. *See p 154.*

Day 7

Drive to the intersection of Diamond Head Rd. and 18th Ave. Follow the road through the tunnel (which is closed 6pm–6am) and park in the lot. Bus: 58 (from the Ala Moana Shopping Center).

⑭ ★ kids Diamond Head. On your last day on Oahu, get a bird's-eye view of the island from atop this 760-foot (232m) extinct volcano. *See p 163.*

Retrace your steps back to Waikiki.

⑮ ★★★ kids Atlantis Submarine. Now that you've seen Oahu from the top, plunge beneath the waves and see it underwater in this high-tech submarine. *See p 182.*

Gauguin's Two Tahitian Woman on the Beach, *at the Honolulu Academy of Arts.*

Hawaii's Early History

Paddling outrigger sailing canoes, the first ancestors of today's Hawaiians followed the stars, waves, and birds across the sea to Hawaii, which they called "the land of raging fire." Those first settlers were part of the great Polynesian migration that settled the vast triangle of islands stretching among New Zealand, Easter Island, and Hawaii. No one is sure when they arrived in Hawaii from Tahiti and the Marquesas Islands, some 2,500 miles to the south, but recent archaeological digs at the Maluuluolele Park in Lahaina date back to A.D. 700 to 900.

All we have today are some archaeological finds, some scientific data, and ancient chants to tell the story of Hawaii's past. The chants, especially the *Kumulipo*, which is the chant of creation and the litany of genealogy of the *alii* (high-ranking chiefs) who ruled the islands, discuss the comings and goings between Hawaii and the islands of the south, presumed to be Tahiti. In fact, the channel between Maui, Kahoolawe, and Lanai is called *Kealaikahiki* or "the pathway to Tahiti."

Around 1300, the transoceanic voyages stopped for some reason, and Hawaii began to develop its own culture in earnest. The settlers built temples, fishponds, and aqueducts to irrigate taro plantations. Each island was a separate kingdom, and the *alii* created a caste system and established taboos. Violators were strangled, and high priests asked the gods Lono and Ku for divine guidance. Ritual human sacrifices were common.

Take Ala Moana Blvd. in the Ewa direction, right on Ward Ave., and another right on Kinau St. to the parking lot. Bus: 2.

⑯ ★★★ kids Honolulu Academy of Arts. After feasting on the beauty of the island in the morning, feed your soul with an incredible art and cultural collection, located at one of Hawaii's most prestigious galleries. I recommend taking a guided tour. *See p 63, bullet ❸.*

⑰ ★★ Pavilion Café. Take a break at this intimate cafe, which is shaded by a 70-year-old monkey-pod tree and faces a landscaped garden with a rushing waterfall and sculptures by Jun Kaneko. Sip a glass of merlot or enjoy a chocolate walnut tart with a cup of green tea. *Honolulu Academy of Art, 900 Beretania St.* ☎ *808/532-8734. $$.*

Turn left, towards the ocean, on Ward Ave., then make a left on Ala Moana Blvd. Bus: 3.

⑱ ★★ Ala Moana Shopping Center. Spend your last few hours on the island wandering through Hawaii's largest shopping center. It's the perfect place to find souvenirs and gifts for your friends and relatives back home. *See p 122.*

The Best of Oahu in Two Weeks

0   5 mi

0   5 km

Kauai Channel

THE NORTH SHORE

KOOLAU RANGE

WAIANAE RANGE

CENTRAL OAHU (EWA PLAIN)

LEEWARD OAHU (WAIANAE COAST)

THE WINDWARD COAST

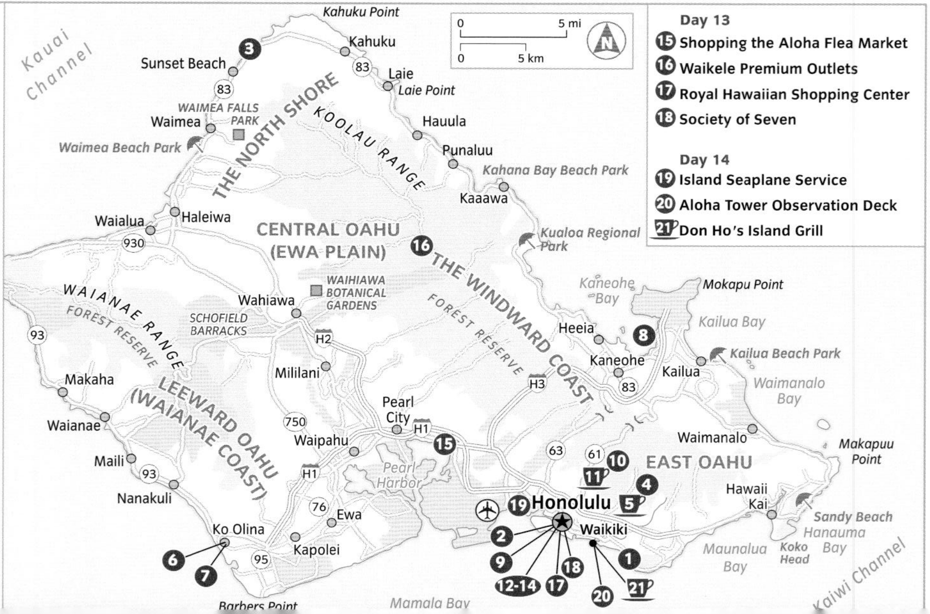

EAST OAHU

Honolulu

Waikiki

Kaiwi Channel

Pearl Harbor

Two weeks on Oahu is perfect: It gives you enough time to see all the sites and experience the true flavor of Hawaii with plenty of time left to relax and really enjoy your vacation. For the first week, follow my "The Best of Oahu in One Week" tour, which starts on p 18. On the second week of your holiday you can explore a tropical rainforest, see more incredible beaches, sail on the windward side, have a day of retail therapy, discover Hawaii's nightlife, and even take in a luau. START: **Waikiki. Trip Length: 467 miles (752km).**

Day 8

Walk in the Diamond Head direction down Kalakaua Ave. Bus: 20.

1 ★★ kids **Kapiolani Park.** Spend a lazy day just a coconut's throw from the high-rise concrete jungle of Waikiki in this 133-acre (54ha) grassy park. You'll find plenty of open space, jogging paths, tennis courts, soccer and cricket fields, and even an archery range. For more information, see my "Kapiolani Park" tour starting on p 84.

Head Ewa (west) on Ala Moana Blvd., which becomes Nimitz Hwy. Right on Bethal St. and left on Merchant St. Bus: B (City Express! B).

2 ★ **Kumu Kahua Theatre.** Shows here offer an intriguing glimpse at island life. *See p 132.*

Local musicians perform at Kapiolani Park's bandstand.

Day 9

Take H-1 west out of Waikiki, then take the H-2 north exit (Exit 8A) towards Mililani/Wahiwa. After 7 miles (11km) H2 becomes Kamehameha Hwy. (Hwy. 80). Look for the turnoff to Haleiwa town. Bus: 19, then transfer to no. 52.

3 ★★★ kids **North Shore Beaches.** Spend the day beaching. Start with breakfast in Haleiwa with stops at North Shore's best beaches: Waimea, Pupukea, Sunset, and Bonsai Pipeline. They're all reviewed in chapter 6, "The Best Beaches."

Retrace your route back to Waikiki.

Day 10

Take Manoa Rd. past Lyon Arboretum and park in the residential area below Paradise Park. Bus: 5.

4 ★ kids **Manoa Falls Hike.** Just 15 minutes from Waikiki you can lose yourself in a tropical rainforest. *See p 165.*

Retrace your route back down Manoa Rd., turn left on Oahu Ave., then left again on E. Manoa Rd.

5 ★ kids **Andy's Sandwiches & Smoothies.** This neighborhood fixture is a terrific place to stop for a smoothie and a healthy snack (try the mango muffins) after your hike. *2904 E. Manoa Rd., opposite Manoa Marketplace.* ☎ 808/988-6161. $.

From Manoa Rd. drive toward the ocean and get on the H-1 West. Stay on H-1 until it ends and becomes Farrington Hwy. Take the Ko Olina Exit and turn left on Aliinui Dr., then turn right on Olani St. No bus service.

6 ★★★ Ihilani Spa. Spend the rest of the day being pampered in this luxury spa. For details on the sensuous options to choose from, see the box "Pampering in Paradise" on p 105.

Retrace your route to Aliinui Dr.

7 Paradise Cove Luau. While you're out in Ko Olina, experience a luau. Don't expect an intimate affair—Paradise Cove generally has some 600 to 800 guests a night. In fact, the small thatched village feels a bit like a Hawaiian theme park. But you're getting more than just a luau: Paradise Cove provides an entire cultural experience, with Hawaiian games, craft demonstrations, and a beautiful shoreline looking out over what is usually a storybook sunset. Tahitian dancing and both ancient and modern hula make this a fun-filled evening for those spirited enough to join in. The food is not breathtaking: You'll find typical luau cuisine (Hawaiian kalua pig, lomi salmon, poi, and coconut pudding and cake) and basic American fare (salads, rice, pineapple, chicken, and so on). ⏲ 3½ hr. Aliinui Dr., Ko Olina. ☎ 808/842-5911. www.paradise covehawaii.com. Packages: $73–$123 for adults. Nightly 5–8:30pm.

Retrace your route back to H-1, then take H-1 into Waikiki.

Day 11
Take Captain Bob's shuttle from Waikiki (it's included in the price of the following cruise).

8 ★ kids Captain Bob's Adventure Cruises. Spend the

My favorite luau on Oahu is the one at Paradise Cove.

day on the water seeing the majestic Windward Coast the way it should be seen—from a boat. Captain Bob will take you on a 4-hour, lazy-day sail of Kaneohe Bay aboard his 42-foot catamaran. You'll skim across the almost-always calm water above the shallow coral reef; land at the disappearing sandbar Ahu o Laka; and cruise past two small islands to snorkel spots full of tropical fish and, sometimes, turtles. ⏲ All day (9am pick up, return 4pm). Kaneohe Bay. ☎ 808/942-5077. $79 adults, $60 children 3–14, free for under 3. Rates include all-you-can-eat barbecue lunch and transportation from Waikiki hotels. No cruises Sun and holidays.

9 ★ kids Cirque Hawaii. End your day by taking in this enthralling show. See p 130.

Day 12
For directions to today's stops, see the "Oahu's Best Gardens" tour on p 58 and "Honolulu for Art Lovers" on p 62.

10 ★★ kids Contemporary Museum. Start your day of culture and the arts at this incredible museum that was once an elegant home. It features cutting-edge art and inspiring views of Honolulu and Waikiki. *See p 62, bullet* ➊.

⓫ ★ Contemporary Museum Café. After you've nourished your soul, nourish your body at this relaxing, intimate cafe. I recommend the crostini of the day (a toasted baguette with a savory topping) or the sinfully delicious flourless chocolate cake. Pair your choice with a just-brewed latte or some fresh lemonade. *Contemporary Museum, 2411 Makiki Heights Dr.* ☎ *808/523-3362. www.tcmhi.org. $$.*

⓬ ★★ Hawaii State Art Museum. Don't miss this art center, which displays works by artists living in Hawaii. It's housed in the original Royal Hawaiian Hotel. *See p. 63, bullet* ➍.

⓭ Foster Botanical Garden. In Hawaii, art can also be made by Mother Nature, and this historical garden is one of her best displays. *See p 60, bullet* ➍.

Take Ala Moana Blvd. to Ward Ave. and turn right. Turn left on King St. for entrance to the parking lot. Bus: 2 or 13.

⓮ Honolulu Symphony Orchestra/ Hawaii Opera Theatre. Complete your day of culture

Heliconia, one of many native plants you can see in the Foster Botanical Gardens.

with either a visit to the Symphony, which performs from September to May, or the Opera, which takes to the stage from January to March. *Honolulu Symphony Orchestra, Neal Blaisdell Concert Hall, 444 Ward Ave.* ☎ *808/524-0815; www.honolulu symphony.com or hawaiiopera.org. Symphony tickets start at $15; opera tickets start at $27.*

Day 13
For maps covering all the shopping areas below, see p 2, p 26, and p 111.

⓯ 🅺🅸🅳🆂 Shopping the Aloha Flea Market. More than just bargain shopping, this giant outdoor bazaar is an adventure full of strange food, odd goods, and incredible bargains. Nobody ever leaves this place empty-handed—or without having had lots of fun. *See p 6.*

It's worth visiting the Contemporary Museum just to stroll the grounds and take in the views.

You can find all kinds of Hawaiian trinkets at the Aloha Flea Market.

16 Waikele Premium Outlets.
The second stop on your bargain hunting day is at these discount outlet shops. This is retail therapy at frugal prices. Just say the word *Waikele* and my eyes glaze over. So many shops, so little time!

17 Royal Hawaiian Shopping Center.
After you've seen the bargains, it's time to wander in luxury at the newly renovated 293,000-square-foot open-air mall (17,000-square-feet larger than before). There are more than 100 stores and restaurants spread across four levels. Go bananas. *See p 123.*

18 ★ Society of Seven.
This nightclub act, which is a blend of skits, Broadway hits, popular music, and costumed musical acts, is so popular it has been playing for more than 3 decades in a town where most shows barely make it 1 year. It's a great way to spend your last evening in paradise. ⏱ *1½–2½ hr. Outrigger Waikiki on the Beach, 2335 Kalakaua Ave.* ☎ *808/922-6408. Tues–Sun, dinner $72 (7pm); cocktail seating $47 (8pm).*

Day 14
I suggest taking Island Seaplane's complimentary van from your hotel in Waikiki. They will even drop you at the Aloha Tower on your way back.

19 ★★ kids Island Seaplane Service.
Spend your last day seeing why Oahu was the island of kings—and the only way to do it is from the air. You'll never forget the slapping sound of the waves as the seaplane skims across the water and then effortlessly lifts off into the air. I recommend taking the full hour tour and seeing the entire island. ⏱ *1 hr. 85 Lagoon Dr., Keehi Lagoon.* ☎ *808/836-6273. www.island seaplane.com. $119 ½-hr. tour; $220 1-hr. tour.*

20 ★ kids Aloha Tower Observation Deck.
This 10-story building was the tallest in the islands when it was built in 1926. It welcomed thousands of visitors who arrived in Hawaii via boat. In the 1920s and '30s, "Boat Day," the arrival of a passenger ship, became a festive celebration shared by the whole community. Take in the panoramic view of Honolulu and Waikiki before you bid the island aloha. *10th floor of Aloha Tower, 1 Aloha Tower Dr.* ☎ *808/528-5700. Daily 9am–5pm.*

21 kids Don Ho's Island Grill.
Raise a glass of good cheer to your fabulous vacation as you look out over Honolulu Harbor. Order the Molokai Seafood Martini, with *he'e* (squid) poke, lomi salmon, and seared ahi (tuna) served in a martini glass, and start planning your next trip to Hawaii. *Aloha Tower Marketplace, 1 Aloha Tower Dr.* ☎ *8808/528-0807. www.donho.com/grill/grill.htm. $$$.* ●

Honolulu & Oahu with Kids

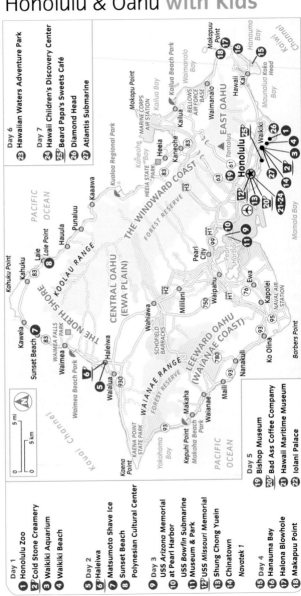

Day 1
1. Honolulu Zoo
2. Cold Stone Creamery
3. Waikiki Aquarium
4. Waikiki Beach

Day 2
5. Haleiwa
6. Matsumoto Shave Ice
7. Sunset Beach
8. Polynesian Cultural Center

Day 3
9. USS Arizona Memorial at Pearl Harbor
10. USS Bowfin Submarine Museum & Park
11. USS Missouri Memorial
12. Shung Chong Yuein
13. Chinatown
14. Navatek 1

Day 4
15. Hanauma Bay
16. Halona Blowhole
17. Makapuu Point

Day 5
18. Bishop Museum
19. Bad Ass Coffee Company
20. Hawaii Maritime Museum
21. Iolani Palace

Day 6
23. Hawaiian Waters Adventure Park

Day 7
24. Beard Papa's Sweets Café
25. Diamond Head
26. Atlantis Submarine

Previous page: Tropical flowers at Foster Botanical Garden.

Families flock to Oahu not only for the island's breathtaking beauty, but also for the abundance of activities. Waikiki is famous for every type of ocean activity you can think of, plus there's the Honolulu Zoo, the Waikiki Aquarium, and fun-filled Kapiolani Park. Dotted around the rest of the island are great family outings like Sea Life Park, the Polynesian Cultural Center, and even a water adventure park. This tour gives families a fun-filled week with something for everyone. START: **Waikiki. Length: 7 days and 196 miles (315km).**

Travel Tip

See chapter 4 for kid-friendly hotel, dining, and shopping recommendations.

Day 1

① ★★ kids **Honolulu Zoo.** If the kids aren't too tired, head for this 43-acre (17ha) municipal zoo. My favorite section is the 10-acre (4ha) African Savannah, with more than 40 African critters roaming around in the open. *Best time to go is when the gates open; the animals are more active in the morning.* ⏱ *2–3 hrs.151 Kapahulu Ave. (between Paki and Kalakaua aves.), at entrance to Kapiolani Park.* ☎ *808/971-7171. www.honoluluzoo.org. $8 adults, $1 kids 6–12, free 5 and under. Daily 9am–4:30pm.*

Walk along Kapahulu Ave. towards Kalakaua Ave., then turn right on Kalakaua.

②' kids **Cold Stone Creamery.** It's not cheap, but it's close, it's air-conditioned, and it does have dreamy ice cream with about a zillion top-pings to choose from (I love their brownies). *ResortQuest Waikiki Beach Hotel, 2570 Kalakaua Ave. (at Paoakalani St.)* ☎ *808/923-1656. $.*

Backtrack on Kalakaua Ave.

③ ★★ kids **Waikiki Aquarium.** *See p 13, bullet* ②.

Kids will love the hands-on exhibits at the Waikiki Aquarium.

Walk Ewa (west) along the beach until you find a spot you like.

④ ★★★ kids **Waikiki Beach.** Finish off your day with some fun in the sun. *See p 159.*

Day 2

Spend your second day on Oahu on the North Shore. Take H-1 west out of Waikiki, then take the H-2 north exit (Exit 8A) towards Mililani/Wahiwa. After 7 miles (11km) H2 becomes Kamehameha Hwy. (Hwy. 80). Look for the turnoff to Haleiwa town. Bus: 19, then transfer to no. 52.

⑤ ★★★ kids **Haleiwa.** Start your day exploring this famous North

Shore surfing town. *See p 136, bullet* ④.

⑥ ★ kids **Matsumoto Shave Ice.** Take time out for a cool, sweet treat at Matsumoto's. *See p 16, bullet* ⑪.

Continue down Kamehameha Hwy. for about 6½ miles (10.5km). Bus: 52.

⑦ ★★★ kids **Sunset Beach.** Spend the rest of the morning playing on Sunset Beach. During the summer months this is a safe beach for swimming. During the winter, it's best to just sit and watch the big wave surfers. *See p 159.*

Drive another 11½ miles (18.5km) down Kamehameha Hwy. to the town of Laie. Bus: 52 to Turtle Bay Resort, then 55.

⑧ ★★ kids **Polynesian Cultural Center.** Spend the rest of the afternoon and evening at this "living museum" of Polynesia. *See p 17, bullet* ⑬.

Day 3
Get an early start to beat the crowds at Pearl Harbor. Drive west on H-1 past the airport to

There's nothing like slurping up a cone of shave ice on a hot day.

the USS *Arizona* Memorial exit, then follow the green-and-white signs; there's ample free parking. Or take the *Arizona* Memorial Shuttle Bus VIP (☎ 808/839-0911), which picks up at Waikiki hotels 6:50am–1pm ($9/person round-trip). Bus: 20.

⑨ ★★★ kids **USS *Arizona* Memorial at Pearl Harbor.** This unforgettable memorial is Oahu's top attraction. Parents should note that strollers and diaper bags are not allowed at the memorial (you

Seeing the Zoo by Moonlight

For a real treat, take the **Honolulu Zoo by Twilight Tour,** which offers a rare behind-the-scenes look into the lives of the zoo's nocturnal residents. Tours are Saturday from 5:30 to 7:30pm; the cost is $12 for adults and $8 for children ages 4 to 12 years. Other great family programs include **Snooze in the Zoo:** Discover "who is roaring and who is snoring" during the night with pizza, tours, and campfire time with s'mores, plus breakfast and a morning stroll; and **Star Gazing at the Zoo,** an evening tour of the zoo that also explores the night sky above Hawaii. Check the website for details on these special events, or call ☎ 808/971-7171.

can store them at the visitor center). Also, there are no restrooms at the memorial, so be sure everyone uses the ones at the visitor center. *See p 14, bullet* ④.

⑩ ★ kids **USS *Bowfin* Submarine Museum & Park.** *See p 47, bullet* ②.

⑪ ★ kids **USS *Missouri* Memorial.** *See p 47, bullet* ③.

From Arizona Memorial Dr. turn right on Kamehameha Hwy. (Hwy. 99). Take the ramp on to H-1 East toward Honolulu. Take Exit 21A and turn towards the ocean on Bishop. Stay right at the fork onto Fort St. Turn right on Beretania St. then left on Maunakea St. There's a parking garage on the corner of Maunakea and Hotel sts. Bus: 42.

⑫ ★ kids **Shung Chong Yuein.** Before you start your tour of Chinatown, take a break at this small pastry shop. *See p 15, bullet* ⑧.

⑬ ★★ kids **Chinatown.** Plan to spend several hours in this exotic part of Honolulu The colorful open markets, Buddhist temples, waterside walkway, and plenty of

If you're lucky, your visit might coincide with the colorful spectacle of a Chinatown parade.

tempting restaurants should keep you occupied for a while. For complete descriptions, see my Chinatown tour on p 72.

From Shung Chong Yuein, continue down Maunakea St., turn left on N. King St., then right on Nuuanu Ave. Make a slight left on Nimitz Hwy. (Hwy. 92). Look for the sign for Pier 6 just after Aloha Tower, and turn right. Bus: 56.

⑭ ★ kids ***Navatek 1.*** Say aloha to the sun from the ocean. For details on this sunset dinner cruise see p 15, bullet ⑨.

The calm waters of Hanauma Bay make it a great place to bring novice snorkelers.

Family-Friendly Events

Your trip may be a little more enjoyable with the added attraction of attending a celebration, festival, or party in Honolulu, Waikiki, or other parts of the island. Check out the following events.

- **Morey World Bodyboarding Championship,** Banzai Pipeline, North Shore (☎ 808/396-2326). Early January. Participants are judged on the best wave selection and maneuvers on the wave.
- **Ala Wai Challenge,** Ala Wai Park, Waikiki (☎ 808/923-1802). Last weekend in January. This event features ancient Hawaiian games such as *ulu maika* (bowling a round stone through pegs), *oo ihe* (spear-throwing), *huki kaula* (tug of war), and an outrigger canoe race. It's also a great place to hear Hawaiian music.
- **Chinese New Year,** Chinatown (☎ 808/533-3181). Late Jan or early Feb (depending on the lunar calendar). Chinatown rolls out the red carpet for this important event with a traditional lion dance, fireworks, food booths, and a host of activities.
- **Punahou School Carnival,** Punahou School, Honolulu (☎ 808/944-5753). February. This private school has everything you can imagine in a school carnival, from high-speed rides to homemade jellies. All proceeds go to scholarship funds.
- **Hawaii Challenge International Sportkite Championship,** Kapiolani Park (☎ 808/735-9059). First weekend in March. The longest-running sportkite competition in the world attracts top kite pilots from around the globe.
- **Outrigger Canoe Season,** Ala Wai Canal (☎ 808/261-6615). Weekends May to September. Canoe paddlers across the state participate in outrigger canoe races.
- **World Fire-Knife Dance Championships and Samoan Festival,** Polynesian Cultural Center, Laie (☎ 808/293-3333). Mid-May. Fire-knife dancers from around the world gather for one of the most amazing performances you'll ever see. Authentic Samoan food and cultural festivities round out the fun.
- **Ukulele Festival,** Kapiolani Park Bandstand, Waikiki (☎ 808/732-3739). Last Sunday in July. This free concert features some 600 kids (ages 4–92) strumming the ukulele. Hawaii's top musicians all pitch in.
- **Triple Crown of Surfing,** North Shore (☎ 808/638-7266). Mid-November to late December. The North Shore is on "wave watch" during this period, and when the big, monster waves roll in, the world's top professional surfers compete in events for more than $1 million in prize money.

Day 4
From Waikiki, take H-1 East, which becomes the Kalaniaole

Hwy. Look for the Koko Head Regional Park on the left; the beach is on the right (oceanside).

Avoid the crowds by going early, about 8am, on a weekday morning; once the parking lot's full, you're out of luck. The Hanauma Bay Shuttle Bus runs from Waikiki to Hanauma Bay every half-hour from 8:45am to 1pm. You can catch it at any city bus stop in Waikiki. It returns every hour from noon to 4pm.

⑮ ★★★ kids Hanauma Bay. Spend the morning at Oahu's best snorkeling beach (note that the beach is closed on Tues). *See p 175.*

Continue to drive east on Kalanianaole Hwy.; look for mile marker 11.

⑯ kids Halona Blowhole. *See p 141, bullet ❸.*

Continue to drive east on Kalanianaole Hwy.; look for the sign for Makapuu Point.

⑰ kids Makapuu Point. Here's a chance to get out of the car and stretch your legs on a hike out to this 647-foot-high cliff and functioning lighthouse. *See p 142, bullet ❻.*

Kids can see dolphins, whales, sea lions, penguins, and more at Sea Life Park.

Continue east on Kalanianaloe Hwy. Bus: 58.

⑱ ★ kids Sea Life Park. This 62-acre (25ha) ocean theme park is one of the island's top attractions. Swim with dolphins, get up close to the sea lions, or just relax and watch the marine mammal shows. *See p 19, bullet ❹.*

To get back to Waikiki, continue on Kalanianaole Hwy. (Hwy. 72), turn left on Pali Hwy. (Hwy. 61), then take H-1 east to Waikiki. Bus: 58.

Day 5
Take Ala Wai Blvd. out of Waikiki. Turn right at Kalakaua Ave., then left on S. Beretania St. and right at Piikoi St. Make a left on to Lunalilo St., and bear left on to H-1 West. Take Exit 20B, which puts you on Haloma St. Turn right at Houghtailing St., and then left on to Bernice St. Bus: 2.

⑲ ★★★ kids Bishop Museum. This entrancing museum may be the highlight of your trip. It covers everything you've always wanted to know about Hawaii, from grass shacks to how a volcano works. *See p 15, bullet ❼.*

Turn right out of the parking lot onto Bernice St., left at Kapalama Ave., and right again on N. School St. Make a right on Liliha St., a left on N King St., and right on River St. Turn left on Nimitz Hwy. and then right at Aloha Tower Drive. Bus: A (City Express A).

⑳ Bad Ass Coffee Company. Take a break at this gourmet Hawaiian coffee. My favorite is the delicious Kona coffee, but they also offer java from Molokai, Kauai, and Maui. *Aloha Tower MarketPlace, 1 Aloha Tower Dr.* ☎ *808/524-0888. $.*

Spend a hot day splashing around at Hawaiian Waters Adventure Park.

Walk towards Diamond Head along the waterfront.

㉑ ★★ kids Hawaii Maritime Center. Hawaii's rich maritime history comes alive at this museum. *See p 22, bullet* **9**.

Walk mauka (inland) up Bishop St., right on S. King, and left on Richards St.

㉒ ★ kids Iolani Palace. If you want to really understand Hawaii, I suggest taking the Grand Tour of this royal palace, built by King David Kalakaua in 1882. Parents take note: Kids under 5 are only allowed on the self-guided tour of the basement galleries (which includes the crown

This humpback whale skeleton hangs over the exhibits at the Hawaii Maritime Center.

jewels, ancient feather cloaks, royal china, and more). *See p 22, bullet* **10**.

To get back to Waikiki, pick up your car at Aloha Tower Marketplace and turn right on Nimitz Hwy., which becomes Ala Moana Blvd. and leads into Waikiki. TheBus: 13.

Day 6
Take H-1 west to exit 1 (Campbell Industrial Park). Make an immediate left turn to Farrington Hwy., and you will see the park on your left. Bus: B (City Express B), transfer to C (Country Express C).

㉓ ★ kids Hawaiian Waters Adventure Park. Kids love this 29-acre (12ha) water-theme amusement park, which opened in spring 1999. Plan to spend the whole day here. Highlights are a football field–size wave pool for bodysurfing, two 65-foot-high (20m) free-fall slides, two water-toboggan bullet slides, inner-tube slides, body flume slides, a continuous river for floating inner tubes, and separate pools for adults, teens, and children. Restaurants, Hawaiian performances, and shops top it all off. ⏲ *All day. 400 Farrington Hwy. (at Kalaeloa Blvd.), Kapolei.* ☎ *808/674-9283. www.hawaiian waters.com. Admission $36 adults,*

$15 seniors; $26 children 3–11, free for children under 3. Hours vary, but generally the park is open daily 10:30am–4 or 5pm in peak season (summer); during off-peak season 10:30am–3:30 or 4pm; closed some weekdays.

Day 7

Take Ala Moana Blvd. out of Waikiki. Turn left on Koula St., then right on Olomehani St. and another right on Ohe St. Bus: 42.

㉔ ★★ kids Hawaii Children's Discovery Center. Perfect for children ages 2 to 13, this 37,000-square-foot (3,437m sq.) museum of color, motion, and activities will entertain them for hours with hands-on exhibits and interactive stations. Where else can kids play volleyball with a robot, don sparkling costumes from India, or dress up as a purple octopus? Lots of summer classes and activities range from playing with clay to painting (most of them invite adults to participate, too). *The Discovery Center closes at 1pm most days, so be sure to make this your first stop of the day.* ⏲ 2 hrs. 111 Ohe St. (at Olomehane St.), Honolulu. ☎ 808/524-5437. www.discoverycenter hawaii.org. Admission: $8 adults, $6.75 ages 2 to 17, free under 2. Tues–Fri 9am–1pm, Sat–Sun 10am–3pm.

Atlantis Submarine.

Retrace your route back to Ala Moana Blvd. and turn right towards Waikiki. Make a left on Ward Ave. and a right on Auahi St., then turn into the parking lot in Ward Center. Bus: 56.

㉕ kids Beard Papa's Sweets Café. The specialty here, made popular in Japan, is a baked (as opposed to fried) cream puff, made of a double-layer of soft French "choux" and "pie crust" outside. The whipped-cream custard filling isn't put inside until you order it—so each one is fresh. *Ward Center, 1200 Ala Moana Blvd.* ☎ 808/593-0107. $

Continue toward Waikiki on Ala Moana Blvd. Turn right on Kalakaua Ave., then right on Diamond Head Rd. Just after 18th Ave. turn into Diamond Head Crater parking. Bus: 3.

㉖ ★ kids Diamond Head. On your last day on Oahu, get a bird's-eye view of the island from atop this 760-foot (232m) extinct volcano. *See p 163.*

Retrace your route back to Waikiki.

㉗ ★★★ kids Atlantis Submarine. Now that you've seen Oahu from the top, plunge beneath the waves and see it underwater in this high-tech submarine. *See p 182.*

A Week of Oahu History & Culture

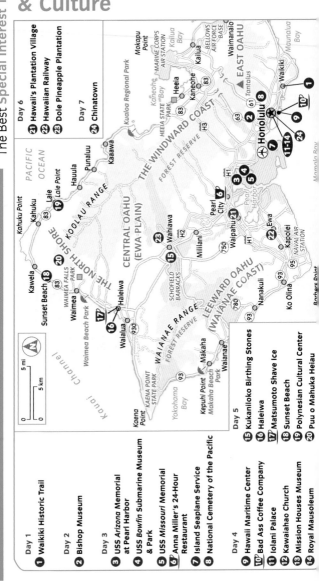

Day 1
① Waikiki Historic Trail

Day 2
② Bishop Museum

Day 3
③ USS Arizona Memorial at Pearl Harbor
④ USS Bowfin Submarine Museum & Park
⑤ USS Missouri Memorial
⑥ Anna Miller's 24-Hour Restaurant
⑦ Island Seaplane Service
⑧ National Cemetery of the Pacific

Day 4
⑨ Hawaii Maritime Center
⑩ Bad Ass Coffee Company
⑪ Iolani Palace
⑫ Kawaiahao Church
⑬ Mission Houses Museum
⑭ Royal Mausoleum

Day 5
⑮ Kukaniloko Birthing Stones
⑯ Haleiwa
⑰ Matsumoto Shave Ice
⑱ Sunset Beach
⑲ Polynesian Cultural Center
⑳ Puu o Mahuka Heiau

Day 6
㉑ Hawaii's Plantation Village
㉒ Hawaiian Railway
㉓ Dole Pineapple Plantation

Day 7
㉔ Chinatown

This tour covers Oahu's most sacred and historically important spots. You'll see ancient sites where wizards once healed
people, visit the birthplaces of Hawaiian royalty, learn about the days
of the missionaries and plantations, and reflect on the attack on
Pearl Harbor. You'll visit Waikiki, downtown Honolulu, Chinatown,
Central Oahu, and Pearl Harbor. START: **Waikiki. Trip Length: 7 days
and 69 miles (111km).**

Day 1

1 ★★ kids **Waikiki
Historic Trail.** To get
an overview of Waikiki's
history, take this 4.5-mile
(7km) walk, with stops
marked by 6-foot-tall
(1.8m) surfboards explaining the history of today's
favorite resort area. For a
full description of the trail,
see my Historic Waikiki
tour starting on p 50.

Day 2

Take Ala Wai Blvd. out of
Waikiki. Turn right at
Kalakaua Ave., then left
on S. Beretania St. and
right at Piikoi St. Make a
left on to Lunalilo St.,
and bear left on to H-1
West. Take Exit 20B,
which puts you on
Haloma St. Turn right at Houghtailing St., and then left on to Bernice St. Bus: 2.

*One of many historic
artifacts at the
Bishop Museum.*

2 ★★★ kids **Bishop Museum.**
Take the entire day to see this
entrancing museum, which could be
the highlight of your trip. You'll find
out about everything from grass
shacks to how a volcano works. *See
p 15, bullet* **7**.

Day 3

Get an early start to beat the
crowds at Pearl Harbor. Drive
west on H-1 past the airport to
the USS *Arizona* Memorial exit,
then follow the green-and-white

signs; there's ample free
parking. Or take the *Arizona* Memorial Shuttle
Bus VIP (☎ 808/839-
0911), which picks up at
Waikiki hotels 6:50am–
1pm ($9/person round-
trip). Bus: 20.

3 ★★★ kids **USS
Arizona Memorial
at Pearl Harbor.** Start
off your day of viewing
wartime Honolulu by see-
ing these three important
reminders of World War II.
See p 14, bullet **4**.

4 ★ kids **USS *Bowfin*
Submarine Museum &
Park.** *See p 47, bullet* **2**.

5 ★ kids **USS *Missouri*
Memorial.** *See p 47,
bullet* **3**.

Turn right on Arizona Rd.
and then left on Kamehameha
Hwy. (Hwy. 99). Turn right on
Kaonohi St. Bus: A (City Express A).

6 ★ kids **Anna Miller's 24-Hour
Restaurant.** Just a couple of miles
away, in Pearlridge, is this always-
busy casual dining restaurant. Treat
yourself to the best fresh strawberry pie on the island (with a generous helping of fluffy whipped
cream). *Pearlridge Centre, 98-115
Kaonohi St. (Kamehameha Hwy.).*
☎ *808/487-2421. $.*

Turn left on Kamehameha Hwy. (Hwy. 99) and merge on Hwy. 78 East. Take Exit 3 toward the Airport (Puuloa Rd., which becomes Lagoon Dr.).

7 ★★ kids Island Seaplane Service. See the box "See World War II History From the Air" on p 48 for details.

From Lagoon Dr. turn right on Nimitz Hwy., take H-1 East to exit 21A (Pali Hwy.). Turn right on Kuakini St., then left on Lusitana St. Right again on Concordia St. and left on Puowaina Dr., then stay on Puowaina Dr. to the end of the road. Bus: 62, transfer to 6.

8 National Cemetery of the Pacific. End the day seeing the final outcome of war. The National Cemetery of the Pacific (also known as "the Punchbowl") is an ash-and-lava tuff cone that exploded about 150,000 years ago—like Diamond Head, only smaller. Early Hawaiians called it *Puowaina,* or "hill of sacrifice." The old crater is a burial ground for 35,000 victims of three American wars in Asia and the Pacific: World War II, Korea, and Vietnam. Among the graves, you'll find many unmarked ones with the date December 7, 1941 carved in the headstone. ⏱ *1 hr. Punchbowl Crater, 2177 Puowaina Dr. (at the end of the road).* ☎ *808/541-1434.*

Gardens of the Missing at the Punchbowl.

Free admission. Daily 8am–5:30pm (Mar–Sept to 6:30pm).

Day 4
Start off at the Hawaii Maritime Center, next to Aloha Tower.

9 ★★ kids Hawaii Maritime Center. Hawaii's rich maritime history comes alive at this museum. *See p 22, bullet* **9**.

Walk next door to the Aloha Tower Market Place.

10 Bad Ass Coffee Company. Take a break at this gourmet Hawaiian coffee. My favorite is the delicious Kona coffee, but they also offer java from Molokai, Kauai, and Maui. *Aloha Tower MarketPlace, 1 Aloha Tower Dr.* ☎ *808/524-0888. $.*

Walk up Bishop St. to King St. and make a right. At Richards St. turn left.

11 ★ kids Iolani Palace. If you want to really understand Hawaii, I suggest taking the Grand Tour of this royal palace, built by King David Kalakaua in 1882. *See p 22, bullet* **10**.

Continue to walk towards Diamond Head on S. King St. to Punchbowl St.

Mission Houses Museum.

⑫ ★ Kawaiahao Church. Don't miss the crowning achievement of the first missionaries in Hawaii—the first permanent stone church, complete with bell tower and colonial colonnade. *See p 23, bullet* ⑪.

Continue in the Diamond Head direction on S. King St.

⑬ Mission Houses Museum. Step into life in 1820 among the 19th-century American Protestant missionaries. *See p. 23, bullet* ⑫.

Retrace your steps to your car at the Aloha Tower. Drive in the Diamond Head direction on Nimtz Hwy. and turn left on Alakea St. Turn left on Beretania St., right on Punchbowl St., then get on the Pali Hwy. north. Exit at Wylolie St. and turn left on Nuuana Ave. Bus: 4.

⑭ Royal Mausoleum. In the cool uplands of Nuuanu, on a 3.7-acre (1.5ha) patch of sacred land dedicated in 1865, is the final resting place of King Kalakaua, Queen Kapiolani, and 16 other Hawaiian royals. Only the Hawaiian flag flies over this grave, a remnant of the kingdom. 🕐 1 hr. 2261 Nuuanu Ave. (between Wyllie and Judd sts.). ☎ 808/536-7602. Free admission. Mon–Fri 8am–4:30pm.

Take Nuuanu Ave. down to Nimitz Hwy., which becomes Ala Moana Blvd., into Waikiki. Bus: 4

Day 5
Take H-1 west out of Waikiki. Take the H-2 north exit (Exit 8A) towards Mililani/Wahiwa. After 7 miles (11km) H2 becomes Kamehameha Hwy. (Hwy. 80). Look for the sign between Wahiawa and Haleiwa, on Plantation Rd., opposite the road to Whitmore Village. No bus.

⑮ Kukaniloko Birthing Stones. The most sacred site in central Oahu, this is where women of ancient Hawaii gave birth to potential *alii* (royalty). *See p 135, bullet* ②.

Retrace your route back to Kamehameha Hwy. (Hwy. 80) and turn

Many Hawaiian royals were born at this site.

Approach the Puu o Mahuka Heiau with respect; many Hawaiians consider it sacred.

left. At the fork in road, remain right, on Kamehameha Hwy. (which now becomes Hwy. 99). Follow the signs into Haleiwa.

16 ★★★ **kids** **Haleiwa.** Start your day exploring this famous North Shore surfing town. *See p 136, bullet* **4**.

17 ★ **kids** **Matsumoto Shave Ice.** Take time out for a cool, sweet treat at Matsumoto's. *See p 16, bullet* **11**.

Continue down Kamehameha Hwy. for about 6½ miles (10.5km). Bus: 52.

18 ★★★ **kids** **Sunset Beach.** Spend the rest of the morning playing on Sunset Beach. During the summer months this is a safe beach for swimming. During the winter, it's best to just sit and watch the big wave surfers. *See p 159.*

Drive another 11½ miles (18.5km) down Kamehameha Hwy. to the town of Laie. Bus: 52 to Turtle Bay Resort, then 55.

19 ★★ **kids** **Polynesian Cultural Center.** Spend the rest of the afternoon and evening at this "living museum" of Polynesia. *See p. 17, bullet* **13**.

Retrace your route back towards Haleiwa. Take Pupukea Rd. mauka (inland) off Kamehameha Hwy. at Foodland, and drive .7 miles (1.1km) up a switchback road. Bus: 52, then walk up Pupukea Rd.

20 ★ **kids** **Puu o Mahuka Heiau.** Go at sunset to feel the *mana* (sacred spirit) of this 18th-century *heiau,* known as the "hill of escape." Sitting on a 5-acre (2ha), 300-foot (91m) bluff overlooking Waimea Bay and 25 miles (40km) of Oahu's wave-lashed North Coast, this sacrificial temple (the largest on Oahu) appears as a huge rectangle of rocks twice as big as a football field, with an altar often covered by the flower and fruit offerings left by native Hawaiians. *Warning:* Never walk on, climb, or even touch the rocks at a *heaiu.* ⏱ *30 min. Pupukea Rd.*

Day 6
Take H-1 west to Waikele-Waipahu exit (Exit 7); get in the left lane on exit and turn left on Paiwa St. At the 5th light, turn right onto Waipahu St.; after the 2nd light, turn left. Bus: 58, transfer 43.

21 **kids** **Hawaii's Plantation Village.** The tour of this restored 50-acre (20ha) village offers a glimpse back in time to when sugar planters shaped the land, economy, and culture of Hawaii. From 1852, when the first contract laborers arrived here from China, to 1947, when the plantation era ended, more than 400,000 men, women, and children from China, Japan, Portugal, Puerto Rico, Korea, and the Philippines came to work the sugarcane fields. ⏱ *1½ hr. Waipahu Cultural Garden Park, 94–695 Waipahu St. (at Waipahu Depot Rd.), Waipahu.* ☎ *808/677-0110. www.hawaii plantationvillage.org. Admission (including escorted tour) $13 adults; $10 seniors; $7 military personnel; $5 children 4–11; children 3 and under free. Mon–Sat 10am–2pm.*

Take Farrington Hwy. to Fort Weaver Rd. (Hwy. 76) toward Ewa Beach. Turn right on Renton Rd.

㉒ kids Hawaiian Railway. All aboard! This is a train ride back into history. Between 1890 and 1947 the chief mode of transportation for Oahu's sugar mills was the Oahu Railway and Land Co.'s narrow-gauge trains. The line carried not only equipment, raw sugar, and supplies, but also passengers from one side of the island to the other. You can relive those days every Sunday with a narrated ride through Ko Olina Resort and out to Makaha. On the second Sunday of the month, you can ride on the nearly 100-year-old, custom-built, parlor-observation car (no kids under 13 on this ride). The fare is $20. ⏱ *2 hrs. 91-1001 Renton Rd., Ewa Beach.* ☎ *808/681-5461. www. hawaiianrailway.com. Admission $10 adults, $7 seniors and children 2–12. Departures Sun 1 and 3pm.*

Retrace your route to Fort Weaver Rd. and take the H-1 East (Honolulu direction). Take exit 8B on the left and merge into H-2 North (Miilani/Wahiawa). Take Exit 8 on to Kamehameha Hwy.

㉓ kids Dole Pineapple Plantation. Concluding this day of Plantation Hawaii, this agricultural exhibit/retail area is a modern pineapple plantation with a few adventures for kids. *See p 60, bullet* ❻.

Retrace your route back on Kamehamea Hwy. to H-1, then take to H-1 to Waikiki.

Day 7
㉔ ★★ kids Chinatown. Plan to spend the entire day in this exotic part of Honolulu. Colorful open markets, Buddhist temples, a waterside walkway, and plenty of tempting restaurants will keep you occupied for hours. For complete descriptions, see my Chinatown tour beginning on p 72.

The Hawaii Plantation Village features 30 restored camp houses.

Wartime Honolulu

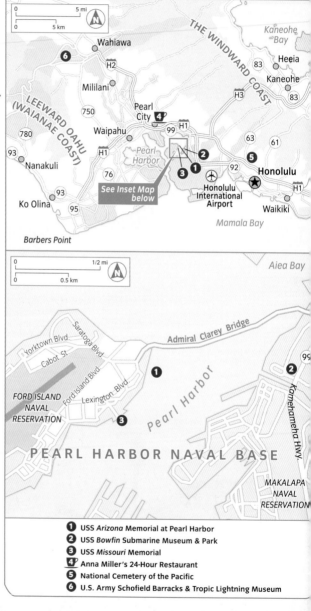

1 USS *Arizona* Memorial at Pearl Harbor
2 USS *Bowfin* Submarine Museum & Park
3 USS *Missouri* Memorial
4 Anna Miller's 24-Hour Restaurant
5 National Cemetery of the Pacific
6 U.S. Army Schofield Barracks & Tropic Lightning Museum

On December 7, 1941, Hawaii's historic "day of infamy," Pearl Harbor was bombed by the Japanese and the United States entered World War II. Honolulu has a rich history during the war years and this 1-day tour covers the highlights. START: **Waikiki.** Length: 1 day and 73 miles (117km).

Drive west on H-1 past the airport to the USS *Arizona* Memorial exit, then follow the green-and-white signs; there's ample free parking. Or take the *Arizona* Memorial Shuttle Bus VIP (☎ 808/839-0911), which picks up at Waikiki hotels 6:50am–1pm ($9/person round-trip). Bus: 20.

❶ ★★★ kids USS *Arizona* Memorial at Pearl Harbor. No trip to Honolulu would be complete without a visit to the this memorial at Pearl Harbor. Get there early, preferably by the 7:30am opening— otherwise face long lines (waits up to 3 hours). *See p 14, bullet* ❹.

❷ ★ kids USS *Bowfin* Submarine Museum & Park. This is a great opportunity to see what life was like on a submarine. You can go below deck of this famous vessel— nicknamed the "Pearl Harbor Avenger" for its successful attacks on the Japanese—and see how the 80-man crew lived during wartime.

The *Bowfin* Museum has an impressive collection of submarine-related artifacts. The Waterfront Memorial honors submariners lost during World War II. ⏱ *1 hr. 11 Arizona Memorial Dr. (next to the USS Arizona Memorial Visitor Center).* ☎ *808/423-1341. www.bowfin.org. Admission $10 adults, $6 active-duty military personnel and seniors, $3 children 4–12 (children under 4 are not permitted for safety reasons). Daily 8am–5pm.*

❸ ★ kids USS *Missouri* Memorial. On the deck of this 58,000-ton (52,616 metric ton) battleship (the last one the navy built), World War II came to an end with the signing of the Japanese surrender on September 2, 1945. I recommend taking the tour, which begins at the visitor center. Guests are shuttled to Ford Island on military-style buses while listening to a 1940s-style radio program. Once on the ship, guests watch an informational film and are

Historical photo of USS Arizona *sinking into Pearl Harbor.*

The USS Missouri provided firepower in the battles of Iwo Jima and Okinawa.

then free to explore on their own or take a guided tour. Highlights of this massive battleship include the forecastle (or *fo'c's'le*, in Navy talk), where the 30,000-pound anchors are dropped on 1,080 feet (329m) of anchor chain; the 16-inch (41cm) guns, which can accurately fire a 2,700-pound (1,225kg) shell some 23 miles (37km) in 50 seconds; and the spot where the Instrument of Surrender was signed as Douglas MacArthur, Chester Nimitz, and "Bull" Halsey looked on. 🕐 *1½ hr. 11 Arizona Memorial Rd.,* ☎ *808/423-2263. www.ussmissouri.com. Admission $16 adults, $8 children 4–12. Guided Tours: $22 adults, $14 children (admission included). Daily 9am–5pm; guided tours 9:30am–4:30pm. Check in at the visitor center of the USS Bowfin Memorial.*

Turn right on Arizona Rd. and then left on Kamehameha Hwy. (Hwy. 99). Turn right on Kaonohi St. Bus: A (City Express A).

4 ★ **kids Anna Miller's 24-Hour Restaurant.** Just a couple of miles away, in Pearlridge, is this always-busy casual dining restaurant. Treat yourself to the best fresh strawberry pie on the island (with a generous helping of fluffy whipped cream). *Pearlridge Centre, 98-115 Kaonohi St. (Kamehameha Hwy.).* ☎ *808/487-2421. $.*

Turn left on Kam Hwy. (Hwy. 99) and merge on Hwy. 78 East, which merges into H-1 East. Take Exit 21A (Pali Hwy.). Turn left on Pali Hwy., right on School St., left

See World War II History from the Air

For a unique perspective on Oahu's historical sites, I highly recommend the **Island Seaplane Service's** (☎ **808/836-6273;** www.islandseaplane.com) 1-hour tour of the island. The tour gives you aerial views of Waikiki Beach, Diamond Head Crater, Kahala's luxury estates, and the sparkling waters of Hanauma and Kaneohe bays and continues on to Chinaman's Hat, the Polynesian Cultural Center, and the rolling surf of the North Shore. The flight returns across the island, over Hawaii's historic wartime sites. Tours cost $220 per person.

on Lusitana St., then right on Puowaina Dr. Stay right on Puowaina Dr. to the end of the road. Bus: 62, transfer to 6.

5 ★ **National Cemetery of the Pacific.** The National Cemetery of the Pacific (also known as "the Punchbowl") is an ash-and-lava tuff cone that exploded about 150,000 years ago—like Diamond Head, only smaller. Early Hawaiians called it *Puowaina,* or "hill of sacrifice." The old crater is a burial ground for 35,000 victims of three American wars: World War II, Korea, and Vietnam. Among the graves, you'll find many unmarked ones with the date December 7, 1941, carved in stone. ⏱ *1 hr. Punchbowl Crater, 2177 Puowaina Dr. (at the end of the road).* ☎ *808/541-1434. Free admission. Daily 8am–5:30pm (Mar–Sept to 6:30pm).*

The attack on Pearl Harbor outraged Americans and launched the country into World War II.

Retrace your route on Puowaina Dr., then go left on Lusitana St., and right on School St. Take H-1 West to H-2 North, which becomes Hwy. 99. Turn left on

Kunia Rd., then right on Lyman Rd. (through the gate). Turn right on Flagler Rd., then left on Waianae Ave. Museum is in Bldg. 361. Bus: 6, transfer to 52, transfer to 72.

6 kids **U.S. Army Schofield Barracks & Tropic Lightning Museum.** With its broad, palm-lined boulevards and Art Deco buildings, this old army cavalry post is still the largest operated by the U.S. Army outside the continental United States. You can no longer visit the barracks themselves, but the history of Schofield Barracks and the 25th Infantry Division is told in the small Tropic Lightning Museum. Displays range from a 1917 bunker exhibit to a replica of Vietnam's infamous Cu Chi tunnels. ⏱ *1 hr. Schofield Barracks, Building 361, Waianae Ave.* ☎ *808/655-0497. www.25idl.army. mil/Tropic%20Lightning%20Museum/ history.htm. Free admission. Tues–Sun 1–4pm.*

Retrace your route back to H-2, then take H-1 back to Waikiki.

A bird's-eye view of the Punchbowl.

Historic Waikiki

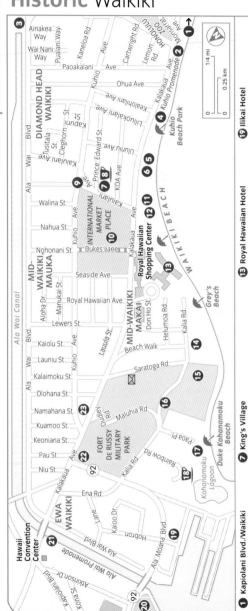

1 Kapiolani Blvd./Waikiki
2 Kapahulu Groin
3 Ala Wai/Lili'uokalani Estate
4 Kuhio Beach Park
5 Duke Kahanamoku Statue
6 Wizard Stones of Kapaemahu
7 King's Village
8 Rock Island Café
9 Aina Hau Park Triangle
10 International Marketplace Banyan Tree
11 Westin Moana Hotel Banyan Tree
12 Duke's, Outrigger Waikiki on the Beach
13 Royal Hawaiian Hotel
14 Outrigger Reef Hotel
15 US Army Museum
16 Kalia Road
17 Paoa Park
18 Lappert's Ice Cream
19 Ilikai Hotel
20 Ala Moana Park
21 Ala Wai Canal
22 Fort DeRussy
23 King Kalaukaua Statue

Spend a morning strolling through history. Each of the 21 Waikiki Historic Trail Markers, 6-foot-tall surfboards, explains the history of Hawaii's favorite resort area, focusing on the time before Westerners came to its shores (I've thrown in a few extra stops along the way). You could probably speed-walk the entire route in a couple of hours, but I recommend taking all morning, stopping at each one and appreciating this culturally rich area. START: **Kapiolani Ave. (near Monsarrat Ave.). Length: 4½ miles (7km).**

❶ Kapiolani Blvd./Waikiki. In ancient times there were two *heiau* (temples) in this area that covered San Souci and Queen's Surf beaches and all of Kapiolani Park. One was *Kupalaha*, located on the shoreline at Queen's Beach and thought to be part of the *Papa'ena'ena* Heiau, where Kamehameha I made the last human sacrifice in Waikiki. The other, *Makahuna*, near Diamond Head, was dedicated to *Kanaloa*, the god of the ocean. *Kalakaua Ave. (near the Natatorium, close to Monsarrat Ave.).*

Walk Away from Diamond Head to the Groin at Kapahulu Ave.

❷ Kapahulu Groin. Waikiki has always been a popular surfing site. Near here, on the slopes of Diamond Head, a *heiau* (temple) was dedicated to *he'e nalu,* or surfing, and the priests there were responsible for announcing the surfing conditions to the village below by flying a kite. *Kalakau and Kapahulu aves.*

Turn mauka (towards the mountains) up Kapahulu Ave. to Ala Wai Blvd.

❸ Ala Wai/Lili'uokalani Estate. This was the site of the estate of Queen Liliuokalani, who was overthrown by the U.S. government in 1893. She had two homes here, *Paoakalani* (royal perfume), located where the canal now stands, and another *Kealohilani* (the brightness of heaven), located opposite Kuhio Beach. *Kapahulu Ave. and Ala Wai Blvd.*

Continue in the Ewa direction on Ala Wai Blvd. and turn left on Paokalani Ave. Walk down to the beach.

❹ Kuhio Beach Park. This beach park is named in honor of Prince Jonah Kalanianaole, Hawaii's second delegate to the U.S. Congress, 1902–22. Kalanianaole successfully got the passage of the Homes Commission Act, giving native Hawaiians some 200,000 acres (80,640ha) of land. His home, *Pualeilani* (flower from the wreath of heaven), was located on the beach here, and was given to the city when he died. *2453 Kalakaua Ave. (between Keaohilani and Liliuokalani sts.).*

Continue walking in the Ewa direction down Kalakaua Ave.

Queen Liliuokalani, Hawaii's last monarch.

Fans of Duke Kahanamoku drape his statue with leis.

⑤ Duke Kahanamoku Statue.
Olympic swimming champion, internationally known surfer, movie actor, and Hawaii's ambassador of Aloha, Duke Paoa Kahanamoku won three gold metals, two silvers, and a bronze in four Olympics. He introduced surfing to Europe, Australia, and the East Coast of the U.S., and appeared in movies from 1925 to 1933. There's no surfboard marker here, just the statue of Duke. *Kalakaua Ave. (between Liliuokalani and Uluniu sts.).*

One of the Wizard Stones.

Continue walking in the Ewa direction down Kalakaua Ave.

⑥ Wizard Stones of Kapaemahu. According to legend, four healers from Tahiti (Kapaemahu, Kahaloa, Kapuni, and Kinohi) came to Hawaii in perhaps the 15th century. Before they left they transferred their healing powers into these stones, which were located in Kaimuki, 2 miles (3.2km) away. No one knows how the stones, which weigh approximately 8 tons (7 metric tons), got to Waikiki. *Diamond Head side of the Waikiki Police Sub-Station, 2405 Kalakaua Ave.*

At Kaiulani Ave. turn towards the mountain to Koa Ave.

⑦ King's Village. The home of King David Kalakaua (1836–1891) once stood here, surrounded by towering coconut trees. The King loved dancing and revived the hula tradition, which the missionaries had just about succeeded in stamping out. He also loved to give parties and earned the nickname The Merrie Monarch. The official name for the block-long shopping center that stands here today is King's Village, but everyone calls it King's Alley. *131Kaiulani Ave. (between Koa Ave. and Prince Edward St.).*

Inside King's Village.

8 **kids** **Rock Island Café.** Order a cherry coke at this nostalgic soda fountain filled with memorabilia from when "Elvis was King, Marilyn was Queen, and they both drank Coca-Cola." *King's Village. 131 Kaiulani Ave. (between Koa Ave. and Prince Edward St.).* ☎ 808-923-8033. $.

Continue mauka on Kaiulani Ave. to Prince Edward St.

9 **Aina Hau Park Triangle.** This tiny park was once part of the palm tree–lined grand entrance to the 10-acre (4ha) estate of Governor Archibald Scott Cleghorn and, his wife, Hawaiian Chiefess Miriam Kapili Likelike. The Chiefess (like her sister, Liliuokalani, and her brother, Kalakaua) was a composer and wrote the song *"Ainahau"* (land of the hau tree), describing the estate of 3 lily ponds, 500 coconut trees, 14 varieties of hibiscus, 8 different kinds of mango, and a giant banyan tree. The huge, 2-story Victorian home stood between what today are Cleghorn and Tusitala streets. *Kaiulani/Kuhio aves.*

Turn left on Kuhio and enter the International Marketplace.

10 **International Marketplace Banyan Tree.** At one time this area fronted the Apuakehau Stream and was the summer home of King William Kanaina Lunalilo (1835–1874), who was the first elected king of Hawaii. The Hawaiians called him *ke alii lokomaikai,* or "the kind chief." His reign was only 1 year and 25 days—he died due to poor health. *Duke's Lane (between Kuhio and Kalakua aves.).*

Walk through the International Marketplace, toward the ocean. At Kalakaua Ave. cross the street.

11 **Westin Moana Hotel Banyan Tree.** The first hotels in Waikiki were just bathhouses that offered rooms for overnight stays. The first oceanfront hotel, the Park Beach, was a home converted into a hotel with 10 rooms, 1 bathroom, and 1 telephone. Then the Moana Hotel opened its doors on March 11, 1901, with four stories (the tallest structure in Hawaii), and 75 rooms (with a bathroom and a telephone in each room). What put Waikiki on the map was Harry Owens and Webley Edwards's radio show, "Hawaii Calls," which started in 1935. At the peak of the show's popularity, in 1952, it was broadcast to 750 stations around the globe. *2365 Kalakaua Ave. (near Kaialani St.).*

The Westin Moana's Banyan tree.

Next door on the Ewa side.

⓬ Duke's, Outrigger Waikiki on the Beach. The outside lanai of Duke's Canoe Club was once where the Apuakehau ("basket of dew") Stream, which flowed through the middle of Waikiki, emptied into the ocean. *Paradise of the Pacific* magazine described the river as flowing through "taro patches, rice and banana fields . . . (with) canoes gliding along the shining surface . . . (and) women and children catching shrimp in long narrow baskets, often stopping to eat a few." *3553 Kalakaua Ave. (across the street from Duke's Lane and Kaiulani St.).*

Continue down Kalakaua Ave. in the Ewa direction, turn toward the ocean at Royal Hawaiian Ave.

⓭ Royal Hawaiian Hotel. At one time, this area, known then as Helumoa, was a royal coconut grove filled with 10,000 coconut trees, first planted in the 16th century by Chief Kakuhihewa. Later Kamehameha I camped here before his conquest of Oahu. After winning battles in Nuuanu, he made Waikiki the capital of the Hawaiian islands. In 1927, the Royal Hawaii Hotel opened with 400 rooms. It cost $5 million to build. *2365 Kalakaua Ave. (Royal Hawaiian Ave.).* ☎ *808/922-3111.*

Retrace your steps back to Kalakaua Ave. and turn left. Turn left (toward the ocean) at Lewers St. Turn right at Kalia Rd.

⓮ Outrigger Reef Hotel. Waikiki is known today for its incredible beauty, but in the olden days, it was known by the Hawaiians as a powerful place of healing. Very successful *kahuna la'au lapa'au* (medical physicians) lived in this area and the royal families often came here to convalesce. The beach, stretching from where the Halekkulani Hotel is today to the Outrigger Reef, was called *Kawehewehe* (removal) because if you bathed in the waters, your illness would be removed. *2169 Kalia Rd. (Lewers St.).* ☎ *808/923-3111.*

⓯ U.S. Army Museum. The grounds where the museum stands today was once the 3-acre (1.2ha) estate and villa of Chung Afong, Hawaii's first Chinese millionaire and member of King David Kalakaua's privy council. Afong arrived in Honolulu in 1849 and in just 6 years made a fortune in retailing, real estate, sugar, rice, and opium (he had the only government license to sell it). In 1904 the U.S. Army Corp of Engineers bought the property for $28,000 to defend Honolulu Harbor. On December 7, 1976, it became a museum. *Ft. DeRussy, near Saratoga and Kalia rds.* ☎ *808/955-9552.*

Continue in the Ewa direction on Kalia Rd.

The Royal Hawaiian Hotel, also known as the "Pink Palace."

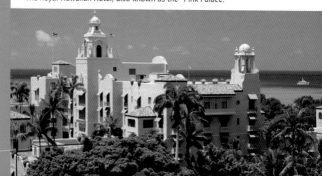

The U.S. Army museum houses everything from ancient Hawaiian warfare items to high-tech munitions.

16 Kalia Road. In 1897, Fort DeRussy, from Kalia Road mauka (towards the mountain) some 13 acres (5.3ha), was the largest fish pond in Waikiki. Called *Ka'ihikapu*, this pond, like the hundreds of others in Waikiki, functioned as "royal iceboxes" where *'ama'ama* (mullet) and *awa* (milkfish) were raised in brackish water. Hawaiians have lots of legends about fishponds, which they believed were protected by *mo'o* (lizards), that could grow to some 12 to 30 feet (4–9m) long. 1908, it took the U.S. military more than 250,000 cubic yards of landfill and 1 year to cover Ka'ihikapu. *Kalia Rd. (between Saratoga Rd. and Ala Moana Blvd.) malka to Kalakaua Ave.*

Continue in the Ewa direction on Kalia Rd.

17 Paoa Park. The 20 acres (8.1ha) where the Hilton Hawaiian Village stands today was home to Olympic champion Duke Kahanamoku's mother's family, the Paoas. Duke's grandfather, Ho'olae Paoa, was a descendant of royal chiefs and got the land from King Kamehameha III in the Great Mahele of 1848, which allowed the king, chiefs, and commoners to claim private title to lands, and for the first time allowed foreigners to own land in Hawaii. *Kalia Rd. (bordered by Paoa Rd. and Ala Moana Ave.).*

Walk inside the Hilton Hawaiian Village to the Rainbow Bazaar.

18 Lappert's Ice Cream. Before you leave the Hilton Hawaiian Village, take an ice cream break at this yummy local shop, where they have some 33 different flavors. (My favorite is the Kona coffee.) *Rainbow Bazaar, Hilton Hawaiian Village, 2005 Kalia Rd. (Ala Moana Blvd.).* ☎ *808/949-4321. $.*

The Hilton Hawaiian Village stands on land once owned by Duke Kamehameha's family.

Make a left on Ala Moana Blvd.

⑲ Ilikai Hotel. Waikiki's third stream, Pi'inaio, once originated here, where the hotel's lanai is today. However, unlike the other two streams (Kuekkaunahi and Apuakehau), Pi'inaio was a muddy delta area with several smaller streams pouring in. It also was a very productive fishing area filled with reef fish, crabs, shrimp, lobster, octopus, eels, and limu (seaweed). However, today, Waikiki is nearly fished out. *1777 Ala Moana Blvd. (at Hobron Ln.).*

Continue in the Ewa direction down Ala Moana Blvd. After you cross the bridge look for the marker on the corner of Atkinson Dr. at the entrance to the park.

⑳ Ala Moana Park. In the late 1800s, Chinese farmers moved into Waikiki and converted the area now occupied by the park and shopping center into duck ponds. In 1931, the city and county of Honolulu wanted to clean up the waterfront and built a park here. In 1959, the 50 acres (20ha) across the street opened as one of the largest shopping centers in the U.S. *Diamond Head corner of the entrance to the park, Ala Moana Blvd. (at Atkinson Dr.).*

Turn right toward the mountains on Atkinson Dr. Bear right on Kapiolani Blvd. The Convention Center is on the corner of Kapiolani Blvd. and Kalakaua Ave. Go around the back of the Center by the Ala Wai Canal for the marker.

㉑ Ala Wai Canal. At the turn of the 20th century, people on Oahu were not very happy with Waikiki. The smelly duck farms, coupled with the zillions of mosquitoes from the stagnant swamp lands, did not make it a pretty picture. Work began on the Ala Wai (fresh water) Canal in 1922 and was completed in 1928. Once the canal had drained the wetlands, the taro and rice fields dried up and the duck farms and fish ponds disappeared. *Ala Wai Canal Side of the Convention Center, 1801 Kalakaua Ave. (Ala Wai Canal).* ☎ *808/943-3500.*

Continue in the Diamond Head direction down Kalakaua to the park on the corner of Ala Moana Blvd.

㉒ Fort DeRussy. This green recreation area was named after Brigadier General Rene E. DeRussy, Corps of Engineers, who served in the American-British War of 1812.

The shady lawns and gold-sand beach of Ala Moana make it one of the island's most popular playgrounds.

All of Fort DeRussy and all the land from here to the foothills of Manoa Valley were planted with taro. By 1870, the demand for taro had diminished and the Chinese farmers began planting rice in the former taro fields. *Near the corner of Ala Moana Blvd. and Kalakaua Ave.*

Continue towards Diamond Head on Kalakkaua Ave. to the intersection of Kuhio Ave.

㉓ King Kalakaua Statue.
Next to Kamehameha I, King David Kalakaua is Hawaii's best-known king and certainly lived up to his nickname, the Merrie Monarch. He was born to royal parents in 1836, raised in the court of King Kamehameha IV, and elected to the position of King in 1874, after King William Lunalilo died. During his 17-year reign he restored Hawaii's rapidly fading culture of chanting, music, and hula (which had been banned by the missionaries for years). He was also forced to sign what has been termed the "Bayonet Constitution," which

King David Kalakaua.

restricted his royal powers, in1887. In 1890, he sailed to California for medical treatment and died in San Francisco due to a mild stroke, kidney failure, and cirrhosis. *No marker (yet); statue is located at Kuhio and Kalakaua aves. intersection.*

Waikiki: It Ain't What It Used to Be

Before Westerners showed up on Oahu, Waikiki was a 2,000-acre (809ha) swamp (compared to the 500 acres/202ha it occupies today). Waikiki (which means spouting water) was a very important area because it held the drainage basin for the 5 million gallons (18.9l million) of daily rainfall from the Koolau Mountains. When Hawaiians settled in Waikiki (which historians estimate was around A.D. 600) they slowly turned the swamp into a Hawaii version of a breadbasket: taro fields, fishponds, and gardens for fruits and vegetables. When Western boats began calling at Honolulu Harbor they brought the pesky mosquito, which loved the swamps of Waikiki. In 1927, the just completed Ala Wai Canal not only drained the swamps, but opened up lands that eventually became the resort area of today.

The Best Special Interest Tours

Oahu's Best **Gardens**

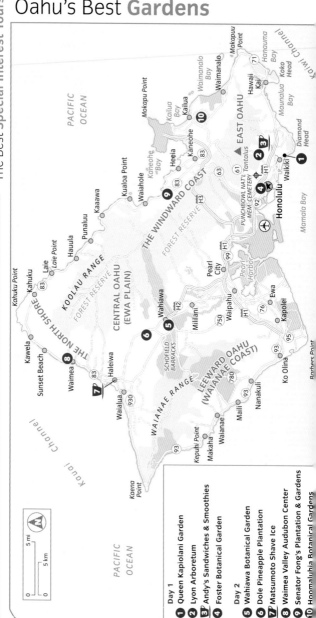

Day 1
1 Queen Kapiolani Garden
2 Lyon Arboretum
3 Andy's Sandwiches & Smoothies
4 Foster Botanical Garden

Day 2
5 Wahiawa Botanical Garden
6 Dole Pineapple Plantation
7 Matsumoto Shave Ice
8 Waimea Valley Audubon Center
9 Senator Fong's Plantation & Gardens
10 Hoomaluhia Botanical Garden

Stop and smell the tuberoses. Or the plumeria. Spend a couple of days exploring the various gardens of Hawaii, from native Hawaiian plants to orchids, palms, aroids, tree ferns, heliconias, calatheas, and myriad trees. START: **Waikiki. Length: 2 Days and 112-miles (180km).**

Located in Waikiki next door to Kapiolani Park, on Monsarrat Ave. (between Paki and Leahi aves.). Parking entrance on Leahi Ave. Bus: 19 or 20.

Day 1

❶ Queen Kapiolani Garden. Wander into this tiny garden and smell the tropical ornamentals, hibiscus cultivars, and a small collection of native Hawaiian plants. ⏱ *30 min. Kapiolani Park, on Monsarrat Avenue (between Paki Ave. and Leahi Ave.). Free admission. Open daily 24 hrs.*

Take McCully St. out of Waikiki, turn right on Kapiolani Blvd., left at University Ave., and right on Oahu. Look for the slight right at Manoa Rd. Bus: B (City Express B), transfer to 5.

❷ ★ Lyon Arboretum. Six-story-tall breadfruit trees. Yellow orchids no bigger than a bus token. Ferns with fuzzy buds as big as a human head. Lyon Arboretum is 194 budding acres (79ha) of botanical wonders. Take the self-guided 20-minute hike through this cultivated rainforest to Inspiration Point and you'll pass more than 5,000 exotic tropical plants full of birdsong. ⏱ *2–3 hrs. 3860 Manoa Rd. (near the top of the road).* ☎ *808/988-0456. www.hawaii.edu/lyonarboretum. $7 adults, $4 seniors, $5 students, $3 children 12 and under. Mon–Fri 9am–4pm.*

Retrace your route back down Manoa Rd., turn left on Oahu Ave. and then left again on E. Manoa Rd. Bus: 5

Water lily.

❸ ★ **kids** **Andy's Sandwiches & Smoothies.** On the way down the hill, stop at this friendly neighborhood eatery. Their smoothies are terrific—try the Hi Pro (peanut butter, bananas, and apple juice with protein powder). *2904 E. Manoa Rd., opposite Manoa Marketplace.* ☎ *808/988-6161. $.*

Take East Manoa Rd. to Oahu Ave. and turn left, then left again at University and get on H-1 West to Exit 22, Vineyard Blvd. Bus: 6, transfer to City Express B.

❹ ★★ Foster Botanical Garden. The giant trees that tower over the main terrace of this leafy oasis were planted in the 1850s by William Hillebrand, a German physician and botanist, on royal land leased from Queen Emma. Today, this 14-acre (5.6ha) public garden, on the north edge of Chinatown, is a living museum of plants, some rare and endangered, collected from the tropical regions of the world. Of

Cannonball tree at Foster Botanical Garden.

special interest are 26 "Exceptional Trees" protected by state law, a large palm collection, a primitive cycad garden, and a hybrid orchid collection. ⏱ 2–3 hrs. 50 N. Vineyard Blvd. (at Nuuanu Ave.). ☎ 808/522-7066. www.co.honolulu.hi.us/parks/hbg/fbg.htm. Admission $5 adults, $1 children 6–12. Daily 9am–4pm; guided tours Mon–Fri at 1pm (reservations recommended).

To get back to Waikiki drive towards Diamond Head on Vineyard Blvd., then turn right on Liliha St. Merge on to H-1 East into Waikiki. Bus: B City Express.

Day 2

Take H-1 from Waikiki to H-2, which becomes Kamehameha Hwy. (Hwy. 99). Turn right at California Ave. Bus: City Express B, transfer to 62.

⑤ Wahiawa Botanical Garden.

Originally begun as an experimental arboretum by sugar planters in the 1920s, this 27-acre (11ha) tropical rainforest garden provides a cool, moist environment for native Hawaiian plants, palms, aroids, tree ferns, heliconias, calatheas, and epiphytic plants. Guided tours can be arranged (call in advance), but there's probably no need for it unless you're an avid gardener. Bring mosquito repellant.

⏱ 1½–2hrs. 1396 California Ave. (at Iliwa Dr.), Wahiawa. ☎ (808) 621-7321. Free admission. Daily 9am–4pm.

Continue on Kamehameha Hwy. to the Dole Plantation, 3 miles (5km) past Wahiawa. Bus: 62, transfer to 52.

⑥ kids Dole Pineapple Plantation.

This rest stop/retail outlet/exhibit area also has an interesting self-guided tour through 8 minigardens totaling about 1½ acres (.6ha). The Plantation also has a single-engine diesel locomotive that takes a 22-minute tour around 2¼ miles (3.6km) of the plantation's grounds, and the Pineapple Garden Maze, which covers more than 2 acres (.8ha) with a 1.7-mile (3km) hibiscus-lined path. ⏱ 1–2 hrs. 64–1550 Kamehameha Hwy. ☎ 808/621-8408. www.dole-plantation.com. Admission to gardens $4 adults, $3.25 kids (4–12); train tickets $7.75 adults, $5.75 kids; pineapple maze $6 adults, $4 kids. Daily 9am–5:30pm.

Continue north on Kamehameha Hwy. At the traffic circle make a left into Haleiwa. Bus: 52.

⑦ ★ kids Matsumoto Shave Ice.

Take a break to enjoy a cool Hawaiian treat. See p 16, bullet ⑪.

Wahiawa Botanical Garden is a lovely place for a stroll.

Continue north on Kamehameha Hwy. Bus: 52.

8 ★ kids Waimea Valley Audubon Center. This 1,875-acre (759ha) park (home to 36 botanical gardens, with about 6,000 rare species of plants and numerous Hawaiian archeological sites) has until recently been under the management of the National Audubon Society, which provided well-marked trails and educational exhibits in this quiet oasis. As we went to press, the National Audubon Society has said it is pulling out of managing the park, leaving the valley's future up in the air. I recommend calling ahead to check on hours and admission prices. ⏱ *2–3 hrs. 59–864 Kamehameha Hwy. (Waimea Valley Rd.).* ☎ *808/638-9199. www.audubon. org/local/sanctuary/Brochures/ Waimea.html. Admission $8 adults, $5 children 4–12 and seniors. Daily 10am–5:30pm.*

Continue on Kamehameha Hwy. for 30 miles (48km), then turn right on Pulama Rd. Bus: 52, which becomes 55 (stay on board), then walk about a mile (1.6km) uphill from the stop.

9 Senator Fong's Plantation & Gardens. Senator Hiram Fong, the first Chinese American elected to the U.S. Senate, served 17 years before retiring to this 725-acre (293ha) tropical garden. The landscape you see today is very much like what early Polynesians saw hundreds of years ago, with forests of kukui, hala, koa, and ohia-'ai (mountain apple). Ti and pili grass still cover the slopes. It's definitely worth the hour guided tour. ⏱ *1 hr. 47–285 Pulama Rd., Kaneohe.* ☎ *808/239-6775. www.fonggarden.net. Admission $15 adults, $13 seniors, $9 children 5–12. Daily 10am–2pm.*

Turn right back on Kamehameha Hwy. Continue on Kahekili Hwy.,

then turn left on Kulukeoe St. and right on Keneke St. Turn left to stay on Keneke St., then right on Anoi Rd. and right on Luluku Rd. Bus: 55 on Kamehameha Hwy.; it's about a mile walk to the visitor center.

10 ★ Hoomaluhia Botanical Gardens. This 400-acre (162ha) botanical garden at the foot of the steepled Koolau Mountains is the perfect place for a picnic. Its name means "a peaceful refuge," and that's exactly what the Army Corps of Engineers created when they installed a flood-control project here, which resulted in a 32-acre (13ha) freshwater lake and garden. The gardens feature geographical groupings of plantings from the major tropical regions around the world, with a special emphasis on native Hawaiian plants. ⏱ *2–3 hrs. 45–680 Luluku Rd. (Visitor Center), Kaneohe.* ☎ *808/233-7323. www.co. honolulu.hi.us/parks/hbg/hmbg.htm. Free admission. Daily 9am–4pm. Guided nature hikes Sat 10am and Sun 1pm.*

Continue on Luluku Rd., then turn right on Kamehameha Hwy. (Hwy. 83). Turn right on Pali Hwy. then take H-1 East back to Waikiki. Bus: 55, transfer to City Express B.

Ti leaves.

Honolulu for **Art Lovers**

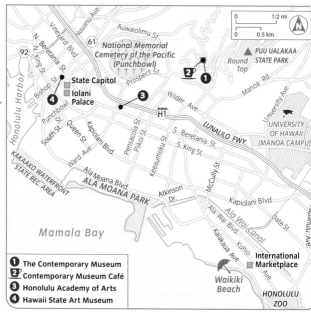

1 The Contemporary Museum
2 Contemporary Museum Café
3 Honolulu Academy of Arts
4 Hawaii State Art Museum

Even if you're not a die-hard art lover, you won't regret giving up a day for this tour. Hawaii's top three cultural galleries aren't just depositories of art work—each is an incredible edifice in its own right. It's a part of Hawaii you won't want to miss. START: **Waikiki. Length: 11 miles (18km).**

Take McCully St. out of Waikiki, then turn left on Dole St. and right on Punahou St. Turn left on Nehoa St., right on Makiki St., then left on Makiki Heights Dr. Bus: 4, then about a ¾ mile (1.2km) walk up Makiki Heights Dr.

1 ★★ **kids** The Contemporary Museum. Honolulu's best contemporary art gallery is nestled up on the slopes of Tantalus, one of Honolulu's upscale residential communities, and is renowned for its 3 acres (1.2ha) of Asian gardens (with reflecting pools, sun-drenched terraces, and views of Diamond Head. Even if

you don't venture inside any of the Museum's buildings, exploring the grounds alone is worth the trip. ⏱ 1½–2hrs. 2411 Makiki Heights Dr. (near Mott-Smith Dr.). ☎ 808/526-0232. www.tcmhi.org. Tickets: $5 for adults, $3 for seniors and students, and free for children 12 and under (The 3rd Thurs of each month is free.) Tues–Sat 10–4pm, Sun noon–4pm.

2 ★ Contemporary Museum Café. After you've wandered the grounds and the exhibits, treat yourself to the sinfully delicious

Shangri La in Hawaii

In the late 1930s, heiress Doris Duke developed her dream property and dubbed it "Shangri La." It reflects Duke's love of both Hawaii and the Middle East by featuring an extensive collection of Islamic art and architecture blended with Hawaii's sweeping ocean views, exotic gardens, and water features. Tours originate at the Honolulu Academy of Arts, 900 South Beretania Street (at Ward Ave.), and cost $25. Reservations are required. For more information, visit www.shangrilahawaii.org or call ☎ 808/532 DUKE.

flourless chocolate cake and a just-brewed latte at this intimate cafe. *Contemporary Museum, 2411 Makiki Heights Dr. (near Mott-Smith Dr.). ☎ 808/523-3362. www.tcmhi.org. $$.*

Turn left at Mott-Smith Dr. then right on Piikoi St., left on Pensacola St., and right on Beretania St. Bus: Walk 1 mile (1.6km) to the stop at Pensacola St. and Wilder Ave. to catch bus 18.

③ ★★★ kids Honolulu Academy of Arts. The state's only general fine-arts museum features one of the top Asian art collections in the country. Also on exhibit are American and European masters and prehistoric works of Mayan, Greek, and Hawaiian art. The museum's award-winning architecture is a

Antoine Bourdelle's La Grande Penelope at the Honolulu Academy of Arts.

paragon of graciousness, featuring magnificent courtyards, lily ponds, and sensitively designed galleries. ⏲ *2–3hrs. 900 S. Beretania St. (at Ward Ave.). ☎ 808/532-8700, or 808/532-8701 for recording. www.honoluluacademy.org. $7 adults, $4 students, seniors, and military personnel; children under 12 free. Tues–Sat 10am–4:30pm, Sun 1–5pm; tours Tues–Sat 11am and Sun 1:15pm.*

Drive Ewa on Beretania St. and turn left on Richards St. Park at a meter on the street. Bus: Walk about a half mile down Beretania St. to Punchbowl St., get on bus 13.

④ ★★ kids Hawaii State Art Museum. This historic building was once the Royal Hawaiian Hotel, built in 1872 during the reign of King Kamehameha V. All of the 360 works on display were created by artists who live in Hawaii. ⏲ *2–3hrs. 250 S. Hotel St. (at Richards St.). ☎ 808/586-0900. www.state.hi.us/sfca. Free admission. Tues–Sat 10am–4pm.*

From Richards St. turn left on King St., then take a slight right at Kapiolani Blvd., right on Piikoi, and left on Ala Moana Blvd. into Waikiki. Bus: Walk 1 block toward the ocean to King St., then walk toward Diamond Head 2 blocks to Punchbowl St. to catch City Express B.

The Best Special Interest Tours

Romantic Honolulu & Oahu

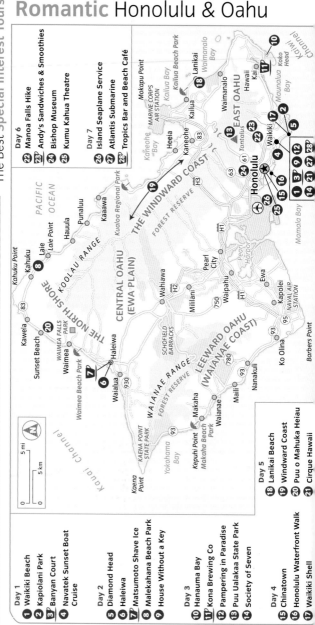

Day 1
1. Waikiki Beach
2. Kapiolani Park
3. Banyan Court
4. Navatek Sunset Boat Cruise

Day 2
5. Diamond Head
6. Haleiwa
7. Matsumoto Shave Ice
8. Malekahana Beach Park
9. House Without a Key

Day 3
10. Hanauma Bay
11. Kona Brewing Co
12. Pampering in Paradise
13. Puu Ualakaa State Park
14. Society of Seven

Day 4
15. Chinatown
16. Honolulu Waterfront Walk
17. Waikiki Shell

Day 5
18. Lanikai Beach
19. Windward Coast
20. Puu o Mahuka Heiau
21. Cirque Hawaii

Day 6
22. Manoa Falls Hike
23. Andy's Sandwiches & Smoothies
24. Bishop Museum
25. Kumu Kahua Theatre

Day 7
26. Island Seaplane Service
27. Atlantis Submarine
28. Tropics Bar and Beach Café

What could be more romantic that a vacation in Waikiki, where the gentle breezes caress your skin, the sensuous aroma of tropical flowers wafts through the air, and the relaxing sound of the rolling surf beckons lovers from around the globe? Below is a suggested tour for discovering not only the exotic isle of Oahu, but also discovering each other. START: **Waikiki. Length: 7 days and 271 miles (436km).**

Day 1

1 ★★★ Waikiki Beach. Your vacation starts when the warm sand covers your toes and the salt air kisses your face. Take a stroll hand-in-hand down this famous beach. *See p 159.*

Walk down Kalakaua Ave.

2 ★★ Kapiolani Park. If you aren't too tired from your trip, take a stroll around this tropical park. Stop to smell the flowers and kiss your sweetie. See my tour of the park beginning on p 84.

Walk back to Waikiki on Kalakaua Ave. Just across the street from Kaiulani St.

3 Banyan Court. After all that walking, sit oceanside at this outdoor bar and order an exotic drink like a mai tai. *Moana Surfrider. 2365 Kalakaua Ave. (Kaiulani St.). ☎ 808/ 921-4600. $$.*

From Waikiki take Ala Moana Blvd. to Aloha Tower Marketplace, Pier 6. Bus: 19 or 20.

4 ★ Navatek I. Spend your first evening in Paradise watching the sun set in the Pacific offshore on a dinner cruise. *See p 15, bullet 9.*

Day 2

Drive to the intersection of Diamond Head Rd. and 18th Ave. Follow the road through the tunnel (which is closed 6pm–6am) and park in the lot. Bus: 58 (from the Ala Moana Shopping Center).

5 ★ Diamond Head. You'll probably be up early on your first day in Hawaii before you get used to the time difference. So get up and greet the sun by hiking up to Waikiki's most famous landmark. You'll get a bird's-eye view of the island from atop this 760-foot extinct volcano. *See p 163.*

A couple enjoying some time on the beach.

Float among the abundant brightly colored fish in Hanauma Bay.

Take H-1 west out of Waikiki, then take the H-2 north exit (Exit 8A) towards Mililani/Wahiwa. After 7 miles (11km) H2 becomes Kamehameha Hwy. (Hwy. 80). Look for the turnoff to Haleiwa town. Bus: 19, then transfer to no. 52.

6 ★★★ **kids Haleiwa.** Spend the rest of your morning exploring this famous North Shore surfing town. *See p 136, bullet* **4**.

7 ★ **kids Matsumoto Shave Ice.** For a tropical taste of the islands, stop at this nearly 50-year-old shop where Hawaii's rendition of a snow cone is served. *See p 16, bullet* **11**.

Continue down Kamehameha Hwy. Bus: 52.

8 ★★★ **Malaekahana Bay State Recreation Area.** Take a picnic lunch to this secluded beach park. (I suggest getting a burger or sandwich from Kua Aina, 66-160 Kamehameha Hwy. in Haleiwa, ☎ 808/637-6067.) If you go during the week, you may have a stretch of beach all to yourself. Plan to spend the entire afternoon here relaxing on the beach, swimming, or snorkeling. *See p 165.*

Retrace your route back to Honolulu: Take Kamehameha Hwy. (Hwy. 83) to Hwy. 99 to H-2 to H-1 to Waikiki. Bus: 52, transfer to City Express B.

9 ★★★ **House Without a Key.** Watch the sunset from the beach at this exquisitely beautiful resort in Waikiki. *See p 129, bullet* **3**.

Day 3
From Waikiki, take H-1 East, which becomes the Kalaniaole Hwy. Look for the Koko Head Regional Park on the left; the beach is on the right (oceanside). Avoid the crowds by going early, about 8am, on a weekday morning; once the parking lot's full, you're out of luck. The Hanauma Bay Shuttle Bus runs from Waikiki to Hanauma Bay every half-hour from 8:45am to 1pm. You can catch it at any city bus stop in Waikiki. It returns every hour from noon to 4pm.

10 **Hanauma Bay.** Rent a mask, snorkel, and fins and head out to Oahu's premiere snorkeling area to discover the incredible beauty of Hawaii's underwater world. ***Note:*** the beach is closed on Tuesdays. *See p 175.*

Oahu's spas offer unique Hawaiian treatments.

The Lei

There's nothing like a lei. The stunning tropical beauty of the delicate garland, the deliciously sweet fragrance of the blossoms, the way the flowers curl softly around your neck. There's no doubt about it: Getting lei'd in Hawaii is a sensuous experience. Leis are much more than just a decorative necklace of flowers; they're also one of the nicest ways to say hello, good-bye, congratulations, I salute you, my sympathies are with you, or I love you. The custom of giving leis can be traced back to Hawaii's very roots; according to chants, the first lei was given by Hiiaka, the sister of the volcano goddess Pele, who presented Pele with a lei of lehua blossoms on a beach in Puna. Leis are the perfect symbol for the islands: They're given in the moment and their fragrance and beauty are enjoyed in the moment, but even after they fade, their spirit of aloha lives on.

Return to Kalanianaole Hwy. (Hwy. 72) heading back to Waikiki.

11 **Kona Brewing Co.** Stop by this local brewing company to sample some of their locally made beer, like the Fire Rock Pale Ale or the Lilikoi Wheat Ale (or the non-alcoholic Gingerade, made from organic ginger). *Koko Marina Center, 7192 Kalanianaole Hwy. (Lunalilo Home Rd.).* ☎ *808/394-5662. $$.*

Trace your route back to Waikiki.

12 **Pampering in Paradise.** Spend the afternoon at a spa getting your body pampered. For my top spa picks, see the box "Pampering in Paradise" on p 105.

From Waikiki, take Ala Wai Blvd. to McCully St., turn right, and drive mauka (inland) beyond the H-1 on-ramps to Wilder St. Turn left and go to Makiki St. Turn right and continue onward and upward about 3 miles (4.8km).

13 ★ **Puu Ualakaa State Park.** One of the island's most romantic

sunset views is from this 1,048-foot (27m) hill named for sweet potatoes. Get there before sunset to see the panoramic view of the entire coastline. *See p 21, bullet* **6**.

Retrace your route to back to Waikiki.

14 ★ **Society of Seven.** Spend the evening with your honey at this popular nightclub featuring a blend of skits, Broadway hits, popular music, and costumed musical acts. *See p 30.*

Chinatown is one of the best places to shop for leis.

Day 4

⓯ ★★★ Chinatown. Explore this exotic neighborhood with the help of the tour starting on p 72. Be sure to shop for a lei for your sweetie.

Walk down Bethel St. toward the ocean to the Aloha Tower.

⓰ ★ Honolulu Waterfront Walk. Continue your day of exploring Honolulu with the tour on p 76. But start out by going up to the top of the Aloha Tower and seeing Honolulu from this bird's-eye view. Finish your tour of the Waterfront by having dinner at Cassis Honolulu (see p 92).

Take Ala Wai Blvd. into Waikiki. TheBus: 19 or 20.

⓱ ★★ Waikiki Shell. Find out if there's anything playing at Waikiki's best outdoor venue, this open amphitheater in Kapiolani Park. *See p 86.*

Day 5
Take the H-1 to the Pali Hwy. (Hwy. 61) to Kailua, where it then becomes Kailua Rd. as it proceeds through town. At Kalaheo Ave., turn right and follow the coast about 2 miles (3.2km) to Kailua Beach Park; just past it, turn left

at the T-intersection and drive uphill on Aalapapa Dr., a one-way street that loops back as Mokulua Dr. Park on Mokulua, and walk down any of the eight public-access lanes to the shore. Bus: 20, transfer to 57, transfer to 70.

⓲ ★★ Lanikai Beach. Escape to the windward side and spend the morning (when the sun is the best) at this tiny, off–the-beaten-track beach. *See p 155.*

From Lanikai take Kawailoa Rd., which becomes Kalaheo Ave., which becomes Kaneohe Bay Dr. Turn left on Kamehameha Hwy. (Hwy. 83). Bus: 57, transfer to 55, transfer to 52.

⓳ ★★ Windward Coast. After a morning at the beach, take a drive along the windy windward coast. Have fun trying to pronounce the tongue-twisting names of the towns. See the tour starting on p 140.

From Kahana continue on Kamehameha Hwy. (Hwy. 83) to Pupukea Rd., just after Pupukea Beach Park. Turn toward the mountain on Pupukea Rd. to Puu o Mahuka Heiau.

Lanikai Beach.

Steal a kiss and a great photo op at Manoa Falls.

(1.2km; one-way) hike in a warm, tropical rainforest just minutes from Waikiki. In less than an hour you'll be at the idyllic Manoa Falls. *See p 165.*

Retrace your route back down Manoa Rd., turn left on Oahu Ave., then left again on E. Manoa Rd.

23 ★ **kids Andy's Sandwiches & Smoothies.** After hiking in the rainforest, stop by this neighborhood eatery and grab a smoothie and a healthy snack (try the mango muffins). *2904 E. Manoa Rd., opposite Manoa Marketplace.* ☎ *808/988-6161. $.*

Drive down E. Manoa Rd., turn left on Oahu Ave., take a slight left on University Ave., then get on H-1 West. Take exit 20A (Likelike Hwy.), then turn right on Bernice St. Bus: 5, transfer to City Express B.

24 ★★★ **Bishop Museum.** Spend the rest of the day wandering through this treasure trove of Hawaiian culture, flora, and fauna. *See p 15, bullet* **7**.

Almost half of the 20,000 couples who get married in Hawaii every year come from somewhere else.

20 ★ **Puu o Mahuka Heiau.** It will take you about 30 to 45 minutes to drive here from Kahana Bay; time your drive so you can be at this historic heiau (temple) as the sun sets. *See p 44, bullet* **20**.

Take Kamehameha Hwy. (Hwy. 83) to Hwy. 99, to H-2, to H-1, to Waikiki. Bus: 52, transfer to City Express B.

21 ★ **Cirque Hawaii.** Back in Waikiki, watching Hawaii's answer to Cirque du Soleil will leave you breathless. *See p 130.*

Day 6

Take McCully St. out of Waikiki toward the mountains. Turn right onto Kapiolani Blvd., then left onto University Ave. and drive through the University of Hawaii campus. Turn right onto Manoa Rd. The trailhead, marked by a footbridge, is at the end of Manoa Rd., past Lyon Arboretum. Park in the Paradise Park neighborhood. TheBus no. 5.

22 **Manoa Falls Hike.** Take your sweetheart on this easy, ¾-mile

Getting Married in Paradise

Honolulu and Waikiki are a great place for a wedding. Not only does the entire island exude romance and natural beauty, but after the ceremony, you're only a few steps away from the perfect honeymoon.

The easiest way to plan your wedding is to let someone else handle it at the resort or hotel where you'll be staying. Most Waikiki resorts and hotels have wedding coordinators who can plan everything from a simple (relatively) low-cost wedding to an extravaganza that people will talk about for years.

You will need a marriage license: Contact the Marriage License Office, Room 101 (1st floor) of the Health Department Building, 1250 Punchbowl St. (corner of Beretania and Punchbowl sts.; ☎ 808/586-4545; www.state.hi.us/doh/records/vr_marri.html). Open Monday through Friday from 8am to 4pm. Once in Hawaii, the prospective bride and groom must go together to the marriage-licensing agent to get a license. A license costs $60 and is good for 30 days. The only requirements for a marriage license are that both parties are 15 years of age or older (couples 15–17 years old must have proof of age, written consent of both parents, and the written approval of the judge of the family court) and are not more closely related than first cousins.

From Bernice turn right on Houghtailing St., then left at N. King St. Turn right on Nuuanu Ave., then left on Merchant St. Bus: 1.

㉕ ★★ Kumu Kahua Theatre. Check out a local play at this intimate theater, which features local playwrights. *See p 132.*

Continue on Merchant St., then turn right on Bishop St. Go left at Ala Moana Blvd. back to Waikiki. Bus: B (City Express B).

Day 7
㉖ ★★ Island Seaplane Service. On your last day on Oahu, take to the air and see this magnificent island from a seaplane. *See p 30.*

Retrace your route down Lagoon Dr., then turn right on Nimitz Hwy., which becomes Ala Moana Blvd. into Waikiki. Bus: 31, transfer to 19.

㉗ ★★★ Atlantis Submarine. After seeing the island from the air, plunge beneath the waves (without getting wet) and see the island from the Neptunian prospective. *See p 182.*

Walk back to the Hilton Hawaiian Village Resort.

㉘ Tropics Bar and Beach Café. Plop down in this beachfront outdoor cafe and order a latte or a mai tai to toast your Hawaiian vacation and start planning your next trip to Paradise. *Hilton Hawaiian Village, beachfront Alii Tower, 2005 Kalia Rd.* ☎ *808/949-4321. $$.* ●

4

The Best of
Honolulu & Waikiki

Historic **Chinatown**

1. Hotel Street
2. Bank of Hawaii
3. Yat Tung Chow Noodle Factory
4. Viet Hoa Chinese Herb Shop
5. Oahu Market Place
6. River Street Pedestrian Mall
7. Chinatown Cultural Plaza
8. Izumo Taishakyo Mission Cultural Hall
9. Kuan Yin Temple
10. Maunakea Street
11. Shung Chong Yuein
12. Lai Fong Department Store
13. Pegge Hopper Gallery
14. Hawaii Theatre

Honolulu's historic Chinatown is a mix of Asian cultures all packed into a small area where tangy spices rule the cuisine, open-air markets have kept out the mini-malls, and the way to good health is through acupuncture and herbalists. The jumble of streets bustles with residents and visitors from all over the world; a cacophony of sounds, from the high-pitched bleating of vendors in the market to the lyrical dialects of the retired men "talking story" over a game of mah-jongg. No trip to Honolulu is complete without a visit to this exotic, historic district. Plan at least 2 hours, more if you love to browse. START: **North Hotel and Maunakea streets. Parking is scarce, so I recommend taking bus 2 or 20. If you insist on driving, take Ala Moana Blvd. and turn right on Smith St.; make a left on Beretania St. and a left again at Maunakea St. The city parking garage is on the Ewa (west) side of Maunakea St., between North Hotel and North King streets.**

1 ★ kids **Hotel Street.** During World War II, Hotel Street was synonymous with good times. Pool halls and beer parlors lined the blocks, and prostitutes were plentiful. Nowadays,

Previous page: Waikiki Beach and Diamond Head.

the more nefarious establishments have been replaced with small shops, from art galleries to specialty boutiques. Wandering up and down this street, head to the intersection with Smith Street. On the Diamond Head

You can easily spend half a day exploring the colorful streets of Chinatown.

(east) side of Smith, you'll notice stones in the sidewalk; they were taken from the sandalwood ships, which came to Hawaii empty of cargo except for these stones, which were used as ballast on the trip over. *Hotel Street, between Maunakea St. and Bethal St.*

When you've finished exploring Hotel St., head back to Maunakea St. and turn toward the ocean.

2 kids **Bank of Hawaii.** This unusual-looking bank is not the conservative edifice you might expect—it's guarded by two fire-breathing-dragon statues. *101 N. King St. (Maunakea St.).* ☎ *808/532-2480.*

Turn right onto King St.

3 ★ kids **Yat Tung Chow Noodle Factory.** The delicious, delicate noodles that star in numerous Asian dishes are made here. There aren't any tours of the factory, but you can look through the window, past the white cloud of flour that hangs in the air, and watch as dough is fed into rollers at one end of the noodle machines, and perfectly cut noodles emerge at the other end. *150 N. King St. (Maunakea St.).* ☎ *808/531-7982. Mon–Sat 6am–3pm.*

4 kids **Viet Hoa Chinese Herb Shop.** Here, Chinese herbalists act as both doctors and dispensers of herbs. There's a wall of tiny drawers all labeled in Chinese characters; the herbalist pulls out objects ranging from dried flowers to mashed antelope antler. The patient then takes the concoction home to brew into a strong tea. *162 N. King St. (Maunakea St.).* ☎ *808/523-5499. Mon–Sat 8:30am–5pm; Sun 8:30am–2pm.*

Cross to the south side of King St., where, just west of Kekaulike St., you'll come to the most-visited part of Chinatown, the open-air market.

5 ★★ kids **Oahu Market Place.** Those interested in Asian cooking will find all the necessary ingredients here, including pigs' heads, poultry (some still squawking), fresh octopi, pungent fish sauce, and 1,000-year-old eggs. The friendly vendors are happy to explain their wares and give instructions on how to prepare these exotic treats. The market has been at this spot since 1904. ⏲ *1 hr. N. King & Kekaulike sts. Daily 6am–6pm.*

Follow King down to River St. and turn right toward the mountains. A range of inexpensive restaurants lines River St. from King to Beretania sts. You can get the best Vietnamese and Filipino food in town in these blocks, but go early—lines for lunch start at 11:15am.

6 kids **River Street Pedestrian Mall.** The statue of Chinese revolutionary leader Sun Yat-sen marks the beginning of this wide mall, which borders the Nuuanu Stream. It's lined with shade trees, park benches, and tables where seniors gather to play mah-jongg and checkers. There are plenty of takeout restaurants nearby if you'd like to eat lunch outdoors. *N. Beretania St. to Vineyard Blvd.*

7 ★ kids **Chinatown Cultural Plaza.** This modern complex is

Bargaining: A Way of Life in Chinatown

In Chinatown, nearly every purchase—from chicken's feet to an 18-carat gold necklace—is made by bargaining. It's the way of life for most Asian countries—and part of the fun and charm of shopping in Chinatown. The main rule of thumb when negotiating a price is respect. The customer must have respect for the merchant and understand that he's in business to make money. This respect is coupled with the understanding that the customer does not want to be taken advantage of and would like the best deal possible.

Keep in mind two rules when bargaining: cash and volume. Don't even begin haggling if you're not planning to pay cash. The second you pull out a credit card (if the merchant or vendor will even accept it), all deals are off. And remember, the more you buy, the better the deal the merchant will extend to you.

Significant savings can be realized for high-ticket items like jewelry. The price of gold in Chinatown is based on the posted price of the *tael* (a unit of weight, slightly more than an ounce), which is listed for 14-, 18-, and 24-carat gold, plus the value of the labor. There's no negotiating on the tael price, but the cost of the labor is where the negotiations begin.

filled with shops featuring everything from tailors to calligraphers (most somewhat more expensive than their street-side counterparts), as well as numerous restaurants, Asian magazine vendors, and even a small post office for those who want to mail cards home with the "Chinatown" postmark. The best

Shop for delicacies like dragon fruit at Chinatown markets.

feature of the plaza is the **Moongate Stage** in the center, the site of many cultural presentations, especially around the Chinese New Year. 🕐 *30 min. 100 N. Beretania St. (Vineyard Blvd.).* ☎ *808/521-4934.*

Continue up the River Street Mall and cross the Nuuanu Stream via the bridge at Kukui St.

8 kids Izumo Taishakyo Mission Cultural Hall. This small, wooden Shinto shrine, built in 1923, houses a male deity (look for the X-shaped crosses on the top). Members of the faith ring the bell out front as an act of purification when they come to pray. Inside the temple is a 100-pound sack of rice, symbolizing good health. 🕐 *15 min. 215 N. Kukui St. (Kukui St.).* ☎ *808/538-7778.*

Walk a block toward the mountains to Vineyard Blvd.; cross back over

The Izumo Shinto shrine.

Nuuanu Stream, past the entrance of Foster Botanical Gardens.

9 kids Kuan Yin Temple. This Buddhist temple, painted in a brilliant red with a green ceramic-tiled roof, is dedicated to Kuan Yin Bodhisattva, the goddess of mercy, whose statue towers in the prayer hall. The temple is still a house of worship, not an exhibit, so enter with respect and leave your shoes outside. You may see people burning paper "money" for prosperity and good luck, or leaving flowers and fruits at the altar (gifts to the goddess). 🕐 *15 min. 170 N. Vineyard Blvd. (Nuunau St.).* ☎ *808/533-6361.*

Continue down Vineyard and then turn right (toward the ocean) on:

10 ★★ kids Maunakea Street. Numerous lei shops line this colorful street, which is this the best place in all of Hawaii to get a deal on leis. The size, color, and design of the leis made here are exceptional. *Between Beretania and King sts.*

11′ ★ kids Shung Chong Yuein. Grab an Asian pastry (my picks: moon cakes and almond cookies) at this tempting shop, which also has a wide selection of dried and sugared candies (ginger, pineapple, and lotus root) that you can eat as you stroll or give as an exotic gift to friends back home. *1027 Maunakea St. (near Hotel St.).* ☎ *808/531-1983. Daily 6am–4:30pm. $.*

Turn left on Hotel St. and walk in the Diamond Head (east) direction to:

12 ★ Lai Fong Department Store. Before you enter this classic Chinatown store, owned by the same family for more than 80 years, check out the sidewalks on Nuuanu Avenue—they're made of granite blocks used as ballast on ships that brought tea from China to Hawaii in the 1800s. This store sells everything from precious antiques to god-awful knickknacks to rare Hawaiian postcards from the early 1900s. But it has built its reputation on its fabulous selection of Chinese silks, brocades, and custom dresses. *118 Nuuanu Ave. (Hotel St).* ☎ *808/537-3497. Mon–Sat 9am–7:30pm.*

13 ★ Pegge Hopper Gallery. One of Hawaii's best known artists. See p. 115.

At Pauahi St., turn toward Diamond Head and walk up to Bethel St.

14 ★★★ kids Hawaii Theatre. This restored 1920 Art Deco theater is a work of art in itself. It hosts a variety of programs, from the Hawaii International Film Festival to Hawaiian concerts. *1130 Bethel St. (at Pauahi St.).* ☎ *808/528-0506.*

You'll find leis of all description in the shops on Maunakea Street.

The Honolulu **Waterfront**

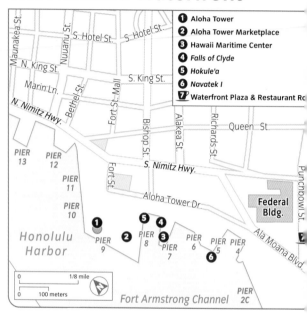

1. Aloha Tower
2. Aloha Tower Marketplace
3. Hawaii Maritime Center
4. *Falls of Clyde*
5. *Hokule'a*
6. *Navatek I*
7. Waterfront Plaza & Restaurant Ro

Honolulu Harbor

Fort Armstrong Channel

0   1/8 mile
0   100 meters

Honolulu's waterfront area has played a vital role in the city's history. King Kamehameha I moved his royal court here in 1809 to keep an eye on the burgeoning trade from the numerous ships that were coming here. The royal residence was at the makai end of Bethel Street, just 1 block from the start of our tour at the Aloha Tower. Plan to spend 2 to 3 hours on this tour. START: **Aloha Tower.** Take Ala Moana Boulevard in the Ewa direction to Nimitz Highway, then turn left. There is parking on the ocean side of Nimitz at Bishop Street. Bus: 19 or 20.

---

1 ★ kids Aloha Tower. Built in 1926 (for the then-outrageous sum of $160,000), this 184-foot (56m), 10-story tower (until 1959, the tallest structure in Hawaii) has clocks on all four of its sides with the word *aloha* under each clock. Aloha, which has come to mean both "hello" and "farewell," was the first thing steamship passengers saw when they entered Honolulu Harbor. In the days when

tourists arrived by steamer, "boat days" were a very big occasion. The Royal Hawaiian band would be on hand to play, crowds would gather, flower leis were freely given, and Honolulu came to a standstill to greet the visitors. Go up the elevator inside the Aloha Tower to the 10th floor observation deck for a bird's-eye view that encompasses Diamond Head and Waikiki, the downtown and

Aloha Tower.

Chinatown areas, and the harbor coastline to the airport. On the ocean side you can see the harbor mouth, Sand Island, the Honolulu reef runway, and the Pearl Harbor entrance channel. ⏱ *15 min. 1 Aloha Tower Dr.* ☎ *808/ 528-5700. Daily 9am–5pm.*

❷ Aloha Tower Marketplace. In the early 1990s, city officials came up with the idea to renovate and

Diving helmet at the Hawaii Maritime Center.

restore the waterfront with shops, restaurants, and bars to bring back the feeling of "boat days." The two-story Aloha Tower Marketplace offers an array of cuisines, one-of-a-kind shops, and even a microbrewery. *1 Aloha Tower Dr.* ☎ *808/ 528-5700. Daily 9am–9pm.*

From the Aloha Tower Marketplace, walk in the Diamond Head direction along the waterfront to Pier 7.

❸ ★ kids Hawaii Maritime Center. *See p 22, bullet ❾.*

Moored next door is the:

❹ ★ kids Falls of Clyde. The world's only remaining fully rigged, four-masted ship is on display as a National Historic Landmark. Still afloat, the 266-foot (81m), iron-hulled ship was built in 1878 in Glasgow, Scotland. Matson Navigation bought the ship in 1899 to carry sugar and passengers between Hilo and San Francisco. When that became economically unfeasible, in 1906 the boat was converted into a sail-driven oil tanker. After 1920, it was dismantled and became a floating oil depot for fishing boats in Alaska. She was headed for the scrap

The Falls of Clyde.

Next door.

⑤ ★ kids *Hokule'a*. If you're lucky, the 60-foot (18m) Polynesian canoe will be docked during your visit, but it's often out on jaunts. In 1976, this reproduction of the traditional double-hulled sailing canoe proved to the world that the Polynesians could have made the 6,000-mile (9,656km) round-trip from Tahiti to Hawaii, navigating only by the stars and the

In stark contrast to its neighbor, the Hokule'a, the Navatek *embodies cutting-edge naval engineering.*

pile when a group of Hawaiian residents raised the money to bring her back to Hawaii in 1963. Since then she has been totally restored, and now visitors can wander across her decks and through the cargo area below. ⏱ *30 min. Hawaii Maritime Center. Pier 7 (next to Aloha Tower).* ☎ *808/ 536-6373. Daily 8:30am–5pm.*

Hawaii's Early History

Paddling outrigger sailing canoes, the first ancestors of today's Hawaiians followed the stars, waves, and birds across the sea to Hawaii, which they called "the land of raging fire." Those first settlers were part of the great Polynesian migration that settled the vast triangle of islands stretching between New Zealand, Easter Island, and Hawaii. No one is sure when they arrived in Hawaii from Tahiti and the Marquesas Islands, some 2,500 miles (4,023km) to the south, but recent archaeological digs at the Maluuluolele Park on Maui date back to A.D. 700–900

All we have today are some archaeological finds, some scientific data, and ancient chants to tell the story of Hawaii's past. The chants, especially the *Kumulipo,* which is the chant of creation and the litany of genealogy of the *alii* (high-ranking chiefs) who ruled the islands, talk about comings and goings between Hawaii and the islands of the south, presumed to be Tahiti. In fact, the channel between Maui, Kahoolawe, and Lanai is called *Kealaikahiki* or "the pathway to Tahiti."

wave patterns. Living on an open deck (9 ft. wide × 40 ft. long/2.7m × 12m), the crew of a dozen, along with a traditional navigator from an island in the Northern Pacific, made the successful voyage. Since then there has been growing interest among native islanders in learning the art of navigation. ⏱ *15 min. Hawaii Maritime Center. Pier 7 (next to Aloha Tower).* ☎ *808/ 536-6373. Daily 8:30am–5pm.*

Next door, at Pier 6.

6 ★ **kids** *Navatek I.* In contrast to the ancient Polynesian sailing canoe next door, *Navatek I* is the latest development in naval engineering. The 140-foot-long (43m) vessel isn't even called a boat; it's actually a SWATH (Small Waterplane Area Twin Hull) vessel. That means the ship's superstructure—the part you ride on—rests on twin torpedo-like hulls that cut through the water so you don't bob like a cork. It's the smoothest ride in town and guarantees you will not get seasick or spill your mai tai. *Pier 6.* ☎ *808/973-1311.*

From May to September, Hawaiians keep the tradition of outrigger canoeing alive with a series of races.

Walk down Ala Moana Blvd. and turn mauka at Punchbowl.

7 ★ **kids** **Waterfront Plaza & Restaurant Row.** Shops, theaters, and eateries serving an array of cuisines (from gourmet Hawaii regional to burgers) fill this block-long complex. This is a great place to stop for lunch or dinner, or for a cool drink at the end of your walk. *500 Ala Moana Blvd. (between Punchbowl and South sts).*

Historians think Tahitians sailed to Hawaii on a canoe much like the Hokule'a.

Historic Honolulu

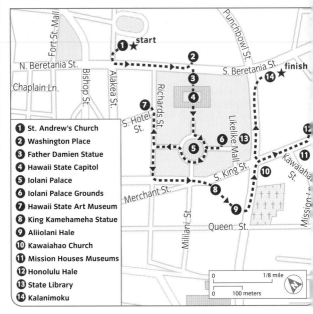

1. St. Andrew's Church
2. Washington Place
3. Father Damien Statue
4. Hawaii State Capitol
5. Iolani Palace
6. Iolani Palace Grounds
7. Hawaii State Art Museum
8. King Kamehameha Statue
9. Aliiolani Hale
10. Kawaiahao Church
11. Mission Houses Museums
12. Honolulu Hale
13. State Library
14. Kalanimoku

The 1800s were a turbulent time in Hawaii. By the end of the 1790s, Kamehameha the Great had united all the islands. Foreigners then began arriving by ship—first explorers, then merchants, and in 1820, missionaries. By 1872, the monarchy had run through the Kamehameha line and in 1873 David Kalakaua was elected to the throne. Known as the "Merrie Monarch," Kalakaua redefined the monarchy by going on a world tour, building Iolani Palace, having a European-style coronation, and throwing extravagant parties. By the end of the 1800s, however, the foreign sugar growers and merchants had become extremely powerful in Hawaii. With the assistance of the U.S. Marines, they orchestrated the overthrow of Queen Liliuokalani, Hawaii's last reigning monarch, in 1893. The United States declared Hawaii a territory in 1898. You can witness the remnants of these turbulent years in just a few short blocks. Allow 2 to 3 hours for this tour. START: **St. Andrew's Church, Beretania and Alakea sts. Take Ala Moana Boulevard in the Ewa direction to Nimitz Highway. Turn right on the next street on your right (Alakea St.). After you cross Beretania St., there's a parking garage across from St. Andrews Church. Bus: 1, 2, 3, 4, 11, 12, or 50.**

Stained-glass window at St. Andrew's.

❶ St. Andrew's Church. The Hawaiian monarchs were greatly influenced by the royals in Europe. When King Kamehameha IV saw the grandeur of the Church of England, he decided to build his own cathedral. He and Queen Emma founded the Anglican Church of Hawaii in 1858. The king, however, didn't live to see the church completed; he died on St. Andrew's Day, 4 years before King Kamehameha V oversaw the laying of the cornerstone in 1867. This French-Gothic structure was shipped in pieces from England and reassembled here. Don't miss the floor-to-eaves hand-blown stained-glass window that faces the setting sun. In the glass is a mural of Reverend Thomas Staley (Hawaii's first bishop), King Kamehameha IV, and Queen Emma. *224 Queen Sq. (between Beretania and Alakea sts.).* ☎ *808/524-2822.*

Next, walk down Beretania St. in the Diamond Head direction.

❷ Washington Place. Once the residence of the Governor of Hawaii (sorry, no tours; just peek through the iron fence), this house occupies a distinguished place in Hawaii's history. The Greek revival–style home was built in 1842 by a U.S. sea captain named John Dominis. The sea captain's son, also named John, married a beautiful Hawaiian princess, Lydia Kapaakea, who later became Hawaii's last queen, Liliuokalani. When the queen was overthrown by U.S. businessmen in 1893, she moved out of Iolani Palace and into her husband's inherited home, Washington Place, where she lived until her death in 1917. On the left side of the building, near the sidewalk, is a plaque inscribed with the words to one of the most popular songs written by Queen Liliuokalani, "Aloha Oe" ("Farewell to Thee"). *Beretania St. (between Queen Emma and Punchbowl sts.).* ☎ *808/586-0240.*

Cross the street and walk to the front of the Hawaii State Capitol.

❸ ★ Father Damien Statue. The people of Hawaii have never forgotten the sacrifice this Belgian priest made to help the sufferers of leprosy when he volunteered to work with them in exile on the Kalaupapa Peninsula on the island of Molokai. After 16 years of service,

Washington Place.

The Hawaii State Capitol.

Father Damien died of leprosy, at the age of 49. *Beretania St. (between Queen Emma and Punchbowl sts.).*

Behind Father Damien's statue.

4 ★ **kids Hawaii State Capitol.** Here's where Hawaii's state legislators work from mid-January to the end of April every year. The building's unusual design has palm tree–shaped pillars, two cone-shaped chambers (representing volcanoes) for the legislative bodies, and in the inner courtyard, a 600,000-tile mosaic of the sea created by a local artist. A reflecting pool (representing the sea) surrounds the entire structure. You are welcome to go into the rotunda and see the woven hangings and murals at the entrance, or take the elevator up to the fifth floor for a spectacular view. *415 Beretania St.* ☎ *808/586-0034.*

Walk down Richards St. toward the ocean.

5 ★ **kids Iolani Palace.** If you want to really understand Hawaii, I suggest taking the "Grand Tour" of this royal palace. *See p 22, bullet* **10**.

6 ★ **kids Iolani Palace Grounds.** You can wander around the grounds at no charge. The ticket window to the palace and the gift shop are in the former barracks of the Royal Household Guards. The domed pavilion on the grounds was

originally built as a Coronation Stand by King Kalakaua. Later he used it as a Royal Bandstand for concerts (King Kalakaua, along with Herni Berger, the 1st Royal Hawaiian Bandmaster, wrote "Hawaii Pono'i," the state anthem). Today the Royal Bandstand is still used for concerts by the Royal Hawaiian Band. *At S. King and Richards sts.* ☎ *808/522-0832.*

Turn in the Ewa direction, cross Richards St., and walk to the corner of Richards and Hotel sts.

7 ★ **kids Hawaii State Art Museum.** *See p 63, bullet* **4**.

Walk makai down Richards St. and turn left (toward Diamond Head) on S. King St.

8 ★ **kids King Kamehameha Statue.** The striking black-and-gold bronze statue is a replica of the man who united the Hawaiian Islands. The best day to see the statue is on June 11 (King Kamehameha Day), when it is covered with leis in honor of Hawaii's favorite son. *Juncture of King, Merchant, and Mililani sts.*

9 **Aliiolani Hale.** The name translates to "House of Heavenly Kings." This distinctive building, with a clock tower, now houses the State Judiciary Building. King Kamehameha V originally wanted to build a palace here and commissioned the Australian architect Thomas Rowe in

The construction of Iolani Palace nearly bankrupted the Hawaiian kingdom.

Statue of King Kamehameha, draped with leis.

1872. However, it ended up as the first major government building for the Hawaiian monarchy. Kamehameha V didn't live to see it completed, and King David Kalakaua dedicated the building in 1874. Ironically, less than 20 years later, on January 17, 1893, Stanford Dole, backed by other prominent sugar planters, stood on the steps to this building and proclaimed the overthrow of the Hawaiian monarchy and the establishment of a provisional government. *417 S. King St. (between Mililani and Punchbowl sts.).* ☎ *808/ 539-4999. Mon–Fri 9am–4pm. Tours: Tues–Thurs 10am–3pm.*

Walk toward Diamond Head on King St.; at the corner of King and Punchbowl, stop in at:

🔟 ★ **Kawaiahao Church.** Don't miss this crowning achievement of the first missionaries in Hawaii—the first permanent stone church, complete with bell tower and colonial colonnade. *See p 23, bullet* ⓫.

Cross the street, and you'll see the:

⓫ ★ **Mission Houses Museum.** Step into 1820 and see what life was like among the 19th-century American Protestant missionaries. *See p 23, bullet* ⓬.

Cross King St. and walk in the Ewa direction to the corner of Punchbowl and King sts.

⓬ **Honolulu Hale.** The Honolulu City Hall, built in 1927, was designed by Honolulu's most famous architect, C. W. Dickey. His Spanish mission–style building has an open-air courtyard, which is used for art exhibits and concerts. *530 South King St. (Punchbowl St.).* ☎ *808/523-4385. Mon–Fri 8am–5pm.*

Cross Punchbowl St. and walk mauka.

⓭ **State Library.** Anything you want to know about Hawaii and the Pacific can be found here, the main branch of the state's library system. Located in a restored historic building, it has an open garden courtyard in the middle, great for stopping for a rest on your walk. *478 South King St. (Punchbowl St.).* ☎ *808/586-3617. Tues–Wed 9am–5pm, Thurs noon–8pm, Fri–Sat 9am–5pm.*

Head mauka up Punchbowl to the corner of Punchbowl and Beretania sts.

⓮ **Kalanimoku.** A beautiful name, "Ship of Heaven," has been given to this dour state office building. Here you can get information on hiking and camping in state parks (from the Department of Land and Natural Resources). *1151 Punchbowl St. (Beretania St.).* ☎ *808/587-0320. Mon–Fri 8am–5pm.*

Retrace your steps in the Ewa direction down Beretania to Alakea back to the parking garage.

Kawaiahao Church was built from 14,000 coral blocks.

Kapiolani Park

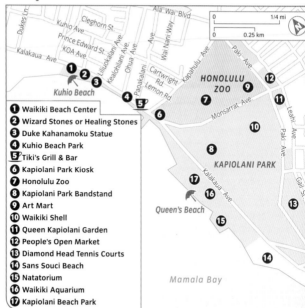

1. Waikiki Beach Center
2. Wizard Stones or Healing Stones
3. Duke Kahanamoku Statue
4. Kuhio Beach Park
5. Tiki's Grill & Bar
6. Kapiolani Park Kiosk
7. Honolulu Zoo
8. Kapiolani Park Bandstand
9. Art Mart
10. Waikiki Shell
11. Queen Kapiolani Garden
12. People's Open Market
13. Diamond Head Tennis Courts
14. Sans Souci Beach
15. Natatorium
16. Waikiki Aquarium
17. Kapiolani Beach Park

On June 11, 1877 (King Kamehameha Day), King David Kalakaua donated some 140 acres (57ha) of land to the people of Hawaii for Hawaii's first park. He asked that the park be named after his beloved wife, Queen Kapiolani, and he celebrated the opening of this vast grassy area with a free concert and "high stakes" horse races (the king loved gambling). The horse races, and the gambling that accompanied it, were eventually outlawed, but the park lives on. Just a coconut's throw from the high-rise concrete jungle of Waikiki lies this grassy oasis dotted with spreading banyans, huge monkeypod trees, blooming royal poincianas, and swaying ironwoods. From Waikiki, walk toward Diamond Head on Kalakaua Avenue. If you're coming by car, the cheapest parking is metered street parking on Kalakaua Avenue adjacent to the park. **START: Waikiki Beach Center, Kalakaua Ave., Diamond Head side of the Westin Moana Hotel, across the street from the Hyatt Regency. Bus: 19 or 20.**

1 Waikiki Beach Center. On the ocean side of Kalakaua Avenue, next to the Westin Moana Hotel, is a complex of restrooms, showers, surfboard lockers, rental concessions, and the Waikiki police substation. *2435 Kalakaua Ave., Diamond Head side of the Westin Moana Hotel.*

2 Wizard Stones or Healing Stones. These four basalt boulders,

A tranquil pond in Kapiolani Park.

which weigh several tons apiece and sit on a lava rock platform, are held sacred by the Hawaiian people. The story goes that sometime before the 15th century, four powerful healers from Moaulanuiakea (in the Society Islands) named Kapaemahu, Kahaloa, Kapuni, and Kihohi, lived in Waikiki. After years of healing the people and the *alii* of Oahu, they wished to return home. They asked the people to erect four monuments made of bell stone, a basalt rock that was found in a Kaimuki quarry and that produced a bell-like ringing when struck. The healers spent a ceremonious month transferring their spiritual healing power, or *mana*, to the stones. The great mystery is how the boulders were transported from Kaimuki to the marshland near Kuhio Beach in Waikiki. *Diamond Head side of the police substation, Kalakaua Ave.*

③ Duke Kahanamoku Statue. Here, cast in bronze, is Hawaii's most famous athlete, also known as the father of modern surfing. Duke (1890–1968) won Olympic swimming medals in 1912, 1920, 1924, and 1928. He was enshrined in both the Swimming Hall of Fame and the Surfing Hall of Fame. He also traveled around the world promoting surfing. *Just Diamond Head side (west) of the stones, Kalakaua Ave.*

④ Kuhio Beach Park. The two small swimming holes here are great, but heed the warning sign: Watch out for holes. There actually are deep holes in the sandy bottom, and you may suddenly find yourself in very deep water. The best pool for swimming is the one on the Diamond Head end, but the water circulation is questionable—there sometimes appears to be a layer of suntan lotion floating on the surface. If the waves are up, watch the Boogie boarders surf by the seawall. They ride toward the wall and at the last minute veer away with a swoosh. *2453 Kalakaua Ave. (between Liliuokalani to Paoakailani aves.).*

Cross Kalakaua Ave. and walk towards Paoakalani St. **⑤ Tiki's Grill & Bar.** Stop for lunch at this casual eatery on the second floor of the ResortQuest Waikiki Beach Hotel overlooking Waikiki Beach. The menu is American with Pacific Rim influences; seafood dishes are especially good. *2570 Kalakaua Ave. (at Paoakalani St.).* ☎ *808-923-TIKI. Daily 10:30am–midnight. $$.*

Kuhio Beach Park.

Walk mauka down Kalakaua Ave. to Kapahulu Ave., then walk towards Diamond Head to the entrance of Kapiolani Park.

6 Kapiolani Park Kiosk.
This small display stand contains brochures and actual photos of the park's history. It also carries information on upcoming events at the various sites within the park (the aquarium, the zoo, Waikiki Shell, and Kapiolani Bandstand). An informative map will help to orient you to the park grounds. *Corner of Kalakaua and Kapahulu aves.*

Continue up Kapahulu Ave.

7 Honolulu Zoo.
The best time to see the city's 42-acre (17ha) zoo is as soon as the gates open at 9am—the animals seem to be more active and it's a lot cooler than walking around at midday in the hot sun. *See p 33, bullet* 1.

Trace your steps back to Kapahulu and Kalakaua aves. and head mauka down Monsarrat Ave.

8 Kapiolani Park Bandstand.
Once upon a time, from 1937 to 2002, the Kodak Hula Show presented the art of hula to visitors, with some 3,000 people filling bleachers around a grassy stage area every day. The Kodak Hula Show is gone now, but the Bandstand is still used for concerts and special events. *Inside Kapiolani Park.*

If you're traveling with kids, plan to spend at least half a day at the Honolulu Zoo.

Back on Monsarrat Ave., on the fence facing the zoo.

9 Art Mart.
The Artists of Oahu Exhibit is the new official name of this display, where local artisans hang their artwork on a fence for the public to view and buy. Not only do you get to meet the artists, but you also have an opportunity to purchase their work at a considerable discount from the prices you'll see in galleries. *Monsarrat Ave. Sat, Sun & Wed, 10am–4pm.*

Cross Monsarrat Ave.

10 Waikiki Shell.
This open-air amphitheater hosts numerous musical shows, from the Honolulu

The Waikiki Shell.

Symphony to traditional Hawaiian music. *2805 Monsarrat Ave.* ☎ *808/527-5400.*

Continue walking down to the end of the block to the corner of Monsarrat and Paki aves.

⓫ Queen Kapiolani Garden. You'll see a range of hibiscus plants and dozens of varieties of roses, including the somewhat rare Hawaiian rose. The tranquil gardens are always open and are a great place to wander and relax. *Corner of Monsarrat and Paki aves.*

Across the street.

⓬ People's Open Market. The farmer's market with its open stalls is an excellent spot to buy fresh produce and flowers. *Monsarrat and Paki aves. Wed 10–11am.*

Continue in the Diamond Head direction down Paki Ave.

⓭ Diamond Head Tennis Courts. Located on the mauka side of Paki Avenue, the nine free city and county tennis courts are open for play daily during daylight hours. Tennis etiquette suggests that if someone is waiting for a court, limit your play to 45 minutes. *3908 Paki Ave.* ☎ *808/971-7150.*

Turn onto Kalakaua Ave., and begin walking back toward Waikiki.

⓮ Sans Souci Beach. This is one of the best swimming beaches in Waikiki. The shallow reef, which is close to shore, keeps the waters calm. Farther out there's good snorkeling in the coral reef by the Kapua Channel. Facilities include outdoor showers and a lifeguard. *Next door the New Otani Kaimana Beach Hotel, 2863 Kalakaua Ave.*

Keep walking toward Waikiki.

⓯ Natatorium. This huge concrete structure next to the beach is both a memorial to the soldiers of World War I and a 100-meter saltwater swimming pool. Opened in 1927, when Honolulu had hopes of hosting the Olympics, the ornate swimming pool fell into disuse and disrepair after World War II, and was finally closed in 1979. *2815 Kalakaua Ave.*

Next door.

⓰ Waikiki Aquarium. Try not to miss this stop—the tropical aquarium is worth a peek if only to see the only living chambered nautilus born in captivity. *See p 13, bullet ❷.*

⓱ Kapiolani Beach Park. Relax on the stretch of grassy lawn alongside the sandy beach, one of the best-kept secrets of Waikiki. This beach park is much less crowded than the beaches of Waikiki, plus it has adjacent grassy lawns, barbecue areas, picnic tables, restrooms, and showers. The swimming is good here year-round, there's a surfing spot known as "Public's" offshore, and there's always a game going at the volleyball courts. The middle section of the beach park, in front of the pavilion, is known as Queen's Beach or Queen's Surf and is popular with the gay community. *2745 Kalakaua Ave.*

Explore Hawaii's underwater world at the Waikiki Aquarium.

Dining Best Bets

Best **Bistro**
★★★ Cassis Honolulu $$ 66 Queen St. (p 92)

Best **Breakfast**
★★ kids Hula Grill Waikiki $$ 2335 Kalakaua Ave. (p 95)

Best **Buffet**
★ Prince Court $$$ 100 Holomoana St. (p 97)

Best **Burger**
★ kids Kua Aina $ 1116 Auahi St. (p 95)

Best **Casual Chinese**
★★ Little Village Noodle House $ 1113 Smith St. (p 96)

Best **Upscale Chinese**
★★ Golden Dragon $$$ 2005 Kalia Rd. (p 94)

Best **Dim Sum**
★ Legend Seafood Restaurant $ 100 N. Beretania St. (p 96)

Best **for Families**
★★ Kaka'ako Kitchen $ 1200 Ala Moana Blvd. (p 95)

Best **French/Vietnamese**
★★ Duc's Bistro $$ 1188 Maunakea St. (p 93)

Best **Hawaii Regional Cuisine**
★★★ Alan Wong's Restaurant $$$$ 1857 S. King St. (p 92)

Best for **under $10**
★★ Nico's At Pier 38 $ 1133 N. Nimitz Hwy. (p 97)

Best **Steakhouse**
★ d.k. Steakhouse $$$ 2552 Kalakaua Ave. (p 93)

Best **Late-Night Meals**
★ Eggs 'n Things $ 1911-B Kalakaua Ave. (p 93)

Most **Romantic**
★★★ La Mer $$$$ 2199 Kalia Rd. (p 96)

Best **Splurge**
★★★ Chef Mavro Restaurant $$$$ 1969 S. King St. (p 93)

Best **Sunday Brunch**
★★★ Orchids $$$$ 2199 Kalia Rd. (p 97)

Best **Sushi**
★★ Sansei Seafood Restaurant & Sushi Bar $$$ 2552 Kalakaua Ave. (p 98)

Best **Sunset Views**
★ Duke's Canoe Club $$ 2335 Kalakaua Ave. (p 93)

Best **View of Waikiki**
★ Hau Tree Lanai $$ 2863 Kalakaua Ave. (p 94)

You'll find beautiful food and beautiful people at the Diamond Head Grill.

Waikiki's Best **Dining**

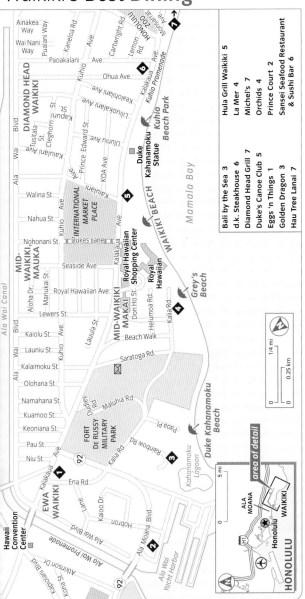

Bali by the Sea **3**
d.k. Steakhouse **6**
Diamond Head Grill **7**
Duke's Canoe Club **5**
Eggs 'n Things **1**
Golden Dragon **3**
Hau Tree Lanai **7**

Hula Grill Waikiki **5**
La Mer **4**
Michel's **4**
Orchids **4**
Prince Court **2**
Sansei Seafood Restaurant
& Sushi Bar **6**

Honolulu's Best **Dining**

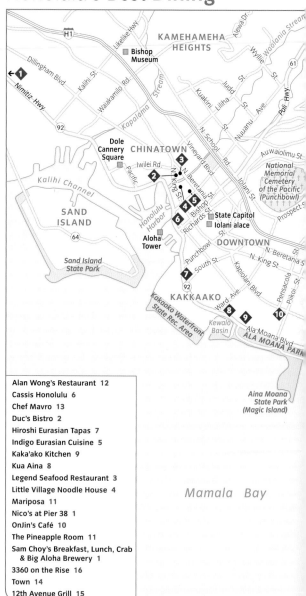

Alan Wong's Restaurant 12
Cassis Honolulu 6
Chef Mavro 13
Duc's Bistro 2
Hiroshi Eurasian Tapas 7
Indigo Eurasian Cuisine 5
Kaka'ako Kitchen 9
Kua Aina 8
Legend Seafood Restaurant 3
Little Village Noodle House 4
Mariposa 11
Nico's at Pier 38 1
OnJin's Café 10
The Pineapple Room 11
Sam Choy's Breakfast, Lunch, Crab
  & Big Aloha Brewery 1
3360 on the Rise 16
Town 14
12th Avenue Grill 15

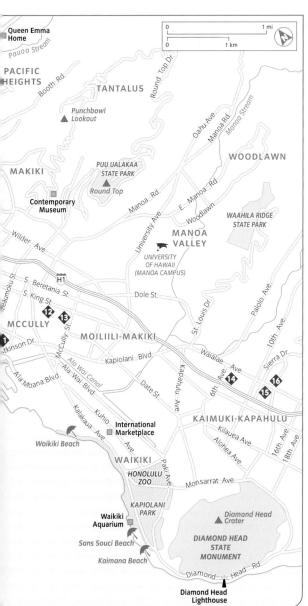

Honolulu and Waikiki Restaurants **A to Z**

★★★ Alan Wong's Restaurant

MCCULLY *HAWAII REGIONAL CUISINE* James Beard Award–winner Chef Alan Wong, worshipped by foodies across the state, serves brilliantly creative and irresistibly cutting-edge cuisine in a casual, sometimes noisy room that is always packed, so book in advance. I love the ginger-crusted onaga. *1857 S. King St. (between Kalakaua Ave. and McCully St.).* ☎ *808/949-2526. Entrees $26–$48; 5-course sampling menu $65 ($90 w/wine); Chef's tasting menu $85 ($120 w/ wine). AE, DC, MC, V. Dinner daily. TheBus 13. Map p 90.*

★★ Bali by the Sea WAIKIKI

CONTINENTAL/PACIFIC RIM Get a window seat at sunset for oceanfront dining on herb-infused rack of lamb or Kona lobster. Choose from a host of mouthwatering desserts. Best time to dine: Fridays to see the 7:30pm fireworks. *Hilton Hawaiian Village, 2005 Kalia Rd. (Ala Moana Blvd.)* ☎ *808/941-2254. Entrees $23–$62. AE, DC, DISC, MC, V. Dinner Mon–Sat. Bus: 19 or 20. Map p 89.*

★★★ Cassis Honolulu HARBOR

FRENCH/HAWAII BISTRO Hawaii's

Kona Kampachi at Bali by the Sea.

top chef, George Mavro, opened this casual bistro in 2007. It features many of the island-influenced dishes from his upscale Chef Mavro Restaurant (see below) that he no longer serves because he changes that menu every 3 months. The trendy eatery (packed at lunch) also has a very hip wine bar (featuring the wine pairings of the day). *66 Queen St. (Nimitz Hwy.).* ☎ *808/545-8100. Entrees: $18–$25 lunch, $25–$33 dinner. AE, DC, DISC, MC, V. Lunch Mon–Fri, dinner Mon–Sat. Bus: 19 or 20. Map p 90.*

Room Service from 50 Different Restaurants

Don't let the room service menu in your hotel room limit you; **Room Service in Paradise** (☎ **808/941-DINE;** www.941-dine. com) delivers almost a dozen different cuisines (from American/ Pacific Rim to Italian to sandwiches and burgers) from oodles of restaurants to your hotel room. You can check out menus online or pick up one of its magazines in various Waikiki locations. There's a $6.50 delivery charge in Waikiki (more in outlying areas).

★★★ Chef Mavro Restaurant
MCCULLLY PROVENÇAL/HAWAII REGIONAL If you only have 1 night on Oahu, splurge at this intimate dining experience in a non-touristy neighborhood. James Beard Award–winner Chef George Mavro's inspired menu (roast pork with apple quinoa or poached fresh fish with sago-coconut nage, Thai herbs, limu, and lime froth) features perfect wine pairings. 1969 S. King St. (McCully St.). ☎ 808/944-4714. Prix fixe $66–$102 ($99–$208 w/wine pairings). AE, DC, DISC, MC, V. Dinner Tues–Sun. Bus: 13, transfer to 1. Map p 90.

★ Diamond Head Grill WAIKIKI
ECLECTIC Three good reasons to dine here: new executive chef Eric Sakai's usual menu (from lobster ravioli to pork chops with risotto), sinful desserts, and a place to party—after 10pm on Friday and Saturday, it becomes a hot nightspot. W Honolulu, 2885 Kalakaua Ave. (across from Kapiolani Park). ☎ 808/922-3734. Entrees $23–$39 dinner. AE, DC, DISC, MC, V. Dinner daily. Bus: 19 or 20. Map p 89.

★ d.k. Steakhouse WAIKIKI STEAK
Attention carnivores: This is the ultimate steakhouse for the 21st century at very reasonable prices (especially for Waikiki). Book an outside table on the lanai to see the sunset on Waikiki Beach. Waikiki Beach Marriott Resort, 2552 Kalakaua Ave. (Ohua Ave.). ☎ 808/931-6280. Main courses $19–$59. AE, DISC, MC, V. Dinner daily. Bus: 19 or 20. Map p 89.

★★ Duc's Bistro CHINATOWN
FRENCH/VIETNAMESE Dine on Honolulu's best French/Vietnamese cuisine (from seafood spring rolls to steak au poivre) in a quietly elegant restaurant that features live music nightly. 1188 Maunakea St. (Beretania St.). ☎ 808/531-6325. Entrees $13–$22 lunch, $15–$33 dinner. AE, DC, DISC, MC, V. Lunch Mon–Fri, dinner Mon–Sat. Bus: 19 or 20. Map p 90.

★ kids Duke's Canoe Club
WAIKIKI STEAK/SEAFOOD This open-air dining room (outfitted in surfing memorabilia) overlooking Waikiki Beach is the best spot to watch the sunset. Hawaiian musicians serenade diners lingering over a menu ranging from burgers to fresh fish. Outrigger Waikiki on the Beach, 2335 Kalakaua Ave. (next door to Royal Hawaiian Shopping Center). ☎ 808/922-2268. Entrees $18–$38. AE, DC, DISC, MC, V. Breakfast, lunch, & dinner daily. Bus: 19 or 20. Map p 89.

★ kids Eggs 'n Things WAIKIKI
BREAKFAST This popular breakfast-only eatery is famous for its huge plates of food and its all-night hours on weekends. 1911-B Kalakaua Ave. (at Ala Moana Blvd.).

d.k. Steakhouse, one of Chef D. K. Kodama's popular restaurants (also check out Sansei Seafood).

Duc's Bistro.

few yards from the waves), this informal eatery has the best view of Waikiki Beach. Breakfast is my favorite—especially the taro pancakes. *New Otani Kaimana Beach Hotel, 2863 Kalakaua Ave. (across from Kapiolani Park).* ☎ *808/ 921-7066. Entrees $18–$39. AE, DC, DISC, MC, V. Breakfast, lunch & dinner daily. Bus: 19 or 20. Map p 89.*

☎ *808/949-0820. Breakfast entrees $7–$12. No credit cards. Mon–Wed 6am–2pm; Thurs–Sun 11pm–2pm the next day. Bus: 19 or 20. Map p 89.*

kids Golden Dragon WAIKIKI *CHINESE* The place to go to celebrate a special occasion that calls for the finest Chinese cuisine (I love the nine-course "lotus dinner," a showcase of the chef's creativity). *Hilton Hawaiian Village Beach Resort & Spa, 2005 Kalia Rd. (Ala Moana Blvd.)* ☎ *808/946-5336. Entrees $12–$35; prix-fixe dinners $38–$55. AE, DC, DISC, MC, V. Dinner Wed–Sun. Bus: 19 or 20. Map p 89.*

★ **kids Hau Tree Lanai** WAIKIKI *PACIFIC RIM* Located under a giant hau tree right on the beach (just a

★ **Hiroshi Eurasian Tapas** RESTAURANT ROW *EURO-ASIAN FUSION* This is my pick for the best tapas (small plates) on the island. Go with as many people as possible so you can sample more— some favorite items include truffled crab cake and kampachi carpaccio. *Restaurant Row, 500 Ala Moana Blvd. (between Punchbowl and South sts.).* ☎ *808/533-HIRO. Tapas $6–$22. AE, DISC, MC, V. Dinner daily. Bus: 19 or 20. Map p 90.*

Duke's Canoe Club.

Dining in Waikiki 24-7

If you get the late-night munchies, your best bet in Waikiki is **MAC 24-7** at the **Hilton Waikiki Prince Kuhio Hotel,** 2500 Kuhio Ave. (at Liliuokalani Ave.; ☎ 808/921-5564). The menu features hotel coffee shop "comfort" food, reasonably priced for Waikiki (most entrees in the $11–$16 range).

★★ kids Hula Grill Waikiki

WAIKIKI *HAWAIIAN REGIONAL* This is the best place for breakfast in Waikiki: Not only does this bistro have a terrific ocean view (clear to Diamond Head), but the food is fabulous (crab cake eggs Benedict, Maui pineapple and coconut pancakes) and prices are reasonable. *Outrigger Waikiki on the Beach, 2335 Kalakaua Ave. (next to Royal Hawaiian Shopping Center).* ☎ *808/923-HULA. Entrees: breakfast $5–$11, dinner $17–$29. AE, DC, MC, V. Breakfast & dinner daily. Bus: 19 or 20. Map p 89.*

★★ Indigo Eurasian Cuisine

CHINATOWN *EURASIAN* Dine in an elegant indoor setting or in a tropical garden, with an East-West menu ranging from pot stickers to plum-glazed baby back ribs. *1121 Nuuanu Ave. (Pauahi St.).* ☎ *808/521-2900. Entrees: lunch $17–$23, dinner $23–$37. DC, DISC, MC, V. Lunch Tues–Fri, dinner Tues–Sat. Bus: 19 or 20. Map p 90.*

★★ kids Kaka'ako Kitchen

HONOLULU *GOURMET PLATE LUNCHES* Bring the family for local home-style cooking at budget prices. (It's owned by chef Russell Siu of 3660 on the Rise; see p 98.) The catch: It's served on Styrofoam plates in a warehouse

Get breakfast all day (and all night on weekends) at Eggs 'n Things.

ambience. *Ward Centre, 1200 Ala Moana Blvd. (Kamakee St.).* ☎ *808/ 596-7488. Entrees: breakfast $5–$8, lunch & dinner $7–$13. AE, MC, V. Breakfast & lunch daily, dinner Mon–Sat. Bus: 19 or 20. Map p 90.*

★ kids Kua Aina

HONOLULU *AMERICAN* This branch of the ultimate sandwich shop (the original is on the North Shore) is very popular—I recommend calling ahead for takeout and going to the beach. The excellent sandwich selection includes burgers and a legendary mahimahi with Ortega chile and cheese. *Ward Village, 1116 Auahi St. (Kamakee St.).* ☎ *808/591-9133. Sandwiches and burgers $4.40–$7.15. No credit cards. Lunch & dinner daily. Bus: 19 or 20. Map p 90.*

Don't be deterred by the Styrofoam plates: Kaka'ako Kitchen serves fabulous Hawaiian home-style food.

★★★ **La Mer** WAIKIKI *NEOCLASSIC FRENCH* This second-floor ocean-front bastion of haute cuisine is the place to go for a romantic evening. Michelin award–winning chef Yves Garnier prepares classical French dishes with fresh island ingredients (hamachi with pistachio, shrimp on black risotto, and scallops with ratatouille served with a saffron sauce). *Halekulani Hotel, 2199 Kalia Rd. (Lewers St.).* ☎ *808/923-2311. Entrees $39–$58, 9-course prix fixe $125, 4-course prix fixe $89. AE, DC, MC, V. Dinner daily. Bus: 19 or 20. Map p 89.*

★ kids **Legend Seafood Restaurant** CHINATOWN *DIM SUM/SEAFOOD* This is my favorite dim sum eatery. It's not fancy, but who cares with the creative dim sum coming out of the kitchen (ranging from deep-fried taro puffs to prawn dumplings). The clientele are mainly Chinese-speaking diners, so you know it's authentic. *Chinese Cultural Plaza, 100 N. Beretania St. (Maunakea St.).* ☎ *808/532-1868. Dim sum under $15. AE, DC, MC, V. Breakfast Sat–Sun, lunch & dinner daily. Dim sum served at lunch only. Bus: 19 or 20. Map p 90.*

★★ kids **Little Village Noodle House** CHINATOWN *CHINESE* My pick for the best Chinese food served "simple and healthy" (its motto), is this tiny neighborhood restaurant with helpful waitstaff and even parking in the back (unheard of in Chinatown). Try the honey-walnut

Steamed clams at Mariposa.

Kua Aina is a great place to get a sandwich on the go.

shrimp or the garlic eggplant. The menu includes Northern, Canton, and Hong Kong–style dishes. *1113 Smith St. (between King and Pauahi sts.).* ☎ *808/545-3008. Entrees under $10. AE, DISC, MC, V. Lunch & dinner daily. Bus: 19 or 20. Map p 90.*

★★ kids **Mariposa** ALA MOANA *AMERICAN HERITAGE* High ceilings inside and outside tables with views of Ala Moana Park pair beautifully with a menu of Pacific and American specialties (from a king crab, shrimp, and mussel risotto, to pan-roasted Hawaiian snapper). At lunch, order the signature starter: the popover with *poha* (gooseberry) butter. *Neiman Marcus, Ala Moana Center, 1450 Ala Moana Blvd. (Piikoi St.).* ☎ *808/951-3420. Entrees: lunch $12–$24, dinner $25–$58. AE, DC, MC, V. Lunch & dinner daily. Bus: 19 or 20. Map p 90.*

★★ **Michel's** WAIKIKI *FRENCH/ HAWAII REGIONAL* One side of this 45-year-old classic French restaurant opens to the ocean view (get there for sunset), but the food is the real draw. Tuxedo-clad waiters serve classic French cuisine with an island infusion (lobster bisque, steak Diane, and a Caesar salad made at your table) in an elegantly casual atmosphere. *Colony Surf Hotel, 2895 Kalakaua Ave. (across from Kapiolani Park).*

☎ 808/923-6552. Entrees $36–$49. AE, DC, DISC, MC, V. Dinner daily. Bus: 19 or 20. Map p 89.

★★ kids **Nico's At Pier 38** IWILEI *FRESH FISH* I never miss a chance to eat at this tiny take-out place, which serves up gourmet French cuisine produced island-style in Styrofoam take-out containers at frugal prices. My favorite is the furikake–pan-seared ahi with the addicting ginger garlic cilantro dip, served with greens or macaroni salad for $8.75. *Pier 38, 1133 N. Nimitz Hwy. (Alakawa St.).* ☎ 808/540-137. Entrees: breakfast $2.45–$6.95, lunch $5.75–$8.75. Breakfast & lunch Mon–Sat. Bus: 19 or 20. Map p 90.

★★ kids **OnJin's Café** HONOLULU *FRENCH/ASIAN* OnJin's is fabulously inexpensive for lunch, when it serves gourmet fare at plate-lunch prices. Evenings are more sophisticated, but still reasonably priced. OnJin Kim is a brilliant chef who serves excellent fare, such as charred ahi with seven Japanese spices, lobster ravioli, and a top-of-the-line bouillabaisse. *401 Kamakee St. (Queen St.).* ☎ 808/589-1666. Entrees: lunch $7.25–$13, dinner $13–$22. MC, V. Lunch & dinner daily. Bus: 19 or 20. Map p 90.

★★★ kids **Orchids** WAIKIKI *INTERNATIONAL/SEAFOOD* This is the best Sunday brunch in Hawaii, with an outstanding array of dishes from popovers to sushi to an omelet station. The setting is extraordinary (right on Waikiki Beach), and the food is excellent. *Halekulani Hotel, 2199 Kalia Rd. (Lewers St.).* ☎ 808/923-2311. Entrees: dinner $24–$40, Sunday brunch $47. AE, DC, MC, V. Breakfast, lunch & dinner Mon–Sat, brunch & dinner Sun. Bus: 19 or 20. Map p 89.

★★ kids **The Pineapple Room** ALA MOANA *HAWAII REGIONAL* Culinary icon Chef Alan Wong's bistro features gustatory masterpieces that will probably leave you wanting to come back to try breakfast, lunch, and dinner, just to see what else he will present. Expect anything from *moi* (served whole and steamed Chinese-style) to apple curry–glazed pork chops with pumpkin and mascarpone puree and mango chutney. *Macy's, 1450 Ala Moana Blvd. (Piikoi St.).* ☎ 808/945-6573. Entrees: lunch $11–$18, dinner $26–$38. AE, DC, MC, V. Breakfast Sat–Sun, lunch daily, dinner Mon–Sat. Bus: 19 or 20. Map p 90.

★ kids **Prince Court** WAIKIKI *CONTEMPORARY ISLAND CUISINE* Floor-to-ceiling windows, sunny views of the harbor, and top-notch buffets are Prince Court's attractions. The best are the Friday and Saturday seafood buffets featuring sushi, Vietnamese pho, crab, oysters, shrimp, scallops, and even prime rib. *Hawaii Prince Hotel Waikiki, 100 Holomoana St. (Ala Moana Blvd.).* ☎ 808/944-4494. Breakfast buffet $20; weekend brunch $33; luncheon buffet $24; dinner buffets $40–$42. AE, DC, MC, V. Breakfast, lunch (or brunch) and dinner daily. Bus: 19 or 20. Map p 89.

The Pineapple Room.

kids Sam Choy's Breakfast, Lunch, Crab & Big Aloha Brewery IWILEI ISLAND CUISINE/ SEAFOOD

Chef/restaurateur Sam Choy's crab house features gigantic meals (fried poke, Cajun seared ahi) and several varieties of Big Aloha beer, brewed on-site. The unusual decor includes a sampan boat smack in the middle of the 11,000-sq.-ft. (1,022m sq.) restaurant. *580 Nimitz Hwy. (between Pacific and Kukahi sts.).* ☎ *808/545-7979. Entrees: breakfast $5–$13, lunch $9–$40, dinner $19–$45. AE, DC, DISC, MC, V. Breakfast, lunch & dinner daily. Bus: 19 or 20. Map p 90.*

Ahi Katsu at 3660 On the Rise.

★★ Sansei Seafood Restaurant & Sushi Bar WAIKIKI

SUSHI/ASIAN–PACIFIC RIM Perpetual award-winner D. K. Kodama's Waikiki restaurant is known not only for its extensive menu but also for Kodama's outrageous sushi creations (he's my favorite sushi chef). Examples include seared foi gras nigiri sushi (duck liver lightly seared over sushi rice, with caramelized onion and ripe mango) or the wonderful mango crab salad hand roll (mango, blue crab, greens, and peanuts with a sweet Thai-chili vinaigrette). *Waikiki Beach Marriott Resort, 2552 Kalakaua Ave.* *(Paoakalani Ave.).* ☎ *808/931-6286. Sushi $3–$17, entrees $17–$40. AE, DISC, MC, V. Dinner daily. Bus: 19 or 20. Map p 89.*

★★★ 3660 On the Rise KAIMUKI

EURO-ISLAND In his elegant 200-seat restaurant, chef Russell Siu adds Asian and local touches to the basics: rack of lamb with macadamia nuts, filets of catfish in *ponzu* (a Japanese sauce), and seared ahi salad with grilled shiitake mushrooms. Save room for the warm chocolate cake. *3660 Waialae Ave. (Koko Head Ave.).* ☎ *808/737-1177. Entrees $25–$55,*

The sushi bar at Sansei's.

Tasty Tours for the Hungry Traveler

See Honolulu one restaurant at a time. Former Honolulu newspaper food critic and chef Mathew Gray has put together **"Hawaii Food Tours"** to show you a side of Hawaii that you wouldn't discover on your own. He offers three different types of tours, all with transportation from your Waikiki hotel in an air-conditioned van and all with running commentary on Hawaii's history, culture, and architecture. I love the "Hole-in-the-Wall Tour," which runs from 10am to 2pm ($99 per person). You'll visit at least four different ethnic restaurants during the tour (Vietnamese, Indian, local food, and dessert) and dine from the best dishes on their menus, preordered by Mathew. For information and booking, call ☎ **800/715-2468** or 808/926-FOOD (www.hawaiifoodtours.com).

prix fixe $40. AE, DC, DISC, MC, V. Dinner Tues–Sun. No bus service. Map p 90.

★ **Town** KAIMUKI *CONTEMPORARY ITALIAN* The latest hip restaurant along Waialae's miracle mile of "in" spots is a surprisingly delicious place to eat. Dine on ahi tartar on risotto cakes or outstanding gnocchi in a metro high-tech atmosphere (highly polished concrete floors, stainless steel tables, and incredibly uncomfortable chairs). Lunches consist of sandwiches, salads, and pastas, and the recently added breakfast menu includes frittata of the day, eggs, and wonderful baked goods. *3435 Waialae Ave. (at 9th St.).* ☎ *808/735-5900. Entrees: breakfast $3.75–$6.50, lunch $7.50–$13, dinner $15–$24. AE, MC, V. Breakfast Mon–Thurs, lunch & dinner Mon–Sat. No bus service. Map p 90.*

★ **kids** **12th Avenue Grill**
KAIMUKI *RETRO-AMERICAN*
All 14 tables in this tiny, upscale neighborhood diner are packed every night with people hungry for good ol' American food, but a little more sophisticated than what mom

used to make. Try gourmet macaroni and smoked parmesan cheese, smoked trout, or grilled pork chop with apple chutney. *1145-C 12th Ave. (at Wailalea Ave.).* ☎ *808/732-9469. Entrees $17–$27. MC, V. Dinner Mon–Sat. No bus service. Map p 90.*

Poi, that humble Hawaiian staple, is often served at luaus; I recommend the one at the Royal Hawaiian (p 108).

Lodging Best Bets

Most **Romantic**
★★ Royal Hawaiian $$$$ 2259 Kalakaua Ave. (p 107)

Most **Historic**
★★ Moana Surfrider, a Westin Resort $$$$ 2365 Kalakaua Ave. (p 104)

Most **Luxurious**
★★★ Halekulani $$$$ 2199 Kalia Rd. (p 103)

Best **Moderately Priced**
★ Ilima Hotel $$ 445 Nohonani St. (p 104)

Best **Budget Hotel**
★ Royal Grove Hotel $ 151 Uluniu Ave. (p 107)

Best **for Kids**
★★★ Embassy Suites Hotel—Waikiki Beach Walk $$$$ 201 Beach Walk (p 102)

Best **Value**
★ The Breakers $$ 250 Beach Walk (p 102)

Hippest Hotel
★★ Waikiki Parc $$$ 2233 Helumoa Rd. (p 109)

Best **View of Waikiki Beach**
★★ Hilton Hawaiian Village Beach Resort & Spa $$$ 2005 Kalia Rd. (p 103)

Best **View of Ala Wai Harbor**
★★ Hawaii Prince Hotel Waikiki $$$$ 100 Holomoana St. (p 103)

Best **View of Ft. DeRussy Park**
★ Outrigger Luana Waikiki $$$ 2045 Kalakaua Ave. (p 106)

Best **Service**
★★★ W Honolulu $$$$ 2885 Kalakaua Ave. (p 109)

Most **Hawaiian**
★ Hawaiiana Hotel $$ 260 Beach Walk (p 103)

Most **Serene**
★ Royal Garden at Waikiki $$ 440 Olohana St. (p 107)

Best **Hi-Tech Gadgets**
★★ Hotel Renew $$$ 129 Paoakalani Ave. (p 104)

Best **Hidden Gem**
★ New Otani Kaimana Beach Hotel $$$ 2863 Kalakaua Ave. (p 105)

Best **Boutique Hotel**
★ DoubleTree Alana Hotel Waikiki $$ 1956 Ala Moana Blvd. (p 102)

Best **Family Condo**
★★ Outrigger Waikiki Shore Condominium $$$ 2161 Kalia Rd. (p 106)

Vera Wang suite at the Halekulani.

Waikiki's Best **Lodging**

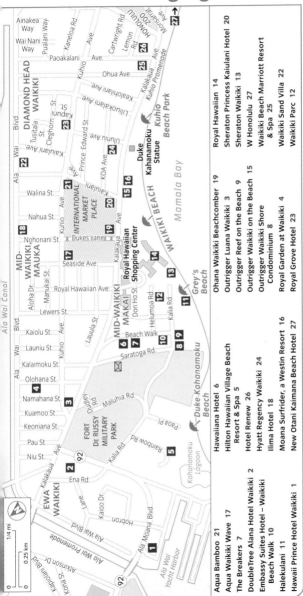

Aqua Bamboo 21
Aqua Waikiki Wave 17
The Breakers 7
DoubleTree Alana Hotel Waikiki 2
Embassy Suites Hotel – Waikiki Beach Walk 10
Halekulani 11
Hawaii Prince Hotel Waikiki 1

Hawaiiana Hotel 6
Hilton Hawaiian Village Beach Resort & Spa 5
Hotel Renew 26
Hyatt Regency Waikiki 24
Ilima Hotel 18
Moana Surfrider, a Westin Resort 16
New Otani Kaimana Beach Hotel 27

Ohana Waikiki Beachcomber 19
Outrigger Luana Waikiki 3
Outrigger Reef on the Beach 9
Outrigger Waikiki on the Beach 15
Outrigger Waikiki Shore Condominium 8
Royal Garden at Waikiki 4
Royal Grove Hotel 23

Royal Hawaiian 14
Sheraton Princess Kaiulani Hotel 20
Sheraton Waikiki 13
W Honolulu 27
Waikiki Beach Marriott Resort & Spa 25
Waikiki Sand Villa 22
Waikiki Parc 12

Waikiki Hotels **A to Z**

★ **Aqua Bamboo** MID-WAIKIKI MAUKA I love the intimacy of this boutique hotel, decorated with an Asian flair (with kitchenettes or kitchens). Other pluses: only a block from Waikiki beach, complimentary continental breakfast, spa on property, and personal service. Minus: not enough parking for all rooms. *2425 Kuhio Ave. (at Kaiulani Ave.).* ☎ *800/367-5004 or 808/922-7777. www.aquaresorts.com. 90 units. Doubles: $195–$207 hotel room; $218–$253 studio; $276–$310 1-bedroom w/breakfast. AE, DISC, MC, V. Bus: 19 or 20. Map p 101.*

★ **Aqua Waikiki Wave** MID-WAIKIKI MAUKA Recently renovated rooms with hip decor, flatscreen TVs, and free Wi-Fi have put this formerly dreary hotel on the map. Located in a not-very-hip neighborhood next door to International Marketplace, about a 10-minute walk to the beach. *2299 Kuhio Ave. (at Duke's Lane), Honolulu, HI 96817.* ☎ *866/406-2782 or 808/922-1262. www.aquaresorts.com. 247 units. Doubles: $200–$265 w/breakfast. AE, DISC, MC, V. Bus: 19 or 20. Map p 101.*

★ **kids The Breakers** MID-WAIKIKI MAKAI One of Waikiki's best deals: This two-story 1950s budget hotel is a terrific buy for a family (kitchenette in all rooms) and just a 2-minute walk to the beach, numerous restaurants, and shopping. Expect comfortable budget accommodations with tropical accents. *250 Beach Walk (between Kalakaua Ave. and Kalia Rd.).* ☎ *800/426-0494 or 808/923-3181. www.breakers-hawaii.com. 64 units. Doubles: $125–$185. AE, DC, MC, V. Bus: 19 or 20. Map p 101.*

★ **DoubleTree Alana Hotel Waikiki** EWA This boutique hotel (operated by the Hilton Hawaiian Village) is a welcome oasis of small, but comfortable rooms, and offers amenities of a more luxurious hotel at more affordable prices. Great location, too: Waikiki Beach is a 10-minute walk away, and the convention center is about a 7-minute walk. *1956 Ala Moana Blvd. (near Kalakaua Ave.).* ☎ *800/222-TREE or 808/941-7275. www.doubletree.com. 317 units. Doubles: $169–$349. AE, DC, DISC, MC, V. Bus: 19 or 20. Map p 101.*

★★★ **kids Embassy Suites Hotel—Waikiki Beach Walk** MID-WAIKIKI MAKAI Opened in 2007, this ultra-luxurious one- and two-bedroom hotel chain, famous for its complimentary "cooked to order" breakfast and evening cocktail reception, has a great location just 1 block from the beach. The newly opened Waikiki Beach Walk provides plenty of shops and restaurants on property as well. Prices may seem high, but it

DoubleTree Alana Hotel.

Hawaiiana Hotel.

pencils out to a deal for families. *201 Beach Walk (at Kalia Rd).* ☎ *800/ EMBASSY or 808/921-2345. www. waikikibeach.embassysuites.com. 421 suites. Doubles: $399–$469 1-bedroom; $549–$649 2-bedroom. AE, DC, DISC, MC, V. Bus: 19 or 20. Map p 101.*

★★★ **kids** **Halekulani** MID-WAIKIKI MAKAI   This is my favorite hotel in all Hawaii; the ultimate heavenly Hawaii luxury accommodation, spread over 5 acres (2ha) of prime Waikiki beachfront. Some 90% of the large rooms (620 sq. ft./58m sq.) face the ocean, and all have furnished lanais and top-drawer amenities. This is the best Waikiki has to offer. *2199 Kalia Rd. (at Lewers St.).* ☎ *800/367-2343 or 808/923-2311. www.halekulani.com. 455 units. Doubles: $405–$705. AE, DC, MC, V. Bus: 19 or 20. Map p 101.*

★ **kids** **Hawaiiana Hotel** MID-WAIKIKI MAKAI   This older hotel, with a 1950s feel, offers plenty of aloha spirit to its loyal guests at great prices. The concrete, hollow-tiled guest rooms have kitchenettes and two beds—great for families. The hotel is about a block from the beach and within walking distance of Waikiki shopping and nightlife. *260 Beach Walk (near Kalakaua Ave.).* ☎ *800/367-5122 or 808/923-3811. www.hawaiianahotelatwaikiki.com. 95 units. Doubles: $125–$235. AE, DC, DISC, MC, V. Bus: 19 or 20. Map p 101.*

★★ **Hawaii Prince Hotel Waikiki** EWA   For a vacation with a view and the feel of a palace, stay in these striking, twin, 33-story high-tech towers, where service is priority. All bedrooms face the Ala Wai Yacht Harbor, with floor-to-ceiling sliding-glass windows (sorry, no

Waikiki Neighborhoods

The neighborhoods in Waikiki can be divided up into four districts: **Ewa** (the western end of Waikiki from Ala Wai Canal to Fort DeRussy Park), **Mid-Waikiki Makai** (from the ocean up to Kalakaua Ave. and from Fort DeRussy Park to Kaiulani St.), **Mid-Waikiki Mauka** (mountain side of Kalakaua Ave. to Ala Wai Blvd. and from Kalaimoku St. to Kaiulani St.), and **Diamond Head** (from the ocean to Ala Wai Blvd. and from Kaiulani to Diamond Head).

lanais). The higher the floor, the higher the price. Ala Moana Center is a 10-minute walk away and Waikiki's beaches are just a 5-minute walk. *100 Holomoana St. (just across Ala Wai Canal Bridge).* ☎ *800/321-OAHU or 808/956-1111. www.princeresortshawaii.com. 521 units. Doubles: $375–$520. AE, DC, DISC, MC, V. Bus: 19 or 20. Map p 101.*

★★ **kids** **Hilton Hawaiian Village Beach Resort & Spa** EWA Sprawling over 20 acres (8ha), this is Waikiki's biggest resort—with tropical gardens dotted with exotic wildlife (flamingos, peacocks, and even penguins), award-winning restaurants (the Golden Dragon, p 94, and Bali by the Sea, p 92), 100 different shops, a secluded lagoon, two minigolf courses, and a gorgeous stretch of Waikiki Beach. A wide choice of accommodations, from simple hotel rooms to ultradeluxe, are housed in five towers. *2005 Kalia Rd. (at Ala Moana Blvd.).* ☎ *800/HILTONS or 808/949-4321. www.hiltonhawaiianvillage.com. 2,860 units. Doubles: $229–$609. AE, DISC, MC, V. Bus: 19 or 20. Map p 101.*

★★ **Hotel Renew** DIAMOND HEAD This boutique is a gem among aging Waikiki hotels; an oasis of tranquility and excellent taste in a sea of schlock. True to its name, Hotel Renew recently underwent several millions of dollars' worth of renovations—every single surface was redone. The result is a quiet, Zen-like decor, just a block from the beach, with complimentary gourmet breakfast, lots of hi-tech gadgets, and a free fitness center and yoga classes. *129 Paoakalani Ave. (at Lemon Rd.).* ☎ *866-406-2782 or 808/687-7700. www.aquaresorts.com. 70 units. Doubles: $300–$350. AE, DC, MC, V. Bus: 19 or 20. Map p 101.*

★ **kids** **Hyatt Regency Waikiki** DIAMOND HEAD This is one of Waikiki's largest hotels, with two 40-story towers covering nearly an entire city block, located across the street from Waikiki Beach. The location is great, there's a good children's program, and guest rooms are large and luxuriously furnished, but personally I find it too big and too impersonal, with service to match. *2424 Kalakaua Ave. (between Kaiulani St. and Uluniu Ave.).* ☎ *800/233-1234 or 808/923-1234. www.waikiki.hyatt.com. 1,230 units. Doubles: $260–$730. AE, DC, DISC, MC, V. Bus: 19 or 20. Map p 101.*

★ **kids** **Ilima Hotel** MID-WAIKIKI MAUKA Local residents frequent this 17-story, condo-style hotel that offers value for your money: huge rooms (with full kitchen), walking distances to restaurants and shops, and low prices. The only two caveats: It's a 15-minute hike to the beach, and there aren't any ocean views. *445 Nohonani St. (near Ala Wai Blvd.).* ☎ *800/801-9366 or 808/923-1877. www.HotelWaikiki.com. 99 units. Doubles: $135–$165 studio; $169–$219*

Lobby of the Moana Surfider.

Pampering in Paradise

Hawaii's spas have raised the art of relaxation and healing to a new level, as traditional Greco-Roman–style spas have evolved into airy, open facilities that embrace the tropics. Today's spas offer a wide diversity of treatments, many including traditional Hawaiian massages and ingredients. There are even side-by-side massages for couples, and duo massages—two massage therapists working on you at once.

Of course, all this pampering doesn't come cheap. Massages are generally $150 to $250 for 50 minutes and $250 to $295 for 80 minutes; body treatments are in the $150 to $250 range; and alternative healthcare treatments can be as high as $200 to $300. But you may think it's worth the expense to banish your tension and stress.

My picks for Waikiki's best spas are:

- **Most Relaxing: SpaHalekulani** From the time you step into the elegantly appointed, intimate spa and experience the foot massage to the last whiff of fragrant maile, their signature scent, you will be transported to nirvana. Spa connoisseurs should try something unique, like the Polynesian Nonu, a Samoan-inspired massage using stones. Halekulani Hotel, ☎ **808/923-2311,** www.halekulani.com.
- **Best Facial: Abhasa Waikiki Spa** This contemporary spa, spread out over 7,000 square feet (650m sq.), concentrates on natural, organic treatments in a soothing atmosphere, where the smell of eucalyptus wafts through the air. Their specialty is an anti-aging facial using caviar that promises to give you a refreshed, revitalized face immediately. Royal Hawaiian Hotel, ☎ **808/922-8200,** www.abhasa.com.
- **Best Spa Menu: Mandara Spa** A great selection of 300 different treatments from around the globe, ranging from a Balinese facial to a Javanese Lulur rub to a Shirodhara Ayurvedic Massage, plus each of the 25 luxury treatment rooms has its own exotic private garden. Hilton Hawaiian Village Beach Resort & Spa, ☎ **808/947-9750,** www.mandaraspa.com.

1-bedroom; $245–$285 2-bedroom; $375–$395 3-bedroom. AE, DC, DISC, MC, V. Bus: 19 or 20. Map p 101.

★★ kids **Moana Surfrider, a Westin Resort** MID-WAIKIKI MAKAI Old Hawaii reigns here; I recommend staying in the historic Banyan Wing, where rooms are modern replicas of Waikiki's first hotel (built in 1901). Outside is a prime stretch of beach and an oceanfront courtyard centered around a 100-year-old banyan tree, where there's live music in the evenings. 2365 Kalakaua Ave. (across from Kaiulani St.). ☎ 800/325-3535 or 808/922-3111. www.moana-surfrider.com. 793 units. Doubles: $380–$710. AE, DC, MC, V. Bus: 19 or 20. Map p 101.

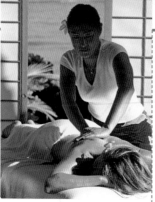

Enjoying a massage as ocean breezes caress your skin is pure bliss.

★ **kids** **New Otani Kaimana Beach Hotel** DIAMOND HEAD
This is one of Waikiki's best-kept secrets: a boutique hotel nestled on the beach at the foot of Diamond Head, with Kapiolani Park just across the street. Skip the inexpensive, teeny-tiny, barely-room-for-two rooms and go for the park-view studios with kitchens. *2863 Kalakaua Ave. (near Waikiki Aquarium, across from Kapiolani Park).* ☎ *800/356-8264 or 808/923-1555. www.kaimana.com. 124 units. Doubles: $150–$375. AE, DC, DISC, MC, V. Bus:19 or 20. Map p 101.*

kids **Ohana Waikiki Beachcomber** MID-WAIKIKI MAUKA
One of the main pluses here is the location—a block from the beach, across the street from the upscale Royal Hawaiian Shopping Center, and walking distance to restaurants.

Outrigger Reef on the Beach.

Rooms are stylish and contemporary. *2300 Kalakaua Ave. (at Duke's Lane).* ☎ *800/622-4646 or 808/922-4646. www.waikikibeachcomber.com. 495 units. Doubles: $269–$339. AE, DC, MC, V. Bus: 19 or 20. Map p 101.*

★ **kids** **Outrigger Luana Waikiki** EWA   Families take note: This mid-size hotel offers studios with kitchenettes and 1-bedrooms with full kitchens. You also get terrific views of Fort DeRussey park and the ocean in the distance. *2045 Kalakaua Ave. (at Kuhio Ave.).* ☎ *800/OUTRIGGER or 808/955-6000. www.outrigger.com. 205 units. Doubles: $255–$285; 1-bedroom: $375–$475. AE, DC, DISC, MC, V. Bus: 19 or 20. Map p 101.*

★ **kids** **Outrigger Reef on the Beach** MID-WAIKIKI MAKAI   This three-tower mega-hotel's prime beachfront location and loads of facilities (including a 5,000-sq.-ft./465m sq. spa) make it one of the chain's most attractive properties. A recent multi-million dollar renovation upgraded furniture and spruced up the bathrooms. Even the standard rooms are large and comfortable. *2169 Kalia Rd. (at Beach Walk).* ☎ *800/OUTRIGGER or 808/923-3111. www.outrigger.com. 883 units. Doubles $289–$609. AE, DC, DISC, MC, V. Bus: 19 or 20. Map p 101.*

★★ **kids** **Outrigger Waikiki on the Beach** MID-WAIKIKI MAKAI
I'd pick this Outrigger to stay in: not only does it have an excellent location on Waikiki Beach, but with some

The Royal Garden room at the Royal Hawaiian Hotel.

$20 million invested into guest room renovations and upgrades (oversize Jacuzzi bathtubs with ocean views in some rooms), coupled with the great dining (Duke's and Hula Grill, see p 93 & p 95), it offers more for the money. *2335 Kalakaua Ave. (between the Royal Hawaiian Shopping Center and the Moana Surfrider).* ☎ *800/OUTRIGGER or 808/923-0711. www.outrigger. com. 525 units. Doubles $359–$749. AE, DC, DISC, MC, V. Bus: 19 or 20. Map p 101.*

★★ kids **Outrigger Waikiki Shore Condominium** MID-WAIKIKI MAKAI One of the few condominiums on Waikiki Beach offers guests a terrific location (right on Waikiki Beach, close to shopping and restaurants), a spectacular panoramic view, daily maid service, and fully equipped kitchens. *2161 Kalia Rd. (at Saratoga Rd.).* ☎ *800/OUTRIGGER. www. outrigger.com. 168 units. Doubles: $265–$275 studio; $355–$485 1-bedroom; $480–$670 2-bedroom. AE, DC, DISC, MC, V. Bus: 19 or 20. Map p 101.*

★ **Royal Garden at Waikiki** EWA For people looking for a quieter stay, this elegant boutique hotel, tucked away on a side street, offers rooms with pantry kitchenettes. The beach is a few blocks away, but at these prices, it's worth the hike. *440 Olohana St. (between*

Kuhio Ave. and Ala Wai Blvd.). ☎ *800/367-5666 or 808/943-0202. www.royalgardens.com. 210 units. Doubles: $185–$300. AE, DC, DISC, MC, V. Bus: 19 or 20. Map p 101.*

★ kids **Royal Grove Hotel** DIAMOND HEAD This is a great bargain for frugal travelers and families; the budget accommodations are no-frill (along the lines of a Motel 6) but the family-owned hotel has genuine aloha for all the guests and Waikiki Beach is a 3-minute walk away. *151 Uluniu Ave. (between Prince Edward and Kuhio aves.), Honolulu, HI 96815.* ☎ *808/ 923-7691. www.royalgrovehotel. com. 85 units. Doubles $47–$64, 1-bedroom $80. AE, DC, DISC, MC, V. Bus: 19 or 20. Map p 101.*

W Honolulu.

Waikiki Parc.

★★ **kids** **Royal Hawaiian** MID-WAIKIKI MAKAI   The symbol of Waikiki, this flamingo-pink oasis, nestled in tropical gardens, offers rooms in both the 1927 historic wing (my favorites, with carved wooden doors, four-poster canopy beds, flowered wallpaper, and period furniture) as well as modern oceanfront towers. The beach outside is the best in

Take a Healthy Vacation: Have Your Next Medical Checkup in Waikiki

Souvenirs from your next vacation to Waikiki could include more than pictures of the sunset: How about photos of your colon? Holistica Hawaii Health Center, Hawaii's only high-tech, preventative medical facility, offers a way for you to see the full picture (literally, in CD format) of your "inner" self.

Set in the tropical resort atmosphere of the Hilton Hawaiian Village Beach Resort and Spa, the Holistica features the Electron Beam Tomography scanner, which offers a safe, rapid, and noninvasive way to detect heart disease, lung cancer, aneurysm, stroke, osteoporosis, colorectal disorders, cancerous abnormalities, and other diseases—all without even taking your clothes off.

This $2-million EBT scanner is considered the "gold standard" in detection. The doctors at Holistica can cite case histories where the scanner revealed potential problems that 10 years down the road could have been fatal, but thanks to early detection, the clients had time to change high-risk behaviors and reverse the harmful effects. For more information, call ☎ **808/951-6546,** or visit www.holistica.com.

Waikiki for sunbathing. *2259 Kalakaua Ave. (at Royal Hawaiian Ave.).* ☎ *800/ 325-3535 or 808/923-7311. www. sheraton.com. 527 units. Doubles: $445–$775. AE, MC, V. Bus: 19 or 20. Map p 101.*

★ kids **Sheraton Princess Kaiulani Hotel** MID-WAIKIKI MAUKA   Across the street from the beach, this moderately priced (for Waikiki), 29-story, three-tower hotel features double-insulated doors with soundproofing (Waikiki can be noisy at night) in their modestly decorated rooms. *120 Kaiulani Ave. (at Kalakaua Ave.).* ☎ *800/325-3535 or 808/922-5811. www.sheraton.com. 1,150 units. Doubles: $205–$400. AE, DC, MC, V. Bus: 19 or 20. Map p 101.*

★ kids **Sheraton Waikiki** MID-WAIKIKI MAKAI   Sitting right on Waikiki Beach, it's hard to get a bad room here: a whopping 1,200 units have ocean views, and 650 overlook Diamond Head. However, this is a mega-hotel, with two 30-story towers and an immense lobby. It's a frequent favorite of conventions and can be crowded, noisy, and overwhelming (not to mention the long wait at the bank of nearly a dozen elevators). *2255 Kalakaua Ave. (at Royal Hawaiian Ave.).* ☎ *800/325-3535 or 808/922-4422. www.sheraton.com. 1,852 units. Doubles: $350–$680. AE, DC, DISC, MC, V. Bus: 19 or 20. Map p 101.*

kids **Waikiki Beach Marriott Resort & Spa** DIAMOND HEAD Pluses: It's across the street from the beach, has renovated rooms, and boasts great restaurants (Sansei Seafood Restaurant and Sushi Bar and d.k. Steakhouse, see p 98 & p 93). The Minus: Rack rates are way too high—check their website for 40% off. *2552 Kalakaua Ave. (at Ohua Ave.).* ☎ *800/367-5370 or 808/922-6611. www.marriottwaikiki.com. 1,310 units. Doubles: $425–$700. AE, DC, DISC, MC, V. Bus: 19 or 20. Map p 101.*

★★ **Waikiki Parc** MID-WAIKIKI MAKAI   Recently redesigned and renovated, especially for the 20s and 30s crowd, this "hidden" luxury hotel (operated by the Halekulani) offers lots of bonuses: It's just 100 yards (91m) from the beach, has modern hi-tech rooms, hosts frequent wine-party receptions, and offers first-class service. *2233 Helumoa Rd. (at Lewers St.).* ☎ *800/422-0450 or 808/921-7272. www.waikikiparchotel.com. 297 units. Doubles $275–$415. AE, DC, MC, V. Bus: 19 or 20. Map p 101.*

kids **Waikiki Sand Villa** MID-WAIKIKI MAUKA   Budget travelers, take note: This very affordable 10-story hotel is located on the quieter side of Waikiki, with medium-size rooms and studio apartments with kitchenettes (fridge, stove, and microwave). It's a 10-minute walk to the beach. *2375 Ala Wai Blvd. (at Kanekapolei Ave.), Honolulu, HI 96815.* ☎ *800/247-1903 or 808/922-4744. www.waikiki sandvillahotel.com. 214 units. Doubles: $139–$205 and $261–$347 studio w/kitchenette. AE, DC, DISC, MC, V. Bus: 19 or 20. Map p 101.*

★★★ **W Honolulu** DIAMOND HEAD   This luxury hotel, located in a quieter, more residential neighborhood on the outskirts of Waikiki, is for visitors looking for peace and quiet in upscale accommodations. It's a 60-second walk to a remote end of Waikiki Beach, and about a 15-min. walk to shops and restaurants. The location coupled with the famous "W" pledge (whatever, whenever) make this a memorable place to stay. *2885 Kalakaua Ave. (between the Waikiki Aquarium and Outrigger Canoe Club).* ☎ *888/528-9465 or 808/922-1700. www.starwood.com/hawaii. 51 units. Doubles: $495–$610 double. AE, DC, DISC, MC, V. Bus: 19 or 20. Map p 101.*

The Best of Honolulu & Waikiki

Shopping Best Bets

Best **Alohawear**
★★ Bailey's Antiques & Aloha Shirts, *517 Kapahulu Ave.* (p 114)

Best **Antiques**
★ Antique Alley, *1347 Kapiolani Blvd.* (p 115)

Best **Place to Browse**
★★★ Native Books Na Mea Hawaii, *1050 Ala Moana Blvd.* (p 121)

Best **Cookies**
Yama's Fish Market, *2332 Young St.* (p 120)

Best **European Bakery**
★ Mary Catherine's, *2820 S. King St.* (p 116)

Best **Exotic Foods**
★ Asian Grocery, *1319 Beretania St.* (p 117)

Best **Fashion Deals**
★★ The Ultimate You, *449 Kapahulu Ave.* (p 117)

Best **Gifts**
Nohea Gallery, *1050 Ala Moana Blvd.* (p 121)

Best **Hawaii Artist**
★ Pegge Hopper Gallery, *1164 Nuuanu Ave.* (p 115)

Best **Hawaiian Books**
★ Rainbow Books and Records, *1010 University Ave.* (p 117)

Best **Hawaiian CDs**
★★ Shop Pacifica, *1525 Bernice St.* (p 121)

Best **Hawaiian Memorabilia**
★ Hula Supply Center, *2346 S. King St.* (p 121)

Best **Place for a Lei**
★ Cindy's Lei Shoppe, *1034 Maunakea St.* (p 120)

Best **Made-in-Hawaii Products**
★★ It's Chili in Hawaii, *2080 S. King St.* (p 118)

Best **Shopping Center**
★★ Ala Moana Center, *1450 Ala Moana Blvd.* (p 122)

Best **Shopping-as-Entertainment**
★★ Honolulu Fish Auction, *Pier 38, 1131 N. Nimitz Hwy.* (p 119)

Best **Sinfully Delicious Bakery**
★★ Honolulu Chocolate Co., *1200 Ala Moana Blvd.* (p 118)

Best **Sushi Takeout**
★ Sushi Company, *1111 McCully St.* (p 119)

Best **T-Shirt**
★ Local Motion, *1958 Kalakaua Ave.* (p 123)

Best **Wine & Liquor**
Fujioka's Wine Merchants, *2919 Kapiolani Blvd.* (p 118)

Aloha shirts at Bailey's Antiques.

Waikiki's Best **Shopping**

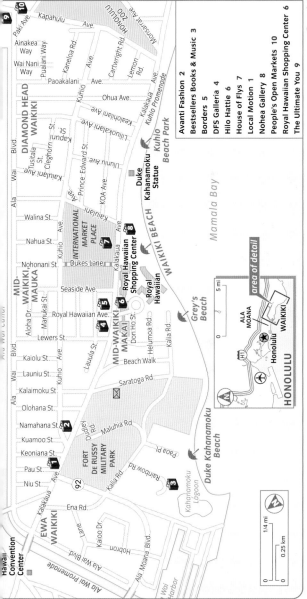

Avanti Fashion 2
Bestsellers Books & Music 3
Borders 5
DFS Galleria 4
Hilo Hattie 6
House of Flys 7
Local Motion 1
Nohea Gallery 8
People's Open Markets 10
Royal Hawaiian Shopping Center 6
The Ultimate You 9

Honolulu's Best **Shopping**

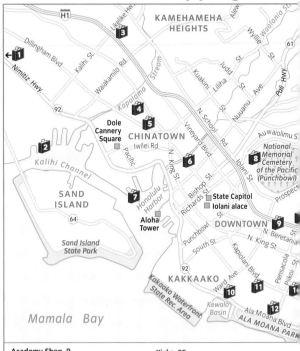

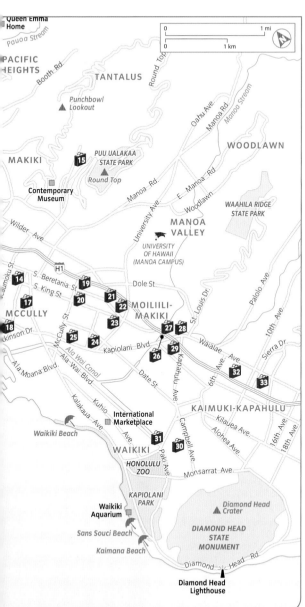

Chinatown's Best **Shopping**

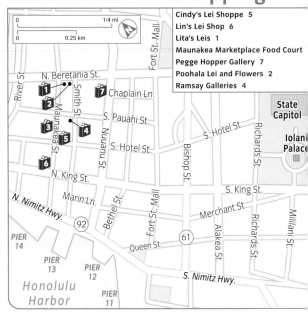

Cindy's Lei Shoppe 5
Lin's Lei Shop 6
Lita's Leis 1
Maunakea Marketplace Food Court
Pegge Hopper Gallery 7
Poohala Lei and Flowers 2
Ramsay Galleries 4

Honolulu & Waikiki Shopping **A to Z**

Alohawear

★ **Avanti Fashion** WAIKIKI This leading retro aloha shirt label turns out stunning hip and nostalgic silk shirts and dresses in authentic 1930s to 1950s fabric patterns. *2160 Kalakaua Ave. (at Kuhio St.).* ☎ *808/ 924-3232. www.avantishirts.com. AE, DC, DISC, MC, V. Bus: 19 or 20. Map p 111.*

★★ **Bailey's Antiques & Aloha Shirts** KAPAHULU Honolulu's largest selection (thousands) of vintage, secondhand, and nearly new aloha shirts and other collectibles fill this eclectic emporium, as well as old ball gowns, feather boas, fur stoles, leather jackets, 1930s

dresses, and scads of other garments. *517 Kapahulu Ave. (at Castle St.)* ☎ *808/734-7628. www.alohashirts.com. DISC, MC, V. Bus: 13 or 14. Map p 112.*

Antique Alley.

Pegge Hopper is known for her paintings of Hawaiian women.

★ **kids Hilo Hattie** IWILEI, ALA MOANA, WAIKIKI   Hawaii's largest manufacturer of Hawaiian fashions has become "hip" in the last few years with inexpensive silk aloha shirts as well as brand-name aloha shirts like Tommy Bahama and the store's own Hilo Hattie label. *700 N. Nimitz Hwy. (at Pacific St.).* ☎ *808/535-6500; Ala Moana Center 1450 Ala Moana Blvd. (at Piikoi),* ☎ *808/973-3266, Bus: 19 or 20; and Royal Hawaiian Shopping Center, 2201 Kalakaua Ave., (at Lewers St.),* ☎ *808/922-0588, Bus: 19 or 20. www.hilohattie. com. AE, DISC, MC, V. Map p 111, 112, & p 113.*

Macy's ALA MOANA   If it's aloha wear, Macy's has it. The extensive aloha shirt and muumuu departments here feature just about every label you can think of, with a selection—in all price ranges—that changes with the times. *Ala Moana Center, 1450 Ala Moana Blvd. (at Atkinson Dr.).* ☎ *808/941-2345. www.macys.com. AE, DISC, MC, V. Bus: 19 or 20. Map p 113.*

Reyn's ALA MOANA   Reyn's used to be a prosaic line but has stepped up its selection of women's and men's aloha wear with contemporary fabric prints and stylings that appeal to a trendier clientele. *Ala Moana Center, 1450 Ala Moana Blvd. (at Piikoi).* ☎ *808/949-5929.*

www.reyns.com. AE, DC, DISC, MC V. Bus: 19 or 20. Map p 113.

Antiques & Collectibles
★ **Antique Alley** KAKAAKO   This narrow shop is chockablock with collections ranging from old Hawaiian artifacts and surfing and hula nostalgia to estate jewelry, antique silver, Hawaiian bottles, collectible toys, pottery, cameras, Depression glass, linens, plantation photos, and a wide selection of nostalgic items from Hawaii and across America. *Located behind America's Mattress. 1347 Kapiolani Blvd. (at Piikoi).* ☎ *808/941-8551. AE, MC, V. Bus: 2. Map p 112.*

T. Fujii Japanese Antiques MOILILI   This is a long-standing icon in Hawaii's antiques world and an impeccable source for ukiyo-e prints, scrolls, obis, Imari porcelain, tansus, tea-ceremony bowls, and screens, as well as contemporary ceramics from Mashiko and Kasama, with prices from $25 to $18,000. *1016-B Kapahulu Ave. (King St. and H1).* ☎ *808/732-7860. ww.tfujiiantiques. com. MC, V. Bus: 14. Map p 113.*

Art
Gallery at Ward Centre ALA MOANA   This cooperative gallery of Oahu artists features fine works in all media, including paper, clay, scratchboard, oils, watercolors, collages, woodblocks, lithographs, glass, jewelry, and more. *Ward Centre, 1200 Ala Moana Blvd. (at Auahi St.)* ☎ *808/597-8034. www.gwcfineart.com. AE, DC, DISC, MC, V. Bus: 19 or 20. Map p 112.*

★ **Pegge Hopper Gallery** CHINATOWN   One of Hawaii's most popular artists, Hopper displays her widely collected paintings in her attractive gallery, which has become quite the gathering place for exhibits ranging from Tibetan sand-painting by saffron-robed monks to the most avant-garde printmaking in the islands. *1164 Nuuanu Ave. (between Beretania and Pauahi sts.)* ☎ 808/524-1160. www.peggehopper.com. *AE, DC, MC, V. Bus: B, 19 or 20. Map p 114.*

★ **Ramsay Galleries** CHINATOWN Nationally known quill-and-ink artist Ramsay, who has drawn everything from the Plaza in New York to most of Honolulu's historic buildings, maintains a vital monthly show schedule featuring her own work as well as shows of her fellow Hawaiian artists. *Tan Sing Building, 1128 Smith St. (between Hotel and Pauahi sts.)* ☎ 808/537-2787. www.ramsay museum.org. *AE, DISC, MC, V. Bus: 2, 3, 12, or 13. Map p 114.*

Tennent Art Foundation Gallery PUNCHBOWL Hawaii's most unusual gallery, listed on the Hawaii Register of Historic Places, is perched on the slopes of Punchbowl. It's devoted to artist Madge Tennent, whose paintings hang in the National Museum of Women alongside the work of Georgia O'Keeffe, and whose much-imitated style depicts Polynesians from the 1920s to the 1940s in bold, modernist strokes that left an indelible influence on Hawaiian art. Open limited hours and by appointment, so call

Finger sandwiches at Cafe Laufer.

before you go. *203 Prospect St. (San Antonio Ave.)* ☎ 808/531-1987. *MC, V. Map p 112.*

Bakeries

★ **kids Cafe Laufer** WAIALAE This small, cheerful cafe features frilly decor and sublime pastries—from apple scones and Linzer tortes to fruit flan, decadent chocolate mousse, and carrot cake—to accompany the latte and espresso. *3565 Waialae Ave. (at 11th Ave)* ☎ 808/735-7717. www.cafelaufer.com. *AE, DISC, MC, V. Map p 113.*

Foodland KAKAAKO This grocery story flies in dough from Los Angeles's famous La Brea bakery and bakes it fresh at this location, so you can pick up fresh-from-the-oven organic wheat, rosemary-olive oil, roasted garlic, potato-dill, and other spectacular breads. *1460 S. Beretania St. (between Kalakaua Ave. and Makiki St.)* ☎ 808/949-4365. www.foodland.com. *AE, DISC, MC, V. Bus: 2. Map p 112.*

★ **kids Mary Catherine's Bakery** MOILILI Local residents love this top-notch European bakery, which sells everything from lavishly tiered wedding cakes to killer carrot cakes, chocolate decadence cakes, and all manner of baked sweets that line the counters calling your name. *2820 S. King St., across from the Hawaiian Humane Society (at Waialae Ave.)* ☎ 808/946-4333. *MC, V. Bus: 4. Map p 113.*

Sconees WAIALAE Formerly Bea's Pies, this unique bakery has fantastic scones, yummy pumpkin-custard pies, and tempting Danishes. *1117 12th Ave. (at Harding).* ☎ 808/734-4024. *No credit cards. Map p 113.*

Bookstores
Bestsellers Books & Music DOWNTOWN/WAIKIKI Hawaii's

A sugar cookie from Mary Catherine's.

largest independent bookstore has a complete selection of nonfiction and fiction titles with an emphasis on Hawaiian books and music. *1001 Bishop St. (at Hotel St.).* ☎ *808/ 528-2378. Bus: 4. www.bestsellers. com. AE, MC, V. Also in the Hilton Hawaiian Village, 2005 Kalia Rd. (at Ala Moana Blvd.).* ☎ *808/953-2378. Bus: 19 or 20. Maps p 111 & p 112.*

Borders WAIKIKI/ALA MOANA
Borders is a beehive of literary activity, with weekly signings, prominent local and mainland musicians at least monthly, and special events almost daily that make this store a major Honolulu attraction. *2250 Kalakaua Ave. (between Royal Hawaiian and Seaside aves.).* ☎ *808/922-4154. Bus: 19 or 20. Also in the Ward Centre, 1200 Ala Moana Blvd. (at Auahi St.).* ☎ *808/591- 8995. www.bordersstores.com. AE, DC, DISC, MC, V. Bus: 19 or 20. Maps p 111 & p 112.*

Rainbow Books and Records
MOILIILI A little weird but totally lovable, especially among students and eccentrics (and insatiable readers), this tiny bookstore is notable for its selection of popular fiction, records, and Hawaii-themed books, secondhand and reduced. *1010 University Ave. (at King St.).* ☎ *808/955-7994. www.rainbow bookshawaii.com. AE, DISC, MC, V. Bus: 4. Map p 113.*

Consignment Shops
★★ **The Ultimate You** WAIKIKI
At this resale boutique, the clothes are relatively current (fashion of the last 2 years) and not always cheap, but they're always 50% to 90% off retail. You'll find brand names such as Escada, Chanel, Prada, Gianfranco Ferre, Donna Karan, Yves St. Laurent, Armani, Ralph Lauren, Laura Ashley, and Ann Taylor. *449 Kapahulu Ave. (at Ala Wai Blvd.).* ☎ *808/734-7724. www.theultimateyou.com. DISC, MC, V. Bus: 2. Map p 111.*

Edibles
★ **Asian Grocery** KAKAAKO
This store supplies many of Honolulu's Thai, Vietnamese, Chinese, Indonesian, and Filipino restaurants with authentic spices, rice, noodles, produce, sauces, herbs, and other adventurous ingredients. Heaven for foodies. *1319 S. Beretania St. (between Piikoi and Keeaumoku sts.).* ☎ *808/593-8440. www.asian foodtrading.com. MC, V. Bus: 2. Map p 112.*

Don Quijote KAKAAKO You can find everything at this huge emporium, ranging from takeout sushi, Korean *kal bi,* pizza, Chinese food, flowers, and Mrs. Fields cookies to Kau navel oranges, macadamia nuts, Kona coffee, Chinese taro, and

You'll find all kinds of Hawaiian goodies at Don Quijote.

Rocky Road bites from Honolulu Chocolate Co.

other Hawaii products. *801 Kaheka St. (at Kahunu St.).* ☎ *808/973-4800. AE, DISC, MC, V. Bus: 2. Map p 113.*

Fujioka's Wine Merchants

MOILIILI Oenophiles flock here for a mouthwatering selection of wines, single-malt Scotches, and affordable, farm-raised caviar—food and libations for all occasions. *Market City Shopping Center, 2919 Kapiolani Blvd. (at S. King St.), lower level.* ☎ *808/739-9463. AE, DC, DISC, MC, V. Bus: 14. Map p 113.*

★★ Honolulu Chocolate Co.

ALA MOANA Life's greatest pleasures are dispensed here with abandon: expensive gourmet chocolates made in Honolulu, Italian and Hawaiian biscotti, boulder-size turtles (caramel and pecans covered with chocolate), truffles, and my favorites—the dark-chocolate-dipped macadamia-nut clusters (heavenly). *Ward Centre, 1200 Ala Moana Blvd. (at Auahi St.).* ☎ *808/591-2997. www.honoluluchocolate.com. AE, DC, MC, V. Bus: 19 or 20. Map p 112.*

★★ It's Chili in Hawaii

MCCULLY This is *the* oasis for chile-heads, a house of heat with endorphins aplenty and good food to accompany the hot sauces from around the world, including a fabulous selection of made-in-Hawaii products. Every Saturday free samples of green-chile stew are dished up to go with the generous hot-sauce tastings. *2080 S. King St., Suite 105 (between McCully and Wiliwili sts.).* ☎ *808/945-7070. MC, V. Bus: 6. Map p 113.*

Maunakea Marketplace Food Court

CHINATOWN Hungry patrons line up for everything from pizza and plate lunches to quick, authentic, and inexpensive Vietnamese, Thai, Italian, Chinese, Japanese, and Filipino dishes. The best seafood fried rice comes from the woks of **Malee Thai/Vietnamese Cuisine**—it's perfectly flavored, with morsels of fish, squid, and shrimp. **Tandoori Chicken Cafe** serves a fount of Indian culinary pleasures, from curries and jasmine-chicken rice balls to spiced rounds of curried potatoes and a wonderful lentil dal. **Masa's** serves bento and Japanese dishes, such as miso eggplant, that are famous. You'll find the best dessert around at **Pho Lau,** which serves haupia (coconut pudding), tapioca, and taro in individual baskets made of pandanus. Join in the spirit of discovery at the produce stalls (pungent odors, fish heads, and chicken feet on counters—not for the squeamish). Vendors sell everything from fresh ahi and whole snapper to yams and taro, seaweed, and fresh fruits and vegetables. *1120 Maunakea St. (between N. Hotel St. and Pauahi St.), Chinatown.* ☎ *808/524-3409. No credit cards. Bus: 2. Map p 114.*

Mazal's Kosherland Israeli Grocery Store

IWILEI Now it is

Hawaiian hot sauces at It's Chili in Hawaii.

possible to keep kosher while in Hawaii with this tiny, two-aisle (950-sq.-ft./88m sq.) shop, with familiar products: Angel Bakery, Ossem Passover foods, Pereq spices, tzfatit, stuffed bureka pastries, canned goods from Israel, frozen kosher meats, and chilled dairy products from the mainland. *Kingsgate Plaza, 555 N. King St., (at Dillingham Blvd.).* ☎ *808/848-1700. www.kosherlandhawaii.com. No credit cards. Bus: 2. Map p 112.*

★ People's Open Market

WAIKIKI   Truck farmers from all over the island bring their produce to Oahu's neighborhoods in regularly scheduled, city-sponsored open markets, held Monday through Saturday at various locations. *Paki/ Monsarrat aves.* ☎ *808/527-5167. www.honolulu.gov/parks/programs/ pom/index1.htm. Map p 111.*

R. Field Wine Co. KAKAAKO

Richard Field—oenophile, gourmet, and cigar aficionado—moved his wine shop and thriving gourmet store into this grocery store. You'll find all manner of epicurean delights, including wines and single-malt Scotches. *Foodland Super Market, 1460 S. Beretania St. (between Kalakaua Ave. and Makiki St.).* ☎ *808/596-9463. AE, DISC, MC, V. Bus: 2. Map p 112.*

★ Sushi Company MCCULLY

Forget about going to a sushi bar when you can get takeout at this small, incredible sushi store. You'll get fast-food sushi of non-fast-food quality, all at great prices. *1111 McCully St. (between King and Beretania sts.).* ☎ *808/947-5411. No credit cards. Bus: 6. Map p 113.*

Fashion

House of Flys WAIKIKI   This store, owned by local surfers and sports enthusiasts, draws in the 20-something crowd with events such as DJ nights or a skateboard-a-thon

Sushi Company has great takeout at bargain prices.

in the nearby parking lot. Come here for hip sports clothing. *2330 Kalakaua Ave., (between Duke Ln. and Kaiulani Ave.), upper floor of the International Marketplace.* ☎ *808/923-3597. AE, DC, DISC, MC, V. Bus: 19 or 20. Map p 111.*

Kicks KAKAAKO   Attention sneaker aficionados, collectors, and those looking for shoes as a fashion statement: This is your store. You'll find limited editions and classic footwear by Nike and Adidas, plus trendy clothing lines. *1530 Makaloa St. (between Keeaumoku and Amana sts.).* ☎ *808/941-9191. www.kickshawaii.com. AE, DISC, MC, V. Bus: 13. Map p 113.*

Modern Amusement

KAPAHULU   One of only four MA stores in the world, this store draws artsy types and non-conformist surfers, skateboarders, and clubbers looking for both cutting-edge surf wear and classic club outfits. *449 Kapahulu Ave., Suite 102 (between Ala Wai Blvd. and Kanainoa Ave.).* ☎ *808/738-2769. www.masoldhere.com. AE, DC, DISC, MC, V. Bus: 13. Map p 113.*

Fish Markets

★★ kids Honolulu Fish Auction IWILEI   If you want to experience the high drama of fish buying, head to this auction at the United Fishing Agency, where fishermen bring their fresh catch in at 5:30am

(sharp) Monday through Saturday, and buyers bid on a variety of fish, from fat tunas to weird-looking hapupu. *Pier 38, 1131 N. Nimitz Hwy.* ☎ *808/536-2148. No credit cards. Bus: 42. Map p 112.*

★ Tamashiro Market IWILEI
Good service and the most extensive selection of fresh fish in Honolulu has made this the granddaddy of fish markets. You'll find everything from live lobsters and crabs to fresh slabs of ahi to whole *onaga* and *ehu. 802 N. King St. (between Palama St. and Austin Ln.), Kalihi.* ☎ *808/841-8047. MC, V. Bus: 42. Map p 112.*

Yama's Fish Market MOILIILI
Known for its inexpensive fresh fish, tasty poke, lomi salmon, and many varieties of prepared seafood, Yama's also has a variety of pre-pared foods and bakery items (their chocolate-chip/mac-nut cookies are peerless). *2332 Young St. (Hoawa Ln).* ☎ *808/941-9994. www.yamas fishmarket.com. DC, DISC, MC, V. Bus: 6. Map p 113.*

Flowers & Leis
★ kids Cindy's Lei Shoppe
CHINATOWN I love this lei shop because it always has unusual leis such as feather dendrobiums, fire-cracker combinations, and everyday

Rudy's Flowers.

Modern Amusement.

favorites like ginger, tuberose, orchid, and pikake. Its "curb service" allows you to phone in your order and pick up your lei curbside—a great convenience on this busy street. *1034 Maunakea St. (at Hotel St.).* ☎ *808/536-6538. MC, V. Bus: 2. Map p 114.*

Lin's Lei Shop CHINATOWN
Features creatively fashioned, unusual leis. *1017-A Maunakea St. (at King St.).* ☎ *808/537-4112. AE, DISC, MC, V. Bus: 19 or 20. Map p 114.*

Lita's Leis CHINATOWN This small lei shop features fresh puakenikeni, gardenias that last, and a supply of fresh and reasonable leis. *59 N. Bere-tania St. (between Maunakea and Smith sts.).* ☎ *808/521-9065. AE, DISC, MC, V. Bus: 19 or 20. Map p 114.*

Poohala Lei and Flowers CHI-NATOWN If you're looking for a worthy selection of the classics at fair prices, this is the shop. *69 N. Beretania St. (between Smith and Maunakea sts.).* ☎ *808/537-3011. MC, V. Bus: 19 or 20. Map p 114.*

★ Rainforest Plantes et Fleurs KAPAHULU For special-occasion designer bouquets or leis, this is the place. Custom-designed leis and special arrangements come com-plete with cards in Hawaiian, with

English translations. *1016 Kapahulu Ave. (between H1 and Kehei Pl.).* ☎ *808/591-9999. AE, DC, DISC, MC, V. Map p 112.*

Rudy's Flowers MOILIILI The best prices on roses, Micronesian ginger leis, and a variety of cut blooms. *2357 S. Beretania St. (at Isenburg St.).* ☎ *808/944-8844. www.rudysflowers.com. AE, DISC, MC, V. Bus: 6. Map p 113.*

Hawaiiana Gifts

★ kids **Hula Supply Center** MOILIILI Hawaiiana meets kitsch. This shop's marvelous selection of souvenirs and memorabilia of Hawaii includes Day-Glo cellophane skirts, bamboo nose flutes, T-shirts, hula drums, shell leis, feathered rattle gourds, lauhala accessories, fiber mats, and a wide assortment of pareu fabrics. *2346 S. King St. (at Isenberg St.).* ☎ *808/941-5379. www.hulasupplycenter.com. MC, V. Bus: 6. Map p 113.*

★★★ kids **Native Books Na Mea Hawaii** ALA MOANA This is a browser's paradise, featuring a variety of Hawaiian items from musical instruments to calabashes, jewelry, leis, and books to contemporary Hawaiian clothing, Hawaiian food products, and other high-quality gift items. *Ward Warehouse, 1050 Ala Moana Blvd. (at Ward Ave.).* ☎ *808/596-8885. www. nativebookshawaii.com. AE, DISC, MC, V. Bus: 19 or 20. Map p 112.*

★★★ kids **Nohea Gallery** ALA MOANA/WAIKIKI A fine showcase for contemporary Hawaii art, Nohea celebrates the islands with thoughtful, attractive selections like pit-fired raku, finely turned wood vessels, jewelry, handblown glass, paintings, prints, fabrics (including Hawaiian-quilt cushions), and furniture. *Ward Warehouse, 1050 Ala Moana Blvd. (at Ward Ave.).* ☎ *808/596-0074. www.noheagallery.com. Bus: 19 or*

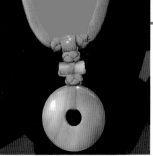

Academy Shop, at the Honolulu Academy of Arts.

20. AE, DC, DISC, MC, V. Also at Moana Surfrider, 2365 Kalakaua Ave. (at Kaiulani Ave.). ☎ *808/923-6644. Maps p 111 & p 112.*

Museum Stores

★ kids **Academy Shop** KAKAAKO The place to go for art books, jewelry, basketry, ethnic fabrics, native crafts from all over the world, posters and books, and fiber vessels and accessories. *Honolulu Academy of Arts, 900 S. Beretania St. (at Ward Ave.).* ☎ *808/532-8703. www.honolulu academy.org. AE, DISC, MC, V. Bus: 2, 13, or City Express B. Map p 112.*

★ **Contemporary Museum Gift Shop** MAKIKI HEIGHTS I love the glammy selection of jewelry and novelties, such as the twisted-wire wall hangings, at this browser-friendly shop. Pick up avant-garde jewelry, cards and stationery, books, home accessories, and gift items made by artists from Hawaii and across the country. *2411 Makiki Heights Rd. (between Round Top Dr. and Mott-Smith Dr.).* ☎ *808/ 523-3447. www.tcmhi.org. AE, DC, DISC, MC, V. Map p 112.*

★★ kids **Shop Pacifica** KALIHI Plan to spend time browsing through the local crafts (including terrific Niihau shell leis), lauhala and Cook Island woven products, Hawaiian music tapes and CDs, pareu, and a vast selection of Hawaii-themed

You'll find everything from upscale boutiques to mainland chains at Ala Moana Shopping Center.

books that anchor this gift shop. *Bishop Museum, 1525 Bernice St. (between Kalihi St. and Kapalama Ave.).* ☎ *808/848-4158. www.bishopmuseum.org. AE, DC, DISC, MC, V. Bus: 2. Map p 112.*

Shopping Centers

★★ kids **Ala Moana Center** ALA MOANA   Nearly 400 shops and restaurants sprawl over several blocks, making this Hawaii's largest shopping center catering to every imaginable need, from upscale (**Neiman Marcus, Tiffany,** and **Chanel**) to mainland chains (**Gap, Banana Republic, DKNY,** and **Old Navy**), to department stores (**Macy's, Sears**), to practical touches, such as banks, a foreign-exchange service (**Travelex**), a U.S. Post Office, several optical companies (including 1-hr. service by **LensCrafters**), and a handful of smaller locally owned stores (**Islands' Best** and **Splash! Hawaii**). The **food court** is abuzz with dozens of stalls purveying Cajun food, pizza, plate lunches, vegetarian fare, green tea, panini, and countless other treats. *1450 Ala Moana Blvd. (between Kaheka and Piikoi sts.).* ☎ *808/955-9517. www.alamoanacenter.com. AE, DC, DISC, MC, V. Bus: 8, 19, or 20. Map p 113.*

Aloha Tower Marketplace

HONOLULU HARBOR   Dining and shopping prospects abound here: **Hawaiian Pacific Crafts, Hawaiian Ukulele Company, Sunglass King, Don Ho's Island Grill, Chai's Island Bistro,** and **Gordon Biersch Brewery Restaurant.** *1 Aloha Tower Dr. (at Bishop St.).* ☎ *808/528-5700. www.alohatower.com. AE, DC, DISC, MC, V. Bus: 19 or 20. Map p 112.*

DFS Galleria WAIKIKI   "Boat days" is the theme at this Waikiki emporium, a three-floor extravaganza of shops ranging from the superluxe (like **Givenchy** and **Coach**) to the very touristy, with great Hawaii food

Bad Ass Coffee Cafe at the Aloha Tower Marketplace.

products (**Big Island Candies**), aloha shirt and T-shirt shops, surf and skate equipment, a terrific Hawaiian music department, and a labyrinth of fashionable stores thrown in to complete the retail experience. *330 Royal Hawaiian Ave. (at Kalakaua Ave.).* ☎ *808/931-2655. www.dfsgalleria.com. AE, DC, MC, V. Bus: 19 or 20. Map p 111.*

★ **Royal Hawaiian Shopping Center** WAIKIKI After 2 years and $84 million in remodeling and renovations, a larger, upscale shopping center opened in 2007 with new shops, restaurants, a nightclub and theater, entry porte-cochere, and even a garden grove of 70 coconut trees with an entertainment area. The result is a 293,000-square-foot (27,220m sq.) open-air mall with 110 stores, restaurants, and entertainment options on four levels. Shops range from **Hilo Hattie** to **Cartier, Hermès,** and **Salvatore Ferragamo.** *2201 Kalakaua Ave., (at Royal Hawaiian Ave.).* ☎ *808/922-0588. www.shopwaikiki.com. AE, DC, DISC, MC, V. Bus: 19 or 20. Map p 111.*

★ **kids Ward Centre** ALA MOANA Great restaurants (**Kakaako Kitchen, Kua Aina**) and shops (**Crazy Shirts Factory Outlet, Paper Roses, Honolulu Chocolate Co., The Gallery,** and **Borders**) make this a popular place, bustling with browsers. *200 Ala Moana Blvd. (at Kamakee St.).* ☎ *808/591-8411. www.victoria ward.com. AE, DC, DISC, MC, V. Bus: 19 or 20. Map p 112.*

kids Ward Entertainment Center ALA MOANA This is the place for eating, drinking, and entertainment. You'll find a 16-movie megaplex; eateries such as **Dave & Buster's, Buca di Beppo,** and **Cold Stone Creamery;** retail therapy including **Nordstrom Rack, Office Depot,** and **Pier 1 Imports;** and the ubiquitous **Starbucks Coffee.** *At the corner of Auahi and Kamakee sts.*

☎ *808/591-8411. www.victoriaward. com. AE, DC, DISC, MC, V. Bus: 19 or 20. Map p 112.*

★ **kids Ward Warehouse** ALA MOANA Older than its sister properties (see above), Ward Warehouse remains a popular stop for dining (**Old Spaghetti Factory, Honolulu Cookie Company**) and shopping (**Native Books & Beautiful Things, Nohea Gallery**). *1050 Ala Moana Blvd. (at Ward Ave.).* ☎ *808/591-8411. www.victoriaward.com. AE, DC, DISC, MC, V. Bus: 19 or 20. Map p 112.*

T-Shirts

Hawaiian Island Creations ALA MOANA This super-cool surf shop offers sunglasses, sun lotions, surf wear, surfboards, skateboards, and accessories galore. *Ala Moana Center, 1450 Ala Moana Blvd. (between Piikoi and Kaheka sts.).* ☎ *808/973-6780. www.hicsurf.com. AE, DISC, MC, V. Bus: 19 or 20. Map p 112.*

★ **kids Local Motion** WAIKIKI The icon of surfers and skateboarders, both professionals and wannabes, has everything from surfboards, T-shirts, aloha and casual wear, to countless accessories for life in the sun. *1958 Kalakaua Ave. (between Pau and Keoniana sts.).* ☎ *808/979-7873. www.localmotion hawaii.com. AE, DISC, MC, V. Bus: 19 or 20. Map p 111.*

Hawaiian Island Creations.

Nightlife & Performing Arts
Best Bets

Best Place to **Celebrate St. Patrick's Day**
★ Murphy's Bar & Grill, *2 Merchant St.* (p 127)

Best for **Hawaiian Music**
★★★ House Without a Key, *Halekulani Hotel, 2199 Kalia Rd.* (p 129)

Best **Club for Jazz**
★★ Indigo's, *1121 Nuuanu Ave.* (p 127)

Best **Club for Concerts**
★ Pipeline, *805 Pohukaina St.* (p 128)

Most **Romantic Place for Sunset**
★★ Banyan Veranda, *Moana Surfrider, 2365 Kalakaua Ave.* (p 129)

Best Place to **People-Watch at Sunset**
★★ Duke's Canoe Club, *Outrigger Waikiki on the Beach Hotel, 2335 Kalakaua Ave.* (p 129)

Most **Amazing Performance**
★ Cirque Hawaii, *325 Seaside Ave. (Kalakaua Ave.; p 130)*

Best **Luau**
Royal Hawaiian Hotel, *2259 Kalakaua Ave.* (p 130)

Best **Performing Arts Center**
★★ Neal Blaisdell Center, *777 Ward Ave.* (p 131)

Best for **Outdoor Concerts**
★★ Waikiki Shell, *2805 Monsarrat Ave.* (p 132)

Best for **Film Buffs**
★★ The Movie Museum, *3566 Harding Ave.* (p 128)

Best **Magic Show**
★ *"The Magic of Polynesia,"* Ohana Waikiki Beachcomber, *2300 Kalakaua Ave.* (p 131)

Best **Musical Show**
★ Society of Seven, *777 Ward Ave.* (p 131)

Most **Historic Theater**
★★★ Hawaii Theatre, *1130 Bethel St.* (p 132)

Best Place to See **Locally Written and Produced Plays**
★★ Kumu Kahua Theatre, *46 Merchant St.* (p 132)

Watch the sun set and listen to Hawaiian music at Duke's Canoe Club.

Waikiki's Best **Nightlife**

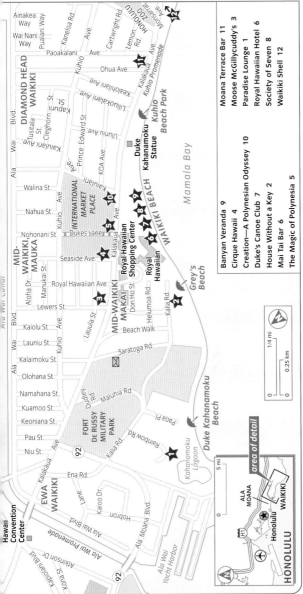

Banyan Veranda 9
Cirque Hawaii 4
Creation—A Polynesian Odyssey 10
Duke's Canoe Club 7
House Without a Key 2
Mai Tai Bar 6
The Magic of Polynesia 5

Moana Terrace Bar 11
Moose McGillycuddy's 3
Paradise Lounge 1
Royal Hawaiian Hotel 6
Society of Seven 8
Waikiki Shell 12

Honolulu's Best **Nightlife**

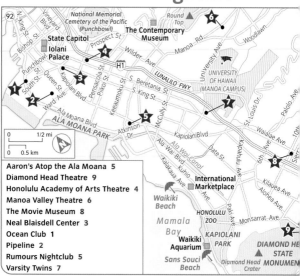

Aaron's Atop the Ala Moana 5
Diamond Head Theatre 9
Honolulu Academy of Arts Theatre 4
Manoa Valley Theatre 6
The Movie Museum 8
Neal Blaisdell Center 3
Ocean Club 1
Pipeline 2
Rumours Nightclub 5
Varsity Twins 7

Chinatown & Downtown Honolulu's Best **Nightlife**

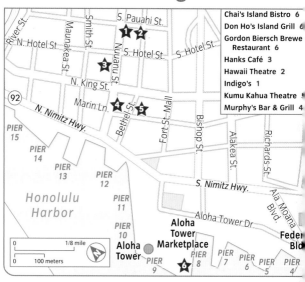

Chai's Island Bistro 6
Don Ho's Island Grill 6
Gordon Biersch Brewe
    Restaurant 6
Hanks Café 3
Hawaii Theatre 2
Indigo's 1
Kumu Kahua Theatre
Murphy's Bar & Grill 4

Nightlife & Performing Arts A to Z

Bars & Cocktail Lounges

Aaron's Atop the Ala Moana

ALA MOANA   For the more mature set: Take in the best view in town (from the 36th floor of the hotel), watch the Honolulu city lights wrap around the room, and cha-cha-cha to the vertigo! There's live music and dancing nightly, a lengthy dinner menu, and an appetizer menu nightly from 5pm. *In the Ala Moana Hotel, 410 Atkinson Dr. (next to the Ala Moana Shopping Center).* ☎ 808/955-4466. Bus: 19 or 20. Map p 126.

★ Gordon Biersch Brewery Restaurant ALOHA TOWER

A new stage area allows diners to swing to jazz, blues, and island riffs. *1 Aloha Tower Dr., on the waterfront between piers 8 and 11, Honolulu Harbor (at Bishop St.).* ☎ 808/599-4877. www.gordonbiersch.com. Map p 126.

Hanks Café DOWNTOWN   This

tiny, kitschy, friendly pub has live music nightly, open-mic nights, and special events that attract great talent and a supportive crowd. On some nights the music spills out into the streets, and it's so packed you have to press your nose against the window to see what you're missing. *1038 Nuuanu Ave. (between Hotel and King sts.).* ☎ 808/526-1410. www.hankscafehonolulu.com. Bus: 2. Map p 126.

★ Murphy's Bar & Grill DOWN-

TOWN   One of Honolulu's most popular downtown ale houses and media haunts. Over a dozen beers on tap, including (of course) Murphy's and Guinness. *2 Merchant St. (at Nuuanu Ave.).* ☎ 808/531-0422. www.gomurphys.com. Bus: 19 or 20. Map p 126.

Clubs

★★ Indigo's CHINATOWN   This

Chinatown spot serves sizzling food during the day, turns to cool jazz in the early evening, and progresses to late-night DJs spinning Top 40, disco, rock, funk, and more. *1121 Nuuanu Ave. (between Hotel and Pauahi sts.).* ☎ 808/521-2900. www.indigo-hawaii.com. No cover. Bus: 13. Map p 126.

Moose McGillycuddy's WAIKIKI

The 20-something crowd, visitors, and military tend to gather here. Downstairs is a cafe serving breakfast, lunch, and dinner; upstairs is a happening live entertainment and dance club. *310 Lewers St. in Waikiki (at Kalakaua Ave.).* ☎ 808/923-0751. www.maui.net/~mooses/mooses_waikiki. No cover. Bus: 19 or 20. Map p 125.

Murphy's Bar & Grill.

Get Down with ARTafterDark

The last Friday of every month (except Nov and Dec) the place to be after the sun goes down is **ARTafterDark**, a *pau-hana* (after work) mixer in the **Honolulu Academy of Arts**, at 900 S. Beretania St. Each gathering has a theme combining art with food, music, and dancing. In addition to the exhibits in the gallery, ARTafterDark also features visual and live performances. Last year the themes ranged from "Plant Rice" (with rice and sake tastings, rice dishes, Asian beers, live Asian fusion music, and a tour of the *Art of Rice* exhibit) to "'80s Night," "Turkish Delights," "Cool Nights, Hot Jazz and Blues," and "Havana Heat."

Entry fee is $7; the party gets going about 6pm and lasts to 9pm, the crowd age ranges from 20s to 50s, the dress is everything from jeans and T-shirts to designer cocktail party attire. For more information, call ☎ 808/532-6091 (www.artafterdark.org).

★ **Pipeline** KAKAAKO This huge club/concert venue has dancing, darts, pool, and a sports bar with larger-than-life TV screens. Patrons here tend to be younger (you can get in at 18 years old) and are dressed to go clubbing. *805 Pohukaina St. (between Koula and Kamani sts.).* ☎ *808/589-1999. www.pipelinecafe.net. Cover $1–$3; concerts around $15. Map p 126.*

Rumours Nightclub ALA MOANA The disco of choice for those who remember Paul McCartney as something other than Stella's

Rumours Nightclub.

father, with "themes" that change monthly. A spacious dance floor, good sound system, and Top-40 music draw a mix of generations. *Lobby, Ala Moana Hotel, 410 Atkinson Dr. (next to Ala Moana Shopping Center).* ☎ *808/955-4811. Cover $5–$12. Bus: 19 or 20. Map p 126.*

Film
★ **Honolulu Academy of Arts Theatre** KAKAAKO This is the film-as-art center of Honolulu, offering special screenings, guest appearances, and cultural performances, as well as noteworthy programs in the visual arts. *900 S. Beretania St. (at Ward Ave.).* ☎ *808/532-8703. www.honoluluacademy.org. Ticket prices vary. Bus: 2 or 13. Map p 126.*

★★ **The Movie Museum** KAIMUKI Film buffs and esoteric movie lovers can enjoy special screenings as they recline comfortably on brown vinyl–stuffed recliners, or rent from a collection of 3,000 vintage and hard-to-find films. *3566 Harding Ave. (between 11th and 12th aves.).* ☎ *808/735-8771.*

Brothers Cazimero playing at Chai's.

www.kaimukihawaii.com/business/
entertainment. Tickets: $5. Bus: 22,
transfer to 14. Map p 126.

★★ Varsity Twins MCCULLY
Near the University of Hawaii, this
art theater specializes in avant-
garde, artistically acclaimed
releases. *1106 University Ave.
(Beretania St.).* ☎ *808/593-3000.
Tickets: $9. Bus: 4. Map p 126.*

Hawaiian Music
★★ Banyan Veranda WAIKIKI
Enjoy a romantic evening sitting on
the back porch of this historic hotel,
overlooking an islet-size canopy of
banyan trees, as you watch the sun
set and sip a liquid libation to the
sounds of live Hawaiian music playing softly in the background. You'll
be in good company; Robert Louis
Stevenson once loved to linger here.
*Moana Surfrider, 2365 Kalakaua Ave.
(between Duke's Ln. and Kaiulani
Ave.).* ☎ *808/922-3111. www.
sheratonmoanasurfrider.com. 2-drink
minimum. Bus: 19 or 20. Map p 125.*

★ Chai's Island Bistro ALOHA
TOWER **Brothers Cazimero**
remain one of Hawaii's most gifted
duos (Robert on bass, Roland on
12-string guitar), appearing every
Wednesday at 7pm at this leading
venue for Hawaiian entertainment.
Also at Chai's: Robert Cazimero plays
by himself on the piano on Tuesday
at 7pm, and **Jerry Santos** and

Olomana perform on Monday at
7pm. *Aloha Tower Marketplace, 1
Aloha Tower Dr., on the waterfront
between piers 8 and 11, Honolulu
Harbor (at Bishop St.).* ☎ *808/585-
0011. www.chaisislandbistro.com.
No cover, $25 drink minimum. Bus:
19 or 20. Map p 126.*

Don Ho's Island Grill ALOHA
TOWER   Hawaii's best known musi-
cian helped design this relaxed
island bar/eatery, where live music
is always on tap. Aloha Tower Marketplace. *1 Aloha Tower Dr., on the
waterfront between piers 8 and 11,
Honolulu Harbor (at Bishop St.).*
☎ *808/528-0807. www.donho.com/
grill/aboutus.htm. No cover. Bus:19
or 20. Map p 126.*

★★ Duke's Canoe Club WAIKIKI
The outside Barefoot Bar is perfect
for sipping a tropical drink, watching
the waves and sunset, and listening
to music. It can get crowded, so get
there early. Hawaii sunset music is
usually from 4 to 6pm on weekends,
and there's live entertainment nightly
from 10pm to midnight. *Outrigger
Waikiki on the Beach Hotel, 2335
Kalakaua Ave. (between Duke's Ln.
and Kaiulani Ave.).* ☎ *808/922-2268.
www.dukeswaikiki.com. No cover, no
minimum. Bus: 19 or 20. Map p 125.*

★★★ House Without a Key
WAIKIKI   This is my favorite place
to relax at sunset. Watch the breathtaking Kanoelehua Miller dance hula

Cirque Hawaii performers.

to the riffs of Hawaiian steel-pedal guitar under a century-old kiawe tree with the sunset and ocean glowing behind her—a romantic, evocative, nostalgic scene. It doesn't hurt, either, that the Halekulani happens to make the best mai tais in the world. This place has the after-dinner hours covered, too, with light jazz by local artists from 10:15pm to midnight nightly. *Halekulani Hotel, 2199 Kalia Rd. (at Lewers St.).* ☎ *808/923-2311. www.halekulani.com. No cover. Bus: 19 or 20. Map p 125.*

Mai Tai Bar WAIKIKI This circular bar, right down at beach level, features live Hawaiian music from 4:30 to 10:30pm nightly. *Royal Hawaiian Hotel, 2259 Kalakaua Ave. (at Seaside Ave.).* ☎ *808/923-7311. www.royal-hawaiian.com. 1-drink minimum. Bus: 19 or 20. Map p 125.*

★ **Moana Terrace Bar** WAIKIKI Hawaii's queen of falsetto, **Genoa Keawe,** can be heard from 5:30 to 8:30pm every Thursday. The rest of the week, except Monday, other contemporary Hawaiian musicians fill in. *Waikiki Beach Marriott, 2552 Kalakaua Ave. (between Ohua and Paoakalani aves.).* ☎ *808/922-6611. www.marriottwaikiki.com. No cover. Bus: 19 or 20. Map p 125.*

★ **Paradise Lounge** WAIKIKI Impromptu hula and spirited music from the family and friends of the performers are an island tradition and often seen in this lounge, which serves as a large living room for the full-bodied music of **Olomana.** The group plays Friday and Saturday from 8pm to midnight. *Hilton Hawaiian Village, 2005 Kalia Rd. (at Ala Moana Blvd.).* ☎ *808/949-4321. www.hilton hawaiianvillage.com. 2-drink minimum. Bus: 19 or 20. Map p 125.*

Luau

Royal Hawaiian Hotel WAIKIKI Waikiki's only oceanfront luau features a variety of traditional Hawaiian as well as continental American dishes: roasted kalua pig, mahimahi, teriyaki steak, poi, sweet potatoes, rice, vegetables, haupia (coconut pudding), and a selection of desserts. Entertainment includes songs and dances from Hawaii and other Polynesian island nations. *Royal Hawaiian Hotel, 2259 Kalakaua Ave. (at Seaside Ave.).* ☎ *888-808-4668. www.honu hawaiiactivities.com. Mon & Thurs, 5:30pm. Adults $97, children (5–12) $54. AE, DISC, MC, V. Bus: 19 or 20. Map p 125.*

Shows

★ **kids Cirque Hawaii** WAIKIKI This 70-minute performance will inspire you, enthrall you, and make you laugh out loud. A series of acts highlighting the performers' athletic prowess, stunning choreography, and flamboyant costumes will keep you on the edge of your seat. Watch the acrobats float, tumble, and fly through the air on a bungee or using silk fabrics; the trapeze artists flitter from one trapeze to another; the gymnasts launch themselves as high as a three-story building from a teeter board; and a contortionist fluidly bends her incredibly flexible body into seemingly impossible positions. *325 Seaside Ave.* ☎ *808/ 922-0017. www.cirquehawaii.com. Thurs–Tues 6:30 & 8:30pm. Packages: $55–$130 adults, $42–$98 children ages 3–11. Map p 125.*

★ kids **"Creation—A Polynesian Odyssey"** WAIKIKI Don't miss this theatrical journey of fire dancing, special effects, illusions, hula, and Polynesian dances from Hawaii and the South Pacific. *Sheraton Princess Kaiulani, 2nd-floor Ainahau Showroom, 120 Kaiulani Ave. (at Kalakaua Ave.).* ☎ *808/931-4660. Shows 7:20pm Tues and Thurs–Sun. $70–$115 w/dinner; $38 for just cocktails. Bus: 19 or 20. Map p 125.*

★ kids **"The Magic of Polynesia"** WAIKIKI This is not your typical dinner theater. This stage show combines magic, illusions, and Polynesian dance, song, and chant with International Magician Society's Merlin award-winning master illusionist John Hirokawa. Amazing magic with a pinch of pyrotechnics, lasers, and other special effects thrown in. *Ohana Waikiki Beachcomber, 2300 Kalakaua Ave. (at Duke's Ln.).* ☎ *808/ 971-4321. www.robertshawaii.com. 8pm show nightly. $80 w/dinner; $51 w/cocktails. Bus: 19 or 20. Map p 125.*

★ **Society of Seven** WAIKIKI This nightclub act (a blend of skits, Broadway hits, popular music, and costumed musical acts) is into

its third decade, no small feat. *Outrigger Waikiki on the Beach, 2335 Kalakaua Ave. (between Duke's Ln. and Kaiulani Ave.).* ☎ *808/ 922-6408. www.outriggeractivities. com. 8:30pm shows Tues–Sun; $72 w/dinner; $47 w/cocktails. Bus: 19 or 20. Map p 125.*

Symphony, Opera & Dance Performances

★★ **Neal Blaisdell Center** KAKAAKO Hawaii's premier performance center for the best in entertaining. This arena/concert hall/exhibition building can be divided into an intimate 2,175-seat concert hall or an 8,805-seat arena, serving everyone from symphony-goers to punk rockers. Playing here from September to May is the **Honolulu Symphony Orchestra** (☎ 808/524-0815; www.honolulusymphony.com). From January to March, the highly successful **Hawaii Opera Theatre** takes to the stage with hits like *La Bohème, Carmen, Turandot, Romeo and Juliet, Rigoletto,* and *Aïda.* Also performing at this concert hall are Hawaii's four ballet companies: **Hawaii Ballet Theatre, Ballet Hawaii, Hawaii State Ballet,** and **Honolulu Dance Theatre.** *Neal Blaisdell Center, 777 Ward Ave. (between Kapiolani Ave. and King St.).* ☎ *808/591-2211. www.blaisdell center.com. Bus: 19 or 20. Map p 126.*

Hawaii Opera Theatre's performance of Madame Butterfly.

Comedy Tonight

Local comics tend to move around a lot, so the best way to see comedy is to check their websites. The best in comedy acts are **Andy Bumatai** (www.andybumatai.com), **Augie T** (www.augietulba.com), and **Frank Delima** (www.frankdelima.com); who perform "local" stand-up sketches that will have you not only understanding local residents, but also screaming with laughter.

★★ kids **Waikiki Shell** WAIKIKI This outdoor venue in the middle of Kapiolani Park allows concertgoers to watch the sunset and see the stars come out before the concert begins. A range of performers, from Hawaiian to jazz musicians, have graced this stage. *2805 Monsarrat Ave. (between Kalakaua and Paki aves.).* ☎ *808/527-5400. www.waikikishell.com. Bus: 19 or 20. Map p 125.*

Theater

★ **Diamond Head Theatre** DIAMOND HEAD Hawaii's oldest theater (since 1915), this community theater presents a sort of "Broadway of the Pacific," producing a variety of performances from musicals to comedies to classical dramas. *520 Makapu'u Ave. (at Alohea Ave.).* ☎ *808/733-0274. www.diamond headtheatre.com. Tickets $12–$42. Bus: 58. Map p 126.*

★★★ **Hawaii Theatre** CHINATOWN Audiences here have enjoyed performances ranging from the big off-Broadway percussion hit *Stomp* to the talent of *Tap Dogs,* Momix, the Jim Nabor's Christmas show, the Hawaii International Jazz Festival, the American Repertory Dance Company, barbershop quartets, and John Ka'imikaua's halau. The neoclassical Beaux Arts landmark features a 1922 dome, 1,400 plush seats, a hydraulically elevated organ, and gilt galore. *1130 Bethel St. (between Hotel and Pauahi sts.).* ☎ *808/528-0506. www.hawaii theatre.com. Ticket prices vary. Bus: 2 or 13. Map p 126.*

★★ **Kumu Kahua Theatre** DOWNTOWN For an intimate glimpse at island life, take in a show at Kumu Kahua. This tiny theater (100 seats) produces plays dealing with today's cultural experience in Hawaii, often written by residents. *46 Merchant St.* ☎ *808/536-4222. www.kumukahua.org. Tickets $13. Map p 126.*

Manoa Valley Theatre MANOA Honolulu's equivalent of Off-Broadway, with performances of well-known shows—anything from *Urinetown* to *Who's Afraid of Virginia Woolf. 2833 E. Manoa Rd. (between Keama Pl. and Huapala St.).* ☎ *808/988-6131. www.manoa valleytheatre.com. Tickets: $20–$25. Map p 126.* ●

A detail of the Hawaii Theatre's architecture.

5 The Best **Regional Tours**

The **North Shore**

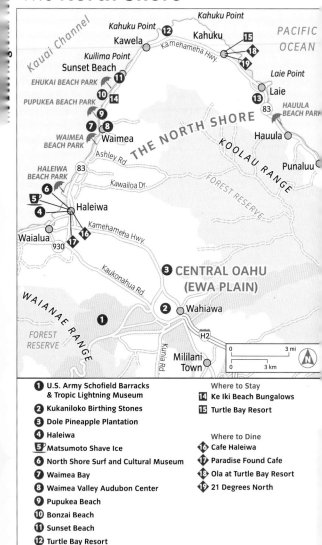

1 U.S. Army Schofield Barracks & Tropic Lightning Museum

2 Kukaniloko Birthing Stones

3 Dole Pineapple Plantation

4 Haleiwa

5 Matsumoto Shave Ice

6 North Shore Surf and Cultural Museum

7 Waimea Bay

8 Waimea Valley Audubon Center

9 Pupukea Beach

10 Bonzai Beach

11 Sunset Beach

12 Turtle Bay Resort

13 Polynesian Cultural Center

Where to Stay

14 Ke Iki Beach Bungalows

15 Turtle Bay Resort

Where to Dine

16 Cafe Haleiwa

17 Paradise Found Cafe

18 Ola at Turtle Bay Resort

19 21 Degrees North

Previous page: Hiking near Haleiwa.

In Hawaii, half the fun is getting there. That's especially true of a drive up through the center of the island on to the famous North Shore. If you can afford the splurge, rent a bright, shiny convertible—the perfect car for Oahu, since you can tan as you go. Majestic sandalwood trees once stood in the central plains; the Hawaiian chiefs ordered them cut down, and now they're covered with tract homes, malls, and factory outlets. Beyond that is the North Shore and Hawaii's surf city: Haleiwa, a quaint turn-of-the-20th-century sugar-plantation town designated a historic site. A collection of faded clapboard stores with a picturesque harbor, Haleiwa has evolved into a surfer outpost and major roadside attraction with art galleries, restaurants, and shops that sell hand-decorated clothing, jewelry, and sports gear. START: **Waikiki. Trip length: 95 miles (153km).**

Take H-1 West to H-2 North, which becomes Hwy. 99. Turn left on Kunia Rd., then right on Lyman Rd. (through the gate), right on Flagler Rd., and left on Waianae Ave. Museum is in Bldg. 361. Bus: 6, transfer to 52, transfer to 72.

1 kids **U.S. Army Schofield Barracks & Tropic Lightning Museum.** This is the largest cavalry post operated by the U.S. Army outside the continental United States. *See p 49, bullet* **6**.

Retrace your route back to Hwy. 99, make a right at the next intersection to stay on Hwy. 99, then another right at Whitemore Ave. The Stones are about a half mile down this road on the left, before the intersection of Kamehameha Hwy. (Hwy. 80). Bus: 52.

2 **Kukaniloko Birthing Stones.** This is the most sacred site in central Oahu. Two rows of 18 lava rocks once flanked a central birthing stone, where women of ancient Hawaii gave birth to potential *alii* (royalty). Used by Oahu's *alii* for generations of births, many of the *pohaku* (rocks) have bowl-like shapes. Some think the site also may have served ancient astronomers—like a Hawaiian Stonehenge. Look for the two interpretive signs, one explaining why this was chosen as a birth site and

The Kukaniloko Birthing Stones lie within a grove of trees in a pineapple field.

Signs mark the entrance to the North Shore Surf and Cultural Museum.

the other telling how the stones were used to aid in the birth process. ⏱ *30 min. Whitemore Ave. (between hwys. 99 and 80).*

Make a left on Kamehameha Hwy. (Hwy. 80), then a right at the intersection to Kamehamaha Hwy. (Hwy. 99). Bus: 52.

❸ kids Dole Pineapple Plantation. Make this a quick rest stop or spend a couple hours exploring the gardens and wandering through the maze. *See p 60, bullet* **❻**.

Continue on Kamehameha Hwy. Bus: 52.

❹ ★★★ kids Haleiwa. Only 34 miles (55km) from Waikiki is Haleiwa, the funky ex-sugar-plantation town that's the world capital of big-wave surfing. This beach town really comes alive in winter, when waves rise up, light rain falls, and temperatures dip into the 70s; then, it seems, every surfer in the world is here to see and be seen. Officially designated a historic cultural and scenic district, Haleiwa thrives in a time warp recalling the turn of the 20th century, when it was founded by sugar baron Benjamin Dillingham. He opened a Victorian hotel overlooking Kaiaka Bay and named it Haleiwa, or "house of the Iwa," the tropical seabird often seen here. The

hotel is gone, but Haleiwa, which was rediscovered in the late 1960s by hippies, resonates with rare rustic charm. Tofu, not taro, is a staple in the local diet. Arts and crafts, boutiques, and burger stands line both sides of the town. There's also a busy fishing harbor full of charter boats. ⏱ *2–3 hrs.*

❺ ★★ kids Matsumoto Shave Ice. Since 1951, this small, humble shop operated by the Matsumoto family has served a popular rendition of the Hawaii-style snow cone (for a real exotic treat try the azuki beans—sweet red beans—in the shave ice). *See p 16, bullet* **⓫**.

❻ kids North Shore Surf and Cultural Museum. Oahu's only surf museum tells the history of this Hawaiian sport of kings. The collection of memorabilia traces the evolution of surfboards from an enormous, weathered redwood board made in the 1930s to the modern-day equivalent—a light, sleek, racy, foam-and-fiberglass board. Other items include classic 1950s surf-meet posters, 1960s surf-music album covers, old beach movie posters, historic photographs, and trophies won by surfing's greatest. ⏱ *30 min. North Shore Marketplace, 66–250 Kamehameha Hwy. (behind Kentucky Fried Chicken), Haleiwa.* ☎ *808/637-8888. www.captainrick.com/surf_museum. htm. Free admission. Tues–Sun noon–5pm.*

Continue on Kamehameha Hwy. Bus: 52.

❼ ★★ kids Waimea Bay. From November to March, monstrous waves—some 30 feet (9m) tall—roll into Waimea. When they break on the shore, the ground actually shakes. The best surfers in the world paddle out to challenge these freight trains—it's amazing to see how small they appear in the lip of the giant waves. *See p 160.*

Turn toward the mountain on Waimea Valley Rd.

⑧ ★ kids Waimea Valley Audubon Center. This 1,875-acre (759ha) park is home to 36 botanical gardens, with about 6,000 rare species of plants and numerous Hawaiian archeological sites. *See p 61, bullet ⑧.*

Continue on Kamehameha Hwy. and spend some time at one of the following three beaches. Bus: 52.

⑨ ★ kids Pupukea Beach. This 80-acre (32ha) beach park, excellent for snorkeling and diving, is a Marine Life Conservation District with strict rules about taking marine life, sand, coral, shells, and rocks. *See p 157.*

Continue on Kamehameha Hwy.; access is via Ehukai Beach Park, off Kamehameha Hwy. on Ke Nui Rd. in Pupukea. Bus: 52

⑩ ★ kids Banzai Beach. In the winter, this is a very popular beach with surfers, surf fans, curious residents, and visitors; it's less crowded in the summer months. *See p 153.*

Waimea Bay.

Continue on Kamehameha Hwy. Bus: 52.

⑪ ★★ kids Sunset Beach. If it's winter, just people-watch on this sandy beach, as the waves are huge here. But during the summer it's safe to go swimming. *See p 159.*

Continue on Kamehameha Hwy. Bus: 52.

⑫ ★★★ kids Turtle Bay Resort. The resort is spectacular—an hour's drive from Waikiki, but eons away in its country feeling. Sitting on 808 acres (327ha), this place is loaded with activities and 5 miles (8km) of shoreline with secluded white-sand coves. Even if you don't stay here, check out the beach activities, golf, horseback riding, tennis, and spa. 🕐 *depends on your activity. 57–091 Kamehameha Hwy., Kahuku.* ☎ *808/293-6000. www. turtlebayresort.com.*

Continue on Kamehameha Hwy. Bus: 55.

⑬ ★ kids Polynesian Cultural Center. Visit all the islands of the Pacific in a single day at the Polynesian Cultural Center. *See p 17, bullet ⑬.*

Continue on Kamehameha Hwy. Turn right on Likelike Hwy. Take the Kalihi St./H-1 exit and continue on H-1 to Waikiki. Bus: 55, transfer to City Express B.

The North Shore's Best Spa

The Zen-like **Spa Luana,** at the Turtle Bay Resort, has a thatched hut treatment room right on the water, plus a meditation waiting area, an outdoor workout area, and a complete fitness center. Best of all, you can book a room on the second floor and use the private elevator reserved for guests getting spa treatments.

Where to **Stay**

★ kids **Ke Iki Beach Bungalows** BONSAI BEACH This collection of studio, one-, and two-bedroom cottages, located on a 200-foot (61m) stretch of beautiful white-sand beach, is affordable and perfect for families (plus all units have full kitchens and their own barbecue areas). *59–579 Ke Iki Rd. (off Kamehameha Hwy.).* ☎ *866/638-8229 or 808/638-8829. www.keiki beach.com. 11 units. Double $120–$135 studio; $135–$210 1-bedroom; $155–$230 2-bedroom. AE, MC, V. Bus: 52.*

★★★ kids **Turtle Bay Resort** KAHUKU Located in the "country" on 5 miles (8km) of shoreline with secluded white-sand coves, this is the place to stay to get away from everything. The resort offers lots of activities, and all rooms have ocean views and balconies. It also boasts one of the best spas on the island. *57–091 Kamehameha Hwy. (at Kuhuku Dr.).* ☎ *800/203-3650 or 808/293-6000. www.turtlebay resort.com. 443 units. Doubles $440–$520. AE, DC, DISC, MC, V. Bus: 52 or 55.*

Where to **Dine**

★ kids **Cafe Haleiwa** HALEIWA *BREAKFAST/MEXICAN* Haleiwa's legendary breakfast joint is a big hit with surfers, urban gentry with weekend country homes, reclusive artists, and anyone who loves mahimahi plate lunches and heroic

sandwiches in a Formica-casual setting. *66–460 Kamehameha Hwy. (near Paalaa Rd.).* ☎ *808/637-5516. Main courses $6–$11. AE, MC, V. Breakfast & lunch daily.*

★★ kids **Ola at Turtle Bay Resort** KAHUKU *ISLAND STYLE*

Turtle Bay Resort.

CUISINE & SEAFOOD The location (literally on the beach), the view (lapping waves), the romantic atmosphere (tiki torches at sunset), and the food (slow-poached salmon; fishermen's stew with lobster, shrimp, scallops and fresh fish; and a kiawe-smoked beef tenderloin) make this open-air eatery one of the best on the North Shore. *Turtle Bay Resort, 57–091 Kamehameha Hwy. (at Kuhuku Dr.).* ☎ *808/293-0801. Entrees $9–$16 lunch & $17–$53 dinner. AE, DC, DISC, MC, V. Lunch Sun–Thurs, dinner daily. Bus: 52 or 55.*

Giovanni's Shrimp Truck.

kids Paradise Found Cafe
HALEIWA *VEGETARIAN* This tiny hole-in-the-wall offers organic, healthy breakfast and lunch to eat in or take out. *66–443 Kamehameha Hwy. (near Paalaa Rd.).* ☎ *808/637-4540. All items less than $12. No credit cards. Breakfast & lunch daily.*

★★★ **kids 21 Degrees North**
KAHUKU *PACIFIC RIM CUISINE* The signature restaurant at Turtle Bay Resort boasts floor-to-ceiling windows overlooking the North Shore's famous rolling surf. The contemporary island cuisine is just as inspiring as the view, with items such as crab-crusted Hawaiian sea bass, salmon with Molokai mashed sweet potatoes, and roasted Peking duck. *57–091 Kamehameha Hwy. (at Kuhuku Dr.).* ☎ *808/293-8811. Entrees $29–$42. AE, DC, DISC, MC, V. Dinner Tues–Sat. Bus: 52 or 55.*

The Shrimp Trucks

The best, sweetest, juiciest shrimp you'll ever eat will be from a shrimp truck on Oahu's North Shore. Several trucks line up around the entry to Haleiwa, just off the Kamehameha Hwy., but my two favorites are **Giovanni's Original White Shrimp Truck** and **Holy Smokes: Hawaiian Meats and Seafood.**

Giovanni's (☎ 808/293-1839, usually parked across the street from the Halewai Senior Housing) claims to be the first shrimp truck to serve the delicious aquaculture shrimp farmed in the surrounding area. The menu is simple: spicy, garlic, or lemon-and-butter shrimp for $12. The battered white truck has picnic tables under the awning outside, so you can munch away right there.

Holy Smokes (parked in the same area) has a bit more of an extensive menu; in addition to the famous shrimp, they also have pork spare ribs ($8.95), smoked chicken ($7.95), and a steak plate ($11).

The trucks are usually in place before noon and stay until about sunset.

Southern Oahu & the **Windward Coast**

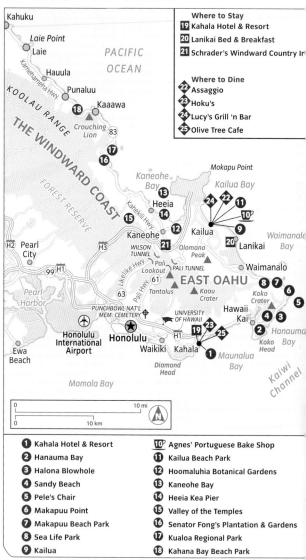

Kahuku

Laie Point
Laie

PACIFIC
OCEAN

Hauula

Punaluu

Kaaawa

Crouching
Lion

THE WINDWARD COAST

KOOLAU RANGE

FOREST RESERVE

Mokapu Point

Kaneohe Bay

Kailua Bay

Heeia

Kahekili Hwy

Kaneohe

Kailua

Lanikai

Waimanalo Bay

WILSON TUNNEL

Olomana Peak

Pali Lookout

PALI TUNNEL

Waimanalo

Likelike Hwy

Pali Hwy

Tantalus

Kaau Crater

EAST OAHU

Koko Crater

H2 Pearl City

Pearl Harbor

PUNCHBOWL NAT'L MEM. CEMETERY

UNIVERSITY OF HAWAII

Hawaii Kai

Koko Head

Honolulu International Airport

Honolulu

Waikiki

Kahala

Hanauma Bay

Ewa Beach

Diamond Head

Maunalua Bay

Kaiwi Channel

Mamala Bay

0   10 mi

0   10 km

Where to Stay
19 Kahala Hotel & Resort
20 Lanikai Bed & Breakfast
21 Schrader's Windward Country Inn

Where to Dine
22 Assaggio
23 Hoku's
24 Lucy's Grill 'n Bar
25 Olive Tree Cafe

1 Kahala Hotel & Resort
2 Hanauma Bay
3 Halona Blowhole
4 Sandy Beach
5 Pele's Chair
6 Makapuu Point
7 Makapuu Beach Park
8 Sea Life Park
9 Kailua
10 Agnes' Portuguese Bake Shop
11 Kailua Beach Park
12 Hoomaluhia Botanical Gardens
13 Kaneohe Bay
14 Heeia Kea Pier
15 Valley of the Temples
16 Senator Fong's Plantation & Gardens
17 Kualoa Regional Park
18 Kahana Bay Beach Park

From the high-rises of Waikiki, venture to a very different Oahu, the arid south shore and lush windward coast. The landscape on the south side is like a moonscape, with prickly cacti onshore and, in winter, spouting whales cavorting in the water. Hawaiians call this area *Ka Iwi*, which means "the bone"—no doubt because of all the bone-cracking shore breaks along this popular bodyboarding coastline. The South gives way to the lush Windward side, where lots of rain keeps the vegetation green and growing and a string of white-sand cove beaches promises a great outing. START: Waikiki. Length: 85 miles (137km).

From Waikiki, take Kalakaua Ave. to Poni Moi Rd. and turn left. Go right on Diamond Head Rd., which becomes Kahala Ave.; go to the end of the street. Bus: 14.

❶ ★★ kids Kahala Hotel & Resort. Stop by and check out this lush, tropical resort where the grounds include an 800-foot (244m) crescent-shaped beach and a 26,000-square-foot (2,415m sq.) lagoon (home to two bottle-nosed dolphins, sea turtles, and tropical fish), plus great dining and a fabulous spa. 🕐 1 hr. 5000 Kahala Ave. (next to the Waialae Country Club). ☎ 800/367-2525 or 808/739-8888.

Backtrack on Kahala Ave., then turn right on Kealaolu Ave. Take a slight right at Waialae Ave., which becomes Kalanianaole Hwy., then go right at Hanauma Bay. Bus: Walk about 1 mile (1.6km) to Kilauea Ave. and Makaiwa St. to catch bus 22.

❷ ★★★ kids Hanauma Bay. This marine preserve is a great place to stop for a swim; you'll find the friendliest fish on the island here. The beach park is closed on Tuesdays. *See p 153.*

Continue about a mile down Kalaniaole Hwy. (Hwy. 72) to around mile marker 11. Bus: 58.

❸ Halona Blowhole. I'll give you two reasons to pull over at this scenic lookout: You get to watch the ocean waves forced through a hole in the rocks shoot up 30 feet (9m) in the air, and there's a great view of

Hanauma Bay.

Pele's Chair.

Sandy Beach and across the 26-mile (42km) gulf to neighboring Molokai, with the faint triangular shadow of Lanai on the far horizon. Be sure to obey all the signs warning you to stay away from the blowhole. ⏱ *15 min. Kalaniaole Hwy. (Hwy. 72) to around mile marker 11.*

Continue about ½ mile (.8km) down Kalaniaole Hwy. Bus: 58.

④ ★ Sandy Beach. This is Oahu's most dangerous beach—it's the only one with an ambulance always standing by to whisk injured wave catchers to the hospital. Bodyboarders just love it. I suggest you just sit on the sand and watch. *See p 157.*

Dolphin encounter at Sea Life Park.

Continue on Kalaniaole Hwy. Bus: 58.

⑤ Pele's Chair. Just after you leave Sandy's, look out to sea for this famous formation, which from a distance looks like a mighty throne; it's believed to be the fire goddess's last resting place on Oahu before she flew off to continue her work on other islands.

Continue on Kalaniaole Hwy. Bus: 58.

⑥ Makapuu Point. As you round the bend, ahead lies a 647-foot-high (197m) hill, with a lighthouse that once signaled safe passage for steamship passengers arriving from San Francisco. Today it lights the south coast for passing tankers, fishing boats, and sailors. You can take a short hike up here for a spectacular vista.

Continue on Kalaniaole Hwy. Bus: 58.

⑦ Makapuu Beach Park. In summer, the ocean here is as gentle as a Jacuzzi, and swimming and diving are perfect; come winter, however, Makapuu is hit with big, pounding waves that are ideal for expert bodysurfers, but too dangerous for regular swimmers. *See p 156.*

Across Kalaniaole Hwy. Bus: 58.

8 ★ **kids** **Sea Life Park.** This 62-acre (25ha) ocean theme park is one of the island's top attractions, with marine animal shows, exhibits, and displays. Don't miss the Hawaiian reef tank full of tropical fish; a "touch" pool, where you can touch a real sea cucumber; and a bird sanctuary, where you can see birds like the red-footed booby and the frigate bird. ⏲ *2–4 hrs. 41–202 Kala-nianaole Hwy. (at Makapuu Point).* ☎ *808/259-7933. www.sealifepark hawaii.com. Admission $29 adults, $19 children 4–12, plus $3 for parking. Daily 9:30am–5pm.*

Continue on Kalaniaole Hwy., right at Kailua Dr. Bus: 58, transfer to 57.

9 **Kailua.** This is Hawaii's biggest beach town, with more than 50,000 residents and two special beaches, Kailua and Lanikai, begging for visitors. Funky little Kailua is lined with million-dollar houses next to tarpaper shacks, antiques shops, and bed-and-breakfasts.

From Kailua Dr. left on Hoolai St. Bus: 56.

10 ★ **kids** **Agnes' Portuguese Bake Shop.** Take a break at this old-fashioned tea shop with the best baked goods in Kailua. My faves are the chocolate brownie and the homemade bread pudding. *40 Hoolai St.* ☎ *808/262-5367. $$.*

Left on Kailua Dr., which becomes Kuulei Rd., then left on Kalaheo Ave., which becomes Kawailoa Rd. No bus service.

11 ★ **kids** **Kailua Beach Park.** Windward Oahu's premier beach is a 2-mile-long (3km), wide golden strand with dunes, palm trees, panoramic views, and offshore islets that are home to seabirds and every type of ocean activity you can think of. *See p 154.*

Retrace your route back to Kalaheo Ave., then turn left on Kuulei Rd., right on Oneawa St., and left at Mokapu Blvd., which becomes Mokapu Saddle Rd. Make a slight left on Kaneohe Bay Dr., left on Kamehameha Hwy., and right on Luluku Rd. Bus: 70, transfer to 57, transfer to 65 and walk 1 mile.

Kailua Beach Park.

⑫ ★ kids Hoomaluhia Botanical Gardens. If you have had enough time at the beach and exposure to the sun, stop by this 400-acre (162ha) botanical garden, the perfect place for a picnic or hike. *See p 61, bullet ⑩.*

Retrace your route back to Kamehameha Hwy., turn right, and immediately get on H-3 East. Take the Kaneohe Bay Dr. Exit. Drive down Kaneohe Bay Dr., then turn right on Kamehameha Hwy. No bus service.

⑬ Kaneohe Bay. Take an incredibly scenic drive around Kaneohe Bay, which is spiked with islets and lined with gold-sand beach parks. The bay has a barrier reef and four tiny islets, one of which is known as Moku o loe, or Coconut Island. Don't be surprised if it looks familiar—it appeared in *Gilligan's Island.* ⏱ *15 min.*

Turn right out on Heeia Kea Pier off Kamehameha Hwy.

⑭ Heeia Kea Pier. This old fishing pier jutting out into Kaneohe Bay is a great place to view the bay. Take a snorkel cruise here, or sail out to a sandbar in the middle of the bay for

Kualoa Park.

an incredible view of Oahu. ⏱ *30 min.; longer if you snorkel or sail.*

Retrace your route on Kamehameha Hwy., then turn right at Haiku Rd. Take a right at Kahekili Hwy. (Hwy. 83), then a left at Avenue of the Temples. Bus: 65

⑮ Valley of the Temples. This famous site is stalked by wild peacocks and about 700 curious people a day, who pay to see the 9-foot (2.8m) meditation Buddha, 2 acres (.8ha) of ponds full of more than 10,000 Japanese koi carp, and a replica of Japan's 900-year-old Byodo-In Temple. A 3-ton (2,722kg)

The Byodo-In Temple.

Hawaiian Seafood Primer

The seafood in Hawaii has been described as the best in the world. And why not? Without a doubt, the islands' surrounding waters and a growing aquaculture industry contribute to the high quality of the seafood here.

Although some menus include the Western description for the fresh fish used, most often the local nomenclature is listed. To help familiarize you with the menu language of Hawaii, here's a basic glossary of island fish:

ahi   yellowfin or big-eye tuna, important for its use in sashimi and poke at sushi bars and in Hawaii Regional Cuisine

aku   skipjack tuna, heavily used in home cooking and poke

ehu   red snapper, delicate and sumptuous, yet lesser known than opakapaka

hapuupuu   grouper, a sea bass whose use is expanding

hebi   spearfish, mildly flavored, and frequently featured as the "catch of the day" in upscale restaurants

kajiki   Pacific blue marlin, also called *au*, with a firm flesh and high fat content that make it a plausible substitute for tuna

mahimahi   dolphin fish (the game fish, not the mammal) or dorado, a classic sweet, white-fleshed fish

monchong   big-scale or sickle pomfret, an exotic, tasty fish, scarce but gaining a higher profile on Hawaiian Island menus

nairagi   striped marlin, also called *au;* good as sashimi and in poke, and often substituted for ahi in raw-fish products

onaga   ruby snapper, a luxury fish, versatile, moist, and flaky

ono   wahoo, firmer and drier than the snappers, often served grilled and in sandwiches

opah   moonfish, rich and fatty, and versatile—cooked, raw, smoked, and broiled

opakapaka   pink snapper, light, flaky, and luxurious, suited for sashimi, poaching, sautéing, and baking

papio   jack trevally, light, firm, and flavorful

shutome   broadbill swordfish, of beeflike texture and rich flavor

tombo   albacore tuna, with a high fat content, suitable for grilling

uhu   parrotfish, most often encountered steamed, Chinese style

uku   gray snapper of clear, pale-pink flesh, delicately flavored and moist

ulua   large jack trevally, firm fleshed and versatile

brass temple bell brings good luck to those who can ring it. 🕐 *1 hr. 47–200 Kahekili Hwy. (across the street from Temple Valley Shopping Center).* ☎ *808/239-8811. Admission $2 adults, $1 children under 12 & seniors 65 & over. Daily 8:30am–4:30pm.*

Continue on Kahekili Hwy., which becomes Kamehameha Hwy., then turn left on Pulama Rd. Bus: 65, transfer to 55, then walk about 1 mile (1.6km) uphill.

🔟 kids **Senator Fong's Plantation & Gardens.** You can ride an

Oahu's Best Spa

The Kahala Hotel & Resort has taken the concept of spa as a journey into relaxation to a new level with **Spa Suites at the Kahala** (☎ 808/739-8938). The former garden guest rooms have been converted into individual personal spa treatment rooms, each with a glass-enclosed shower, private changing area, infinity-edge deep soaking Jacuzzi tub, and personal relaxation area. No detail is overlooked, from the warm foot bath when you arrive to the refreshing hot tea served on your personal enclosed garden lanai after your relaxation treatment.

open-air tram through five gardens on former U.S. Senator Hiram Fong's 725-acre (293ha) private estate, which includes 75 edible nuts and fruits. *See p 61, bullet* **9**.

Turn left on Kamehameha Hwy. for 1 mile (1.6km). Bus: 55.

17 ★★ **kids** **Kualoa Regional Park.** This 150-acre (61ha) coconut palm–fringed peninsula is the biggest beach park on the windward side and one of Hawaii's most scenic. The long, narrow, white-sand beach is perfect for swimming, walking, beachcombing, kite flying, or just sunbathing. *See p 155.*

Continue on Kamehameha Hwy. about 10 miles (16km). Bus: 55.

18 ★★ **kids** **Kahana Bay Beach Park.** This white-sand, crescent-shaped beach has a picture-perfect backdrop: a huge, jungle-cloaked valley with dramatic, jagged cliffs. The bay's calm water and shallow, sandy bottom make it a safe swimming area for children. *See p 154.*

Retrace your route on Kamehameha Hwy. to Kahekili Hwy. Turn right on Likelike Hwy. Take the Kahilli St./H-1 Exit. Merge on to H-1 and continue into Waikiki. Bus: 55, transfer to City Express B.

Where to **Stay**

Kahala Resort.

★★ **kids** **Kahala Hotel & Resort** KAHALA   Located in one of Oahu's most prestigious residential areas, the Kahala offers elegant rooms and the peace and serenity of a neighbor-island resort, with the conveniences of Waikiki just a 10-minute drive away. The lush, tropical grounds include an 800-foot (244m) crescent-shaped beach and a 26,000-square-foot (2,415m sq.) lagoon that's home to sea turtles, tropical fish, and two bottle-nosed dolphins. Activities range from Hawaiian cultural

Schrader's Windward Country Inn.

programs to daily dolphin-education talks by a trainer from Sea Life Park. *5000 Kahala Ave. (next to the Waialae Country Club). ☎ 800/367-2525 or 808/739-8888. www.kahalaresort.com. 343 units. Double $405–$820. AE, DC, DISC, MC, V.*

★ Lanikai Bed & Breakfast

LANIKAI   Choose from a 1,000-square-foot (93m sq.) 2-bedroom apartment or a 540-square-foot (50m sq.) honeymooner's studio in this B&B tucked away in the swank beach community. They also have a booking agency to help you with other B&B and vacation rentals nearby. *1277 Mokulua Dr. (between Onekea and Aala drs.). ☎ 800/258-7895 or 808/261-1059. www.lanikaibb.com. 2 units. Double $155–$175.*

kids Schrader's Windward Country Inn

KANEOHE   Despite the name, the ambience here is more motel than "country inn," but Schrader's offers a great buy for families. Nestled in the tranquil, tropical setting on Kaneohe Bay, the complex is made up of aging cottage-style motels and a collection of older homes, all with cooking facilities. *Tip:* When booking, ask for a unit with a lanai; that way you'll end up with at least a partial view of the bay. *47–039 Lihikai Dr. (off Kamehameha Hwy.). ☎ 800/735-5071 or 808/239-5711. www.hawaiiscene.com/schrader. 20 units. Doubles: $72–$143 1-bedroom; $127–$215 2-bedroom for 4; $226–$358 3-bedroom for 6; $446–$501 4-bedroom for 8, w/breakfast. AE, DC, DISC, MC, V.*

Assaggio.

Where to **Dine**

★ **Assaggio** KAILUA *ITALIAN*
Assaggio's affordable prices, attentive service, and winning menu items won this neighborhood bistro many loyal fans. You can choose linguine, fettuccine, or ziti with 10 different sauces in small or regular portions, or any of the extensive list of seafood or chicken dishes. *354 Uluniu St. (at Aulike St.). 808/261-2772. Entrees $10–$25. AE, DC, DISC, MC, V. Lunch Mon–Fri, dinner daily.*

★★★ **Hoku's** KAHALA *HAWAIIAN REGIONAL*   Elegant without being stuffy, and creative without being overwrought, the upscale dining room of the Kahala Hotel & Resort combines European finesse with an island touch, with dishes like steamed whole fresh fish, pan-seared foie gras, rack of lamb, ahi steak, and the full range of East-West specialties. Sunday brunch is not to be missed. *Kahala Hotel, 5000 Kahala Ave. (end of street). 808/739-8780. Entrees $32–$94. AE, DC, DISC, MC, V. Dinner daily; brunch Sun.*

★★ **kids** **Lucy's Grill 'n Bar.**
KAILUA *HAWAII REGIONAL CUISINE*
This is one of Kailua's most popular restaurants, not just because of the open-air bar and the outdoor lanai seating, but because of the terrific food. I recommend the Szechuan-spiced jumbo tiger prawns with black-bean cream and penne pasta, or the lemon grass–crusted scallops with yellow Thai curry. *33 Aulike St.*

Salmon at Hoku's.

(at Kuulei Rd.). 808/230-8188. Entrees $14–$28. MC, V. Dinner daily.

★★ **kids** **Olive Tree Cafe.**
KAHALA *GREEK/EASTERN MEDITER-RANEAN*   This is Honolulu's best restaurant for a meal under $20, a totally hip hole-in-the-wall eatery with divine Greek fare. There are umbrella tables outside and a few seats indoors, and you order and pay at the counter. Winners include mussel ceviche; creamy, tender chicken saffron; and the generous Greek salad. *4614 Kilauea Ave., across from Kahala Mall. 808/737-0303. Entrees $8–$15. No credit cards. Dinner daily.* ●

6 The Best **Beaches**

Oahu's Best **Beaches**

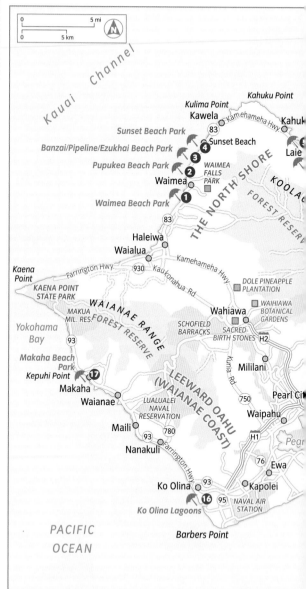

Kauai Channel

Kahuku Point

Kulima Point

Kawela

Kamehameha Hwy.

Kahuk

Sunset Beach Park

83

Banzai/Pipeline/Ezukhai Beach Park

Sunset Beach

3

4

Laie

Pupukea Beach Park

2

WAIMEA FALLS PARK

THE NORTH SHORE

KOOLA

Waimea

1

FOREST RESERV

Waimea Beach Park

83

Haleiwa

Waialua

Kamehameha Hwy.

930

Kaukonahua Rd.

DOLE PINEAPPLE PLANTATION

Kaena Point

Farrington Hwy.

WAIHIAWA BOTANICAL GARDENS

KAENA POINT STATE PARK

WAIANAE RANGE

FOREST RESERVE

MAKUA MIL. RES.

Wahiawa

SCHOFIELD BARRACKS

SACRED BIRTH STONES

H2

Yokohama Bay

93

Kuna Rd.

Mililani

Makaha Beach Park

Kepuhi Point

17

LEEWARD OAHU (WAIANAE COAST)

Pearl Ci

Makaha

Waianae

LUALUALEI NAVAL RESERVATION

Waipahu

H1

Maili

93

780

Farrington Hwy.

Pea

Nanakuli

Ewa

76

Ko Olina

93

16

95

Kapolei

NAVAL AIR STATION

Ko Olina Lagoons

Barbers Point

PACIFIC OCEAN

Ala Moana Beach Park 15
Banzai/Pipeline/Ehukai Beach Park 3
Hanauma Bay 13
Kahana Bay Beach Park 7
Kailua Beach 9
Ko Olina Lagoons 16
Kualoa Regional Park 8
Lanikai Beach 10
Makaha Beach Park 17
Makapuu Beach Park 11
Malaekahana Bay State Recreation Area 5
Pounders Beach 6
Pupukea Beach Park 2
Sandy Beach 12
Sunset Beach Park 4
Waikiki Beach 14
Waimea Beach Park 1

PACIFIC
OCEAN

Hauula

Punaluu

Kahana Bay Beach Park

Kaaawa

7

RANGE

THE WINDWARD COAST

FOREST RESERVE

8 Kualoa Regional Park

Mokapu Point

Kaneohe
Bay

HEEIA STATE
PARK

MARINE CORPS
AIR STATION

Kailua Bay

Heeia

83

Kaneohe

Kailua Beach Park

Kailua 9

83

BELLOWS
AIR FORCE
BASE

Waimanalo
Bay

H3

WILSON TUNNEL

PALI
TUNNEL

10

Makapuu
Beach Park

99 H1

USS ARIZONA
MEMORIAL

Pali Hwy.

Likelike Hwy.

Waimanalo

EAST OAHU

11

Harbor
HICKAM
AFB

92 H1

63 61

Tantalus

PUNCHBOWL NAT'L
MEM. CEMETERY

HALONA BLOW
HOLE

Sandy Beach

12

Honolulu

Hawaii
Kai

13 Hanauma
Bay

Honolulu
International
Airport

Ala Moana
Beach Park

15

14

Waikiki
Beach

Diamond
Head

Maunalua
Bay

Koko
Head

Mamala Bay

Kaiwi Channel

Beaches Best Bets

Best for a **Picnic**
★★ Ala Moana Beach Park, *1200 Ala Moana Blvd.* (p 153)

Best Place to **"Shoot the Tube"**
★ Banzai/Pipeline/Ehukai Beach Park, *59–337 Ka Nui Rd.* (p 153)

Best **Snorkeling**
★★★ Hanauma Bay, *7455 Koko Kalanianaole Hwy.* (p 153)

Best Place to **Kayak**
★★ Kahana Bay Beach Park, *52–222 Kamehameha Hwy.* (p 154)

Best **Windsurfing**
★★★ Kailua Beach, *450 Kawailoa Rd.* (p 154)

Best for **Kids**
Ko Olina Lagoons, *Aliinui Dr.* (p 154)

Best **Scenic Beach Park**
★★ Kualoa Regional Park, *49–600 Kamehameha Hwy.* (p 155)

Best for **Swimming**
★★ Lanikai Beach, *Mokulua Dr.* (p 155)

Best for **Expert Body Surfing**
★ Makapuu Beach Park, *41–095 Kalanianaole Hwy.* (p 156)

Best **Secluded Beach**
★★★ Malaekahana Bay State Recreation Area, *Kamehameha Hwy.* (p 156)

Best **Diving**
★ Pupukea Beach Park, *59–727 Kamehameha Hwy.* (p 157)

Best Beach for **Watching Bodyboarders**
★ Sandy Beach, *8800 Kalanianaole Hwy.* (p 157)

Best for **People-Watching**
★★ Sunset Beach Park, *59–100 Kamehameha Hwy.* (p 159)

Best for **Sunbathing & Partying**
★★★ Waikiki Beach, *from Ala Wai Yacht Harbor to Diamond Head Park* (p 159)

Best for **Big Waves**
★★ Waimea Bay Beach Park, *51–031 Kamehameha Hwy.* (p 160)

Lanikai Beach.

Oahu Beaches **A to Z**

A Word of Warning

Wherever you are on Oahu, remember that you're in an urban area. Never leave valuables in your car. Thefts do occur at Oahu's beaches, and locked cars are not a deterrent.

★★ kids Ala Moana Beach Park HONOLULU

The gold-sand Ala Moana ("by the sea") stretches for more than a mile along Honolulu's coast between downtown and Waikiki. This 76-acre (31ha) midtown beach park, with spreading lawns shaded by banyans and palms, is one of the island's most popular playgrounds, with its own lagoon, yacht harbor, tennis courts, music pavilion, bathhouses, picnic tables, and plenty of wide-open green spaces. The water is calm almost year-round, protected by black lava rocks set offshore. There's a large parking lot as well as metered street parking. *1200 Ala Moana Blvd. (between Kamakee St. and Atkinson Dr.).*

★ Banzai/Pipeline/Ehukai Beach Park NORTH SHORE

There are three separate areas here, but because the sandy beach is continuous, most people think of it as one beach park. Located near Pupukea, **Ehukai Beach Park** is 1 acre (.4ha) of grass with a parking lot, great for winter surfing and summer swimming. **Pipeline** is about 100 yards (91m) to the left of Ehukai. When the winter surf rolls in and hits the shallow coral shelf, the waves that quickly form are steep— so steep, in fact, that the crest of the wave falls forward, forming a near-perfect tube, or "pipeline." Just west of Pipeline is the area surfers call **"Banzai Beach."** The Japanese word *banzai* means "10,000 years;"

it's given as a toast or as a battle charge, meaning "go for it." In the late 1950s, filmmaker Bruce Brown was shooting one of the first surf movies ever made, *Surf Safari,* when he saw a bodysurfer ride a huge wave. Brown yelled: "Banzai!" and the name stuck. In the winter, this is a very popular beach with surfers and surf fans. *Access is via Ehukai Beach Park, 59-337 Ka Nui Rd. (off Kamehameha Hwy.), Pupukea. TheBus: 52.*

★★★ kids Hanauma Bay KOKO HEAD

This small, curved, 2,000-foot (610m) gold-sand beach is packed elbow-to-elbow with people year-round. The bay's shallow shoreline water and abundant marine life draw snorkelers, but this good-looking beach is also popular for sunbathing and people-watching. The deeper water outside the bay is great for scuba diving. Hanauma Bay is a conservation district; don't touch any marine life or feed the fish. Facilities include parking, restrooms, a pavilion, a grass volleyball court, lifeguards, barbecues, picnic

Ala Moana Beach Park.

tables, and food concessions. Alcohol is prohibited in the park; no smoking past the visitor center. Expect to pay $1 per vehicle to park and a $3 per person entrance fee (children 12 and under are free). Avoid the crowds by going early on a weekday morning; once the parking lot's full, you're out of luck. *7455 Koko Kalanianaole Hwy. (at Hanauma Bay Rd.). Closed Tues. Take TheBus to escape the parking problem: The Hanauma Bay Shuttle runs from Waikiki to Hanauma Bay every half hour from 8:45am–1pm; you can catch it at the Ala Moana Hotel, the Ilikai Hotel, or any city bus stop. It returns every hour noon–4:30pm.*

★★ kids Kahana Bay Beach Park WINDWARD

This white-sand, crescent-shaped beach is backed by a huge, jungle-cloaked valley with dramatic, jagged cliffs and is protected by ironwood and kamani trees. The bay's calm water and shallow, sandy bottom make it a safe swimming area for children. The surrounding park has picnic areas, camping, and hiking trails. The wide sand-bottom channel that runs through the park and out to Kahana Bay is one of the largest on Oahu—it's perfect for kayakers. *52–222 Kamehameha Hwy. Kahana. TheBus: 55.*

★★★ kids Kailua Beach WINDWARD

Windward Oahu's premier beach is a 2-mile-long (3km), wide golden strand with dunes, palm trees, panoramic views, and offshore islets that are home to seabirds. The swimming is excellent, and the warm, azure waters are usually decorated with bright sails; this is Oahu's premier windsurfing beach as well. It's also a favorite spot to sail catamarans, bodysurf the gentle waves, or paddle a kayak. Water conditions are quite safe, especially at the mouth of Kaelepulu Stream, where toddlers play in the freshwater shallows at the middle of the beach park. Facilities include lifeguards, picnic tables, barbecues, restrooms, a volleyball court, a public boat ramp, and free parking. *450 Kawailoa Rd., Kailua. TheBus: 56 or 57, transfer 70.*

Ko Olina Lagoons LEEWARD

The developer of the 640-acre (259ha) Ko Olina Resort has created four white-sand lagoons to make the rocky shoreline more attractive and accessible. The lagoons offer

You'll see Oahu's biggest waves off the North Shore in winter.

Kailua Beach.

calm, shallow waters and a powdery white-sand beach bordered by a broad, grassy lawn. No lifeguards are present, but the generally tranquil waters are great for swimming, perfect for kids, and offer some snorkeling opportunities around the boulders at the entrance to the lagoons. Two lagoons have restrooms, and there's plenty of public parking. *Off Aliinui Dr. (between Olani and Mauloa pls.), Ko Olina Resort.*

★★ kids **Kualoa Regional Park** WINDWARD   This 150-acre (61ha) coconut palm–fringed peninsula is the biggest beach park on the windward side and one of Hawaii's most scenic. The park has a broad, grassy lawn and a long, narrow, white-sand beach ideal for swimming, walking, beachcombing, kite flying, or sunbathing. The waters are shallow and safe for swimming year-round, and at low tide, you can swim or wade out to the islet of Mokolii (popularly known as Chinaman's Hat), which has a small sandy beach and is a bird preserve. Lifeguards are on duty, and picnic and camping areas are available. *49–600 Kamehameha Hwy., Kualoa. TheBus: 55.*

★★ **Lanikai Beach** WINDWARD One of Hawaii's best spots for

Staying Safe in the Water

From 1999 to 2004 the number of drownings of non-residents in Hawaii more than doubled from 18 deaths to 40. Below are some tips to keep in mind when swimming in Hawaii's gorgeous waters:

- Never swim alone.
- Always supervise children in the water.
- Always swim at beaches with lifeguards.
- Know your limits—don't swim out farther than you think you can.
- Read the posted warning signs before you enter the water.
- Call a lifeguard or 911 if you see someone in distress.

Kualoa Regional Park.

swimming, gold-sand Lanikai's crystal-clear lagoon is like a giant saltwater swimming pool. The beach is a mile (1.6km) long and thin in places, but the sand is soft and onshore trade winds make this an excellent place for sailing and windsurfing. Kayakers often paddle out to the two tiny offshore Mokulua islands, which are seabird sanctuaries. Sun worshipers: arrive in the morning; the Koolau Mountains block the afternoon rays. *Mokulua Dr., Kailua. TheBus: 56 or 57, transfer to 70.*

Makaha Beach Park LEEWARD When surf's up here, it's spectacular: Monstrous waves pound the beach from October through April. Nearly a mile (1.6km) long, this half-moon gold-sand beach is tucked between 231-foot (70m) Lahilahi Point, which locals call Black Rock, and Kepuhi Point, a toe of the Waianae mountain range. Summer is the best time for swimming. Children hug the shore on the north side of the beach, near the lifeguard stand, while surfers dodge the rocks and divers seek an offshore channel full of big fish. Facilities include restrooms, lifeguards, and parking. *84–369 Farrington Hwy. (near Kili Dr.), Waianae. TheBus: 51.*

★ **Makapuu Beach Park** WINDWARD   Hawaii's most famous bodysurfing beach is a beautiful 1,000-foot-long (305m) gold-sand beach cupped in the stark black Koolau cliffs. In summer, the ocean here is as gentle as a Jacuzzi, and swimming and diving are perfect; come winter, however, Makapuu is hit with big, pounding waves that are ideal for expert bodysurfers, but too dangerous for regular swimmers. Small boards—no longer than 3 feet (.9m), and no skeg (bottom fin)—are permitted; regular board surfing is banned. Facilities include restrooms, lifeguards, barbecue grills, picnic tables, and parking. *41–095 Kalanianaole Hwy. (across the street from Sea Life Park), Waimanalo. TheBus: 57 or 58.*

★★★ kids **Malaekahana Bay State Recreation Area** NORTH SHORE   This almost mile-long white-sand crescent lives up to just about everyone's image of the perfect Hawaiian beach: excellent for swimming and at low tide you can wade offshore to Goat Island, a sanctuary for seabirds and turtles. Facilities include restrooms, barbecue grills, picnic tables, outdoor showers, and parking.

Kamehameha Hwy. 83 (2 miles/3km north of the Polynesian Cultural Center). TheBus: 52.

Pounders Beach NORTH SHORE This wide beach, extending a quarter mile (.4km) between two points, has easy access from the highway and is very popular on weekends. At the west end of the beach, the waters usually are calm and safe for swimming (during May–Sept). However, at the opposite end, near the limestone cliffs, there's a shore break that can be dangerous for inexperienced bodysurfers; there the bottom drops off abruptly, causing strong rip currents. Go on a weekday morning to have the beach to yourself. *Kamehameha Hwy. (about ½ mile/.8km south of Polynesian Cultural Center). Laie. TheBus: 55.*

★ **Pupukea Beach Park** NORTH SHORE   This 80-acre (32ha) beach park, very popular for snorkeling and diving, is a Marine Life Conservation District. Locals divide the area into two: **Shark's Cove** (which is *not* named for an abundance of sharks), great for snorkeling, and outside the cove, good diving; and at the southern end **Three Tables** (named for the three flat sections of reef visible at low tide), also great for snorkeling where the water is about 15 feet (4.6m) deep, and diving outside the tables, where the

Three Tables beach at Pupukea Beach Park.

water is 30 to 45 feet (9–14m) deep. It's packed May to October, when swimming, diving, and snorkeling are best; the water is usually calm but watch out for surges. In the winter, when currents form and waves roll in, this area is very dangerous, even in the tide pools, and also much less crowded. No lifeguards. *59–727 Kamehameha Hwy. (Pupukea Rd.), Pupukea. TheBus: 52.*

★ **Sandy Beach** KOKO HEAD Sandy Beach is one of the best bodysurfing beaches on Oahu. It's also one of the most dangerous. The 1,200-foot-long (366m) gold-sand beach is pounded by wild waves and haunted by a dangerous shore break and strong backwash; the experienced bodysurfers make wave-riding look easy, but it's best just to watch the daredevils risking their necks. Weak swimmers and

Makapuu Beach Park.

Don't Get Burned: Smart Tanning Tips

Hawaii's Caucasian population has the highest incidence of malignant melanoma (deadly skin cancer) in the world. And nobody is completely safe from the sun's harmful rays: All skin types and races can burn. To ensure that your vacation won't be ruined by a painful sunburn, here are some helpful tips:

- **Wear a strong sunscreen at all times.** Use a sunscreen with an SPF of 15 or higher; people with light complexions should use SPF 30. Apply it liberally and reapply every 2 hours.
- **Wrinkle prevention.** Wrinkles, sagging skin, and other signs of premature aging can be caused by Ultraviolet A (UVA) rays. Some sunscreens only block out Ultraviolet B (UVB) rays. Look for a sunscreen that blocks both. Zinc oxide, benzophenone, oxybenzone, sulisobenzone, titanium dioxide, or avobenzone (also known as Parsol 1789) all protect against UVA rays.
- **Wear a hat and sunglasses.** The hat should have a brim all the way around to cover not only your face but also the sensitive back of your neck. Make sure your sunglasses have UV filters.
- **Protect children from the sun.** Infants under 6 months should not be in the sun at all. Older babies need zinc oxide to protect their fragile skin, and all children should be slathered with sunscreen frequently.
- **If it's too late.** The best remedy for a sunburn is to stay out of the sun until all the redness is gone. Aloe vera, cool compresses, cold baths, and anesthetic benzocaine also help with the pain of sunburn.

Sandy Beach.

Sunset Beach Park.

children should definitely stay out of the water here—Sandy Beach's heroic lifeguards make more rescues in a year than those at any other beach on Oahu. Lifeguards post flags to alert beachgoers to the day's surf: Green means safe, yellow caution, and red indicates very dangerous water conditions; always check the flags before you dive in. Facilities include restrooms and parking. Go weekdays to avoid the crowds, weekends to catch the bodysurfers in action. *8800 Kalanianaole Hwy. (about 2 miles/3km east of Hanauma Bay). TheBus: 22.*

★★ **Sunset Beach Park** NORTH SHORE   Surfers around the world know this famous site for its spectacular winter surf—the huge thundering waves can reach 15 to 20 feet (5–6m). During the winter surf season (Sept–Apr) swimming is very dangerous here, due to the alongshore currents and powerful rip currents. The only safe time to swim is during the calm summer months. A great place to people-watch is on the wide sandy beach, but don't go too near the water when the lifeguards have posted the red warning flags. *59–100*

Kamehameha Hwy. (near Paumalu Pl.). TheBus: 52.

★★★ kids **Waikiki Beach** WAIKIKI   No beach anywhere is so widely known or so universally sought after as this narrow, 1½-mile-long (2.4km) crescent of imported sand (from Molokai) at the foot of a string of high-rise hotels. Home to the world's longest-running beach party, Waikiki attracts nearly five million visitors a year from every corner of the planet. Waikiki is actually a string of beaches that extends

Waimea Bay Beach Park.

Waikiki Beach.

from **Sans Souci State Recreational Area,** near Diamond Head to the east, to **Duke Kahanamoku Beach,** in front of the Hilton Hawaiian Village Beach Resort & Spa, to the west. Great stretches along Waikiki include **Kuhio Beach,** next to the Moana Surfrider, which provides the quickest access to the Waikiki shoreline; the stretch in front of the Royal Hawaiian Hotel known as **Grey's Beach,** which is canted so it catches the rays perfectly; and **Sans Souci,** the small, popular beach in front of the New Otani Kaimana Beach Hotel that's locally known as "Dig Me" Beach because of all the gorgeous bods who strut their stuff here. Waikiki is fabulous for swimming, board- and bodysurfing, outrigger canoeing, diving, sailing, snorkeling, and pole fishing. Every imaginable type of marine equipment is available for rent here. Facilities include showers, lifeguards, restrooms, grills, picnic tables, and pavilions at the **Queen's Surf** end of the beach (at Kapiolani Park, between the zoo and the aquarium). *Stretching from Ala Wai Yacht Harbor to Diamond Head Park. TheBus: 19 or 20.*

★★ Waimea Bay Beach Park

NORTH SHORE   This deep, sandy bowl has gentle summer waves that are excellent for swimming, snorkeling, and bodysurfing. To one side of the bay is a huge rock that local kids like to climb up and dive from. The scene is much different in winter, when waves pound the narrow bay, sometimes rising to 50 feet (15m) high. When the surf's really up, very strong currents and shore breaks sweep the bay—and it seems like everyone on Oahu drives out to Waimea to get a look at the monster waves and those who ride them. Weekends are great for watching the surfers; to avoid the crowds, go on weekdays. Facilities include lifeguards, restrooms, showers, parking, and nearby restaurants and shops in Haleiwa town. *51–031 Kamehameha Hwy., Waimea. TheBus: 52.* ●

7 The Great Outdoors

Oahu's Best Hiking & Camping

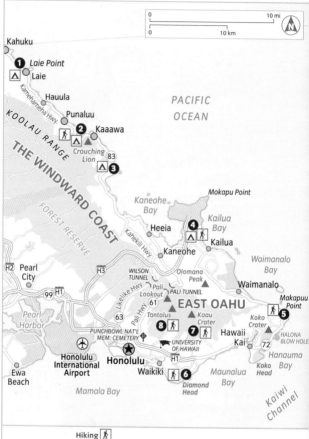

Hiking 🚶

Diamond Head Crater 6

Hoomaluhia Botanical Gardens 4

Kahana Bay Beach Park 2

Makapuu Lighthouse Trail 5

Makiki Valley–Tantalus–Round Top–Nuuanu Valley Trails 8

Manoa Falls Trail 7

Camping ◬

Hoomaluhia Botanical Gardens 4

Kualoa Regional Park 3

Kahana Bay Beach Park 2

Malaekahana Bay State Recreation Area 1

Previous page: Windsurfer.

On Oahu you can camp by the ocean, hike in a tropical rainforest, and take in scenic views that will imprint themselves on your memory forever. Just a couple of warnings: If you plan to camp, you must bring your own gear—no one on Oahu rents it. If you plan to go hiking, take a fully charged cell phone, in case of emergency.

★★★ kids Diamond Head Crater

Hiking This is a moderate (but steep) walk to the summit of the 750-foot (23m) volcanic cone, Hawaii's most famous landmark with a reward of a 360-degree view of the island. The 1.4-mile (2.3km) round-trip takes about 1½ hours and the entry fee is $1. Wear decent shoes (rubber-soled tennies are fine) and take a flashlight (you'll walk through several dark tunnels), binoculars, water, a hat to protect you from the sun, and a camera. You might want to put all your gear in a pack to leave your hands free for the climb. Go early, preferably just after the 6:30am opening, before the midday sun starts beating down. *Monsarrat and 18th aves. Bus: 58.*

Safety Tip

When planning sunset activities, be aware that Hawaii, like other places close to the Equator, has a very short (5–10 min.) twilight period after the sun sets. After that, it's dark. If you hike out to watch the sunset, be sure you can make it back quickly, or take a flashlight.

★ kids Hoomaluhia Botanical Gardens

Hiking & Camping This relatively unknown windward-side camping area, outside Kaneohe, is a real find. *Hoomaluhia* means "peace and tranquility," an apt description for this 400-acre (162ha) lush, botanical garden. Standing among the rare plants, with craggy cliffs in the background, it's hard to believe you're just a half-hour from downtown Honolulu. A 32-acre (13ha) lake sits in the middle of the scenic park (no

The climb up Diamond Head is steep, but anyone reasonably fit can do it.

swimming or boating is allowed), and there are numerous hiking trails. The Visitors Center can suggest a host of activities, ranging from guided walks to demonstrations of ancient Hawaiian plant use. Facilities include a tent-camp area, restrooms, cold showers, dishwashing stations, picnic tables, grills, and water. Permits are free, but you have to get here on a Friday no later than 3pm, as the office is not open on weekends. Stays are limited to Friday, Saturday, and Sunday nights only. *Hoomaluhia Botanical Gardens, 45–680 Luluku Rd. (at Kamehameha Hwy.), Kaneohe.* ☎ *808/233-7323. Bus: 55.*

★★ kids Kahana Bay Beach Park

Camping Under Tahiti-like cliffs, with a beautiful, gold-sand crescent beach framed by pine-needle casuarina trees, Kahana Bay Beach Park is a place of serene beauty. You can swim, bodysurf, fish, hike, and picnic, or just sit and listen to the trade winds whistle through the beach pines. Both tent and vehicle camping are allowed at this oceanside oasis. Facilities include restrooms, picnic tables, drinking water, public phones, and a boat-launching ramp.

Hiking Spectacular views of this verdant valley and a few swimming holes are the rewards of a 4.5-mile (7km) loop trail above the beach. The downside to this 2- to 3-hour,

somewhat ardent adventure are mosquitoes (clouds of them) and some thrashing about in dense forest where a bit of navigation is required along the not-always-marked trail. The trail starts behind the Visitor's Center at the Kahana Valley State Park. *52–222 Kamehameha Hwy. (between Kaaawa and Kahana). Bus: 55.*

★★ kids Kualoa Regional Park

Camping Located on a peninsula in Kaneohe Bay, this park has a spectacular setting right on a gold-sand beach, with a great view of Mokolii Island. Facilities include restrooms, showers, picnic tables, drinking fountains, and a public phone. *49–600 Kamehameha Hwy., across from Mokolii Island (between Waikane and Kaaawa). Bus: 55.*

★ kids Makapuu Lighthouse Trail

Hiking It's a little precarious at times, but anyone in reasonably good shape can handle this 45-minute (one-way) hike, which winds around the 646-foot-high (197m) sea bluff to the Lighthouse. The rewards are the views: the entire Windward Coast, across the azure Pacific and out to Manana (Rabbit) Island. *Kalanianaole Hwy. (half a mile/.8km down the road from the Hawaii Kai Golf Course), past Sandy Beach. Bus: 57 or 58.*

Kahana Valley.

The Makapuu Lighthouse.

Water Safety

Water might be everywhere in Hawaii, but it more than likely isn't safe to drink. Most stream water is contaminated with *bacterium leptospirosis,* which produces flulike symptoms and can be fatal. Make sure that your drinking water is safe by vigorously boiling it, or if boiling is not an option, use tablets with hydroperiodide; portable water filters will not screen out *bacterium leptospirosis.*

★★ Makiki Valley–Tantalus–Round Top–Nuuanu Valley Trails

Hiking This is the starting place for some of Oahu's best hiking

trails—miles of trails converge through the area. The draws here are the breathtaking views, historic remains, and incredible vegetation. Stop at the Hawaii Nature Center, by the trailhead, for information and maps. *2131 Makiki Heights Dr.* ☎ *808/955-0100. Mon–Fri, 8am–4:30pm. Bus: 4.*

★★★ kids Malaekahana Bay State Recreation Area

Camping This beautiful beach camping site has a mile-long (1.6km) gold-sand beach. Facilities include picnic tables, restrooms, showers, sinks, drinking water, and a phone. *Kamehameha Hwy. between Laie and Kahuku. Bus: 55.*

★★ kids Manoa Falls Trail

Hiking This easy, ¾-mile (1km) hike (one-way) is terrific for families; it takes less than an hour to reach idyllic Manoa Falls. The often-muddy trail follows Waihi Stream and meanders through the forest reserve past guavas, mountain apples, and wild ginger. The forest is moist and humid and is inhabited by giant bloodthirsty mosquitoes, so bring repellent. If it has rained recently, stay on the trail and step carefully, as it can be very slippery. The trailhead is marked by a footbridge. *End of Manoa Rd., past Lyon Arboretum. Bus: 5.*

Camping Permits

You must get a permit for all camping in all parks on Oahu. For Honolulu County Parks (like Kualoa Regional Park) contact Honolulu Department of Parks and Recreation, 650 S. King St., Honolulu, HI 96713 (☎ 808/523-4525; www.co.honolulu.hi.us). For state parks (like Kahana Bay Beach Park and Malaekahana Bay State Recreation Area), contact any state parks office, including the Department of Land and Natural Resources, State Parks Division, P.O. Box 621, Honolulu, HI 96809 (☎ 808/587-0300; www.hawaii.gov/dlnr/dsp/fees.html). County and state parks do not allow camping Wednesday and Thursday.

Oahu's Best Golf Courses

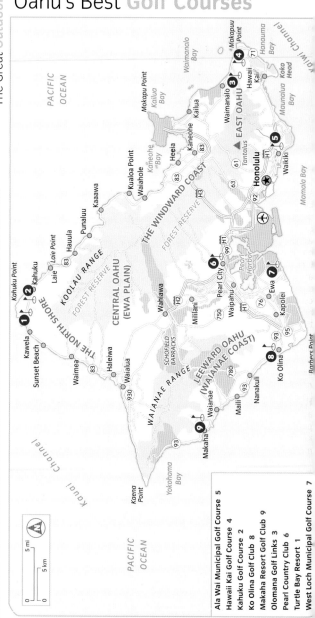

Oahu has nearly three dozen golf courses, ranging from bare-bones municipal courses to exclusive country-club courses with membership fees running to six figures a year. Below are the best of a great bunch. As you play Oahu's courses, you'll come to know that the windward courses play much differently than the leeward courses. On the windward side, the prevailing winds blow from the ocean to shore, and the grain direction of the greens tends to run the same way—from the ocean to the mountains. Leeward golf courses have the opposite tendency: The winds usually blow from the mountains to the ocean, with the grain direction of the greens corresponding.

Ala Wai Municipal Golf Course   The *Guinness Book of World Records* lists this as the busiest golf course in the world; duffers play some 500 rounds a day on this 18-hole municipal course, within walking distance of Waikiki's hotels. It is a challenge to get a tee time (you can book only 3 days in advance). Ala Wai has a flat layout and is less windy than most Oahu courses, but pay attention; some holes are not as easy as you may think. *404 Kapahulu Ave., Waikiki.* ☎ *808/733-7387 (golf course), or 808/296-2000 tee time reservations. www.co.honolulu.hi.us/des/golf/alawai.htm. Greens fees: $42; twilight rate $21. Bus: 19, 20, or 22.*

Hawaii Kai Golf Course   This is actually two golf courses in one. The par-72, 6,222-yard (5,689m) Hawaii Kai Championship Golf Course is moderately challenging, with scenic vistas. The course is forgiving to high-handicap golfers, although it does have a few surprises. The par-3 Hawaii Kai Executive Golf Course is fun for beginners and those just getting back in the game after a few years. The course has lots of hills and valleys, with no water hazards and only a few sand traps. *8902 Kalanianaole Hwy., Honolulu.* ☎ *808/395-2358. www.hawaiikai golf.com. Greens fees: Champion Course $100 Mon–Fri, $110 Sat–Sun, twilight rates $70; Executive Course $37 Mon–Fri, $42 Sat–Sun. Check the website for discounts. Bus: 58.*

Kahuku Golf Course   This 9-hole budget golf course is a bit funky: no club rentals, no clubhouse, and no facilities other than a few pull carts that disappear with the first handful of golfers. But a round at this scenic oceanside course amid the tranquility of the

Ko Olina Golf Club.

North Shore is quite an experience. Duffers will love the ease of this recreational course, and weight watchers will be happy to walk the gently sloping greens. Don't forget to bring your camera for the views. No reservations are taken; tee times are first-come, first-served, and with plenty of retirees happy to sit and wait, the competition is fierce for early tee times. Bring your own clubs and call ahead to check the weather. *56–501 Kamehameha Hwy., Kahuku.* ☎ *808/293-5842. Greens fees: $10 for 9 holes. Bus: 55.*

★★★ **Ko Olina Golf Club** The Ted Robinson–designed course (6,867-yard/6,279m, par-72) has rolling fairways and elevated tee and water features. The signature hole—the 12th, a par-3—has an elevated tee that sits on a rock garden with a cascading waterfall. At the 18th hole, you'll see and hear water all around you—seven pools begin on the right side of the fairway and slope down to a lake. Book in advance; this course is crowded all the time. Facilities include a driving range, locker rooms, Jacuzzi, steam rooms, and a restaurant and bar. Lessons are available. *92–1220 Aliinui Dr., Kapolei.* ☎ *808/676-5309. www.koolinagolf.com. Greens fees: $170 ($150 for Ihilani Resort guests); twilight rates $110 (after 1pm in winter and 2:30pm in summer; $90 for guests). Men and woman are asked to wear a collared shirt. No bus service.*

★★ **Makaha Resort Golf Club** This challenging course sits some 45 miles (72km) west of Honolulu, in Makaha Valley. Designed by William Bell, the par-72, 7,091-yard (6,484m) course meanders toward the ocean before turning and heading into the valley. Sheer volcanic walls tower 1,500 feet (457m) above the course, which is surrounded by swaying palm trees and neon-bright bougainvillea; an occasional peacock will even strut across the fairways. The beauty here could make it difficult to keep your mind on the game if it weren't for the course's many challenges: eight water hazards, 107 bunkers, and frequent brisk winds. This course is packed on weekends, so it's best to try weekdays. Facilities include a pro shop, bag storage, and a snack shop. *84–627 Makaha Valley Rd., Waianae.* ☎ *808/695-7111 or 808/695-5239. www.makahavalley cc.com. Greens fees: $80 (check the website for specials). Bus: 51.*

Olomana Golf Links Low-handicap golfers may not find this gorgeous course difficult, but the striking views of the craggy Koolau mountain ridge alone are worth the fees. The par-72, 6,326-yard (5,784m) course is popular with locals and visitors alike. The course

Olomana Golf Links.

starts off a bit hilly on the front 9 but flattens out by the back 9, where there are some tricky water hazards. This course is very, very green; the rain gods bless it regularly with brief passing showers. You can spot the regular players here—they all carry umbrellas, wait patiently for the squalls to pass, and then resume play. Facilities include a driving range, practice greens, club rental, pro shop, and restaurant. *41–1801 Kalanianaole Hwy., Waimanalo.* ☎ *808/259-7926. ww.olomanagolflinks.com. Greens fees: $80; twilight fees $26 weekdays, $28 weekends. Bus: 57.*

Pearl Country Club Looking for a challenge? You'll find one at this popular public course, located just above Pearl City in Aiea. Sure, the 6,230-yard (5,697m), par-72 looks harmless enough, and the views of Pearl Harbor and the USS *Arizona* Memorial are gorgeous, but around the 5th hole, you'll start to see what you're in for: water hazards, forest, and dog legs that allow only a small margin of error between the tee and the steep out-of-bounds hillside. Oahu residents can't get enough of it, so don't even try to get a tee time on weekends. Facilities include a driving range, practice greens, club rental, pro shop, and restaurant. *98–535 Kaonohi St., Aiea.* ☎ *808/487-3802. www.pearlcc.com. Greens fees: $75 Mon–Fri; $85 Sat–Sun; after 4pm 9 holes are $25. Bus: 32 (stops at Pearlridge Shopping Center at Kaonohi and Moanalua sts.; you'll have to walk about ½ mile/.8km uphill from here).*

★★ Turtle Bay Resort This North Shore resort is home to two of Hawaii's top golf courses: the 18-hole Arnold Palmer Course (formerly the Links at Kuilima) was designed by Arnold Palmer and Ed Seay, and the par-71, 6,200-yard (5,669m)

Turtle Bay Resort.

George Fazio Course. Palmer's is the most challenging, with the front 9 playing like a British Isles course (rolling terrain, only a few trees, and lots of wind). The back 9 has narrower, tree-lined fairways and water. Fazio is a more forgiving course, without all the water hazards and bunkers of the Palmer course. Facilities include a pro shop, driving range, putting and chipping green, and snack bar. Weekdays are best for tee times. *57–049 Kamehameha Hwy., Kahuku.* ☎ *808/ 293-8574 or 808/293-9094. www.turtlebayresort.com. Greens fees: Palmer Course $175 ($145 for resort guests); Fazio Course $155 ($115 for guests). Bus: 52 or 55.*

West Loch Municipal Golf Course This par-72, 6,615-yard (6,049m) course located just 30 minutes from Waikiki, in Ewa Beach, offers golfers a challenge at bargain rates. The difficulties on this unusual municipal course, designed by Robin Nelson and Rodney Wright, are water (lots of hazards), constant trade winds, and narrow fairways. To help you out, the course features a "water" driving range (with a lake) to practice your drives. Facilities include a driving range, practice greens, pro shop, and restaurant. *91–1126 Okupe St., Ewa Beach.* ☎ *808/675-6076. Greens fees: $50; $25 after 4pm. Book a week in advance. Bus: 50.*

Adventures **on Land**

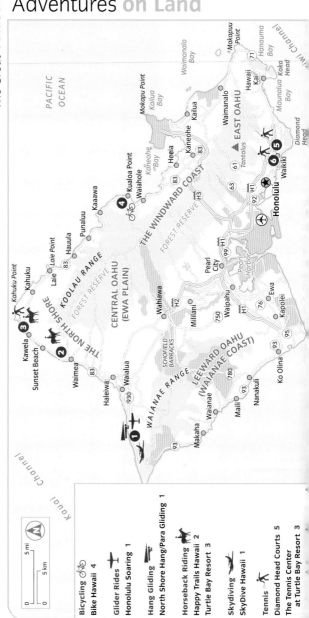

Bicycling
Bike Hawaii 4

Glider Rides
Honolulu Soaring 1

Hang Gliding
North Shore Hang/Para Gliding 1

Horseback Riding
Happy Trails Hawaii 2
Turtle Bay Resort 3

Skydiving
SkyDive Hawaii 1

Tennis
Diamond Head Courts 5
The Tennis Center
at Turtle Bay Resort 3

Honolulu isn't just sparkling ocean water and rainbow-colored fish; it's also the land of adventure—you can cycle back through history to an ancient, terraced taro field, soar through the air in a glider, gallop along a deserted sandy beach, or even leap from a plane and float to earth under a parachute.

Bicycling

Get off the street and get dirty with an off-road, guided mountain bike tour from **Bike Hawaii,** through the 1,000 acre (405ha) Kaaawa Valley on Oahu's northeast shore. The tour is the same site as the annual 24 Hours of Hell Mountain Bike Race; you'll follow dirt roads and single-track through verdant tropical landscape, dotted with mountain streams. Stops on the 6-mile (9.5km), 2-hour ride include: an ancient Hawaiian house site in the midst of a terraced taro field, an old military bunker converted into a movie museum for films shot within this historical valley *(Jurassic Park, Godzilla, Mighty Joe Young, Windtalkers)*, and views of sheer valley walls, panoramic ocean vistas, and lush Hawaiian vegetation. ☎ 877/MTV-RIDE or 808/734-4214.

www.bikehawaii.com. Adults $105, children 13yrs and under $76 (includes mountain bike, van transportation, helmet, lunch, snacks, water bottle and guide).

Glider Rides

Imagine soaring through silence on gossamer wings, a panoramic view of Oahu below you. A glider ride is an unforgettable experience, and it's available from **Honolulu Soaring,** at Dillingham Air Field, in Mokuleia, on Oahu's North Shore. The glider is towed behind a plane; at the proper altitude, the tow is dropped, and you (and the glider pilot) are left to soar in the thermals. *Dillingham Air Field, Mokuleia.* ☎ *808/677-3404. www.honolulu soaring.com. From $59 for 10 minutes.*

Soar silently over the North Shore's breathtaking landscape in a glider.

You can explore Oahu by bike on your own or with a tour.

Hang Gliding

See things from a bird's-eye view as you and your instructor float high above Oahu on a tandem hang glider with **North Shore Hang/Para Gliding.** *Dillingham Air Field.* ☎ *808/637-3178. www.kailuablue.com. Ground school plus 30 minutes in the air $175.*

Horseback Riding

★ **kids Happy Trails Hawaii** NORTH SHORE   This small operation welcomes families (kids as young as 6 years are okay) on these guided trail rides on a hilltop above Pupukea Beach and overlooking Waimea Valley, on the North Shore. *59-231 Pupukea Rd.* ☎ *808/638RIDE. www.happytrailshawaii.com. From $58 for 1-hr. rides.*

★ **Turtle Bay Resort** NORTH SHORE   You can gallop along a deserted North Shore beach with spectacular ocean views and through a forest of ironwood trees or take a romantic evening ride at sunset with your sweetheart.

Biking on Your Own

Bicycling is a great way to see Oahu, and most streets here have bike lanes. For information on bikeways and maps, contact the **Honolulu City and County Bicycle Coordinator** (☎ 808/527-5044; www.state.hi.us/dot/highways/bike/oahu).

If you're in Waikiki, you can rent a bike for as little as $10 for a half-day and $20 for 24 hours at **Big Kuhuna Rentals,** 407 Seaside Ave. (☎ 808/924-2736; www.bigkahunarentals.com). On the North Shore, for a full-suspension mountain bike, try **Raging Isle,** 66–250 Kamehameha Hwy., Haleiwa (☎ 808/637-7707; www.raging isle.com), which rents bikes for $40 for 24 hours.

Rolling through Waikiki on a Segway

One of my favorite ways to tour Waikiki is on a Segway Personal Transporter, one of those two-wheeled machines that look like an old push lawn mower (big wheels and a long handle). It only takes a few minutes to get the hang of this contraption (which works through a series of high-tech stabilization mechanisms that read the motion of your body to turn or go forward or backwards), and it's a lot of fun (think back to the first time you rode your bicycle—the incredible freedom of zipping through space without walking). **Glide Ride Tours and Rentals,** located in the Hawaii Tapa Tower of the Hilton Hawaiian Village Beach Resort & Spa, 2005 Kalia Rd. (☎ **808/ 941-3151;** www.segwayofhawaii.com), offers instruction and several tours ranging from a 40-min. introductory tour for $49 per person to a 2½-hour tour of Waikiki, Kapiolani Park, and Diamond Head for $125 per person.

57–091 Kamehameha Hwy., Kahuku. ☎ 808/293-8811. www.turtlebay resort.com. Bus: 52 or 55. Beach ride (45 min.): $50 adults, $30 for children 7–12 (they must be at least 4 ft. 4 in./1.3m tall); Sunset rides: $80.

Skydiving

SkyDive Hawaii offers a once-in-a-lifetime experience: leap from a plane and float to earth in a tandem jump (where you're strapped to an expert who wears a chute big enough for the both of you). 68–760 Farrington Hwy., Waiawa. ☎ 808/637-9700. www.hawaiiskydiving.com. $225.

Tennis

Free Tennis Courts Oahu has 181 free public tennis courts. The courts are available on a first-come, first-served basis; playing time is limited to 45 minutes if others are waiting. The closest courts to Waikiki are the **Diamond Head Courts.** 3908 Paki Ave. (across from Kapiolani Park). ☎ 808/971-7150.

The Tennis Center at Turtle Bay Resort Turtle Bay has eight plexipave courts, two of which are lit for night play. Instruction, rental equipment, player matchup, and even a ball machine are available here. You must reserve the night courts in advance; they're very popular. 57–091 Kamehameha Hwy., Kahuku. ☎ 808/293-6024. www. turtlebayresort.com. Bus: 52 or 55. Court time: $10/person (complimentary for guests); equipment rental $8; lessons $35 for 30 min. & $60 for 1 hr.

Waikiki Tennis Courts and Lessons If you are staying in Waikiki, one of the most accessible courts is tucked away at the entrance to Waikiki, just across the bridge over Ala Wai Canal at **Aqua Marina Hotel.** 1700 Ala Moana Blvd. ☎ 808/551-9438. Bus: 19 or 20. Daily 9am–9pm. Court rental: $10 person/hour; Racket rental $8 per day; private lessons $60/hour, semi-private $75/hour for 2 or more.

Oahu's Best Snorkeling

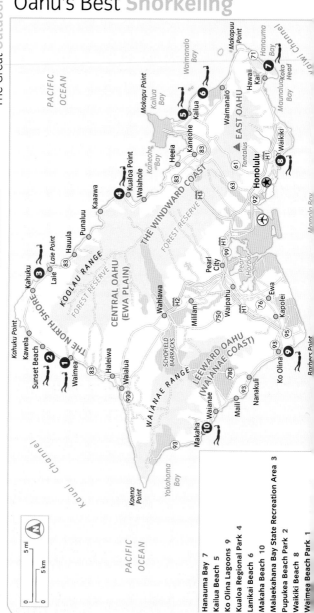

Hanauma Bay 7

Kailua Beach 5

Ko Olina Lagoons 9

Kualoa Regional Park 4

Lanikai Beach 6

Makaha Beach 10

Malaekahana Bay State Recreation Area 3

Pupukea Beach Park 2

Waikiki Beach 8

Waimea Beach Park 1

Snorkeling is a huge attraction on Oahu—just relax as you float over underwater worlds populated with colorful clouds of tropical fish. If you've never snorkeled before, most resorts and excursion boats offer instruction, but it's plenty easy to figure it out for yourself. All you need are a mask, a snorkel, fins, and some basic swimming skills. In many places all you have to do is wade into the water and look down. Below are Oahu's best snorkeling beaches.

★★★ kids **Hanauma Bay** KOKO HEAD   Oahu's most popular snorkeling spot is a curved, 2,000-foot (610m) gold-sand beach packed elbow-to-elbow with people year-round. Part of an old crater that fell into the sea, the bay's shallow shoreline water and abundant marine life are the main attractions to snorkelers. A shallow reef outside the bay protects it from the surf, keeping the waters very calm. Hanauma Bay is a conservation district; you may look at but not touch or take any marine life here. Feeding the fish is also prohibited. *7455 Koko Kalanianaole Hwy. (at Hanauma Bay Rd.). Or take TheBus to escape the parking problem: The Hanauma Bay Shuttle runs from Waikiki to Hanauma Bay every half hour from 8:45am–1pm.*

★★★ kids **Kailua Beach** WINDWARD   Stretched out between two points, this 2-mile-long (3km) golden strand (with dunes, palm trees, panoramic views, and offshore islets) offers great snorkeling (along with a host of other ocean activities) with safe water conditions most of the year. *450 Kawailoa Rd., Kailua. Bus: 56 or 57, transfer 70.*

Ko Olina Lagoons LEEWARD   When the developer of the 640-acre (259ha) Ko Olina Resort blasted four white-sand lagoons out of the shoreline to make the rocky shoreline more attractive and accessible, he created a great snorkeling area around the boulders at the entrance to each lagoon. The man-made lagoons offer calm, shallow waters and a powdery white-sand beach bordered by a broad, grassy lawn. No lifeguards are present, but the generally tranquil waters are safe. *Off Aliinui Dr. (between Olani and Mauloa pls.), Ko Olina Resort. No bus.*

★★ kids **Kualoa Regional Park** WINDWARD   This 150-acre (61ha) coconut palm–fringed peninsula is the biggest beach park on the windward side and one of Hawaii's most scenic. The sandy waters off shore

Snorkeling with a sea turtle in Hanauma Bay.

Kualoa Park.

are safe and have snorkeling areas. Just 500 yards (457m) off shore is the tiny islet, Mokoli'i Island (popularly known as Chinaman's Hat), which has a small sandy beach and is a bird preserve—so don't spook the red-footed boobies. *49-600 Kamehameha Hwy., Kualoa. Bus: 55.*

★★ **Lanikai Beach** WINDWARD One of Hawaii's best spots for snorkeling is off the gold-sand Lanikai's crystal-clear lagoon (it feels like a giant saltwater aquarium there are so many fish). The reef extends out for about ½ mile (.8km), with snorkeling along the entire length. *Mokulua Dr., Kailua. Bus: 56 or 57, transfer to 70.*

★ **Makaha Beach** LEEWARD During the summer, the waters here are clear and filled with a range of sealife (from green sea turtles to schools of tropical fish to an occasional manta ray). Plus the underwater landscape has arches and tunnels just 40 feet (12m) down, great habitats for reef fish. *84-369 Farrington Hwy., Makaha. Bus: City Express B, transfer to Country Express C.*

★★★ **kids** **Malaekahana Bay State Recreation Area** NORTH SHORE This almost mile-long (1.6km) white-sand crescent lives up to just about everyone's image of the perfect Hawaiian beach. I head for the rocky areas around either of

Where to Rent Beach Equipment

If you want to rent beach toys (snorkeling equipment, boogie boards, surfboards, kayaks, and more), check out the following rental shops: **Snorkel Bob's,** on the way to Hanauma Bay at 700 Kapahulu Ave. (at Date St.), Honolulu (☎ **808/735-7944;** www.snorkelbob. com); and **Aloha Beach Service,** in the Moana Surfrider, 2365 Kalakaua Ave. (☎ **808/922-3111,** ext. 2341), in Waikiki. On Oahu's windward side, try **Kailua Sailboards & Kayaks,** 130 Kailua Rd., a block from the Kailua Beach Park (☎ **808/262-2555;** www.kailuasail boards.com). On the North Shore, get equipment from **Surf-N-Sea,** 62–595 Kamehameha Hwy., Haleiwa (☎ **808/637-9887;** www. surfnsea.com).

the two points (Makahoa Pt. and Kalanai Pt) that define this bay. *Kamehameha Hwy. (2 miles/3km north of the Polynesian Cultural Center). Bus: 52.*

★ **Pupukea Beach Park** NORTH SHORE   This 80-acre (32ha) beach park, very popular for snorkeling in the summer, is a Marine Life Conservation District with strict rules about taking marine life, sand, coral, shells, and rocks. Locals divide the area into two: Shark's Cove (which is *not* named for an abundance of sharks), great for snorkeling, and at the southern end Three Tables (named for the three flat sections of reef visible at low tide), also great for snorkeling, where the water is about 15 feet deep. Snorkeling is best from May to October, when the water is calm; nevertheless, watch out for surges. In the winter, when currents form and waves roll in, this area is very dangerous, even in the tide pools, and there are no lifeguards. *59–727 Kamehameha Hwy. (Pupukea Rd.), Pupukea. Bus: 52.*

★★★ **kids** **Waikiki Beach** WAIKIKI This famous 1½-mile-long (2.4km) crescent of imported sand (from Molokai) has great snorkeling spots along nearly the entire length of the beach, but my favorite snorkeling spot is Queen's Beach or Queen's

The shallow waters at Pupukea are ideal for beginners.

Surf Beach, between the Natatorium and the Waikiki Aquarium. It's less crowded here, the waters are calm, and the fish are plentiful. I usually get in the water behind the Waikiki Aquarium and snorkel up to the Natatorium and back. *Stretching from Ala Wai Yacht Harbor to Diamond Head Park. Bus: 19 or 20.*

★★ **Waimea Beach Park** NORTH SHORE   In summer, this deep, sandy bowl has gentle waves that allow access to great snorkeling around the rocks and reef. Snorkeling isn't an option in the winter, when huge waves pummel the shoreline. *51-031 Kamehameha Hwy., Waimea. Bus: 52.*

Swimming with butterfly fish at Hanauma Bay.

The Great Outdoors

Adventures in the Ocean

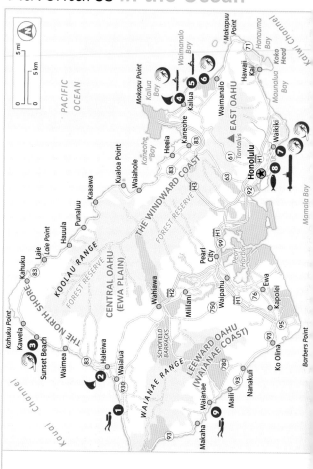

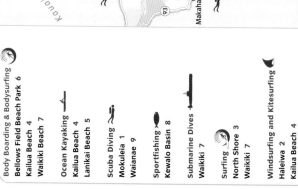

Body Boarding & Bodysurfing
Bellows Field Beach Park 6
Kailua Beach 4
Waikiki Beach 7

Ocean Kayaking
Kailua Beach 4
Lanikai Beach 5

Scuba Diving
Mokuleia 1
Waianae 9

Sportfishing
Kewalo Basin 8

Submarine Dives
Waikiki 7

Surfing
North Shore 3
Waikiki 7

Windsurfing and Kitesurfing
Haleiwa 2
Kailua Beach 4

o really appreciate Oahu, you need to get off the land.
Strap on some scuba gear and plunge beneath the ocean, skip across the water in a sailing charter, go sportfishing and battle a 1,000-pound (454kg) marlin, glide over the water in the kayak, or ride the waves body surfing, board surfing, or windsurfing. Whatever ocean adventure thrills you, you will find it here.

Bodyboarding (Boogie Boarding) & Bodysurfing

Riding the waves without a board, becoming one with the rolling water, is a way of life in Hawaii. Some bodysurfers just rely on their hands to ride the waves; others use hand boards or a boogie board or body board. Both bodysurfing and bodyboarding require a pair of open-heeled swim fins to help propel you through the water. Good places to learn to body board are in the small waves of **Waikiki Beach** and **Kailua Beach** (both reviewed in chapter 6), and Bellows Field Beach Park, off Kalanianaole Hwy. 72 (Hughs Rd.), in Waimanalo (bus 57), which is open to the public on weekends (noon Fri–midnight Sun and holidays).

Ocean Kayaking

Gliding silently over the water, propelled by a paddle, seeing Oahu from the sea the way the early Hawaiians did—that's what ocean kayaking is all about. Early mornings are always best, because the wind comes up around 11am, making seas choppy and paddling difficult. For a wonderful adventure, rent a kayak, arrive at **Lanikai Beach** just as the sun is appearing, and paddle across the emerald lagoon to the pyramid-shaped islands called Mokulua—it's an experience you won't forget. A second favorite kayak launching area is **Kailua Beach.** Kayak equipment rental starts at $10 an hour for a single kayak, and $16 an hour for a double kayak. See the box "Where to Rent Beach Equipment" on p 176.

A bodyboarder takes on some North Shore waves.

Sailing & Snorkeling Tours

A funny thing happens to people when they come to Hawaii. Maybe it's the salt air, the warm tropical nights, or the blue Hawaiian moonlight, but otherwise-rational people who have never set foot on a boat in their life suddenly want to go out to sea. You can opt for a "booze cruise," jammed with loud, rum-soaked strangers, or you can sail on one of these special yachts, all of which will take you out whale-watching in season (roughly Jan–Apr).

With ★ **Captain Bob's Adventure Cruises** (☎ 808/942-5077) you can see the majestic Windward Coast the way it should be seen—from Kaneohe Bay. The 42-foot (13m) catamaran skims across the almost always calm water above the shallow coral reef, lands at the disappearing sandbar Ahu o Laka, and takes you past two small islands to snorkel among abundant tropical fish and, sometimes, turtles. The trip costs $79 adults, $60 children 3 to 14 (free for kids under 3).

The 140-foot-long (43m) ★★ *Navatek I* (☎ 808/973-1311) isn't even called a boat; it's actually a SWATH (Small Waterplane Area Twin Hull) vessel, which guarantees that you'll be "seasick-free." It's the smoothest ride in Waikiki. In fact, *Navatek I* is the only dinner cruise ship to receive U.S. Coast Guard certification to travel beyond Diamond Head. They offer both lunch ($63 adults, $56 kids 2–11) and sunset dinner cruises ($80–$112 adults, $74–$95 kids 2–11), and during the whale season (roughly Jan–Apr), you get whales to boot. Both cruises include live Hawaiian music. The cruise leaves from Aloha Tower Marketplace, Pier 6.

Picture this: floating in the calm waters off the Waianae coast, where your 42-foot (13m) sailing catamaran has just dropped you off. You watch turtles swimming in the reef below, and in the distance, a pod of spinner dolphins appears. In the winter, you may spot humpback whales on the morning cruise, which also includes continental breakfast and other refreshments and snorkel gear, instruction, and a floatation device. Sound good? Call **Wild Side Tours** (☎ 808/306-7273; www.sailhawaii.com). Tours leave from the Waianae Boat Harbor. The morning sail/snorkel tour costs $95 (ages 6 and up; not recommended for younger children).

★★ **kids** **Kailua Sailboards & Kayaks** First-timer kayakers can learn a lot on the "excursion" tour, designed for the novice. The fee covers lunch, all equipment, lessons, transportation from Waikiki hotels, and 2 hours of kayaking in Kailua Bay. *130 Kailua Rd. ☎ 808/ 262-2555. www.kailuasailboards. com. Excursion tour $89 adults, $75 kids 8–12.*

Scuba Diving

Oahu is a wonderful place to scuba dive, especially for those interested in wreck diving. One of the more famous wrecks in Hawaii is the *Mahi*, a 185-foot (56m) former minesweeper easily accessible just south of Waianae. Abundant marine life makes this a great place to shoot photos—schools of lemon butterfly fish and taape (blue-lined snapper) are so comfortable with divers and photographers that they practically pose. Eagle rays, green sea turtles, manta rays, and white-tipped sharks occasionally cruise by as well, and eels peer out from the wreck.

For nonwreck diving, one of the best dive spots in summer is Kahuna Canyon, a massive amphitheater located near Mokuleia. Walls rising from the ocean floor create the illusion of an underwater Grand Canyon. Inside the amphitheater, crabs, octopi, slippers, and spiny lobsters abound (be aware that taking them in summer is illegal), and giant trevally, parrotfish, and unicorn fish congregate as well. Outside the amphitheater, you're likely to see an occasional shark in the distance.

Because Oahu's greatest dives are offshore, your best bet is to book a two-tank dive from a dive boat. Hawaii's oldest and largest outfitter is **Aaron's Dive Shop,** 307 Hahani St., Kailua (☎ **808/262-2333;** www.hawaii-scuba.com). A two-tank boat dive costs $115, including transportation from the Kailua shop. **Dive Oahu,** 1085 Ala Moana Blvd., Waikiki (☎ **808/922-3483;** www.diveoahu.com), has two-tank boat dives for $129. **Surf-N-Sea,** 62–595 Kamehameha Hwy., Haleiwa (☎ **808/637-9887;** www.surfnsea.com), has two-tank boat dives for $110.

Diving Tips

A great resource for diving on your own is the University of Hawaii Sea Grant's *Dive Hawaii Guide* (www.hawaii scubadiving.com), which describes nearly every dive site on the various Hawaiian islands, including Oahu.

Kayaking on the windward coast.

Sportfishing

Marlin (as big as 1,200 lb./544kg), tuna, ono, and mahimahi await the baited hook in Hawaii's coastal and channel waters. No license is required, just book a sportfishing vessel out of Kewalo Basin, on Ala Moana Boulevard (at Ward Ave.), the main location for charter fishing boats on Oahu, located between the Honolulu International Airport and Waikiki. When the fish are biting, the captains display the catch of the day in the afternoon. Or contact **Sportfish Hawaii.** This sportfishing booking agency helps match you with the best fishing boat; every vessel they book has been inspected and must meet rigorous criteria to guarantee that you will have a great time. ☎ *877/388-1376 or 808/396-2607. www.sportfishhawaii.com. Prices range from $750–$932 for a full-day exclusive charter (you, plus five friends, get the entire boat to yourself); $621–$717 for a half-day exclusive; or from $187 for a full-day share charter (you share the boat with five other people).*

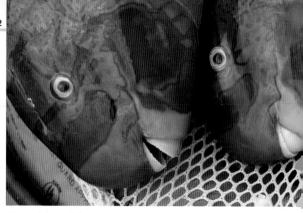

Spectacled parrotfish.

Submarine Dives

Here's your chance to play Jules Verne and experience the underwater world from the comfort of a submarine. ★★ **Atlantis Submarine** will take you on an adventure below the surface in high-tech comfort, narrating your tour as you watch tropical fish and sunken ships just outside the sub; if swimming's not your thing, this is a great way to see Hawaii's spectacular sea life. *Warning:* Skip this if you suffer from claustrophobia. *Shuttle boats to the sub leave from Hilton Hawaiian Village Pier.* ☎ *800/548-6262 or 808/973-9811. www.atlantis submarines.com. Adults $90–$113, children 12 and under $80–$98 (children must be at least 36 in./.9m tall). Budget tip: Book online for discount reservation rates of $84 adults and $78 kids.*

Surfing

The ancient Hawaiian sport of *hee nalu* (wave sliding) is probably the sport most people picture when they think of the islands. In summer, when the water's warm and there's a soft breeze in the air, the south swell comes up. It's surf season in Waikiki, the best place on Oahu to learn how

to surf. For lessons in Waikiki, go early to **Aloha Beach Service,** next to the Moana Surfrider, 2365 Kalakaua Ave. (☎ **808/922-3111**). Lessons are $30 an hour and rentals $10 for the first hour; $5 for every hour after that. On the North Shore, contact the **Hans Hedemann Surf School** at the Turtle Bay Resort (☎ **808/924-7778;** www.hhsurf. com); Hedemann has been a champion surfer for some 34 years. Lessons start at $50 an hour.

Surf's Up!

To find out where the waves are call the **Surf News Network Surfline** (☎ **808/596-SURF**) to get the latest surf conditions.

Windsurfing & Kitesurfing

Windward Oahu's Kailua Beach is the home of champion and pioneer windsurfer Robbie Naish; it's also the best place to learn to windsurf. The oldest and most established windsurfing business in Hawaii is **Naish Hawaii/Naish Windsurfing Hawaii,** 155-A Hamakua Dr., Kailua (☎ **800/767-6068** or 808/262-6068; www.naish.com). Private lessons

Experiencing *Jaws:* Up Close & Personal

You're 4 miles (6km) out from land, surrounded by open ocean. Suddenly from out of the blue depths a shape emerges: the sleek, pale shadow of a 6-foot-long (1.8m) gray reef shark, followed quickly by a couple of 10-foot-long (3m) Galapagos sharks. Within a couple of heartbeats, you are surrounded by sharks on all sides. Do you panic? No—you paid $120 to be in the midst of these jaws of the deep. And, of course, you have a 6×6×10-foot (1.8m×1.8m×3m) aluminum shark cage separating you from all those teeth. If this sounds like your idea of a good time, call **North Shore Shark Adventures** (☎ **808/256-2769;** www.hawaiisharkadventures.com). The shark cage, connected to the boat with wire line, holds up to four snorkelers (it's comfortable with two but pretty snug at full capacity). You can stay on the boat and view the sharks from a more respectable distance for just $60.

start at $75 for a 90-minute session. Kite-surfing lessons are also available at $125 for 1½ hours. Another option is **Kailua Sailboards & Kayaks,** 130 Kailua Rd. (☎ **808/ 262-2555;** www.kailuasailboards. com). Group lessons cost $89 per person for 3 hours (including all gear and lunch). On the North Shore, windsurfer wannabes should contact **Surf-N-Sea,** 62–595 Kamehameha Hwy., Haleiwa (☎ **808/637-9887;** www.surfnsea.com). Private lessons cost $75 for 2 hours. These companies also rent equipment.

Waikiki is the ideal place to learn to hang ten.

Sea Life Primer

You're likely to spot one or more of the following fish while underwater:

Angelfish can be distinguished by the spine, located low on the gill plate. These fish are very shy; several species live in colonies close to coral.

Blennies are small, elongated fish, ranging from 2 to 10 inches long, with the majority in the 3- to 4-inch range. Blennies are so small that they can live in tide pools; you might have a hard time spotting one.

Butterfly fish, among the most colorful of the reef fish, are usually seen in pairs (scientists believe they mate for life) and appear to spend most of their day feeding. Most butterfly fish have a dark band through the eye and a spot near the tail resembling an eye, meant to confuse their predators (moray eels love to lunch on them).

Moray and **conger eels** are the most common eels seen in Hawaii. Morays are usually docile except when provoked or when there's food around. Although morays may look menacing, conger eels look downright happy, with big lips and pectoral fins (situated so that they look like big ears) that give them the appearance of a perpetually smiling face.

Parrotfish, one of the largest and most colorful of the reef fish, can grow up to 40 inches long. They're easy to spot—their front teeth are fused together, protruding like buck teeth that allow them to feed by scraping algae from rocks and coral. Native parrotfish species include yellowbar, regal, and spectacled.

Scorpion fish are what scientists call "ambush predators." They hide under camouflaged exteriors and ambush their prey. Several kinds sport a venomous dorsal spine. These fish don't have a gas bladder, so when they stop swimming, they sink—that's why you usually find them "resting" on ledges and on the ocean bottom. They're not aggressive, but they very careful where you put your hands and feet in the water so as to avoid those venomous spines.

Surgeonfish, sometimes called *tang,* get their name from the scalpel-like spines located on each side of the body near the base of the tail. Several surgeonfish, such as the brightly colored yellow tang, are boldly colored; others are adorned in more conservative shades of gray, brown, or black.

Wrasses are a very diverse family of fish, ranging in length from 2 to 15 inches. Wrasses can change gender from female to male. Some have brilliant coloration that changes as they age. ●

The
Savvy Traveler

Before You Go

Government Tourist Offices

The **Hawaii Visitors and Convention Bureau (HVCB)** has an office at 2270 Kalakaua Ave., Seventh Floor, Honolulu, HI 96815 (☎ **800/GO-HAWAII** or 808/923-1811; www.gohawaii.com). The **Oahu Visitors Bureau** is at 735 Bishop St., Suite 1872, Honolulu, HI 96813 (☎ **877/525-OAHU** or 808/524-0722; www.visit-oahu.com).

The Best Time to Go

Most visitors don't come to Honolulu when the weather's best in the islands; rather, they come when it's at its worst everywhere else. Thus, the **high season**—when prices are up and resorts are booked to capacity—generally runs from mid-December through March or mid-April (depending when Easter falls). The last 2 weeks of December in particular are the prime time for travel. If you're planning a holiday trip, make your reservations as early as possible, count on holiday crowds, and expect to pay top dollar for accommodations, car rentals, and airfare. Whale-watching season begins in January and continues through the rest of winter, sometimes lasting into May.

The **off seasons,** when the best bargain rates are available, are spring (mid-Apr–mid-June) and fall (Sept–mid-Dec)—a paradox, since these are the best seasons in terms of reliably great weather. If you're looking to save money, or if you just want to avoid the crowds, this is the time to visit. Hotel rates tend to be significantly lower during these off seasons. Airfares also tend to be lower—again, sometimes substantially—and good packages and special deals are often available.

Note: If you plan to come to Honolulu between the last week in April and the first week in May, be sure to book your accommodations, air reservations, and car rental in advance. In Japan the last week of April is called **Golden Week,** because three Japanese holidays take place one after the other. The islands are especially busy with Japanese tourists during this time.

Due to the large number of families traveling in **summer** (June–Aug), you won't get the fantastic bargains of spring and fall. However, you'll still do much better on packages, airfare, and accommodations than you will in the winter months.

Festivals & Special Events

WINTER. At the **Triple Crown of Surfing,** the world's top professional surfers compete in events for more than $1 million in prize money. Competition takes place on the North Shore whenever the surf's up from late November to December. Call ☎ **808/739-3965** (www.triplecrownofsurfing.com). The second Sunday in December is the **Honolulu Marathon,** one of the largest marathons in the world, with more than 30,000 competitors. Call ☎ **808/734-7200** (www.honolulumarathon.org). In late January or early February (depending on the lunar calendar), the red carpet is rolled out for **Chinese New Year** with a traditional lion dance, fireworks, food booths, and a host of activities. Call ☎ **808/533-3181.** Depending on surf conditions, February or March brings the **Buffalo's Big Board Classic** at Makaha Beach. You'll see traditional Hawaiian surfing, long boarding, and canoe-surfing. Call ☎ **808/951-7877.**

SPRING. The **Annual Easter Sunrise Service** is celebrated with the century-old sunrise services at the

National Cemetery of the Pacific, Punchbowl Crater, Honolulu. Call ☎ **808/566-1430.** May 1 means Lei Day in Hawaii and the largest celebration is the **Annual Lei Day Concert** with the Brothers Cazimero at the Waikiki Shell. Call ☎ **808/597-1888,** ext. 232. Mid-May brings the **World Fire-Knife Dance Championships and Samoan Festival,** Polynesian Cultural Center, Laie, where junior and adult fire-knife dancers from around the world converge for one of the most amazing performances you'll ever see. Authentic Samoan food and cultural festivities round out the fun. Call ☎ **808/293-3333** (www.polynesian culturalcenter.com).

SUMMER. In June, the **King Kamehameha Celebration,** a state holiday, features a massive floral parade, *hoolaulea* (party), and much more. Call ☎ **808/586-0333** (www.state. hi.us/dags/kkcc). The third weekend in June brings the **King Kamehameha Hula Competition** to the Neal Blaisdell Center; it's one of the top hula competitions in the world, with dancers from as far away as Japan. Call ☎ **808/586-0333** (www. hawaii.gov). In late July, head for the annual **Ukulele Festival,** Kapiolani Park Bandstand, Waikiki, a free concert with a ukulele orchestra of

some 600 students (ages 4–92). Hawaii's top musicians all pitch in. Call ☎ **808/732-3739** (www. roysakuma.net). Late July is the annual **Queen Liliuokalani Keiki Hula Competition** at the Neal Blaisdell Center, Honolulu. More than 500 *keiki* (children) representing 22 *halau* (hula schools) from the islands compete in this dance fest. Call ☎ **808/521-6905.** In August, the **Hawaii International Jazz Festival,** The Hawaii Theatre, Honolulu, includes evening concerts and daily jam sessions plus scholarship giveaways, the University of Southern California jazz band, and many popular jazz and blues artists. Call ☎ **808/941-9974;** www.hawaiijazz.com.

FALL. In September and October are the statewide **Aloha Festivals,** with parades and other events celebrating Hawaiian culture and friendliness throughout the state. Call ☎ **808-589-1771** (www.aloha festivals.com) for a schedule of events. The annual **Hawaii International Film Festival** takes place the first 2 weeks in November. This cinema festival with a cross-cultural spin features filmmakers from Asia, the Pacific Islands, and the United States. Call ☎ **808/550-8457** (www. hiff.org).

HONOLULU'S AVERAGE TEMPERATURES & RAINFALL

MONTH	HIGH (F/C)	LOW (F/C)	WATER TEMP (F/C)	RAIN (IN/CM)
January	80/27	66/19	75/24	3.5/9
February	81/27	65/18	75/24	2.5/6.5
March	82/28	67/19	76/24	2.5/6.5
April	83/28	68/20	77/25	1.5/4
May	85/29	70/21	79/26	1/2.5
June	87/31	72/22	81/27	0.5/1.5
July	88/31	74/23	81/27	0.5/1.5
August	89/32	75/24	81/27	0.5/1.5
September	89/32	74/23	81/27	1/2.5
October	87/31	73/23	81/27	2.5/6.5
November	84/29	71/22	79/26	3/7.5
December	82/28	68/20	76/24	4/10

The Weather

Because Honolulu lies at the edge of the tropical zone, it technically has only two seasons, both of them warm. The dry season corresponds to summer, and the rainy season generally runs during the winter, from November to March. It rains every day somewhere in the islands at any time of the year, but the rainy season can cause "gray" weather and spoil your tanning opportunities. Honolulu and Waikiki generally may have a brief rain shower, followed by bright sunshine and maybe a rainbow. The **year-round temperature** usually varies no more than about 10°F (6°C), but it depends on where you are. Honolulu's **leeward** sides (the west and south, where Waikiki and Honolulu are located) are usually hot and dry, whereas the **windward** sides (east and north) are generally cooler and moist. If you want arid, sunbaked, desertlike weather, go leeward. If you want lush, often wet, junglelike weather, go windward. If you want to know how to pack just before you go, check CNN's online 5-day forecast at www.cnn.com/weather. You can also get the local weather by calling ☎ 808/871-5111.

Restaurant & Activity Reservations

I can't say it enough: Book well in advance if you're determined to eat at a particular spot or participate in a certain activity. For popular restaurants, if you didn't call in advance, try asking for early or late hours—often tables are available before 6:30pm and after 9pm. You could also call the day before or first thing in the morning, when you may be able to take advantage of a cancellation.

Cell (Mobile) Phones

In general it's a good bet that your phone will work in Honolulu,

Useful Websites

- **www.gohawaii.com**: An excellent, all-around guide to activities, tours, lodging, and events by the members of the Hawaii Visitors and Convention Bureau.
- **www.planet-hawaii.com**: Click on "Island" for an island-by-island guide to activities, lodging, shopping, culture, the surf report, and weather.
- **www.hotspots.hawaii.com**: Lists most of the radio stations in Hawaii, with links to their websites and the type of format.
- **www.visit-oahu.com**: Oahu chapter of the state visitors bureau lists activities, dining, lodging, parks, shopping, and more.
- **www.hawaiian105.com**: Hawaiian music radio station.
- **www.geocities.com/~olelo**: Hawaiian language website with easy lessons on Hawaiian and a cultural calendar.
- **www.honoluluadvertiser.com**: Honolulu's daily newspaper with a section on entertainment.
- **www.honoluluweekly.com**: The alternative weekly newspaper, a good source to find out entertainment listings.
- **www.weather.com**: Up-to-the-minute worldwide weather reports.

although coverage may not be as good as in your home town. You'll be appalled at the poor reach of our GSM (Global System for Mobiles) wireless network, which is used by much of the rest of the world. (To see where GSM phones work in the U.S., check out www.t-mobile.com/coverage/national_popup.asp). And you may or may not be able to send SMS (text messages) overseas. Assume nothing—call your wireless provider and get the full scoop. In a worst-case scenario, you can always rent a phone from InTouch USA (☎ **800/872-7626**; www.intouch global.com), but beware that you'll pay $1 a minute or more for airtime.

Getting There

By Plane

Fly directly to Honolulu. **United Airlines** (☎ 800/225-5825; www.ual. com) offers the most frequent service from the U.S. mainland. **Aloha Airlines** (☎ 800/367-5250 or 808/484-1111; www.alohaairlines.com) has direct flights from Oakland, Orange County, and Las Vegas. **American Airlines** (☎ 800/433-7300; www.americanair.com) offers flights from Dallas, Chicago, San Francisco, San Jose, Los Angeles, and St. Louis. **ATA** (www.ata.com), code sharing with **Southwest Airlines,** has direct flights from Oakland, Los Angeles, Orange County, Las Vegas, and Phoenix. **Continental Airlines** (☎ 800/231-0856; www.continental.com) offers the only daily nonstop from the New York area (Newark) to Honolulu. **Delta Air Lines** (☎ 800/221-1212; www.delta.com) flies nonstop from the West Coast and from Houston and Cincinnati. **Hawaiian Airlines** (☎ **800/367-5320;** www.hawaiian air.com) offers nonstop flights to Honolulu from several West Coast cities (including new service from San Diego). **Northwest Airlines** (☎ 800/225-2525; www.nwa.com) has a daily nonstop from Detroit to Honolulu.

Airlines serving Honolulu from places other than the U.S. mainland include **Air Canada** (☎ 800/776-3000; www.aircanada.ca); **Air New Zealand** (☎ 0800/737-000 in Auckland, 643/379-5200 in Christchurch, 800/926-7255 in the U.S.; www.air newzealand.com); **Air Pacific Airways** (☎ 808/833 5582 in the US; www.airpacific.com); **Continental Air Micronesia** (☎ 800-231-0856; www.continental.com); **Qantas** (☎ 008/177-767 in Australia, 800/227-4500 in the U.S.; www.qantas. com.au); **Japan Air Lines** (☎ 03/5489-1111 in Tokyo, 800/525-3663 in the U.S.; www.japanair.com); **Jetstar** (☎ 866/397-8170, www.jet star.com) from Syndey; **All Nippon Airways (ANA;** ☎ 03/5489-1212 in Tokyo, 800/235-9262 in the U.S.; www.fly-ana.com); **China Airlines** (☎ 02/715-1212 in Taipei, 800/227-5118 in the U.S.; www.china-airlines. com); **Air Pacific,** serving Fiji, Australia, New Zealand, and the South Pacific (☎ 800/227-4446; www.air pacific.com); **Korean Air** (☎ 02/656-2000 in Seoul, 800/223-1155 on the East Coast, 800/421-8200 on the West Coast, 800/438-5000 from Hawaii; www.koreanair.com); and **Philippine Airlines** (☎ 631/816-6691 in Manila, 800/435-9725 in the U.S.; www.philippineair.com).

Getting Around

Really, the only way to get around Honolulu and the entire island is to rent a car. There is bus service, but you must be able to put all your luggage under the seat (no surfboards or golf clubs), plus the bus service is set up for local residents and many visitor attractions do not have direct routes from Waikiki. The best way to get a good deal on a car rental is to book online. Surprisingly Honolulu has one of the least expensive car-rental rates in the country—about $47 a day (including all state tax and fees); the national average is about $56. Cars are usually plentiful, except on holiday weekends, which in Hawaii also means King Kamehameha Day (June 10 or the closest weekend), Prince Kuhio Day (March 26), and Admission Day (third weekend in August). All the major car-rental agencies have offices in Honolulu: **Alamo** (☎ 800/327-9633; www.goalamo.com), **Avis** (☎ 800/321-3712; www.avis.com), **Budget** (☎ 800/572-0700; www.budget.com), **Dollar** (☎ 800/800-4000; www.dollarcar.com), **Enterprise** (☎ 800/325-8007; www.enterprise.com), **Hertz** (☎ 800/654-3011; www.hertz.com),

National (☎ 800/227-7368; www.nationalcar.com), and **Thrifty** (☎ 800/367-2277; www.thrifty.com). It's almost always cheaper to rent a car at the airport than in Waikiki or through your hotel (unless there's one already included in your package deal).

To rent a car in Hawaii, you must be at least 25 years old and have a valid driver's license and a credit card. Hawaii is a no-fault state, which means that if you don't have collision-damage insurance, you are required to pay for all damages before you leave the state, whether or not the accident was your fault. Your personal car insurance back home may provide rental-car coverage; read your policy or call your insurer before you leave home. Bring your insurance identification card if you decline the optional insurance, which usually costs from $12 to $20 a day, and obtain the name of your company's local claim representative before you go. Some credit card companies also provide collision-damage insurance for their customers; check with yours before you rent.

Fast Facts

ATMS Hawaii pioneered the use of **ATMs** nearly 3 decades ago, and now they're everywhere. You'll find them at most banks, in supermarkets, at Long's Drugs, and in most resorts and shopping centers. **Cirrus** (☎ 800/424-7787; www.mastercard.com) and **PLUS** (☎ 800/843-7587; www.visa.com) are the two most popular networks; check the back of your ATM card to see which network your bank belongs to (most banks belong to both these days).

BABYSITTING The first place to check is with your hotel. Many

hotels have babysitting services or will provide you with lists of reliable sitters. If this doesn't pan out, call **People Attentive to Children** (PATCH; ☎ **808/839-1988;** www.patchhawaii.org), which will refer you to individuals who have taken their training courses on child care.

BANKING HOURS Bank hours are Monday through Thursday from 8:30am to 3pm, Friday from 8:30am to 6pm; some banks are open on Saturday.

BED & BREAKFAST, CONDOMINIUM, AND VACATION HOMES RENTALS The top reservations service for bed-and-breakfasts is **Hawaii's Best Bed & Breakfasts** (☎ 800/262-9912; www.bestbnb.com). For condos, I recommend **Hawaii Condo Exchange** (☎ 800/442-0404; http://hawaiicondoexchange.com); for vacation rentals, contact **Hawaiian Beach Rentals** (☎ 808/262-69368; www.hawaiianbeachrentals.com).

BUSINESS HOURS Most offices are open from 8am to 5pm. Most shopping centers are open Monday through Friday from 10am to 9pm, Saturday from 10am to 5:30pm, and Sunday from 10am to 5 or 6pm.

CLIMATE See "The Weather" on p 188.

CONSULATES & EMBASSIES Honolulu has the following consulates: **Australia,** 1000 Bishop St., Penthouse Suite, Honolulu, HI 96813 (☎ 808/524-5050); **Federated States of Micronesia,** 3049 Ualena St., Suite 908, Honolulu, 96819 (☎ 808/836-4775); **Japan,** 1742 Nuuanu Ave., Honolulu, HI 96817 (☎ 808/543-3111); and **Republic of the Marshall Islands,** 1888 Lusitana St., Suite 301, Honolulu, 96813 (☎ 808/545-7767).

CREDIT CARDS Credit cards are a safe way to carry money, they provide a convenient record of all your expenses, and they generally offer good exchange rates. You can also withdraw cash advances from your credit cards at banks or ATMs, provided you know your PIN.

CUSTOMS Depending on the city of your departure, some countries (like Canada) clear customs at the city of their departure, while other countries clear customs in Honolulu.

DENTISTS If you have dental problems, a nationwide referral service known as 1-800-DENTIST (☎ 800/336-8478) will provide the name of a nearby dentist or clinic.

Emergency dental care is available from Dr. Ronald Kashiwada,

3049 Ualena St., Ste 716, Honolulu (☎ 808/836-3348); Dr Dino Dee, 1441 Kapiolani Blvd., Suite 1112, Honolulu (☎ 808/942-8877); and Dr. Herman Zampetti, 1441 Kapiolani Blvd., Suite 518, Honolulu (☎ 808/941-6222).

DINING With a few exceptions at the high-end of the scale, dining attire is fairly casual. It's a good idea to make reservations in advance if you plan on eating between 7 and 9pm.

DOCTORS **Doctors On Call** offers daily, 24-hr. office visits and house calls, as well as 24-hr. courtesy pick-up service; 2335 Kalakaua Ave., #207 Honolulu (☎ 808/971-6000 [English] or ☎ 808/923-9966 [Japanese]). They also have offices in the following Waikiki hotels: **Outrigger Waikiki Hotel,** 2335 Kalakaua Ave. (☎ 808/971-6000, open daily 24 hours); **Hilton Hawaiian Village,** 2005 Kalia Rd. Rainbow Bazaar, upper level (☎ 808/973-5252, daily 8am–5pm); **Hyatt Regency Waikiki,** 2424 Kalakaua Ave., Diamond Head Tower, 4th Floor (☎ 808/971-8001, open Mon–Fri 8am–4pm); and **Royal Hawaiian Hotel,** 2259 Kalakaua Ave., Lower Arcade (☎ 808/923-4499, daily 8am–5pm).

ELECTRICITY Like Canada, the United States uses 110–120 volts AC (60 cycles), compared to 220–240 volts AC (50 cycles) in most of Europe, Australia, and New Zealand. If your small appliances use 220 to 240 volts, you'll need a 110-volt transformer and a plug adapter with two flat parallel pins to operate them here. Downward converters that change 220–240 volts to 110–120 volts are difficult to find in the United States, so bring one with you.

EMBASSIES See "Consulates & Embassies" above.

EMERGENCIES Dial ☎ **911** for the police, an ambulance, or the fire department. For the **Poison Control Center,** call ☎ 800/362-3585.

EVENT LISTINGS The best sources for listings are the Friday edition of the local daily newspaper, *Honolulu Advertiser* (www.honoluluadvertiser.com); the weekly alternative newspaper, *Honolulu Weekly* (www.honoluluweekly.com); and the weekly shopper, *MidWeek* (www.midweek.com). There are also several tourist publications, such as *This Week on Oahu* (www.thisweek.com).

GAY & LESBIAN TRAVELERS The International Gay & Lesbian Travel Association (IGLTA; ☎ **800/448-8550** or 954/776-2626; www.iglta.org) is the trade association for the gay and lesbian travel industry, and offers an online directory of gay-and lesbian-friendly travel businesses. For information on gay-friendly business, accommodations, and gay-owned and gay-friendly lodgings, contact **Pacific Ocean Holidays,** P.O. Box 88245, Honolulu, HI 96830 (☎ **800/735-6600;** www.gayhawaii.com). **The Center,** P.O. Box 22718, Honolulu, 96823 (mailing address) or 2424 S. Beretania St. (between Isenberg and University), Honolulu (☎ **808/951-7000;** http://thecenterhawaii.org), is a referral center for nearly every kind of gay-related service you can think of, including the latest happenings on Oahu. Open Monday through Friday from 10am to 6pm, Saturday from noon to 4pm. Check out their quarterly community newspaper, *Outlook,* which covers local issues concerning the islands' gay community.

INSURANCE Trip-Cancellation Insurance helps you get your money back if you have to back out of a trip, if you have to go home early, or if your travel supplier goes bankrupt. Allowed reasons for cancellation can range from sickness to natural disasters to the State Department declaring your destination unsafe for travel. In this unstable world, trip-cancellation insurance is a good buy if you're getting tickets well in advance. Insurance policy details vary, so read the fine print—and especially make sure that your airline or cruise line is on the list of carriers covered in case of bankruptcy. For information, contact one of the following insurers: **Access America** (☎ 866/807-3982; www.accessamerica.com); **Travel Guard International** (☎ 800/826-4919; www.travelguard.com); **Travel Insured International** (☎ 800/243-3174; www.travelinsured.com); and **Travelex Insurance Services** (☎ 888/457-4602; www.travelex-insurance.com). Although it's not required of travelers, health insurance is highly recommended. Unlike many European countries, the United States does not usually offer free or low-cost medical care to its citizens or visitors. Doctors and hospitals are expensive, and in most cases will require advance payment or proof of coverage before they render their services. Though lack of health insurance may prevent you from being admitted to a hospital in non-emergencies, don't worry about being left on a street corner to die: The American way is to fix you now and bill the living daylights out of you later.

Insurance for British Travelers: Most big travel agents offer their own insurance and will probably try to sell you their package when you book a holiday. Think before you sign. Britain's Consumers' Association recommends that you insist on seeing the policy and reading the fine print before buying travel insurance. **The Association of British Insurers** (☎ 020/7600-3333; www.abi.org.uk) gives advice by phone and publishes *Holiday Insurance,* a free guide to policy provisions and prices. You might also shop around for better deals: Try **Columbus Direct** (☎ 020/7375-0011; www.columbusdirect.net).

Insurance for Canadian Travelers: Canadians should check with their provincial health plan offices or call Health Canada (☎ 613/957-2991; www.hc-sc.gc.ca) to find out the extent of your coverage and what documentation and receipts you must take home in case you are treated in the United States.

Lost-Luggage Insurance: On domestic flights, checked baggage is covered *up to* $2,800 per ticketed passenger. Key words "up to," which does not mean you collect $2,800 if they lose your bag. When you read the fine print on your ticket you often wonder what the heck they do cover as they explicitly state they have no liability for damage or loss of protruding baggage parts (wheels, straps, pockets, pull handles, etc.), and no liability for photographic equipment, computers, VCRs, and any other electronic equipment including software or components, jewelry, cash, documents, furs, works of art, or other similar valuable items. On international flights (including U.S. portions of international trips), baggage liability is limited to $9.07 per pound ($20 per kg) or a maximum of 70lbs/32 kgs ($635) per checked bag. If you plan to check items more valuable than the standard liability, see if your valuables are covered by your homeowner's policy or get baggage insurance as part of your comprehensive travel-insurance package. Don't buy insurance at the airport, as it's usually overpriced. Be sure to take any valuables or irreplaceable items with you in your carry-on luggage. If your luggage is lost, immediately file a lost-luggage claim at the airport, detailing the luggage contents (always carry a list in your carry-on). For most airlines, you must report delayed, damaged, or lost baggage within 4 hours of arrival. The airlines are required to deliver luggage, once found, directly to your house or destination free of charge.

INTERNET CENTERS Every major hotel and even many small B&Bs have Internet access. Many of them offer high-speed wireless; check ahead of time, the charges can be exorbitant. The best Internet deal in Hawaii is the service at the **public libraries** (to find the closest location near you, check www.public libraries.com/hawaii.htm), which offer free access if you have a library card. You can purchase a 3-month visitor card for $10. **ShakaNet,** Hawaii's largest wireless Internet service provider, has completed the first phase of its free Wireless Waikiki network. Phase I covers a significant portion of Waikiki and includes an estimated 1,000 hotel rooms, portions of the Honolulu Zoo, Kapi'olani Park, Queens Beach, Kuhio Beach, and the adjacent shoreline. The boundaries of Phase I are roughly Kalakaua Ave. from Liliuokalani Ave. to Queen's Beach in the Diamond Head direction, and Liliuokalani Ave./Kuhio Ave. on the Ewa side, down Kuhio Ave. across Kapiolani Park to Monsarrat Ave. If you are outside that area, try: **Caffé Giovannini,** 1888 Kalakaua Ave C-106 (☎ **808/979-2299,** www.caffegiovannini.com).

LOST PROPERTY Check **Travelers Aid International,** Waikiki Shopping Plaza, 2250 Kalakaua Ave., Suite 403-3, Waikiki (☎ **808/926-8274;** www.visitoralohasocietyof hawaii.org).

MAIL & POSTAGE To find the nearest post office, call ☎ **800/ASK-USPS** or log on to www.usps.gov. In Waikiki, the post office is located at 330 Saratoga Rd. (☎ **808/973-7515**).

Mail can be sent to you, in your name, c/o General Delivery, at the post office. Most post offices will hold your mail for up to 1 month. At press time, domestic postage rates were 26¢ for a postcard and 41¢ for a letter. For international mail, a first-class letter of up to 1 ounce costs 63¢ and a first-class postcard costs 55¢.

MONEY Don't carry a lot of cash in your wallet. Many small restaurants won't accept credit cards, so ask upfront if you plan to pay with plastic. Traveler's checks are something of an anachronism from the days before ATMs; **American Express** (☎ 800/221-7282), **Visa** (☎ 800/732-1322), and **MasterCard** (☎ 800/223-9920) all offer them. If you choose to carry traveler's checks, be sure to keep a record of their serial numbers separate from your checks in the event that they are stolen or lost.

PASSPORTS Always keep a photocopy of your passport with you when you're traveling. If your passport is lost or stolen, having a copy significantly facilitates the reissuing process at your consulate. Keep your passport and other valuables in your room's safe or in the hotel safe.

PHARMACIES There are no 24-hour pharmacies in Honolulu or Waikiki. Pharmacies I recommend are **Longs Drugs**: in Waikiki at 1450 Ala Moana Blvd. at Atkins Dr. (☎ 808/941-4433); in Honolulu at 330 Pali Hwy. near Vineyard Blvd. (☎ 808/536-7302); or at 4211 Waialae Ave. near Hunakai St. (☎ 808/732-0781).

SAFETY Although Hawaii is generally a safe tourist destination, visitors have been crime victims, so stay alert. The most common crime against tourists is rental-car break-ins. Never leave any valuables in your car, not even in your trunk. Be especially careful at high-risk areas such as beaches and resorts. Never carry large amounts of cash with you. Stay in well-lighted areas after dark. Don't hike on deserted trails or swim in the ocean alone. If you are a victim of crime, contact The **Visitor Aloha Society of Hawaii (VASH),** Waikiki Shopping Plaza, 2250 Kalakaua Ave., Suite 403-3 (☎ **808/926-8274;** www.visitor alohasocietyofhawaii.org).

SENIOR TRAVELERS Discounts for seniors are available at almost all major attractions, and occasionally at hotels and restaurants. Always inquire when making hotel reservations, and especially when you're buying your airline ticket—most major domestic airlines offer senior discounts. Members of **AARP** (☎ **800/424-3410** or 202/434-2277; www.aarp.org) are usually eligible for such discounts. AARP also puts together organized-tour packages at moderate rates. Some great, low-cost trips to Hawaii are offered to people 55 and older through **Elderhostel,** 75 Federal St., Boston, MA 02110 (☎ **617/426-8056;** www. elderhostel.org), a nonprofit group that arranges travel and study programs around the world. You can obtain a complete catalog of offerings by writing to Elderhostel, P.O. Box 1959, Wakefield, MA 01880-5959.

SPECTATOR SPORTS You've got your choice of **golf tournaments** (☎ **808/792-9300**); **Hawaiian outrigger canoe races,** from May to September (☎ **808/383-7790;** www.y2kanu.com); and **surfing** (☎ **808/739-3965;** www.triple crownofsurfing.com).

TAXIS Taxis are abundant at the airport; an attendant will be happy to flag one down for you. Fares are standard for all taxi firms; from the airport, expect to pay about $28 to $35 to Waikiki and about $25 to downtown Honolulu (plus tip). For a flat fee of $25, **Star Taxi ★**

(☎ **800/671-2999** or 808/942-STAR; www.hawaiistartaxi.net) will take up to five passengers from the airport to Waikiki (with no extra charge for baggage); however, you must book in advance, and call Star again after you've arrived and before you pick up your luggage to make sure a cab will be outside waiting for you. All taxis in Honolulu take cash and traveler's checks, no credit cards.

TELEPHONE   For directory assistance, dial ☎ 411; for long-distance information, dial 1, then the appropriate area code and 555-1212. Pay phones cost 50¢ for local calls (all calls on the island of Oahu are local calls). The area code for all of Hawaii is 808. Calls to other islands are considered long distance, so you have to dial 1+ 808+ the 7-digit phone number.

TIPPING   Tipping is ingrained in the American way of life. Here are some rules of thumb: In hotels, tip bellhops at least $1 per bag ($2–$3 if you have a lot of luggage) and tip the chamber staff $1 to $2 per person per day (more if you've left a disaster area for him or her to clean up, or if you're traveling with kids and/or pets). Tip the doorman or concierge only if he or she has provided you with some specific service (like calling a cab). In restaurants, bars, and nightclubs, tip service staff 15% to 20% of the check, and tip bartenders 10% to 15%. Tipping is not expected in cafeterias and fast-food restaurants. Tip cab drivers 15% of the fare and tip skycaps at airports at least $1 per bag ($2–$3 if you have a lot of luggage).

TOILETS   Your best bet is Starbucks or a fast food restaurant. You can also head to hotel lobbies and shopping centers. Parks have restrooms, but generally they are not very clean and in need of major repairs.

TOURIST OFFICES   The **Hawaii Visitors and Convention Bureau**

(HVCB) is at 2270 Kalakaua Ave., Seventh Floor, Honolulu, HI 96815 (☎ **800/GO-HAWAII** or 808/923-1811; www.gohawaii.com). The **Oahu Visitors Bureau** is at 735 Bishop St., Suite 1872, Honolulu, HI 96813 (☎ **877/525-OAHU** or 808/524-0722; www.visit-oahu.com).

TRAVELERS WITH DISABILITIES   Travelers with disabilities are made to feel very welcome in Hawaii. Hotels are usually equipped with wheelchair-accessible rooms, and tour companies provide many special services. The only travel agency in Hawaii specializing in needs for travelers with disabilities is **Access Aloha Travel** (☎ 800/480-1143; www.accessalohatravel.com), which can book anything, including rental vans, accommodations, tours, cruises, airfare, and just about anything else you can think of.

Handicabs of the Pacific (☎ **808/524-3866**) is a private company offering wheelchair taxi services in air-conditioned vehicles that are specially equipped with ramps and wheelchair lockdowns. Handicabs offers a range of taxi services (airport pickup to Waikiki hotels is $47 one-way for two). To rent wheelchair accessible vans, contact **Accessible Vans of Hawaii** (☎ **800/303-3750;** www.accessible vanshawaii.com/index.htm). For hand-controlled cars contact **Avis** (☎ **800/331-1212;** www.avis.com) and **Hertz** (☎ **800/654-3131;** www. hertz.com). The number of hand-controlled cars in Hawaii is limited, so be sure to book well in advance. Vision-impaired travelers who use a Seeing Eye dog need to present documentation that the dog is a trained Seeing Eye dog and has had rabies shots. For more information, contact the Animal Quarantine Facility (☎ 808/483-7171; www.hawaii.gov).

Hawaii: **A Brief History**

AROUND 250–700 Paddling outrigger canoes, the first ancestors of today's Hawaiians followed the stars and birds across the sea to Hawaii, which they called "the land of raging fire."

AROUND 1300, the transoceanic voyages stopped for some reason, and Hawaii began to develop its own culture in earnest. The settlers built temples, fishponds, and aqueducts to irrigate taro plantations. Sailors became farmers and fishermen. Each island was a separate kingdom. The *alii* created a caste system and established taboos. Violators were strangled. High priests asked the gods Lono and Ku for divine guidance. Ritual human sacrifices were common.

1778 Captain James Cook, trying to find the mythical Northwest Passage to link the Pacific and Atlantic oceans, sailed into Waimea Bay on Kauai, where he was welcomed as the god Lono. Overnight, Stone Age Hawaii entered the age of iron. Nails were traded for fresh water, pigs, and the affections of Hawaiian women. The sailors brought syphilis, measles, and other diseases to which the Hawaiians had no natural immunity, thereby unwittingly wreaking havoc on the native population.

FEB. 14, 1779 Cook and four of his crew were killed in Kealakekua Bay on the Big Island.

1782 Kamehameha I begins his campaign to unify the Hawaiian islands.

1804 King Kamehameha I conquers Oahu in a bloody battle fought the length of Nuuanu Valley, then moves his court from the island of Hawaii to Waikiki. Five years later, he relocates to what is now downtown Honolulu, next to Nimitz Highway at Queen and Bethel streets.

1810 Kamehameha I unites the Hawaiian Islands under a single leader.

1819 This year brings events that change the Hawaiian Islands forever: Kamehameha I dies, his son Liholiho is proclaimed Kamehameha II, and under the influence of Queen Kaahumanu, Kamehameha II orders the destruction of heiaus and an end to the *kapu* (taboo) system, thus overthrowing the traditional Hawaiian religion. The first whaling ship, *Bellina,* drops anchor in Lahaina.

1823 The whalers met their rivals for this hedonistic playground: the missionaries, who arrive from New England bent on converting the pagans. Intent on instilling their brand of rock-ribbed Christianity in the islanders, the missionaries clothe the natives, ban them from dancing the hula, and nearly dismantle their ancient culture. They try to keep the whalers and sailors out of the bawdy houses, where a flood of whiskey quenches fleet-size thirsts and where the virtue of native women is never safe.

1845 King Kamehameha III moves the capital of Hawaii from Lahaina to Honolulu, where more commerce can be accommodated due to the natural harbor there.

1848 The Great Mahele is signed by King Kamehameha III, which allows commoners and foreigners to own land outright or in "fee simple," a concept that continues today.

1850 Kamehameha III proclaims Honolulu the capital city of his kingdom. It is still the capital and dominant city of the nation's 50th State.

1882 America's only royal residence, Iolani Palace, is built on Oahu.

1885 The first contract laborers from Japan arrive to work on the sugar-cane plantations.

JAN. 17, 1893 A group of American sugar planters and missionary descendants, with the support of U.S. Marines, imprison Queen Liliuokalani in her own palace in Honolulu and illegally overthrow the Hawaiian government.

1898 Hawaii is annexed to the United States.

1900 Hawaii becomes a United States territory. The Great Chinatown fire leaves 7,000 people homeless in Honolulu.

1922 Prince Jonah Kalanianaole Kuhio, the last powerful member of the royal Hawaiian family, dies.

1927 First nonstop air flight from the mainland to Honolulu.

DEC. 7, 1941 Japanese Zeros bomb American warships based at Pearl Harbor, plunging the United States into World War II.

MAR. 18, 1959 Hawaii becomes the last star on the Stars and Stripes, the 50th state of the union. This year also sees the arrival of the first jet airliners, which bring 250,000 tourists to the fledgling state.

1967 The state of Hawaii hosts 1 million tourists this year.

1990S Hawaii's state economy goes into a tailspin following a series of events: First, the Gulf War severely curtails air travel to the island; then Hurricane Iniki slams into Kauai, crippling its infrastructure; and finally, sugar-cane companies across the state began shutting down, laying off thousands of workers.

The Hawaiian **Language**

Almost everyone here speaks English. But many folks in Hawaii now speak Hawaiian as well. All visitors will hear the words *aloha* (hello/goodbye/love) and *mahalo* (thank you). If you've just arrived, you're a *malihini*. Someone who's been here a long time is a *kamaaina*. When you finish a job or your meal, you are *pau* (finished). On Friday it's *pau hana*, work finished. You eat *pupu* (Hawaii's version of hors d'oeuvres) when you go *pau hana*.

The Hawaiian alphabet, created by the New England missionaries, has only 12 letters: the five regular vowels (a, e, i, o, and u) and seven consonants (h, k, l, m, n, p, and w). The vowels are pronounced in the Roman fashion, that is, *ah, ay, ee, oh,* and *oo* (as in "too")—not *ay, ee, eye, oh,* and *you,* as in English. For example, *huhu* is pronounced *who-who*. Most vowels are sounded separately, though some are pronounced together, as in Kalakaua: *Kah-lah-cow-ah*.

Useful Words & Phrases
Here are some basic Hawaiian words that you'll often hear in Hawaii and see throughout this

book. For a more complete list of Hawaiian words, point your Web browser to www.geocities.com/~olelo/hltableofcontents.html or www.hisurf.com/hawaiian/dictionary.html.

alii Hawaiian royalty

aloha greeting or farewell

halau school

hale house or building

heiau Hawaiian temple or place of worship

kahuna priest or expert

kamaaina old-timer

kapa tapa, bark cloth

kapu taboo, forbidden

keiki child

lanai porch or veranda

lomilomi massage

mahalo thank you

makai a direction, toward the sea

mana spirit power

mauka a direction, toward the mountains

muumuu loose-fitting gown or dress

ono delicious

pali cliff

paniolo Hawaiian cowboy(s)

wiki quick

Eating in **Honolulu**

In the mid-1980s, Hawaii Regional Cuisine (HRC) ignited a culinary revolution. Waves of new Asian residents have planted the food traditions of their homelands in the fertile soil of Hawaii, resulting in unforgettable taste treats true to their Thai, Vietnamese, Japanese, Chinese, and Indo-Pacific roots. Traditions are mixed and matched—and when combined with the fresh harvests from sea and land for which Hawaii is known, these ethnic and culinary traditions take on renewed vigor and a cross-cultural, yet uniquely Hawaiian, quality.

At the other end of the spectrum is the vast and endearing world of "local food." By that I mean plate lunches and poke, shave ice and saimin, bento lunches and *manapua*—cultural hybrids all. A **plate lunch,** usually ordered from a lunch wagon, consisting of fried mahimahi (or teriyaki beef or shoyu chicken), "two scoops rice," macaroni salad, and a few leaves of green—typically julienned cabbage. Heavy gravy is often the condiment of choice, accompanied by a soft drink in a paper cup or straight out of the can. Another favorite is **saimin**—the local version of noodles in broth topped with scrambled eggs, green onions, and sometimes pork.

The **bento,** another popular quick meal available throughout Hawaii, is a compact, boxed assortment of picnic fare usually consisting of neatly arranged sections of rice, pickled vegetables, and fried chicken, beef, or pork. From the plantations come **manapua,** a bready, doughy sphere filled with tasty fillings of sweetened pork or sweet beans. The daintier Chinese delicacy **dim sum** is made of translucent wrappers filled with fresh seafood, pork hash, and vegetables, served for breakfast and lunch. For dessert or a snack, the prevailing choice is **shave ice,** the island version of a snow cone.

Recommended Reading

Fiction

The first book people think about is James A. Michener's *Hawaii* (Fawcett Crest, 1974). This epic novel manages to put the island's history into chronological order, but remember, it is still fiction, and very sanitized fiction, too. For a more contemporary look at life in Hawaii today, one of the best novels is *Shark Dialogue*, by Kiana Davenport (Plume, 1995). The novel tells the story of Pono, the larger-than-life matriarch, and her four daughters of mixed races. Lois-Ann Yamanaka uses a very "local" voice and stark depictions of life in the islands in her fabulous novels *Wild Meat and the Bully Burgers* (Farrar, Straus, Giroux, 1996), *Blu's Hanging* (Avon, 1997), and *Heads by Harry* (Avon, 1999).

Nonfiction

Mark Twain's writing on Hawaii in the 1860s offers a wonderful introduction to Hawaii's history. One of his best books is *Mark Twain in Hawaii: Roughing It in the Sandwich Islands* (Mutual Publishing, 1990). Another great depiction of the Hawaii of 1889 is *Travels in Hawaii* (University of Hawaii Press, 1973), by Robert Louis Stevenson. For contemporary voices on Hawaii's unique culture, one of the best books to get is *Voices of Wisdom: Hawaiian Elders Speak*, by M. J. Harden (Aka Press, 1999). Some 24 different Kahuna (experts) in their fields were interviewed about their talent, skill, or artistic practice.

The recently rereleased *Native Planters in Old Hawaii: Their Life, Lore and Environment* (Bishop Museum Press, Honolulu, 2004) was originally published in 1972 but is still one of the most important ethnographic works on traditional Hawaiian culture, portraying the lives of the common folk and their relationship with the land before the arrival of Westerners.

History

There are many great books on Hawaii's history, but one of the best places to start is with the formation of the Hawaiian islands, vividly described in David E. Eyre's *By Wind, By Wave: An Introduction to Hawaii's Natural History* (Bess Press, 2000). In addition to chronicling the natural history of Hawaii, Eyre describes the complex interrelationships among the plants, animals, ocean, and people that are necessary.

For a history of "precontact" Hawaii (before Westerners arrived), David Malo's *Hawaiian Antiquities* (Bishop Museum Press, 1976) is the preeminent source. Malo was born around 1793 and wrote about the Hawaiian lifestyle at that time, as well as the beliefs and religion of his people. It's an excellent reference book, but not a fast read. For more readable books on old Hawaii, try *Stories of Old Hawaii* (Bess Press, 1997), by Roy Kakulu Alameide, on myths and legends; *Hawaiian Folk Tales* (Mutual Publishing, 1998), by Thomas G. Thrum; and *The Legends and Myths of Hawaii* (Charles E. Tuttle Company, 1992), by His Hawaiian Majesty King David Kalakaua.

The best story of the 1893 overthrow of the Hawaiian monarchy is told by Queen Liliuokalani, in her book *Hawaii's Story by Hawaii's Queen Liliuokalani* (Mutual Publishing, 1990). When it was written, it was an international plea for justice for her people, but it is a poignant read even today. It's also a "must-read" for people interested in current events and the recent rally in the 50th state for sovereignty. Two contemporary books on the question of Hawaii's sovereignty are Tom Coffman's *Nation Within—The Story of America's Annexation of the Nation of Hawaii* (Epicenter, 1998), and *Hawaiian Sovereignty: Do the Facts Matter?* (Goodale, 2000), by Thurston Twigg-Smith, which explores the opposite view. Twigg-Smith, former publisher of the statewide newspaper *The Honolulu Advertiser,* is the grandson of Lorrin A. Thurston, one of the architects of the 1893 overthrow of the monarchy. His so-called "politically incorrect" views present a different look on this hotly debated topic.

For more recent history, Lawrence H. Fuchs's *Hawaii Pono* (Bess Press, 1991) is a carefully researched tome on the contributions of each of Hawaii's main immigrant communities (Chinese, Japanese, and Filipino) between 1893 and 1959.

An insightful look at history and its effect on the Hawaiian culture is *Waikiki, A History of Forgetting and Remembering*, by Andrea Feeser (University of Hawaii Press, 2006). A beautiful art book (designed by Gaye Chan), this is not your normal coffee-table book, but a different look at the cultural and environmental history of Waikiki. Using historical texts, photos, government documents, and interviews, this book lays out the story of how Waikiki went from a self-sufficient agricultural area to a tourism mecca.

Another great cultural book just released is Davianna Pomaikai McGreggor's *Na Kua'aina, Living Hawaiian Culture* (University of Hawaii Press, 2007). McGregor, a professor of ethnic studies at UH, examines how people lived in rural lands and how they kept the Hawaiian traditions alive. She describes the cultural significance of each area (the island of Molokai; Hana, Maui; and Puna, Hawaii), the landscape, the Hawaiian gods who lived there, the chants and myths about the area, and how the westernization of the area has changed the land and the Hawaiian people.

Index

See also Accommodations and Restaurant indexes, below.

Photo **Credits**

p. viii: © Douglas Peebles/Jupiterimages; p. 3: © Douglas Peebles/Jupiter images; p. 4: © David Fleetham/Mira.com/drr.net; p. 5: © Ryan Siphers; p. 6: © Photo Resource Hawaii/DanitaDelimont.com; p. 7: © David R. Frazier/Danita Delimont.com; p. 9: © Thorsten Indra/Alamy; p. 10 top: © Photo Resource Hawaii/DanitaDelimont.com/drr.net; p. 10 bottom: © Photo Resource Hawaii/ DanitaDelimont.com/drr.net; p. 11: © Karl Lehmann/Lonely Planet Images; p. 13 center: © James Montgomery/Jon Arnold Images/Alamy; p. 13 bottom: © Jonathan Blair/Corbis; p. 14: © Photo Resource Hawaii/DanitaDelimont.com; p. 15: © SIME s.a.s./eStock Photo; p. 16 top: © Andrew Woodley/Alamy; p. 16 bottom: © Kord.com/AGE Fotostock; p. 17: © John Borthwick/Lonely Planet Images; p. 19 center: © Andre Seale/Alamy; p. 19 bottom: © Visionsof Paradise.com/Alamy; p. 20: © P. Narayan/AGE Fotostock; p. 21 top: © David L. Moore/Alamy; p. 21 bottom: © David Franzen Photography; p. 22 : © Photo Resource Hawaii/DanitaDelimont.com; p. 23: © David L. Moore/Alamy; p. 24 top: © Photo Resource Hawaii/DanitaDelimont.com; p. 24 bottom: © Honolulu Academy of Arts, Hawaii, USA, Giraudon/The Bridgeman Art Library International; p. 27: © David L. Moore/Alamy; p. 28: © Ryan Siphers; p. 29 top: © Bruce Behnke/DanitaDelimont.com; p. 29 bottom: Courtesy The Contemporary Museum; p. 30: © Ryan Siphers; p. 31: © Richard Cummins/Lonely Planet Images; p. 33: © Photo Resource Hawaii/DanitaDelimont.com/drr.net; p. 34: © Ryan Siphers; p. 35 top: © Douglas Peebles/Corbis; p. 35 bottom: © Photo Resource Hawaii/DanitaDelimont.com/drr.net; p. 37: © Photo Resource Hawaii/ DanitaDelimont.com/drr.net; p. 38 top: © Ryan Siphers; p. 38 bottom: © David Franzen Photography; p. 39: Courtesy Atlantis Adventures; p. 41: © Photo Resource Hawaii/DanitaDelimont.com; p. 42: © Kord.com/AGE Fotostock; p. 43 top: © nagelestock.com/Alamy; p. 43 bottom: © Photo Resource Hawaii/ DanitaDelimont.com; p. 44: © Photo Resource Hawaii/DanitaDelimont.com; p. 45: © Michele Burgess/Index Stock Imagery; p. 47: © Corbis; p. 48: © Walter Bibikow/AGE Fotostock; p. 49 center: © David J. & Janice L. Frent Collection/ Corbis; p. 49 bottom: © Douglas Peebles/AGE Fotostock; p. 51: © Bettmann/ Corbis; p. 52 top: © David L. Moore/Alamy; p. 52 bottom: © Photo Resource Hawaii/DanitaDelimont.com/drr.net; p. 53: Courtesy Lodging: Westin Moana Surfrider; p. 54: © JTB/drr.net; p. 55 top: © Photo Resource Hawaii/Danita Delimont.com/drr.net; p. 55 bottom: © David Franzen Photography; p. 56: © Douglas Peebles/Jupiterimages; p. 57: © Historical Picture Archive/Corbis; p. 59: © VisionsofParadise.com/Alamy; p. 60 top: © Douglas Peebles Photography/Alamy; p. 60 bottom: © Ryan Siphers; p. 61: © Mark Johnson/Mira.com/ drr.net; p. 63: © David L. Moore/Alamy; p. 65: © Dave Bartruff/Index Stock Imagery; p. 66 top: © Photo Resource Hawaii/DanitaDelimont.com/drr.net; p. 66 bottom: © Photo Resource Hawaii/DanitaDelimont.com; p. 67: © Douglas Peebles Photography/Alamy; p. 68: © Douglas Peebles Photography/Alamy; p. 69 top: © Photo Resource Hawaii/DanitaDelimont.com; p. 69 bottom: © Craig Ellenwood/Alamy; p. 71: © Gisela Damm/eStock Photo; p. 73: © Photo Resource Hawaii/DanitaDelimont.com; p. 74: © John Oeth/Alamy; p. 75 top: © John Elk III/Lonely Planet Images; p. 75 bottom: © Ryan Siphers; p. 77 top: © Stuart Westmorland/Corbis; p. 77 bottom: © David Franzen Photography; p. 78 top: © Phil Mislinski/SuperStock; p. 78 center: © Sam Mircovich/Reuters/ Corbis; p. 79 top: © Photo Resource Hawaii/Alamy; p. 79 bottom: © Lee Foster/ drr.net; p. 81 top: © Mervyn Rees/Alamy; p. 81 bottom: © David Franzen

ADMINISTRATIVE LAW AND PROCESS

IN A NUTSHELL

Third Edition

By

ERNEST GELLHORN

Jones, Day, Reavis & Pogue
Los Angeles, California

RONALD M. LEVIN

Professor of Law
Washington University

ST. PAUL, MINN.
WEST PUBLISHING CO.
1990

COPYRIGHT © 1972, 1981 By WEST PUBLISHING CO.
COPYRIGHT © 1990 By WEST PUBLISHING CO.
610 Opperman Drive
P.O. Box 64526
St. Paul, MN 55164–0526

Library of Congress Cataloging-in-Publication Data

Gellhorn, Ernest.
Administrative law and process in a nutshell / by Ernest Gellhorn
and Ronald M. Levin. — 3rd ed.
p.   cm.
Includes index.
ISBN 0–314–76184–5
1. Administrative law—United States.   I. Levin, Ronald M., 1950–
II. Title.
KF5402.Z9G4   1990
342.73'06—dc20
[347.3026]   90–38837
                                                          CIP

ISBN 0–314–76184–5

PRINTED WITH
SOY INK

(G. & L.) Admin.Law 3rd Ed. NS
2nd Reprint—1994

OUTLINE

Appendices

*

TABLE OF CASES

References are to Pages

IX

TABLE OF CASES

TABLE OF CASES

TABLE OF CASES

*

TABLE OF STATUTES

References are to Pages

UNITED STATES CONSTITUTION

FEDERAL STATUTES

ADMINISTRATIVE PROCEDURE ACT

TABLE OF STATUTES

FEDERAL RULES OF CIVIL PROCEDURE

FEDERAL RULES OF EVIDENCE

TABLE OF STATUTES

EXECUTIVE ORDERS

TABLE OF AGENCIES

References are to Pages

*

ADMINISTRATIVE LAW AND PROCESS

IN A NUTSHELL

Third Edition

*

INTRODUCTION

Administrative agencies usually are created to deal with current crises or to redress serious social problems. Throughout the modern era of administrative regulation, which began approximately a century ago, the government's response to a public demand for action has often been to establish a new agency, or to grant new powers to an existing bureaucracy. Near the turn of the century, agencies like the Interstate Commerce Commission and the Federal Trade Commission were created in an attempt to control the anticompetitive conduct of monopolies and powerful corporations. The economic depression of the 1930's was followed by a proliferation of agencies during the New Deal which were designed to stabilize the economy, temper the excesses of unregulated markets, and provide some financial security for individuals. Agencies were also established or enlarged in wartime to mobilize manpower and production, and to administer price controls and rationing. The development of new technologies, ranging from radio broadcasting to air transportation to nuclear energy, often led to creation of new government bureaus to promote and supervise these emerging industries. In the 1960's when the injustices of poverty and racial discrimination became an urgent national concern, the development of programs designed to redress these grievances expanded the scope of government administration. More recently, increased public concern about risks to human health and safety and threats to the natural environment have resulted in new agencies and new regulatory programs.

The primary reason why administrative agencies have so frequently been called upon to deal with such diverse social problems is the great flexibility of the regulatory process. In comparison to courts or legislatures or elected executive officials, administrative agencies have several institutional strengths that equip them to deal with complex problems. Perhaps the most important of these strengths is specialized staffing: an agency is authorized to hire people with whatever mix of talents, skills and experience it needs to get the job done. Moreover, because the agency has responsibility for a limited area of public policy, it can develop the expertise that comes from continued exposure to a problem area. An agency's regulatory techniques and decisionmaking procedures can also be tailored to meet the problem at hand. Agencies can control entry into a field by requiring a license to undertake specified activities; they can set standards, adjudicate violations, and impose penalties; they can dispense grants, subsidies or other incentives; they can set maximum or minimum rates; and they can influence conduct through a wide variety of informal methods.

However, these potential strengths of the administrative process can also be viewed as a threat to other important values. Administrative "flexibility" may simply be a mask for unchecked power, and in our society unrestrained government power has traditionally been viewed with great and justifiable suspicion. Thus, the fundamental policy problem of the administrative process is how to design a system of checks which will minimize the risks of bureaucratic arbitrariness and overreaching, while preserving for the agencies the flexibility they need to act effectively. Administrative law concerns the legal checks that are used to control and limit the powers of government agencies.

Moreover, continued exposure to the same issues may lead not only to agency expertise but also to rigidity and ineffectiveness. Indeed, scholars and other critics have identified a wide variety of causes for regulatory failure: the basic theory of the regulatory program may be wrong, or the state of knowledge not adequate to support wise decisions; there may be a mismatch between the regulatory objective and the technique chosen to achieve it; the agency may be unduly influenced or "captured" by a powerful constituency group; agency officials may be incompetent or corrupt or lack incentives to produce quality work; and regulatory programs may simply be politically unacceptable in a particular time and place.

These substantive problems of administrative regulation are important and interesting, but they are largely beyond the scope of this text. This explanation of the administrative process will concentrate on how it operates, on "the rules of the game." There is admittedly artificiality and oversimplification in this approach. Administrative law as applied by the agencies and the courts cannot be separated from the particular mix of factors that make each agency unique—factors such as the nature of the agency's legislative mandate, its structure and traditions, the values and personalities of the people who work in the agency or deal with it regularly, and, most importantly, its substantive law. Even the procedural uniformity imposed on the federal agencies by the Administrative Procedure Act, 5 U.S.C.A. §§ 551–706 (see statutory appendix), seems to have weakened, as the Congress has at times been willing to prescribe detailed codes of procedure in enabling legislation. Thus, it is an open question whether the differences among agencies are more important than the similarities.

Still, there is something useful to be gained from the effort to view the administrative process as a whole. The student, the lawyer or the citizen who is trying to penetrate the workings of an unfamiliar bureaucracy needs a general framework of principles and doctrines in order to understand— let alone to criticize or try to change—the particular agency decisionmaking process confronting him. It is also important to remember that, despite their many differences, agencies also share several broad challenges. One is to design procedures that will strike a workable compromise among important and potentially conflicting public values. These values can be grouped into four categories.

(1) *Fairness.* Concern with the fairness of government decisionmaking procedures is a primary feature of Anglo–American legal systems. The basic elements of fairness, embodied in the concept of due process, are assurances that the individual will receive adequate notice and a meaningful opportunity to be heard before an official tribunal makes a decision that may substantially affect her interests.

(2) *Accuracy.* The administrative decisionmaking process should also attempt to minimize the risk of wrong decisions. The real difficulty, however, is in defining and measuring accuracy. Since the goals of many regulatory programs are not simple or clearly stated, and the consequences of agency decisions may be difficult to identify, there will often be differences of opinion as to whether a particular decision was accurate or wise—and how the procedures may have influenced the result. Nevertheless, there is widespread agreement that different procedures are more suitable for some kinds of decisions than for others. For example, trial procedures are generally considered most useful for resolving disputes over specific facts concerning past events, and least useful for making general predictions or policy judgments about the future.

(3) *Efficiency.* Efforts to increase the fairness of an administrative decision by expanding opportunities to participate, or to improve accuracy by gathering and evaluating additional information, can be very costly in time, money and missed opportunities. Since agency resources are always limited and usually insufficient to accomplish the full range of duties imposed by statute, it becomes necessary to consider the efficiency of decision-making procedures. Typically, this takes the form of an inquiry into whether additional procedural safeguards are likely to increase the fairness or accuracy of decisions enough to warrant the costs and delays they will create.

(4) *Acceptability.* Because the legitimate exercise of official power ultimately depends upon the consent of the governed, it is necessary to consider the attitudes of constituency groups and the general public toward the regulatory process. That is, administrative procedures should be judged not only on their actual effects, but also on the ways they will be perceived by affected interest groups. There are probably few situations in which public attitudes toward agency procedures play a determinative role in shaping beliefs about the basic legitimacy of the regulatory decision or program. Still, it seems clear that a widespread feeling that a government bureaucracy makes decisions arbitrarily or unfairly can undermine the public's confidence in the agency and the regulated industry's willingness to comply with its decisions.

The administrative law system does not rely solely on procedural controls to ensure that officials will perform their functions satisfactorily. It also expects the legislative, executive, and judicial branches to supervise the substance of what agencies do. For example, the President appoints officeholders and chooses the overall goals of his Administration; Congress conducts oversight hearings and, when necessary, rewrites enabling statutes; courts enforce legal requirements and place outer limits on agencies' use of discretion.

The primary focus of this text is on federal administrative agencies, although some discussions of state administrative practice are included. There are several reasons for this emphasis. As a practical matter, the numerous variations in state law make it impossible to cover the subject adequately in a brief survey. Moreover, most of the standard teaching materials in the field deal primarily with the federal system. In any case, the basic objective of this book is to help the student of the administrative process develop a framework of general principles, policy considerations and methods of analysis that will be useful in understanding a wide variety of administrative agency procedures, regardless of whether they are found at the federal, state or local level.

CHAPTER I

THE DELEGATION OF
AUTHORITY TO AGENCIES

The study of administrative law can be viewed as an analysis of the limits placed on the powers and actions of administrative agencies. These limits are imposed in many ways, and it is important to remember that legal controls may be supplemented or replaced by political checks on agency decisions. One set of legal controls that we will examine at length is the procedures that reviewing courts have required the agencies to use. Another is the rules specified by Congress in the Administrative Procedure Act (APA). Conceptually, however, the first question that should be examined is the amount of legislative or judicial power that can be delegated initially to the agency by the legislature—the governmental body creating it.

A. THE DELEGATION ISSUE

Throughout the modern era of administrative regulation, agencies have been delegated sweeping powers. Some of these powers are assigned on an industry-wide basis, as with the Interstate Commerce Commission, the Federal Communications Commission, and the Nuclear Regulatory Commission. Other agencies are charged with enforcing certain norms of conduct throughout the economy.

8

These range from the Federal Trade Commission, which since 1914 has enforced a ban on "unfair methods of competition," to newer health and safety regulators, such as the Environmental Protection Agency and the Occupational Safety and Health Administration.

What makes the delegations more dramatic is that these agencies typically wield powers that are characteristic of each of the three principal branches of government. Many agencies operate under statutes that give them *legislative power* to issue rules which control private behavior, and which carry heavy civil or criminal penalties for violations; *executive power* to investigate potential violations of rules or statutes and to prosecute offenders; and *judicial power* to adjudicate particular disputes over whether an individual or a company has failed to comply with the governing standards.

For example, the Securities Exchange Commission (SEC) formulates law by writing rules which spell out what disclosures must be made in a stock prospectus; these rules may have the same effect as a law passed by the legislature. The SEC then enforces these rules by prosecuting those who violate its regulations through disciplinary actions against broker-dealers or through stop order proceedings against corporate issuers. Finally, the SEC also acts as judge and jury in deciding whether its rules have been violated; it conducts adjudicatory hearings to determine guilt and mete out punishment. In addition, administrative agencies are often unattached to any of the three branches of government (executive, legislative, or judicial). Although the Commissioners—agency members—of the SEC are presidential appointees (subject to Senate approval), the SEC is an independent agency; it is not attached to the Congress nor is it a part of any executive department.

Such delegations raise fundamental questions concerning the constitutional distribution of authority in our system of government. The federal Constitution, and most state constitutions as well, are based on the principle of separation of powers. Generally, law-making power is assigned to the legislature, law-enforcing power to the executive, and law-deciding power to the judiciary. With responsibility divided in this fashion, each branch theoretically provides checks and balances on the exercise of power by the other two branches. The image of administrative agencies as a "fourth branch" seems, at least formally, at odds with this three-part paradigm of government.

Justifications for these broad delegations of combined powers can be found in the institutional advantages of the administrative agency. Particularly in novel or rapidly changing fields of activity, the legislature may be unable to specify detailed rules of conduct. An agency, armed with flexible decision-making procedures and charged with continuing responsibility for a limited subject matter, may be better equipped to develop sound and coherent policies. Moreover, effective development and implementation of regulatory policy may require the exercise of all three kinds of power. A rule or a policy decision can be quickly nullified in practice if investigations and prosecutions are not vigorously pursued, or if adjudications are decided by tribunals which do not understand or support the regulatory goals. When the subject matter of a regulatory program is technical or complex, or when detailed knowledge of the regulated industry is essential to the formulation of sound policy, administrative agencies can bring to bear their superior experience and expertise. Uniformity and predictability are also important in many areas of economic regulation. Businesses need to plan their operations and make their investment decisions with some assurance that the ground rules will not be changed abruptly or applied inconsistently—problems which might well arise if decisionmaking power were dispersed among the three branches of government.

It should also be noted, however, that a substantial number of legislators, judges, and commentators are unpersuaded by these arguments. They argue that little real justification exists for continued sweeping delegations or for the combination of prosecutorial, rulemaking and adjudicative powers within one agency. See pp. 18–20 infra. Thus there is pressure to separate such functions, to establish an administrative court, or otherwise to limit the delegation of broad authority to the agencies.

B. DEVELOPMENT OF DOCTRINE

The language of the Constitution suggests that the delegation doctrine should not be regarded as an absolute or unqualified principle. While Article I, § 1 provides that "All legislative Powers herein granted shall be vested in a Congress of the United States," § 8, paragraph 18 of the same Article empowers the Congress "To make all Laws which shall be necessary and proper." These and other provisions, as well as the structure of the Constitution, suggest that the delegation doctrine's objective of dividing the responsibilities of government to provide checks on abuses of power must be counterbalanced by the need for effective government.

However, the earliest judicial decisions interpreting the delegation doctrine contained broad, uncompromising statements. A classic example is the Supreme Court's statement in Field v. Clark, 143 U.S. 649, 692 (1892): "That Congress cannot delegate legislative power . . . is a principle universally recognized as vital to the integrity and maintenance of the system of government ordained by the Constitution." Nevertheless, the Court in its early decisions did consistently uphold delegations, by minimizing their significance. Typically the Court would claim that, in the cases presented to it, the executive branch had been granted nothing more than a power to "ascertain and declare the event upon which . . . [the legislative] will was to take effect" (*Field*), or a power to "fill up the details," United States v. Grimaud, 220 U.S. 506 (1911). In truth, the executive branch was not merely finding facts or supplying details in these cases; it was exercising a substantial measure of policy judgment. The *Field* case involved a congressional authorization for the President to impose retaliatory tariffs when foreign nations raised their duties on agricultural products; *Grimaud* upheld the power of the Secretary of Agriculture to issue regulations, backed by criminal penalties, governing the use and preservation of the national forests. The holdings of the cases, therefore, belied the Court's absolutist language.

However, as the modern industrial economy developed and demands for regulation grew, it became apparent that these narrow formulas were too restrictive, even with a liberal interpretation. Gradually the focus of judicial inquiry shifted to whether the legislature had provided *sufficient standards* to limit the scope of agency discretion. The Supreme Court's decision in Buttfield v. Stranahan, 192 U.S. 470 (1904), was the first case to articulate this modern version of the delegation doctrine. Later cases adopted this line of analysis, and in J.W. Hampton, Jr. & Co. v. United States, 276 U.S. 394, 409 (1928), the Court refined it in the often-quoted statement that a permissible delegation must contain an "intelligible principle to which the [agency must] . . . conform."

Throughout this early evolution of the doctrine, the Supreme Court had never invalidated a congressional grant of authority to an administrative agency on delegation grounds. However, the Great Depression of the 1930's brought a wave of new regulatory agencies, armed with broad statutory delegations of authority, to control the economy. In the rush to find solutions for this overwhelming economic crisis, some regulatory statutes were poorly designed, poorly drafted, and poorly implemented as well. One of the most visible and controversial of these New Deal regulatory agencies, the National Recovery Administration, provided the Supreme Court with an opportunity to demonstrate that the delegation doctrine could become a very real constraint on the powers of administrative agencies.

The first major test came in the "Hot Oil" case, Panama Refining Co. v. Ryan, 293 U.S. 388 (1935). The National Industrial Recovery Act (NIRA) had authorized the President to prohibit interstate shipments of "contraband" oil. The purpose of this provision was to reduce economic disruptions in the oil industry, which was faced with falling demand and an increasing supply from newly discovered oil fields. The Court found that the statute gave the President absolutely no guidance as to the circumstances under which he should impose the prohibition. Accordingly, for the first time in its history, the Supreme Court struck down an Act of Congress as an overly broad delegation of legislative power.

The regulation that was challenged in *Panama Refining* also had a serious procedural defect. The "code" in question had been issued without prior notice or opportunity for public participation. Just before the case was argued in the Supreme Court, it was discovered that the code had accidentally been amended out of existence. One beneficial side effect of the *Panama Refining* decision was the passage of legislation requiring the federal agencies to publish official texts of their regulations in the Federal Register. See L. Jaffe, *Judicial Control of Administrative Action* 62 (1965); 5 U.S.C.A. § 552(a)(1). However, the opinion did not resolve the central questions about the constitutionality of the system of regulation created by the National Industrial Recovery Act.

Those questions arose a few months later in the decision that is usually referred to as the "Sick Chicken" case. It involved a criminal prosecution for violations of the Live Poultry Code issued under another section of the NIRA. A.L.A. Schechter Poultry Corp. v. United States, 295 U.S. 495 (1935). As in the Hot Oil case, the Court was concerned by the lack of both substantive and procedural standards. The statute had empowered the agency (acting on behalf of the President) to issue "codes of fair competition" for particular industries if the code "tend[ed] to effectuate the policy of this title."

However, the Court could not find a clear policy directive in the legislation; indeed, the congressional statements of policy seemed to pull in several different directions. The Act adopted the policies of preventing monopolies while promoting cooperative actions among trade groups, and of encouraging increased production while improving the wages and conditions of labor; it gave no indication of how these potentially conflicting values should be weighed or reconciled. The Court also gave considerable emphasis to the procedural deficiencies in the Act. In contrast to prior delegations of authority to the Interstate Commerce Commission or the Federal Trade Commission, the NIRA did not require the agency to hold trial-type hearings, or even to provide interested persons with notice and a right to participate in the challenged decision. Nor did it provide an opportunity for judicial review to those who might be adversely affected. Thus, the Court concluded that the delegation was unconstitutionally broad.

A third Supreme Court decision invalidating a delegation on constitutional grounds was also decided in the 1930's. Carter v. Carter Coal Co., 298 U.S. 238 (1936), involved a system of industry "codes" for the coal industry, roughly similar to the "codes of fair competition" that were at issue in the *Schechter* case. In *Carter Coal,* however, the Court noted an additional factor which made the delegation suspect: decisionmaking power had effectively been granted to committees of industry

representatives rather than to government officials. Because these private parties had "interests
[which] may be and often are adverse to the interests of others in the same business," the statute
was "legislative delegation in its most obnoxious
form."

In retrospect, these three decisions were the
high-water mark for the delegation doctrine.
While the Congress has continued to grant sweeping, vaguely defined powers to administrative
agencies in the intervening decades, the Supreme
Court has not invalidated any other statutes on
delegation grounds. The Court's present leniency
is exemplified by Yakus v. United States, 321 U.S.
414 (1944). There the system of wartime price
controls was challenged on delegation grounds.
The statute empowered an Administrator to promulgate standards that would be "generally fair
and equitable and . . . effectuate the [enumerat-
ed] purposes of this Act." The Court upheld the
statute, noting that constitutional problems would
arise only if the legislation were so lacking in
standards "that it would be impossible in a proper
proceeding to ascertain whether the will of Congress has been obeyed." This tolerance has continued right up until the present day. See Skinner v.
Mid–America Pipeline Co., 109 S.Ct. 1726 (1989)
(upholding statute authorizing agency to set "user
fees" for pipeline companies); Mistretta v. United
States, 488 U.S. 361 (1989) (upholding statute authorizing commission to write criminal sentencing

guidelines). The Court's unwillingness for over fifty years to require precise standards in legislative delegations has led some commentators to conclude that this branch of the delegation doctrine is simply unworkable, and ought to be abandoned altogether. See Davis, *A New Approach to Delegation,* 36 U.Chi.L.Rev. 713 (1969). But, as discussed in the next section, there is no shortage of proposals for a reinvigoration of the doctrine.

C. MODERN CONTROVERSY OVER THE DELEGATION DOCTRINE

A decision involving the Occupational Safety and Health Act of 1970 has spurred discussion of whether the Court should begin anew to hold broad delegations unconstitutional. Section 6(b)(5) of that Act directed the Secretary of Labor to issue rules requiring employers to protect their workers, "to the extent feasible," from harm due to toxic substances in the workplace. The Secretary subsequently promulgated a regulation that called for expensive measures to minimize workers' exposure to benzene, a cancer-causing chemical. The Supreme Court struck down the rule in Industrial Union Dep't, AFL–CIO v. American Petroleum Inst., 448 U.S. 607 (1980), commonly known as the *Benzene* case. Four Justices, led by Justice Stevens, believed that the Secretary had not made all of the findings required by the statute. The fifth vote against the Secretary was that of Justice (now Chief Justice) Rehnquist, who would have held that

the statute contained an unconstitutional delegation to the Secretary. He regarded the statutory
phrase "to the extent feasible" as a "legislative
mirage" by which Congress had simply avoided
resolving the hard questions about the circumstances in which employers could be allowed to
take some risks of injury to workers because of the
high costs of protective measures. Resolving fundamental, politically divisive policy issues, he insisted, is the very essence of legislative authority
and could not "unnecessarily" be left to a politically unresponsive administrator. See also American
Textile Mfrs. Inst. v. Donovan, 452 U.S. 490 (1981),
in which Justice Rehnquist repeated his position
and was joined by Chief Justice Burger.

Some commentators, believing that the legislative abdication that Justice Rehnquist perceived in
Benzene is a common phenomenon, have urged the
Court to make more frequent use of the delegation
doctrine to invalidate regulatory legislation. In
the present climate, they say, Congress has too
great a temptation to make use of open-ended
delegations, so that it will be able to divert public
blame from itself to the bureaucracy when regulatory decisions prove controversial. See, e.g., J. Ely,
Democracy and Distrust 131–32 (1980); Wright,
Review—Beyond Discretionary Justice, 81 Yale L.J.
575, 582–87 (1972). Furthermore, it is argued,
delegation makes it all too easy for Congress to
enact, or allow continuation of, regulatory schemes
that work against the public interest. This theory

notes the tendency of much economic regulation to transfer wealth from one private interest group to another, without any particular public benefit. Judicial toleration of vague substantive standards fosters this tendency, it is argued, by allowing major decisions to be made by administrators, without the glare of publicity that would be generated if Congress itself took on the policymaking responsibility. See Aranson, Gellhorn & Robinson, *A Theory of Legislative Delegation,* 68 Cornell L.Rev. 1 (1982).

While the courts have not articulated why they have failed to accept the challenge of Justice Rehnquist and others, three possible explanations can be suggested. First, some courts may continue to believe that broad delegations are on the whole desirable, because they make maximum use of the flexibility that the administrative process affords. See pp. 10–11 supra. Indeed, it has been argued that broad delegations are not even necessarily undemocratic, as Rehnquist claimed. Many of them can be seen as simply shifting policymaking discretion to appointees of the President, who has his own electoral base. In other words, vague delegations can at times be defended as a means of giving an incumbent Administration the latitude it needs if it is to implement the President's electoral mandate. See Mashaw, *Prodelegation: Why Administrators Should Make Political Decisions,* 1 J.L.Econ. & Org. 81 (1985).

Second, the courts may believe that they cannot devise a workable test with which to implement the delegation doctrine. It might be very difficult for judges to identify those delegations that involve "fundamental" issues or that are motivated by a congressional desire to avoid political accountability. If the standards for applying the delegation doctrine were too subjective, every new regulatory statute would be under serious threat of being held unconstitutional; it would be all too easy for private parties to make a credible argument, especially with hindsight, that Congress should have spoken in more detail than it did.

Finally, and perhaps most important, courts may have refrained from using the delegation doctrine to strike down statutes because they have found alternative methods of preventing broad grants of power from becoming instruments of administrative oppression. These are discussed in the next section.

D. CONSTRUCTION TO SAVE A DELEGATION

While the requirement that delegations of legislative authority must contain substantive standards has been relaxed since the 1930's, courts are still very much concerned with the limits Congress has imposed on agency powers. However, the analysis has become more comprehensive and sophisticated in comparison to the rather mechanical formulas used in some of the early delegation

cases. This contemporary approach is best illustrated by Amalgamated Meat Cutters v. Connally,
337 F.Supp. 737 (D.D.C.1971). Like the *Yakus*
case, *Meat Cutters* involved a broad grant of discretion to the President to set limits on wages and
prices throughout the national economy. The
court recognized that the delegation question could
not be answered by a simple inquiry into whether
the governmental function being exercised was
"legislative" in nature, or whether the Congress
had enacted an "intelligible" substantive standard.
This was true because the fundamental objective of
the delegation doctrine—assuring adequate control
and accountability in the exercise of official power—could be achieved by either substantive or procedural constraints, or by some combination of the
two.

Starting from this premise, the *Meat Cutters*
opinion looked beyond the text of the statute itself.
The court carefully reviewed the legislative history
and the experience under previous price control
programs to give content to the vague statutory
language. In addition, the court noted that Congress would closely monitor the program; the
agency would have to develop its own administrative standards over time; and judicial review was
available pursuant to the Administrative Procedure Act. This combination of limitations and
safeguards convinced the court that the statutory
scheme, taken as a whole, provided adequate
means by which the public, the Congress, and

(perhaps most importantly) reviewing courts could check the agency's exercise of discretion. Accordingly, the delegation was sustained.

According to the approach exemplified in *Meat Cutters,* therefore, the delegation doctrine requires a court to examine not only whether an administrative statute contains an "intelligible standard" on its face, but also the total system of controls, both substantive and procedural, that limit agency power. In a more rudimentary form, this analysis is discernible in a number of other modern opinions.

1. *Implying Substantive Limitations.* Even when a statute has not been directly challenged as violating the delegation doctrine, courts sometimes adopt a relatively narrow view of an agency's powers, intimating that a broad view might constitute an unlawful delegation of legislative power. This device was employed to save a questionable delegation in Kent v. Dulles, 357 U.S. 116 (1958), where the Court construed the relevant statutes to prohibit the Secretary of State from denying a passport because of the applicant's political beliefs. Since the administrator's decision curtailed the constitutionally protected freedom to travel, and prior administrative practice had not included similar restraints, the Court would not presume that the agency had been granted the power in question without a clear statement of congressional intention. See also Zemel v. Rusk, 381 U.S. 1 (1965).

The Court again used this approach to avoid a delegation issue in National Cable Television Ass'n v. United States, 415 U.S. 336 (1974). The FCC had imposed substantial charges on cable television systems, relying on a broad delegation of authority to regulate the communications industry. The relevant statute could be read narrowly as permitting the agency only to collect "fees," which recouped the costs of regulatory benefits it was conferring, or it could be interpreted broadly as conferring the power to assess "taxes" that were unrelated to the benefits received by the regulated industry. The Court chose the narrow reading, noting that it would be "a sharp break with our traditions to conclude that Congress had bestowed on a federal agency the taxing power." The Court was apparently concerned that the power to tax implied the authority to make broad policy judgments about whether certain private activities should be encouraged by subsidies, or discouraged by high taxes. These kinds of basic value choices or resource allocation decisions are typically made by the political branches of government, which most closely reflect the preferences and values of the populace. By construing the statute narrowly, the Court was able to postpone deciding whether this sensitive power could be transferred to an administrative agency.[1]

1. Eventually, however, the Court had to face this question. A statute empowered the Secretary of Transportation to set "user fees" to cover the costs of administering pipeline safety programs. Although the fees were largely intended to benefit

Finally, the narrow construction device played a role in the *Benzene* case, discussed at pp. 18–19 supra. Justice Stevens, writing for a plurality, declined to accept Justice Rehnquist's conclusion that the Occupational Safety and Health Act was unconstitutionally vague. Instead, he maintained that the benzene rule was flawed because the agency had not found that the requirements would cure a "significant risk" in the workplace, as he claimed the Act required. Most commentators agree that this construction of the Act was rather forced. But Stevens declared that he was adopting it partly because of the possibility that, without this limitation, the Act would have violated the delegation doctrine.

2. *Procedural Safeguards.* The *Meat Cutters* case was not the first to suggest that procedural safeguards to assure fair, informed decisionmaking can be crucial to the validity of a possibly overbroad delegation. In the *Schechter* and *Panama Refining* decisions, the Court placed considerable emphasis on the fact that the statutes did not require the agency to use fair and open administrative procedures. This theme was also reflected in the *Carter Coal* case. Where governmental power has been delegated to a private group, some mem-

the public, not just the pipeline operators who paid the charges, the Court unanimously upheld the statute, declaring that "the delegation of discretionary authority under Congress' taxing power is subject to no constitutional scrutiny greater than that we have applied to other nondelegation challenges." Skinner v. Mid–America Pipeline Co., 109 S.Ct. 1726 (1989).

bers of the industry may attempt to use this grant
of authority to harm or exclude their competitors.
Thus, the absence of an impartial decisionmaker
may be fatal under the delegation doctrine, just as
it may also violate the due process clause. See pp.
231–34 infra.

The *Meat Cutters* decision expanded the range of
procedural safeguards that are considered relevant
to the delegation question. In contrast to earlier
cases like *Schechter,* the *Meat Cutters* opinion did
not assume that trial-type hearings were required.
But it did warn the agency of "an on-going requirement of intelligible administrative policy." Development of administrative standards would minimize the risks of inadequate notice to the
regulated, or of inconsistent and arbitrary decisionmaking in particular cases. Finally, the availability of judicial review meant that administrative
standards could be tested for rationality and compliance with the congressional intent, and that the
agency's consistency in interpreting and applying
those standards in particular cases could be
checked.

Concerns about delegation also played a role in
the unorthodox decision in Hampton v. Mow Sun
Wong, 426 U.S. 88 (1976). The Supreme Court
invalidated a Civil Service Commission rule ban-
ning resident aliens from government employment.
The Court assumed that, because of foreign policy
considerations, the federal government might be
able to subject aliens to disabilities that would

violate normal equal protection standards. The Court was also willing to assume that this power could be delegated to an agency—but only under limited conditions. Specifically, the Court reasoned that "due process requires that there be a legitimate basis for presuming that the rule was actually intended to serve" a valid governmental interest. Since the Commission was concerned solely with promoting the efficiency of the federal service and the rule had no clear relationship to that purpose, the agency would be required to articulate a justification for the rule. The Court indicated that it would not have imposed this duty of explanation on the President or Congress had either of them taken the action. *Mow Sun Wong* is a puzzling decision that has had little if any influence. It does, however, show how procedural requirements can be the direct consequence of a court's reservations about the delegation of legislative power.

3. *Conclusion.* The *Meat Cutters* approach, in which a reviewing court considers the entire range of procedural and substantive limits on agency authority and construes the statute to minimize delegation problems, is an effort to reconcile a broad range of conflicting concerns. The delegation doctrine raises sensitive questions about the relationships among the three co-equal branches of government. Ever since the Supreme Court asserted the power to declare legislation unconstitutional in Marbury v. Madison, 5 U.S. (1 Cranch) 137

(1803), the exercise of this power has involved at least a potential conflict between the judiciary and the political branches. At times, this potential has escalated into actual confrontations. Perhaps the most familiar example is President Franklin Roosevelt's plan to "pack" the Supreme Court as a means of overcoming the obstacles to New Deal legislation that were created by decisions like *Schechter* and *Panama Refining*. A judicial holding that a delegation is unconstitutional invites a similar confrontation, for it may require radical restructuring or even abandonment of the entire program. Statutory interpretations or judicial directives that the agencies improve their procedures are less disruptive and more easily correctable if the court has misread the will of the Congress.

The contemporary emphasis on controlling discretion at the agency level, rather than striking down entire regulatory programs under the delegation doctrine, also represents an effort to accommodate the needs of a complex modern economy. Rigid insistence on the legislative specification of detailed standards is thought to be unsound and unworkable. For many regulatory problems, the legislature can neither foresee what actions the agency should take, nor constantly revise the statutory mandate as conditions change. Even when the policy alternatives are reasonably clear, an attempt to write highly detailed standards in the legislature may delay the passage of desired legislation, or jeopardize its chances for enactment.

The delegation doctrine remains available to use in truly extreme cases. For the present, however, the more immediate—and more pragmatic—task for Administrative Law is to evaluate and further refine the doctrines and techniques for making bureaucratic power accountable, without destroying the effectiveness of those administrative agencies considered necessary.

E. DELEGATION OF JUDICIAL POWER

The discussion thus far has concerned delegation of *legislative* power. A distinct question is the extent to which Congress may grant an agency *judicial* power, i.e., the power to adjudicate controversies between individual litigants. A strict reading of Article III of the Constitution would foreclose this option, because it provides that the "judicial Power of the United States" shall be exercised by judges with lifetime tenure and salary protection.

The propriety of using administrative agencies to adjudicate was long considered settled by Crowell v. Benson, 285 U.S. 22 (1932), which allowed an agency to resolve workers' compensation claims brought by maritime workers. The Court recognized that the case involved "private rights," i.e., rights between private parties, and thus closely resembled cases traditionally heard in Article III courts. Nevertheless, the Court saw no objection to administrative adjudication, so long as Congress permitted full judicial review of the agency's legal conclusions and deferential judicial review of its fact findings.[2] The Court indicated that Article III was even less of a constraint in controversies involving "public rights," i.e., rights between a private party and the government.

In 1982, however, the Court raised doubts about the survival of *Crowell's* permissiveness when it held unconstitutional the system of bankruptcy courts that Congress had established in 1978. Northern Pipeline Construction Co. v. Marathon Pipe Line Co., 458 U.S. 50 (1982). Although there was no opinion for the Court, the prevailing Justices expressed concern that Congress had authorized the bankruptcy judges to adjudicate a wide range of private rights questions, including rights that derived from state law rather than from Congress itself. *Northern Pipeline* was widely regarded as potentially applicable to administrative agencies as well as specialized courts.

But subsequent cases have removed many of these apprehensions. First, the Court upheld the EPA's use of an arbitrator to decide how much one pesticide manufacturer should pay another for using the latter's research data in a registration

2. The Court insisted, however, that there must be de novo judicial review of certain "jurisdictional facts." Later cases have never extended this perplexing holding, and seven Justices pronounced it dead in the *Northern Pipeline* case discussed just below. A related notion, that courts must be allowed to review de novo the fact findings on which a constitutional right depends, may have more vitality today. See p. 107 infra.

proceeding under the Federal Insecticide, Fungicide and Rodenticide Act. Thomas v. Union Carbide Agric. Products Co., 473 U.S. 568 (1985). Although this was in one sense a private rights case, the Court considered the distinction between public and private rights unhelpful. Instead, it stressed that Congress must have the flexibility to adopt innovative procedures to implement a complex regulatory scheme. Furthermore, the manufacturer that would be making the payment had effectively consented to the use of arbitration; and the Act provided for judicial review of the arbitrator's decision for fraud, misconduct, misrepresentation, or constitutional error. Later, the Court sustained the jurisdiction of the Commodities Futures Trading Commission to resolve a dispute between a commodities broker and his customer, including a counterclaim based on state law. CFTC v. Schor, 478 U.S. 833 (1986). Again the Court emphasized that the private nature of the claims should not prevent the Court from weighing a number of factors in deciding whether Congress had fatally compromised the independence of the judiciary. Given that the parties had voluntarily chosen to litigate their claims before the CFTC rather than in court, that traditional judicial review was available, and that the CFTC's jurisdiction over private rights was strictly limited to what Congress believed necessary to make the regulatory scheme effective, there was no reason to invalidate this minor transfer of Article III business.

Thus, Congress's power to delegate judicial power to agencies seems fairly secure. Nearly all administrative cases involve "public rights," which are universally considered appropriate for agency adjudication; and even though the Court has declined to embrace any bright line rules for private rights cases, *Northern Pipeline* increasingly appears to have little relevance to the administrative state. Similarly, the Seventh Amendment right to jury trial is no bar to administrative adjudication, at least in "public rights" cases. Atlas Roofing Co. v. OSHRC, 430 U.S. 442 (1977). Indeed, although the Court has recently upheld a creditor's right to jury trial in a bankruptcy trustee's suit to recover a fraudulent conveyance, it was careful to reaffirm that an administrative agency may adjudicate a dispute between private citizens if the claim is "closely intertwined with a federal regulatory program Congress has power to enact." Granfinanciera, S.A. v. Nordberg, 492 U.S. 109 (1989). But cf. Tull v. United States, 481 U.S. 412 (1987) (when government brings penalty action *in court*, jury determines defendant's liability).

If anything, the Court may have become too permissive: *Thomas* has disturbed some commentators, because the parties were allowed less judicial review than is customarily available against administrative agencies. But in any event, the current doctrine on delegation of judicial power, which avoids flat prohibitions and focuses on the net effect of a variety of factors, is broadly similar to the *Meat Cutters* approach, as well as to the balancing approach found in some of the separation of powers cases that will be examined in the next chapter.

F. THE DELEGATION DOCTRINE IN THE STATES

Since many state constitutions are based on the principle of separation of powers and provide for due process of law, delegation questions also arise at the state level. As might be expected, the delegation doctrine that has evolved in the states is more variable than the current federal law on the subject. Some states—a relatively large proportion, judging from the reported cases—still adhere to a relatively stringent version of the doctrine and require that statutes contain detailed standards confining agency discretion. See, e.g., People v. Tibbitts, 56 Ill.2d 56, 305 N.E.2d 152 (1973). The states have also been more resistant than the federal courts to allowing agencies to determine what acts will be punished criminally. See Lincoln Dairy Co. v. Finigan, 170 Neb. 777, 104 N.W.2d 227 (1960). One reason for this divergence between the state and federal approaches may be the fact that the scope of administrative regulation has increased much more rapidly in the federal government than in the states in recent decades. As a result, the federal courts may be more sensitive to the need for broad delegations than their state counterparts. Another reason might be the kinds of regulatory activities undertaken by the states. A large part of state regulation consists of occupational licensing. The fairness of these licensing programs is often suspect, particularly when the regulatory board is dominated by members of the regulated industry. As in the *Carter Coal* case, due process concerns become more compelling when the administrative process is controlled by private individuals who might use government power to protect themselves from competition, rather than to protect the public from incompetent practitioners. See, e.g., Allen v. California Board of Barber Examiners, 25 Cal.App.3d 1014, 102 Cal.Rptr. 368 (1972).

At the other extreme from the states which still adhere to the standards doctrine are a few that place little or no emphasis on statutory standards as such. This latter approach is illustrated by Sun Ray Drive–In Dairy, Inc. v. Oregon Liquor Control Comm'n, 16 Or.App. 63, 517 P.2d 289 (1973). The court in that case reversed an administrative order refusing to treat a convenience store as a "grocery store" eligible for a liquor license. It remanded the case to the Commission with a directive not to act on the petitioner's application until the agency had adopted general rules giving content to the vague statutory standard. The *Sun Ray* decision follows the federal pattern of tolerating broad delegations but insisting on safeguards. Here, as in *Meat Cutters*, the court reasoned that the development of administrative standards through rulemaking would ensure fair notice to applicants of what they must prove, would promote consistent application of the law, and would facilitate legislative and judicial oversight.

CHAPTER II

POLITICAL CONTROLS OVER AGENCY ACTION

In a constitutional democracy, government institutions which set and enforce public policy must be politically accountable to the electorate. When the legislature delegates broad lawmaking powers to an administrative agency, the popular control provided by direct election of decisionmakers is absent. However, this does not mean that administrative agencies are free from political accountability. In many areas, policy oversight by elected officials in the legislature or the executive branch is a more important check on agency power than judicial review.

Formally, agencies are dependent upon the legislature and the executive for their budgets and their operating authority. If an agency loses the support of these bodies or oversteps the bounds of political acceptability, it may be subjected to radical restructuring. During the 1970's the Atomic Energy Commission came under intense criticism for overemphasizing the promotion of nuclear power while underemphasizing safety and environmental protection. The political branches responded by transferring the AEC's promotional functions to the new Department of Energy, and by reconstituting the agency as the Nuclear Regulatory Commis-

sion, whose functions are solely regulatory. Another important form of political control over the
agencies is a statutory directive to change their
traditional ways of making decisions, either by
using different procedures or by taking account of
new values and interests. The National Environmental Policy Act of 1969, 42 U.S.C.A. §§ 4321–61,
is one of the clearest examples of significant substantive change in the agencies' mandates: for the
first time, it forced all federal agencies to consider
the environmental impacts of their major decisions. Similarly, the Regulatory Flexibility Act, 5
U.S.C.A. §§ 601–12, requires agencies to study the
economic effects of their regulations on small businesses and to consider ways to minimize those
effects.

While there are numerous examples of legislatures and chief executives taking formal action to
bring regulatory policy into accord with changing
political realities, the network of less formal and
less visible political "oversight" mechanisms is
probably more important in the day-to-day functioning of the administrative process. There are
numerous procedures and practices which bring
the activities of the agencies to the attention of
elected officials and their staffs, and in most regulatory settings the continuing dialogue which results from this process is an important determi-
nant of public policy. Here, the role of law and
legal rules has been to channel this interaction
within limited boundaries—for example, by re-

stricting *ex parte* contacts—rather than to determine final results.

Another significant dimension of agency accountability is the political acceptance of administrative policy among those who will be affected or
regulated. Public dissatisfaction not only triggers
the oversight of the political branches; it also may
determine the practical effectiveness of an entire
regulatory program. The Internal Revenue Service would require a much larger staff, and a much
different approach to enforcement, if it could not
count on a substantial measure of honest self-
reporting and voluntary compliance among taxpayers. Thus, an accurate understanding of the methods used to assure the control and accountability of
administrative agencies must begin with an appre-
ciation of the political environment within which
the agencies function.

In considering the mechanisms for assuring political control over agency policy, it is useful to
keep in mind some basic differences between judicial and political methods for making regulatory
bureaucracies accountable. Judicial review seeks
to assure that agency action is consistent with the
will of the political branches, as that will is expressed in constitutional mandates or properly enacted statutes. Political oversight is not limited to
these formal directives; a newly elected President,
for example, is expected to bring new people and
new policies into the regulatory process, even if the
basic statutes remain the same. Moreover, judicial

review usually is based on the premise that agency actions are reasoned decisions which result from a process of finding facts and applying generally accepted principles to them. Courts cannot easily review decisions that are the result of bargaining, or compromise, or pure policy choice. Compromise and choice among competing values are the essence of the political process, and for these kinds of issues, political methods for making and legitimizing decisions are essential. Indeed, the "political question doctrine" and other related judicial principles are designed to prevent the courts from making political choices that are conferred upon the other two branches of government. See, e.g., Baker v. Carr, 369 U.S. 186, 277–97 (1962) (Frankfurter, J., dissenting). The difficulty in the administrative process is that agency decisions range across the spectrum, from pure policy choice to reasoned application of settled principles, with most of them falling somewhere in between. Thus, there is often conflict over the proper scope of judicial and political accountability.

A. LEGISLATIVE OVERSIGHT BY FORMAL ACTION

Although the modern delegation doctrine puts few limits on the legislature's ability to grant broad powers to administrative agencies, Congress can always revoke or narrow the authority it has granted through subsequent legislation. At times, Congress moves quickly and explicitly to reverse or postpone a controversial agency action. When large numbers of consumers complained to their congressional representatives about the National Highway Traffic Safety Administration's automobile seat belt "interlock" rule, the legislature promptly amended the agency's organic act to provide that NHTSA safety standards could not require belt systems which prevented the car from starting or sounded a continuous buzzer when seat belts were unfastened. 15 U.S.C.A. § 1410b. Similarly, the Food and Drug Administration's attempts to ban the only approved artificial sweetener, saccharin, aroused such strong popular opposition that the Congress imposed a moratorium on regulatory action, and substituted a warning label for products containing the chemical. 91 Stat. 1451 (1977).

During the 1970's, many members of Congress began to feel that the normal process of legislation was too cumbersome for effective control of administrative action. The solution they favored was increased reliance on an old device: the so-called "legislative veto." These provisions took a variety of forms, but most of them directed agencies to transmit final administrative rules to the Congress for review before they became effective. The vote of two chambers, or sometimes only one (or even a committee or a committee chairman) would be enough to kill the rule.

Just as this approach to regulatory reform was gathering speed, the Supreme Court dealt it a fatal blow in INS v. Chadha, 462 U.S. 919 (1983). Under the Immigration and Nationality Act, a decision by the Attorney General suspending deportation of an alien could be nullified by vote of either House of Congress. When the House of Representatives exercised this power in Chadha's case, he brought suit. The Supreme Court held that this "one-house veto" scheme violated Art. I, § 7, of the Constitution. Under that section, no legislation can be valid unless it is passed by both houses of Congress and signed by the President (or, if he vetoes it, repassed by two-thirds of each house). The House's veto should be presumed to be an exercise of legislative power, the Court explained, and thus the Art. I, § 7 requirements applied. The veto's "legislative purpose and effect" was all the more clear, according to the Court, because it was intended to have the force of law and to affect Chadha's legal rights.[1] *Chadha* appeared to invalidate all of the nearly 200 legislative veto devices that were then on the books. That implication was underscored two weeks later, when the Court summarily upheld challenges to two other legislative vetoes, involving rulemaking by the Federal Trade Commission and the Federal Energy Regulatory Commission.

1. The Court also held that the veto was severable from the rest of the Immigration Act, so that the latter could remain in effect. The severability of legislative veto provisions in other regulatory statutes has had to be resolved on a case-by-case basis. See, e.g., Alaska Airlines, Inc. v. Brock, 480 U.S. 678 (1987) (airline deregulation statute).

The *Chadha* opinion has been severely criticized as formalistic. Commentators have questioned the Court's premise that Congress can act only in a legislative capacity. It was not self-evident that the procedural requirements of Art. I, § 7 were applicable to a congressional device—created by a duly enacted statute—that was only intended to constrain the executive branch's use of delegated authority. And although the Court assumed that the legislative veto had altered Chadha's rights, it would have been equally logical to conclude that his rights were at all times contingent on the nonoccurrence of a legislative veto. A more practical analysis, it is argued, would have paid more attention to the need of the people's representatives to exert more control over policymaking by the unelected bureaucracy.

The ruling may appear in a more sympathetic light, however, if one assumes that the Court was motivated by functional concerns. Prior studies of the legislative veto had suggested that it tended to bring out some of the less admirable aspects of congressional decisionmaking. The abbreviated procedure and the purely negative character of the vote seemed to encourage Congress to override well-considered agency decisions thoughtlessly—as apparently happened in Chadha's case—or on the basis of lobbyists' influence rather than deliberation. Moreover, since agencies issue far too many rules for the entire legislature to review in a meaningful fashion, the legislative veto actually tended to reinforce the power of oversight committees and their staffs, which themselves are often unrepresentative of Congress as a whole.

Even when *Chadha* is rationalized on these grounds, however, there are lingering doubts about whether the decision was too broad. Some potential uses for the legislative veto are so unlike the ones reviewed by the Court that they might deserve a different analysis. For instance, the War Powers Resolution of 1973 provides that the President must withdraw military forces in an undeclared war if Congress so directs in a resolution passed by both chambers. This measure seems far removed from the regulatory contexts in which the validity of the legislative veto has been litigated, but its legality is in doubt after *Chadha.*

The demise of the legislative veto stimulated interest in other approaches to regulatory reform. One such approach, expressly approved in *Chadha,* is a "report-and-wait" procedure, under which the effective date of an agency's proposed rule is delayed for a period of time so that Congress can consider whether to pass a statute overriding the rule. This type of congressional review has long been part of the process for amending the Federal Rules of Civil Procedure and other federal court rules. Another regulatory reform idea that was in vogue at about the same time as the legislative veto was the "sunset" law, under which a given agency would go out of existence after a fixed period of time unless the legislature reenacted its statutory charter. Sunset proposals differed greatly in their details, but they all shared the common assumption that it is useful to compel the Congress to undertake a thorough reexamination of its delegations of authority periodically, and to assess their utility in the light of experience. In this respect, sunset laws would have resembled budget authorizations that are limited to a fixed period of time. Although many state governments have adopted the sunset concept, it appears to have passed from favor at the federal level.

Regulatory "reform" aside, much congressional review of agency actions occurs as part of the routine legislative process. Indeed, since Congress retains the power of the purse, it has ample opportunity to influence implementation of regulatory statutes when it can muster the will. There are two required stages for Congressional approval of agency funding. First, there must be a legislative *authorization* for appropriations, which is usually contained in the basic delegation of power to the agency. The authorization for a particular program may expire after a fixed period of years, or it may be permanent. Similarly, it may set a ceiling on future appropriations, or permit the appropriation of such sums as are necessary to carry out the purposes of the statute. For example, when the Federal Trade Commission instituted a series of sweeping consumer protection proposals which many members of Congress believed were unnecessary or ill conceived, the legislature used its budg-

etary powers to prohibit the FTC from taking final
action on the pending rules until new statutory
controls on the agency's authority could be enacted. See FTC Improvements Act of 1980, 94
Stat. 374 (1980), amending 15 U.S.C.A. § 41 et seq.
On the other hand, when the Environmental Protection Agency came under political attack for
being too lenient with those responsible for toxic
waste dumps, Congress responded with numerous
"hammer" provisions, requiring the agency to ban
certain practices or impose specified performance
standards by a fixed date unless it could find that
the statutory limits were unnecessary to protect
health or the environment. Hazardous and Solid
Waste Amendments of 1984, 98 Stat. 3221 (1984).

More commonly, funding controls are imposed in
the annual *appropriations* process. Each year,
agencies must submit budget requests which are
reviewed by the President (acting through the Office of Management and Budget) and are transmit-
ted to the appropriations committees of the House
and Senate. These committees then hold hearings
and report bills allocating funds among the various
agencies and programs, which must be voted on by
both houses of Congress. Generally, the appropriations committees are responsible for "fiscal" oversight of agency spending, while the authorizing
committees are primarily concerned with "legislative" oversight or substantive policy. In practice,
however, the two functions tend to overlap, and
both committees may become involved in review-

ing the wisdom or desirability of agency policy. Since 1974, moreover, the House and Senate have each maintained a committee to draw up an overall budget for the government's activities. These committees have become still another arena in which battles over regulatory policy can be waged.

B. INFORMAL LEGISLATIVE OVERSIGHT

In addition to its formal legislating and funding powers, Congress has broad authority to investigate implementation of statutory programs and to expose corrupt or ineffective administration. Primary responsibility for investigating the efficiency and effectiveness of the administrative agencies is lodged in the House and Senate Government Operations committees, but any committee which has jurisdiction over some aspect of the agency's program may conduct investigations. Congress may also use an ad hoc committee to inquire into a particularly delicate problem, as it did in the case of the Watergate investigation in 1973 and the Iran–Contra scandal in 1987. By mobilizing public and political pressure on the agency, and by raising the threat of future legislation, investigative oversight can greatly affect agency behavior.

Congressional demands for information can often come into conflict with the executive branch's interest in the confidentiality of its internal deliberations. The doctrine of executive privilege, which has roots in the Constitution, gives agencies a limited right to withhold information for this reason. See generally United States v. Nixon, 418 U.S. 683 (1974). However, the scope of the privilege is ill-defined, because disputes over executive privilege are ordinarily resolved through political compromise rather than court litigation.

To facilitate the oversight process, Congress normally requires agencies to report back periodically on their activities. Agency reports to the Congress may be limited to a particular function, or they may range more broadly over a variety of activities and programs. Most reports are submitted on an annual basis, but occasionally the Congress will request a special report. Agencies may also submit special reports to Congress on their own initiative, particularly if the agency needs additional legislative authority to deal with a particular problem.

There are also several permanent organizations which Congress has created to assist its own legislative and oversight responsibilities. Congressional support agencies like the Congressional Research Service or the Office of Technology Assessment may conduct studies of agency activities. These studies can trigger more formal oversight mechanisms, or induce the agencies to modify their practices. The support agency which is most influential in the legislative oversight process is the General Accounting Office, headed by the Comptroller General. The GAO was originally created to conduct financial audits of the agencies' use of public funds, but in recent years it has taken on considerable responsibility for program review and evaluation. The Supreme Court made clear in Bowsher v. Synar, 478 U.S. 714 (1986), that there are limits beyond which the GAO may not go if it is to avoid infringing on the constitutional powers of the executive branch. See pp. 59–60 infra. However, the location of those limits remains unsettled. See Ameron, Inc. v. U.S. Army Corps of Eng'rs, 809 F.2d 979 (3d Cir.1986) (upholding constitutionality of Comptroller General's authority to delay performance of defense procurement contract, pending GAO scrutiny of its propriety), cert. dismissed, 109 S.Ct. 297 (1988).

Another method by which the legislature influences agency activities is through the institution of congressional "casework," which is the general name given to legislators' attempts to assist their constituents in dealing with the bureaucracy. Ideally, congressional casework puts the legislator in the role of an "ombudsman" checking up on the quality of administration and helping citizens to obtain fair treatment from the agencies. It can also help the representatives identify problem areas which are appropriate for oversight hearings or statutory correction. In its less-than-ideal manifestations, however, casework can become either an attempt by a legislator to pressure the bureaucrats into making an improper decision in favor of his constituent, or a paper shuffle in which the citizen's complaint is simply "bucked" back to the

agency topped by a form letter from the congressman. See generally W. Gellhorn, *When Americans
Complain* (1966).

Since legislative oversight is basically political in
nature, and often operates through pressure or
bargaining, it may come into conflict with legal or
constitutional requirements for agency decisionmaking. This is particularly true in administrative adjudications, where an agency passes upon
the legality of private conduct. In Pillsbury Co. v.
FTC, 354 F.2d 952 (5th Cir.1966), the commissioners of the Federal Trade Commission were subjected to prolonged and hostile questioning by congressional oversight committees regarding a legal
interpretation they had issued in an interlocutory
order during a pending adjudication. The court
held that this intrusion into the agency's decisionmaking process had deprived the respondent of a
fair adjudication. Even when the decision is not
adjudicative in nature, however, some kinds of
congressional oversight may be improper. The
"Three Sisters Bridge" case, D.C. Federation of
Civic Ass'ns v. Volpe, 459 F.2d 1231 (D.C.Cir.1971),
cert. denied, 405 U.S. 1030 (1972), is an example of
legal limits on political intervention. There, the
powerful chairman of a House appropriations committee brought pressure to bear on the Secretary of
Transportation to grant approval of a controversial
bridge construction project. The court concluded
that the Secretary's consideration of this pressure
in making his decision was grounds for reversal.

In its basic grant of authority to the Secretary, the Congress as a whole had directed him to consider the project "on its merits" and to make a reasoned analysis of the facts. Thus, political pressures were technically irrelevant to that kind of decision; oversight activities by one congressman or one committee could not override the will of the Congress as a whole, as expressed in the underlying legislation. In Sierra Club v. Costle, 657 F.2d 298 (D.C.Cir.1981), however, the court distinguished *D.C. Federation.* A Senator from a coal mining state had forcefully expressed his constituents' concerns to the EPA during a rulemaking proceeding to set limits on emissions from coal-fired power plants. Since there was no hard evidence that the Senator had brought irrelevant considerations into the deliberations, and since rulemaking is by its nature a political process, the EPA rules were upheld.

C. CONTROL OVER PERSONNEL

1. PRESIDENTIAL APPOINTMENT

Like the Congress, the President has a variety of powers and techniques he can use to oversee and influence the operations of administrative agencies. One of the President's most important instruments of control, at least potentially, is his power to appoint federal officers. The Appointments Clause of the Constitution (Art. II, § 2, cl. 2) contains some fairly specific guidance on the staffing of federal administrative agencies. It provides that the President generally appoints all "Officers of the United States," with the advice and consent of the Senate. For the most part, Presidents have not made very effective use of the appointment power to shape policy. See generally V. Kramer & J. Graham, *Appointments to the Regulatory Agencies,* Senate Comm. on Commerce, 94th Cong., 2d Sess. (Comm. Print 1976). It is generally agreed, however, that President Reagan was able to bring about significant policy changes by appointing agency heads who shared his objective of reducing the burdens of regulation on business.

Congress tested the limits of the Appointments Clause in 1974 when it passed a statute creating the Federal Election Commission. The statute required that four of the FEC's six voting members would be appointed by the Speaker of the House and the President *pro tempore* of the Senate. The Supreme Court struck down this legislation in Buckley v. Valeo, 424 U.S. 1, 118–43 (1976). The Court explained that the constitutional term "Officers of the United States," identifying those officeholders who must be chosen pursuant to the Appointments Clause, includes all appointees exercising significant authority pursuant to the laws of the United States, such as rulemaking, adjudication, or enforcement functions. Thus the FEC, a typical agency wielding all of those powers, was clearly covered by the clause. The Court noted, however, that it would have reached a different result if the FEC had merely been assigned powers of an investigative and informative nature. (The Civil Rights Commission is an example of such an agency; some of its members are chosen by the President and some by Congress.)

A significant limitation on the President's appointment power is found in a proviso to the Appointments Clause itself: "Congress may by Law vest the Appointment of such inferior Officers, as they think proper, in the President alone, in the Courts of Law, or in the Heads of Departments." This exemption makes it possible for agencies to hire rank-and-file civil servants using a merit system of competitive examinations, without Presidential involvement.

The same proviso came into play in a celebrated recent case concerning the constitutionality of the Ethics in Government Act. The Act authorizes a federal court of appeals to appoint a special prosecutor, or "independent counsel," to investigate allegations of criminal wrongdoing by high officials of the Executive Branch. The Court upheld the statute, finding that the independent counsel was an "inferior Officer" and thus could properly be appointed by one of the "Courts of Law," rather than by the President. Morrison v. Olson, 487 U.S. 654 (1988). Without laying down any general test for identifying an inferior officer, the Court concluded that the independent counsel fell within that category because she was removable by the Attorney General (although only under strictly limited conditions) and because her duties were limited to handling a single case and would terminate at the end of that case. The Court indicated that, in some situations, judicial appointment of an executive officer would create a fatal "incongruity"—for example, if a court were charged with appointing officials in the Agriculture Department. But the Act was not vulnerable on that ground, because courts have appointed prosecutors in various circumstances for many years. The Court's concern about avoiding "incongruity" suggests that *Morrison* was not intended to cast doubt on the President's exclusive right to appoint most agency heads and high ranking policymakers.

2. PRESIDENTIAL REMOVAL

Except in the clauses dealing with impeachment, the Constitution does not address the circumstances under which agency personnel may be removed from office. There is, however, a substantial case law on this subject, applying generalized separation of powers notions. Indeed, these cases are the source of one of the central puzzles of Administrative Law: the concept of the "independent agency." Independent agencies tend to be multimember boards and commissions, such as the SEC, FCC, and NLRB. A major difference between these agencies and the "executive agencies" (the familiar Cabinet departments) is that the heads of independent agencies do not serve "at the pleasure of the President." Their governing statutes may provide, for example, that commissioners are appointed for a fixed period of years which does not correspond with the President's term of office. There may also be statutory provisions protecting the commissioners from arbitrary removal during their terms of office.

The paradox inherent in this situation is easy to state. The independent agencies perform functions that one would normally associate with the executive branch, yet they are not under the full control of the President, in whom Article II of the Constitution vests "the executive Power." On the other hand, if they are not part of the executive branch, there seems to be no constitutional basis for them to exist at all. Thus, independent agencies are sometimes described as "arms of Congress" or as members of a "headless fourth branch."

For a long time, two cases dominated discussion of these matters. The first, involving the dismissal of a postmaster at a time when the Post Office was still a Cabinet department, suggested that Congress could not limit the President's removal power without violating Article II. Myers v. United States, 272 U.S. 52 (1926). The Court reasoned that the President needed the power to fire any agency head at will if he was to fulfill his constitutional duty to "take Care that the Laws be faithfully executed." However, a decade later the Court limited *Myers*. The issue came to a head when President Roosevelt sought to remove a chairman of the Federal Trade Commission who was unsympathetic to some of the New Deal programs that

the FTC was responsible for administering. The
statute provided that FTC commissioners were to
serve for a fixed term of years, and that they could
be removed during their term only for "inefficiency, neglect of duty, or malfeasance in office." The
President did not claim that the recalcitrant chairman was guilty of any of these offenses; he simply
wanted to change the policy direction of the agency. When the discharged chairman brought suit to
challenge the legality of his removal, the Supreme
Court held that the statutory removal-for-cause
provision was a constitutionally proper limit on the
President's removal power. Humphrey's Executor
(Rathbun) v. United States, 295 U.S. 602 (1935).
The Court distinguished *Myers* as a case involving
a "purely executive" officer. As such, it did not
apply to officers of the FTC, which "occupies no
place in the executive department" and "acts in
part quasi-legislatively and in part quasi-judicial-
ly."

The Court's desire to shield "quasi-judicial" officers from executive domination has obvious appeal. Adjudication of individual disputes is often
thought to call for independent, apolitical judgment. The Court relied on this rationale in Wiener v. United States, 357 U.S. 349 (1958), to prevent a member of the War Claims Commission
from being dismissed without cause. The *Wiener*
holding was striking because the statute said nothing about removal of commissioners. Because the
commissioners were expected to "adjudicate ac-

cording to law," the Court felt that it could *infer* a congressional desire to protect them from arbitrary removal.

Other aspects of the *Humphrey's Executor* reasoning, however, have been roundly criticized in subsequent years. To the extent that an agency exercises "quasi-legislative" or policymaking powers, a substantial measure of political responsiveness and accountability to elected officials seems highly desirable. More fundamentally, it is not possible to pigeonhole functions as neatly as the Court seemed to assume. As the delegation cases illustrate, there is considerable overlap between "quasi-legislative" and "executive" power, and no good way to draw the line. In practice, scholars have found no consistent difference separating the work of the independent commissions from that of the Cabinet departments.

The Court explicitly abandoned the analysis of *Humphrey's Executor* in 1988, when it decided *Morrison v. Olson,* 487 U.S. 654 (1988), discussed at pp. 51–52 supra. The Court recognized that the duties of the independent counsel were clearly "executive" in nature. Nevertheless, the Court upheld the provision in the Ethics in Government Act allowing the independent counsel to be removed only for "good cause." The proper inquiry, the Court said, was whether removal restrictions "impede the President's ability to perform his constitutional duty." The good cause standard in the Act did not constitute such an impediment, especially in light of the limited nature of the independent counsel's responsibilities and the congressionally perceived need for her to function independently. The Court added that the good cause standard was equivalent to the statutory protections enjoyed by many independent agency heads. The clear implication was that the removal protections applicable to traditional independent agencies would also survive scrutiny under the *Morrison* test.

There have been suggestions in recent years that *Humphrey's Executor* should be overruled, so that all agencies would be under the complete control of the President. After *Morrison* the independent agency concept appears to be alive and well. This ratifies the status quo: even before the decision, Presidents were generally cautious about trying to make independent agencies adhere to Administration policy. What *Morrison* does appear to change is the theory on which the independent agencies are justified. The Court endorses Congress's power to innovate, pursuant to the necessary and proper clause, so long as the President's "ability to perform his constitutional duty" is not impaired. Future cases, applying this vague test, will have to work out which other agencies can be shielded from presidential control, and how far.

Another unsettled matter concerns several agencies, including the FCC and the SEC, that are in an ambiguous position because they were created after the *Myers* decision suggested that the President's removal power could not be limited by Congress, but before the *Humphrey* opinion made it clear that some limits were possible. Thus, the commissioners of the SEC serve for fixed terms of years, but they have no explicit statutory protection against summary removal from office. It is not clear whether the President would be able to remove them without cause.

As a practical matter, the distinction between independent and executive agencies should not be overemphasized. Even fixed terms of office and removal-for-cause statutes do not pose serious obstacles to the President's ability to influence regulatory policy through the appointments process. Since regulators' terms of office are typically staggered in the multimember agencies and many commissioners do not serve out their terms, a newly elected President almost always has the opportunity to make key appointments early in his administration. Moreover, if the President formally requests an administrator's resignation, even an "independent" commissioner is not very likely to resist or to face the prospect of a removal-for-cause controversy. The President also has the statutory power to designate one of the commissioners of an independent agency to serve as chairman, and to "demote" the chairman back to the rank of commissioner without cause. Since the chairman of a regulatory agency has the primary responsibility for managing its operations, including the hiring of new personnel, a change in agency leadership often results in policy changes. This was evident in the "revitalization" of the FTC during the early 1970's when the President responded to public criticism of the agency by appointing activist chairmen who initiated sweeping changes in staffing and regulatory policy.

On the other hand, Presidents sometimes have to put up with high-ranking executive officials whom they have the legal right to fire, because a dismissal would be politically costly, particularly if the administrator has the support of a powerful constituency. Finally, it should be noted that both executive and independent agencies follow roughly the same procedures and are reviewed in the same fashion by the courts. Thus, the distinction between the two has little relevance to the vast majority of the principles of administrative law.

3. THE CONGRESSIONAL ROLE

In light of *Buckley v. Valeo,* discussed at pp. 50–51 supra, Congress cannot make appointments to the agencies itself. It can, however, set qualifications for various offices. One type of restriction is a statutory provision requiring that a multimember commission be politically balanced; for example, no more than three of the five members of the SEC may be members of one political party. The Senate also must decide whether to "advise and consent" to the President's appointees. Occasionally, the Senate rejects a nominee. In 1989, for example, President Bush failed in his effort to install a former senator as Secretary of Defense; the nomination

collapsed amid a swirl of allegations that the nominee was guilty of alcoholism, conflicts of interest,
and loose living. Such cases are exceptional, however, because the Senate generally recognizes a
President's strong interest in filling high government positions with personnel of his own choosing.
Thus, Senators normally use confirmation hearings
for more intangible purposes: to air their concerns
about regulatory matters and to extract policy commitments from nominees.

Except by impeachment, Congress also has no
power to remove agency officials, as the Court held
in Bowsher v. Synar, 478 U.S. 714 (1986). The
Gramm–Rudman–Hollings Act provided that if
Congress and the President failed to agree on fiscal
policies that would hold federal budget deficits
down to a specified target figure, across-the-board
reductions in program funding would go into effect.
Final responsibility for calculating these reductions rested with the Comptroller General, an official who is removable by joint resolution of Congress. The Supreme Court found the Act
unconstitutional, declaring that separation of powers principles prevent Congress from taking "an
active role . . . in the supervision of officers
charged with the execution of the laws it enacts."
Thus, Congress cannot remove an executive official
except for impeachable offenses. Although the
Comptroller General normally performs legislative
support functions, see pp. 46–47 supra, the responsibilities he might have to exercise in implement-

ing the new Act were "executive" in nature; he could not be asked to fulfill those responsibilities under threat of a congressional ouster.

Like *Chadha, Bowsher* has been criticized for relying on an overly formal model of the congressional role in the checks and balances system. It would have been hard for the Court to make a case in pragmatic terms that *any* threat of congressional removal of an "executing" official disrupts the balance of power among the branches. (In the case of the Comptroller General, the threat was only abstract; the removal power had never been exercised.) Some of the Court's language was surely overbroad: the exclusion of Congress from any "supervision," if taken literally, would even condemn routine congressional oversight activity. On a more concrete level, however, *Bowsher* may have been justified in regarding the Comptroller General's role under the Act as an improper attempt by Congress to exert influence over the budget reduction process without taking the political risks that substantive budget-cutting legislation would have entailed. By its holding, the Court ensured that one or more elected officials (Congress, the President, or both) would ultimately be accountable for making the quintessentially political choices about how much to fund various programs.

In view of the relatively flexible analysis embraced by the Court in *Morrison* two years later, one might doubt whether the Court would still adhere to *Bowsher*'s strict notions of Congress' role (although the cases are distinguishable, as *Morrison* did not involve Congress adding to its own power). However that may be, Congress is by no means as impotent in practice as it is in constitutional theory. Every agency needs a minimum degree of legislative support if it is to maintain its programs and obtain funding for them. When legislators' confidence in an administrative official drops too far, a resignation is likely to follow.

D. OTHER EXECUTIVE OVERSIGHT

In the day-to-day functioning of the administrative process, the President's power of persuasion and the other less drastic tools of executive oversight are usually more significant factors than the threat of removal. Exercise of these oversight powers often takes the form of an executive order, a formal directive from the President to federal agencies or officials. Depending upon the context, a particular executive order may be based either on an inherent constitutional power of the President, or on an express or implicit delegation from Congress. See generally Fleishman & Aufses, *Law and Orders: The Problem of Presidential Legislation,* 40 L. & Contemp.Prob. 1, 11 (Summer 1976).

One technique which has been used more frequently than the removal power is the President's authority to modify the organizational structure of the bureaucracy. Under the Reorganization Act, 5 U.S.C.A. §§ 901–12, the President may submit a "reorganization plan" to the Congress, transferring functions from one department to another. If the legislature endorses the plan within ninety days, the transfer becomes effective. Thus, for example, the Environmental Protection Agency was created by Reorganization Plan No. 3 of 1970, 5 U.S.C.A. App. 1, which consolidated in one new agency a variety of programs that had been scattered among several executive departments.

Much of the work of executive oversight takes place within the organizations which comprise the Executive Office of the President, commonly referred to as "The White House." The Executive Office of the President includes not only the President's personal advisors, who comprise the White House Office, but also permanent organizations like the National Security Council and the Council of Economic Advisers. See 3 U.S.C.A. § 101. The most important of these units to the regulatory agencies is the Office of Management and Budget (OMB). As its name suggests, OMB has primary responsibility for formulating the annual executive budget which the President transmits to the Congress. In performing this task, OMB receives budget requests from the individual agencies and modifies them in accordance with the administration's priorities. 31 U.S.C.A. § 16. Similarly, OMB reviews the agencies' requests for substantive legislation, including agency officials' proposed testimony before congressional committees, for consistency with the Administration's position. Both of these "clearance" procedures typically give rise to extensive negotiations between OMB staff and agency officials, and usually a compromise solution is reached. However, major disagreements are sometimes resolved by the President. In addition, the Paperwork Reduction Act, 44 U.S.C.A. § 3501 et seq., provides that OMB must approve any new information demand that an agency wishes to impose on the private sector. The Act applies only to information that the government seeks for its own purposes; it does not authorize OMB to review rules that require companies to disclose information to the public, such as consumer product labeling regulations. Dole v. United Steelworkers of America, 110 S.Ct. 929 (1990).

Since 1971, the White House has attempted to exert direct supervision and control over major rulemaking proceedings through a regulatory analysis program. This technique was first formalized in the Ford and Carter Administrations, but reached its most fullblown form when President Reagan issued Executive Order 12291, 46 Fed.Reg. 13193 (1981). The order instructs *executive* agencies, "to the extent permitted by law," to take regulatory action only if "the potential benefits to society for the regulation outweigh the potential costs to society." They must also prepare a "regulatory impact analysis" or assessment of anticipated costs and benefits for any proposed rule that is likely to have a significant economic impact. OMB then conducts its own review of the agency's cost-benefit analysis, and the agency may not issue the rule without OMB's clearance. A related directive, Executive Order 12498, 50 Fed.Reg. 1036 (1985), requires executive agencies to submit their anticipated regulatory programs to OMB each year. This "regulatory planning process" is intended to give OMB and the agency heads themselves an opportunity to consider carefully at the outset whether the ideas being developed by the agency's staff are intrinsically sound and are consistent with the administration's priorities. The two executive orders exempt independent agencies, although some of those agencies voluntarily participate in the oversight program.

The effect of E.O. 12291 is to put a staff with close ties to the President into a strong position to press its views on pending regulations, and thereby to influence their contents. OMB's analysts typically raise questions about whether particular aspects of a proposed regulation are really necessary, and whether the rule's objectives can be met in a less intrusive way than the agency's proposal contemplates. OMB usually gives a quick clearance to simple regulations, but it sometimes studies a relatively complex or controversial one at length, extending the rule's gestation period by several months or more. When OMB objects to a proposed rule, it generally enters into negotiations with the agency over specific points, with each side deploying whatever technical arguments and political weaponry it can muster. In these exchanges, the agency usually has the edge in technical expertise, but OMB's ability to delay the issuance of a rule that the agency wants to promulgate as quickly as possible can give the reviewing office considerable leverage with which to extract concessions. See Bruff, *Presidential Management of Agency Rulemaking,* 57 Geo.Wash.L.Rev. 533 (1989).

To date, the courts have not directly ruled on the legality of E.O. 12291. The legal case for the order rests on the supervisory power that inheres in the President's status as head of the executive branch. The Constitution (Art. II, § 2, cl. 1) specifically authorizes him to "require the Opinion, in writing, [of department heads] upon any Subject relating to the Duties of their respective Offices." Moreover, because of the President's electoral base, his participation in the process can be seen as legitimizing a rule. See Sierra Club v. Costle, 657 F.2d 298 (D.C. Cir.1981). The countervailing consideration is that both agencies and the President must execute the laws enacted by Congress. Critics of the order maintain that, in some cases, conformity with the regulatory analysis program prevents an agency from fulfilling the duties assigned to it by the legislature. The clearest case would be one in which the statute forbids the agency to act on the basis of a cost-benefit analysis, as the Supreme Court has found to be true of the Occupational Safety and Health Act. See American Textile Mfrs. Inst. v. Donovan, 452 U.S. 490 (1981). Another decision has held that OMB review must not be used to keep an agency from meeting a statutory deadline. EDF v. Thomas, 627 F.Supp. 566 (D.D.C.1986). Since E.O. 12291 by its terms applies only "to the extent permitted by law," it leaves questions about the allowable scope of the program to be resolved on a case-by-case basis.

Underlying the legal questions about the oversight program are conflicting perceptions about its practical value. Supporters of the program stress the President's unique vantage point as a national leader who can coordinate conflicting governmental objectives and resist the parochial demands of a department's particular constituency. They also cite OMB's expertise in sophisticated policy analysis techniques. Opponents respond that the order effectively takes power away from the agency that has the greatest expertise in the relevant subject area. They also say that OMB involvement causes unwarranted delays in the rulemaking process and breeds procedural unfairness, because key decisions will be made behind closed doors, where opposing parties cannot correct OMB's misapprehensions. (To meet these latter criticisms, however, OMB has recently taken steps to bolster the procedural regularity of its processes. See pp. 342–43 infra.)

The regulatory analysis provides an essentially negative check on agency decisions, in the sense that the reviewers are looking for errors and deficiencies in the agency's proposals. For some years, commentators have suggested that the President ought to have a more affirmative role in initiating

and directing agency policy. One proposal recommends enactment of a statute generally authorizing the President to issue executive orders modify-
ing or reversing agency policy, or directing an
agency to consider and decide a particular matter
within a fixed period of time. See Cutler & Johnson, *Regulation and the Political Process,* 84 Yale
L.J. 1395 (1975). The President's order would have
a delayed effective date, and during this waiting
period either house of Congress could pass a resolution setting it aside. This approach is intended to
provide greater political legitimacy for agency policymaking, by bringing the elected branches of government more directly into the process. However,
the Congress generally has not been receptive to
proposals that would increase executive power over
the agencies, particularly the independent regulatory commissions, which have remained partially
insulated from executive oversight.

A final tool of executive oversight, which is often
overlooked, is the President's power to control litigation affecting the agencies through the Department of Justice. See 5 U.S.C.A. § 3106. Although
there are significant exceptions, most agencies lack
the statutory authority to litigate on their own
behalf. Rather, they must obtain representation
from the Department of Justice, and the Department's refusal to advocate or defend a particular
agency policy may mean that the agency's decision
has no practical effect. Cf. United States v. Provi-
dence Journal Co., 485 U.S. 693 (1988) (case dis-

missed because Justice Department had not authorized the appeal). One notable instance in which
the Department used this power occurred in 1977.
Then Attorney General Griffin Bell sent an open
letter to the heads of all departments and agencies,
advising them that the government would not defend an agency against suits to compel disclosure
of documents under the Freedom of Information
Act, 5 U.S.C.A. § 552, even if the documents were
exempt, unless the agency could show that disclosure was "demonstrably harmful." This directive
was designed to implement the Carter Administration's belief that greater openness in government
was desirable, and it appears to have been an
effective means of compelling the agencies to abide
by that policy.

Despite the wide array of formal oversight techniques and the considerable informal "powers of
persuasion" that a President can bring to bear,
direct Presidential involvement in many areas of
regulatory policy is still rare or nonexistent. Part
of the reason may be the sheer pressure of time
and workload; the President and his personal advisors may often find that more pressing matters
prevent them from getting too deeply involved in
the intricacies of administrative regulation. On
the other hand, when a regulatory policy issue is
truly controversial and any decision is likely to
offend some powerful interest group, the White
House may think it prudent to avoid direct involve-

ment that could make the President personally responsible for the final decision.

E. THE FUTURE OF SEPARATION OF POWERS

The 1980's have seen an extraordinary revival of litigation raising fundamental separation of powers issues—issues that courts had scarcely reexamined since the 1930's. But the courts have not analyzed these issues in a consistent manner. *Chadha* and *Bowsher* perceived absolute constitutional limitations on the activities of the legislative branch; they assumed that liberty can be best preserved if the courts will strictly enforce the division of responsibilities implied by the tripartite structure of the Constitution. In contrast, *Morrison* assumed that courts can best decide on a case-by-case basis whether a given innovation will disrupt the balance of powers among the branches: the question becomes whether the challenged action disables any branch from performing its core functions, and whether it would allow any branch (including the agency itself) to acquire so much power that there would be insufficient checks against possible abuses. Scholars describe these two styles of reasoning as "formalist" and "functionalist," respectively. The functionalist premises of *Morrison* became evident when the Court ruled that the Ethics in Government Act as a whole did not violate separation of powers principles: the Court reasoned that the Act did not significantly enhance the powers of Congress or the courts at the expense of the executive branch, nor did it unduly weaken the Presidency. The *Morrison* approach closely resembles the modern approach to another separation of powers issue: whether particular powers can be delegated to agencies in the first place. See the discussion of *Meat Cutters* and *Schor* at pp. 21–29, 31 supra.

As the 1980's came to an end, the Court appeared to have become converted to the functional approach. In Mistretta v. United States, 488 U.S. 361 (1989), the Court considered the constitutionality of the United States Sentencing Commission, which Congress had created to write guidelines that would establish, within narrow limits, the allowable sentences for most federal criminal offenses. The structure of the Commission was unconventional, because the statute referred to it as "an independent commission in the judicial branch," and some of its members were federal judges. In upholding this unusual arrangement, the Court reasoned that the statute did not unduly strengthen the judicial branch: the judiciary had traditionally been deeply involved in criminal sentencing, and there was historical precedent for judicial branch rulemaking and for individual judges to perform nonjudicial government functions. On the other hand, the statute did not unduly weaken the judicial branch: the fact that the President could appoint judges to the commission, and remove them for good cause, posed only a negligible threat of compromising the impartiality of the courts as they performed their normal adjudicatory functions. Yet, despite the reasoning of *Mistretta*, the formalist approach to separation of powers analysis—under which each branch of government is deemed to hold certain powers that are absolutely protected against encroachment by other branches—still retains some support within the Court. See *Morrison*, 487 U.S. at 733–34 (Scalia, J., dissenting); Public Citizen v. United States Department of Justice, 109 S.Ct. 2558, 2580–84 (1989) (Kennedy, J., joined by Rehnquist, C.J., and O'Connor, J., dissenting) (statute limiting President's freedom to consult with citizens concerning his judicial nominees violates Appointments Clause).

In the years ahead, new questions of political oversight will surely arise: how closely the President may supervise the agencies (both executive and independent), and what supervisory role remains for Congress. No doubt the courts will continue to rely heavily on the constitutional text. In some contexts, as *Buckley* illustrates, that type of argument can be nearly conclusive. But it seems likely that courts will usually be receptive to more functional arguments as well. In context, this means that arguments about the value of political supervision will have to be weighed against arguments for keeping some matters "out of politics." This flexible approach surely gives rise to a lack of predictability in constitutional law, as its critics contend; but, at least some of the time, the Court seems to regard uncertainty as a price that it must pay if it is to accommodate new structural arrangements in the administrative state.

CHAPTER III

THE SCOPE OF JUDICIAL REVIEW

The courts' review of agency action (or inaction) furnishes an important set of controls on administrative behavior; indeed, these are the controls that are most often at issue in administrative law. Unlike the political oversight controls, which generally influence entire programs or basic policies, judicial review regularly operates to provide relief for the individual person who is harmed by a particular agency decision. Judicial review also differs from the political controls in that it attempts to foster reasoned decisionmaking, by requiring the agencies to produce supporting facts and rational explanations. Thus, judicial oversight may work at cross-purposes with the oversight activities of the political branches, which depend heavily on pressure, bargaining, and compromise rather than on reasoned analysis. Yet judicial review can also serve as an essential supplement to political controls on administration: one of its major functions is to assure that the agency is acting in accord with the will of the political branches, as expressed in the enabling legislation. At the same time, judicial review may contribute to the political legitimacy of bureaucratic regulation, by providing an independent check on the validity of administrative decisions.

Like the regulatory process, judicial review has evolved over a period of years into a complex and not completely coherent system. A series of statutory, constitutional, and judicial doctrines have been developed to define the proper boundaries on judicial oversight of administration. In some areas, the courts may lack institutional competence to review an administrative action because the decision in question is political, or the plaintiff is asking the court to render an advisory opinion; in other instances, the court may decline to intervene until the administrative process has had a chance to run its course. On the whole, however, the trend in the recent judicial decisions and in modern statutes like the APA is to make judicial review more widely and easily available. This trend, and its limits, will be examined in Chapter 10 of this text.

Where judicial review is available, the question then becomes: how far can the court go in examining the agency decision? Technically, this issue is known as "scope of review" and, as Professor Davis has observed, the scope of review for a particular administrative decision may range from zero to a hundred percent. That is, the reviewing court may be completely precluded from testing the merits of an agency action, or it may be free to decide the issues de novo, with no deference to the agency's determination. Usually, however, the function of the reviewing court falls somewhere between these extremes.

Inherent in judicial review are many functional limitations. It is designed only to maintain minimum standards, not to assure an optimal or perfect decision. Thus, above the threshold of minimum fairness and rationality, the agencies may still make unsatisfactory decisions or use poor procedures. Even a judicial reversal may have little impact on administrative policy, if there are strong bureaucratic or political reasons for the agency to persist in its view. On remand, the agency may simply produce a better rationalization for its action, or reach the same result using different procedures, or misinterpret the court's directives (perhaps intentionally). And, of course, there are many decisions in which judicial review is not even sought. Judicial review is expensive and slow, and the outcome is never certain. These factors often combine to prevent parties from bringing even a meritorious claim, particularly when the person aggrieved is not wealthy or does not have a large financial stake in the outcome. Yet, despite the "limited office" of judicial review, it is generally regarded as the most significant safeguard available to curb excesses in administrative action.

A. LAW, FACT, AND DISCRETION

To understand the complex assortment of administrative law doctrines on judicial review, one must begin with the realization that most administrative decisions result from a series of determinations on the agency's part. Typically, an agency starts by *interpreting the law* it is supposed to implement; it *finds facts* about the situation it will address; and it *uses discretion* in applying the law to the factual situation that it has found to exist. These distinctions matter because the courts will review some types of determinations more intensively than others.

These same distinctions are reflected in 5 U.S. C.A. § 706, the Administrative Procedure Act's scope of review provision. Section 706(2) lists a variety of grounds on which an agency decision can be reversed. Two clauses deal exclusively with questions of law: whether the Constitution has been violated (§ 706(2)(B)), and whether the agency has exceeded its statutory authority (§ 706(2)(C)). Two other clauses deal exclusively with fact issues: § 706(2)(E) codifies the "substantial evidence" test, which is most often applied in proceedings in which there has been a formal, trial-type hearing; and § 706(2)(F) provides for de novo fact review (a rarity in administrative law). Section 706(2)(A) contains the APA's "arbitrary and capricious" test, which, depending on the context, can involve legal, factual, or discretionary issues. Finally, § 706(2) (D) permits a court to reverse an agency because of procedural error. (Procedural issues are discussed in subsequent chapters of this book; the present chapter is concerned exclusively with judicial review of substantive issues.)

The general rule of thumb is that a reviewing court will give less deference to an agency's legal conclusions than to the agency's factual or discretionary determinations. Some of the reasons for this distinction can be briefly stated. The courts' relative independence in declaring the law is a natural outgrowth of their traditional role in the American legal system; in administrative law, as in other subject areas, courts have always been "the final authorities on issues of statutory construction." SEC v. Sloan, 436 U.S. 103, 118 (1978). This judicial independence, however, has to coexist with the reality that Congress regularly delegates broad authority to administrative agencies. Sometimes Congress does so explicitly; sometimes it delegates by merely leaving a statutory term openended, in the expectation that the agency will flesh out the legislation. In either case, judicial deference to the administrator's discretionary choices is considered essential: it allows the agency to exercise the kind of creativity that the legislature intended. Thus, the court has two tasks: to ensure, through a relatively intrusive examination of the agency's legal conclusions, that the agency does not exceed the outer bounds of the delegation; and also to ensure, through a more deferential examination of the agency's factual and discretionary determinations, that the delegated power is exercised in a rational fashion.

Of course, the scope of Congress' delegation is often indeterminate. Thus, the courts often look to additional policy arguments as they consider how ready they should be to overturn various agency findings and conclusions. These considerations tend to reinforce the practice of giving less deference on legal issues than on factual and discretionary issues.

One factor is the relative competence of the courts and the agencies. As a general matter, the courts ought to be at least as expert as the agencies in interpreting constitutional and statutory requirements, and they are comparatively disinterested. An agency may tend to misinterpret a jurisdictional limitation in order to expand its power and authority, for example, and full judicial review of legal issues can counteract this tendency toward bureaucratic empire building. On the other hand, when the agencies are dealing with highly technical issues of fact or policy—whether the airborne pollutants generated by leaded gasoline are absorbed by human beings in sufficient quantities to pose a health hazard, or whether emergency core cooling systems on nuclear reactors are adequate to prevent releases of radiation in certain hypothesized accidents—one would expect the courts, staffed by generalist lawyers, to be less well equipped to make the basic decision. Even if the issue is as simple as whether a welfare recipient has outside sources of income, however, the agency fact-finder who has heard the testimony and observed the demeanor of the witnesses may be in a better position to assess their credibility and decide where the truth lies.

Considerations of economy and efficiency are also pertinent. When a court announces an interpretation of the law, it sets forth a standard that an agency can apply in all future cases of the same general type. A one-time decision of this kind consumes few judicial resources. But if, in every individual case, the court were obliged to duplicate the agency's work in finding facts and applying the law to them, the burden on the courts would be enormous and the delays intolerable. The costs to the participants and the government would also be formidable.

Despite these theoretical and practical factors leading the courts to review legal issues more intensively than factual and discretionary issues, one must not overstate the differences in the rigor of the various standards of review. While courts regard themselves as the final authorities on legal questions, they do give significant deference to administrators' views in resolving those questions. On the other hand, judicial review of factual findings and exercises of discretion, although basically quite deferential, includes a significant supervisory role for the courts. Indeed, this latter type of review has become particularly probing in recent years. Nevertheless, distinctions between law, fact, and discretion are vital starting points if one is to make sense out of contemporary case law on scope of review.

While the importance of these distinctions is well recognized, courts sometimes have difficulty knowing how to classify particular agency findings. The most confusion seems to result from their efforts to review agencies' application of law to fact; this problem involves what are revealingly known as "mixed questions of law and fact." The courts' perplexity is understandable, because law-applying judgments are supposed to be reviewed about as deferentially as issues of fact, although they frequently call for judgments that are plainly more legal than factual. See, e.g., O'Leary v. Brown–Pacific–Maxon, Inc., 340 U.S. 504 (1951) (agency's conclusion that employee died "in the course of [his] employment" was reviewed as a finding of "fact," although the underlying factual circumstances were undisputed).

Furthermore, courts often seem to dispose of mixed questions in inconsistent ways. In NLRB v. Hearst Publications, Inc., 322 U.S. 111 (1944), the Board ruled that "newsboys" who sold Hearst newspapers on street corners were "employees" within the meaning of the National Labor Relations Act, and hence entitled to bargain collectively under the Act. The Supreme Court upheld the decision, but not by finding on its own authority that the newsboys were "employees." Instead, the Court said that its function as a reviewing court was "limited," because "the question [was] one of specific application of a broad statutory term." Three years later, the Court upheld the Board's decision that foremen could unionize, notwithstanding their ties to management. Packard Motor Car Co. v. NLRB, 330 U.S. 485 (1947). Here, however, the Court made no reference to the deferential standard of review mentioned in *Hearst,* even though the same statutory term "employee" was involved; the Court resolved the labor law question on its own authority.

The apparently contradictory approaches of these and similar decisions has long been a source of puzzlement and dissatisfaction. See Pittston Stevedoring Corp. v. Dellaventura, 544 F.2d 35 (2d Cir.1976) (protesting two lines of authority "which are analytically in conflict"), aff'd, 432 U.S. 249 (1977); NLRB v. Marcus Trucking Co., 286 F.2d 583 (2d Cir.1961) (classifying decisions involving mixed questions into categories with "fuzzy boundaries"). Other observers approve of the doctrinal uncertainties, on the ground that they give judges (and advocates) some room to maneuver, and to adjust the intensity of judicial scrutiny in particular cases to reflect factors such as the perceived competence of court and agency decisionmakers and the impact of the decision on affected interests.

Much of the confusion can be dispelled, however, by a careful analysis of the precise issues that comprise a "mixed question." An agency's application of law to fact requires it to make two distinct determinations: it must decide what legal constraints govern the problem at hand, and then it

must decide what action to take within those constraints. The former of these two steps involves a
determination of law—the kind of question on
which courts are the "final authorities." Only if
the agency's view survives a relatively independent
judicial examination does a court proceed to the
second step: the task of law application, in which
the reviewing court's function is considerably more
deferential.

Thus, in *O'Leary,* the Court first satisfied itself
that the agency had correctly understood its obligation under the federal workers' compensation law.
Since the agency had correctly appreciated that
the proper inquiry was whether the " 'obligations
or conditions' of employment create[d] the 'zone of
special danger' out of which the injury arose," the
Court was able to proceed to the next step and
review the agency's application of law with the
same kind of deference that it would have given to
a pure finding of fact. Similarly, in the *Hearst*
case, the Court first considered whether the
NLRB's understanding of its duty was consistent
with the congressional mandate. The Court answered this question on its own authority (just as
in *Packard*), agreeing with the Board that the
correct inquiry was whether the newsboys suffered
from economic conditions of a kind that deserved
labor law protection, not whether they would have
been considered "employees" at common law. Only because the Board had applied proper legal
standards, in the Court's view, did the Court pro-

ceed to the second step in the inquiry, where its function was "limited."

When closely analyzed, therefore, these decisions display a pattern that can serve as a general guide to scope of review problems. The reviewing court's first task is to consider, in a relatively independent fashion, whether the agency misapprehended its legal obligations. The principles by which the court should conduct this inquiry are discussed in the following section. If the agency decision survives this scrutiny, the next question is whether the agency applied the law in a rational (or "reasonable") way. Subsequent sections of the chapter explain this more deferential component of the reviewing court's job.

B. LEGAL ISSUES

As just explained, judicial review of an agency's legal rulings, such as statutory interpretations, is *relatively* independent. Nevertheless, the courts do show significant deference to administrative constructions, as the Supreme Court emphasized in Chevron U.S.A., Inc. v. NRDC, 467 U.S. 837 (1984). *Chevron* involved a challenge to the EPA's "bubble" policy, a new method of measuring discharges of industrial pollution. Adoption of the plan would have reduced the costs to manufacturers of installing pollution controls. The legality of the plan turned on whether the agency could define the Clean Air Act term "stationary source" to refer to an entire manufacturing plant, rather than an individual device within the plant. The Court upheld the policy, prescribing two inquiries that a reviewing court should conduct when reviewing an agency's construction of a statute. The first was whether "Congress has directly spoken to the precise question at issue." If so, the court would have to "give effect to the unambiguously expressed intent of Congress." However, if the statute were to prove "silent or ambiguous with respect to the specific issue," the remaining question was whether the agency's answer was "permissible"—or, as the Court also phrased it, a "reasonable interpretation."

Chevron is the most widely cited of a long line of cases requiring courts to defer to agencies' legal interpretations. Although this principle may seem anomalous in light of the courts' traditional supremacy in statutory interpretation, it is supported by a number of policies, including the following: (1) Agencies tend to be familiar with, and sophisticated about, the statutes they administer; they understand the relationships among various provisions, the practical implications of adopting one interpretation as opposed to another, etc. (2) As unforeseen problems develop in the administration of a complex regulatory scheme, the agency needs flexibility if it is to make the program function effectively. (3) As *Chevron* noted, an agency has ties to the incumbent administration, and thus is politically accountable for its choices in a way that a court cannot be. (4) Deference promotes uniformity in the law, because it makes reviewing courts scattered across the country less likely to adopt differing readings of a statute; instead, the view taken by a single centralized agency will usually control.

Yet the American legal system has never fully embraced these arguments. There remains a lingering feeling that administrative agencies cannot be trusted to be the final arbiters of their own power, that the courts' independence is a necessary check, and that courts are at least as competent as agencies in matters of legal interpretation. These sentiments became particularly evident in the early 1980's, when Congress nearly enacted the "Bumpers Amendment," a proposed amendment to the APA that would have eliminated, or sharply reduced, courts' duty to defer to administrative views on legal issues. The proposal failed, but the support that it attracted testifies to our society's unease about claims of bureaucratic expertise.

Because of this ambivalence, courts have striven to avoid carrying the principle of deference represented by *Chevron* too far. First, they have used considerable imagination in defining what *Chevron* calls the "precise question at issue." Second, they have remained willing to reject administrators' interpretations on the strength of their own analyses of the disputed statutory provisions.

1. *The "Precise Question at Issue."* There are many situations in which a court can properly hold that an agency neglected its statutory duties, even

though the legislature did not foresee the specific
policy issues that underlie the agency action.
Most statutory delegations of power direct an agency to take account of particular factors or interests
in making its decisions, and these instructions can
be enforced by reviewing courts.   In Citizens to
Preserve Overton Park, Inc. v. Volpe, 401 U.S. 402
(1971), the relevant statute provided that the Secretary of Transportation could not grant federal
funds to finance construction of highways through
public parks if a "feasible and prudent" alternative
route existed.   The Court gave the seemingly broad
term "prudent" a stringent interpretation that limited the Secretary's discretion.   The Court reasoned that the legislature had given primary importance to the preservation of park land; thus,
the Secretary could not approve a route through a
park unless he found that alternatives presented
"unique problems" or would impose cost and community disruption of "extraordinary magnitude." [1]
Similarly, the Court in the *Benzene* case found that
the Occupational Safety and Health Act required
the Secretary of Labor to find that a given toxic
substance created a "significant risk" to workers
before he could regulate it.   Industrial Union
Dep't, AFL–CIO v. American Petroleum Inst., 448

---

1.   Although the opinion did not explain why it did not give
the Transportation Department's more permissive interpretation the usual deference, the Court may have felt that an
agency that had been established for the purpose of building
highways might not be fully attentive to Congress's environmental concerns.

U.S. 607 (1980). If the "precise question" raised by a party is whether the agency adhered to the statutorily relevant factors, a negative answer on the court's part would warrant reversal pursuant to the first step of *Chevron.*

Moreover, when a statute directs an agency to consider certain factors in making a particular type of decision, it may implicitly prohibit the administrator from taking other factors into account. A classic example is Addison v. Holly Hill Fruit Prods. Co., 322 U.S. 607 (1944): the Court remanded a regulation of the Wage–Hour Administrator classifying companies on the basis of size, because the underlying statute had required the Administrator to classify them on the basis of geography only. Similarly, in a follow-up case to *Benzene,* the Court held that the Secretary has a statutory duty to protect workers from dangerous toxic substances to the maximum extent that is technologically and economically feasible; therefore, the Secretary would not be free to rely on a cost-benefit analysis in setting the level of protection. American Textile Mfrs. Ass'n v. Donovan, 452 U.S. 490 (1981). In this type of case, the "precise question at issue" could be whether the agency's decision rested on a factor that Congress had clearly indicated should be irrelevant.

2. *"Unambiguous" Intents and "Unreasonable" Interpretations.* Once a court has identified the "precise question at issue," it must decide how much significance the agency's view should carry

pursuant to *Chevron*. In the language of the Court's opinion, when is an agency's interpretation "unreasonable" or one that Congress has addressed "unambiguously"?

On its face, *Chevron* did not impose an extremely strong level of deference: the Court acknowledged that "the judiciary is the final authority on issues of statutory construction." But many observers believe that courts are even less hesitant about discerning "unambiguous" mandates in regulatory laws than one would expect from a reading of the *Chevron* opinion. In one case, for example, the Federal Reserve Board attempted to regulate financial institutions that offered "NOW accounts." As a matter of practice, these firms permitted their customers to withdraw funds from the accounts on demand. But the Board's statutory jurisdiction extended only to institutions that offered checking accounts from which depositors had a "legal right" to withdraw funds on demand. The Court held that the firms' voluntary practice simply could not be equated with a "legal right" to payment on demand. Board of Govs. v. Dimension Fin. Corp., 474 U.S. 361 (1986). The Court thought the statute so clear that no claim of expertise could overcome that meaning.

Not all rejections of agency interpretations rely so heavily on the "plain meaning" of the statutory language. *Chevron* itself said that courts may draw upon "traditional tools of construction," and in our legal system courts have traditionally inquired into the intent of Congress by looking at the overall structure of a statute, related provisions, the legislative history, and the underlying purposes of the statute. *Overton Park* and *Benzene* are examples of cases in which courts have creatively used what they regarded as the general purposes of regulatory legislation to identify a congressional intent that the agency had failed to observe. See also, e.g., Dole v. United Steelworkers of America, 110 S.Ct. 929 (1990) (rejecting Secretary's interpretation of statutory language largely on the basis of inferences drawn from other provisions of same Act). Moreover, the second step of the *Chevron* test allows reversal of an agency interpretation that is "unreasonable." As one court has explained, an agency interpretation should not be considered unreasonable in this sense merely because a reviewing court finds that some other interpretation would better promote the statute's goals; but if the agency's interpretation would actually frustrate Congress' goals, a reversal would be warranted. Continental Air Lines v. Department of Transp., 843 F.2d 1444, 1453 (D.C.Cir.1988). Courts also draw freely on traditional maxims of construction. For example, they may say that an otherwise reasonable agency interpretation must be rejected because it would raise a serious constitutional question and thus cannot be attributed to a statute without a "clear statement" from Congress. See Edward J. DeBartolo Corp. v. Florida Gulf Coast Bldg. & Constr. Trade Council, 485 U.S. 568 (1988).

Indeed, judges have been so ingenious at finding "unambiguous" statutory mandates and "frustrations" of congressional purposes that some writers suspect that the *Chevron* doctrine is a fraud: the courts invoke it when they wish to defer, and ignore it when they wish to go their own way. That assessment may be too cynical, but it seems fair to say that the *Chevron* opinion, if read in isolation, would give an exaggerated picture of the deference that courts actually give to administrative constructions.

3. *Variations in the Level of Deference.* A final complication in the *Chevron* doctrine is that courts appear to regard some administrative interpretations as worthy of more deference than others. One important variable is the nature of the agency's responsibilities. In a classic 1944 case, the Court examined the deference due to interpretations of the Administrator of the Fair Labor Standards Act. Skidmore v. Swift & Co., 323 U.S. 134 (1944). The Administrator had no delegated lawmaking authority, and thus courts were not bound by his interpretive guidelines.[2] Even so, said the

2. "Interpretive rules," like those discussed in *Skidmore,* are sometimes contrasted for scope of review purposes with "legislative rules." The latter, which implement a grant of delegated lawmaking power, are said to command much more deference from the courts. The distinction is somewhat oversimplified, however, because when a court considers whether a legislative rule is beyond statutory authority, it will examine congressional intent in about the same manner as when it reviews an interpretive rule. See, e.g., the opinions invalidating legislative rules in *Benzene, Addison,* and *Dimension,* discussed above.

Court, he did conduct investigations under the Act, issue guidelines, and initiate injunction actions. Therefore, courts should give significant weight to his interpretations, out of respect for the knowledge and experience that shaped them and the need for uniform standards governing the public and private sectors. Similarly, the Court has said that interpretations of the Truth in Lending Act by the staff of the Federal Reserve Board deserve great deference, because the staff has expertise in the highly technical issues raised by the Act and because Congress itself has provided that creditors who rely on staff interpretations will be immune from subsequent damage liability. Ford Motor Credit Corp. v. Milhollin, 444 U.S. 555 (1980). In contrast, courts have shown relatively little deference to administrative tribunals that have purely adjudicative duties, without any responsibility for making policy or managing the regulatory program. Pittston Stevedoring Corp. v. Dellaventura, 544 F.2d 35 (2d Cir.1976), aff'd, 432 U.S. 249 (1977).

Skidmore went on to say that the weight given to an individual interpretation would "depend on the thoroughness evident in its consideration, the validity of its reasoning, its consistency with earlier and later pronouncements, and all those factors which give it power to persuade." Applying this reasoning, courts have sometimes held that an agency's interpretation deserves little or no deference if it is in conflict with the agency's previous, long-held views. See, e.g., General Electric Co. v.

Gilbert, 429 U.S. 125 (1976); NLRB v. Bell Aerospace Co., 416 U.S. 267 (1974).

In summary, the *Chevron* doctrine is less absolute and more complex than it would at first appear to be. Properly understood, however, it plays a useful and influential role in administrative law. Its concepts are also important when the court is construing a legal norm other than a statute; but there are significant variations. On constitutional questions, judges rarely display any deference at all to administrative views. On the other hand, when an agency construes its own regulation, deference is said to be "even more clearly in order" than when the meaning of a statute is in dispute. See, e.g., Udall v. Tallman, 380 U.S. 1, 16 (1965).

C. SUBSTANTIAL EVIDENCE REVIEW

When an agency's legal premises survive judicial scrutiny, the reviewing court must go on to consider whether to sustain the agency's factual findings. The APA contains three standards of review that potentially can govern this inquiry. The "substantial evidence" test, 5 U.S.C.A. § 706(2)(E), comes into play in "a case subject to sections 556 and 557 of this title or otherwise reviewed on the record of an agency hearing provided by statute." In other words, it is triggered if the agency decision was made after a trial-type, on-the-record hearing (a "formal adjudication" or "rulemaking on a record"). In most other proceedings, the facts are reviewed under the "arbitrary and capricious" test of § 706(2)(A), although in a handful of cases the court finds the facts for itself in a de novo trial, as provided in § 706(2)(F). This section explains the substantial evidence test, the most traditionally recognized and easily comprehended of the three. This discussion will provide the groundwork for an analysis of the other two standards, which are considered at pp. 105–09 infra.

A court applying the substantial evidence test is supposed to assess the reasonableness of the agency's factfinding, and not find the "right" or "true" facts itself. The test is sometimes analogized to appellate review of jury verdicts: in this view, substantial evidence is "enough to justify, if the trial were to a jury, a refusal to direct a verdict when the conclusion sought to be drawn from it is one of fact for the jury." NLRB v. Columbian Enameling & Stamping Co., 306 U.S. 292, 300 (1939). Another frequently quoted formulation states that substantial evidence is "such relevant evidence as a reasonable mind might accept as adequate to support a conclusion." Consolidated Edison Co. v. NLRB, 305 U.S. 197, 229 (1938). These verbal glosses on the text of the APA are admittedly not very helpful in applying the substantial evidence test to particular cases. Perhaps the most that can be said is that a court reviewing agency action under the substantial evidence test should make sure that the agency has done a careful, workmanlike job of collecting and evaluating the available data—or, as Judge Leventhal put it, that the agency has taken a "hard look" at the important factual issues. When the action being reviewed is a rule rather than an order, however, other complications enter the picture, as discussed at pp. 115–17 infra.

In reviewing agency findings under the substantial evidence test, the court is obliged to consider the "whole record." Universal Camera Corp. v. NLRB, 340 U.S. 474 (1951). That is, the court is not supposed to look only for evidence that supports the agency's decision; it is required to consider all of the relevant evidence for and against the agency's findings, and determine whether they are within the zone of reasonableness. In the federal system, and in many states as well, uncorroborated hearsay can constitute substantial evidence. See, e.g., Richardson v. Perales, 402 U.S. 389 (1971) (hearsay reports of examining physicians were substantial evidence for denial of disability claim, even though opposed by live testimony on behalf of the claimant). The old "legal residuum rule," which required that there be a residuum of legally competent evidence to support agency findings, is now generally regarded as an overly technical doctrine which can work substantial injustice when hearsay is the only, or best, available evidence. See Carroll v. Knickerbocker Ice Co., 218 N.Y. 435, 113 N.E. 507 (1916) (workers' compensation claim denied because the only evidence that the injuries had been sustained on the job was statements by the injured worker, who had died as a result of his injuries).

Another question that can arise when courts review agency findings under the substantial evidence test is how the court should view an agency's reversal of an administrative law judge's initial decision. Section 557(b) of the APA gives the agency heads broad power to find the facts de novo when they are reviewing an initial decision. See pp. 277–78 infra. At the same time, however, § 557(c) declares that the initial decision is part of the official record of the proceeding, and the substantial evidence test requires the reviewing court to consider the "whole record." The *Universal Camera* decision relied on these provisions in explaining the proper role of the ALJ's decision during judicial review: The substantial evidence test applies to the agency's decision, not the ALJ's. However, since the ALJ's decision is part of the record, the reviewing court must consider it in evaluating the evidentiary support for the final agency decision. Thus, a contrary initial decision may undermine the support for the agency's ultimate determination. In this context, the weight to be accorded the ALJ's findings may depend upon the kind of issues that are involved in the proceeding. When the case turns on eyewitness testimony, as the *Universal Camera* case did, the initial decision should be given considerable weight: the ALJ was able to observe the demeanor of the witnesses and assess their credibility and veracity first hand. See, e.g., Penasquitos Village, Inc. v. NLRB, 565 F.2d 1074 (9th Cir.1977). On the other hand, if the decision depends primarily upon expert testimony or policy considerations, the ALJ's decision may deserve little deference; the agency heads may be the best equipped to deal with this kind of testimony, and the reviewing court should be less concerned about their reversal of the ALJ.

Of course, the substantial evidence test becomes meaningful only in conjunction with a substantive standard against which the agency's fact findings will be evaluated. An agency can sometimes lighten its evidentiary burdens, in effect, by interpreting the governing statute in a way that makes the requirements for a prima facie case very lenient. This device will be effective if (but only if) the court finds that the agency's interpretation of the statute is reasonable and consistent with the statutory purpose, as required by *Chevron.* See, e.g., NLRB v. Transportation Mgmt. Corp., 462 U.S. 393 (1983) (in "mixed motive" discharge cases, Board may put burden on employer to disprove causation in fact). Agencies often use rulemaking for this purpose. See pp. 296–300 infra.

D. ABUSE OF DISCRETION REVIEW

Once the reviewing court has found that the agency correctly understood the law and adopted a rational view of the facts, it must still consider whether the action was "arbitrary, capricious, an abuse of discretion, or otherwise not in accordance with law." 5 U.S.C.A. § 706(2)(A).[3] This inquiry is sometimes nicknamed review for "arbitrariness," sometimes review for "abuse of discretion," and sometimes "rational basis" review.

Supreme Court guidance as to the nature of abuse of discretion review has been sparse. For years, the Court's most prominent statement on the subject was a brief remark in Citizens to Preserve Overton Park, Inc. v. Volpe, 401 U.S. 402 (1971): the Court called for inquiry into "whether the decision was based on a consideration of the relevant factors and whether there has been a clear error of judgment." In Motor Vehicle Mfrs. Ass'n v. State Farm Mut. Auto. Ins. Co., 463 U.S. 29 (1983), the Court was a little more specific: "Normally, an agency rule would be arbitrary and capricious if the agency has relied on factors which Congress has not intended it to consider, entirely failed to consider an important aspect of the problem, offered an explanation for its decision that runs counter to the evidence before the agency, or is so implausible that it could not be ascribed to a difference in view or the product of agency expertise." Both formulas have been considered confusing. Generally speaking, the "relevant factors" for an administrative decision come from the underly-

3. In most cases in which the substantial evidence test does not apply, the court will also rely on § 706(2)(A) in reviewing the agency's fact findings. See pp. 105–09 infra. The present discussion, however, is concerned with the arbitrariness standard in its nonfactual aspect, which governs all reviewable agency actions.

ing statute; thus, both formulas create an overlap between arbitrariness review and the *legal* question of whether the agency acted beyond its statutory authority—a question that the court logically should confront *before* reaching the issue of arbitrariness. In any event, neither of these two formulas has been interpreted as stating an all-encompassing test of arbitrariness. On the contrary, the case law has established a number of other situations in which a reviewing court can properly hold that an agency has abused its discretion, including the following:

First, even when an administrator's discretionary decision is in accord with governing statutes, it may be unlawful if it is inconsistent with the agency's own rules. Since a legislative regulation has the "force of law," it is normally binding on an agency in the same way that a statute is. This point was at issue in litigation resulting from the famous "Saturday Night Massacre" incident. The Justice Department had issued formal regulations providing that the Watergate Special Prosecutor would not be removed from his duties "except for extraordinary improprieties on his part." Nevertheless, Acting Attorney General Bork followed President Nixon's directive to dismiss the prosecutor without cause. The court held that this violation of a valid administrative regulation made the firing illegal. Nader v. Bork, 366 F.Supp. 104 (D.D.C.1973). The court did not actually reinstate the prosecutor (in part because a successor had already been appointed), but its legal reasoning was later adopted by the Supreme Court in a closely related context. United States v. Nixon, 418 U.S. 683 (1974).

Second, departure from agency precedents embodied in prior adjudicative decisions can constitute an abuse of discretion, if the reasons for the failure to follow precedent are not adequately explained. See, e.g., Atchison, T. & S.F. Ry. v. Wichita Bd. of Trade, 412 U.S. 800 (1973); Contractors Transp. Corp. v. United States, 537 F.2d 1160 (4th Cir.1976). Differential treatment of parties who are similarly situated raises questions as to whether the agency is administering its program in a fair, impartial, and competent manner. However, reviewing courts have refrained from requiring agencies to follow precedent mechanically. Since conditions in a regulated industry may change rapidly and the agency often needs some latitude to adjust and develop its policies, rigid adherence to precedent would sometimes frustrate the objectives of the regulatory program. Furthermore, when one administration replaces another, it may have a legitimate desire to alter existing policies to fulfill what it sees as its political mandate. Thus, when a reviewing court finds that a particular administrative decision is inconsistent with the agency's own precedents, it will remand the matter to the agency for a fuller statement of reasons instead of reversing outright. If the agency supplies a reasonable explanation for its new direction, its action should survive review.

Third, an agency can abuse its discretion by breaching certain principles of judge-made law. Equitable estoppel is one such area, although the Supreme Court has confined this doctrine within very narrow limits. See pp. 186–88 infra. Res judicata and collateral estoppel may also limit an agency's discretion. In United States v. Stauffer Chem. Co., 464 U.S. 165 (1984), Stauffer secured a court decision rejecting an EPA interpretation of the Clean Air Act. When the agency tried to relitigate the identical issue against Stauffer in another court, the Supreme Court held that the agency was precluded by collateral estoppel. On the other hand, in United States v. Mendoza, 464 U.S. 154 (1984), the Court held that collateral estoppel may not be asserted against the United States by persons who were not parties to the earlier case. The Court explained that to allow such "nonmutual" collateral estoppel "would substantially thwart the development of important questions of law by freezing the first final decision rendered on a particular legal issue." [4]

4. *Mendoza*'s suggestion that the law should develop gradually, through litigation in multiple forums, has been read as indirectly supporting the practice of "nonacquiescence," by which an agency declines to give stare decisis effect to lower court decisions with which it disagrees. Too much nonacquiescence, however, would interfere with the courts' ability to prevent an agency from violating its statutory mandate. The practice is generally upheld, but is considered questionable when an agency adheres to its legal position in a case that could

Fourth, a court will sometimes hold that a particular remedy is too harsh, if the agency has not explained satisfactorily why it did not choose a less drastic sanction. See, e.g., Jacob Siegel Co. v. FTC, 327 U.S. 608 (1946) (remanding case in which FTC ordered company to abandon allegedly deceptive brand name but did not seriously consider whether an informational label would have been adequate). More specifically, courts may intervene when an agency adopts a retroactive decision, if they think that the public interest in enforcement is outweighed by the unfairness of imposing a sanction for conduct that the respondent had reasonably believed to be lawful. See, e.g., NLRB v. E & B Brewing Co., 276 F.2d 594 (6th Cir.1960), cert. denied, 366 U.S. 908 (1961). Still, review of an agency's remedial decisions tends to be fairly deferential: usually courts are reluctant to second-guess the agency's choice of sanctions, which falls close to the core of the executive branch's enforcement discretion. See Butz v. Glover Livestock Comm'n Co., 411 U.S. 182 (1973) (upholding strict sanction).

Finally, courts measure agency actions against a loosely defined "reasoned decisionmaking" standard. Its classic articulation was by Judge Leventhal in Greater Boston Television Corp. v. FCC, 444 F.2d 841, 850–52 (D.C.Cir.1970), cert. de-

only be reviewed in a circuit that has already rejected the agency's stance. When the Social Security Administration made frequent use of the latter kind of nonacquiescence in the administration of its disability benefits program in the 1980's, it was widely criticized.

nied, 403 U.S. 923 (1971): the court will intervene if it "becomes aware, especially through a combination of danger signals, that the agency has not really taken a 'hard look' at the salient problems, and has not genuinely engaged in reasoned decision-making." This inquiry is clearly susceptible of abuse by the courts, which might easily use a critique of an agency's reasoning process as an excuse to overturn a policy judgment with which they simply happen to disagree. Notwithstanding its dangers, however, the "reasoned decisionmaking" standard, also known as the "hard look" doctrine, is firmly established. It has been especially prominent in review of rulemaking, as will be seen in a later section. See pp. 110–13 infra.

E. FINDINGS AND REASONS

The review standards for legal, factual, and discretionary determinations, as set forth in the preceding three sections, all presuppose that the court will examine the agency's reasoning with a good deal of care. In practice, however, agencies often take action without explaining the precise grounds on which they have made their determinations. To overcome this difficulty, the courts have developed the device of remanding administrative actions to the agency for fuller explanation. See, e.g., Schaffer Transp. Co. v. United States, 355 U.S. 83 (1957). The courts often remark that they do not need great detail; the basic requirement is that the agency reveal enough of its reasoning to permit meaningful judicial review. (At times, however, it appears that no amount of explanation would suffice, because the court is using a remand for "reconsideration" as a diplomatic way of expressing its disapproval of the agency's substantive policy.)

Actually, a focus on the agency's reasoning is inescapable, because it is axiomatic that a discretionary agency action may be upheld *only* on the strength of the agency's own rationale. In the leading case, the Supreme Court remanded an SEC order disapproving a corporate reorganization plan, because the Commission had reasoned from incorrect legal premises. SEC v. Chenery Corp., 318 U.S. 80 (1943) (*Chenery I*). In doing so, however, the Court indicated that it might uphold the SEC's position if the Commission justified it on a lawful basis; and when the SEC issued a revised opinion, the Court did exactly that. SEC v. Chenery Corp., 332 U.S. 194 (1947) (*Chenery II*). The reason why a reviewing court may not affirm on a basis other than the agency's is that only the agency has authority to make discretionary determinations that Congress has delegated to it. Similarly, "courts may not accept appellate counsel's post hoc rationalizations for agency action," Burlington Truck Lines v. United States, 371 U.S. 156, 168–69 (1962), because it is the agency heads, not the attorneys who defend their decisions in court, who have the legislatively conferred responsibility to make discretionary judgments on regulatory policy.

Although under *Chenery* the courts must carefully scrutinize administrative opinions, they generally will not probe for motives hidden beneath the surface of those opinions. The principle was established in lengthy litigation involving ratesetting by the Secretary of Agriculture. Initially, the Court authorized the district court to investigate allegations that the Secretary had issued his decision without reading the briefs or considering the evidence. After remand, however, the Court reconsidered, declaring that "it was not the function of the court to probe the mental processes of the Secretary in reaching his conclusions if he gave the hearing that the law required." Morgan v. United States, 304 U.S. 1, 18 (1941) (*Morgan II*). The Court stated this point even more forcefully when the *Morgan* controversy came before it for a fourth time several years later. Just as a judge cannot be deposed or cross-examined about his decisions, "so the integrity of the administrative process must be equally respected." United States v. Morgan, 313 U.S. 409, 422 (1941) (*Morgan IV*). Without this presumption of regularity, agency officials would constantly be called away from their duties to answer questions about their decisions.

Special problems arise, however, when an agency acts without issuing any explanation at all for its decision. In that situation, said the Supreme Court in the familiar *Overton Park* case, the reviewing court must make a factual inquiry into the agency's rationale, either by obtaining affidavits from the officials who made the decision or by calling them into court to testify. (On remand, the district court conducted a 25–day trial to determine why the Secretary of Transportation had approved a highway route through Overton Park.) On the other hand, *Overton Park* made clear—and Camp v. Pitts, 411 U.S. 138 (1973), reaffirmed— that where an agency *does* provide a contemporaneous explanation for its decision, the *Morgan* rule is still good law; the agency opinion must be taken at face value unless the challenger makes a "strong showing of bad faith or improper behavior" (a standard that is seldom met). Obviously, the net effect of these cases is to give agency decisionmakers a strong incentive to write opinions to accompany their actions, even when procedural law does not compel them to do so.

F. REVIEW ON THE ADMINISTRATIVE RECORD

Most of the scope of review principles discussed in preceding sections were originally developed for courts to use when an agency acts after formal, trial-type proceedings. For cases in which there is no such formality, including most rulemaking cases, additional principles must be examined. Since the substantial evidence test normally does not apply, the court could potentially turn to either of two other provisions of § 706 as the basis for reviewing the agency's fact findings: it could review the facts de novo, without any deference to the agency's findings (§ 706(2)(F)); or it could review the agency's findings pursuant to the arbitrariness standard (§ 706(2)(A)).

Citizens to Preserve Overton Park v. Volpe, 401 U.S. 402 (1971), definitively established the relative scope of these two clauses. The Court held that an informal action, such as the Secretary of Transportation's highway funding decision, must be reviewed for abuse of discretion under § 706(2)(A), on the basis of "the full administrative record that was before the Secretary at the time he made his decision." Although the Court asserted that the APA required this approach, scholars agree that the concept of an exclusive "administrative record" for review of informal agency actions was not contemplated by the framers of the APA. Prior to *Overton Park,* any facts that the courts needed in order to review such actions were typically developed through judicial trial.

At the same time, the Court accomplished a drastic narrowing of § 706(2)(F). Relying on what is generally agreed to have been a misreading of the legislative history of the APA, the *Overton Park* opinion asserted that independent judicial factfinding pursuant to clause (2)(F) is available in only two circumstances: where "the action is adjudicatory in nature and the agency factfinding procedures are inadequate," or where "issues that were not before the agency are raised in a proceeding to enforce nonadjudicatory agency action." Scholars have puzzled about what these phrases might mean; but the debate has little practical significance, because judicial decisions finding *either* of the two conditions applicable are virtually nonexistent. De novo review of the substance of agency actions has essentially vanished from administrative law, except in the handful of situations in which a statutory or constitutional guarantee outside of the APA requires such treatment. For example, the Court early held that an individual facing deportation has a constitutional right to an independent judicial decision as to whether he is a citizen. Ng Fung Ho v. White, 259 U.S. 276 (1922). Congress has since codified this holding. 8 U.S.C.A. § 1105(a)(5). A case from the same era called for de novo review of whether a ratesetting order was confiscatory. Ohio Valley Water Co. v. Ben Avon Borough, 253 U.S. 287 (1920). This holding may still be valid, but it is unimportant, because the constitutional limits on ratemaking have become very lenient today. See also p. 30 supra.

The *Overton Park* holding that review would take place on an "administrative record" was soon extended to informal rulemaking cases. Under the prior practice, courts were willing to presume the existence of facts supporting the validity of an administrative rule, unless the challenging party proved at trial that the rule was arbitrary. Pacific States Box & Basket Co. v. White, 296 U.S. 176

(1935).   Since any litigation over the factual basis of the rule would occur in court, agency decisionmakers did not take time *during* the rulemaking proceeding to compile a "record" for judicial review.   After *Overton Park,* however, both agencies and regulated parties came to realize that they would have to make their case at the administrative level, because the reviewing court would disregard any evidence submitted subsequently.   See United States v. Nova Scotia Food Prods. Corp., 568 F.2d 240 (2d Cir.1977) (in proceeding to enforce FDA rule, courts refused to examine new evidence casting doubt on need for rule).

In an informal rulemaking proceeding, the administrative record will generally consist of the notice of proposed rulemaking, the final rule and accompanying statement of basis and purpose, the comments filed by the public, and any unprivileged working papers prepared by the agency itself.   The rule will pass muster under the arbitrary and capricious test if this record contains evidence that could lead a reasonable person to accept the factual premises of the regulation (taking into account the evidence submitted by opponents of the rule).[5] The agency's obligation to assemble such evidence has turned modern rulemaking into a more formalized, adversarial process than the framers of the

5.   However, the agency need not supply complete record support for scientific conclusions and other propositions that are inherently unprovable.   See pp. 113–15 infra.   Also, under some circumstances an agency can dispense with proof by invoking the doctrine of official notice.   See pp. 303–08 infra.

APA anticipated. However, *Overton Park*'s administrative record concept was an essential step in the development of "hard look" review of rulemaking. Intensive scrutiny of an agency's reasoning process would scarcely be meaningful if the agency did not have to defend its exercise of discretion by reference to facts that were actually before it at the time the rule was written.

G. REVIEW OF RULES

On a general level, most of the scope of review principles described above are fully applicable to judicial review of rules. Like all other forms of agency action reviewed under the APA, rules must be consistent with the agency's statutory mandate (§ 706(2)(C)), the Constitution (§ 706(2)(B)) and procedural requirements (§ 706(2)(D)). They also must not be "arbitrary and capricious" (§ 706(2)(A)), a standard that is breached if the agency lacked support in the administrative record for its factual assumptions, or otherwise misused its discretion.[6]

However, courts have had to struggle to apply these standards satisfactorily in the rulemaking context. In those situations, many of the central issues concern policy judgments and "legislative facts," which often are not susceptible of "proof" in the same way as the facts in a typical adjudicative

6. Of course, in the relatively rare case of a rule issued after a trial-type hearing, the substantial evidence test (§ 706(2)(E)) would also apply.

proceeding are. Moreover, the issues involved in the rulemaking proceeding can be highly technical, notably in the newer fields of health and safety regulation. Finally, an informal rulemaking record is fundamentally different from the adjudicative records that judges have traditionally reviewed. As Judge McGowan noted, an informal rulemaking record "is indistinguishable in its content from [materials collected in] the proceedings before a legislative committee hearing on a proposed bill—letters, telegrams, and written statements from proponents and opponents, including occasional oral testimony not subjected to adversary cross-examination." In reviewing this kind of record, there is a risk that the judges will "vote their policy preferences in the same manner as does the legislator" and "thereby risk nullification of the principle that democracies are to be run in accordance with the majority will." McGowan, Congress and the Courts, 62 A.B.A.J. 1588, 1589–90 (1976). Thus, courts have had to develop a method of review that would enable them to prevent abuses of power in the rulemaking process (which agencies are using more and more frequently to implement their mandates), but that would not permit them to make essentially legislative or political judgments.

1. *Hard Look Review.* In Automotive Parts & Accessories Ass'n v. Boyd, 407 F.2d 330 (D.C.Cir. 1968), the court faced up to some of these complications. Judge McGowan stated that judicial review

of rulemaking "need be no less searching and strict [than in a case of formal adjudication], but because it is addressed to different materials, it inevitably varies from the adjudicatory model. The paramount objective is to see whether the agency, given an essentially legislative task to perform, has carried it out in a manner calculated to negate the dangers of arbitrariness and irrationality. . . ." To that end, the agency's statement of basis and purpose (the written explanation accompanying the rule) must "enable us to see what major issues of policy were ventilated by the informal proceedings and why the agency reacted to them as it did." In other words, the court would examine whether the agency had engaged in what Judge Leventhal was soon to call "reasoned decisionmaking," including whether the agency explained its position cogently and thoroughly, and whether it responded to significant criticisms by participants in the rulemaking proceeding.

The rule reviewed in the *Automobile Parts* case itself survived this type of scrutiny. But in other cases, where an agency had stated its position obscurely or failed to answer cogent criticisms, regulations fell victim to the growing power of the "hard look." For example, in National Tire Dealers & Retreaders Ass'n v. Brinegar, 491 F.2d 31 (D.C.Cir.1974), the court set aside a safety standard governing retreaded tires. Under the regulation, safety information had to be permanently molded into the tire, rather than disclosed on a removable label. The Secretary had barely justified this requirement; and, despite much record evidence that permanent molding would be prohibitively expensive, he had asserted without record support that the requirement was "practicable," as the statute required it to be. See also Kennecott Copper Co. v. EPA, 462 F.2d 846 (D.C.Cir.1972) (remanding to allow Administrator to explain why he had set a limit on sulphur oxide emissions at a level that was lower than any of the studies in the record had shown to be dangerous); Portland Cement Ass'n v. Ruckelshaus, 486 F.2d 375 (D.C.Cir.1973), cert. denied, 417 U.S. 921 (1974) (remanding cement dust regulations because EPA had failed to respond to significant methodological criticisms); United States v. Nova Scotia Food Prods. Corp., 568 F.2d 240 (2d Cir.1977) (remanding FDA rules that instructed manufacturers how to prevent botulism in whitefish, because agency had ignored cogent comments that its approach would render the product commercially unsaleable).

Ultimately, the Supreme Court gave its approval to the developing case law insisting on reasoned decisionmaking in Motor Vehicle Mfrs. Ass'n v. State Farm Mut. Auto. Ins. Co., 463 U.S. 29 (1983). In 1981, the Department of Transportation rescinded a 1977 rule requiring the installation of "passive restraints" in automobiles—either airbags or automatic seatbelts. The agency explained this action by saying that "detachable" automatic seatbelts, the industry's favored method of meeting the requirement, would not necessarily promote safety, because consumers would detach them. The *State Farm* Court found two flaws in this explanation. First, the agency's doubts about the effectiveness of automatic seatbelts ignored the factor of inertia: consumers who would not bother to fasten manual belts might well allow self-fastening belts to remain in place. The agency had to address this crucial point. Second, even if those belts were ineffective, the agency did not explain why it had not fallen back on a requirement of airbags or "nondetachable" seatbelts, both of which the agency itself had found in 1977 to be effective.

The Court in *State Farm* was careful to point out that the alternatives ignored by the agency were clearly presented on the record, and that the administrator was reversing a settled course of action. It also emphasized that a rule is not arbitrary simply because there is no direct evidence in support of the agency's conclusion. But the agency must explain the evidence that is available and "provide a rational connection between the facts found and the choice made."

2. *Scientific Uncertainty.* Regulations in highly technical areas have proved troublesome for courts that must review them. The problems in this area surfaced in Ethyl Corp. v. EPA, 541 F.2d 1 (D.C.Cir.) (en banc), cert. denied, 426 U.S. 941 (1976), which upheld an EPA rule reducing the use of lead additives in gasoline on the ground that the

additives created a health hazard. Judge Bazelon, in a concurring opinion, argued that judicial review of the facts should be extremely restrained, because "substantive review of mathematical and scientific evidence by technically illiterate judges is dangerously unreliable." At most, reviewing courts could assure rationality indirectly, by making sure that the agency had strictly complied with applicable procedural requirements and had exposed its factual premises to public scrutiny. Judge Leventhal, however, cautioned against judicial abdication: court review of the substance of agency rules, even in technical areas, was crucial to the legitimacy of agency rulemaking. Yet even Leventhal joined the opinion of the majority, written by Judge Wright, which demonstrated keen awareness of the importance of judicial restraint in such cases. First, the court interpreted the Clean Air Act permissively: the EPA's mandate to regulate emissions that "will endanger" public health was satisfied if the agency showed a significant risk of harm, not necessarily proof of actual harm. Second, the court showed a willingness to defer to the agency's factfinding, so long as it was not based on "hunches" or "wild guesses." Judge Wright concluded: "Where a statute [delegating rulemaking authority] is precautionary in nature, the evidence difficult to come by, uncertain, or conflicting because it is on the frontiers of scientific knowledge, . . . and the decision that of an expert administrator, we will not demand rigorous step-by-step proof of cause and effect."

The Supreme Court has also called for judicial restraint in this area. In the *Benzene* case, although the plurality read the statute to require a showing of significant risk before toxic substances could be regulated, it also concluded that the Secretary was not required to support his finding "with anything approaching scientific certainty"; the finding of risk need only be supported by "a body of reputable scientific thought." (The dissenters would have allowed even more leeway to the Secretary.) Similarly, in Baltimore Gas & Elec. Co. v. NRDC, 462 U.S. 87 (1983), the Court remarked that "a reviewing court must generally be at its most deferential" when an agency is "making predictions, within its area of special expertise, at the frontiers of science." Accordingly, the Court sustained an NRC rule that permitted licensing boards to ignore the possibility of environmental harm from long-term storage of spent nuclear fuel, despite considerable uncertainty about whether a safe method of storing nuclear waste would ever be found.

3. *Substantial Evidence Review.* In several regulatory statutes enacted in the early 1970's, such as the Occupational Safety and Health Act, Congress provided that agency rules should be reviewed under a substantial evidence test. This trend evidently resulted from a desire for particularly probing judicial review; historically, the substantial evidence test had been regarded as significantly more rigorous than the arbitrariness test,

which ordinarily governs rulemaking. But this approach created an "anomaly," Judge McGowan later wrote, because these new rulemaking statutes generally contemplated "informal" (notice-and-comment) rulemaking, while the substantial evidence test has traditionally been understood as a test for judging the evidence in a record compiled during a trial-type hearing. Industrial Union Dep't, AFL–CIO v. Hodgson, 499 F.2d 467 (D.C.Cir. 1974). He went on to say that, no matter how the standard of review was phrased, a court could not be expected to demand solid factual support for predictive or scientific fact findings, let alone for policy judgments. Congress now seems to have ceased creating this type of statutory provision— partly because it has become more aware of the inherent limits of the judicial function, as explained by Judge McGowan, and partly because the "hard look" that courts provide under the arbitrariness test has become just as intrusive as the rigorous review that Congress had hoped to achieve through a substantial evidence test. See National Lime Ass'n v. EPA, 627 F.2d 416, 452 (D.C.Cir. 1980) (in 1977 revision of Clean Air Act, substantial evidence test for rulemaking was rejected as unnecessary).

Indeed, courts increasingly see a "convergence" between the arbitrariness test and the substantial evidence test. As Judge (now Justice) Scalia explained in Association of Data Processing Serv. Orgs. v. Board of Govs., 745 F.2d 677 (D.C.Cir.1984), the real difference between the two tests is that in substantial evidence review the court seeks support for factual findings in the record of a formal hearing, while in arbitrariness review it does not. But, he continued, this does not mean that an agency needs more factual support to pass one test than to pass the other. The *Data Processing* analysis is likely to prevail in the long run. Traditionally, the substantial evidence test was regarded as a more stringent standard because it occurred on a record. But now that informal actions are reviewed on the "administrative record," that functional distinction has lost its force. Moreover, agencies are now using informal rulemaking to implement policies that formerly would have been handled through trial-type proceedings, and courts perceive no reason why this shift in procedure should result in a diminished scope of review on substantive issues. In any event, the debate over which test is stricter is somewhat fruitless. Both tests really contemplate a standard of "reasonableness," which no one can define with precision. Under either test, ultimately, the court is likely to be influenced by a variety of subtle factors, such as the nature and complexity of the issues involved, the consequences of an erroneous determination, the agency's reputation for competence and fairness, and the judge's philosophy of judicial review.

H. AGENCY INACTION AND DELAY

The APA's definition of "agency action" includes "failure to act." 5 U.S.C.A. § 551(13). Nevertheless, when courts are asked to review administrative inaction, they are usually much more deferential than when affirmative acts are challenged. A modern example of this attitude is Heckler v. Chaney, 470 U.S. 821 (1985). There, eight death row prisoners wrote to the Food and Drug Administration, contending that states' use of lethal drug injections in human executions violated the Food, Drug, and Cosmetics Act. They urged the FDA to bring suit to stop this practice, but the FDA refused. The Supreme Court declined to intervene, declaring broadly that an agency's refusal to initiate an enforcement proceeding is "presumptively unreviewable." Although this holding rested in part on an analogy to the tradition of prosecutorial discretion in the criminal justice system, the Court laid greater emphasis on some of the practical difficulties that judicial review of nonenforcement decisions can entail. Enforcing agencies usually do not have sufficient personnel or funds to pursue all possible violations of the laws they administer. As they allocate their investigative and litigating resources, they must make judgments about such factors as the seriousness of the offense, the nature and quality of proof available, the likelihood of obtaining a consent settlement or a favorable decision, the deterrent value of a prosecution, and the "opportunity cost" of other cases that will not be brought if resources are invested in this one. Courts have little competence to evaluate the rationality of discretionary choices such as these.[7]

The *Chaney* opinion added, however, that when Congress lays down specific guidelines cabining an agency's enforcement discretion, the court can require the agency to respect its legislative mandate. In this regard, the Court cited with approval Dunlop v. Bachowski, 421 U.S. 560 (1975), in which it had upheld judicial review of the Secretary of Labor's refusal to challenge a union election under the Labor–Management Reporting and Disclosure Act. In *Dunlop* the Act itself had directed the Secretary to bring suit if he found probable cause to believe that a violation had occurred.

Although the lower courts have adhered to the core holding of *Chaney,* they have usually striven not to extend it beyond its necessary limits. See Levin, *Understanding Unreviewability in Administrative Law*, 74 Minn.L.Rev. 689 (1990). For example, when a plaintiff contends that an agency's nonenforcement decision resulted from a misunderstanding of the substantive law, rather than from an exercise of managerial judgment, the courts have consistently been willing to reach

7. For similar reasons, courts have held that an agency may bring an enforcement action against one suspected violator, without immediately pursuing similarly situated competitors; this enforcement strategy will stand in the absence of a "patent abuse of discretion." Moog Industries, Inc. v. FTC, 355 U.S. 411 (1958); see F.T.C. v. Universal–Rundle Corp., 387 U.S. 244 (1967) (similar ruling).

these legal issues. See, e.g., UAW v. Brock, 783 F.2d 237 (D.C.Cir.1986). Similarly, courts have adhered to their pre-*Chaney* view that an agency's refusal to institute a rulemaking proceeding is subject to judicial review. American Horse Protection Ass'n v. Lyng, 812 F.2d 1 (D.C.Cir.1987) (reaffirming WWHT, Inc. v. FCC, 656 F.2d 807 (D.C.Cir. 1981)). They do insist, however, that in this latter situation the agency will be reversed "only in the rarest and most compelling of circumstances." Id. In practice, therefore, judicial oversight of agency inaction in the rulemaking context is probably not much more intrusive than it is in the context of individual enforcement decisions.

After a proceeding has been launched, participants may ask the courts to intervene if the agency does not render a decision within a reasonable period of time. Courts resolve unreasonable delay claims through a "rule of reason," balancing hardships to the agency and to the complaining party. Telecommunications Research & Action Center v. FCC, 750 F.2d 70 (D.C.Cir.1984). Nevertheless, courts try to remain sensitive to the agencies' problems of resource allocation, and so their responses usually take the form of exhortation rather than direct compulsion. See generally Eisner, *Agency Delay in Informal Rulemaking,* 3 Ad.L.J. 7 (1989).

I. CONCLUSION

In the final analysis, the scope of review standards examined in this chapter—both those of the APA and those created by case law—leave a great deal of discretion in the hands of individual judges. Phrases like "substantial evidence" and "arbitrary and capricious" can never be defined with precision, and courts have their own reasons for wanting to keep the governing standards rather vague. One explanation for this preference is that judges like to have flexibility to respond to the equities of individual fact patterns. Another explanation is that the courts disagree among themselves about the proper degree of deference that they should give to various administrative decisions. This disagreement, in turn, can be traced to differing assessments of the ultimate utility of judicial review in the control of agency action.

To some minds, judicial review should be highly prized for its contribution to the rule of law: it is the best means to ensure that agencies' policies adhere to the terms of their statutory mandates, and that individuals receive fair and evenhanded treatment in the implementation of those policies. On the other hand, overly intrusive judicial review is sometimes criticized for its undemocratic character. When courts use their review powers aggressively, they may undermine the agencies' ability to make legitimate responses to the will of the public. As the Court in *Chevron* observed, "federal judges—who have no constituency—have a duty to respect legitimate policy choices made by those who do."

Defenders of judicial review also emphasize that it can serve a quality control function, remedying carelessness and corner-cutting at the administrative level. Moreover, courts can supply a generalist perspective that single-mission agencies often lack. However, those who are more skeptical about the value of judicial review point out that administrative agencies possess technical sophistication and experience that courts simply cannot duplicate. They also note that the courts, with their limited sources of information, do not always grasp the realities of program administration that lurk in the background of some agency policy choices.

Supporters of judicial review also argue that the courts' openness to a wide variety of suitors is one of their strengths. Groups that obtain aid from the courts sometimes represent interests that the agency should have heeded at an earlier stage. And courts are often the only hope for individuals who lack access to the mechanisms of political oversight. Critics see the courts as too often serving as pawns in interest groups' campaigns of delay and obstructionism, sabotaging the coherence of orderly program administration. History records many incidents in which an agency simply gave up on a project because it was exhausted by efforts to overcome judicial roadblocks.

In the years ahead, these and other competing arguments will undoubtedly shape the continuing development of scope of review doctrine, as courts endeavor to maintain meaningful controls over administrative actions without usurping the functions that Congress intended the agencies to perform.

CHAPTER IV

ACQUIRING AND DISCLOSING INFORMATION

Without information, administrative agencies could not regulate industry, protect the environment, prosecute fraud, collect taxes, or issue grants. Good decisions require good data, and if an agency does not fully understand the nature of the problems confronting it or the consequences of possible actions, its programs are likely to be either unduly burdensome or ineffective. Indeed, one of the strongest arguments for "deregulating" major sectors of the economy is the claim that agencies often cannot learn enough about the regulated industry to make sound policy.

Much of the information needed to make the administrative process work is freely available from published sources, voluntary submissions by regulated persons and organizations, citizen complaints, and studies conducted by agency staff or outside parties. Frequently, however, the necessary information can be obtained only from members of the regulated industry or other private parties who are not willing to give it to the government. A substantial legal battle may then develop. Personal privacy and freedom from governmental intrusion have long been considered fundamental elements of liberty, and these interests are constitutionally protected by the Fourth Amendment's prohibition of unreasonable searches as well as the Fifth Amendment's ban on compulsory self-incrimination. The growth of regulatory and benefit programs in recent years has greatly increased the government's demand for sensitive private information, and the computerization of files has heightened popular fears that agencies may misuse personal data.

Beyond these legitimate concerns about abuse of official power, however, there are some strong practical incentives for regulated persons and firms to resist disclosure. Withholding requested information is often an effective way of avoiding unwanted regulation or delaying it; even if the agency ultimately succeeds in forcing disclosure, conditions may have changed sufficiently to make the data useless or irrelevant. Moreover, some of the data sought by the regulatory agencies may be commercially valuable material such as trade secrets, and companies may fear that information will "leak" from the agencies' files to their competitors. Cost is also an important factor in many situations where private parties refuse to provide information voluntarily. When the FTC ordered large manufacturing firms to provide detailed financial information broken down by product category or "line of business," some companies fought the demand through the courts for years, because they did not keep records according to the categories requested by the agency. As a result, it would have been extremely costly for them to generate the data from existing business records. See In re FTC Line of Business Report Litigation, 595 F.2d 685 (D.C.Cir.1978), cert. denied, 439 U.S. 958 (1978).

Just as agencies thrive on information, citizens have a vital need for information *from* the agencies. Many of the procedural protections found in judicial and administrative proceedings are designed to give interested persons a fair opportunity to discover, present, and challenge relevant information. In addition, disclosure of information about the government serves the interest of public and political accountability, by revealing areas where administration is ineffective and reform is necessary. Because of several disclosure statutes enacted during the 1960's and 1970's, a great deal of the business of government in the United States is open to public view, and much of the data on which agency decisions rest is available for the asking to interested citizens.

A. JUDICIAL CONTROLS ON INVESTIGATORY POWERS

The power to compel private parties to submit information, like other administrative powers, must be based upon a valid legislative delegation of authority, and the agency must observe the standards and procedures specified in the relevant statutes. Traditionally, however, Congress has granted the agencies wide discretion to investigate and compel disclosure of information; many statutes impose only minimal constraints on the agency's use of compulsory process. Another source of legal limitations on agency data gathering is the Constitution. Because the government's attempts to gather information can threaten constitutionally protected privacy interests, the agency's activities must be measured against the requirements of the Fourth and Fifth Amendments. Applying these established general principles has often proven difficult, however, because the agencies engage in widely diverse activities, and the constitutional protections, which were designed primarily to deal with criminal law enforcement proceedings, cannot be mechanically applied to all agency activities. Administrative inquiries may be directed towards an eventual criminal prosecution, as in the case of an IRS tax fraud investigation, but they may also be designed to support a civil penalty, or a cease and desist order, or the setting of rates for the future, or the formulation of general policy. Moreover, much of the work of the regulatory agencies takes place outside of formal proceedings. The Equal Employment Opportunity Commission mediates discrimination complaints; the Food and Drug Administration negotiates "voluntary" recalls of potentially hazardous food products; the Federal Reserve Board exercises continuing supervision over banks. The agency's (and the public's) need to compel disclosure of information may vary in each of these settings, and so also may the potential harm to the regulated if that power is unchecked. See generally Freedman, *Summary Ac-*

tion by Administrative Agencies, 40 U.Chi.L.Rev. 1 (1972).

Another source of difficulty is the fact that agencies use a variety of techniques for gathering data, and these techniques vary in their burdensomeness and intrusion on protected interests. In some Federal Trade Commission investigations, for example, the Commission can issue subpoenas for documents or testimony, or it can demand to inspect records in the office where they are kept, or it can require companies to fill out special "report orders"; in other instances, the FTC can issue "civil investigative demands" that are subject to different standards and procedures; and presiding officers in adjudicative proceedings can issue discovery orders much like those used in federal courts. Other agencies, particularly those enforcing health and safety regulations, have the power to inspect facilities and seize suspicious goods. As might be expected, the courts' attempts to adapt the constitutional protections to the administrative process have produced a large and not entirely consistent body of law.

A threshold question in disputes over agency access to information is how the party who is presented with an agency demand for records or other data may contest the legality of the request. In many agencies, rules or statutes explicitly provide a procedure similar to the motion to quash a subpoena that is used in the courts. When such a procedure is available, the party served with a subpoena must present her objections before the agency or she may be barred from raising them in the courts under the doctrine of exhaustion of administrative remedies. McClendon v. Jackson Television, 603 F.2d 1174 (5th Cir.1979); see also pp. 378–83 infra.

While courts can enforce their own subpoenas directly by use of the contempt power, most agencies cannot; they must bring an enforcement action and obtain a court order directing compliance with the subpoena. In this enforcement action, the party who is resisting disclosure may present her objections to the subpoena, and the court will review the legality of the agency's use of compulsory process. If the court upholds the subpoena, it will issue an order enforcing it, and a violation of this order is punishable as contempt of court. Thus, a party resisting an agency subpoena typically does not incur any risk of penalties or legal liability until after court review. On the other hand, some statutes do provide that a party who refuses to comply without just cause is subject to fines or criminal penalties from the time the agency subpoena is issued. See, e.g., Securities Exchange Act, 15 U.S.C.A. § 78u(c) (failure to comply with SEC subpoena is a misdemeanor). These immediate sanctions are rarely enforced, however, and a party can usually obtain judicial review of administrative subpoenas with no risk that substantial penalties will accrue. Of course, if the subpoena is directed to a third party, the "target" may have no remedy because she may not even know that she is under investigation. See SEC v. Jerry T. O'Brien, Inc., 467 U.S. 735 (1984) (SEC has discretion not to notify target).

B. SUBPOENAS: GENERAL PRINCIPLES

When a private party contests an agency's demand for records, testimony, or other information, the reviewing courts will test the legality of the agency's demand by applying general principles that have evolved to control the use of compulsory process. These basic standards can be divided into four categories.

1. *The Investigation Must Be Authorized by Law and Undertaken For a Legitimate Purpose.* Because administrative agencies can exercise only those powers that the legislature has delegated to them, the first inquiry is whether the relevant statutes have conferred the power to conduct the investigation in question. See 5 U.S.C.A. § 555(c) (compulsory process may not be issued or enforced "except as authorized by law"). In practice, however, this jurisdictional limit on administrative investigations is generally easy to satisfy. Both the substantive delegation of regulatory power to the agency and the grant of investigative authority may be drafted in such broad terms that the reviewing court will find it difficult to conclude that the investigation is *ultra vires*. Even when the issue of agency jurisdiction is arguable or unclear,

the court is likely to perceive several reasons to let the investigation go forward. First, an injured party will generally have an opportunity to challenge the scope of the agency's power on review of a final decision. Second, a judicial attempt to fix the boundaries of agency jurisdiction at the preliminary stage of subpoena enforcement may be premature, because the issues may be more clearly defined if review is postponed until there is a final administrative decision. Third, the question may become moot if the agency ultimately decides not to exercise regulatory power over the complaining party. Thus, the courts generally conclude that the question of statutory coverage is to be determined by the agency in the first instance. See, e.g., Oklahoma Press Pub. Co. v. Walling, 327 U.S. 186 (1946).

A jurisdictional argument may succeed where the complaining party is able to show a clear congressional intent not only to exempt it from regulation, but also to protect it from particular agency investigations. A common carrier that was subject to regulation by the ICC and explicitly exempted from investigative or regulatory activities of the FTC was able to resist compliance on this ground in FTC v. Miller, 549 F.2d 452 (7th Cir. 1977). Another situation in which reviewing courts are likely to take a close look at agency demands for information is where the complaining party can make a convincing showing that the investigation was undertaken in bad faith for some improper purpose such as harassing or persecuting the respondent. United States v. Powell, 379 U.S. 48 (1964). However, if the administrator has a colorable basis for requesting the information in question, the complaining party will have to satisfy a substantial burden of pleading and proof in establishing an improper motive. Id.

2. *The Information Sought Must Be Relevant to a Lawful Subject of Investigation.* The Fourth Amendment prohibits the issuance of search warrants unless there is probable cause to believe that a specific violation of law has occurred, and during the early years of administrative regulation a similar standard was applied to administrative subpoenas. The leading case was FTC v. American Tobacco Co., 264 U.S. 298 (1924), where the Court strictly construed the FTC's investigative authority in order to avoid the constitutional question: if the statute did not require "[s]ome evidence of the materiality of the papers demanded," it might well violate the Fourth Amendment.

A few years later, however, the Court relaxed this seemingly stringent requirement. In Endicott Johnson Corp. v. Perkins, 317 U.S. 501 (1943), the Secretary of Labor had requested payroll data from a government contractor for the purpose of determining whether certain factories were covered by the minimum wage law. The Court concluded that the issue of whether the factories were covered should not be litigated in the subpoena enforcement proceeding; so long as "[t]he evidence sought by the subpoena was not plainly incompetent or irrelevant to any lawful purpose of the Secretary in the discharge of her duties under the Act," the district court should grant enforcement.

The constitutional basis for this result was further explained in Oklahoma Press Pub. Co. v. Walling, 327 U.S. 186 (1946). There, the Court distinguished actual searches and seizures, like those commonly used in criminal law enforcement, from the "figurative" or "constructive" search that takes place when a regulatory agency demands to see the records of a regulated company. The *Oklahoma Press* opinion emphasized that there was a long history of legislative provisions requiring corporations to maintain records that were open to public and government scrutiny, while individuals had been protected against "officious intermeddling" in their affairs. In essence, the threat to legitimate expectations of privacy was less in the regulatory setting, while the public interest in access to corporate records was strong. In many fields of regulation, the only evidence of possible violations of law may be the records of regulated companies. In this situation, a strict probable cause requirement could make enforcement impossible. The Supreme Court recognized this necessity in United States v. Morton Salt Co., 338 U.S. 632 (1950), when it analogized the agency's investigative power to a grand jury's: an agency with a proper legislative authorization "can investigate merely on suspicion that the law is being violated, or even just because it wants assurance that it is not." Furthermore, many agencies' responsibilities extend beyond the enforcement of existing laws and rules. When administrators are delegated the power to make policy through rulemaking or are authorized to report to the Congress on matters that may require legislation, they will often need to obtain information from unwilling private parties. Rigid application of the probable cause standard could undermine the quality of agency policymaking. See also Donovan v. Lone Steer, Inc., 464 U.S. 408 (1984) (reaffirming *Oklahoma Press*).

While the constitutional standard of relevance has become easy to satisfy, particular statutes may impose more rigorous requirements on agency investigations. An EEOC subpoena, for example, may only inquire into matters that are "relevant to [a] charge under investigation." 42 U.S.C.A. § 2000e–8(a); see EEOC v. Shell Oil Co., 466 U.S. 54 (1984). It is also important to remember that physical inspections and other administrative searches are subject to more intensive judicial scrutiny than agency demands to produce records or witnesses. See pp. 142–48 infra.

3. *The Investigative Demand Must Be Sufficiently Specific and Not Unreasonably Burdensome.* The Fourth Amendment's prohibition of unreasonable searches and seizures has also been modified in its application to administrative investigations. As the Court noted in the *Oklahoma Press* case,

this requirement implies that the subpoena must adequately describe the materials sought; however, the sufficiency of the specifications is "variable in relation to the nature, purposes, and scope of the inquiry." Other factors bearing on the reasonableness of the subpoena are the cost of assembling and copying the requested materials; the disruption of the data source's business or activities that will result from compliance with the agency's request; the repeated or excessive nature of the agency's demands for data; and the risk of competitive harm if trade secrets or other commercially valuable information is released by the agency. While claims of unreasonable burden are frequently made, they are rarely successful. At most, the reviewing court may inquire whether there is adequate assurance, through protective orders or other procedural devices, that the respondent will be protected against the loss of proprietary information.

4. *The Information Sought Must Not Be Privileged.* The extent to which constitutional, common law, or statutory privileges limit the agencies' powers of compulsory process has been the subject of continuing debate. Much of the controversy has concerned the Fifth Amendment's privilege against self-incrimination. The extent of this protection is discussed in the next section. Other testimonial privileges, such as the common law protection for husband-wife and lawyer-client communications, as well as the more recent state statutes such as those

protecting journalists and their sources or accountants and their clients, have rarely been litigated in the administrative context. Agency statutes and regulations are usually silent on this point. In Upjohn Co. v. United States, 449 U.S. 383 (1981), however, the Court held that a taxpayer could assert both the attorney-client privilege and the work product privilege in resisting enforcement of an IRS summons. But see United States v. Arthur Young & Co., 465 U.S. 805 (1984) (no accountant-client privilege). In some instances, the common law privileges and the constitutional protection against self-incrimination may both be relevant to a subpoena enforcement action. In Fisher v. United States, 425 U.S. 391 (1976), the IRS sought to subpoena documents that taxpayers had given to their lawyers while seeking legal advice. The Court held that the documents were covered by the attorney-client privilege, but only to the extent that they would have been protected from disclosure if they had remained in the custody of the taxpayers. Because these documents could have been subpoenaed from the taxpayers without violating the Fifth Amendment (see pp. 139–40 infra), and no other privilege was applicable, the subpoena to the lawyers was enforced.

C. SELF–INCRIMINATION

When an agency seeks to compel a witness to testify, its attempts may conflict with the Fifth Amendment's assurance that no person "shall be compelled in any criminal case to be a witness against himself." Although the agency that is seeking the testimony will not have the power to impose criminal sanctions itself, a witness may fear that the information she provides will later be used against her in a criminal prosecution. When there is a risk that criminal sanctions will be imposed, the witness may refuse to answer questions that could incriminate her or provide a link in a chain of evidence against her. However, there are some significant limitations on the use of the privilege in administrative investigations or hearings.

1. *The Threatened Penalty Must Be Criminal Rather Than Civil in Nature.* In many regulatory areas, the sanction the witness fears may be labeled a "civil penalty," a "forfeiture," or some similar term rather than a crime. When this occurs, the court must determine whether the statutory penalty is sufficiently punitive in purpose or effect to be considered criminal. See Flemming v. Nestor, 363 U.S. 603, 613–21 (1960). In making this determination, the court will consider a variety of factors, such as whether the penalty is designed to promote retribution and deterrence rather than to compensate for damage, and whether the sanction in question is excessive in relation to its claimed purpose. United States v. Ward, 448 U.S. 242 (1980) (requirement that persons responsible for oil spills in navigable waters must report the spills to appropriate government agencies was

not a violation of Fifth Amendment despite civil penalties of $5000 for each spill); see also Kennedy v. Mendoza–Martinez, 372 U.S. 144, 168–69 (1963).

2. *The Privilege Is Available Only to Natural Persons and Cannot Be Asserted on Behalf of Corporations or Associations.* Since the purpose of the self-incrimination privilege is to protect individuals from the government's use of the "third degree" and similar coercive tactics to extract confessions of personal wrongdoing, a corporation has no Fifth Amendment privilege. Thus, the officers of corporations and other business associations may not withhold testimony that might incriminate their firms. Bellis v. United States, 417 U.S. 85 (1974). A related principle, known as the collective entity rule, provides that a corporate officer who has custody of the firm's records must produce them in response to a subpoena, even though this response might incriminate the custodian herself. "[T]he custodian's act of production is not deemed a personal act, but rather an act of the corporation." Braswell v. United States, 487 U.S. 99 (1988).

3. *The Privilege Attaches Only to Compelled Testimonial Utterances and Not to Other Communications.* To receive Fifth Amendment protection, a communication must be coerced and must be testimonial in nature. Generally, however, modern cases have narrowed the protection afforded by these two related requirements. Thus, in Couch v. United States, 409 U.S. 322 (1973), a subpoena for documents that were in the hands of the taxpayer's

accountant did not violate the taxpayer's privilege, because it did not compel the taxpayer to do anything.[1] Conversely, in Fisher v. United States, 425 U.S. 391 (1976), the Court concluded that taxpayers could be required to produce the work papers their accountants had created in preparing their tax returns. Such papers would contain testimonial declarations by the accountants, not by the taxpayers. The Court extended *Fisher* in United States v. Doe, 465 U.S. 605 (1984), holding that the contents of even the respondent's own business records were unprivileged: since he had prepared these records voluntarily (in the ordinary course of business), their contents did not constitute *compelled* testimony.

The Court did recognize in *Fisher* that the very act of producing records can be self-incriminating, because the response in effect admits that the subpoenaed documents exist and are genuine. On the facts of that case, the Court did not believe that production of the accountants' work papers would be the equivalent of testifying to damaging information: "The existence and location of the papers are a foregone conclusion, and the taxpayer adds little or nothing to the sum total of the govern-

1. Similarly, even if the documents sought are personal records that are in the possession of the individual and contain handwritten notations, the agency may still be able to obtain them by using a search warrant rather than a subpoena. Here, also, the individual is not compelled to testify against herself, and so the Fifth Amendment does not apply. Andresen v. Maryland, 427 U.S. 463 (1976).

ment's information by conceding that he in fact has the papers." Where, however, compliance with a subpoena would effectively admit to the existence and authenticity of numerous documents of which the government is otherwise unaware, the act of production may have testimonial aspects that come within the privilege. *United States v. Doe,* supra (privilege claim upheld).

The Fifth Amendment analysis may be different if the agency seeks to compel an individual to report information rather than trying to get access to existing records or documents. One early case, Shapiro v. United States, 335 U.S. 1 (1948), suggested that the government had broad power to require that individuals keep business records and make them available to the government on demand, so long as the underlying regulatory program was a proper exercise of governmental power. The recordkeeping requirement was viewed as a less drastic form of regulation than a complete prohibition of the activity in question. However, this broad power to compel disclosure was later narrowed by a series of cases involving requirements that criminal conduct be reported to the government. In Marchetti v. United States, 390 U.S. 39 (1968), the Court relied on the Fifth Amendment in striking down a requirement that persons whose income resulted from accepting wagers must provide information about their activities to the Internal Revenue Service. Since bookmaking was a criminal offense under state and federal laws, Marchetti was forced either to violate the law by not registering or to incriminate himself. The Court found several bases for distinguishing Marchetti's situation from the *Shapiro* decision. *Shapiro* had involved a price control program in which the individual was only required to preserve and make available business records that he normally kept; Marchetti, by contrast, was required to report information that was unrelated to his customary business records. In addition, the records at issue in the *Shapiro* case had "public" rather than private aspects, and they involved "an essentially non-criminal and regulatory area of activity." Neither factor was present in Marchetti's situation; instead, he was part of a group that had been singled out as "inherently suspect of criminal activities." See also Grosso v. United States, 390 U.S. 62 (1968); Haynes v. United States, 390 U.S. 85 (1968). The scope of the *Marchetti* exception to the required records rule is somewhat unclear, but it seems likely that most administrative reporting requirements would be more closely analogous to the *Shapiro* provisions than to the unusual facts of the *Marchetti* case. Cf. Baltimore City Dept. of Social Services v. Bouknight, 110 S.Ct. 900 (1990) (upholding, under *Shapiro,* juvenile court order directing mother to produce allegedly abused child).

4. *The Privilege Can Be Defeated by a Grant of Immunity From Prosecution.* Even if the Fifth Amendment has been validly invoked by the sub-

ject of an administrative investigation, the agency
can still compel the individual to testify by granting her immunity from prosecution. Under 18
U.S.C.A. § 6004, the agency must find that the
testimony is "necessary to the public interest," and
it must obtain the approval of the Attorney General before immunizing the witness. A grant of
immunity will not prevent the government from
bringing a criminal prosecution based on independent evidence, see Kastigar v. United States, 406
U.S. 441 (1972), and it will not protect the witness
against use of the information in a noncriminal
administrative proceeding, see Burley v. U.S. Drug
Enforcement Administration, 443 F.Supp. 619
(M.D.Tenn.1977).

D. SEARCHES AND INSPECTIONS

Many agencies gather information through direct observation. Administrative inspections cover
a wide range of activity, including safety tests of
commercial equipment and personal cars, sanitary
inspections of restaurants and hotels, environmental monitoring of factory emissions, and fire and
health checks of apartments and homes. Although
they are occasionally used for law enforcement
purposes, the primary function of administrative
inspections is to prevent and correct undesirable
conditions. Physical inspections or tests may also
take the place of formal hearings. The Administrative Procedure Act provides an exception to the
Act's trial-type hearing procedures when an adjudi-

cative decision "rest[s] solely on inspections [or] tests." 5 U.S.C.A. § 554(a)(3). Regardless of the reason for which it is undertaken, however, an administrative inspection must not violate the Fourth Amendment's prohibition of unreasonable searches and seizures, nor its requirement that search warrants may be issued only upon a showing of probable cause. Much of the litigation on administrative searches has involved the application of the warrant clause to agency inspections.

At one time administrative inspections were considered exempt from the constitutional warrant requirement. Thus, a health inspector did not need a search warrant to enter a house in search of a source of rats that had been infesting the neighborhood, if the authorizing statute imposed reasonable safeguards such as a requirement that the inspector adequately identify himself and conduct his inspections only during normal business hours. Frank v. Maryland, 359 U.S. 360 (1959). Prior judicial authorization for this kind of limited investigation was unnecessary, because the strong public interest in sanitation and the historic acceptance of such inspections outweighed the individual's interest in privacy. However, this view was rejected in two later inspection cases, Camara v. Municipal Court, 387 U.S. 523 (1967) (apartment building), and See v. Seattle, 387 U.S. 541 (1967) (commercial warehouse). Although routine fire and health inspections may be less hostile and less intrusive than the typical police search for evidence of a crime, the Court reasoned, "[i]t is surely anomalous to say that the individual and his private property are fully protected by the Fourth Amendment only when the individual is suspected of criminal behavior." Moreover, health and fire codes are frequently enforced by criminal processes. Thus, the individual's privacy interests were entitled to the protection of the warrant requirement.

At the same time, the Court in *Camara* and *See* recognized that inspections are essential to effective enforcement of health and sanitary standards and that the concepts of probable cause developed in criminal law enforcement could not be mechanically applied to these administrative searches. In place of the criminal law standard requiring a showing of probable cause to believe that a violation had occurred and that fruits, instrumentalities, or evidence of a crime would be recovered at the place specified, the Court established the rule that an administrative search warrant could issue when "reasonable legislative or administrative standards for conducting an area inspection are satisfied." The standards would vary according to the nature of the regulatory program, and they might be based upon factors such as "the passage of time, the nature of the building . . ., or the condition of the entire area, but they will not necessarily depend upon specific knowledge of the condition of the particular dwelling."

The *See* decision left open the possibility that warrants would not be required for administrative searches in situations where a license was required to conduct the business in question and the grant of a license was effectively conditioned on the applicant's consent to warrantless searches. Two later cases, Colonnade Catering Corp. v. United States, 397 U.S. 72 (1970) (licensed retail liquor establishment), and United States v. Biswell, 406 U.S. 311 (1972) (firearms dealer), confirmed that warrantless searches were permissible in industries subject to a licensing system that involved intensive regulation.

This trend toward judicial approval for warrantless administrative inspections was interrupted by the Supreme Court's decision in Marshall v. Barlow's, Inc., 436 U.S. 307 (1978). The Occupational Safety and Health Administration, defending a statute that explicitly authorized it to conduct warrantless searches, argued that surprise inspections of workplaces were both necessary for effective protection of workers, and reasonable within the meaning of the Fourth Amendment. The Court, however, described the *Colonnade–Biswell* exception to the warrant requirement as a narrow one, applicable only when the target of the search was part of a "pervasively regulated" industry that has been subject to a "long tradition of close supervision." For all other inspections, a warrant was still necessary. As in *Camara* and *See,* the warrant would not require "specific evidence of an existing violation"; it could be based on reasonable legislative or administrative standards, including "a general administrative plan for the enforcement of the Act derived from neutral sources such as . . . dispersion of employees in various types of industries across a given area." In the Court's view, the warrant requirement would protect employers against arbitrary or harassing invasions of their privacy, and give them notice of the proper scope of the inspection.

In its most recent decisions, however, the Court has aggressively expanded the *Colonnade–Biswell* exception to the warrant requirement for "closely regulated" businesses. In Donovan v. Dewey, 452 U.S. 594 (1981), the Court upheld a statute authorizing warrantless inspections in the mining industry. Although there was no "long tradition" of regulation throughout this industry, as in *Colonnade* and *Biswell*, the Court noted that the legislation created a "comprehensive and defined" regulatory scheme that would make mine operators aware that they would face periodic inspections. The Court also based its decision on the gravity of the social problem (health and safety hazards in mines); the legislature's determination that surprise inspections were essential to detect violations; and the existence of statutes and regulations that defined the circumstances in which inspections could be conducted, so that individual inspectors would not wield unchecked discretion. Using essentially the same reasoning, the Court later held that police had validly conducted a warrant-less search of an automobile junkyard, pursuant to a New York statute that "closely regulated" the vehicle dismantling business in order to curb automobile theft. New York v. Burger, 482 U.S. 691 (1987). In fact, however, the scope of the state's regulation in *Burger* was slight, consisting of minimal registration and record-keeping duties; and the constraints that the statute placed on the police's discretion were also minor.

To judge from the most recent cases, therefore, Congress can apparently subject a wide variety of industries to warrantless searches. The Court has perhaps effectively limited the reach of *Barlow's* to agencies like OSHA, which has jurisdiction over almost the entire range of workplaces in American society. Of course, even when an agency is subject to the *Barlow's* rule, the scope of the protection afforded by the warrant requirement will largely depend on the diligence of reviewing courts in scrutinizing agency requests for warrants. Experience in the field of criminal law enforcement suggests that some courts may be willing to grant approvals routinely, with only a perfunctory review of the agency's justification.

Administrative inspections also may fall within exceptions to the warrant requirement that have evolved in the context of criminal law enforcement. If the individual consents to the search of the premises, no warrant is required. *Barlow's,* supra. The consent may be valid even if permission to search is a condition to receiving important benefits. Wyman v. James, 400 U.S. 309 (1971) (requirement that recipients of welfare benefits consent to home visits by caseworkers not a violation of the Fourth Amendment). Nor is a warrant necessary if the evidence gathered by the inspector is in "plain view" from roadways or other public space. Air Pollution Variance Bd. of Colorado v. Western Alfalfa Corp., 416 U.S. 861 (1974) (emissions from smokestack visible from public areas of factory grounds); Dow Chemical Co. v. United States, 476 U.S. 227 (1986) (inspection of industrial complex by aerial photography).

E. DISCLOSURE OF AGENCY RECORDS

The public interest in a liberal disclosure policy is generally strong. Effective public and political oversight requires detailed knowledge of agency activities; and without disclosure of records in the government's possession, citizens may be unable to determine whether the agency is ignoring violations of law. Moreover, when administrative powers are exercised in secrecy, they can readily be abused to subvert fundamental rights. The exposure during the 1970's of the FBI's extensive efforts to suppress political dissent graphically illustrates this risk. In addition, disclosure of unpublished "secret law" can serve the public interest by helping citizens know whether their conduct is likely to lead to enforcement action. But disclosure of government data also carries with it some very substantial risks. Premature release of information about pending investigations can impede the enforcement of regulatory laws by alerting wrongdoers to hide or destroy evidence, or by discouraging potential witnesses from cooperating with investigators. Public disclosure can invade personal privacy and damage the reputations of persons or firms before they have had a chance to establish their innocence. It may also destroy commercially valuable trade secrets, or give competitors an unjustifiable advantage.

In contemporary administrative practice, these conflicting concerns are addressed through a series of information disclosure statutes. The most important of these is the Freedom of Information Act (FOIA), 5 U.S.C.A. § 552, which was enacted in 1966 and has been amended several times since. FOIA's major provision directs each agency to release identifiable records in its possession to "any person" who requests them, unless the material in question falls within one of the exemptions listed in the Act. Id. § 552(a)(3).[2] When the government refuses a request, the citizen may obtain de novo review in a district court, with the burden on the

2. Other FOIA provisions require agencies to publish their rules and statements of general policy in the Federal Register, 5 U.S.C.A. § 552(a)(1), and to make available for public inspection their final opinions, interpretations, staff manuals, and instructions that affect an individual's rights. Id. § 552(a)(2). When an agency fails to comply with these requirements, the undisclosed pronouncements may not be relied on or used against citizens who did not have actual notice of them.

government to justify the withholding. The court may examine the requested agency records "in camera" (privately) to determine whether they should be released; and if the court finds that only a portion of the document is exempt, it may order release of the remainder. Id. § 552(a)(4)(B). Parties who sue successfully under the Act may recover their costs and attorneys' fees. Id. § 552(a)(4)(E).

Some of the primary users of FOIA are the organized constituency groups that are sufficiently concerned about regulatory policy to conduct continuous monitoring of agency activities. The most familiar—and often the most numerous and influential—of these constituency groups are the regulated industries and their trade associations, but environmental, consumer, and other "public interest" groups have also become a significant factor in the administrative arena. By following agency activities and learning the basis of proposed actions, these constituency groups can often use persuasion or pressure to mold regulatory policy at the early stages of a proceeding, when participation is most effective. In many regulatory areas, FOIA, supplemented by personal contact within the agencies, functions as a kind of informal "discovery" system that constituency groups use in preparing to make their "case" to the agency.

Section 552(b) of FOIA lists nine categories of information that are exempt from disclosure, and most litigation under the Act has concerned the scope of one or more of these categories. The exemptions were designed to permit the withholding of records only when disclosure would harm some important governmental function or private interest, and the reviewing courts have usually construed them narrowly. The nine exemptions are often known by their subsection numbers; for example, the provision that permits agencies to deny requests for classified information that must be kept secret in the interest of national security, 5 U.S.C.A. § 552(b)(1), is usually called "Exemption 1." Case law on the exemptions is voluminous, and only a few illustrative issues can be treated here.

Exemption 5 of FOIA, § 552(b)(5), permits an agency to withhold information "which would not be available by law to a [private] party . . . in litigation with the agency." The provision is interpreted as preserving the evidentiary privileges that the government has traditionally enjoyed in litigation, such as the attorney-client and work product privileges. Particularly significant is the so-called "executive privilege," which protects internal deliberative documents that contain advice or recommendations. The rationale for this privilege is that the threat of eventual disclosure might inhibit candid discussion within the agencies. See EPA v. Mink, 410 U.S. 73 (1973) (evaluative portions of policy memoranda are exempt, although segregable factual portions are not). This privilege, however, exempts only *predecisional* documents.

When an agency reaches a final decision and writes a memorandum explaining it, the document cannot be considered part of the deliberative process; it is part of the law itself, and must be disclosed. For example, requesters are entitled to obtain memoranda of the General Counsel of the NLRB explaining why he did *not* commence an unfair labor practice proceeding. NLRB v. Sears, Roebuck & Co., 421 U.S. 132 (1975). However, a General Counsel's memorandum explaining why he *will* commence a proceeding is protected as work product, because its release could reveal his litigation strategy. Id.

The government's interest in effective law enforcement is acknowledged in Exemption 7, § 552(b)(7), which protects against forced disclosure of "records or information compiled for law enforcement purposes" when the release could cause such harms as revealing the identity of a confidential source or endangering any individual's physical safety. (A newly enacted subsection of FOIA, § 552(c), strengthens these safeguards.) Exemption 7 also authorizes the withholding of investigatory records when disclosure "could reasonably be expected to interfere with enforcement proceedings." Thus, in NLRB v. Robbins Tire & Rubber Co., 437 U.S. 214 (1978), the Court upheld the Board's policy of refusing to give access to witness statements gathered during unfair labor practice investigations. The Court noted that disclosure would permit employers or unions to coerce potential witnesses into changing their testimony, or not testifying at all. In addition, some persons might refuse to provide information to investigators if they knew that their statements would become public documents. In light of these possibilities, it was not necessary for the Board or the courts to conduct a burdensome case-by-case inquiry into the harm that was likely to result from a particular disclosure of witness statements; the agency could treat them as exempt on a generic basis.

Other FOIA provisions protect the privacy rights of individuals whose personal data is incorporated into agency records. Exemption 6, § 552(b)(6), authorizes agencies to withhold personnel and medical records if disclosure would constitute a "clearly unwarranted invasion of personal privacy," and a comparable provision in Exemption 7 is designed to prevent invasions of privacy through the release of investigatory records. Both of these provisions enable the reviewing court to balance the threat to the data subject's privacy interests against the public's interest in access to the data in question. For example, in Department of the Air Force v. Rose, 425 U.S. 352 (1976), the government relied on Exemption 6 in denying a request for access to summaries of disciplinary actions taken under the Honor Code at the Air Force Academy. The Supreme Court, however, refused to uphold this blanket denial, stressing that the language of the exemption compels disclosure unless the invasion of privacy is "clearly unwarranted." The Court remanded so that the district court could consider, through in camera inspection, whether the cadets' privacy could be protected if the case summaries were released with identifying details edited out. This solution, the Court suggested, would respect privacy interests and at the same time allow some public scrutiny of the Air Force's administration of the Honor Code.[3]

Another private interest that could be threatened by indiscriminate release of government files is the commercial value of trade secrets and other proprietary information. Exemption 4 of FOIA, § 552(b)(4), allows the agencies to withhold "trade secrets and commercial or financial information obtained from a person and privileged or confidential." A leading case holds that commercial information is "confidential" within the meaning of this clause if its disclosure would be likely "(1) to impair the Government's ability to obtain necessary information in the future; or (2) to cause substantial harm to the competitive position of the person from whom the information was obtained." Na-

---

3. A separate source of protection for individuals is the Privacy Act, 5 U.S.C.A. § 552a. It applies to all agency systems of records in which files can be retrieved by the individual's name or identifying number. The Act permits the individual citizen to inspect government agencies' files relating to her and to seek correction of erroneous or incomplete records. In addition, the Act requires agencies to publish notice of all "routine uses" of personal information, and it provides damages and injunctive relief for the record subject if the agency makes unauthorized disclosures of her file. This is one of the few situations in which Congress has provided injured persons with a damage remedy for the government's misuse of information.

tional Parks & Conservation Ass'n v. Morton, 498 F.2d 765 (D.C.Cir.1974). Further protection is provided by the Trade Secrets Act, 18 U.S.C.A. § 1905, which makes it a crime for government officials to disclose trade secrets.

During the early years of FOIA, however, companies submitting proprietary information often felt unprotected. Even if the material requested under FOIA were exempt from disclosure, the agency might still decide to release it as a matter of discretion. They also feared that the Trade Secrets Act would not be a very powerful deterrent in this situation, because the Justice Department would be unlikely to prosecute a bureaucrat for releasing documents to the public. These apprehensions were fueled by anecdotal evidence that some firms had in fact been injured when their competitors obtained valuable proprietary information by simply filing a FOIA request. During the 1970's, suppliers of business information began initiating court actions—soon dubbed "reverse FOIA" suits—in an effort to find some way to prevent the government from disclosing such data.

One of these "reverse FOIA" plaintiffs scored a partial victory in Chrysler Corp. v. Brown, 441 U.S. 281 (1979). There, several Chrysler employees had sought copies of affirmative action compliance reports submitted by the company to the Department of Defense Logistics Agency; Chrysler in turn sued to enjoin the release of these reports on the ground that they were exempt from disclosure under

FOIA. The Court rejected the company's claim that the exemptions to the Freedom of Information Act were mandatory; FOIA is a disclosure statute, and it does not affect the agencies' discretion to release material that falls within the statutory exemptions. But, the Court continued, this discretion is not unbounded. A decision to release exempt documents is a final agency action subject to judicial review under the APA, and the reviewing court must decide whether the administrative determination was "arbitrary, capricious, an abuse of discretion, or otherwise not in accordance with law." See pp. 96–102 supra. Since a disclosure that violated the Trade Secrets Act would not be "in accordance with law," the reviewing court could prohibit disclosure.

The Court did not attempt to define the scope of the Trade Secrets Act in *Chrysler*. Subsequently, however, the D.C. Circuit has held that the Trade Secrets Act is as broad as Exemption 4 is; therefore, that Act *requires* agencies to withhold any commercial information that Exemption 4 *permits* them to withhold. CNA Financial Corp. v. Donovan, 830 F.2d 1132 (D.C.Cir.1987). Another new safeguard, Executive Order 12600, 52 Fed.Reg. 23781 (1987), issued by President Reagan, instructs agencies that when they are considering granting a FOIA request for information that arguably could be withheld under Exemption 4, they must notify the company that supplied the information and permit it to present objections. These recent developments will probably go far to deter agencies from granting FOIA requests for business information. That result is not necessarily a matter for regret, however, because the basic purpose of the Act was to promote openness and accountability in government operations, not to help one firm gain commercial advantage over another.

F. OPEN MEETINGS

Just as the Freedom of Information Act calls upon agencies to adhere to standards of openness and accountability when they act on requests for written materials, the Government in the Sunshine Act of 1976, 5 U.S.C.A. § 552b, requires officials to follow similar principles when they hold live proceedings. Under the latter act, most meetings of the multimember regulatory agencies must be open to public scrutiny. Meetings must usually be publicly announced at least a week before they are held; and when an agency holds a closed meeting, it must keep a recording or transcript that it can release to the public if a court later decides that the meeting should have been conducted openly. The Act does not apply to agencies headed by a single individual, such as a Secretary. It also contains a list of exemptions closely resembling the FOIA exemptions. Id. § 552b(c). As in FOIA cases, however, courts sometimes respond skeptically to agency pleas for secrecy. See, e.g., Common Cause v. NRC, 674 F.2d 921 (D.C.Cir.1982) (agency's strategy meetings to decide how it will present budget requests to OMB are not always exempt).

The merits of the Sunshine Act are controversial. The virtues of conducting "government in the sunshine" are obvious; but critics contend that the open meetings requirement impairs the quality of agency deliberations, because in a private session commissioners are more likely to raise tentative ideas, explore compromises, and interact in a truly collegial manner. To date the Supreme Court has not addressed the scope of the exemptions. It has, however, made clear that the Act applies only to meetings that an agency holds as it proposes to take official action on specific proposals or issues—not to exploratory background sessions, or to gatherings organized by outside groups. FCC v. ITT World Communications, Inc., 466 U.S. 463 (1984).

Still another disclosure statute is the Federal Advisory Committee Act of 1972 (FACA), 5 U.S. C.A.App. 2, which governs the activities of advisory committees.[4] Typically, these committees are groups of private citizens who are asked to provide an agency with advice and recommendations re-

4. On its face the Act applies to all groups that are "established or utilized" to advise the executive branch. The Supreme Court has cautioned, however, that this language must not be read too literally, lest FACA be held to constrain informal consultations that Congress could not have meant to regulate. Public Citizen v. U.S. Department of Justice, 109 S.Ct. 2558 (1989) (FACA does not apply to ABA committee that advises Justice Department on Supreme Court nominees).

garding a particular issue or program. Some advisory committees are comprised of technical experts, like the scientific committees that advise the EPA on proposals to cancel the registrations of pesticides as safety or environmental hazards. Others may be designed to represent diverse political constituencies, as in the presidential committee that was appointed to investigate the nuclear reactor accident at Three Mile Island: it was composed not only of scientists and technicians, but also environmentalists, industry members, and citizens from the community where the accident occurred. Under FACA, advisory committees must hold their meetings in public (subject to the same exemptions that apply to meetings of multimember agencies under the Sunshine Act). The Act resulted in part from a congressional belief that the advisory committees had proliferated excessively, wasting taxpayer dollars and enabling favored private interests to wield undue influence over the early stages of executive policymaking. The sponsors assumed that broader public scrutiny of the committees' activities would ameliorate these problems—and might induce agencies to create fewer such committees in the future.

CHAPTER V

THE INFORMAL
ADMINISTRATIVE PROCESS

The Administrative Procedure Act sets forth several procedural models for federal agency decision-making, but these APA models do not even apply to the largest and probably most important category of agency actions—the informal administrative process. The APA specifies the procedures to be used only when the agency is formulating policy for the future through substantive rulemaking (5 U.S.C.A. § 553), or when the statute being implemented requires that the decision in question be made after a formal trial-type hearing (5 U.S.C.A. §§ 554, 556–57). See pp. 242–43, 320–29 infra. Generally speaking, the remaining administrative decisions comprise the legal category of "informal action."

The term "informal" is somewhat misleading, because many of the activities that technically fall within this category are subject to significant legal controls. Agencies often impose procedural constraints on their own discretion by issuing rules of practice, staff manuals, or instructions to the public. These procedural requirements may create opportunities for interested persons to be heard, and they may be legally binding, so that a failure to observe them can be reversed by a reviewing court.   Moreover, the due process clauses of the Constitution require the agencies to meet basic standards of fairness when they affect the life, liberty, or property of individuals.   The application of procedural due process to informal administrative action is treated in Chapter 6.   The discussion in this chapter provides context and background for that analysis, by reviewing the most common types of informal administrative decisions.

In addition to procedural checks on discretion, informal action is usually subject to judicial review.   Thus, courts can generally determine whether the agency has acted within the bounds of its statutory jurisdiction, has properly exercised its discretion, and has developed a reasonable factual basis for its action.   There may also be a variety of nonlegal controls on discretion, such as statistical "quality control" checks to reduce error rates, supervision by higher-level officials, oversight by the legislative and executive branches, and publicity from the media.

In short, informal action often is subject to significant safeguards against abuse or overreaching. Nevertheless, certain characteristics of informal agency processes give special cause for concern. Many informal programs, such as those dispensing welfare or veterans' benefits, process a high volume of cases.   In this situation, the difficult or unusual case may get less attention than it deserves, and pressure to move cases along may overcome the desire to decide them correctly.   The risks of error and arbitrariness are compounded when the program affects relatively powerless classes of clients who are unable to make effective use of any procedures that are available to them. Moreover, some kinds of informal action have far less visibility than formal proceedings generally do; media exposure of corruption or incompetence in these fields is unlikely and effective political oversight is a rarity.

A. SETTLEMENT, NEGOTIATION, AND ALTERNATIVE DISPUTE RESOLUTION

Since many agencies have a huge caseload of claims, hearings, and penalty actions to resolve each year, settlements are a vital part of the administrative process. Like trial courts, most agency adjudicative systems would become hopelessly backlogged if all the cases filed had to go through a full hearing. In recognition of this fact, the agencies have developed a diverse array of settlement practices and procedures. See, e.g., Bermann, *Federal Tort Claims at the Agency Level: The FTCA Administrative Process*, 35 Case W.Res.L.Rev. 509 (1984–85). Several factors contribute to the prevalence of settlements in administrative practice. Regulated industries have to live with the agencies that oversee their operations, and the company accused of a violation may be reluctant to earn the reputation of being uncooperative by resisting when it is in the wrong. At the same time, an agency that has become familiar with the respondent through continuing supervision or prior dealings may have access to ample information establishing the violation. Finally, the costs of litigation, including the harm to the company's reputation among consumers and the uncertainty resulting from prolonged litigation, often create a powerful incentive to settle a pending charge.

Negotiated settlements increase the efficiency of the administrative process, but they may do so at the expense of other interests. In contrast to the typical negotiated compromise between two private litigants, the agency adjudication usually has a strong public interest dimension: the rights and interests of consumers, competitors, or other parties who are not directly represented can be greatly affected by the agency's decision. Decisions made without full testing of the facts and adversary debate on matters of law and policy may reach questionable results, and persons who are indirectly affected may feel that these decisions are less fair to them than actions taken after trial-type hearings. In recognition of these risks, many agencies have codified their settlement procedures in their rules of practice, including the allowance of an opportunity for interested members of the public to comment on proposed settlements. This approach has been extended by statute to the settlement of civil antitrust cases brought by the Department of Justice. 15 U.S.C.A. § 16.

The importance of sound settlement practices to the fulfillment of an agency's statutory mission is illustrated by EPA's implementation of the Comprehensive Environmental Response, Compensation, and Liability Act of 1980, 42 U.S.C.A. § 9601 et seq., more commonly known as "Superfund." The Act imposes liability for cleaning up toxic waste dumps on parties who generated or participated in disposing of the wastes. The costs of remediation can run into millions of dollars at a major Superfund site, and dozens or even hundreds of potentially responsible parties may be involved. As a result, settlement negotiations are typically complex and hard-fought.

EPA's approach to settlement changed radically during the early implementation of Superfund. At first, the agency was willing to accept settlement offers that granted responsible parties broad releases from liability without requiring them to bear the full costs of cleanup operations. This settlement policy was attacked by environmental groups, congressional oversight committees, and the media for failing to provide adequate protection of public health and the environment. The agency responded by going to the opposite extreme and requiring settling parties to assume virtually full joint and several liability for all future costs of remediation. As might be expected, this policy produced few settlements. In the end, Congress enacted settlement guidelines that were intended to steer a middle course between the two opposing approaches. See Superfund Amendments and Reauthorization Act of 1986, 100 Stat. 1678, 42 U.S.C.A. § 9622. See generally Anderson, *Negotiation and Informal Agency Action: The Case of Superfund,* 1985 Duke L.J. 261.

Usually, consent negotiations can take place either before or after the issuance of a formal complaint. The respondent signing a consent order agrees to comply with the order's remedial requirements, but it does not formally admit that it has committed a violation of the applicable laws. As a result, the party signing the consent settlement would not be estopped from denying legal liability if a private party, such as a competitor or a customer, later brought a civil damage action against the respondent based on the same set of facts. This opportunity to avoid a formal adjudication of wrongdoing is often a major incentive for the respondent to settle. Once a consent settlement has been signed, it has the same legal effect as a final agency order. See, e.g., NLRB v. Ochoa Fertilizer Corp., 368 U.S. 318, 322 (1961).

The APA imposes a duty on the agencies to consider settlement offers. See 5 U.S.C.A. § 554(c)(1) (settlement offers from respondents in formal cases must be considered "when time, the nature of the proceeding, and the public interest permit"); cf. id. § 558(c) (licensee must usually be given an "opportunity to demonstrate or achieve compliance with all lawful requirements" before revocation proceedings commence). However, the APA imposes few limits on the agencies' discretion to accept or reject an offer. Thus, judicial review of a decision to settle a pending case will be very narrow or nonexistent. Compare NLRB v. United Food Workers Local 23, 484 U.S. 112 (1987) (General Counsel of NLRB has unreviewable discretion to dismiss an unfair labor practice complaint pursuant to an informal settlement), with Arctic Slope Regional Corp. v. FERC, 832 F.2d 158 (D.C.Cir. 1987) (reviewing termination of rate proceedings for abuse of discretion), cert. denied, 109 S.Ct. 175 (1988). Like decisions not to prosecute (see pp. 118–20 supra), settlements tend to be ill-suited to judicial supervision. Often they are based on factors that a court could not easily review, such as the history of negotiations between the agency staff and the respondent, the need to devote resources to other cases or investigations, the likelihood that the agency would prevail in litigation, or the precedential value of a favorable decision.

In recent years, agencies have shown growing interest in "alternative dispute resolution" processes. Most of the attention has been devoted to "regulatory negotiation" in rulemaking, see pp. 343–45 infra, but there has also been experimentation with informal decisionmaking models in adjudicative settings. See Administrative Conference of the United States, *Sourcebook: Federal Agency Use of Alternative Means of Dispute Resolution* (1987) (collecting materials on agencies' experiments with mediation, arbitration, and summary "minitrials"). One statutory provision requiring pesticide manufacturers to resort to compulsory arbitration in certain disputes at EPA was upheld against a separation of powers challenge in Thomas v. Union Carbide Agric. Products Co., 473 U.S. 568 (1985). See pp. 30–31 supra. It seems likely that these structured but informal methods of conducting administrative adjudications will become increasingly common and important in the future.

B. APPLICATIONS AND CLAIMS

One of the most common reasons for creating administrative agencies is to provide for the fast processing of large numbers of claims and applications. The agencies that are responsible for dispensing social welfare benefits, collecting taxes, and controlling immigration make millions of informal decisions each year, and these decisions significantly affect the lives of virtually all Americans. In a single year, for example, the Social Security Administration disburses about two hundred billion dollars and makes over four million determinations in administering the Old–Age, Survivors, Disability, and Health Insurance programs.

Some benefits programs, such as the veterans' benefits system, rely almost exclusively on informal, nonadversary procedures. In other programs, including most of the social welfare programs administered by SSA, an applicant whose claim is denied in an informally reached decision may then resort to a trial-type "fair hearing." Even when such an opportunity for a formal hearing is available, however, relatively few claimants take advantage of it; the remainder may be uninformed about their options, unable to secure legal services, or unable to represent their own interests adequately—or may simply be satisfied with the informal hearing they received.

Faced with the need to make an enormous number of decisions quickly, many of the agencies that process individual claims have developed sophisticated informal procedures in an effort to minimize the use of formal hearings. One of the most familiar examples is the Internal Revenue Service. Despite the formidable complexity of the tax laws, the IRS has developed forms that are relatively simple to complete, as well as a variety of informational pamphlets and simplified instructions for taxpayers. It also provides direct assistance and advice through regional offices located throughout the country. Computerized audit routines and cross-checks with state tax records "flag" suspicious returns for further analysis. When a question arises, a system of administrative reviews and a simplified "small claims" procedure serve to resolve most disputes. Thus, out of more than a hundred million tax returns filed annually, about one million may be examined; only about 100,000 cases are appealed administratively beyond the examination stage, and all but about 10,000 of these are settled by appeals officers.

An effective system for resolving disputes administratively, and for establishing some quality control over routine decisions, is essential if the claims processing agencies are to avoid paralysis. However, efforts to upgrade the system as a whole through management supervision can also threaten strongly felt commitments to the ideal of resolving individual cases fairly by giving the claimant a trial-type hearing. One example of this tension surfaced during the early 1980's, when the Social Security Administration implemented a statutory directive to improve the consistency of disability benefits decisions by "targeting" for appellate review Administrative Law Judges whose allowance rates exceeded the statistical average for all ALJs. This "Bellmon review" process resulted in a series of suits claiming that the focus on high allowance rates compromised the impartiality of the ALJs, and thereby denied the claimants a fair hearing. See pp. 274–75 infra. This experience illustrates the more general proposition that justice in a mass social welfare system is not a unitary value, but rather a balance among the frequently conflicting goals of carrying out the legislative mandate efficiently, providing assistance to individuals in distress, and evaluating the claimant's moral entitlement to public funds. Outside intervention, whether from courts or from legislatures, may disrupt the existing balance in unforeseen ways, and thereby undermine the quality of administrative justice. See generally J. Mashaw, *Bureaucratic Justice* (1983).

C. TESTS AND INSPECTIONS

A person seeking a driver's license must usually pass a written exam, an eyesight check, and a driving test. All of these are administered by trained inspectors who do not use formal judicialized procedures in making the decision to grant or deny the license. Routine use of trial-type hearings for these kinds of decisions would be not only slow and cumbersome, but also pointless: courtroom procedures such as sworn testimony and cross-examination would contribute relatively little to the straightforward processes of measurement and observation that are the basis of many administrative decisions.

Tests and inspections are used in a variety of regulatory programs where technical criteria or other objective standards are applied. Informal inspections determine whether planes and trains are in compliance with safety rules, agricultural products can meet quality standards, or periodicals can obtain second class mailing privileges. They may also form the basis of agency decisions as to whether foods and drugs are contaminated, pilots are physically fit to operate aircraft, or factories are in compliance with environmental standards. In addition, agencies may conduct tests and publish the results for the purpose of assisting consumer choice, as when the FTC releases statistics on the tar and nicotine content of cigarettes or the EPA measures the gas mileage of automobiles.

Although the savings in time and resources are great and the threat of inaccurate decision is generally small, the widespread use of administrative tests and inspections does give rise to some procedural concerns. Even when the test is simple and the results unambiguous, there is still a risk that the official conducting it will be careless or corrupt, or use defective measuring equipment. The inspector may be under pressure to make a certain number of inspections during the workday, or to maintain production at the inspected facility. Moreover, many decisions based on tests or inspections require a considerable amount of judgment or interpretation. The decision whether to certify a newly designed airplane as "airworthy" to carry passengers requires a series of engineering judgments about the problems that the plane is likely to encounter in operation, and about its ability to withstand a variety of predictable stresses and failures. Tests can provide the basis on which these decisions are made, but they will not necessarily furnish a clear answer. Decisions like the airworthiness certification may also involve an implicit value choice on matters such as whether the public interest is best served by allowing relatively easy certification, so that manufacturers and airlines can bring new airplanes into service quickly and cheaply, or whether the paramount interest in safety requires a high level of prior assurance, even though this may raise prices and stifle innovation. Ideally, basic policy choices of this nature should be made in visible, public proceedings with ample opportunities for interested persons to participate; yet, if the established criteria are vague or incomplete, the policy decisions may actually be made by the technicians who conduct the tests and inspections.

The D.C. Circuit was mindful of these concerns in a case interpreting the APA provision that excuses agencies from holding a trial-type hearing where "decisions rest solely on inspections, tests, or elections." 5 U.S.C.A. § 554(a)(3). In Union of Concerned Scientists v. NRC, 735 F.2d 1437 (D.C. Cir.1984), the Nuclear Regulatory Commission amended its rules to provide that the adequacy of emergency preparedness exercises conducted by communities near a new nuclear power reactor could no longer be litigated in licensing proceedings; instead, the agency would evaluate the required emergency drills as part of its pre-operation inspections of the plant. The court ruled that this was an misuse of the APA hearing exemption, because the agency's decision would not depend "solely" on facts observed by its inspectors. The NRC would also consider reports from other interested persons, and questions of credibility, conflict in testimony, and sufficiency of the evidence were likely to arise. Since the statutory formal hearing had been provided to resolve such conflicts, the court held, it was improper for the NRC to decide these issues outside of the hearing process.

Fairness to regulated parties may also be lacking if a decision is based on a test or inspection that they have no real opportunity to contest. When the environmental inspector takes an incriminating reading of the opacity of smoke rising from the company's stack, or draws a sample of the river water near its drain pipe, there may be no practical or effective way to contest the alleged violation unless there has been prior notice and an opportunity to conduct independent tests, or at least to observe the sampling procedure.

Several steps and strategies have been developed to minimize these risks. The skills and integrity of inspectors can be checked by setting minimum qualifications for these personnel, and by providing expert supervision (especially through unannounced spot checks). Apart from emergency situations—such as where contaminated perishable foods or livestock with contagious diseases have been discovered and must be destroyed immediately—it is usually possible to provide a check on the inspector's discretion by having a second official reinspect the goods, or even by providing the right to a trial-type hearing. Furthermore, although the Fourth Amendment warrant clause has only limited application to administrative searches, it ensures in many situations that the agency will have to submit to an independent review of the need for the inspection, or to other checks on administrative arbitrariness. See pp. 142–48 supra.

Whatever the legal checks on inspectors' behavior, agencies may find it prudent to display a healthy self-restraint in their use of tests and inspections. Experience in agencies like the Occupational Safety and Health Administration suggests that a rigid, penal style of enforcement can be counterproductive. If the inspector mechanically cites all violations without regard to the actual risks created or the reasons for noncompliance, he may succeed only in creating resentment and resistance among the regulated. E. Bardach & R. Kagan, *Going By the Book* (1983). On the other hand, an inspector who responds intelligently to the problems he encounters can enhance the credibility of the regulatory program, and encourage voluntary compliance from regulated firms.

D. SUSPENSIONS, SEIZURES, AND RECALLS

Many agencies have the authority to remove a product from the market, to seize property, or to suspend a license or a rate pending full adjudication of alleged violations. Federal agencies can summarily seize adulterated or misbranded foods and drugs, stop public trading in securities, and take control of banks that have become fiscally unsound. The licenses of doctors, lawyers, horse trainers, and innumerable others whose occupations are regulated at the state or federal level can usually be suspended when the responsible authorities have reason to believe that the licensee has failed to observe minimum professional standards. This power to issue orders that summarily terminate risks to the public health, safety, or economic welfare has historical antecedents in the common law power to abate public nuisances, but in the modern regulatory state the delegation of powers to take summary action has become widespread.

The justification for summary administrative powers is straightforward. When private conduct is arguably in violation of regulatory statutes and poses an immediate threat to the public, the responsible agency should not have to wait months or years until it can complete a formal trial-type proceeding before protecting the public from harm. But summary action can also have a devastating impact on those who are regulated, both in lost income and in damage to reputation. Recalls of defective or dangerous products or suspensions of occupational licenses for corruption or incompetence are often newsworthy events that carry a lasting stigma. Moreover, since summary action often must be taken on the basis of incomplete or untested information, there can be a high risk that the agency is wrong.

In recognition of these risks, some agencies are required to obtain court approval for summary actions, such as the Consumer Product Safety Commission's decision to remove appliances or other products from the market as imminent hazards. 15 U.S.C.A. § 2061. Another procedural protection against hasty or unauthorized summary action is the requirement that the agency hold a full hearing promptly after it has suspended a license or removed a product from the market. If the agency's rules or the relevant statutes do not provide a prompt post-termination hearing, procedural due process may require it. See Barry v. Barchi, 443 U.S. 55 (1979) (horse trainer's license could be suspended without prior hearing when horse trained by him had been drugged, but trainer had a constitutional right to a prompt postsuspension hearing), discussed pp. 219–20 infra.

In practice, most disputes over hazardous consumer products are resolved through voluntary recalls—although in many instances the manufacturer's "voluntary" participation results from considerable agency prodding and from its desire to avoid the adverse publicity that formal action could entail. From the agency's perspective, a voluntary recall is more attractive than a seizure action because it is usually quicker and requires fewer agency resources. See Schwartz & Adler, *Product Recalls: A Remedy in Need of Repair,* 34 Case W.Res.L.Rev. 401 (1983–84). The desire for expeditious results at low cost also helps to explain why product safety agencies tend to use voluntary recalls as a substitute for rulemaking or other forms of standard-setting. And the courts have inadvertently fostered this tendency, according to one study of automobile safety regulation by the Transportation Department: the agency has scaled back its rulemaking efforts because it is reluctant to commit resources to generating the detailed explanatory statement and comprehensive factual record needed to satisfy a rigorous judicial "hard look." Mashaw & Harfst, *Regulation and Legal Culture: The Case of Motor Vehicle Safety,* 4 Yale J. on Reg. 257 (1987).

Whatever its causes, the agencies' preference for recalls over rulemaking is troubling. Rules setting safety standards for new vehicles prevent injuries far more effectively than recall actions do. Id. at 313. As often as not, car owners do not even respond to recall notices, and neither do the vast majority of owners of other consumer products. Moreover, extensive use of voluntary recalls can undercut agency accountability. When administrators fix the limits of acceptable risk in public rulemaking proceedings, all interested parties have an opportunity to participate in the formulation of policy. To the extent that regulatory action is instead accomplished through informal negotiation, this check on administrative discretion is bypassed.

E. SUPERVISION

In many regulated industries, the agency's constant surveillance of business activities is similar to the physical inspection of regulated products. National bank regulation is one field where pervasive regulation takes place through informal supervision rather than through formal proceedings. Administrators determine who can open a bank, whether a branch bank can be established and where it can be located, what cash reserves must be maintained, what auditing procedures must be followed, whether the bank can enter other businesses, and the like. The administrator may even be empowered to take over a bank at his discretion, without a prior hearing, in order to protect its creditors. Fahey v. Mallonee, 332 U.S. 245 (1947); see also FDIC v. Mallen, 486 U.S. 230 (1988) (summary suspension of bank officer).

Compliance with this extensive regulatory framework is enforced by daily supervision and periodic (often unannounced) visits by bank examiners. When problems or potential violations are uncovered, they are usually resolved quietly by mutual consent. This system of intensive but informal regulation has worked in the banking field because banks are extremely concerned with maintaining public confidence in their fiscal soundness. A bank will surely lose business, and perhaps have to close its doors, if its financial stability is publicly questioned by a regulatory agency. Thus, the agency's decision simply to institute a formal proceeding may be a severe sanction.

The principal risk of continuing supervision is that the agency will have too much or too little "leverage" to enforce compliance with its policies. When the regulated industry is effectively precluded from challenging agency decisions in formal proceedings or on judicial review, as is often the case in bank regulation, the agency may be under little pressure to explain and rationalize its policies, or to apply them consistently. See Scott, *In Quest of Reason: The Licensing Decisions of the*

Federal Banking Agencies, 42 U.Chi.L.Rev. 235 (1975). Here, as elsewhere, the development of "secret law" may result in inadequately considered policy choices and unfair or arbitrary treatment of the regulated. On the other hand, if the agency is unable to back up its supervisory efforts with a credible threat of formal proceedings or other sanctions, the regulatory program may be ineffective. Moreover, when an agency becomes too heavily dependent upon informal supervision, it will not develop the resources and staff expertise required to conduct formal proceedings effectively when the need arises.

F. PUBLICITY

An administrator's decision to issue a press release, hold a news conference, grant an interview, or "leak" a story to the press is usually made informally, yet these publicity-generating activities can be as potent as a formal rule or order. Media coverage of agency activities serves several purposes. Agencies frequently use publicity to warn consumers about dangerous products or fraudulent sales practices. Consumers need to know if cans of a particular brand of soup may cause botulism, or if a new toy on store shelves has a defect that can harm their children. Reports by the press and the broadcast media may be the only effective way to warn people of these risks.

Other uses of publicity may be more questionable. An agency can use the media to enhance, if not exceed, its delegated powers. The EEOC, for example, has reportedly used adverse publicity to supplement weak statutory penalties for employment discrimination. Similarly, the FDA was able to conduct a series of "voluntary" recalls of suspect food products, despite the absence of any explicit statutory authority, because the companies knew that they would be subject to adverse publicity if they refused to cooperate. An official may also exploit press coverage in order to establish his agency's credibility with constituency groups, or to bring pressure to bear on other government agencies. When it was first created, the Environmental Protection Agency vigorously publicized a series of pollution cases it had referred to the Justice Department for prosecution, with the apparent intent of establishing EPA's reputation as a tough enforcement agency (and perhaps also with the idea of making it difficult for the Justice Department to drop the cases). Finally, when the regulated industry is very sensitive to adverse publicity, the agency can threaten disclosure to induce compliance, or use press coverage as a sanction to punish violators for past offenses.

The potential for misuse of agency publicity raises concerns about the fairness of this facet of the administrative process. The effect of unfavorable publicity on the regulated industry can be devastating. Products and companies have been driven out of existence by it, and sometimes the warning turns out to have been a false alarm.

Normally, administrators cannot impose a sanction until the respondent has been afforded notice, an opportunity for a hearing, a reasoned agency decision, and judicial review of final agency action. The publicity sanction has none of these prior safeguards. See, e.g., Industrial Safety Equipment Ass'n v. EPA, 837 F.2d 1115 (D.C.Cir.1988) (agency booklet comparing petitioner's products unfavorably with others was not reviewable agency action). Moreover, the government is not liable for damages caused by adverse publicity, and public denials or even agency recantations cannot cancel out the lingering effects of a damaging public accusation. Thus, the target of adverse publicity will typically have no redress after the fact, unless Congress passes a private bill. Furthermore, the agencies' ability to resort to a publicity sanction may prevent the development of legal penalties and procedures, and leave dubious theories or policies untested.

A few agencies have issued internal rules or guidelines confining their own discretion to publicize pending matters. See, e.g., 28 C.F.R. § 50.2 (Justice Department). Some statutory provisions also confine the agency's discretion to release damaging information. The Consumer Product Safety Commission, for example, cannot disclose information relating to manufacturers of consumer goods unless the agency has first provided the manufacturer with a summary of the information in question and an opportunity to comment on it. The

CPSC also must take "reasonable steps" to assure the accuracy of the information that it releases, and publish a retraction if that information turns out to be wrong. However, these protections do not apply when the agency believes that a product is an imminent hazard to consumers. 15 U.S.C.A. § 2055; cf. CPSC v. GTE Sylvania, Inc., 447 U.S. 102 (1980) (same requirements apply when CPSC releases file information under the Freedom of Information Act).

In the absence of such statutes or administrative rules, a reviewing court would be primarily concerned with whether the agency's informational activities were authorized by statute, and whether prehearing statements by decisionmakers in a formal proceeding constituted a prejudgment of the facts. See pp. 288–93 infra. When adverse publicity is equivalent to a formal accusation of criminal wrongdoing, due process may compel the agency to allow the accused some opportunity to present evidence and cross-examine adverse witnesses. Compare Hannah v. Larche, 363 U.S. 420 (1960) (Civil Rights Commission not required to identify adverse witnesses or permit cross-examination in investigative hearings on racial discrimination), with Jenkins v. McKeithen, 395 U.S. 411 (1969) (state commission holding hearings on labor racketeering required to permit accused individuals to present live testimony and confront and cross-examine witnesses, because commission's investigative hearings were limited to alleged criminal violations).

G. ADVICE AND DECLARATORY ORDERS

The most frequent contacts between private parties and administrators involve requests for advice about agency policies, procedures, or legal interpretations.   Advice-giving can be beneficial to both the regulators and the regulated.   In many situations an administrative statute and the agency's rules and precedents may convey no clear indication of how the agency would deal with a particular act or practice.   Thus, even when a private party has access to good legal advice, she may be unsure about her duties and liabilities.   By learning the agency's current interpretation of the law and perhaps also its enforcement intentions, she can make better decisions and avoid unexpected liabilities.   In addition, when agency personnel have technical expertise in a particular field, they may be able to suggest efficient ways of complying with agency standards or regulations.   A staff member of an environmental agency, for example, might be in a position to share his detailed knowledge of available pollution control technologies with persons working in the affected industries. Access to legal or technical advice from administrators can be particularly important to small businesses, both because they often lack the resources to master the requirements of all of the regulatory programs they encounter, and because they would be more severely damaged if an unwitting violation led to an enforcement action.

From the agency's perspective, advice to the public can be a useful way of inducing voluntary compliance at minimal cost. Giving advice is cheaper and faster than conducting a formal proceeding, or even a major investigation. Moreover, it is usually easier to prevent violations from occurring than to remedy them after the fact. For example, the agency has a definite interest in responding to an inquiry from a private party who is contemplating a major business project, because the requesting party is more likely to acquiesce in the agency's views before she has invested resources and effort in the proposed enterprise.

Agency advisory activities take many forms. At the simplest and most common level, an agency staff person provides information over the telephone or replies to a written inquiry. In some instances, however, the transaction or the point of law involved may be sufficiently important that either the agency or the private party will want a more formal statement of policy from a higher level of the bureaucracy. One of the most formal types of advice is the declaratory order. The APA states that an agency "may issue a declaratory order to terminate a controversy or remove uncertainty," and that these orders are to have "like effect as in the case of other orders." 5 U.S.C.A. § 554(e). Consequently, they are binding on both the agency and the private party. However, the APA declaratory order practice has some significant limitations. One deficiency is that the declaratory order provision is applicable only when the agency decision must be based on a formal trial-type hearing, which eliminates the great majority of situations where advisory opinions are sought. In addition, § 554(e) provides that the issuance of declaratory orders is within the "sound discretion" of the agencies, and apparently none of them has exercised that discretion to make declaratory orders widely available. See generally Powell, *Sinners, Supplicants, and Samaritans: Agency Advice–Giving in Relation to Section 554(e) of the Administrative Procedure Act,* 63 N.C.L.Rev. 339 (1985).

Some agencies, however, have developed elaborate informal processes for rendering advisory opinions. The Internal Revenue Service's revenue ruling procedure is a sophisticated system that issues more than twenty thousand rulings annually. The Service distinguishes between two categories of written advice: unpublished "private letter rulings," which are issued by branch offices; and published rulings, which are approved in the Commissioner's office. The former outnumber the latter by about a hundred to one. Published revenue rulings are official statements of agency policy, and the public may rely on them. However, the Service takes the position that a private letter ruling applies only to the taxpayer to whom it was addressed; other taxpayers should not rely on it, even if their situations are identical, because such rulings have not received thorough consideration at the highest levels of the agency.

The IRS revenue ruling system illustrates some of the dilemmas an agency faces in trying to develop a sound advisory opinion practice. The Service's refusal to be bound by private letter rulings has been criticized for allowing inconsistent treatment of similarly situated taxpayers and for discouraging reliance on administrative precedent. However, a policy of freely authorizing staff members to give binding advice to the public would create a risk that important policy issues would be decided by low level employees without adequate analysis, investigation, or review by supervisors. On the other hand, if the Service undertook to subject more of its advisory opinions to thorough exploration of relevant policy, factual, and legal issues, including high-level review, this administrative function could become so formal as to lose most of the advantages of speed and low cost previously mentioned. The agency would become less willing to give advice, and private parties would less often be able to obtain an answer quickly enough to serve their needs. Ideally, routine inquiries in areas of settled policy should be handled at the staff level, while unresolved issues of law or policy are referred to higher levels of the agency for more formal consideration. In practice, however, it is often difficult to apply this distinction to a particular request—or even to decide who should make the initial assignment.

A related question that arises when agencies give advice to the public is whether even the requesting party can confidently rely upon the advice she receives. Viewing the issue from the administrator's side, is the agency estopped from changing its position if the regulated party relies on advice that is later discovered to be erroneous? The detriment to the private party who sought the advice can be substantial, particularly if she changed her position significantly in reliance on the agency's opinion. On the other hand, when the advice in question was not formally endorsed by the head of the agency, the administrator can argue that any reliance was not reasonable and that the agency should not be bound by the opinions of low level personnel.

Since the purpose of most regulatory programs is to protect the public, it is also possible that the interest in realizing the statutory goals will override the private party's reliance interest. A clear illustration of this principle is Wilmington Chem. Corp. v. Celebrezze, 229 F.Supp. 168 (N.D.Ill.1964), where the manufacturer of a basement waterproofing compound argued that the FDA could not require a more stringent label on cans of its paint that had already been marketed, because the cans had been labeled in reliance on an earlier advisory opinion. The court rejected this contention when the FDA pointed out that it had later learned that a "mere spark"—such as a house furnace starting up—had touched off explosions killing users of the improperly labeled product. Expanding on this theme, the Supreme Court has generally given primacy to the general public interest in effective law enforcement, and has refused to estop the government when it gives erroneous advice. See, e.g., Heckler v. Community Health Services, 467 U.S. 51 (1984) (no estoppel where government's financial intermediary erroneously told health care provider that certain expenses were reimbursable); Schweiker v. Hansen, 450 U.S. 785 (1981) (government not estopped from denying Social Security benefits even though government agent erroneously told applicant she was not eligible and prevented her from filing a claim); Federal Crop Insurance Corp. v. Merrill, 332 U.S. 380 (1947) (government not estopped when private party relied on misrepresentation regarding coverage of crop insurance policy, even though a private insurer would have been estopped under the same circumstances). The Court has not held that the government can never be estopped on the basis of its erroneous advice, but it has clearly indicated that the essential elements of an estoppel—a definite misrepresentation of fact, resulting in reasonable detrimental reliance by the complaining party—will be strictly construed when the government has given bad advice. *Community Health Services,* supra. Fortunately, however, agencies generally do honor reasonable reliance interests as they make enforcement decisions, even where the law does not require them to do so.

Another question that arises when agencies give advice to the public is whether their opinions are subject to judicial review. A declaratory order issued under § 554(e) of the APA is certainly reviewable. See Weinberger v. Hynson, Westcott & Dunning, Inc., 412 U.S. 609, 627 (1973). When a party seeks judicial review of a less formal opinion, however, the question is more difficult. Agencies generally are not required by statute to give advice to the public, and courts have been sensitive to the risk that an agency might write fewer advisory opinions if its pronouncements had to be thorough and polished enough to withstand judicial review. Review can also force the agency to litigate questionable interpretations of law or policy before the administrator's position has fully crystallized, and in a forum and a factual setting not of its choosing. On the other hand, denial of review can mean that the only way a private party can have her rights and liabilities finally determined is by ignoring the agency's advice and risking civil or criminal sanctions. The ripeness doctrine furnishes an apt framework for addressing these competing concerns, although the courts' application of the doctrine is highly discretionary. See pp. 384–87 infra.

Two cases involving SEC "no-action letters" illustrate these difficulties. Companies subject to the securities laws can ask the SEC for advice as to whether certain actions, such as the refusal to include a shareholder's proposal in a proxy statement, would be considered a violation of the Act. If the agency staff concludes that the activity in question would not violate the law, or that at most there might be a technical violation not worthy of corrective action, it will issue a letter stating that the Commission will not take any action against the company. In Medical Committee for Human Rights v. SEC, 432 F.2d 659 (D.C.Cir.1970), vacated as moot, 404 U.S. 403 (1972), a chemical company excluded from its proxy statement a proposal by a group of antiwar stockholders that the company stop manufacturing napalm for use in Vietnam. The SEC issued a no-action letter upholding this refusal, and the court held that this letter was subject to judicial review, noting that the letter had been issued pursuant to well-defined agency procedures, including review by the Commissioners themselves. However, when a similar issue arose in Kixmiller v. SEC, 492 F.2d 641 (D.C.Cir.1974), the court held that there was no reviewable final order. The advice in that case had been given at the staff level, and the Commissioners had declined to examine the controversy. *Kixmiller* seems to establish that an advice letter is unreviewable unless it has been approved by someone who can definitively set policy for the agency. Although only a small fraction of advisory opinions can meet this test, the *Kixmiller* limitation seems appropriate, because it helps to preserve both the free flow of advice and the agency head's control over the evolution of policy within his agency.

H. CONTRACTS AND GRANTS

The federal government spends vast sums of money each year on grants, benefits, and the procurement of goods and services. Grant money pays for programs in fields ranging from education to medical research, and from crime control to pollution control. State and local governments receive most of the grant payments, but universities, hospitals, and community action groups may also be beneficiaries. The federal government is also the primary, or sole, customer for a host of business enterprises. Federal expenditures are largely made through informal action. Agencies are even exempted from the notice-and-comment rulemaking obligations of the APA when they issue rules relating to government "loans, grants, benefits, or contracts," 5 U.S.C.A. § 553(a)(2), although some agencies have adopted regulations declaring that they will not invoke this exemption.

A variety of disputes can arise between the federal government and its contractors or grantees. A disappointed applicant may contend that it was wrongly declared ineligible for funding; an agency may contend that a grant recipient kept inadequate records of its expenditures, or that the goods furnished by a contractor were of insufficient quality. Some agencies have well developed procedures for resolving issues of this kind. For example, the Department of Health and Human Services has long used a Grant Appeals Board, with elaborately defined rules of practice, to hear grievances involving its grantees. See 45 C.F.R. §§ 16.1 et seq. Other agencies have no systematic procedures for resolution of these disputes, although the Administrative Conference has recommended a set of minimum procedures in this area. See 1 C.F.R. § 305.82–2. In extreme cases, the courts have stepped in with due process holdings. See, e.g., Old Dominion Dairy Products, Inc. v. Secretary of Defense, 631 F.2d 953 (D.C.Cir.1980) (defense contractor accused of dishonesty was entitled to notice and opportunity to be heard before contract could be terminated). In practice, however, trial-type hearings are rarely held unless there is a major dispute over performance under a previously awarded grant or contract. Nearly all disputes are resolved informally, through such techniques as compliance reviews prior to awards, reporting requirements and site inspections, and direct negotiation.

I. MANAGEMENT

The government also makes or implements policy in its role as manager, especially through its administration of the public lands. Approximately a third of the nation's land area is in government ownership, and agencies such as the Forest Service, the Bureau of Land Management, and the National Park Service often have considerable discretion in determining how the resources in these federal lands will be used. Issuance of grazing and timber harvesting permits and mineral leases, operation of recreational facilities, construction of public works ranging from backcountry hiking trails to massive dams and reservoirs, and provision of firefighting and rescue services are only a few of the activities that the land management agencies undertake.

Like the grant and contract functions, management activities are exempt from the APA rulemaking procedures (5 U.S.C.A. § 553(a)(2)) and have traditionally been conducted informally. Many of the statutes governing the management of the federal lands recite broad, conflicting objectives (e.g., wilderness preservation *and* economic development), and therefore provide few checks on agency discretion. However, some environmental statutes, particularly the National Environmental Policy Act, 42 U.S.C.A. §§ 4321–61, impose certain procedural requirements and provide opportunities for public participation. Under NEPA, major actions that will significantly affect the environment must be preceded by public release of an environmental impact statement assessing the costs and benefits of the proposal and reviewing alternatives. Interested groups and individuals may submit comments on the impact statement, so that major land use policy decisions are made in a process that resembles the APA's informal rulemaking procedures. However, NEPA does not confine the agencies' substantive discretion, and it does not reach the many decisions that do not constitute "major federal actions." Kleppe v. Sierra Club, 427 U.S. 390 (1976).

CHAPTER VI

PROCEDURAL DUE PROCESS

The Constitution is the source of many of the procedural principles that administrative agencies must observe. The Fifth Amendment, applicable to the federal agencies, provides that no person shall "be deprived of life, liberty, or property, without due process of law," and the Fourteenth Amendment contains a similar limitation on state action. The concept of procedural due process implies that official action must meet minimum standards of fairness to the individual, such as the right to adequate notice and a meaningful opportunity to be heard before a decision is made. This concept gives federal courts a potent tool with which to oversee the decisionmaking procedures of federal agencies when the applicable statutes and regulations permit the administrator to act informally. Equally important, this constitutional doctrine gives the federal judiciary a measure of control over the decisionmaking methods of state and local agencies, which otherwise are governed almost exclusively by state law.

Broadly speaking, judicial decisions applying the due process clauses to administrative action have developed a fairly well defined analytical framework. Since the constitutional language refers to denials of "life, liberty, or property," the threshold question is whether an adverse decision will deprive a person of one of these protected interests. Very few administrative decisions pose threats to life; thus, the usual starting point is to determine whether a protected property or liberty interest exists.

If these and certain other threshold issues are surmounted, the question becomes one of determining what process is "due" under the particular circumstances. This question is often difficult to answer, however, because modern administrative law tries to take account of the enormous diversity of situations in which due process claims can be advanced. Regulatory decisions affect a wide variety of private interests, and the government's justifications for summary action also differ from one setting to the next. In addition, a particular procedural right, such as the opportunity to confront and cross-examine adverse witnesses or the right to be heard by an impartial decisionmaker, may enhance the accuracy and fairness of the process more substantially in one setting than in another. Consequently, due process rights in administrative law can vary enormously, depending on the context in which they are asserted.

A. INTERESTS PROTECTED BY DUE PROCESS

Traditionally, the interests protected by the due process clauses were defined quite narrowly. Many government benefits and grants were consid-

ered mere gratuities or "privileges" rather than
rights; like a private donor, the government could
impose whatever conditions it wished on its gift, or
even remove the benefit at will. This view was
exemplified by Justice Holmes' famous dictum, in
upholding the firing of a police officer for political
activities, that "[t]he petitioner may have a constitutional right to talk politics, but he has no constitutional right to be a policeman." McAuliffe v.
Mayor of New Bedford, 155 Mass. 216, 29 N.E. 517
(1892). Reflecting this attitude, courts held for
many years that government employment was not
an interest protected by due process and thus could
be terminated without any procedural protection.
See Bailey v. Richardson, 182 F.2d 46 (D.C.Cir.
1950), aff'd by equally divided Court, 341 U.S. 918
(1951).

During the 1960's, however, as the size of the
bureaucracy grew and public concern about government's obligations to its citizens became more
acute, the soundness of the right-privilege distinction was questioned. Commentators pointed out
that a wide variety of forms of social wealth, ranging from TV station licenses to truck routes to
occupational licenses to welfare benefits, were the
results of government largess, and thus were "privileges." As government expanded, these new
forms of wealth had become increasingly vital to
the individual; often, the loss of a government job,
or an occupational license, or a welfare payment,
could deprive a person of her livelihood. Thus, to

maintain the balance between government and individual, it was necessary to extend the protections of due process to this "new property." See generally Reich, *The New Property,* 73 Yale L.J. 733 (1964).

Accordingly, the Supreme Court started to edge away from the right-privilege distinction. In Cafeteria & Restaurant Workers Union v. McElroy, 367 U.S. 886 (1961), the Court held that a government employee who was stripped of her security clearance, and thus her ability to work at a naval base, was not entitled to a specification of charges and an opportunity to know and refute adverse evidence. Nevertheless, the Court indicated that the right-privilege distinction was "perhaps [an] oversimplification"; the Court used a more flexible line of reasoning, arguing that the government's proprietary interest in unfettered management of a military base outweighed the employee's interest in keeping her job as a short-order cook at a specific site.

The Court finally abandoned the right-privilege distinction in Goldberg v. Kelly, 397 U.S. 254, 261–63 (1970). In that case, welfare beneficiaries in New York claimed that their payments had been terminated without due process of law. The Court said that these claims could not be defeated by a mere assertion that the benefits were gratuities or privileges. (Actually, the state defendants had made no such assertion, but the Court's dictum was quickly recognized as authoritative.) The welfare program in question was based on a system of statutory entitlements: all applicants who met the conditions defined by the legislature were entitled to receive public assistance. Consequently, the state had to afford due process safeguards—in this instance, an oral hearing—before it could terminate the benefits.

With the demise of the right-privilege distinction, the Court needed to develop a new method for deciding who was entitled to due process protection. The Court unveiled such an approach in Board of Regents of State Colleges v. Roth, 408 U.S. 564 (1972). There an untenured instructor at a state university was held to have no due process right to be heard when the university refused to renew his contract. Emphasizing the language of the Fourteenth Amendment, the Court noted that the requirements of procedural due process extend only to those who have been deprived of "liberty" or "property." The Court went on to explain that the loss of a governmental benefit is a deprivation of "property" only if the individual has a "legitimate claim of entitlement" to the benefit, rather than merely a "unilateral expectation" of it. Since neither state law nor university rules nor the contract itself had given Roth a legitimate basis for claiming that he was "entitled" to a renewal of the contract, he had possessed no "property" interest in continued employment beyond his contract year. Similarly, Roth had not been deprived of "liberty" in the constitutional sense, because, so far as the record showed, he "simply [was] not rehired in one job but remain[ed] as free as before to seek another."

The *Roth* approach of examining initially whether a plaintiff has been deprived of liberty or property has retained its vitality down to the present day. Both of these two pivotal concepts, however, have been refined by subsequent case law developments.

1. PROPERTY

In many administrative settings, it is easy to show that an agency decision has deprived someone of "property." For example, coercive regulation of business enterprises, almost by definition, invades their property interests, because it limits their freedom to engage in profitable activity. Thus, the difficult cases usually involve governmental benefits. In these so-called "new property" cases, *Roth* requires the court to consider whether the plaintiff had a "legitimate claim of entitlement" to the benefit of which she was deprived. The claim of entitlement does not arise from the Constitution itself; it must rest upon "existing rules or understandings that stem from an independent source such as state law." Thus, the plaintiff must demonstrate that, according to some authoritative source of law, she has a *right* to the benefit in question if she meets certain criteria. To state the same point inversely, she must show that the benefit cannot be withheld from her except "for cause." For example, the welfare claimants in *Goldberg* plainly had a property interest at stake, because the underlying federal legislation provided that everyone who satisfied certain criteria had a legal right to receive welfare payments. Similarly, the Court in *Roth* indicated that the teacher in that case would have been entitled to due process protections if he had been dismissed during the term of his contract, because the contract itself had secured his interest in employment during that period.

The companion case of Perry v. Sindermann, 408 U.S. 593 (1972), indicated, however, that an employee's claim of entitlement does not have to be based upon a written contract or a statutory grant of job tenure. There, a dismissed teacher claimed that the college had a de facto tenure system: policy guidelines issued by the state education system provided that teachers who had successfully completed a probationary period, as the respondent had, could expect continued employment. The Court analogized this informal tenure system to an implied contract term, and concluded that it was sufficient to give the dismissed teacher a constitutionally protected property interest.

The Court has extended the "entitlement" concept to many other kinds of cases in which a deprivation of "property" has been alleged. For example, when the state grants all children the right to attend public schools, and establishes rules specifying the grounds for suspension, it cannot suspend a given student for alleged misconduct without affording the student at least a limited prior hearing. Goss v. Lopez, 419 U.S. 565 (1975). Similarly, a horse trainer whose license was suspended had the right to due process (a prompt postsuspension hearing) because, according to the Court, New York law entitled him to keep the license unless it were shown "that his horse had been drugged and that he was at least negligent in failing to prevent the drugging." Barry v. Barchi, 443 U.S. 55 (1979). Even a cause of action can be a constitutionally protected property right. In Logan v. Zimmerman Brush Co., 455 U.S. 422 (1982), an Illinois commission was required by statute to redress all meritorious claims of employment discrimination against the handicapped. Therefore, when the agency denied relief to the plaintiff by invoking a blatantly unfair procedural rule (under state law, the complaint had to be dismissed if the commission did not schedule a hearing within 120 days, although plaintiff had no control over the agency's scheduling), it violated his due process rights.

Of course, when Congress and the states create public benefits, they usually create procedures by which citizens can seek to protect those benefits. It took some time for the courts to work out the relationship between those procedures and the dictates of due process. One aspect of this problem came into focus in Arnett v. Kennedy, 416 U.S. 134 (1974). Kennedy, a federal civil service employee, was fired after accusing his superior of illegal activities. He filed suit, seeking a pretermination evidentiary hearing under the due process clause. The relevant statute, the Lloyd–LaFollette Act, provided that employees in Kennedy's job category could be dismissed "only for such cause as will promote the efficiency of the service"; therefore, he had a protected property interest. But the Act also provided that this right would be protected through a written protest procedure rather than a trial-type hearing. A plurality of three Justices, led by Justice Rehnquist, concluded that the legislatively created right not to be terminated except for cause could not be considered in the abstract, apart from the procedural mechanism that Congress had designed for its implementation. Rehnquist concluded that "where the grant of a substantive right is inextricably intertwined with the limitations on the procedures which are to be employed in determining that right, a litigant in the position of [plaintiff] must take the bitter with the sweet." The other six Justices rejected Rehnquist's theory that the procedures provided by the Act could define civil service employees' due process rights. (Kennedy lost his case, however, because the Court's swing voters thought that due process did not require an evidentiary hearing.)

When the Court again considered the due process rights of government employees in Bishop v. Wood, 426 U.S. 341 (1976), it managed to steer around the question that Justice Rehnquist had raised in *Arnett.* The petitioner in *Bishop* had been fired from his job as a city policeman. A city ordinance provided that a permanent employee like the petitioner could be dismissed for cause, such as for negligence or inefficiency on the job. Although this language seemed to mean that the petitioner could not be fired in the absence of cause, the Court relied heavily on the lower courts' interpretation of state law and concluded that he "held his position at the will and pleasure of the city." Having read the ordinance as not conferring any "sweet," the Court did not need to decide whether the petitioner had to "take the bitter" as well.

Ultimately, the Court squarely rejected the *Arnett* plurality's "bitter with the sweet" theory. In Cleveland Board of Education v. Loudermill, 470 U.S. 532 (1985), the Court insisted upon due process safeguards for a discharged city security guard who, under Ohio statutes, could only have been fired for cause. The Court emphasized that substance and procedure are distinct in due process analysis. Once a state creates entitlements through substantive laws or standards, the adequacy of procedures used to deprive individuals of those entitlements depends on federal constitutional law, and state laws or regulations cannot foreclose the due process inquiry.[1]

1. On the other hand, state-created procedures cannot *expand* federal due process rights, either. Thus, a procedural guarantee in a state statute or regulation does not create a property interest, see *Bishop v. Wood,* supra, and the breach of

2. LIBERTY

The conceptual unity that the Court has reached in its definition of "property" is absent from its approach to the companion concept, "liberty." The *Roth* opinion itself showed the Court's ambivalence. On the one hand, the Court said that the definition of liberty must be "broad," encompassing " 'not merely freedom from bodily restraint but also the right of the individual to contract, to engage in any of the common occupations of life, to acquire useful knowledge, to marry, establish a home and bring up children, to worship God according to the dictates of . . . conscience, and generally to enjoy those privileges long recognized . . . as essential to the orderly pursuit of happiness by free men' " (quoting Meyer v. Nebraska, 262 U.S. 390, 399 (1923)). Yet the holding in *Roth* belied this liberal spirit; at least, the Court did not explain why the opportunity to keep a teaching position at a state university, or another government job, was not comparable to the freedoms on the *Meyer* list. Indeed, the Court seemed to be striving to keep its options open, declaring that an interest would not qualify as "liberty" merely because it was important to the individual: "we must look not to the 'weight' but to the *nature* of the

such a guarantee is not a due process violation. Board of Curators v. Horowitz, 435 U.S. 78 (1978). A claimant in this situation must rely on whatever remedy the state has provided. A federal agency's breach of a federal statute or regulation, of course, can be redressed under the APA. See pp. 98–99 supra.

interest at stake." This unconstrained approach plainly left room for odd disparities—as the Court demonstrated a few years later, when it held, despite *Roth,* that a ten-day suspension from high school *did* implicate a liberty interest. Goss v. Lopez, 419 U.S. 565 (1975).

Despite the *Roth* opinion's reticence, one can perceive various factors that may have made the Court reluctant to extend due process guarantees to all dismissed government employees. One such concern was expressed in Bishop v. Wood, 426 U.S. 341 (1976): a less restrictive approach could involve the federal courts in the impossible task of supervising "the multitude of personnel decisions that are made daily by public agencies." Many of those decisions are made by state or local agencies, so that federalism concerns are also relevant. In addition, many public employees enjoy nonconstitutional protections against arbitrary dismissal, by virtue of the procedures of their civil service systems. With the spread of collective bargaining in government, unions and contractual grievance procedures often provide a further source of protection against improper dismissal or suspension. Finally, recent First Amendment decisions have made clear that government employees cannot be dismissed for their political beliefs or affiliations unless "the hiring authority can demonstrate that party affiliation is an appropriate requirement for the effective performance of the public office involved." Branti v. Finkel, 445 U.S. 507 (1980). But see

Connick v. Myers, 461 U.S. 138 (1983) (public employee's speech on personnel matters can constitute insubordination that justifies dismissal).

The Court did say in *Roth* that the plaintiff would have had a stronger case if the employer, in declining to rehire him, had made a charge against him that might injure his reputation. The Court has adhered to this notion that reputational harm tends to show a deprivation of liberty, but has circumscribed it in a number of ways. First, the *Roth* opinion noted that the purpose of guaranteeing a hearing to a stigmatized employee is simply "to provide the person an opportunity to clear his name"; the employer is free to grant a name-clearing hearing and then to dismiss the employee for other reasons. Later decisions added further qualifications: stigmatizing reasons for a discharge are not actionable unless the employer discloses them to the public, *Bishop v. Wood,* supra, and unless the plaintiff raises a substantial issue about the accuracy of the charge. Codd v. Velger, 429 U.S. 624 (1977).[2]

2. The plaintiff in *Codd* was a policeman who had been terminated for misusing a firearm. He admitted the incident but sought a hearing on the question of whether it justified his discharge. The Court recognized that a party does not normally lose a due process right to a hearing when the underlying facts of his case are undisputed; for example, a parolee threatened with reincarceration who admits the violation with which he is charged is still entitled to a hearing at which he can argue that his parole should nevertheless not be revoked. But, the Court continued, the purpose of a *Roth* name-clearing hearing is solely to enable the individual to refute a stigmatizing charge, not to lay the groundwork for reconsideration of the state's

The most heavily criticized of the Court's opinions on the role of stigma is Paul v. Davis, 424 U.S. 693 (1976). In *Paul*, two local police departments included Davis' name and picture in a flyer listing "active shoplifters," which was distributed to hundreds of merchants in his home town. Despite Davis' claim that distribution of the leaflet impaired his future job opportunities and made him reluctant to enter stores for fear of being apprehended, the Court concluded that he had not suffered any injury to a constitutionally protected liberty interest. The Court said that injury to reputation does not entail a loss of liberty when it stands alone, but only when it is accompanied by some alteration in the plaintiff's legal status, such as the loss of employment in *Roth*. Few writers have thought that this analysis made sense, or that the Court was persuasive in its efforts to demonstrate that this restrictive concept of liberty was consistent with precedent.[3] The Court seemed to be motivated by a desire to keep the federal judiciary from absorbing too much of the business of

adverse action. Since the officer did not dispute the state's account of the facts, there was no basis for a hearing.

3. For example, in Wisconsin v. Constantineau, 400 U.S. 433 (1971), the Court condemned a state's practice of "posting"— causing lists of "excessive" drinkers to be posted in all city liquor stores. The Court found that the state had violated due process by publicly branding petitioner with this "degrading" label without giving her notice and an opportunity to defend herself. In *Paul*, however, the majority explained *Constantineau* as a case in which the stigma was accompanied by a change in legal status, because stores were forbidden to sell liquor to a person who had been "posted."

state courts, which have historically protected reputation through defamation actions. Subsequently, however, the Court has come to understand that it can incorporate the adequacy of state remedies into its due process calculus more straightforwardly, see pp. 220–23 infra; and so, without expressly overruling *Paul,* it has quietly ceased using artificial limitations on the scope of constitutionally protected interests as a means of preventing overlap between the Constitution and state tort law.

Another challenge has been to define the due process interests of prisoners. Prison bureaucracies and parole boards make decisions every day that in some sense affect the "liberty" of incarcerated persons, and the Court has felt a need to prevent the federal courts from being deluged with cases challenging these decisions on due process grounds.

One way in which the Court has sought to identify those prisoners' cases qualifying for constitutional protection is heavy reliance on the *Roth* concept of entitlements. For example, in holding that a disciplinary proceeding to revoke a prisoner's "good time" credits (and thus to increase the time he would actually serve on his sentence) had to meet constitutional requirements of due process, the Court stressed that the statute made accrual of good time a right, subject to forfeiture only for serious misconduct. Wolff v. McDonnell, 418 U.S. 539 (1974). The Court has never explained why the entitlements concept, originally designed as an elaboration of the meaning of the term "property," is an appropriate tool for defining "liberty". However, nothing turns on which label the Court uses, because the tests for identifying entitlements under *Roth* have been followed faithfully in this new context. Thus, the inmate must demonstrate a legal basis for his expectancy, such as a statute or regulation; a mere statistical showing that most similarly situated prisoners have received favorable treatment is not sufficient to create a constitutionally protected liberty interest. Connecticut Board of Pardons v. Dumschat, 452 U.S. 458 (1981). And, as in the case of property interests, state-created *procedures* neither limit the scope of due process protections, Vitek v. Jones, 445 U.S. 480 (1980), nor create an entitlement where none would otherwise exist, Olim v. Wakinekona, 461 U.S. 238 (1983).

Prisoners who cannot point to an entitlement created by law or regulation remain free to rely on the Constitution as the source of an "inherent" liberty interest, but this line of argument has had mixed success. It has prevailed in cases in which a convicted criminal who has been conditionally released is sent back to prison because of some alleged misconduct. Obviously, such reincarceration entails a major loss of personal freedom, and due process protections have been accorded. See Gagnon v. Scarpelli, 411 U.S. 778 (1973) (probation revocation); Morrissey v. Brewer, 408 U.S. 471 (1972) (parole revocation). Yet the Court declined to find that a prisoner loses an inherent liberty interest by being refused parole in the first place. Greenholtz v. Inmates of Nebraska Penal and Correction Complex, 442 U.S. 1 (1979) (noting the "human difference between losing what one has and not getting what one wants").

In some of these cases, the Court has argued that when an individual is validly convicted of a crime and sentenced to incarceration, he loses much of the inherent right to be free from bodily restraint that other citizens enjoy.[4] Thus, in the absence of a statutory liberty entitlement, he may be transferred from one prison facility to another without a due process hearing, Meachum v. Fano, 427 U.S. 215 (1976), even if the transfer takes him out of state and far away from friends and relatives. Olim v. Wakinekona, supra. Such a transfer is within the ambit of his sentence—that is, it is the sort of confinement that inmates should reasonably expect. On the other hand, an inmate's transfer from prison to a mental hospital for involuntary treatment and behavior modification is "qualitatively different" from what would be expected in his sentence, and therefore involves an inherent liberty interest. Vitek v. Jones, 445 U.S. 480 (1980).

---

4. Outside the corrections area, the Court has had no hesitation about finding that direct governmental intrusions on physical freedom and body integrity implicate the "liberty" element of due process. See Parham v. J.R., 442 U.S. 584 (1979) (commitment of minors to mental institution); Ingraham v. Wright, 430 U.S. 651 (1977) (corporal punishment of schoolchildren).

On the whole, the case law dealing with both property and liberty is somewhat unsatisfying, because the Court's conceptual distinctions seem only distantly related to notions of fundamental procedural fairness, the traditional touchstone of due process. However, so long as the courts remain determined to contain the expansive pressure of the "due process explosion," they will probably continue to enforce these occasionally harsh threshold limitations on the right to enjoy due process protection.

B. OTHER THRESHOLD ISSUES

Even where a plaintiff can show a "property" or "liberty" interest that has been infringed, she may face other threshold obstacles to her pursuit of a procedural due process claim. First, an injury to a protected interest does not qualify as a "deprivation" if it was inflicted through mere negligence rather than deliberately. Daniels v. Williams, 474 U.S. 327 (1986) (deputy who negligently left pillow on stairway, where prisoner tripped on it, did not "deprive" him of liberty). The Court observed in *Daniels* that "[h]istorically, [the] guarantee of due process has been applied to *deliberate* decisions of government officials to deprive a person of life, liberty, or property," and that to extend its scope to negligent actions would "trivialize" the Constitution. However, the Court declined to decide whether any kind of unintended conduct, such as reckless or grossly negligent behavior, might qualify as a "deprivation." (Normally, of course, when an agency imposes a penalty or withholds a benefit, it knows that it is causing the individual to suffer a loss; thus, the *Daniels* principle is not an issue in the typical administrative law case.)

Second, a person is entitled to due process only if the challenged order is directed at her; a plaintiff who may be worse off because of government action towards a third party has no constitutional injury. Thus, in O'Bannon v. Town Court Nursing Center, 447 U.S. 773 (1980), the Court held that patients at a subsidized nursing home had no right to participate in proceedings to revoke the home's Medicaid certification and terminate its subsidy. The Court assumed that some of the elderly patients could suffer physical or psychological trauma from being forced to relocate; yet it concluded that this loss was only "an indirect and incidental result of the Government's enforcement action," and thus did not implicate their due process rights. Only the nursing home itself had a right to be heard on the issue of decertification. The Court's reluctance to provide constitutional protection for indirect benefits may reflect its concern that a different result would greatly increase the number of persons entitled to participate in decisions, and thereby disrupt the functioning of welfare or regulatory programs.

A final limitation, which is of vital importance in administrative law, is that procedural due process guarantees are directed primarily at adjudicative action and are rarely applicable to agency rulemaking proceedings. The Court laid the foundations for this doctrine in two early property tax assessment cases. In Londoner v. Denver, 210 U.S. 373 (1908), the city of Denver sought to assess property owners for improvements to their street. Each owner's assessment was based on the amount of benefit accruing to her particular parcel. The Court held that the city had to afford each owner an evidentiary hearing. On the other hand, in Bi–Metallic Inv. Co. v. State Bd. of Equalization, 239 U.S. 441 (1915), the Court upheld an agency regulation increasing the valuation of all taxable property in Denver by 40 percent, even though the board had given no notice or hearing whatever to the affected property owners. "Where a rule of conduct applies to more than a few people," Justice Holmes wrote, "it is impracticable that every one should have a direct voice in its adoption." The *Bi–Metallic* doctrine—limiting due process rights in rulemaking—has been repeatedly reaffirmed in modern decisions. See, e.g., United States v. Florida East Coast Ry., 410 U.S. 224 (1973) (evidentiary hearing unnecessary in ICC proceeding to set uniform nationwide rail charges).

The *Bi–Metallic* principle has been explained on various grounds. One argument stresses the functional similarity between rulemaking and legislation. Since members of the public obviously have no constitutional right to testify or submit evidence to Congress before a statute affecting them can be enacted, the argument runs, they also have no fundamental right to appear before agency officials who are exercising delegated legislative power. A second argument notes the impossibility of granting a hearing to everyone when a regulation applies to numerous individuals. Government "would likely grind to a halt were policymaking constrained by constitutional requirements on whose voices must be heard." Minnesota State Board for Community Colleges v. Knight, 465 U.S. 271 (1984). A third rationale is that rulemaking characteristically turns on "legislative facts" as opposed to "adjudicative facts." The terminology is that of Professor Davis, who defines adjudicative facts as those having to do with the parties to a dispute, while legislative facts are general propositions that a tribunal uses in formulating law or policy. 2 K. Davis, Administrative Law Treatise § 12:3 (2d ed. 1979). Davis argues that the parties to an adjudication should be allowed broad participation rights, because they are normally in the best position to produce information about themselves and their activities. In contrast, he argues, the critical facts in a rulemaking proceeding are unlikely to be any more accessible to one member of the affected class than to another, and it would be wasteful to guarantee each member of the class a right to an individualized hearing.

The *Bi–Metallic* doctrine is certainly authoritative in situations that can be unambiguously characterized as rulemaking. However, it is less clear that the case applies with full force to proceedings that fall into the gray area between rulemaking and adjudication (see pp. 313–15 infra). The *Bi–Metallic* rationales tend to lose force as the number of persons affected by the rule shrinks. For example, when an agency proposes a regulation that would govern an industry in which there are only a few firms, granting a trial-type hearing to all of them might well be feasible. Moreover, the categories of adjudicative and legislative facts tend to merge in cases of this sort, because information about the companies that are to be regulated would probably be crucial to any decision about whether the proposed rule is sound policy. The Court has left the door open to due process protection in such cases. See Vermont Yankee Nuclear Power Corp. v. NRDC, 435 U.S. 519, 542 (1978). For the most part, however, the tradition represented by *Bi–Metallic* remains strong; courts that have insisted that the public be given some right to be heard in rulemaking proceedings have tended to avoid resting their holdings squarely on the due process clause. See pp. 329–36 infra.

C. THE PROCESS THAT IS DUE

Once it has been determined that a constitutionally protected liberty or property interest was infringed, the next stage of the due process analysis is to decide what procedures the Constitution requires. Much of the Supreme Court's case law on this topic can be understood as elaborating upon—

or, more often, reacting against—the Court's expansive ruling in Goldberg v. Kelly, 397 U.S. 254 (1970). There the Court held that welfare recipients in New York had to be afforded an evidentiary hearing before they could be terminated from the program. At the hearing, they would be entitled to many of the procedural safeguards that had historically been available in court proceedings, such as the right to present a case orally, to confront adverse witnesses, to appear through an attorney, and to receive a decision based exclusively on the hearing record.

The *Goldberg* opinion gave rise to concern that the Court might soon impose trial-type procedures in many other programs, including ones in which courtroom methods would be ineffective or too expensive. In Mathews v. Eldridge, 424 U.S. 319 (1976), however, the Court demonstrated that it was determined to maintain flexibility in due process analysis. The Court declared that it would look at three factors in order to decide what due process requires in a given situation: "First, the private interest that will be affected by the official action; second, the risk of an erroneous deprivation of such interest through the procedures used, and the probable value, if any, of additional or substitute safeguards; and finally, the Government's interest, including the function involved and the fiscal and administrative burdens that the additional or substitute procedural requirement would entail." Applying this balancing test, the

Court held that an order terminating a person's Social Security disability benefits need not be preceded by an evidentiary hearing.

The *Mathews* test has been criticized as being so open-ended as to give courts little guidance: judges are put into the position of making policy choices much as a legislator would do. On the other hand, the test has also been criticized as too restrictive: it implies that procedures are to be evaluated solely on the impersonal basis of whether they promote or detract from *accuracy,* without regard to whether the individual is likely to *feel* that she has been treated fairly. But the Court has continued to invoke the three-factor test in a wide variety of factual settings. Indeed, although at first the Court used the test primarily in "new property" cases, where government benefits were at issue, more recently the Court has also applied the *Mathews* analysis in a more tradition-bound area of administrative law—coercive regulation of business. See Brock v. Roadway Express, Inc., 481 U.S. 252 (1987) (using *Mathews* test to decide rights of employer who was ordered by government to reinstate an employee while the latter's allegations of retaliatory discharge were pending).

In applying the *Mathews* formula, a court is not limited to an either-or choice between a full trial-type hearing and the informal procedures the agency is already using. Rather, each procedural right must be analyzed separately, and alternatives or intermediate procedural models must be considered. For purposes of explanation, the procedural rights that have been examined most frequently in due process litigation can be grouped into several broad categories.

1. PRIOR NOTICE AND HEARING

"An elementary and fundamental requirement of due process in any proceeding which is to be accorded finality is notice reasonably calculated, under all the circumstances, to apprise interested parties of the pendency of the action and afford them an opportunity to present their objections." Mullane v. Central Hanover Bank & Trust Co., 339 U.S. 306, 314 (1950). Without proper prior notice to those who may be affected by a government decision, all other procedural rights may be nullified. The exact contents of the notice required by due process will, of course, vary with the circumstances. The *Goldberg* decision stated that welfare beneficiaries were entitled to a notice "detailing the reasons for the proposed termination." In another case, a municipal utility's notice threatening a customer with termination of service was held inadequate because it did not spell out the procedural avenues by which she could protest the proposed termination. Memphis Light, Gas & Water Div. v. Craft, 436 U.S. 1 (1978). On the other hand, the Court sustained the action of Massachusetts officials who sent a form letter to food stamp recipients advising them of a statutory change that could reduce or eliminate their benefits. Atkins v. Parker, 472 U.S. 115 (1985). Even though the notice did not inform recipients of their new benefit levels, it did give them a general awareness of the new law, so that they could make further inquiry and challenge the computations in their respective cases if they wished.

Although prior notice of threatened adverse action is generally required, there are some exceptions to this principle. Most involve a demonstrated need for immediate action to protect the public from serious harm. See generally Freedman, *Summary Action by Administrative Agencies*, 40 U.Chi. L.Rev. 1 (1972). Thus, prehearing seizures of potentially dangerous or mislabeled consumer products have been upheld. Ewing v. Mytinger & Casselberry, Inc., 339 U.S. 594 (1950); North American Cold Storage Co. v. Chicago, 211 U.S. 306 (1908). Serious financial risks to the public or to the government's revenues may also justify summary action. See, e.g., FDIC v. Mallen, 486 U.S. 230 (1988) (upholding statute providing for summary suspension of bank officer who has been indicted for a felony involving dishonesty); Phillips v. Commissioner, 283 U.S. 589 (1931) (summary seizure of taxpayer's property to assure payment of taxes upheld against due process challenge). Even a threat to the integrity of state-sanctioned wagering on horse races has been held sufficient to justify summary suspension of the license of a trainer suspected of drugging horses. Barry v. Barchi, 443 U.S. 55 (1979).

In *Barchi,* the Court added an important qualification: due process required a prompt postsuspension hearing, so that the horse trainer would have a reasonable opportunity to clear his name and the deprivation would not be unnecessarily prolonged. However, the state in that case had not attempted to justify its failure to grant a prompt hearing; and in subsequent cases, where government interests have been more clearly articulated, the Court has been reluctant to extend the *Barchi* holding. For example, in *Mallen,* the Court held that a ninety-day wait between the bank officer's request for a hearing and the final decision would not necessarily violate due process, in light of the public's strong interest in the agency's reaching a well-considered decision about whether to reinstate him. Thus, the question of how quickly an agency must proceed with adjudication following a summary action depends on a careful weighing of competing interests. See United States v. $8,850 in U.S. Currency, 461 U.S. 555 (1983) (applying balancing test to delay in filing of proceedings for forfeiture of illegally imported currency). Even a nine-months' wait for adjudication to run its course is not necessarily too lengthy. Cleveland Board of Education v. Loudermill, 470 U.S. 532 (1985) (no unconstitutional delay in decision on whether to reinstate suspended public employee).

Another consideration that can militate against the right to predeprivation notice and hearing is the availability of statutory or common law remedies that can compensate the individual for her loss of liberty or property. Under the right circumstances, courts will hold that such a remedy itself provides the "process that is due." For example, in Ingraham v. Wright, 430 U.S. 651 (1977), the Court upheld a state statute and local school board regulations which authorized teachers to paddle students for misconduct, even though the students had no right to notice or a hearing before the punishment was inflicted. Under state law an injured student could bring a damage action if the teacher used excessive force, and this was considered adequate protection to satisfy the requirements of due process. Similarly, in Parratt v. Taylor, 451 U.S. 527 (1981), a prisoner claimed that state prison officials had negligently lost a hobby kit (worth $23.50) that had been mailed to him. The Court held that this "deprivation of property" had occurred *with* due process, because the state had made available a small-claims procedure by which he could seek compensation for his loss. The Court extended the *Parratt* holding to deliberate deprivations of property in Hudson v. Palmer, 468 U.S. 517 (1984). The plaintiff in *Hudson* was a prisoner whose personal effects had been intentionally destroyed by a prison guard. Again the Court found no due process violation, because the prisoner could have sought redress through a tort action.[5]

---

5. *Parratt* has since been overruled insofar as it assumed that due process constraints apply to deprivations that are merely negligent. See pp. 211–12 supra. However, this development does not impair the authority of *Hudson*, in which the deprivation was deliberate.

However, the principle that state remedies can provide the "process that is due" has been confined to situations in which the state has strong reasons not to grant a predeprivation hearing. In *Ingraham,* the Court was concerned that a requirement of a prior hearing would deter teachers from paddling students and undermine their disciplinary authority. In *Parratt* and *Hudson,* the Court saw no way in which the prison could have improved its procedures for preventing mistakes or unauthorized misconduct by its personnel; therefore, a compensation system was as good a solution as the state could provide. In contrast, where predeprivation process would be practicable, the Court has insisted on it. For example, the municipal utility in *Memphis Light* could easily have given its customer an explanation of its protest procedure before shutting off her service. Accordingly, the Court found that the customer's due process rights had been violated, even though she theoretically could have retained an attorney and sued for an injunction or refund. The Court noted that it was unrealistic to expect a consumer to engage counsel in a case involving such small monetary stakes. Similarly, in Zinermon v. Burch, 110 S.Ct. 975 (1990), a mental patient sued hospital officials for institutionalizing him through "voluntary" commitment procedures at a time when he was incompetent to give valid consent. Despite the availability of state damage remedies, the Court allowed the plaintiff's due process challenge to proceed, because the state could practicably have devised additional safeguards to reduce the risk of erroneous commitment. See also Logan v. Zimmerman Brush Co., 455 U.S. 422 (1982) (state's use of unfair procedural rule to extinguish plaintiff's employment discrimination claim violated due process, although tort remedy was also available).

2. TRIAL–TYPE HEARINGS

Often a litigant claiming a denial of due process will ask the court to hold that the agency must afford her procedural rights similar to those used in judicial trials or formal administrative trial-type hearings—including the rights to present testimony orally and to confront and cross-examine adverse witnesses. In *Goldberg,* the Court held that welfare recipients facing termination of their benefits were entitled to nearly all of these rights. In subsequent cases, however, the Court has made clear that trial procedures are not essential for every government decision that might affect an individual. The suspended students in Goss v. Lopez, 419 U.S. 565 (1975), for example, were entitled only to an oral statement of the charges against them, and a chance to tell their side of the story. The discharged public employee in Cleveland Board of Education v. Loudermill, 470 U.S. 532 (1985), received a slightly more elaborate version of this informal oral hearing: he was entitled to "oral or written notice of the charges against him, an explanation of the employer's evidence, and an opportunity to present his side of the sto-

ry." The employer subjected to a temporary rein-
statement order in Brock v. Roadway Express, Inc.,
481 U.S. 252 (1987), received similar rights, including the right to support its case with a written
response and witness affidavits. As these examples make clear, the courts are reluctant to impose
the full panoply of trial-type procedures when
there is a reasonable likelihood that less burdensome oral proceedings will adequately protect the
individual's interest.

In deciding what safeguards are required in a
particular situation, courts are heavily influenced
by the nature of the questions that are likely to
arise. In *Goldberg,* the Court considered oral testimony and cross-examination essential in a welfare
termination case, because "written submissions are
a wholly unsatisfactory basis for decision" in proceedings where "credibility and veracity are at
issue." On the other hand, an oral hearing may
not be necessary when the usual questions to be
resolved are relatively straightforward or objective.
The Court relied on this proposition in *Mathews* as
one basis for holding that the Social Security Administration complied with due process when it
used written submissions as the basis for terminating an individual's disability benefits, with an evidentiary hearing available only after the cutoff.
The Court reasoned that the decision in such a
proceeding was likely to turn on medical reports
written by doctors, or on statistical evidence such
as data concerning the availability of jobs in the

national economy. These issues could be effectively aired through an exchange of documents. The *Mathews* opinion also noted that the opportunity to file written submissions had been characterized in *Goldberg* as an "unrealistic option" for most AFDC recipients, because they "lack the educational attainment to write effectively" and often "cannot obtain professional assistance." In *Mathews,* on the other hand, disability claimants could obtain assistance in completing the necessary forms from the local Social Security office, and most of the important medical evidence was provided directly by treating physicians, who presumably were competent to communicate clearly in written reports.[6]

The Court revisited the reasoning of both *Goldberg* and *Mathews* when it decided Califano v. Yamasaki, 442 U.S. 682 (1979), a case involving attempts by the Secretary of Health and Human Services (HHS) to recover overpayments of Social Security disability benefit payments. As prescribed by statute, HHS first determined whether an overpayment had been made, and then decided whether the government's right to recoup the overpayment should be waived. The regulations provided that the waiver decision turned in part on

6. The first factor in the *Mathews* calculus—the private interests at stake—also served to distinguish that case from *Goldberg.* The earlier case had observed that welfare claimants would be deprived of "the very means with which to live" if they were erroneously terminated. In contrast, *Mathews* pointed out that disability benefits recipients were not necessarily poor, and that those who were could fall back on other public assistance programs such as welfare and food stamps.

the applicant's fault—that is, whether she had known or should have known that there was an overpayment. The Court held that, because the fault determination could depend on an assessment of credibility, oral procedures were necessary (although the Court was able to rest this decision on a statutory ground, avoiding an unnecessary constitutional holding).[7] However, HHS's initial determinations as to whether there had been an overpayment did not require an oral hearing, because such determinations usually depended on objective data such as earnings reports.

Another line of cases deals with decisions that are regarded as so intrinsically nonlegal that trial processes would be incongruous. For example, the Court held that a medical school did not need to conduct a formal hearing before dismissing a student from school on account of her inadequate clinical ability. Board of Curators v. Horowitz, 435 U.S. 78 (1978). The decision involved essentially academic judgments and was thus unsuited to courtroom methods. The Court in *Horowitz* also suggested that relationships between faculty and students would suffer if decisionmaking on academic matters were to become too adversarial.

7. Cf. Gray Panthers v. Schweiker, 652 F.2d 146 (D.C.Cir. 1980), appeal after remand, 716 F.2d 23 (D.C.Cir.1983) (to ensure personal attention as well as reliable decisions on credibility issues, HHS must provide some opportunity for oral contact with decisionmakers when it rules on Medicare claims for less than $100; but the contacts may be by toll-free telephone calls instead of face-to-face meetings).

Similarly, the Court declined to require trial-type hearings to test the wisdom of a parental decision to place a child in a state mental hospital. Parham v. J.R., 442 U.S. 584 (1979). The Court thought that review by an independent medical professional would be sufficient, if not more reliable. In addition, a formal hearing might exacerbate tensions between parent and child. (However, in a closely related situation not involving potential danger to family relationships, the Court insisted on a formal hearing, with cross-examination rights afforded. Vitek v. Jones, 445 U.S. 480 (1980) (involuntary commitment of a prisoner to a mental institution).)

Even in administrative settings in which it is clear that trial-type hearings are generally available, such as those subject to the APA's formal adjudication procedures, agencies can decline to conduct a hearing on certain issues without violating due process. In some circumstances, for example, an agency may promulgate a legislative rule, and then refuse during subsequent adjudications to hold a hearing on issues that it has already decided in the rulemaking proceeding; or it may place a burden of going forward on private parties, and enter summary judgment against those who do not satisfy that burden. See pp. 296–303 infra. In addition, the doctrine of official notice allows agencies to rely on certain factual assumptions that have not been tested through the adversary process. See pp. 303–08 infra.

A broader position, long urged by Professor Davis, is that due process generally does not require a trial on issues of "legislative fact" arising during an adjudication. 2 K. Davis, Administrative Law Treatise §§ 12:1–:8 (2d ed. 1979). "Legislative" facts are general facts bearing upon issues of law or policy; they are contrasted with "adjudicative facts," which are facts about the specific parties to the case. The Davis theory has lower court support, see, e.g., Zamora v. INS, 534 F.2d 1055, 1062 (2d Cir.1976) (Friendly, J.), but the Supreme Court has never endorsed it; the Court may believe that trial processes are sometimes a cost-effective means of exploring disputed issues of legislative fact. In any event, the significance of this controversy has waned in recent years, as agencies have increasingly resolved legislative fact controversies through the rulemaking process, where the curtailment of due process rights is more firmly established. See pp. 212–15 supra.

3. RIGHT TO COUNSEL

Section 555(b) of the APA provides that "[a] person compelled to appear in person before an agency or representative thereof is entitled to be accompanied, represented, and advised by counsel." The APA, however, does not apply to state and local bureaucracies, nor to federal agencies that are exempted by statute from APA coverage; and it says nothing about the person who is effectively denied representation because she cannot afford to retain a lawyer. Finally, section 555(b) applies only to those compelled to appear, not those who appear voluntarily. Thus, there are a number of administrative settings in which an asserted due process right to appear through counsel could potentially become an issue.

The Supreme Court recognized such a right in *Goldberg*, holding that welfare beneficiaries facing termination of benefits must be allowed to retain counsel if they wish. Yet it is clear that due process does not guarantee a right to legal representation in every administrative proceeding. In Walters v. National Association of Radiation Survivors, 473 U.S. 305 (1985), the Court rejected a due process challenge to a federal statute which limited the fees payable to lawyers representing veterans' benefit claimants to a maximum of $10. Despite the fact that this fee limit virtually precluded claimants from retaining private attorneys, the Court found no basis for overturning the presumption of constitutionality that should be accorded to a federal statute. Congress's paternalistic objectives of keeping the process nonadversarial and informal and keeping the veteran from having to share his award with an attorney were found to be valid and important government interests that would be frustrated if attorneys routinely became involved. Moreover, it was not clear that lawyers would materially increase the accuracy of decision-making: the key issues were medical rather than legal, and the claimants could obtain representation from lay service representatives whose success rates were high. Given these protections and the existence of a regulation requiring the agency to resolve all doubts in favor of the claimant, the Court concluded that no constitutional right to legal representation was necessary.

Practically speaking, the *Walters* ruling may not be very important. The fee limitation in veterans' cases was repealed in 1988, and there are few if any other administrative schemes in which Congress has expressly taken a position against attorney involvement. Indeed, most state and federal agencies routinely allow parties to be represented by counsel.

Appointment of counsel for those who cannot afford to retain one is another matter. Although such appointments are common in criminal proceedings, they are rare in administrative law. Indeed, the Supreme Court has yet to hold that there is any administrative setting in which indigent parties must routinely be provided with attorneys. In Gagnon v. Scarpelli, 411 U.S. 778 (1973), the Court gave several reasons for rejecting such a right in the context of parole and probation revocation hearings. Providing counsel in all cases would not only be expensive, but would also make the parole board's role "more akin to that of a judge at a trial, and less attuned to the rehabilitative needs of the individual probationer or parolee." Indeed, the presence of counsel and the resulting increase in procedural formality might make the agency "less tolerant of marginal deviant behavior." Thus, although the Court could see a need for appointed counsel in some cases, it held that these determinations "must be made on a case-by-case basis in the exercise of a sound discretion by the state authority," taking into account factors such as the complexity of the case and the individual's ability to speak for himself.

At times, the concerns mentioned in *Gagnon* have led the Court to mandate "assistance" for inmates who need it, while leaving the state free to designate a nonlawyer to serve that function. For example, at a hearing to determine whether to transfer a prisoner to a mental institution, the prisoner has a due process right to qualified and independent assistance, but the advisor may be a mental health professional or a competent lay person rather than an attorney. Vitek v. Jones, 445 U.S. 480 (1980). See also Wolff v. McDonnell, 418 U.S. 539 (1974) (in prison disciplinary proceedings, inmates have no constitutional right to retained or appointed counsel, but should be provided with assistance in certain cases).

4. AN IMPARTIAL DECISIONMAKER

"[O]f course, an impartial decision maker is essential" to an adjudication that comports with due process. Goldberg v. Kelly, supra. There are several kinds of disqualifying bias. For example, an agency official should be disqualified from sitting in an adjudicatory proceeding if his service as an advocate at an earlier stage of the controversy, or his overt comments, suggest that he may have prejudged facts that will be at issue in the case. See pp. 288–93 infra. But even in the absence of direct evidence about a particular officeholder's experiences or views, courts will sometimes discern an unacceptable risk of bias when an adjudicator has strong incentives to decide the case on grounds other than the merits.

For example, one well established ground for disqualification is the administrator's personal financial stake in the outcome. Thus, in Tumey v. Ohio, 273 U.S. 510 (1927), the Court held that a mayor who received a share of the fines levied on persons convicted in the town court could not constitutionally preside over their trials. The same conclusion has been reached when financial benefit accrues to some agency or unit of government and the person making the decision is closely identified with the operation of that agency. See, e.g., Ward v. Village of Monroeville, 409 U.S. 57 (1972) (violation of due process when fines levied in traffic court by the mayor increased village revenues). However, a prosecutorial agency that keeps a portion of the fines collected in the cases it brings is not necessarily disqualified, if those cases will be adjudicated by independent officers who have no stake in the outcome. Marshall v. Jerrico, Inc., 446 U.S. 238 (1980). Nor is it a violation of due process for private insurance carriers to participate (under contract with the government) in making determinations of Medicare benefits, because the carriers pay benefits from federal funds, not their own pockets. Schweiker v. McClure, 456 U.S. 188 (1982).

Another type of indirect financial stake which may require disqualification of the decisionmaker arises when the administrator is affiliated with a business and has the power to eliminate or restrict competition through his official acts. This situation frequently arises in state occupational licensing systems, where the licensing boards are customarily made up of individuals who practice in the regulated industry. See generally W. Gellhorn, *The Abuse of Occupational Licensing*, 44 U.Chi.L.Rev. 6 (1976). In Gibson v. Berryhill, 411 U.S. 564 (1973), a state board composed solely of optometrists who were in practice for themselves had brought a disciplinary action against optometrists who were in practice as employees of a corporation, charging that the corporate business connection was an unethical practice. The Court held that the board members' possible pecuniary interest in excluding competitors was sufficient to render the impartiality of the board constitutionally suspect. In Friedman v. Rogers, 440 U.S. 1 (1979), however, a similar claim was rejected, because no disciplinary proceeding had been brought against the complaining party. The *Friedman* holding is difficult to explain, but it may rest on a belief that states would be unable to find knowledgeable regulators for the professions if they could not look to practitioners in the relevant occupational groups. Thus, the Court is willing to accept some risk of occupational bias in the day-to-day administration of a licensing scheme. At the same time, the Court finds this risk intolerable in a case like *Gibson,* where an individual stands accused of wrongdoing—perhaps because the private interest in procedural fairness is at its zenith in accusatory proceedings.

In many agencies which adjudicate violations of regulatory statutes and regulations, the agency heads who will make the final decision also make the preliminary determination to initiate the proceeding by voting to issue a complaint. In doing so, they may examine evidence gathered by the staff for the purpose of determining whether they have "reason to believe" a violation has occurred. This practice has long been considered constitutional. See, e.g., FTC v. Cement Inst., 333 U.S. 683 (1948). Due process does not require a strict "separation of functions" between prosecuting and decisionmaking officials, and "mere exposure to evidence presented in nonadversary investigative procedures is insufficient in itself" to overcome the presumption that the official will decide impartially. Withrow v. Larkin, 421 U.S. 35 (1975) (permitting members of state board of medical examiners to exercise multiple functions). However, this due process doctrine has its critics. See pp. 283–88 infra.

5. FINDINGS AND CONCLUSIONS

Administrative law sets great store by reasoned findings accompanying agency decisions, and this attitude is reflected in due process doctrine. In a formal adjudication governed by the APA, the agency's decision must include a statement of "findings and conclusions, and the reasons or basis therefor, on all the material issues of fact, law, or discretion presented on the record." 5 U.S.C.A. § 557(c)(A). Even when the agency is engaged in informal rulemaking under the APA, it is required to "incorporate in the rules adopted a concise general statement of their basis and purpose." 5 U.S. C.A. § 553(c). A statement of reasons may be important not only to the perceived fairness of the process, but also to the quality of the decision. The need to prepare a written explanation may impose some discipline on the agency, by pressuring decisionmakers to consider the evidence more carefully and to examine the legal and policy justification for the action more closely. When the grounds for the decision are committed to writing, it is easier for a higher level administrator to review it, and thereby provide a check on the discretion of the lower-level officials. Finally, a reasonably detailed statement of reasons makes it possible for a reviewing court to examine the actual basis of the agency's decision, rather than rationalizations it has produced after the fact. See pp. 102–05 supra; Rabin, *Job Security and Due Process:*

Monitoring Administrative Discretion Through a Reasons Requirement, 44 U.Chi.L.Rev. 60 (1976).

The Supreme Court acknowledged the importance of an agency statement of reasons in *Goldberg,* holding that due process required the welfare agency to give some explanation of its action to affected individuals. The Court added, however, that the statement "need not amount to a full opinion or even formal findings of fact and conclusions of law." Comparable requirements that the administrators inform the accused of the information and evidence relied upon have been imposed in prison disciplinary hearings, Wolff v. McDonnell, supra, and parole revocation proceedings, Morrissey v. Brewer, 408 U.S. 471 (1972). But no written statement of reasons is required when the prescribed due process hearing is extremely informal, as in the presuspension discussion between an accused student and his teacher, Goss v. Lopez, supra, or when the substantive decision has been left to the "unfettered discretion" of the agency: "A state cannot be required to explain its reasons for a decision when it is not required to act on prescribed grounds." Connecticut Board of Pardons v. Dumschat, 452 U.S. 458 (1981) (denial of petition for commutation of sentence).

Related to the reasons requirement is the notion that a constitutionally adequate decision must be supported by some minimum quantity of evidence. For example, in Superintendent, Massachusetts Correctional Institution v. Hill, 472 U.S. 445 (1985), the Court ruled that it would violate due process to revoke an inmate's good time credits without any evidentiary support in the record. However, the opinion emphasized that only a very limited fact review was required. Instead of examining the whole record (as it would do in reviewing an adjudicative decision under the Administrative Procedure Act), the reviewing court was merely to see whether there was "any evidence in the record that could support the conclusion reached."

D. THE FUTURE OF THE "DUE PROCESS REVOLUTION"

No doubt the Supreme Court's due process decisions have their share of seeming inconsistencies. It is hard to understand, for example, why the right to prior notice and hearing applies to some relatively minimal injuries, such as a ten-day suspension from high school (*Goss*), but not to such relatively serious deprivations as a severe beating by one's teacher (*Ingraham*) or the decertification of one's nursing home (*O'Bannon*). Nevertheless, the overall trend is clear: after the initial expansion of procedural rights ushered in by *Goldberg*, the Court has become markedly more reluctant to find that agency action has infringed a constitutionally protected interest, and also more skeptical about the value of trial-type procedures.

As the Court has struggled with a growing workload of procedural due process cases, it has attracted criticism for both the methods and the goals of its analyses. The utilitarian interest-balancing of the *Goldberg* and *Mathews* decisions, which remains the dominant approach to due process today, has the advantage of being flexible in application and functional in approach. It asks important questions about what improvements in accuracy and fairness will result from the use of particular procedural devices, and how much it will cost the agency and the public to provide the requested rights. However, as Professor Mashaw and others have pointed out, the Court's due process analysis has some significant shortcomings as well. J. Mashaw, Due Process in the Administrative State (1985). By looking to positive law—primarily statutes and administrative regulations—as the principal source of the entitlements protected by due process, the Court's approach not only makes it easy for legislators and administrators to deprive claimants of procedural protections, but also creates a positive incentive for them to do so. By keeping their decisionmaking standards vague and discretionary, administrators can avoid the due process obligation to use minimally fair procedures—and also minimize their accountability.

Moreover, even when the claimant can establish a substantive entitlement, the interest-balancing analysis makes it possible—and perhaps too easy—for government to override the individual's interests. Unless the utilitarian calculus is applied with appropriate sensitivity to the worth and dignity of the individual, government's efficiency claims can become a cloak for petty oppression and harassment.

Perhaps the most fundamental argument against the interest-balancing analysis, however, is that the courts lack the competence and the data to make it work properly. According to Professor Mashaw, a court seeking to perform a reasonably complete cost-benefit analysis of a claimant's request for due process rights would need reliable information about "the causes and incidence of error, the social valuation of both positive and negative errors, the error-correcting power of various procedural devices, and the dynamic adjustments that may result" when the bureaucracy tries to compensate for new procedural demands that might be imposed by the courts. Id. at 126. This kind of information is not available in most litigation records—indeed, much of it may not be available anywhere—and if it were, it is not clear that generalist judges would be able to interpret it properly. As a result, the procedural cost-benefit calculus often becomes an exercise in poorly informed guesswork.

If interest-balancing presents these kinds of problems, what alternative approaches might the courts take when presented with a claim that administrative decisionmaking processes are fundamentally unfair? Professor Mashaw identifies two other theories of due process that have historically been used in constitutional adjudication.

One, based on tradition, looks to the usual processes traditionally employed in making similar decisions, and reasons by analogy to determine whether the challenged procedures are constitutionally appropriate. See generally Rubin, *Due Process and the Administrative State,* 72 Cal.L.Rev. 1044 (1984). The second approach is based on a belief in the natural rights of persons. It holds that government cannot pursue its purposes through processes which ignore the dignity and worth of the individual. Starting from this premise, the natural rights analysis seeks to identify core values which must be safeguarded in decisionmaking, such as autonomy, privacy, equality, and comprehensibility, and then tries to realize these values in a particular decisionmaking context.

Regardless of which due process tradition dominates in the courts, it is clear that there can be no concrete, objective constitutional formula for reconciling the myriad conflicts over administrative procedures. As a result, a substantial measure of subjectivity and inconsistency will probably remain part of our procedural due process doctrines. If this is true, then it may be wise in the long run for the courts to be relatively restrained in imposing procedural requirements on the agencies, despite the manifest hardship to some claimants.

Because the Supreme Court speaks with finality in matters of constitutional interpretation, the codes of administrative procedure that it promulgates when it holds that an agency has violated due process are highly resistant to change. Premature constitutionalization of the administrative process can cut short promising improvements and forestall experimentation. Moreover, it is not clear that court-imposed procedures improve the quality of justice dispensed by the agencies, even in the short run.

After a careful study of the Social Security Administration's procedures for adjudicating disability claims, Professor Mashaw concluded that the bureaucracy was doing a superior job of reconciling the conflicting interests in fair, accurate, and efficient decisionmaking, despite clumsy interference of the courts. J. Mashaw, Bureaucratic Justice (1983). Other studies have found that the procedural rights won in *Goldberg* were a rather hollow victory for the welfare recipients, because the vast majority of claimants are not able to make effective use of the trial-type hearing opportunities. E.g., J. Handler, Protecting the Social Services Client (1979). Until we have developed a much fuller understanding of the practical operations of informal administrative decisionmaking, it may be wiser to focus attention on statutory, administrative, and managerial attempts to improve the basic fairness of informal adjudications, while reserving the due process clause for truly severe deprivations of individual rights.

CHAPTER VII

FORMAL ADJUDICATIONS

The procedures used by administrative agencies to adjudicate individual claims or cases are extremely diverse. Hearing procedures are shaped by the subject matter of the controversy, the agency's traditions and policies, the applicable statutes and regulations, and the requirements imposed by reviewing courts. Thus, any general description of administrative adjudications must be subject to numerous exceptions and qualifications.

Within the federal system, sections 554, 556, and 557 of the APA establish some minimum standards for administrative adjudications. However, it is important to remember that the APA's coverage is limited, and that its procedural requirements apply to only a relatively small proportion of agency adjudications. Under the APA, every final agency action that produces an "order" is technically an adjudication. 5 U.S.C.A. § 551(7). The term "order" is defined very broadly to include any final disposition "in a matter other than rule making but including licensing." Id. § 551(6). Thus, adjudication is a broad residual category that includes the great majority of agency decisions affecting private parties. But the fact that a particular agency decision is an adjudication does not imply that the agency must use trial-type procedures, or even that those who will be affected by the decision have any right to be heard. The APA establishes procedural requirements for only one class of adjudications: those which are "required by statute to be determined on the record after opportunity for an agency hearing." Id. § 554(a).[1] This means that the APA's adjudication procedures are mandatory only when some other statute directs the agency to conduct an evidentiary hearing in adjudicating particular kinds of cases.[2] Some courts presume that any statute that prescribes a "hearing" prior to issuance of an adjudicative order is intended to trigger the APA formal adjudication procedures, Seacoast Anti–Pollution League v. Costle, 572 F.2d 872 (1st Cir.), cert. denied, 439 U.S. 824 (1978), but elsewhere the presumption has been rejected. Chemical Waste Mgmt., Inc. v. EPA, 873 F.2d 1477 (D.C.Cir.1989).

1. Section 554(a) of the APA contains a number of specific exemptions to the Act's formal hearing requirements. Trial-type hearings are not required, for example, in "proceedings in which decisions rest solely on inspections, tests, or elections," or in "the conduct of military or foreign affairs functions." 5 U.S. C.A. §§ 554(a)(3), (4).

2. In addition, by virtue of a judicially devised gloss on § 554(a), the APA adjudication procedures come into play when an evidentiary hearing is required by the Constitution rather than by a statute. Wong Yang Sung v. McGrath, 339 U.S. 33 (1950). The consequence of this holding in *Wong Yang Sung* was that officers who presided over deportation hearings could not also be involved in the investigation of deportation cases. However, Congress soon amended the Immigration and Nationality Act to exempt immigration officers from this separation-of-functions requirement. 8 U.S.C.A. § 1252(b); see Marcello v. Bonds, 349 U.S. 302 (1955) (upholding statute).

Formal adjudications under the APA are sometimes called "evidentiary hearings," "full hearings," or "trial-type hearings." The latter term is probably the most accurate and descriptive, although, as will be seen below, there are significant differences between agency trial-type hearings and court trials. Even though formal adjudications comprise only a small proportion of the decisions made by the agencies, the total volume of administrative trial-type hearings is substantial. In 1983, for example, nearly 400,000 new cases were referred to administrative law judges for potential hearing—a figure that exceeds by more than a third the total number of cases filed in all of the federal district courts during the same year. The great majority of the formal administrative proceedings were hearings on welfare and disability benefits conducted by the Social Security Administration, but administrative law judges at other agencies were presented with more than 25,000 new cases. See Lubbers, *Federal Agency Adjudications: Trying to See the Forest and the Trees,* 31 Fed.Bar News & J. 383 (1984).

The following discussion is limited to agency adjudications that are "required by statute to be determined on the record after opportunity for an agency hearing," and therefore are governed by sections 554, 556, and 557 of the APA. Other agency adjudications may be governed by special statutory procedures, and informal adjudications must always comply with the requirements of procedural due process. See pp. 194–241 supra. Beyond those limitations, the procedures used in agency adjudications that are exempt from the APA remain within the administrator's discretion.

A. PARTIES

1. NOTICE

An adversary decisionmaking process like formal adjudication depends upon the litigating parties to gather and present relevant evidence, and to challenge the evidence introduced by other parties. Thus, adequate notice of the other side's contentions is an essential prerequisite to fair and effective adjudication. See also pp. 218–19 supra. The APA provides that "persons entitled to notice of an agency hearing shall be timely informed" of the time and place of the hearing, the legal authority that the agency is relying on, and "the matters of fact and law asserted." 5 U.S.C.A. § 554(b). This language is generally interpreted as adopting the philosophy of "notice pleading": actual notice of the relevant facts and issues is sufficient, so long as the respondent has a fair opportunity to know and challenge the positions taken by adverse parties. Thus, proof may vary from the pleadings, and pleadings may be amended to conform to the proof.

If anything, technical defects in pleadings are less significant in administrative practice than in civil litigation. Many regulated industries have continuous dealings with the staffs of the agencies that oversee their operations, and in the process they often learn informally what facts and issues the agency considers crucial in a pending adjudication. In addition, agencies do not necessarily follow the "continuous hearing" practice of the courts. Instead, they may adopt an "interval hearing" system in which, for example, the government presents its case and the hearing is then recessed for a period of weeks or months so that the respondent can prepare a defense. See, e.g., NLRB v. Remington Rand, Inc., 94 F.2d 862 (2d Cir.), cert. denied, 304 U.S. 576 (1938). However, if the agency changes or conceals its theory so that the respondent is deprived of a reasonable opportunity to challenge it, a reviewing court may set aside an order because of inadequate notice. See, e.g., Morgan v. United States, 304 U.S. 1, 18–19 (1938) (*Morgan II*); Sterling Drug, Inc. v. Weinberger, 503 F.2d 675 (2d Cir.1974).

A common problem for agencies that conduct formal adjudications is determining when a proposed decision will have such a substantial collateral impact on parties other than the respondent that they must be given notice and an opportunity to be heard. Agency adjudications frequently affect competitors, customers, suppliers, or employees of a regulated company. An FCC decision to grant a television broadcasting license may affect not only the listening public and the employees and stockholders of the station, but also advertisers, newspaper publishers, competing broadcasters, performing artists, community groups, and political officials in the station's service area. Usually these indirectly affected persons or organizations are not "indispensable parties" to the adjudication, and they will not receive formal service of pleadings and other documents unless they take the initiative to intervene in the proceedings. However, many agencies make special efforts to assure that potentially interested persons will receive notice of the pending adjudication. In broadcast licensing, for example, an incumbent licensee is required to announce to listeners that its license is due for renewal, and that interested persons may participate in the process. Agencies also use a variety of methods to reach potential participants directly, ranging from Federal Register publication to newspaper advertisements and public service announcements on television or radio.

2. INTERVENTION

When an agency adjudication affects individuals or organizations who are not named parties, they will often seek to participate in the hearing. The methods by which an interested person may participate are generally similar to those available in civil litigation. They include testifying at the request of the agency staff or one of the named parties; supplying documentary evidence to them; requesting permission to file an amicus curiae brief and perhaps to present oral argument; and seeking to intervene as a party. In recent years, as

environmental, consumer, and other "public interest" groups have become more actively involved in
the administrative process, requests to intervene in
agency adjudications have increased. Intervenor
status generally has several advantages over more
limited forms of participation, including the right
to control the presentation of evidence supporting
the intervenor's position, to cross-examine other
parties' witnesses, and to appeal an adverse initial
decision. However, intervention is also more costly to the agency in hearing time and other resources, and named parties in the case may fear
that the intervenor's participation will be harmful
to their interests. As a result, disputes often arise
as to whether an interested person or group should
be allowed to intervene in an agency adjudication.

The APA does not directly deal with the right to
intervene in formal adjudication, and the standards
for intervention set forth in pertinent agency statutes and rules of practice are usually vague. For
example, a provision of the Federal Trade Commission Act simply states that intervention shall be
allowed in formal adjudications "upon good cause
shown." 15 U.S.C.A. § 45(b); see Firestone Tire &
Rubber Co., 77 F.T.C. 1666 (1970). In the absence of
statutory guidance, reviewing courts have often resolved intervention disputes by drawing analogies to
the law of standing to seek judicial review of administrative action, discussed at pp. 368–78 infra. In
both contexts, one prominent argument is that participation by "public interest" groups is an especially

helpful means of furthering the mission of an agency that is itself charged with promoting the public interest. See, e.g., National Welfare Rights Org. v. Finch, 429 F.2d 725 (D.C.Cir.1970); Office of Communication of United Church of Christ v. FCC, 359 F.2d 994 (D.C.Cir.1966).

In addition, courts and commentators have sought to develop functional criteria that can be used to determine whether an intervenor should be allowed to participate in an administrative adjudication, and what the scope of her participation should be. See generally Gellhorn, *Public Participation in Administrative Proceedings,* 81 Yale L.J. 359 (1972). The Administrative Conference of the United States has recommended that administrators and reviewing courts should consider several factors in determining whether a person will be allowed to intervene in an agency adjudication. According to the Administrative Conference, the decisionmaker should take into account not only the intervenor's interest in the subject matter and the outcome of the proceeding, but also the extent to which other parties will adequately represent the intervenor's interest, the ability of the prospective intervenor to present relevant evidence and argument, and the effect of intervention on the agency's implementation of its statutory mandate. Recommendation 71–6, 1 C.F.R. § 305.71–6.

Just as the requirements for standing to challenge agency action in court have become very lenient in recent years, agencies today tend to be receptive to intervention. They have become more aware of the positive contributions that intervenors can make to their decisions, and more sensitized to the practical costs (such as judicial reversals and congressional criticism) that may result from a refusal to permit public participation. The rapid expansion of administrative rulemaking may also be a factor. Important policy questions are increasingly being addressed through general rulemaking proceedings rather than through individual adjudications, and usually there is no doubt that all interested persons have the right to participate in a rulemaking proceeding.

As the right to participate has become more widely accepted, attention has shifted to finding ways to assure that participation will be effective. For many public interest groups, the principal barriers to effective participation are costs and attorneys' fees. A few agencies have explicit statutory power to compensate groups and individuals who lack the resources to present their views in particular proceedings, and the Comptroller General has ruled that many other agencies have implied discretionary authority to do so. However, the latter position has met with a skeptical reception in the courts, see, e.g., Pacific Legal Foundation v. Goyan, 664 F.2d 1221 (4th Cir.1981), and during the 1980's most agencies themselves have lost interest in reimbursing public participants.[3] For the most part,

3. Prevailing parties, including intervenors, may also claim the right to attorney fees under the Equal Access to Justice Act, 5 U.S.C.A. § 504, but only if the government's litigating posi-

therefore, organizations that wish to participate in the administrative process are still dependent on the contributions of their members and occasional support from private foundations to finance their advocacy.

3. CONSOLIDATION AND THE COMPARATIVE HEARING

When an agency conducts adjudications in licensing proceedings, and there are multiple applicants for a single license, the agency's discretion to determine which parties will be heard may be limited by the "*Ashbacker* doctrine." The principle was first articulated in Ashbacker Radio Corp. v. FCC 326 U.S. 327 (1945), where the FCC had received applications from two companies seeking licenses to provide radio broadcast services on the same frequency in adjoining communities. The applications were mutually exclusive, because if both were granted, each station's signal would cause electrical interference with the other's, making it impossible for most listeners to hear the programs. The statute provided that the agency could grant a license without a formal hearing, but it required an opportunity for trial-type hearing before a license application was denied. The FCC granted the first license application without hear-

tion was not "substantially justified," i.e., "justified to a degree that could satisfy a reasonable person." Pierce v. Underwood, 487 U.S. 552 (1988). The Act uses the same standard as the basis for reimbursing litigants for the expense of challenging the government's actions in court. 28 U.S.C.A. § 2412(d)(1)(A).

ing, then set the other down for evidentiary hearing. The Supreme Court concluded that this procedure violated the second broadcaster's statutory right to a "full hearing," because the prior grant to the first applicant made the subsequent hearing a sham. To preserve the hearing rights of both parties, the Commission was required to consolidate the mutually exclusive applications and hold a single "comparative hearing" in which each licensee would have an opportunity to show that he was best qualified to serve the public interest.

The *Ashbacker* principle has been applied not only in FCC broadcast licensing, but also in air route proceedings, gas pipeline certifications, motor carrier route cases, and other fields where multiple applicants compete for valuable operating rights. The doctrine is easy to apply in situations where it is physically impossible to grant both licenses and the second applicant has been summarily denied the right to a hearing. However, difficult questions have arisen when these conditions are not met. One problem has involved "economic mutual exclusivity"—the claim that one or both of the applicants will be driven out of business if both licenses are granted, because there is not enough business in the relevant market area to support both of them. See, e.g., Carroll Broadcasting Co. v. FCC, 258 F.2d 440 (D.C.Cir.1958) (comparative hearing required). Another problem can arise when the agency's procedural rulings or rules of practice do not explicitly prohibit the comparative hearing, but rather make it extremely difficult for the competing applicant to obtain one. This was the essence of the claim made in Citizens Communications Center v. FCC, 447 F.2d 1201 (D.C.Dir. 1971). The FCC had issued a policy statement providing that a broadcaster who wished to challenge the renewal application of an existing licensee could obtain a comparative hearing only if the Commission had first concluded that the incumbent had not rendered "substantial service" to the listening public. The court held that this policy violated the statutory hearing right as interpreted in *Ashbacker,* because it unduly limited the challenger's right to a comparative hearing on all of the relevant issues.

When it is read broadly, the *Citizens* decision seems inconsistent with a basic proposition of administrative law: an agency that has been delegated rulemaking authority may issue substantive standards refining the applicable statutory language, and then use summary judgment or similar procedural devices to deny hearings to those who plainly do not meet the criteria set forth in the rules. See pp. 296–303 infra. However, the *Citizens* opinion does not necessarily repudiate that proposition. Although phrased as a procedural holding, the decision might be better understood in substantive terms: the absolute priority given to any broadcaster who rendered "substantial service" was irreconcilable with the Communications Act's policy that licenses should be awarded to the *best* qualified applicant. Because the FCC's position was invalid on the merits, it could not be used to circumscribe the *Ashbacker* hearing right. From this standpoint, the case may be seen as one episode in the FCC's longstanding struggle to achieve a reasonable balance between the incumbent licensee's expectancy of renewal and the public's interest in quality service. Not until after several additional rounds of litigation did the Commission manage to find a formula that the court could accept, even temporarily, as a rational accomodation of these two goals. See Central Florida Enterprises, Inc. v. FCC, 683 F.2d 503 (D.C.Cir.1982).

B. DISCOVERY

In most civil cases brought in federal and state courts, the litigants are routinely permitted to conduct extensive discovery through a variety of devices such as oral depositions, written interrogatories, bills of particulars, and requests for admissions and stipulations. The advantages of liberal pretrial discovery are widely acknowledged: it assures fairness to the litigants and prevents "trial by surprise"; it encourages settlements; and it can improve the efficiency of the trial and the quality of the decision. Despite its general acceptance in the courts, however, pretrial discovery is not always available in administrative adjudications. Apart from the Freedom of Information Act, the APA contains no provisions relating to discovery against the agency (although it does give parties a limited right to obtain subpoenas against third parties, 5 U.S.C.A. § 555(d)). Nor do many agency enabling acts deal explicitly with the subject of discovery. Agency practice appears to be highly varied; a few agencies, such as the Federal Trade Commission, have adopted broad discovery provisions modeled on those used in the federal courts, but other agencies, such as the NLRB, provide only limited opportunities for a respondent to discover the evidence against her before the hearing.

There are several reasons why agencies may be reluctant to follow the courts' lead and expand the discovery rights available to litigants. Without a specific delegation of power from the legislature to compel discovery from unwilling parties, the agency may lack the power to implement a liberal discovery policy. Compare FMC v. Anglo–Canadian Shipping Co., 335 F.2d 255 (9th Cir.1964) (grant of general rulemaking power to Commission did not imply authorization to adopt discovery rules), with FCC v. Schreiber, 381 U.S. 279 (1965) (grant of authority to conduct proceedings empowers Commission to resolve "subordinate questions of procedure," including rules governing public disclosure of information received in investigations). Agencies may also be hesitant to establish procedures that would create the potential for costly and time-consuming "discovery wars," such as those which have often been fought in complex court litigation. Indeed, one study found that the FTC's liberal discovery rules have "caused significant delays in

FTC proceedings as respondents have sought to depose dozens if not hundreds of third persons on matters which the deponents often insisted deserved confidential treatment"; moreover, Administrative Law Judges' "rulings granting or denying applications for depositions have prompted many interlocutory appeals." Tomlinson, *Report of the Committee on Compliance and Enforcement Proceedings in Support of Recommendation No. 21 of the Administrative Conference of the United States,* 1 A.C.U.S. 577, 600 (1970).

Perhaps the major reason why discovery is limited in many agencies, however, is the availability of alternative methods for disclosing information necessary to assure a fair hearing and a decision based on the best available evidence. Most formal agency adjudications are preceded by a staff investigation, which is usually backed by the subpoena power. In contrast to a private litigant, who is primarily concerned with gathering and presenting information to support her own "theory of the case," the agency staff typically has a broader obligation to collect all relevant information that might be of use to the decisionmakers. If the staff is diligent in performing its duties, it may cover much of the ground that would be relegated to discovery in civil litigation. Moreover, the Freedom of Information Act, 5 U.S.C.A. § 552, is a powerful "discovery" tool which private parties can use to learn what information is available in the agency's files. See generally pp. 148–57 supra.

Since bureaucracies typically commit most significant information to writing, a carefully drafted FOIA request can often give a comprehensive picture of the agency's "case." Another source of discovery is the "*Jencks* rule." First developed in criminal prosecutions, see Jencks v. United States, 353 U.S. 657 (1957), and later codified in the Jencks Act, 18 U.S.C.A. § 3500, the rule requires government attorneys who are acting in a prosecutorial capacity to disclose prior statements made by prosecution witnesses after the witness has testified. See, e.g., NLRB v. Adhesive Products Corp., 258 F.2d 403 (2d Cir.1958). Under these circumstances, respondents in agency adjudications will frequently have the functional equivalent of the protections afforded by a formal discovery system.

C. EVIDENCE

1. PRESENTATION OF CASE

In broad outline, the form of many agency adjudications resembles that of a court trial. After the prehearing stage of pleadings, motions, and prehearing conferences is completed, an oral hearing is held before an official who is called a judge.[4] The agency and the respondent are represented by

---

4. If the agency seeks to compel testimony from an unwilling witness, or attempts to use evidence obtained in violation of constitutional safeguards, claims of privilege may arise. As previously noted, agencies generally follow the constitutional and common law evidentiary privileges observed in the courts. See pp. 135–36 supra.

counsel who introduce testimony and exhibits. Witnesses may be cross-examined, objections may be raised, and rulings issued. At the conclusion of the testimony, the parties submit proposed findings and conclusions and legal briefs to the presiding officer. The Administrative Law Judge then renders his initial decision, which may be appealed to the agency heads. Beneath these surface similarities, however, there are significant differences between judicial and administrative adjudications.

Administrative practice generally follows the judicial model in allocating burdens of proof. The APA adopts the customary common law rule that the moving party—that is, the proponent of a rule or order—has the burden of proof, including both the burden of going forward and the burden of persuasion. 5 U.S.C.A. § 556(d). This provision also establishes that the burden of persuasion in administrative adjudications is met by the "preponderance of the evidence" standard. Steadman v. SEC, 450 U.S. 91 (1981). Where, however, the APA does not apply and Congress has not otherwise prescribed the degree of proof, courts have felt at liberty to impose stricter standards in order to protect important private interests. Thus, in a deportation proceeding, which was exempted from the APA, the Court applied the "clear and convincing evidence" standard, because of the impact of such a proceeding on personal liberty and security. Woodby v. INS, 385 U.S. 276 (1966).

Perhaps the most distinctive feature of many administrative adjudications is the substitution of written evidence for direct oral testimony. The APA explicitly authorizes this practice in formal rulemaking proceedings and in adjudications "determining claims for money or benefits or applications for initial licenses," by providing that "an agency may, when a party will not be prejudiced thereby, adopt procedures for the submission of all or part of the evidence in written form." 5 U.S.C.A. § 556(d). Use of written direct testimony can take several forms. One of the simplest and least productive is the use of "canned dialogue"—previously written questions and answers that are read into the record in place of live testimony. More effective and efficient is the practice originally developed by the ICC, in which verified written statements are prepared by witnesses and submitted to adverse parties for rebuttal. There are also some intermediate methods, such as the practice developed by the FTC in rulemaking hearings. Witnesses in those proceedings are required to submit advance texts of their testimony; then, at the hearings, they are requested to provide a brief oral summary of the principal points in their statements, much as witnesses in congressional hearings are encouraged to do. The bulk of hearing time can then be devoted to questioning and cross-examination designed to clarify and test the witnesses' conclusions.

One reason why written evidence plays such a significant role in administrative practice is the nature of the issues involved in many agency adjudications. In court proceedings, the crucial evidence is frequently eyewitness testimony relating to a particular transaction or event. To assess this type of testimony, the factfinder must make judgments about the witness's perception, memory, and sincerity, as well as the inherent plausibility of his narrative. The witness's demeanor in testifying provides useful guidance in making this assessment. In administrative adjudications, however, the crucial evidence is usually opinion testimony. Sometimes the opinions of lay persons are relevant, such as when residents of a community want to testify at an NRC hearing to determine the location of a proposed nuclear power plant—some supporting the grant of the license because they believe that the plant will bring new employment to the region, others opposing it because they are concerned about the plant's effect on property values or environmental amenities. More commonly, however, agencies require expert opinion testimony on matters such as the medical diagnosis of the injuries suffered by a claimant for disability benefits, the economic justification for a proposed merger of two regulated companies, the impact of a proposed utility power line on wildlife habitat, or the perceptions of a random sample of consumers who responded to a survey questionnaire regarding their understanding of certain sales representations. The demeanor of the witness usually contributes little to the assessment of such evidence; more important are the qualifications and background of the expert, the adequacy of his data base and methodology, and the soundness of the inferences he has drawn from available information. Cross-examination may occasionally be useful in illuminating these matters, but direct oral testimony using the courtroom question-and-answer format is of little value, particularly when the administrator has some expertise in the subject matter of the expert's testimony.

2. CROSS–EXAMINATION

Few issues in administrative law have proven as controversial as the proper role of cross-examination in formal adjudications and rulemakings. The APA is deceptively simple; it merely provides that a party to an evidentiary hearing is entitled "to conduct such cross-examination as may be required for a full and true disclosure of the facts." 5 U.S. C.A. § 556(d). The Act's legislative history indicates that Congress was seeking to draw a line between an unlimited right of cross-examination, with all the cost, delay, and waste that unrestricted questioning can produce, and a reasonable opportunity to test opposing evidence. However, this does not provide much guidance in determining when cross-examination is "required for a full and true disclosure of the facts."

A helpful starting point is to recognize that the utility of cross-examination can vary according to the purpose for which it is used, the nature and importance of the testimony that is being attacked, and the skills and backgrounds of the hearing participants. In general, cross-examination can be used to challenge the credibility of the witness or to test the accuracy and completeness of his testimony. Credibility attacks usually fall into several broad categories. A questioner can challenge the witness's veracity or memory; she can explore factors that might compromise the witness's objectivity, such as a financial stake in the outcome or a strong ideological belief; she can suggest that the testimony is not really the witness's own product, but rather the result of coaching by counsel or some other influence; she can attack the witness's competence, by showing that he lacks the background and formal credentials to speak with authority or does not fully understand the issues; and she can show that the witness's testimony is inconsistent with prior practice or statements, or with recognized authorities. Substantive attacks on the accuracy of testimony also tend to repeat some common themes. A cross-examiner may try to show that the witness has a weak or insufficient basis for conclusions reached in his testimony, by exposing limitations in the witness's data or experience or opportunity to observe the events he has described; she may try to bring out points that were not discussed or not emphasized in the direct testimony; she may attempt to separate valid factual inferences from policy preferences or value judgments; and she may use cross-examination to clarify technical concepts or other unfamiliar matters for the decisionmakers.

When the direct testimony is based upon eyewitness observations, cross-examination that is directed at witness credibility, veracity, and perception may be useful means of testing the truth of the specific factual assertions. However, most observers seem to agree that credibility attacks are rarely successful when the witness is an expert. Questioning that is designed to clarify expert testimony or expose its substantive limitations may sometimes be useful, particularly when the decisionmaker is unfamiliar with the subject matter of the testimony. More frequently, however, it is a waste of time. Few cross-examiners have sufficient technical sophistication to meet an expert on his own ground and challenge his methodology or analysis convincingly. Too often counsel follows the path of least resistance and simply reads passages from treatises or reports, asking the witness whether he agrees or disagrees with the authority quoted—an exercise that is usually both pointless and tedious. In other instances, the cross-examiner adopts a "shotgun" strategy in which her questions skip rapidly from one topic to another, in the hope of uncovering a useful bit of information or at least of making the witness appear confused. "Shotgunning" is easier than careful preparation, but it may generate a chaotic record and actually impede the decisionmakers' understanding of the testimony.

From the presiding officer's perspective, the major difficulty in controlling cross-examination is that these multiple factors affecting the utility of questioning cannot be reduced to a set of simple rules that can be easily and fairly applied in the heat of an adversary hearing. Without clear standards to guide his rulings, the ALJ can be under considerable pressure to allow relatively unconstrained questioning: any attempt to cut off a line of inquiry might invite a reversal and remand by the higher levels of the agency or by the courts, and the hearing time spent in disputes over the permissible scope of cross-examination might well be greater than the time the examination itself would consume. Thus, there are few authoritative rulings here, and the practical situation in the agencies often seems to approach the unrestricted cross-examination that the drafters of the APA sought to avoid.

3. ADMISSIBILITY AND EVALUATION OF EVIDENCE

In comparison with court trials, administrative adjudications generally are governed by liberal evidentiary rules that create a strong presumption in favor of admitting questionable or challenged evidence.[5] This difference between courts and agencies is reflected in the ways in which the two

---

5. See generally Gellhorn, *Rules of Evidence and Official Notice in Formal Administrative Hearings,* 1971 Duke L.J. 1; Pierce, *Use of the Federal Rules of Evidence in Federal Agency Adjudications,* 39 Ad.L.Rev. 1 (1987).

tribunals deal with the problem of hearsay evidence—that is, statements that were made outside the hearing and are subsequently offered in evidence to prove the truth of the matter asserted. The Federal Rules of Evidence, which govern hearings before federal courts and magistrates, adopt the rule that hearsay is inadmissible, and then proceed to carve out more than twenty technical exceptions to that general standard. Rules 802–03. By contrast, the APA establishes a much simpler standard for administrative trial-type hearings. Section 556(d) provides that "[a]ny oral or documentary evidence may be received, but the agency as a matter of policy shall provide for the exclusion of irrelevant, immaterial, or unduly repetitious evidence." This provision opens the door to any evidence that the presiding officer admits and only *suggests* that insignificant or redundant evidence should be rejected. Moreover, the APA pointedly omits "incompetent" evidence, such as hearsay, from the list of evidence that should not be received. As a result, much material that would be inadmissible in court is routinely accepted in a formal administrative adjudication; its exclusion may even be reversible error. NLRB v. Addison Shoe Corp., 450 F.2d 115 (8th Cir.1971).

The reason for the APA's liberal rules of admissibility can be traced to basic differences in the nature of courts and administrative agencies. Judicial rules of evidence are formulated with the understanding that a significant proportion of cases will be tried to a jury. It is generally assumed that lay jurors tend to overestimate the probative value of hearsay testimony, particularly when the litigants are deprived of the opportunity to cross-examine a declarant who is not a witness in the proceeding. Thus, admitting such evidence in the absence of reliable circumstantial guarantees that it is trustworthy could be prejudicial to the party against whom it is offered. However, there is much less risk of unfairness or error when the factfinding is performed by expert administrators. In the administrative context, it makes sense to save the time and effort that would be spent ruling on questions of admissibility, and let the decisionmakers take account of the lesser probative value of hearsay or other questionable evidence in making their findings. In other words, the fact that a particular bit of evidence is hearsay should go to its weight, but not to its admissibility, in a formal agency adjudication.

Thus, in administrative hearings, the crucial question often is whether, after hearsay or other "tainted" evidence has been received, the ALJ or agency heads should *rely* on this evidence in reaching their decisions. It has long been recognized that hearsay can vary greatly in its reliability, ranging from "mere rumor" to "the kind of evidence on which responsible persons are accustomed to rely in serious affairs." NLRB v. Remington Rand, Inc., 94 F.2d 862, 873 (2d Cir.), cert. denied, 304 U.S. 576 (1938). This common sense notion suggests several rules of thumb that can be used in determining whether a particular item of hearsay is sufficiently trustworthy to support a finding of fact.

(a) Are there circumstantial guarantees that the evidence is trustworthy? Some forms of hearsay are generically more reliable than others, because the circumstances surrounding the statements in question give some assurance that the declarants have been careful and accurate in their representations. Business records, agency reports to Congress or the public, and vital statistics are examples of information that is technically hearsay, but likely to be highly accurate; thus, these documents usually fall within an exception to the hearsay rule, even in a jury trial. In other situations, different kinds of information from a single source may have varying degrees of reliability. For example, factual newspaper accounts of significant events are likely to be accurate, because reporters normally do not fabricate news. However, newspaper quotations or summaries of statements made by particular individuals may be much less reliable. The process of hearing, understanding, and summarizing another's oral statements accurately can be very difficult, as any student knows who has reviewed class notes before an important examination. Thus, a newspaper report that an accident took place may be sufficient support for an administrative decision, but a summary of a speech given by a public official might not be. See, e.g.,

Montana Power Co. v. FPC, 185 F.2d 491, 498 (D.C. Cir.1950), cert. denied, 340 U.S. 947 (1951).

(b) Is better evidence available? If the party against whom hearsay is offered has easy access to better information but fails to produce it, an agency could reasonably infer that the hearsay is reliable. See, e.g., United States ex rel. Vajtauer v. Commissioner, 273 U.S. 103 (1927) (deportation order upheld when alien produced no evidence to refute hearsay indicating that he had advocated forcible overthrow of the government); cf. Interstate Circuit, Inc. v. United States, 306 U.S. 208, 225–26 (1939).

(c) Would the cost of acquiring better evidence be justified in relation to the importance of the subject matter? If the hearsay declarant is readily available and the hearing is likely to have a major effect upon an individual's liberty or livelihood—as in a deportation proceeding—then hearsay may not be adequate to support an adverse finding. However, when the subject is a routine disability compensation claim in a program handling thousands of cases annually, and the declarant is a physician who prepared a diagnostic report, then the additional cost and delay of requiring live testimony may not be justified. See Richardson v. Perales, 402 U.S. 389 (1971) (physicians' written reports sufficient to support denial of disability claim even though opposed by live expert testimony on behalf of the claimant).

(d) How precise must the agency's factfinding be? If the agency needs only to make an approximation of the relevant facts, or can support a finding on the basis of a few documented instances, then hearsay evidence may be adequate. Thus, if the Federal Trade Commission can conclude that advertisements are unlawfully deceptive whenever a particular representation has the capacity to deceive even the most vulnerable consumers, it may be sufficient for the agency to produce a hearsay survey showing that a substantial proportion of the consumers interviewed were misled by the advertisements in question. Since the agency could support its findings by weaker evidence—or even by applying its expertise to the text of the advertisements—it would be pointless to require that each of the survey respondents be made available for cross-examination.

(e) What is the policy behind the statute being enforced? In some instances, the structure or purpose of the agency's program may have a bearing on the kind of evidence required to support a decision. For example, social security and workers' compensation programs are designed to provide benefits quickly and at low cost. A refusal to rely upon affidavits and written reports in such hearings could defeat the basic purposes of the programs.

When focusing on these criteria, it is important to remember that evaluation of technically incompetent evidence cannot be accomplished in the abstract. Much depends upon the quantity and quality of the evidence that each side has placed on the record, the kinds of issues being decided, the impact of an adverse decision on the litigants, and other circumstances surrounding the case.

D. THE INSTITUTIONAL DECISION

In court litigation, decisions are essentially personal: the trial judge who issues findings and conclusions has heard the presentation of evidence and has also reviewed the relevant points of law personally, perhaps with the aid of one or two clerks. Even on appeal, the judges who make the decision and the clerks who assist them listen to arguments and review records and briefs themselves. Administrative agencies are not designed to function like courts, however, and even in formal adjudications the process of decision may be much different from the judicial model. The administrative decisionmaking process is often described as an "institutional decision," in recognition of the fact that it is the product of a bureaucracy rather than of a single person or a small group of identifiable people.

Most regulatory agencies are hierarchies, headed by political appointees who have the responsibility for establishing general policies. Technical expertise is found primarily at the lower levels, among the protected civil service employees, and the expertise needed to decide a particular case may be spread among several bureaus or divisions within the agency. Thus, a central problem of the institutional decision is when and how the officials responsible for making the decision can take advantage of this reservoir of expertise without violating the requirements of fairness to the litigating parties. See pp. 283–88 infra. Conversely, issues may arise as to whether an agency head can properly delegate the power to decide a particular controversy or class of cases to subordinate officials instead of personally hearing and deciding.

This latter question (which is technically known as the "subdelegation" problem because it involves a redelegation by the agency heads of powers originally delegated to them by the legislature) has generally been resolved by recognizing a broad power in top administrators to assign responsibilities to their subordinates. This was not always the prevailing view. In a few early cases, courts strictly construed statutory delegations and concluded that powers had to be exercised personally by the agency heads. See, e.g., Cudahy Packing Co. v. Holland, 315 U.S. 357 (1942) (agency head must sign subpoenas). The culmination of this line of decisions was the first *Morgan* case, where the Supreme Court held that a statute that gave a private party the right to a "full hearing" required a personal decision by the agency head. Chief Justice Hughes, writing for the majority, reasoned that the duty to decide "cannot be performed by one who has not considered evidence or argument.

. . . The one who decides must hear." Morgan v.
United States, 298 U.S. 468, 481 (1936).

However, this principle was too broad to be tak-
en literally, and the Court soon began to cut back
on the *Morgan I* decision. The case returned for a
second round of Supreme Court review after a trial
had been held on the details of the agency's decisionmaking process, and the Court made clear that
the administrator was not required to be physically
present at the taking of testimony. Rather, it was
sufficient that he "dipped into [the record] from
time to time to get its drift," read the parties'
briefs, and discussed the case with his assistants.
Morgan v. United States, 304 U.S. 1, 18 (1938)
(*Morgan II*). The Court further declared that reviewing courts should rarely, if ever, probe beneath
the record of an agency decision to uncover flaws
in the process by which the agency reached its
decision. See pp. 104–05 supra. The practical
effect of this presumption of regularity is to make
it virtually impossible for a challenging party to
show that an administrator has failed to give sufficient personal attention to a decision.

Subsequent developments in the law have made
Morgan 's reservations about the institutional decision largely irrelevant. Contemporary statutes
and reorganization plans usually contain broad
grants of authority to subdelegate decisions. The
price control statute that was upheld against a
delegation attack in Amalgamated Meat Cutters v.
Connally, 337 F.Supp. 737 (D.D.C.1971), discussed

pp. 21–23 supra, illustrates how broad a modern subdelegation can be: it provided that "[t]he President may delegate the performance of any function under this title to such officers, departments, and agencies of the United States as he may deem appropriate." 84 Stat. 800, § 203 (1970).

Although this may be an extreme example, it seems clear that the top administrators of a major regulatory agency or program need considerable discretion to assign tasks to their subordinates. The number of formal adjudications heard in many agencies, and the size of the records compiled in major contested proceedings, make it physically impossible for agency heads to conduct more than a selective policy review of staff recommendations.[6] In any event, it is not clear that they should do more than that. Agency heads and top program administrators are typically political appointees who are selected primarily on the basis of their ability to make policy consistent with the goals of the Administration. They are not normally skilled at presiding over trial-type hearings or sifting through volumes of detailed evidence. In the contemporary administrative agency, those functions have been largely taken over by the Administrative Law Judge.

6. An interesting description of the workload pressures confronting a regulatory commissioner during a "typical" day of decisions is provided in Johnson & Dystel, *A Day in the Life: The Federal Communications Commission,* 82 Yale L.J. 1572 (1973).

1. THE PRESIDING OFFICER

One of the significant changes that accompanied the passage of the Administrative Procedure Act in 1946 was the enhancement of the status and independence of the hearing officer. These officials, which were formerly known as "trial examiners" or "hearing examiners" and are now called "Administrative Law Judges" or ALJs, have several statutory protections. They are appointed through a professional merit selection system, which requires both high performance on a competitive examination and, in many instances, experience in the particular regulatory program; they may not be assigned to perform duties inconsistent with their judicial functions; and they are tenured employees who may be removed or disciplined only for good cause. 5 U.S.C.A. §§ 1305, 3105, 3344, 5372, 7521.

The limits of the ALJs' independence were tested by the "Bellmon review program" conducted by the Social Security Administration during the 1980's. The agency, concerned about widespread inconsistency and inaccuracy in ALJs' decisions in disability benefits cases, began making active use of its authority to conduct internal review of decisions by ALJs. Rulings by those ALJs who had been rendering the highest percentage of decisions favorable to claimants were singled out for special attention in this program. The judicial response to the program was mixed. One court concluded that the "targeting" of individual ALJs had compromised their statutorily guaranteed independence by exerting subtle pressure on them to rule against claimants more often. Association of Administrative Law Judges v. Heckler, 594 F.Supp. 1132 (D.D.C.1984). Another court, finding no direct coercion to maintain a fixed percentage of reversals, upheld the program as a legitimate management tool. Nash v. Bowen, 869 F.2d 675 (2d Cir.), cert. denied, 110 S.Ct. 59 (1989). Within a few years the most intrusive features of the program were abandoned, but the scars that it had created in the relationship between the agency and its ALJs were more enduring.

In a formal trial-type hearing, the ALJ has two primary functions: to conduct the hearing, and to render an initial or recommended decision. Both responsibilities are governed by detailed provisions of the APA. Section 556(b) requires that an ALJ preside at the taking of evidence in a formal adjudication, unless one or more of the agency heads personally conduct the hearing. Another section of the Act delegates broad power to the ALJ to control the proceeding. When authorized by statute and agency rules of practice, the ALJ may issue subpoenas and administer oaths, rule on offers of proof, dispose of procedural requests, and otherwise "regulate the course of the hearing." 5 U.S.C.A. § 556(c). As a practical matter, the ALJ may have greater affirmative responsibility than a trial judge to assure that a full and accurate record is developed at the hearing. Most agencies have been given a statutory mission to accomplish, and they have the duty to develop the facts needed to carry out that mandate. Thus, the hearings need not be structured as pure adversary contests in which the presiding officer serves as a passive referee. In some programs, particularly those involving welfare or disability benefit claims, the hearings may be largely "inquisitorial," with the ALJ taking an active part in questioning witnesses and eliciting relevant facts.

After the hearing has concluded, the parties normally submit proposed findings of fact and conclusions of law, see 5 U.S.C.A. § 557(c), and then the ALJ prepares a decision. Under § 557(b), this may be either an initial or a recommended decision. The distinction lies in the effect of the ALJ's determination: an initial decision becomes the final agency action unless it is reviewed by an appeal board or the agency heads, while a recommended decision must be considered and acted upon by the agency leadership before it takes effect. The existence of these two forms of ALJ decisions may be viewed as a recognition of the fact that agency adjudications have a widely varying policy content. If the proceeding involves routine application of settled principles to a particular fact situation, then it may be efficient to let the ALJ's initial decision become final without review by the agency heads. On the other hand, when a proceeding has been brought as a "test case" to develop policy in an area that is currently unsettled, the use of a recommended decision assures that the top leadership will consider the policy implications of the case. Finally, the APA acknowledges that some agency actions are virtually pure policy choices, even though they may have been preceded by a trial-type hearing. In these situations, a tenured ALJ may have much less to contribute to the ultimate determination than the political appointees who head the agency. Thus, § 557(b) provides that in initial licensing cases and formal rulemaking proceedings, the presiding officer may simply certify the record to the agency heads, and they in turn may issue a tentative decision for comment by the parties.

Regardless of whether it takes the form of an initial or a recommended decision, the ALJ's determination in a formal adjudication is likely to carry considerable weight with the ultimate agency decisionmakers. The ALJ has seen and heard the witnesses personally, and he has usually devoted more time and effort to mastering the issues than the higher level officials who will review his determination. However, the APA makes clear that the agency heads are not required to defer to the ALJ's factfinding in the same way that an appellate court must defer to the trial judge's factual determinations. Section 557(b) states that "[o]n appeal from or review of the initial decision, the agency has all the powers which it would have in making the initial decision, except as it may limit the issues on notice or by rule." One reason for this difference between judicial and administrative practice may be the importance of factual matters in the formulation of agency policy. When the agency makes policy through adjudicative decisions, the key policy issues may have a substantial factual component. In this situation the agency heads who have the primary responsibility for formulating policy should not be bound by the factual conclusions of a tenured ALJ, particularly on doubtful issues of general or "legislative" fact. Policymakers should have some accountability to the political process, and the statutory provision giving them plenary authority to find facts may be one way of preserving this allocation of responsibility. However, the power of the agency to find facts *de novo* can cause conceptual problems for a reviewing court when the agency heads and the examiner have reached different conclusions. See pp. 95–96 supra.

2.   EX PARTE CONTACTS

Like a court trial, a formal agency adjudication is supposed to be decided solely on the basis of the record evidence. This principle is embodied in § 556(e) of the APA, which provides that "[t]he transcript of testimony and exhibits, together with all papers and requests filed in the proceeding, constitutes the exclusive record for decision." The primary reason for requiring this "exclusiveness of the record," as it is sometimes called, is fairness to the litigating parties. If the right to a trial-type hearing is to be meaningful, a participant must be able to know what evidence may be used against her, and to contest it through cross-examination and rebuttal evidence. These rights can easily be nullified if the decisionmakers are free to consider facts outside the record, without notice or opportunity to respond.

The most common problem of extra-record evidence occurs when there are ex parte contacts—communications from an interested party to a decisionmaking official that take place outside the hearing and off the record. There are several reasons why ex parte contact issues arise more frequently in agency proceedings than in court trials. Judicial decisions are almost always made on the record, after an adversary proceeding; the few exceptions, such as applications for a temporary restraining order, are clearly defined and relatively well understood. In this setting, litigants and their attorneys generally assume that it is improper to discuss the merits of pending cases with the judge outside of the formal proceedings. However, on-the-record proceedings comprise only a small part of the workload in most administrative agencies.

The great bulk of agency decisions are made through informal action, or through public proceedings like notice-and-comment rulemaking where ex parte contacts may be not just permissible but affirmatively desirable. Frequently, regulated companies or interest group representatives will be involved in several pending proceedings before an agency, perhaps involving related issues. In this continuing course of dealing, it is easy for even the most careful person to slip and touch upon issues that are under consideration in a formal adjudication. This is not to suggest that all improper ex parte contacts between regulators and regulated are inadvertent; but it does seem clear that regulatory officials function in a complex environment where the line between "responsive government" and "backroom dealing" is often indistinct.

The APA as originally enacted did not deal explicitly with ex parte contacts, and as a result claims of improper ex parte influence were generally evaluated under the due process clause of the Constitution. See, e.g. WKAT v. FCC, 296 F.2d 375, 383 (D.C.Cir.), cert. denied, 368 U.S. 841 (1961). In 1976, however, the APA was amended (90 Stat. 1247) and now contains detailed provisions governing ex parte contacts in formal adjudications. Section 557(d)(1) prohibits any "interested person outside the agency" from making, or knowingly causing, "any ex parte communication relevant to the merits of the proceeding" to any decisionmaking official. It also imposes similar restraints on the agency decisionmakers, who are defined to include any "member of the body comprising the agency, administrative law judge, or other employee who is or may reasonably be expected to be involved in the decisional process." The prohibitions on ex parte contacts come into play when a proceeding has been noticed for hearing, unless the agency has designated some earlier time. 5 U.S. C.A. § 557(d)(1)(E).

When an improper ex parte contact does take place, the APA requires that it be placed on the public record; if it was an oral communication, a memorandum summarizing the contact must be filed. Id. § 557(d)(1)(C). Potentially, the APA can trigger an even more severe sanction on parties who improperly try to influence the agency: an outside party who made or caused the improper contact can be required to show cause "why his claim or interest in the proceeding should not be dismissed, denied, disregarded, or otherwise adversely affected on account of such violation." Id. § 557(d)(1)(D). Ultimately, however, the decision whether to impose such a sanction is a matter for judicial discretion. Professional Air Traffic Controllers Org. v. FLRA, 685 F.2d 547 (D.C.Cir.1982). *PATCO* arose out of a Federal Labor Relations Authority proceeding to decertify a union of air traffic controllers that had led its members in an illegal strike against the government. The evidence showed that a prominent labor leader had met privately with a member of the FLRA, urging him not to revoke the union's certification. Although the court was convinced that this contact was illegal, it did not overturn the FLRA's order, because the discussion of PATCO's situation had been brief, the labor leader had made no threats or promises, and the conversation had not affected the outcome of the case.

A case that arose before the APA amendments illustrates that there is a tension between concerns about ex parte contacts and the need for political oversight of agency decisionmaking. In Pillsbury Co. v. FTC, 354 F.2d 952 (5th Cir.1966), the FTC rendered an interlocutory decision on a question of antitrust law in a merger case and remanded the case to the ALJ for further hearings. Shortly afterwards, at a congressional oversight hearing, several senators were extremely critical of the Commission's ruling, and they subjected the FTC chairman and some agency staff members to detailed, hostile questioning. Despite the fact that the chairman disqualified himself from participating in the case when it returned to the Commission for review, the court held that the entire agency was disqualified. In the court's view, the congressional pressure had so interfered with the agency's process of decision that the respondent could not get a fair hearing. However, the passage of time and the consequent changes in agency personnel had diluted the risk of future prejudgment, and so the court remanded the case for further proceedings.

Analytically, the court's decision is somewhat questionable, because the FTC adhered in its final opinion to the same legal position that it had taken originally, a fact indicating that it had not been influenced by congressional pressure. Moreover, the colloquy at the hearing had concerned purely legal issues, not factual ones, and members of Congress surely have a legitimate interest in urging an agency head to follow legislative intent as they interpret it. Arguably, however, the *Pillsbury* opinion serves a useful purpose insofar as it serves generally to discourage congressional intervention in adjudicative proceedings. Such intervention often runs the risk of injecting a political element where it does not belong—in the factfinding and law-applying functions that constitute the usual stuff of administrative adjudication.

3.   SEPARATION OF FUNCTIONS

When an agency is conducting a formal adjudication, a variant of the ex parte contacts problem often arises within the agency. Usually, agency staff members are assigned to act as advocates in trial-type hearings. For example, staff attorneys may be designated "counsel supporting the complaint" in a disciplinary proceeding and instructed to act as prosecutors presenting the case against the respondent. When the proceeding is structured in this fashion, a question may arise as to whether the staff attorneys may consult with the decisionmakers outside the record of the proceeding.

From the perspective of the accused respondent, this sort of consultation is likely to seem just as unfair as any other ex parte communication by an adverse party. On the other hand, there are some valid policy reasons for permitting free communications within the agency. Many administrative decisions, including those made in formal adjudications, involve highly technical issues. The expertise necessary to understand those issues is usually found at the staff levels of the agency rather than among the ALJs and the agency heads; thus, insulating the decisionmakers from expert staff could undermine the quality of the decision.

The APA seeks to resolve this tension by defining a limited class of agency staff members who may not consult with decisionmakers in a formal adjudication. This ban on internal communications is generally referred to as "separation of functions." Section 554(d) provides that any employee who is "engaged in the performance of investigative or prosecuting functions" may not participate in the decision or advise the decisionmakers in that case or any factually related case. Any input from the prosecuting staff must come "as a witness or counsel in public proceedings." Id. Thus, the APA acknowledges that a staff member who acts as an advocate is likely to have strong views on the merits, and that it would be unfair to the respondent to give such persons preferential access to the decisionmakers. However, agency employees who have not taken on an adversary role in the particular hearing will be more objective, and the agency heads should be free to call upon them when they need assistance in interpreting the record evidence. Finally, the APA recognizes that the risk of unfairness is likely to be small when the proceedings do not have an accusatory or adversary tenor. Section 554(d) stipulates that the separation of functions requirements do not apply to initial licensing or ratemaking—proceedings that are designed to decide technical or policy questions rather than to impose sanctions for past conduct.

Although the agency decisionmakers may consult with nonprosecuting staff members when they are evaluating the record of a formal proceeding, this does not mean that they are free to obtain additional, nonrecord evidence from these agency employees. The principle of § 556(e) that the transcript, exhibits, and other formal filings constitute the "exclusive record for decision" still applies, and consideration of nonrecord evidence may be reversible error. A decision by the Administrator of the Environmental Protection Agency authorizing the construction of a nuclear power plant was reversed on this ground in Seacoast Anti–Pollution League v. Costle, 572 F.2d 872 (1st Cir.1978). The Administrator had established a "technical review panel" of agency scientists to assist him in reviewing an initial decision involving the thermal pollution that would result from the proposed reactor. The court held that this review panel had not merely analyzed the record, but rather had supplemented it with additional scientific material which should have been introduced as evidence. Since the Administrator had relied on their assessments, the error was prejudicial and reversal was required.

In addition to the internal separation of functions required by § 554(d) of the APA, it has sometimes been argued that agencies should have a structural separation of functions. That is, some commentators have contended that the system of administrative adjudication is inherently unfair, because a single agency often investigates, decides to issue a complaint, conducts the hearing, reviews the initial decision, imposes the sanctions, and checks compliance with its orders. In extreme form, this line of criticism concludes that an independent system of "administrative courts" should be established solely for the purpose of hearing and deciding cases brought by the agencies. Congress has occasionally responded to these concerns by enacting statutes that require strict separation of prosecuting and deciding functions. The National Labor Relations Board is a good example. In 1947, Congress separated the responsibility for investigating violations and issuing complaints from the Board, and conferred it on an independent General Counsel. The Board members who ultimately hear and decide these cases have no control over the General Counsel or the decision to prosecute. Similarly, when Congress enacted the Occupational Safety and Health Act in 1970, it assigned the adjudicative function to a review commission that has no responsibility for deciding which cases will be brought initially.

Litigants, too, have attacked the institutional combination of functions, claiming that the mixture of prosecuting and deciding powers in a single agency was so unfair as to constitute a denial of due process of law. This argument was unanimously rejected by the Supreme Court in Withrow v. Larkin, 421 U.S. 35 (1975). The Court pointed out that, even in criminal trials, judges make a variety of preliminary determinations that are analogous to the agency's decision to issue a complaint: arrest and search warrants are issued by judges who may later preside at the trial, and "[j]udges also preside at preliminary hearings where they must decide whether the evidence is sufficient to hold a defendant for trial." Moreover, trial judges who are reversed in civil appeals and administrators who have had their decisions remanded by the courts for further consideration are not considered incapable of giving fair and impartial consideration to the merits of the case. Thus, the due process claim fails unless the protesting party can demonstrate some particular bias which goes beyond the mere combination of prosecuting and adjudicating functions in a single agency.

Concerns about the potential unfairness of combining multiple powers in a single agency are not wholly insubstantial. It is probably true, at least in some instances, that an agency head who has reviewed an investigative file and concluded that there was enough evidence to issue a complaint will be more likely to find the respondent guilty when he later reviews the initial decision. Moreover, an administrator who has himself been responsible for committing substantial staff resources to an enforcement proceeding may be reluctant to rule, in the end, that it was all for naught. Nevertheless, the price of total insulation of the adjudicators could often be high, especially where issues are technically complex or there is a need for a coherent national regulatory policy in a particular field. The cost of creating equal expertise in two separate institutions could be high or even prohibitive. Just as troublesome is the likelihood that separate bureaucracies would work at cross purposes; the possibilities for policy stalemate or confusion could increase markedly.

4. BIAS AND PREJUDGMENT

The right to an administrative trial-type hearing would have little meaning if the decisionmaker held a personal grudge against one of the litigants, or had already made up his mind about the facts of the case before any evidence was taken. Thus, in agency adjudications as in court trials, due process combines with statutory provisions to require that the decisionmaker be impartial. See pp. 231–34 supra; 5 U.S.C.A. § 556(b) (procedures for ruling on claims that decisionmakers are biased or otherwise disqualified from participating in formal adjudications).

However, a decision as to whether an administrator has violated the requirement of impartiality is in some ways more complex than a decision as to whether a judge should recuse herself from hearing a case. Courts generally perform only one function, the resolution of disputes in adversary proceedings, while agencies typically have been delegated a variety of managerial and policymaking responsibilities in addition to the power to adjudicate particular cases. The actions taken and the statements made by administrators in the course of these nonadjudicative duties may create the appearance that a particular case has been prejudged, if not the reality. Yet stringent prohibitions on the appearance of prejudgment in formal adjudications could make it difficult for administrators to perform their nonjudicial functions adequately. In addition, most agencies have a statutory mandate to fulfill; rather than simply resolving disputes that are presented to them, agencies are supposed to implement important social policies such as protecting consumers from dangerous foods and drugs or preventing unscrupulous practices in the sale of securities. To this extent, at least, most agencies have what might be considered a "built–in bias."

In responding to these conflicting pressures, the law has generally demonstrated a keen awareness that an agency decisionmaker should be open minded, but not empty headed. The political appointees who head the agencies are chosen in large measure because of the policy positions they have publicly taken, and it would be absurd to require that the Secretary of Transportation have no ideas on the subject of auto safety or that the Administrator of the Environmental Protection Agency be indifferent to the problems of pollution. Thus, an administrator who has taken public positions on controversial matters of law or policy is generally not disqualified from deciding cases that raise those issues. United States v. Morgan, 313 U.S. 409, 421 (1941) (*Morgan IV*). The same rule generally applies to judges who have spoken out on matters that are at issue in pending cases. In Laird v. Tatum, 409 U.S. 824 (1972), Justice (now Chief Justice) Rehnquist refused to disqualify himself from participating in a case concerning the constitutionality of government surveillance of political activity, even though he had testified on behalf of the Administration in congressional hearings dealing with the same activities and had made other public statements in support of the government's position before being appointed to the Court. Since virtually all of the Justices have expressed public opinions on constitutional issues before their appointment to the Court, and have written opinions on these questions as part of their judicial duties, a rule that required disqualification for prior statements on issues of law and policy would prevent the Court from functioning.

Similar reasoning was applied to administrative adjudicators in FTC v. Cement Institute, 333 U.S. 683 (1948). There, the Federal Trade Commission had issued public reports and given testimony in

Congress concluding that a particular system of pricing that was widely used in the cement industry violated the antitrust laws. When the agency later issued a complaint against one of the companies using the pricing system, the respondent claimed that the agency's prior reports showed impermissible prejudgment of the issues. The Court disagreed, noting that Congress' very purpose had been to establish an expert agency that could engage in both reporting and adjudicative functions; adoption of the respondent's theory would have made the congressional plan unworkable. The Court was also concerned that a rigid approach to disqualification would mean that no administrative tribunal would be able to adjudicate the case. This latter consideration is sometimes called the "rule of necessity": an adjudicator should not be disqualified if the case could not be heard otherwise. This principle has enabled the courts to sit in cases involving judicial salaries. United States v. Will, 449 U.S. 200 (1980). Similarly, in *Cement Institute,* there was no provision for substituting commissioners, and no other agency could bring a cease and desist proceeding against the respondents if the FTC were held unable to act.

A more troubling situation arises when a public statement by a regulatory commissioner suggests that he may already have made up his mind on *facts* that are at issue in a pending case. Speeches, articles, and interviews are useful means of informing the public about agency policy and activi-

ties; but careless comments about the facts of
pending cases may tend to entrench the commissioner in his assumptions, making it difficult for
him to consider the evidence impartially when the
case comes before the agency for final decision.
The test applied in this situation emphasizes both
actual and apparent fairness: the reviewing court
will inquire whether a disinterested observer
would conclude that the administrator has in some
measure prejudged the facts of the case. Texaco,
Inc. v. FTC, 336 F.2d 754 (D.C.Cir.1964), vacated
and remanded on other grounds, 381 U.S. 739
(1965); Cinderella Career & Finishing Schools, Inc.
v. FTC, 425 F.2d 583 (D.C.Cir.1970) (*Cinderella II*).
The "rule of necessity" carries less weight in this
context, because an administrator can avoid the
appearance of partiality by simply discussing the
issues in the case more guardedly. See Kennecott
Copper Corp. v. FTC, 467 F.2d 67 (10th Cir.1972)
(neutral description of complaint's allegations was
permissible). By the same token, the issuance of a
factual press release that merely describes the
filing of a complaint does not violate the respondent's right to an impartial decisionmaker. FTC v.
Cinderella Career & Finishing Schools, Inc., 404
F.2d 1308 (D.C.Cir.1968) (*Cinderella I*).

In some situations, disqualifying bias can be
shown by circumstantial evidence rather than by
an overt statement by the official. For example,
an adjudicator who has become personally familiar
with the evidence by serving in an adversary ca-

pacity as an investigator or advocate is disqualified from participating in the decision. Thus, in American Cyanamid Co. v. FTC, 363 F.2d 757 (6th Cir. 1966), a commissioner who had investigated the respondent's practices in his prior job as staff counsel to a congressional committee was held ineligible to participate in an adjudication where the same practices were alleged to be violations of the antitrust laws.

Finally, although ideological commitments are usually not sufficient to disqualify adjudicators, the opposite is true when administrators have a financial or other personal stake in the decision. In this situation disqualification is required not only by due process, see pp. 232–34 supra, but also by statutes, executive orders, and agency regulations prohibiting conflicts of interest. Most of these provisions follow the general approach taken in the federal judicial disqualification statute: a judge must recuse herself in any case in which she "has a financial interest in the subject matter . . . or any other interest that could be substantially affected by the outcome of the proceeding." 28 U.S.C.A. § 455(b)(4). Troublesome questions regarding the applicability of these standards may arise, particularly when an agency adjudicator comes to government service from private practice and his law firm has been active in representing clients before the agency. However, the general principle is well established: a personal stake in the outcome, however small, constitutes grounds for disqualification.

E. FINDINGS, CONCLUSIONS, AND REASONS

A formal adjudication concludes with the issuance of a written decision, and the APA has detailed provisions governing the contents of the agency's final product. Section 557(c) requires that the parties be given an opportunity to submit proposed findings and conclusions, or "exceptions" to the proposed decision (usually in the form of briefs), before the agency renders a recommended, initial, or final decision. The APA then directs that "[a]ll decisions" in formal adjudications, whether preliminary or final, "shall include . . . findings and conclusions, and the reasons or basis therefor, on all the material issues of fact, law, or discretion presented on the record." Id.

There are several reasons for requiring agencies to state in detail the factual, legal, and policy bases of important decisions. Exposure of the agency's reasoning helps to assure that administrators will be publicly accountable for their decisions, and that interested persons will have better guidance on the agency's current policy. The need to prepare a detailed analysis of the evidence and arguments can also exert some discipline on the decisionmaking process, by forcing the responsible officials to deal with each party's points carefully and systematically. Finally, statements of findings, conclusions, and reasons make meaningful judicial review possible: without them, a reviewing court will likely find it very difficult to determine whether the agency has exceeded the bounds of the power conferred by the legislature, or has abused its discretion by taking account of factors not properly relevant to its decision, or has found facts without a sufficient evidentiary basis.

Unfortunately, much of the value of the APA requirements governing findings and statements of reasons is lost when the opinions are not prepared, or at least carefully considered, by the responsible decisionmakers. Traditionally, top administrators in some agencies that have a large volume of adjudications have delegated most of the responsibility for documenting their decisions to specialized opinion writing staffs. The opinions prepared by these staffs may rely heavily on standard "boilerplate" passages, and they may be written with a view towards minimizing the discussion of points that might cause problems on judicial review. In these circumstances, the opinion-writing process does not really impose any discipline on the decision, and a reviewing court cannot be sure that it is considering the actual bases for the agency action: the opinion becomes more of a rationalization for the decision than an explanation.

CHAPTER VIII

PROCEDURAL SHORTCUTS

Many administrative statutes contain clauses conferring broad rights to trial-type hearings. Administrative hearings, however, can be costly in time, manpower, and other resources, and they sometimes make only a marginal contribution to the quality of information available or to the acceptability of the final decision. Thus, agencies often have an incentive to develop procedural techniques for avoiding unnecessary hearings or for narrowing the issues that will be considered in a formal setting. Several such techniques are examined in this chapter.

A. LEGISLATIVE RULEMAKING

Most agencies operate under statutory schemes that permit them to issue legislative rules. Once such a rule has been promulgated, private parties have no further right to be heard at the agency level on the issues addressed in the rule; those issues will remain settled unless the party can show that the rule itself is invalid. (The term "substantive rules" is sometimes used as a synonym for "legislative rules," but it is slightly misleading, because a *procedural* rule can also be "legislative," settling the issues it addresses.) Sometimes it is unclear whether an agency's rulemaking authority applies to a given administrative function; private parties may contend that this authority cannot be used to defeat their own statutory right to a trial-type administrative hearing. In general, however, the Supreme Court has rejected these contentions, preferring to construe agencies' rulemaking powers expansively.

Early experiments in using rulemaking to streamline adjudications were initiated by licensing agencies. The Federal Communications Commission, for example, is required to hold a "full hearing"—a formal adjudication under the APA—before refusing an application for a broadcast license. In United States v. Storer Broadcasting Co., 351 U.S. 192 (1956), the Commission had issued multiple ownership rules reducing the number of television outlets that could be controlled by one licensee. Storer, which exceeded the new maximum limit, had applied for an additional license before the rule became final, but the FCC nonetheless dismissed the application as not conforming to the new rule. Storer claimed that this procedure was a denial of its statutory right to a full hearing, but the Supreme Court held that the rule was valid and therefore the denial of a trial-type hearing was proper. Subsequent decisions made clear that the *Storer* principle was not limited to the communications field. See FPC v. Texaco, Inc., 377 U.S. 33 (1964) (upholding FPC rule that imposed conditions on the grant of gas pipeline certificates); American Airlines, Inc. v. C.A.B., 359 F.2d 624 (D.C.Cir.) (en banc), cert. denied, 385 U.S. 843 (1966) (upholding CAB rule that effectively modified some air carriers' certificates by prohibiting them from transporting cargo through "blocked space" arrangements).[1]

More recently, the Court has extended *Storer* to benefits programs, upholding the "medical-vocational guidelines" used in the Social Security disability program. Heckler v. Campbell, 461 U.S. 458 (1983). Under the Social Security Act, benefits are to be paid to persons who are so severely disabled that they cannot engage in any work available in the national economy. The claimant's job qualifications are to be judged in light of four variables: age, education, work experience, and physical ability. The guidelines, also known as "grid regulations," listed numerous combinations of the four threshold variables and stated, for each combination, whether a worker with those qualifications was employable. Thus, administrative law judges (ALJs) hearing disability benefits claims would no longer rely on expert testimony in deciding whether a claimant was employable; instead, they would simply make findings concerning the four variables, and reference to the guidelines would then

1. The rules challenged in *Storer* and *Texaco* had actually been relatively flexible, for they had provided that companies could ask for a waiver on the basis of individual circumstances. However, a rule that lacks a waiver provision can still be valid. For example, the FCC was allowed to adopt a flat rule that radio stations' changes of format would never be considered during license renewal proceedings. FCC v. WNCN Listeners Guild, 450 U.S. 582 (1981).

automatically determine whether the claimant was entitled to benefits. The Court concluded that, although the Act states that the disability determination is to be made on the basis of evidence adduced at a hearing, this provision "does not bar the Secretary from relying on rulemaking to resolve certain classes of issues."

The rules upheld in *Campbell* were controversial, for they tended to curb ALJs' ability to respond to individual circumstances that might come to light at an evidentiary hearing. As the Court noted, however, use of the guidelines enhanced the efficiency of the program and helped bring about uniform results nationwide. Moreover, the process was not entirely impersonal, because an ALJ still had to use individualized judgment in assessing a claimant's particular abilities. In any event, the Court endorsed rulemaking only with respect to "issues that do not require case-by-case consideration." The guidelines had made findings about the availability of jobs in the national economy—a generic question that could be resolved in an across-the-board fashion. In reasoning reminiscent of the distinction between "legislative" and "adjudicative" facts (see p. 214 supra), the Court indicated that issues that had a closer relationship to unique characteristics of the individual could only be resolved through a hearing. (Indeed, in a later case involving the children's disability benefits program, the Court struck down rules under which a child's eligibility for benefits turned exclusively on whether she had one of the medical conditions listed in the rule; the Court said that each child claimant was entitled to make an individualized showing that she was disabled. Sullivan v. Zebley, 110 S.Ct. 885 (1990).[2] Thus, although the Court has strongly supported the use of rulemaking, it also acknowledges that the scope of rulemaking power must depend on considerations of fairness as well as efficiency.

B. SUMMARY JUDGMENT

Another way in which an agency can avoid unnecessary hearings is to adopt a summary judgment procedure. For the most part, administrative summary judgment rules are similar to Rule 56 of the Federal Rules of Civil Procedure: a judgment on the merits may be rendered without hearing when there is no genuine issue of material fact to be tried.[3] An agency, however, typically has much wider substantive policymaking authority than a court. It can sometimes use this authority to redefine the underlying legal standards, and then enter summary judgment against parties who fail to show a triable issue under the new standards.

2. But cf. Bowen v. Yuckert, 482 U.S. 137 (1987) (upholding, by a divided vote, a regulation providing that if a claimant's impairments did not significantly limit her ability to do most jobs, she would automatically be deemed ineligible for benefits).

3. See generally Gellhorn & Robinson, *Summary Judgment in Administrative Adjudication,* 84 Harv.L.Rev. 612 (1971).

The Supreme Court addressed one example of this technique in Weinberger v. Hynson, Westcott & Dunning, Inc., 412 U.S. 609 (1973). In 1962, Congress directed the Food and Drug Administration to withdraw from the market any therapeutic drug that could not be proved by its manufacturer to be effective. More than 16,000 claims of effectiveness had to be reviewed, yet the statute required the agency to give a manufacturer "due notice and opportunity for hearing" before withdrawing approval of any drug. To cope with its massive assignment, the FDA promulgated rules stating that it would evaluate the effectiveness of a given drug only on the basis of adequate and well-controlled clinical studies, not anecdotal reports from sources such as practicing physicians. The agency also adopted a summary judgment procedure, under which a manufacturer facing disapproval of a drug would be denied a hearing unless it could demonstrate in advance that it could present a "genuine and substantial issue of fact" under the new rules.

In *Hynson,* a company that had been subjected to summary judgment sought judicial review, claiming that the FDA's procedure violated its statutory right to a full hearing. The Court generally upheld the FDA's summary judgment practice. A primary factor in the Court's reasoning was the common sense notion that it would be pointless to hold a hearing if the challenging party had no chance of succeeding on the merits. It was also clear that the FDA could not accomplish its statutory mission of getting ineffective drugs off the market if it were obliged to grant a trial-type hearing on every claim, however insubstantial. But there were also cautionary signals in the *Hynson* opinion. The Court found that the drug company's submissions in the case at bar had been sufficient to require a hearing. Moreover, the Court warned that its approval of summary judgment extended only to situations in which the FDA was applying a "precise" regulation; where the applicable legal standards required the agency to exercise "discretion or subjective judgment" in appraising the applicant's evidence, "it might not be proper to deny a hearing."

Subsequent cases display similar ambivalence about the FDA's use of summary judgment. Courts have required the FDA to give clear notice of the evidence that it believes warrants summary judgment, so that the company has a fair opportunity to respond; and they have carefully scrutinized this evidence to see whether it shows the absence of a triable fact issue. In one case, the FDA granted summary judgment against the manufacturer of an animal drug, reasoning that the presence of carcinogenic residues in cattle treated with the drug conclusively established that the drug was unsafe. The court reversed, because the manufacturer had raised doubts about whether the residues had resulted from the drug or from the agency's own testing procedure. Hess & Clark v.

FDA, 495 F.2d 975 (D.C.Cir.1974). On the other hand, when the FDA found that all evidence indicated that the artificial sweetener aspartame *was* safe, the court declined to order a trial; it was reluctant to second-guess the agency on the technical issues involved. Community Nutrition Institute v. Young, 773 F.2d 1356 (D.C.Cir.1985).

The Supreme Court's support for summary judgment has continued since *Hynson.* See Costle v. Pacific Legal Foundation, 445 U.S. 198 (1980). Nevertheless, agencies seem to make little use of this device. One reason may be that most of the adjudicating agencies have extensive informal mechanisms for resolving cases by voluntary compliance or consent settlement. When a case is reasonably clear on the facts, these mechanisms may often serve the same functions that summary judgment does in court litigation.

C. OFFICIAL NOTICE

In the same manner that courts can bypass the normal process of proof by taking judicial notice of facts, administrative agencies sometimes overcome deficiencies in the record of a formal proceeding by taking "official notice" of material facts. Indeed, agencies enjoy considerably wider power to dispense with formal proof than the courts do. In federal courts, for example, the rules of evidence limit judicial notice of adjudicative facts to propositions that are "beyond reasonable dispute, in that [they are] either (1) generally known within the territorial jurisdiction of the trial court, or (2) capable of accurate and ready determination by resort to sources whose accuracy cannot reasonably be questioned." Federal Rule of Evidence 201(b). These strict limits are unsuitable for administrative agencies, which often are created precisely so that they can become repositories of knowledge and expertise. Because they are continuously active in the fields of their specialties, agency officials are frequently aware of extrarecord facts that bear on cases pending before them. A liberal system of official notice can contribute to the convenience and efficiency of the decisional process, by avoiding the need for repetitive, time-consuming proof of matters that have already been thoroughly investigated.

Official notice, however, is often confused with the application of expertise in the *evaluation of evidence.* In drawing conclusions from a record, administrative law judges and agencies may rely on their special skills in engineering, economics, medicine, etc., just as judges may freely use their legal skills in reading statutes and applying decided cases in the preparation of their opinions. They also resort to theories, predictions, and intuitions that are inherently incapable of exact proof. See pp. 113–15 supra. Properly speaking, however, these evaluations and insights are not within the concept of official notice. Rather, official notice comes into play when an agency that *could* have documented one of its factual premises on the record is allowed to avoid that process for efficiency reasons.

Because of its breadth, official notice has the potential to interfere with the due process right to a fair administrative hearing. One way in which the law addresses this concern is to impose procedural safeguards. First, the noticed material must be specifically identified. The agency cannot rest on a vague claim that it is an expert; it must explain with particularity the sources of its information. Ohio Bell Tel. Co. v. Public Util. Comm'n, 301 U.S. 292 (1937); Air Prods. & Chems., Inc. v. FERC, 650 F.2d 687 (5th Cir.1981). Second, it must give the opposing party a meaningful chance to rebut the information or to present additional arguments that would put the noticed facts into a more favorable light. United States v. Abilene & Southern Ry., 265 U.S. 274 (1924). This latter requirement is codified in the APA: "When an agency decision rests on official notice of a material fact . . . a party is entitled, on timely request, to an opportunity to show the contrary." 5 U.S. C.A. § 556(e).[4] In practice, the APA obligation is not burdensome. An agency may even cite official-

---

4. Similar rights exist in the federal court system, see Federal Rule of Evidence 201(e), but only with regard to "adjudicative facts"—facts concerning the immediate parties to a case. The Rules leave a trial judge completely free to take judicial notice of a "legislative fact" (a general fact bearing on law or policy) without obtaining any input from the parties. It has been argued that courts should follow a procedure like that of the APA, by giving parties an opportunity to contest important legislative facts that are being judicially noticed. See 3 K.

ly noticed facts for the first time in its final opinion, so long as it allows the opposing party to rebut these facts by filing a petition for rehearing.

Even where an agency is willing to allow rebuttal from an opposing party, its efforts to rely on official notice may fail. Courts are wary of allowing this device to cut too far into the agency's obligation to build its case through the normal adversary process. Unfortunately, they have developed no clear guidelines to identify the circumstances in which official notice is permissible. In general, however, the device seems to be accepted most readily in situations in which there are strong reasons to assume that the agency's assertions are trustworthy. For example, in Market Street Ry. v. Railroad Comm'n, 324 U.S. 548 (1945), the agency was setting rates for a streetcar company and needed to know the company's operating revenues for 1943. It took notice of figures in the company's monthly operating reports, which had been filed with it after the record closed. The Supreme Court upheld this procedure, noting that the company had never contended that the figures in its own reports were erroneous or had been cited misleadingly. Similarly, the Federal Trade Commission could take official notice of more than two dozen prior proceedings in which agency counsel had successfully proved that many consumers were deceived when sellers failed to disclose that goods

Davis, Administrative Law Treatise §§ 15:11–15:13 (2d ed. 1980).

had been manufactured in foreign countries. Manco Watch Strap Co., 60 F.T.C. 495 (1962) (endorsed in Brite Mfg. Co. v. FTC, 347 F.2d 477 (D.C. Cir.1965)).[5]

In contrast, the FTC's attempt to take official notice in more questionable circumstances brought a judicial reversal in Dayco Corp. v. FTC, 362 F.2d 180 (6th Cir.1966). The respondent, Dayco, was an automobile parts manufacturer accused of price discrimination. The Commission sought to take official notice of the findings that it had made in an earlier proceeding against one of the company's customers. The findings tended to show that Dayco had used a sham distribution system to grant discounts to certain buyers, and that these customers were in competition with other buyers who did not receive discounts. The FTC's tactic was unfair, the court concluded, even though the Commission had offered Dayco an opportunity to respond. The court implied that an agency may never take official notice of facts that it develops while litigating cases. Although that distinction seems artificial, the result was surely plausible. The officially noticed "facts" in *Dayco* were merely inferences that the FTC had drawn by weighing testimony in a single unappealed case in which Dayco had not been a party. These findings were not reliable enough to justify dispensing with the

5. See also Banks v. Schweiker, 654 F.2d 637 (9th Cir.1981) (ALJ could have taken notice of routine practices at Social Security office, if he had granted claimant an opportunity for rebuttal).

usual safeguards of the adversary process. The court distinguished the case from *Manco,* in which the accumulation of findings in numerous cases had given the FTC a firmer basis for invoking its expertise as a substitute for formal proof.[6]

Judging from the small number of reported cases, the doctrine of official notice has apparently not been used extensively or creatively by many agencies. This reluctance may be partly a result of uncertainties in the applicable legal standards; without clear tests indicating when official notice is proper, agencies may be unwilling to risk reversal by taking notice of nonrecord facts. It remains a potentially useful device for simplifying and expediting hearings.

---

6. The *Dayco* court also intimated that an agency should have more freedom to take official notice of "legislative" facts than "adjudicative" facts. This proposition, which other courts also have endorsed, rests on the widely held belief that trial-type processes are relatively unhelpful in the development of legislative facts, and thus may be foregone more readily when an agency wants to rely on such facts. This does not mean, however, that an agency may never take official notice of an adjudicative fact. See *Market Street,* supra.

CHAPTER IX

RULES AND RULEMAKING

One of the most important developments in administrative law during the past two decades has been the agencies' growing reliance on rulemaking as a means of formulating policy. Administrative rulemaking is not a recent invention; the federal executive departments have issued legally binding rules since the beginning of our national government, and the Administrative Procedure Act as originally passed in 1946 had several provisions dealing with rulemaking procedure. In the 1970's and 1980's, however, the number and significance of decisions being made in agency rulemaking proceedings increased dramatically.

Much can be said in favor of this trend. As commentators have argued, the rulemaking process can be more efficient than case-by-case adjudication, because it can resolve a multiplicity of issues in a single proceeding. A clear general rule can produce rapid and uniform compliance among the affected firms or individuals; the scope of an adjudicative precedent may well be harder to define, because its reach will usually depend to some degree on the facts of a particular case. At the same time, rulemaking can provide individuals with important protection. "When a governmental official is given the power to make discretionary decisions under a broad statutory standard, case-by-case decisionmaking may not be the best way to assure fairness. . . . [The use of rulemaking] provides [regulated persons] with more precise notice of what conduct will be sanctioned and promotes equality of treatment among similarly situated [persons]." Dixon v. Love, 431 U.S. 105 (1977). Furthermore, rulemaking proceedings can put all affected parties on notice of impending changes in regulatory policy, and give them an opportunity to be heard before the agency's position has crystallized.

Despite these advantages of rules over individual adjudications, the agencies probably would not have made such a marked shift towards rulemaking without some external pressures. From the agency's perspective, writing a general rule is often more difficult than deciding a particular case, and the likelihood of producing an undesirable or unintended result is correspondingly greater. Moreover, general rules are more likely to inspire concerted opposition from those who will be covered by them. An individual case isolates one respondent, generally selected because of questionable actions, for possible sanction, but a general rule can inspire the whole industry (whose members may or may not have engaged in similar actions) to fight—not only before the agency but in the courts, the Congress, and the media as well. In short, promulgating a rule can be more costly to the agency in time, effort, and good will than deciding a series of cases.

The major impetus for agencies to make greater use of their rulemaking authority came from Congress. Regulatory statutes enacted during the 1970's often contained express grants of rulemaking authority, and some of them specifically instructed agencies to proceed by general rule. Moreover, agencies' procedural choices were influenced by the changing nature of the tasks they were being asked to perform. In the wave of health, safety, environmental, and consumer-protection legislation that burgeoned during the 1970's, Congress created programs under which administrative officials would be responsible for regulating hundreds of thousands of workplaces or pollution sources, or millions of consumer transactions. The agencies could not hope to accomplish these missions unless they were prepared to make liberal use of rulemaking authority.

The courts, too, encouraged broader use of rulemaking. Where an agency's authority to proceed by rulemaking was in doubt, they tended to find that the agency did have such authority. For example, in National Petroleum Refiners Ass'n v. FTC, 482 F.2d 672 (D.C.Cir.1973), cert. denied, 415 U.S. 951 (1974), the FTC proposed a regulation that would have required service stations to post octane ratings on gasoline pumps. Industry groups brought suit, pointing out that the Commission was attempting to make use of a half-century-old statutory provision that it had never before regarded as a source of authority to issue substantive rules. The court turned this challenge aside, declaring that the agency's power to make rules should be "interpret[ed] liberally" in light of the numerous benefits of administrative rulemaking. Similarly, the courts were unsympathetic to arguments that an agency's rulemaking authority should be construed narrowly in order to preserve regulated parties' right to a full hearing in adjudicative proceedings in which the rule might be applied. See pp. 296–300 supra. Some courts even attempted to *force* agencies to use rulemaking, although the weight of authority strongly disfavors such efforts. See pp. 345–52 infra.

The growth of rulemaking gave rise to a searching reexamination of the adequacy of the procedures that agencies followed in adopting rules. Courts and legislatures became more willing to experiment with new variations on the APA's procedural models, as they sought to accommodate traditional rulemaking practices to the new kinds of decisions that agencies were making. Eventually this wave of procedural reform ebbed in significance, only to be superseded by other innovations, such as negotiated rulemaking and intensified executive oversight. In coming years, there is every likelihood that the rulemaking process will remain one of the most dynamic areas of administrative law.

A. THE TYPES OF ADMINISTRATIVE RULES

The APA divides agency action into the broad categories of adjudication and rulemaking, and creates different procedural models within each category. Thus, to find out what procedures the APA requires an agency to use in promulgating a particular rule or standard, one must first make sure that the decision in question is a rule, and then determine what type of rule it is.

1. *Rules Defined.* According to the APA, a rule is "the whole or a part of an agency statement of general or particular applicability and future effect designed to implement, interpret, or prescribe law or policy" or to establish rules of practice. 5 U.S. C.A. § 551(4). Any other agency action is an adjudicative "order." Id. § 551(6). These definitions, however, are often taken less seriously than one might expect, because they differ significantly from the usual understanding of the two terms.

The APA's reference to rules of "particular applicability," which seems contrary to the very idea of a rule, is something of an historical anomaly. It is designed to preserve the traditional understanding that ratemaking proceedings (that is, those concerned with the approval of "tariffs" or rate schedules filed by public utilities and common carriers) should be regarded as rulemaking proceedings rather than adjudications. In most instances, however, rules can be identified by the fact that they apply to a general *class* of persons or situations. Indeed, the premise that rules tend to be general in their applicability is at the heart of the policy justifications for the distinction between rulemaking and adjudication in administrative procedure. See pp. 212–15 supra.

Another source of difficulty is the language in § 551(4) indicating that rules must be of "future effect." Although the vast majority of administrative rules do concern future standards of conduct, agencies occasionally issue rules that are intended to operate retroactively. In Bowen v. Georgetown University Hospital, 488 U.S. 204 (1988), the Court held that a statute will not be construed to authorize an agency to issue retroactive legislative rules "unless that power is conveyed in express terms." This holding rests on the potential for unfairness that exists when officials impose liability for an act that was legal when it was done. The Court did not suggest, however, that when Congress *has* authorized retroactive regulations (see, e.g., 26 U.S. C.A. § 7805(b) (tax rulings)), the agency's pronouncement is not a "rule" for APA purposes. In any event, the "future effect" language is often unhelpful as a means of distinguishing rulemaking from adjudication, because many, if not most, adjudicative orders—ranging from bargaining orders to awards of broadcast licenses to grants of disability benefits—also operate in a basically prospective fashion. Moreover, agencies frequently use the process of adjudication to develop new legal standards. See SEC v. Chenery Corp., 332 U.S. 194 (1947), discussed at pp. 345–46 infra.

In practice, therefore, the primary factor distinguishing a rule from an adjudicative order is the "general applicability" of the former. This distinction corresponds to the usage that administrative lawyers commonly employ: An agency action that is addressed to *named parties* is an adjudication (except in ratemaking cases); an action that is addressed to a *category* of persons or situations is a rule.[1]

2. *Binding and nonbinding rules.* The most important and familiar type of rule is the *legislative* rule (sometimes called a substantive rule). It has several distinctive characteristics. It has "the force and effect of law" and is always "rooted in a grant of [quasi-legislative] power by the Congress." Chrysler Corp. v. Brown, 441 U.S. 281, 302 (1979). A valid legislative rule conclusively settles the matters it addresses, at least at the administrative level. Of course, to say that such a rule has "the force and effect of law" does not mean that it is immune from judicial review; courts can entertain challenges to the rule on various grounds. See pp. 109–17 supra. It does mean, however, that unless

1. However, when it is apparent that a rule will affect only a few identifiable persons, due process may require the agency to afford procedural safeguards resembling those available in adjudication. Vermont Yankee Nuclear Power Corp. v. NRDC, 435 U.S. 519, 542 (1978); see also Sangamon Valley Television Corp. v. United States, 269 F.2d 221 (D.C.Cir.1959), discussed at p. 337 infra.

the rule is overturned by a court (or rescinded by the agency), it is binding on both private parties and the government itself. This *binding effect* is the chief identifying feature of a legislative rule: its nature and purpose is to alter citizens' legal rights in a decisive fashion.

Of course, not all agency pronouncements that fit within the APA's broad definition of "rule" are legislative rules. The courts have explored the boundaries of the narrower term in the course of applying the APA's rulemaking provisions. The APA generally requires that the issuance of rules be preceded by a public procedure, usually a notice-and-comment process, but it exempts "interpretative rules, general statements of policy, [and] rules of agency organization, procedure, and practice" from this command. 5 U.S.C.A. § 553(b)(A). Congress excluded interpretive rules and policy statements from the APA's procedural obligations because they are *not* legislative rules. Thus, in order to determine whether a given rule was issued in compliance with the APA, courts must regularly distinguish legislative rules from those more informal pronouncements. This has never been an easy task. During the 1970's some courts maintained that an agency is obliged to allow notice and comment before issuing any rule that has a "substantial impact" on the public. See, e.g., Pharmaceutical Mfrs. Ass'n v. Finch, 307 F.Supp. 858, 863 (D.Del.1970). More recently, this test has fallen out of favor, because it is too much at odds with the language of the APA: virtually any significant rule can have a substantial effect on private rights. Energy Reserves Group, Inc. v. DOE, 589 F.2d 1082 (Temp.Emer.Ct.App.1978). Today's courts are more restrained, but the § 553(b)(A) exemptions still give rise to confusion and extensive litigation. Many cases do not carefully distinguish between the various APA exemptions; each, however, has a different focus and calls for a discrete analysis. See American Hospital Ass'n v. Bowen, 834 F.2d 1037 (D.C.Cir.1987).

An *interpretive rule* differs from a legislative rule in that it is not intended to alter legal rights, but to state the agency's view of what existing law already requires. Of course, the issuance of an interpretive rule has some impact on parties' rights, because courts construing administrative statutes generally give some weight to the agency's views. See pp. 83–92 supra. Nevertheless, on judicial review the agency will have to defend its legal position as persuasively as if it had not issued the rule; its power to make law through rulemaking will not strengthen its case. For example, in Morton v. Ruiz, 415 U.S. 199 (1974), the Court observed that the Bureau of Indian Affairs could potentially issue rules to modify Indians' rights to welfare payments in response to a shortage of funding. However, since the Bureau's guidelines contemplating such a reduction had not been accorded the procedural treatment required for a legislative rule (in this case, publication in the Federal Register), they had the status of a mere interpretive rule; the Bureau's attempt to deny payments to the plaintiff could only rest on the relatively weak argument that the underlying statute itself made the plaintiff ineligible for benefits.[2]

A *general statement of policy* states how the agency intends to use its lawmaking power in the future but does not attempt to bind anyone immediately. The APA exempts these pronouncements from public procedure because they do not, in themselves, alter anyone's legal rights. In a subsequent proceeding, however, the agency cannot cite the policy statement as settling any issues; opposing parties have a right to be heard as though the statement had never been issued. The court found this exemption applicable in Pacific Gas & Electric Co. v. FPC, 506 F.2d 33 (D.C.Cir.1974), in which the Commission had tentatively endorsed a particular set of priorities for allocating natural gas in the event of a shortage, but had indicated that in later proceedings it would give further consideration to its suggested approach, in light of any counterarguments presented by companies that favored alternative approaches. However, courts do not always take an agency's representations as to its intentions at face value. If the language of the statement, or the way in which the agency implements it, suggests that the agency will not give opposing

2. Of course, if the agency has no delegated lawmaking authority, its rules are necessarily interpretive. See General Electric Co. v. Gilbert, 429 U.S. 125, 141 (1976) (discussing EEOC guidelines).

parties a genuine opportunity to reopen the issues, the court may conclude that the agency is trying to give the statement the force of law, making notice and comment essential. American Bus Ass'n v. United States, 627 F.2d 525 (D.C.Cir.1980). For example, in Community Nutrition Inst. v. Young, 818 F.2d 943 (D.C.Cir.1987), the FDA issued "action levels" advising corn producers not to exceed certain maximum levels of contamination in their products. On the surface, these statements were mere nonbinding admonitions. In practice, the agency appeared to regard them as binding; it had even established a procedure for "exempting" producers from the prescribed levels in special circumstances. Accordingly, the court held that the action levels were not general statements of policy and could not stand in the absence of APA procedures.

Finally, § 553(b)(A) permits agencies to issue *procedural rules* without prior notice. This exemption reflects "the congressional judgment that such rules, because they do not directly guide public conduct, do not merit the administrative burdens of public input proceedings." United States Dept. of Labor v. Kast Metals Corp., 744 F.2d 1145 (5th Cir.1984). For example, an agency's decision about where it will concentrate its enforcement resources does not alter anyone's substantive rights and thus is within the exemption. Id.; *American Hospital Ass'n,* supra. Unlike the interpretive rule and policy statement exemptions, however, the procedural rules exemption does not rest on an implied contrast with legislative rules, for procedural rules are often "legislative" in character: if written in a way that draws upon the agency's delegated lawmaking power, they are binding on both citizens and the agency. See Schweiker v. Hansen, 450 U.S. 785 (1981) (private persons are bound); Service v. Dulles, 354 U.S. 363 (1957) (government is bound).

B. RULEMAKING PROCEDURES

Agency rulemaking proceedings can take on three different procedural forms under the APA: they may be formal, informal, or exempted completely from the Act's procedural requirements. In addition, the basic APA procedural models have sometimes been supplemented or modified by Congress in particular grants of rulemaking authority, and reviewing courts have, at least in the past, occasionally required agencies to use procedures other than those specified in the APA. Before discussing these latter "hybrid" rulemaking approaches, however, it is necessary to examine the three kinds of rulemaking proceedings contemplated by the APA.

1. THE APA PROCEDURAL MODELS

a. *Exempted Rulemaking.* The general rulemaking provision of the APA, § 553, contains several exemptions that authorize agencies to issue final rules without any public participation. The exemptions for interpretive rules, policy statements, and procedural rules have just been discussed. In addition, § 553(a) completely exempts from public notice and opportunity to comment all rulemaking proceedings relating to "a military or foreign affairs function" or "agency management or personnel or to public property, loans, grants, benefits, or contracts." Commentators have strongly criticized these sweeping exemptions, and the Administrative Conference of the United States has recommended that they be repealed. 1 C.F.R. §§ 305.73–5 (military or foreign affairs), 305.69–8 (proprietary matters). The exemption for proprietary matters, such as grants and benefits, seems particularly difficult to justify. When it was originally enacted, there was a general assumption that private parties had few procedural rights when the government action affected a "privilege" or a "mere gratuity" rather than private property. That distinction has now been rejected as unsound and unworkable in contemporary due process analysis; see pp. 195–98 supra. The government uses the spending power to pursue a wide variety of social objectives, and the effect of the § 553 exemption is to immunize many important policy decisions from public participation.

The final exemption to the APA's notice-and-comment procedures applies when "notice and public procedure . . . are impracticable, unnecessary, or contrary to the public interest." 5 U.S.C.A. § 553(b)(3)(B). In practice, this exception applies primarily when delay in the issuance of the rule would frustrate the rule's purpose, or when the subject matter is so routine or trivial that the value of public participation would be negligible. When an agency invokes this exemption, the APA also requires it to make a "good cause" finding and incorporate a brief statement of its reasons for avoiding public participation in the final rule. The finding is subject to judicial review, and usually encounters a skeptical reception in the courts. See, e.g., New Jersey v. United States EPA, 626 F.2d 1038, 1049–50 (D.C.Cir.1980) (EPA's approval of state plans for compliance with Clean Air Act required public comment, despite time pressure created by statutory deadline). See generally Jordan, *The Administrative Procedure Act's "Good Cause" Exception,* 36 Ad.L.Rev. 113 (1984).

While these exemptions from public participation are quite broad, an agency is generally free to give affected persons more opportunities to participate than the Act requires. Thus it can use notice-and-comment procedures, or confer informally with affected interest groups, or hold public hearings on important rules that are technically exempt from the APA. The Administrative Conference has recommended that agencies provide such opportunities for public participation when an interpretive rule or general policy statement "is likely to have a substantial impact on the public." 1 C.F.R. § 305.76–5; see also id. § 305.83–2 (agencies should provide an opportunity for post-promulgation comment when rules have been issued under the "good cause" exception).

b. *Informal Rulemaking.* The basic rulemaking procedure prescribed by § 553 of the APA is generally called "informal" or "notice-and-comment" rulemaking. In the absence of directives to the contrary in an agency's enabling legislation, the APA's informal rulemaking procedures will apply whenever the agency issues substantive rules. Thus, if the statute merely authorizes the agency to issue regulations and those regulations affect the legal rights of private parties, the agency will be required to follow the notice-and-comment procedure of § 553.

The APA's informal rulemaking process is simple and flexible, consisting of only three procedural requirements. First, the agency must give prior *notice,* which is usually accomplished by publication of an item in the Federal Register. The notice must contain "either the terms or substance of the proposed rule or a description of the subjects and issues involved," as well as a reference to the legal authority for issuing the rule and information about the opportunities for public participation. 5 U.S.C.A. § 553(b). After publication of the notice of rulemaking, the agency must "give interested persons an opportunity to participate" through *submission of written comments* containing data, views, or arguments. 5 U.S.C.A. § 553(c). The agency is not required to hold any oral hearings under this section; it has discretion to decide whether interested persons will be allowed to submit testimony or to present oral argument to the decisionmakers. Finally, after the agency has considered the public comments, it must issue with its final rules "a concise general *statement of . . . basis and purpose.*" Id. Reviewing courts expect the agency to spell out in detail its reasons for issuing a rule; thus, statements of basis and purpose have become increasingly lengthy in recent years. See Automotive Parts & Accessories Ass'n v. Boyd, 407 F.2d 330, 338 (D.C.Cir.1968) (function of statement of basis and purpose in informal rulemaking is to enable the reviewing court "to see what major issues of policy were ventilated by the informal proceedings and why the agency reacted to them as it did").

The simple procedures of notice-and-comment rulemaking provide an efficient means by which administrators can acquire information and reach a prompt decision. From the point of view of a party who opposes a particular rule, however, the procedures may seem much less fair than trial-type hearings, where parties enjoy extensive rights to know and challenge opposing evidence. The APA informal rulemaking provisions do not expressly require the agency to expose its factual, legal, and policy support to public criticism. Unless a challenging party is able to obtain internal agency documents under the Freedom of Information Act, see pp. 148–57 supra, she may not be able to discover the agency's supporting evidence and analysis until the rule has been issued and an action has been brought in court to challenge its validity. Consequently, informal rulemaking may produce inaccurate or misguided decisions if the agency is not sufficiently rigorous or self-disciplined in gathering and analyzing information. For these reasons, regulated industries and other constituency groups have often sought additional procedural safeguards in administrative rulemaking. One strategy they have used is to attempt to invoke the APA's formal rulemaking procedures.

c. *Formal Rulemaking.* Section 553(c) of the APA contains an exception to the general principle that administrative rulemaking requires, at most, a notice-and-comment process. It states that "[w]hen rules are required by statute to be made on the record after opportunity for an agency hearing," the agency must follow sections 556 and 557 of the APA—that is, it must afford most of the procedures required in formal adjudication. Thus, when some other statute (usually the one that delegates rulemaking authority) directs the agency to do so, it must conduct a trial-type hearing and provide interested persons with an opportunity to testify and cross-examine adverse witnesses before issuing a rule. This process is generally called "rulemaking on a record" or "formal rulemaking."

Since legislative drafters are often not attuned to the nuances of the APA, the relevant statutes may be ambiguous with respect to whether Congress intended the agency to use formal or informal rulemaking. This was the situation that the Supreme Court encountered in United States v. Florida East Coast Ry., 410 U.S. 224 (1973). The statute merely provided that the Interstate Commerce Commission "may, after hearing" issue rules establishing incentive per diem charges for the use of freight cars. The protesting railroad argued that this language required the ICC to follow the APA's formal rulemaking procedures, and the legislative history did tend to support this conclusion. The Supreme Court upheld the ICC: although a statute did not have to track verbatim the APA phrase "on the record after opportunity for an agency hearing" in order to trigger the formal rulemaking requirements, a clear expression of congressional intent was necessary. In effect, the *Florida East Coast* decision created a strong presumption in favor of informal rulemaking.

Although the point was not openly discussed in the opinion, the *Florida East Coast* decision may be based upon a belief that trial-type hearings are generally not desirable in rulemaking. Commentators have criticized formal rulemaking as a costly, cumbersome process that contributes little to the quality of decision. The experience of the FDA, which is required to use formal rulemaking in some of its regulatory programs, is often cited as illustrative. In the notorious Peanut Butter rulemaking, for example, the parties consumed weeks of hearing time and hundreds of pages of transcript so that experts could be cross-examined on such issues as whether peanut butter should contain 87 or 90 percent peanuts. See generally Hamilton, *Rulemaking on a Record by the Food and Drug Administration,* 50 Tex.L.Rev. 1132 (1972). Another FDA formal rulemaking dealing with vitamin supplements was an even longer exercise in futility. After it had held 18 months of hearings, the agency lost on appeal because it had unduly restricted cross-examination of a government expert. National Nutritional Foods Ass'n v. FDA, 504 F.2d 761, 792–99 (2d Cir.1974), cert. denied, 420 U.S. 946 (1975). In other agencies, the costs and delays associated with formal rulemaking have led to the virtual abandonment of regulatory programs. Hamilton, *Procedures for the Adoption of Rules of General Applicability: The Need for Procedural Innovation in Administrative Rulemaking,* 60 Cal.L. Rev. 1276, 1283–1313 (1972). Against the background of this experience, the Supreme Court's reluctance to conclude that an ambiguous statute required formal rulemaking is understandable.

Even when the statute does plainly require formal rulemaking, the APA permits some departures from the procedures used in formal adjudications (described at pp. 242–95 supra). Section 556(d) allows the agency to substitute written submissions for oral direct testimony in rulemaking. However, the proviso in the same section that a party is entitled "to conduct such cross-examination as may be required for a full and true disclosure of the facts" still applies, so the agency must make avail-

able for cross-examination the persons who supplied the information contained in the written submissions.   This obligation sometimes proves
onerous. In Wirtz v. Baldor Elec. Co., 337 F.2d 518
(D.C.Cir.1963), the Labor Department had conducted a survey of manufacturers to determine the
prevailing wages in the electrical equipment industry. When the agency used statistics derived from
this survey in a formal rulemaking to set minimum wages for government contractors in the industry, it made available for cross-examination the
statistician who had tabulated the figures from the
questionnaires. However, the Department refused
to disclose individual companies' responses, because it had given them assurances that their
replies would be kept confidential. The reviewing
court concluded that the industry representatives
opposing the rule needed access to the raw data in
order to cross-examine effectively, and since the
agency was unwilling to retract its promises of
confidentiality, the rule had to be set aside. This
data disclosure requirement implies that an agency
that wishes to rely on surveys or other technical
reports in a formal proceeding may incur considerable delay and expense: in addition to the time
spent in hearings, the agency may have to resort to
compulsory process if the persons or companies
supplying the data are not willing to have it disclosed to the public. If any of the subpoenaed
parties resists, as is likely to happen when sensitive commercial information is involved, there may
be lengthy litigation over the legality of the agen-

cy's demand before the data can be collected. See generally pp. 124–36 supra. Perhaps the real lesson is that a "legislative fact" issue of this kind should not be litigated in a formal proceeding in the first place.

Another way in which formal rulemaking differs from formal adjudication is that the process of decision followed within the agency is somewhat less confined. Under § 557(b) of the APA, the agency may omit the presiding officer's initial or recommended decision, and instead issue a tentative agency decision for public comment. In addition, the strict separation of functions requirements of § 554(d) do not apply; decisionmakers in a formal rulemaking are free to consult with staff experts throughout the agency, including those who were responsible for presenting the agency's position at the hearing. Unlike adjudications, rulemaking proceedings are generally not accusatory; consequently, there is less need to isolate the decisionmakers from a potentially adversary staff in order to assure fairness to the accused. However, the § 557(d) ban on ex parte contacts with outside parties does apply to formal rulemaking proceedings.

2. JUDICIALLY IMPOSED PARTICIPATION RIGHTS

In the late 1960's, as rulemaking became an increasingly important form of administrative decisionmaking, dissatisfaction with the rulemaking procedures provided by the APA began to spread. Informal rulemaking was simple and efficient, but it gave interested persons few rights to know and contest the basis of a proposed rule. Formal rulemaking, on the other hand, provided abundant opportunities to participate and to challenge the agency's proposal, but at the cost of near paralysis. As these shortcomings became more apparent, courts, commentators, and legislators attempted to develop intermediate procedural models that would permit effective public participation in rulemaking while avoiding the excesses of trial procedure. These compromise procedures were generally described as "hybrid rulemaking."

Reviewing courts were among the most active proponents of hybrid rulemaking procedures. Although constitutionally based notions of fundamental fairness seemed to underlie this development, the courts generally did not rest their holdings squarely on the Constitution, doubtless because of the traditional understanding that the due process clause has little application in rulemaking cases. See pp. 212–15 supra. Nevertheless, they readily found a variety of other legal bases for imposing hybrid rulemaking procedures. Inartful or ambiguous legislative drafting sometimes provided an opportunity for creative judicial interpretation. For example, in Mobil Oil Corp. v. FPC, 483 F.2d 1238 (D.C.Cir.1973), the court held that the FPC had to employ hybrid procedures, including evidentiary hearings on some contested issues, in setting rates to be charged by pipelines transporting certain kinds of hydrocarbon products. The holding was based on a statute providing that courts should review these rules using the substantial evidence test (a standard of review normally associated with formal proceedings).

In other instances, the courts reinterpreted the APA provisions governing informal rulemaking to enhance the opportunities for meaningful public participation. This approach is illustrated by United States v. Nova Scotia Food Products Corp., 568 F.2d 240 (2d Cir.1977), where the court found an APA violation in the FDA's failure to make a key scientific study available to potential commenters. "To suppress meaningful comment by failure to disclose the basic data relied upon," the court reasoned, "is akin to rejecting comment altogether." Finally, some of the hybrid rulemaking opinions had little direct basis in the texts of statutes or constitutional provisions. In essence, the courts created a judicial common law of rulemaking procedure. See generally Davis, *Administrative Common Law and the Vermont Yankee Opinion*, 1980 Utah L.Rev. 3.

Whatever their legal bases, the hybrid rulemaking requirements generally fell into two broad categories. First, as in *Nova Scotia*, the courts pressed agencies to disclose the data on which a proposed rule rested, so that opposing parties could offer responses. As a well-known case remarked, "It is not consonant with the purpose of a rule-making proceeding to promulgate rules on the basis of inadequate data, or on data that, [to a] critical degree, is known only to the agency." Portland Cement Ass'n v. Ruckelshaus, 486 F.2d 375, 393–94 (D.C.Cir.1973), cert. denied, 417 U.S. 921 (1974). Second, as in *Mobil Oil*, reviewing courts sometimes remanded rules with instructions that the agency allow cross-examination on particular issues, even though the proceeding was generally governed by the APA's informal rulemaking provisions. It was in a case of the latter variety that the Supreme Court ultimately intervened, writing an unusually strong opinion that effectively halted the judicial development of hybrid rulemaking procedures.

Vermont Yankee Nuclear Power Corp. v. Natural Resources Defense Council, Inc., 435 U.S. 519 (1978), arose out of a rulemaking proceeding in which the Atomic Energy Commission (the predecessor of the Nuclear Regulatory Commission) sought to determine the weight that it should assign to the environmental effects of radioactive waste when it conducted individual licensing proceedings for nuclear power plants. The agency was authorized to use informal rulemaking in issuing this kind of rule, but it had voluntarily held an oral hearing at which witnesses were questioned by agency representatives. On judicial review, the District of Columbia Circuit held that the agency had not permitted sufficient exploration of key testimony concerning its plans for disposal of nu-

clear waste: on remand, environmentalist intervenors would be entitled to fuller procedural opportunities, such as discovery or cross-examination.

The Supreme Court unanimously reversed, de-
nouncing the D.C. Circuit's opinion as "Monday
morning quarterbacking." The Court said that,
except in "extremely rare" circumstances, courts
may not force agencies to utilize rulemaking procedures beyond those prescribed in the APA or other
statutory or constitutional provisions. In the
Court's view, the APA enacted " 'a formula upon
which opposing social and political forces have
come to rest' " (quoting Wong Yang Sung v. Mc-
Grath, 339 U.S. 33, 40 (1950)), and it is not the
province of the judiciary to alter that legislative
judgment. The Court also rejected the argument
that additional procedures such as cross-examination would provide a more adequate record for
agency decision and judicial review. On the other
hand, the Court was convinced that judicially imposed hybrid rulemaking requirements would impose real costs. If the courts were free to devise
procedural requirements on an ad hoc basis, "judicial review would be totally unpredictable"; the
agencies, seeking to avoid reversals, would inevitably gravitate towards using highly adversarial procedures in every case.

In general, courts have faithfully adhered to
Vermont Yankee's admonition against imposing
rulemaking procedures beyond those mandated by
statute. This does not mean, however, that judi-

cial supervision of the rulemaking process has become insignificant. In the first place, courts can still enforce the APA's requirements, and they often do so aggressively. Not infrequently, for example, an agency is held to have violated its notice obligations under 5 U.S.C.A. § 553(b) because it promulgated a final rule that is not a "logical outgrowth" of the proposed rule on which it solicited comments. See, e.g., Chocolate Manufacturers Ass'n v. Block, 755 F.2d 1098 (4th Cir. 1985). Indeed, courts have had little difficulty adhering to the *Nova Scotia* principle that basic factual assumptions underlying a proposed rule must be made available for comment by interested parties; this principle is now regarded as implied by § 553(b). See, e.g., Connecticut Light & Power Co. v. NRC, 673 F.2d 525, 530–31 (D.C.Cir.), cert. denied, 459 U.S. 835 (1982).

Moreover, *Vermont Yankee* has not been read as detracting from the courts' ability to engage in rigorous review of the *substance* of agency rulemaking activities.[3] Modern "hard look" review, as exemplified by decisions like *State Farm,* demands that an agency build a record in support of a rule and respond to significant comments

---

3. On remand in the *Vermont Yankee* case itself, the D.C. Circuit set aside the AEC rule on the merits as an abuse of discretion. The Supreme Court again reversed, but did so in a narrowly written opinion that displayed no overall displeasure with the D.C. Circuit's policy of subjecting administrative rules to a "hard look." Baltimore Gas & Electric Co. v. NRDC, 462 U.S. 87 (1983).

made by participants in the rulemaking proceeding. See pp. 109–13 supra. Indeed, the *Vermont Yankee* opinion expressly reaffirmed the principle that the rationality of an agency rule must be judged on the basis of the record that was before the agency when it issued the rule. In a sense, this principle contradicts the Court's emphasis on deference to Congress, because the notion of a rulemaking record is itself a judicial creation that was never envisioned by the framers of the APA. See pp. 105–09 supra. Be that as it may, the Court's stance is understandable in pragmatic terms: the agency has a duty to build a record that demonstrates that it has exercised its discretion seriously and responsibly, but it has wide latitude to determine the best way to assemble that record.

Some agencies, however, still follow hybrid rulemaking procedures because of legislative mandates that obligate them to do so. In several regulatory statutes adopted in the 1970's, Congress showed considerable willingness to experiment with variations on the APA rulemaking models, often borrowing devices that had first been developed in the hybrid rulemaking cases. See, e.g., 42 U.S.C.A. § 7607(d) (EPA rulemaking under Clean Air Act); 15 U.S.C.A. § 57a (FTC consumer protection rulemaking). In the 1980's this legislative trend has largely faded away: Congress, too, seems to have recognized the large differences between writing a rule and trying a case. Indeed, experience with the legislatively imposed hybrid procedures has not been encouraging. The Administrative Conference of the U.S. concluded that its detailed study of hybrid rulemaking procedures used by the FTC provided "compelling evidence" that trial-type hearing procedure "is not an effective means of controlling an agency's discretion in its exercise of a broad delegation of legislative power which has not acquired, in law, specific meaning." Recommendation No. 80–1, 1980 A.C. U.S. 3. Nevertheless, Congress has not repealed many of the 1970's mandates; they remain on the books, as a continuing legacy of the hybrid rulemaking era.

3.   EX PARTE CONTACTS AND PREJUDGMENT

The rise and fall of faith in procedural formality, which was so prominent in the debate over participation rights, has been replicated in other controversies concerning the rulemaking process. For example, § 553 of the APA says nothing about the problems of ex parte contacts and administrative bias. As rulemaking grew in importance during the 1970's, however, it was often argued that courts should devise safeguards in those areas, borrowing from the principles enforced in formal adjudications. See generally pp. 278–94 supra. The debate was a vigorous one, for important procedural values were at stake on both sides of the issues. See generally Gellhorn & Robinson, *Rulemaking Due Process: An Inconclusive Dia-*

logue, 48 U.Chi.L.Rev. 201 (1981). Ultimately, however, the balance seems to have been struck decisively on the side of administrative flexibility in the rulemaking setting.

Even before the era of the hybrid rulemaking decisions, there had been one occasion on which a court overturned a rule issued in notice-and-comment proceedings because the decisionmakers had engaged in off-the-record discussions with an interested party. In Sangamon Valley Television Corp. v. United States, 269 F.2d 221 (D.C.Cir.1959), the court set aside a rule reallocating a television channel from one city to another, because a corporate official of an interested license applicant had met informally with the FCC commissioners to discuss the merits of the proceeding. The court noted that the proceeding involved "conflicting private claims to a valuable privilege": although the rule on its face made only a general determination as to the number of stations that would be available in the two cities, in effect it determined which of several competing applicants would get a license. In this respect, the proceeding was functionally similar to a comparative licensing adjudication. Because of this unusual circumstance, *Sangamon* was viewed for many years as having no application to most rulemaking proceedings.

The situation was less closely analogous to adjudication when the D.C. Circuit set aside another FCC rule on ex parte contact grounds in Home Box Office, Inc. v. FCC, 567 F.2d 9 (D.C.Cir.1977), cert.

denied, 434 U.S. 829 (1978). In the course of developing a rule regulating pay cable television, the commissioners had held a number of private meetings with interested participants. The court felt that it would be "intolerable" if there were one rulemaking record for insiders, and another for the general public. In addition to this concern for the fairness of the process, the court reasoned that nonrecord communications would undermine the effectiveness of judicial review, because the reviewing judges would not have access through the rulemaking record to all of the material considered by the agency.

By the time it decided Sierra Club v. Costle, 657 F.2d 298 (1981), the D.C. Circuit seemed to have come full circle from *HBO* to the belief that ex parte contacts during informal rulemaking are not only permissible, but affirmatively desirable. In rejecting environmentalists' claims that EPA rules governing air pollution from coal-fired power plants should be set aside because of ex parte contacts with industry representatives and others, the court noted: "Under our system of government, the very legitimacy of general policymaking performed by unelected administrators depends in no small part upon the openness, accessibility, and amenability of these officials to the needs and ideas of the public from whom their ultimate authority derives, and upon whom their commands must fall." The court discounted the risk that the agency might be influenced by undisclosed information, because the underlying statute required EPA to justify its rule on the basis of a publicly available administrative record. (The court's reasoning seems equally applicable to other rulemaking situations, because it is now standard practice for courts to review a rule on the basis of the administrative record. See pp. 105–09 supra.) However, the statute did require the agency to put any written communication having "central relevance" to the rule on the public record so that other participants would have an opportunity to respond, and the court reasoned that *oral* communications of equal relevance should be treated in the same way.

The courts have been equally lenient, if not more so, in permitting agency heads to consult freely with their own staffs. In United Steelworkers of America v. Marshall, 647 F.2d 1189 (D.C.Cir.1980), the challenged contacts were between the Occupational Safety and Health Administration and some consultants hired by the agency to analyze the record of a rulemaking proceeding establishing permissible levels of worker exposure to airborne lead. The court recognized that "nothing in the Administrative Procedure Act bars a staff advocate from advising the decisionmaker in setting a final rule," and that *Vermont Yankee* militated against any judicial effort to impose additional procedural requirements in rulemaking. The court then held that, although the consultants had earlier appeared as witnesses in the proceeding, they were "the functional equivalent of agency staff." Inasmuch as there was no strong evidence that the agency had relied on otherwise undisclosed facts or legal arguments supplied by the consultants, their work in summarizing and analyzing the record had been a legitimate part of the agency's deliberative process.

Reluctance to force rulemaking into the mold of adjudicative procedure is also evident in the law's response to the issue of prejudgment in rulemaking. In Ass'n of Nat'l Advertisers, Inc. v. FTC, 627 F.2d 1151 (D.C.Cir.1979), cert. denied, 447 U.S. 921 (1980), the court concluded that the FTC chairman should not be disqualified from participating in a rulemaking proceeding to ban advertisements directed at young children, even though he had made statements and written letters indicating that he strongly favored some regulatory action against the advertisers. The court reasoned that administrators should be encouraged to speak their minds on the issues involved in pending rulemaking proceedings, so that they can engage in direct, candid dialogue with affected interest groups, and thereby assess the political acceptability of different policy choices. In rulemaking, therefore, the test for disqualification should not be whether the decisionmaker appears to have prejudged any fact issue (the test applied in adjudicative proceedings), but whether "clear and convincing evidence" shows that he has an "unalterably closed mind" on the pending matters.[4] One might suspect that the court's test will, as a practical matter, virtually immunize agency officials from the threat of being removed from a rulemaking proceeding for bias, even if they are highly partisan advocates for their cause. The case dramatically illustrates the extent to which courts now view rulemaking as a political process, in which value judgments and unprovable assumptions are more important than the kind of facts that can be found by a neutral, detached adjudicator.

C. EXECUTIVE OVERSIGHT

While courts have been scaling back their attempts to supervise the rulemaking process in the years since *Vermont Yankee,* managerial activity within the executive branch has increased. At present the oversight function is exercised primarily by the Office of Management and Budget, which engages in systematic scrutiny of proposed "major rules" to determine whether they are cost-justified and consistent with administration policy. See pp. 62–66 supra.

To some observers, the extensive involvement of White House officials in rulemaking proceedings implicates the dangers of ex parte contacts in a

4. A further complication in the *National Advertisers* case was that Congress had directed the FTC to exercise its rulemaking authority through relatively formal procedures, resembling those used in adjudication; nevertheless, the proceeding clearly was designed to produce a rule, not an order, and thus the disqualification test for rulemakers was applicable.

particularly glaring fashion: private meetings between OMB and officials at rulemaking agencies have been thought to subvert the essential procedural regularity and openness of the rulemaking process. However, in Sierra Club v. Costle, 657 F.2d 298 (D.C.Cir.1981) (discussed at pp. 338–39 supra), the court defended White House participation in rulemaking proceedings: "Our form of government simply could not function effectively or rationally if key executive policymakers were isolated from each other and from the Chief Executive. Single-mission agencies do not always have the answers to complex regulatory problems." The court thus declined to invalidate a rulemaking proceeding during which EPA officials had met with President Carter and his economic advisors but had not disclosed this meeting in the administrative record.[5] Nevertheless, the court suggested that disclosure of presidential contacts might be essential if the discussion brought important new factual information to the agency's attention. Accordingly, OMB soon adopted a procedure for submitting such facts to the agency for inclusion in the administrative record.

The court's endorsement of executive supervision facilitated the growth of the Reagan oversight program. During the program's initial years, however, there were persistent reports that OMB was pressuring agencies to weaken regulations in ways

---

5. The court was also tolerant of pressures emanating from the legislative branch. See p. 49 supra.

that were antithetical to the spirit of the statutes they were administering. In 1986, under threat of congressional intervention, OMB adopted a set of procedural reforms, including a commitment that its formal written communications to agencies would be released to the public after a final rule was issued. Controls on "conduit communications" (in which OMB passes along to an agency the views of interested outside parties) were also tightened. These reforms served to improve the accountability of a reviewing office that, as a practical matter, usually operates independently of the President himself. Nevertheless, questions about the propriety of OMB's oversight activity have continued to arise. Indeed, the openly political nature of OMB's mission, and the high stakes involved in the proceedings in which it intervenes, virtually guarantee that its work will remain controversial for the indefinite future.

D. RULEMAKING BY NEGOTIATION

The image of rulemaking as a political process, which underlies decisions such as *Sierra Club* and *National Advertisers,* has given impetus to the belief that structured bargaining among competing interest groups might be a desirable means for developing certain rules. Thus, several agencies are exploring ways to introduce a variety of "alternative dispute resolution" techniques into the rulemaking process. The Administrative Conference has strongly supported these experiments in consensus-seeking, which are generally called "regulatory negotiation" or "reg-neg." See 1 C.F.R. § 305.82–4. In a typical regulatory negotiation, concerned interest groups and the agency itself send representatives to bargaining sessions led by a mediator. The resulting agreement is then forwarded to the agency, which publishes it as a proposed rule and follows through with the normal APA rulemaking process. However, the agency is not obligated to accept the participants' compromise in the final rule. See NRDC v. United States EPA, 859 F.2d 156, 194–95 (D.C.Cir.1988).

In theory, regulatory negotiation can provide a superior format for encouraging cooperation rather than confrontation. If all affected interests, including the agency, participate in hammering out a consensual solution, the result is likely to be more acceptable to the participants than any policy that the agency or an external reviewer might seek to impose. See Harter, *Negotiating Regulations: A Cure for Malaise,* 71 Geo.L.J. 1 (1982). Even the proponents of regulatory negotiation acknowledge, however, that in some situations the technique is not worth trying, such as where the number of interests needing representation is unmanageably high, or where agreement would be possible only if some participants compromised on a fundamental issue of principle.

Experience with regulatory negotiation has been fairly limited, and the results somewhat ambiguous. A built-in difficulty with the process is that the negotiating group's proposed rule may contain illogical compromises that were helpful in the search for consensus, but that the agency cannot easily justify as a rational exercise of its discretion under the governing statute. The long-run success of regulatory negotiation may depend in large part on whether the courts prove willing to uphold negotiated rules that might not withstand scrutiny under the usual hard look standards, but that are arguably legitimated by the process from which they emerged.

E. REQUIRED RULEMAKING

Agencies often choose to make policy in an individual adjudication rather than in a rulemaking proceeding, and for the most part the law respects this preference. The APA provides procedural models for both rulemaking and adjudication, but it does not direct an administrator to use one form of proceeding rather than the other. Nor do most substantive regulatory statutes limit an agency's choice of procedural vehicle; typically, they simply authorize the administrator both to issue rules and to adjudicate particular cases. As for judicial constraints, the general rule is well established: "the choice between proceeding by general rule or by individual, ad hoc litigation is one that lies primarily in the informed discretion of the administrative agency." SEC v. Chenery Corp., 332 U.S. 194, 203 (1947) (*Chenery II*).

As *Chenery* recognizes, agencies often have legitimate reasons to make policy through adjudication. The agency may feel a need to consider the policy first in a concrete fact situation, building rules only incrementally in the fashion of common law courts. It may sense that the issues are too complex, or not ripe enough, for across-the-board treatment. Alternatively, the agency may not even have thought that a new policy was needed until the final stages of an adjudication, when the cost and delay of starting a new proceeding would be considerable. Of course, the agency may also have less attractive motives for shunning rulemaking: for example, it may calculate that it can avoid public or congressional criticism if its new policies are buried in fact-specific adjudications instead of being clearly articulated by rule. Usually, however, courts do not attempt to question the agency's motives or to second-guess its judgment as to how to develop policy.

Nevertheless, the *Chenery* principle has long troubled scholars and judges who have believed that rulemaking has sizable advantages in terms of both efficiency and fairness, see pp. 309–10 supra, and that some agencies rely too heavily on case-by-case adjudication to formulate policy. This critique has occasionally prompted courts to attempt to force agencies to make wider use of rulemaking in policy development. To date, however, exceptions to *Chenery* are rare and ill-defined.

A number of cases raising this issue have involved the National Labor Relations Board, an agency that has been exceptionally reluctant to act through rules. In NLRB v. Wyman–Gordon Co., 394 U.S. 759 (1969), the Board ordered an election to enable the company's workers to select a collective bargaining representative. The Board also ordered the company to provide the union organizers with a list of the names and addresses of employees eligible to vote in the election. The latter directive was based on *Excelsior Underwear, Inc.,* 156 N.L.R.B. 1236 (1966), an earlier agency adjudication in which the Board had established the list requirement, but had made it applicable only in future cases. Wyman–Gordon claimed that the *Excelsior* requirement was equivalent to a "rule" and was invalid because it had not been adopted in accordance with the APA rulemaking procedures. In the Supreme Court, the plurality opinion (for four Justices) strongly criticized the NLRB's failure to use rulemaking procedure to establish the *Excelsior* list requirement. Nevertheless, the plurality upheld the Board's action, because the agency had ordered Wyman–Gordon to produce the list during a valid adjudicative proceeding. Although the Board was not entitled to treat the *Excelsior* decision as conclusively settling the propriety of the list requirement (as a rule would have done, see pp. 296–300 supra), it was free to rely on that decision as a precedent while litigating against subsequent employers. That is just what it had done. Thus, *Wyman–Gordon* apparently holds that an agency *may* develop new policies through adjudication, so long as each person to whom those policies are later applied has the right to an adjudicative hearing at which she may challenge them if she wishes to do so.

The issue of choice between adjudication and rulemaking returned to the Court in NLRB v. Bell Aerospace Co., 416 U.S. 267 (1974). The agency certified a bargaining unit of Bell's buyers, who under previous Board policy would have been regarded as "managerial employees" who could not be given such rights. As in *Wyman–Gordon,* the company argued that a significant policy change of this nature had to be made in rulemaking rather than in an individual adjudication. Once again, the Supreme Court disagreed, reaffirming *Chenery* and stating that the Board's preference for adjudication in this case deserved "great weight." (The Court did indicate that a "different result" might have been required if the company had relied to its detriment on prior Board policy. However, this "different result" would probably not have been a demand for rulemaking. Generally, when courts discern unfair retroactivity in an agency order, their response is simply to hold that any attempt to apply the new policy to the respondent would be void as an abuse of discretion. See p. 101 supra.)

Notwithstanding this line of cases, the Court has on one occasion required an agency to engage in rulemaking. In Morton v. Ruiz, 415 U.S. 199 (1974), the Court reversed a decision of the Bureau of Indian Affairs denying benefits to Native Americans under a federal assistance program. The BIA had developed an internal policy of denying assistance to claimants who lived outside of the reservations, but it had never communicated this policy to the public. The Court held that, while this policy might be a reasonable response to limitations in the program's funding, it could not be implemented through ad hoc decisions; the BIA had to issue valid legislative rules, which would be published in the Federal Register, before it could cut off the claimants' eligibility in this fashion. A relatively systematic approach to dispensing public assistance payments was needed "so as to assure that [the agency's policy] is being applied consistently and so as to avoid both the reality and the appearance of arbitrary denial of benefits to potential beneficiaries."

Many commentators consider *Ruiz* irreconcilable with the *Chenery* line of cases. One explanation for these contrasting holdings is that Ruiz was relying on an interest that was not implicated in the other cases: an interest in obtaining fair consideration of his application for benefits that Congress intended to confer on persons such as himself. This, however, is only a partial explanation. The Court did not explain why Ruiz's case differed from that of many other statutory beneficiaries who might feel that an agency has not sufficiently spelled out the criteria by which it will dispense benefits.

While *Ruiz* is a unique case at the Supreme Court level, it was not without antecedents in administrative law. A handful of cases, decided under the due process clause, have held that an agency must make selections among applicants for scarce governmental benefits on the basis of "ascertainable standards." See Holmes v. New York Housing Auth., 398 F.2d 262 (2d Cir.1968) (applications for public housing); Hornsby v. Allen, 326 F.2d 605 (5th Cir.1964) (applications for retail liquor licenses). Similarly, judicial refusals to strike down vague regulatory statutes under the delegation doctrine are sometimes predicated on an expectation that the administering agency will develop standards to particularize the statute. See pp. 26, 34 supra. To be sure, these cases can be read as permitting the agencies to develop the requisite "standards" in adjudicative proceedings, obviating the need for regulations as such. The Court in *Ruiz* may have reasoned, however, that in a large nationwide program like the BIA's, the only real protection for impecunious claimants like Ruiz lay in readily accessible rules that would ensure consistent behavior by the low-level bureaucrats who would effectively be the final decisionmakers in most instances.

An analogous situation in which courts have insisted on rulemaking arose out of a program that Congress created in 1978 for relief of farmers who were unable to make payments on loans issued by the Farmers Home Administration. The Secretary of Agriculture was authorized to defer foreclosure on the loans, but he consistently declined to grant any deferrals. Several courts of appeals, concluding that this refusal to implement the statute was an abuse of the Secretary's authority, directed him to devise standards that would promote the congressional objectives. A few of these decisions also held that, in light of the urgency of the farmers' plight, only the issuance of rules would provide the necessary assurance that the Secretary was implementing the program conscientiously. Curry v. Block, 738 F.2d 1556 (11th Cir.1984); Matzke v. Block, 732 F.2d 799 (10th Cir.1984). But cf. Allison v. Block, 723 F.2d 631 (8th Cir.1983) (Secretary must develop standards but may do so through adjudication if he prefers). These cases indicate that when an agency fails to implement a program in good faith, mandatory rulemaking is a remedy that the courts will at least consider.

In summary, agencies have almost complete freedom, in the absence of statutory restrictions, to choose between rules and orders as vehicles for policymaking. A few decisions have required rulemaking in order to ensure that applications for statutory benefits will be handled in a consistent and rational fashion. When regulated parties have raised the issue of mandatory rulemaking, however, the Supreme Court has been entirely unreceptive. (Regulated parties have prevailed in a few recent lower court cases, but these cases have not seriously attempted to distinguish *Bell Aero-*

space and probably cannot be reconciled with it. See, e.g., Ford Motor Co. v. FTC, 673 F.2d 1008 (9th Cir.1981), cert. denied, 459 U.S. 999 (1982).) Of course, despite the absence of judicial compulsion, most agencies have, as mentioned earlier, expanded their rulemaking activity tremendously during the past two decades. Increasingly, therefore, agencies like the NLRB, which confine themselves to adjudicating, are aberrations in the federal administrative system.

CHAPTER X

OBTAINING JUDICIAL REVIEW

A party seeking court reversal of an administrative decision may be met at the threshold with a series of technical defenses that could bar the court from reaching the merits of her claim. This complex and often overlapping set of doctrines is intended primarily to define the proper boundaries between courts and agencies—that is, to keep the courts from exceeding the limits of their institutional competence and intruding too deeply into the workings of the other branches of government. For example, administrators often make political or bargained decisions that do not readily lend themselves to judicial scrutiny. Parties sometimes seek judicial review of agency decisions in which they have no real stake. Or they seek review prematurely, creating a risk of early judicial intervention that could frustrate or delay the administrative process, and waste judicial resources. To deal with these kinds of problems, the courts have developed doctrines such as unreviewability, standing, and exhaustion of administrative remedies. Still, the trend of the past two decades has been towards breaking down these barriers and allowing liberal access to judicial review. The threshold defenses still have some bite, but review has become freely available to an extent that would have surprised lawyers of a generation ago.

A. JURISDICTION: ROUTES TO REVIEW

The preliminary task in any attempt to obtain judicial review of an agency action in the federal system is to determine the proper court in which to seek relief. The APA contains a general guideline: If Congress has created a "special statutory review proceeding relevant to the subject matter," the party is expected to file her petition in the court specified in the statute; if no statutory review proceeding is available or adequate, the party may utilize "any applicable form of legal action" in a "court of competent jurisdiction." 5 U.S.C.A. § 703. These forms of proceeding are respectively known as "statutory review" and "nonstatutory review." In a given situation, it may be difficult to know which court to select. If a party mistakenly files in a court that lacks jurisdiction, however, the petition need not be dismissed: that court can transfer the case directly to a court that does have jurisdiction. 28 U.S.C.A. § 1631.

1. *Statutory Review.* Since they are individually enacted as part of the legislation prescribing the powers of an agency, special statutory review proceedings can take a variety of forms. Most commonly, however, they follow the pattern set by the Federal Trade Commission Act in 1914: after the agency's decision becomes final, an interested per-

son may file a petition for review in a federal court of appeals. The court reviews the decision on the basis of the record compiled by the administrator, and if the agency action has violated the APA, some other statute, or the Constitution, the reviewing court may vacate the decision or remand it for further proceedings. Under some administrative statutes, such as the Social Security Act, review occurs initially in a federal district court. The modern trend, however, is to allow petitioners to proceed directly to a court of appeals. Since even informal actions are now generally reviewed on an administrative record, the factfinding capabilities of a trial court are not needed; thus, immediate review in the court of appeals promotes judicial economy and has few offsetting disadvantages. See Florida Power & Light Co. v. Lorion, 470 U.S. 729 (1985).

Sometimes two or more parties file for review of a single agency decision in different courts of appeals. Until recently, the first court to receive a petition would automatically acquire jurisdiction over the appeal. This rule occasionally induced rival challengers to engage in frantic "races to the courthouse," each hoping that the case would be heard by a court of appeals that it thought would favor its interests. Now, under a procedure enacted in 1988, a random selection method is used to determine which court will hear the case (subject to a change of venue motion). 28 U.S.C.A. § 2112(a).

2. *Nonstatutory Review.* When Congress has failed to create a special statutory procedure for judicial review, or when the procedure that does exist cannot furnish adequate relief, a party dissatisfied with an agency action must resort to "nonstatutory review." This term is actually a misnomer, because judicial review is always based upon some statutory grant of subject matter jurisdiction. Thus, a party who wishes to invoke nonstatutory review will look to the general grants of original jurisdiction that apply to the federal courts. It should be noted that the APA itself cannot supply the jurisdictional basis for nonstatutory review; the Supreme Court has held that the APA merely tells the reviewing court what to do after it has obtained jurisdiction under some other statute. Califano v. Sanders, 430 U.S. 99 (1977).

One available basis for jurisdiction is the Mandamus and Venue Act, 28 U.S.C.A. § 1361, which permits the federal district courts to hear suits "in the nature of mandamus to compel an officer or employee of the United States or any agency thereof to perform a duty owed to the plaintiff." The Act is a direct outgrowth of the old common law system of writs (such as mandamus, certiorari, and prohibition), which served as the foundation for judicial review of administrative action before the modern system of civil procedure was developed. However, § 1361 applies only when the agency decision is "ministerial" or nondiscretionary, and thus its utility is fairly limited. Plaintiffs usually prefer to proceed under statutory provisions that do not suffer from this defect, such as the general federal question jurisdiction statute, 28 U.S.C.A. § 1331, which authorizes the federal district courts to entertain any case "arising under" the Constitution or laws of the United States. An action for injunctive or declaratory relief under § 1331 is generally the simplest and most straightforward route to obtaining nonstatutory review of an agency action.

Two other varieties of nonstatutory review should also be mentioned. First, instead of challenging an agency rule directly in court, a regulated party can simply choose not to comply with it, and then attack the validity of the rule in an enforcement action if the agency brings one. This strategy may not work, however, if the statute limits judicial review of the rule to direct challenges. See pp. 361–62 infra. Second, the APA provides relief only to litigants whose goal is to compel, enjoin, or set aside agency action. Those who seek to recover damages for harm inflicted by an administrative agency or official must rely on a separate set of remedies. See pp. 391–99 infra.

B. UNREVIEWABLE ADMINISTRATIVE ACTIONS

In the contemporary administrative state, judicial review serves important social functions: it provides redress for persons who have been harmed by arbitrary or illegal government action, and it serves to keep the agencies faithful to the policy objectives and procedural safeguards established by the legislature. To promote these ends, the APA empowers the courts to review nearly all agency actions. At times, however, there are good reasons to exclude the courts from reviewing certain agency actions, or at least some of the findings underlying these actions. Two exceptions to the general availability of judicial review are codified in § 701 of the APA. Under this provision, judicial review is not available "to the extent that (1) statutes preclude judicial review; or (2) agency action is committed to agency discretion by law." 5 U.S.C.A. § 701. The first of these exceptions is primarily concerned with formal expressions of legislative intent, while the latter deals primarily with functional reasons why review would be difficult or harmful.

The words "to the extent" in § 701 are intended as a reminder that an action can be partially rather than totally unreviewable. In reaching any decision, an agency typically makes a series of determinations—some legal, some factual, and some discretionary. To say that an action is partially unreviewable is simply to say that the courts will examine some of these determinations and will not examine others. This qualification is important, because partial unreviewability is much more common than total unreviewability. Courts rarely pronounce an action "unreviewable" without adding that they would, nevertheless, entertain a challenge under limited circumstances—for example, if the action were alleged to be unconstitutional.

1. STATUTORY PRECLUSION OF REVIEW

Since Congress controls the jurisdiction of the federal courts, it is free to write into statutes particular exceptions to the general availability of judicial review—in other words, to "preclude" judicial review by statute. Courts are bound to follow these congressional directives so long as they are constitutional, but statutory preclusions run counter to a strong modern trend toward making judicial review freely available. In Abbott Laboratories v. Gardner, 387 U.S. 136 (1967), the Supreme Court formally acknowledged this presumption of reviewability. It held that judicial review of final agency action "will not be cut off unless there is persuasive reason to believe that [this] was the intention of Congress." Congressional intent to preclude review had to be demonstrated by "clear and convincing evidence."

The strength of the presumption of reviewability is reflected in the extraordinary feats of statutory construction that courts have performed in order to avoid concluding that particular statutes preclude judicial review. For example, in Johnson v. Robison, 415 U.S. 361 (1974), a statute provided that "the decisions of the Administrator on any question of law or fact under any law administered by the Veterans Administration providing benefits for veterans and their dependents or survivors shall be final and conclusive and no . . . court . . . shall have power or jurisdiction to review any such decision." Despite this extraordinarily clear expression of Congressional intent, the Supreme Court found a way to grant limited review. The claimant Robison was a conscientious objector who had performed alternative service, as required by the draft law. The VA concluded that he was ineligible for assistance under a statute that provided educational assistance to veterans who had "served on active duty." Robison asserted that this interpretation denied his constitutional rights to equal protection of the laws and free exercise of religion. The Court held that Robison escaped the statutory preclusion because he was not seeking review of an administrative decision *under* the statute, but rather was challenging the constitutionality of the statute itself.

The *Robison* opinion reflects a tendency of contemporary reviewing courts to seek a functional or institutional reason for prohibiting review, and to bar litigants only when there is a valid policy justification. The legislative history of the statutory preclusion for VA decisions suggested that it was designed to serve two policy goals: preventing burdens on the courts and the agency, and assuring national uniformity in the application of VA standards and policies. The Court reasoned that neither justification applied to constitutional claims like Robison's: the number of constitutional attacks was likely to be small, and the VA admittedly had no special competence in determining constitutional rights. Later, the Court extended *Robison* by permitting judicial review in situations in which a claimant contended that the VA had misinterpreted a statute other than its organic legislation. Traynor v. Turnage, 485 U.S. 535 (1988) (VA allegedly violated Rehabilitation Act by refusing to treat alcoholism as a disease). Finally, in 1988, Congress bowed to criticism of the broad VA preclusion statute, replacing it with a narrow one under which the VA's legal rulings (but not its factual or law-applying rulings) would be freely reviewable. 38 U.S.C.A. § 101.

A different, and perhaps more common, type of statutory preclusion is legislation that imposes a time limit on efforts to obtain review of an administrative decision. A provision of this kind was at issue in Adamo Wrecking Co. v. United States, 434 U.S. 275 (1978). The petitioner had been prosecuted for violating an air pollution emission standard for asbestos dust while demolishing a building, and in defense he attempted to raise a variety of objections to the validity of the rule. However, the relevant section of the Clean Air Act required that challenges must be brought within 30 days of the date when the rule was issued, and the petitioner had missed that deadline. The Court nevertheless granted limited review by directing the court hearing the enforcement action to determine whether the asbestos rule was the kind of emissions standard authorized by the Clean Air Act. On the other hand, that court would be precluded from deciding claims that the standard lacked factual support or was issued through defective procedures. The reasoning of the *Adamo Wrecking* opinion is narrow, but the case does illustrate the Court's reluctance to cut off all access to judicial review. It also reflects the Court's willingness to construe preclusion statutes creatively in order to strike a balance between the competing risks of unfairness to the complaining party and impairment of the regulatory program.

In a few recent cases, the Court has demonstrated that the presumption of reviewability can at times be overcome. In Block v. Community Nutrition Institute, 467 U.S. 340 (1984) (*CNI*), the Court stated that the *Abbott Laboratories* "clear and convincing evidence" standard should not be applied in a "strict evidentiary sense"; rather, congressional intent to preclude review need only be "fairly discernible" in the statutory scheme. Indeed, in *CNI* itself, the Court was willing to find such intent despite the absence of any explicit preclusive language in the statute in controversy. A group of consumers challenged a marketing order in which the Secretary of Agriculture had established minimum prices that dairy farmers could charge to "handlers" (processors) of their milk products. As the Court noted, Congress, in the underlying statute, had designed a complex framework by which handlers could participate in the adoption of milk marketing orders at the administrative level, but it had not provided for consumer participation in those proceedings. Therefore, the Court reasoned, Congress must have meant to exclude consumers from the entire regulatory process, including the use of judicial review. The *CNI* case shows the difficulty of making generalizations about statutory preclusion: ultimately, every case turns on an examination of the meaning of a particular statute. While the presumption of reviewability is certainly well entrenched, and reflects a dominant judicial attitude, one cannot expect it to control the outcome of every case.

2. COMMITTED TO AGENCY DISCRETION

While statutory preclusion is concerned primarily with the legislature's intent to bar review, the exception for actions "committed to agency discretion" is more directly concerned with functional reasons for limiting or denying review. Courts are designed to make and review reasoned decisions—those which result from finding facts, drawing inferences from them, and applying legal principles to them. Agencies perform similar functions in both adjudication and rulemaking, but they also make other kinds of decisions as well—including political judgments or bargained decisions that the courts may not be competent to review. In addition, some areas of administration have a compelling need for speed, flexibility, or secrecy in decisionmaking that is inconsistent with the open and deliberate processes of judicial review. When the court finds that there is some compelling practical justification for avoiding review, it may conclude that the action is wholly or partly committed to the agency's unreviewable discretion. Of course, the fact that an agency has been granted *some* discretion by statute is not enough to trigger this exemption from judicial review. The phrase "committed to agency discretion" is a technical term, and the circumstances in which it is found applicable are actually quite limited.

Administrative decisions affecting national defense and foreign policy are often held to be committed to agency discretion, because of the courts' lack of information about military and diplomatic affairs, the confidentiality of much of that information, and the desire to allow the United States to "speak with one voice" in its foreign relations. Thus, a decision by the Secretary of Defense to use foreign vessels to ship military supplies rather than reactivating the American "mothball fleet" has been held nonreviewable, Curran v. Laird, 420 F.2d 122 (D.C.Cir.1969) (en banc) (Leventhal, J.), and so has the President's decision to approve or modify the CAB's grants of air routes between the United States and foreign countries, Chicago & So. Air Lines v. Waterman S.S. Corp., 333 U.S. 103 (1948). Decisions have also been deemed "committed to agency discretion" where the administrator is acting in a managerial capacity—that is, exercising continuing supervision over an area of responsibility through a series of small decisions which may have to be based on intuition or hunch rather than findings of fact and deductions from legal principles. Examples of regulatory areas where this rationale has been applied to preclude judicial review include supervision of rents charged by private landlords in subsidized housing (Hahn v. Gottlieb, 430 F.2d 1243 (1st Cir.1970); cf. Langevin v. Chenango Court, Inc., 447 F.2d 296 (2d Cir. 1971)), and the decision by the administrator of a VA hospital to transfer a doctor who had "strained personal relationship" with his colleagues (Kletschka v. Driver, 411 F.2d 436 (2d Cir.1969)).

The Supreme Court has provided scant guidance as to when an agency action should be deemed "committed to agency discretion." In its most ambitious effort to clarify the doctrine, the Court stated that this exemption from judicial review comes into play when there is "no law to apply" to the agency's decision. Citizens to Preserve Overton Park, Inc. v. Volpe, 401 U.S. 402 (1971). This emphasis on whether the court has "law to apply" is fairly reliable as far as it goes: when a plaintiff tenders a credible argument that an agency has violated the Constitution, a statute, or a binding regulation, reviewing courts will virtually always listen. Nevertheless, the *Overton Park* test has been criticized for being potentially too restrictive. The absence of legal constraints on an administrative decision does not, in itself, demonstrate that judicial review is unworkable, for a court may still be able to investigate whether the agency's decision is inadequately reasoned, inconsistent with facts in the record, or in some other sense "arbitrary and capricious." Moreover, the assumptions behind *Overton Park* seem somewhat confused: even if it were true in a given case that a court could not possibly find any basis on which to reverse the agency, the notion of unreviewability would be superfluous, because the agency would be bound to win on the merits in any event. In short, the "law to apply" test places undue emphasis on whether a court *can* review a given decision; the focus ought to be on whether a court *should* review it. See Levin, *Understanding Unreviewability in Administrative Law*, 74 Minn.L.Rev. 689 (1990).

In fact, the Court has never used the "law to apply" test as the sole basis for holding any administrative action unreviewable. In Heckler v. Chaney, 470 U.S. 821 (1985), discussed at pp. 118–19 supra, the Court held that agency decisions not to initiate enforcement proceedings are "presumptively unreviewable," and that this presumption is rebutted if Congress has furnished "law to apply" in the form of guidelines limiting the agency's enforcement discretion. But the Court's holding also rested heavily on functional considerations, such as the abstract nature of the issues presented and the intrinsically managerial nature of an agency's decisions about how to allocate scarce human and budgetary resources. Similarly, when the

Court held that a dismissed CIA employee could not challenge his termination in federal court (except on constitutional grounds), it relied not only on the breadth of the underlying statute, but also on the practical point that "employment with the CIA entails a high degree of trust that is perhaps unmatched in government service." Webster v. Doe, 486 U.S. 592 (1988).

In summary, the determination that an administrative decision is committed to agency discretion seems to turn on a variety of factors, such as "the appropriateness of the issues raised for review by the courts; . . . the need for judicial supervision to safeguard the interests of the plaintiffs; and . . . the impact of review on the effectiveness of the agency in carrying out its assigned role." *Hahn v. Gottlieb*, supra. The relatively undeveloped nature of the law in this area is undoubtedly related to the courts' strong allegiance to the *Abbott Laboratories* presumption of reviewability. Mindful of the risks of unchecked administrative power, judges are usually not receptive to government counsel's pleas that particular agency decisions or findings should receive no judicial scrutiny whatever. Generally, therefore, courts rely on deferential scope-of-review principles, rather than applications of the doctrine of unreviewability, as the preferred tool for separating the administrative from the judicial spheres of responsibility.

C. STANDING

A person bringing a court challenge to an administrative decision must have standing to seek judicial review. The standing doctrine is a complex and frequently changing body of law, which has both a constitutional and a common law basis. The constitutional source of the standing doctrine is Article III, § 2 of the Constitution, which limits the federal judicial power to "cases" and "controversies." The American judicial process is an adversary system, which depends upon the litigants to gather and present the information needed for a sound decision. The "case or controversy" limitation, as embodied in the standing doctrine, seeks to assure sufficient opposition between the parties to make this system function properly. In addition, the law of standing is intended to help keep the judiciary within its proper orbit, so that the political branches of government will not be dominated by an "anti-majoritarian" judiciary.

The difficulty, however, is that these considerations of institutional competence and legitimacy conflict with other strongly held values. The individual plaintiff's demand for redress from illegal government action can exert a powerful countervailing claim on the court's sense of justice. Moreover, judicial review serves as a method of assuring that bureaucratic actions are consistent with the Constitution and with mandates established by elected political actors. In light of these conflicting policy pulls, it is perhaps not surprising that the law of standing has had an erratic pattern of development.

The early view was that a person seeking judicial scrutiny of agency action had to show that he had a legally protected interest—that is, one recognized by the Constitution, by statute or common law—that was adversely affected by the agency's decision. A personal or economic interest was not sufficient. E.g., Alabama Power Co. v. Ickes, 302 U.S. 464 (1938). The "legally protected interest" test suffered from a number of deficiencies that led to its eventual rejection. It tended to confuse standing issues with merits issues, because the court was required to consider the merits of the plaintiff's assertions of administrative illegality in order to determine whether he had a sufficient legal interest to confer standing. Moreover, it was excessively rigid because it depended more upon ancient common law concepts than upon policy considerations such as the need for a judicial check on a growing federal bureaucracy. These defects led to a crumbling of the doctrinal barriers in the 1940's.

The first major breakthrough occurred in FCC v. Sanders Bros. Radio Station, 309 U.S. 470 (1940). The Court there held that the statutory language granting judicial review to "persons aggrieved" by an FCC license decision was broad enough to include competitors of a successful applicant, even though the substantive provisions of the Communications Act were intended to protect the public interest, not the economic interests of competitors such as the petitioner. The test of an "aggrieved person," in other words, was not limited to the assertion of a personal legal wrong. The Court reasoned that Congress "may have been of the opinion that one likely to be financially injured by the issuance of a license would be the only person having a sufficient interest to bring to the attention of the appellate court errors of law in the action of the Commission." *Sanders* gave rise to a series of cases in which private parties were granted standing under various statutory review provisions, on the assumption that Congress had viewed them as "private Attorney Generals" to enforce statutory requirements. See, e.g., Associated Indus. of New York v. Ickes, 134 F.2d 694, 704 (2d Cir.), vacated as moot, 320 U.S. 707 (1943). Once a claimant established that he was within the statutory language, he was free to challenge the legality of the agency action on all available grounds, even though some of them might not be relevant to his personal interest.

The adoption of the APA in 1946, providing in § 702 that a person "adversely affected or aggrieved by agency action within the meaning of a relevant statute" could obtain judicial review, eventually contributed to the liberalizing trend. Litigants began to argue that the Act did not merely codify the existing "legal interest" theory but rather expanded the availability of standing by allowing judicial review whenever the complainant could prove that he was adversely affected in fact. This theory met with mixed results in the lower courts. When, two and a half decades later, the Supreme Court finally addressed the meaning of § 702, it did not fully endorse the theory just mentioned, but it did propound a relatively permissive analytical framework that is still in use today. In Association of Data Processing Service Organizations v. Camp, 397 U.S. 150 (1970), the Court reduced the law of standing to seek judicial review of administrative action to two questions: (1) has the complainant alleged "injury in fact"; and (2) is the interest sought to be protected by the complainant "arguably within the zone of interests to be protected or regulated by the statute or constitutional guarantee in question"? Applying this two-pronged test, the Court found that sellers of data processing services could sue to prevent the Comptroller of the Currency from authorizing banks to compete with them, because (a) the Comptroller's ruling would cause them economic harm, and (b) federal banking legislation suggested, at least "arguably," that Congress desired to protect companies from having to compete with banks for nonbanking business.

The "zone of interests" issue has proved to be the less controversial of the two prongs of the *Data Processing* test. On its face it is fairly lenient, because the "relevant statute" need only "arguably" protect the plaintiff's interest. The Court elaborated on the "zone" test in Clarke v. Securities Industry Ass'n, 479 U.S. 388 (1987). The facts closely resembled those of *Data Processing:* securities dealers challenged a ruling of the Comptroller allowing banks to offer discount brokerage services without conforming to federal restrictions on branch banking. The Court again found standing, noting that the zone of interests test is "not meant to be especially demanding" and prevents standing only when "the plaintiff's interests are so marginally related to or inconsistent with the purposes implicit in the statute that it cannot reasonably be assumed that Congress intended to permit the suit."

Unlike the "zone" issue, the injury in fact component of the *Data Processing* test has given rise to numerous bitter debates within the Supreme Court and lower courts. The importance of this issue became clearly evident when the Sierra Club brought suit to block the development of a ski resort in a wilderness area and the construction of a highway through federal lands. Sierra Club v. Morton, 405 U.S. 727 (1972). The Supreme Court conceded that threats to aesthetic, recreational, and environmental interests could constitute sufficient injury in fact to satisfy the standing requirement. See also Scenic Hudson Preservation Conference v. FPC, 354 F.2d 608, 616 (2d Cir.1965). Nevertheless, the Sierra Club's pleadings were inadequate, because it had failed to allege that any of its members actually used the wilderness area that would be affected by the resort development; instead, it had merely relied on its status as a responsible environmentalist organization. This was not enough for standing. To satisfy the APA, the Court said, an organization had to demonstrate that the government was causing specific injury to it or its members.[1] A "mere 'interest in a problem'" (even when possessed by so reputable and expert an entity as the Sierra Club) would not entitle it to bring suit. *Sierra Club* soon gave rise to other cases refusing standing to litigants who could allege only an "abstract injury." E.g., Schlesinger v. Reservists Committee to Stop the War, 418 U.S. 208 (1974) (plaintiff had no individualized stake in whether members of Congress retained membership in the Reserves).

The injury-in-fact test is especially difficult to apply when the threat of harm to the plaintiff's interests is only remotely or indirectly attributable to agency action. This problem is especially likely to emerge when the government program uses subsidies, tax credits, or other such incentives to

---

1. An association has standing to sue on behalf of its members when "(a) its members would otherwise have standing to sue in their own right; (b) the interests it seeks to protect are germane to the organization's purpose; and (c) neither the claim asserted nor the relief requested requires the participation of individual members in the lawsuit." Hunt v. Washington Apple Advertising Comm'n, 432 U.S. 333 (1977). In practice, the latter two criteria are easy to satisfy, and the issue in litigation is usually whether the first is met. See Humane Society v. Hodel, 840 F.2d 45 (D.C.Cir.1988) (lenient interpretation of "germaneness" test).

achieve a desired result, rather than providing for direct regulation or disbursements of benefits to claimants. At first, the Supreme Court seemed untroubled by causation issues of this kind. In United States v. Students Challenging Regulatory Agency Proceedings, 412 U.S. 669 (1973) (*SCRAP*), the plaintiffs were law students who wanted to contest the ICC's approval of a freight rate that they felt would discourage the use of recycled materials and thereby contribute to environmental pollution. To establish standing, they alleged that the rate increase would lead to increased litter and depletion of minerals and other natural resources in forests or parks where they engaged in recreational activities. The Court thought this an "attenuated line of causation," but it did not bar the students from maintaining their action. Instead, it noted that the plaintiffs must be prepared to prove the allegations of harm in their complaint, and it remanded to the district court for further proceedings.

The liberality of *SCRAP*, however, proved short-lived. Later decisions of the Supreme Court have insisted that plaintiffs demonstrate a "substantial likelihood" that the government is causing them harm and that a favorable decision would actually redress that harm. For example, Simon v. Eastern Kentucky Welfare Rights Organization, 426 U.S. 26 (1976), involved tax exemptions for private hospitals providing medical care to indigents. When the IRS issued a revenue ruling reducing the amount of indigent care a hospital must provide in order to qualify for the exemption, a welfare organization and several indigent individuals sought judicial review. Despite allegations that the individual plaintiffs had been denied treatment as a result of the IRS ruling, the Court ordered the case dismissed for lack of standing. In the Court's view, it was purely speculative whether the plaintiffs would have been given any service in the absence of the ruling; nor was it clear that a favorable decision on the merits would be likely to redress the claimed injury, for the hospitals might continue to withhold care for indigents even without the tax incentive. Similarly, in Allen v. Wright, 468 U.S. 737 (1984), parents of black children who attended public schools sued the IRS to force it to deny tax exempt status to racially discriminatory private schools. The parents (whose children had not applied for admission to the schools in question) claimed that the IRS's conduct caused these schools to flourish and thus impaired their children's right to attend an integrated school district. But the Court saw no reason to believe that elimination of the exemptions would make an appreciable difference in public school integration, and thus denied standing.

These new tests of causation and redressability have not always resulted in barring litigants from judicial review when they allege indirect harm. In Duke Power Co. v. Carolina Environmental Study Group, Inc., 438 U.S. 59 (1978), the plaintiffs sought to challenge the constitutionality of a statute that encouraged the development of nuclear power by limiting the liability of utilities for damages caused by a nuclear accident. They alleged that two nuclear power plants that were under construction near their residences would cause thermal pollution and health risks from radioactive discharges; in addition, they claimed that the plants would not be constructed and operated without the statute limiting liability. Thus, when the Nuclear Regulatory Commission executed an agreement entitling the power company to limit its liability in the event of an accident, the NRC was causing the plants to be built and therefore was causing the plaintiffs to suffer environmental injury. The Court concluded that the plaintiffs had standing,[2] although it then went on to uphold the statute on the merits. The Court's relative liberality may be explainable in part on the basis that in *Duke Power,* unlike the more restrictive prece-

2. The Court also said it was irrelevant that the injuries supporting standing (thermal pollution, etc.) had no relationship to the right that the plaintiffs hoped to vindicate (the constitutional right to full compensation in the event of an accident). Although a "subject-matter nexus" between these two variables has been required in the context of taxpayers' suits to prevent unlawful government expenditures, Flast v. Cohen, 392 U.S. 83 (1968), the Court said in *Duke Power* that the requirement is limited to that context. Indeed, the Court seems to regard *Flast* as a unique decision that should be confined to its facts. See Valley Forge Christian College v. Americans United for Separation of Church and State, Inc., 454 U.S. 464 (1982) (taxpayer standing recognized in *Flast* does not apply when government acts by giving away property rather than by spending money).

dents, the necessary causal relationship had been established through evidence in the district court. That court had specifically found that the plants would not have been built "but for" the liability limitation, and the Court did not consider this finding clearly erroneous. Many observers believe, however, that the real explanation for these contrasting results is that in *Duke Power,* unlike the other decisions, the Court was eager to reach the merits, so that it could remove doubts about the constitutionality of the challenged statute.

Whether or not the Court's holdings can be reconciled factually, one can seriously question whether the doctrine provides a coherent approach to defining the scope of judicial power. It does impose some limits on the power of courts to hear and decide claims of administrative illegality, but these limits appear to be few and often unrelated to the policies underlying the doctrine. The evolution of the injury-in-fact test to incorporate causation and redressability has injected complicated factual inquiries into the standing calculus, and resolution of these threshold factual issues can be costly to both courts and litigants. The time seems ripe for a thorough reexamination of the doctrinal and practical bases for standing to seek judicial review of administrative action. The proper solution may be to place less emphasis on injury-in-fact inquiries and more emphasis on whether Congress likely intended for persons in the plaintiff's situation to enforce the regulatory statute at issue. See Sunstein, *Standing and the Privatization of Public Law,* 88 Colum.L.Rev. 1432 (1988).

D. TIMING OF JUDICIAL REVIEW

Even though an agency's decision is reviewable and the plaintiff has standing to litigate, she may still be unable to get judicial review if she has brought the action at the wrong time. A party who comes into court prematurely is likely to be told that she has failed to exhaust her administrative remedies or that the matter is not yet ripe for judicial review. Exhaustion and ripeness are complementary doctrines that are designed to prevent unnecessary or untimely judicial interference in the administrative process. The two terms are sometimes used interchangeably (and the term "finality" is sometimes used in place of either of them). In general, however, a party's effort to derail an ongoing administrative proceeding at an early stage is analyzed as raising an issue of exhaustion. The notion of ripeness, on the other hand, usually implies that the agency's program is unfolding in a series of discrete actions; the plaintiff seeks review of one of these actions, and the question is whether she must wait until the agency has taken further action.

1. EXHAUSTION

If review is sought while an agency proceeding is still under way, a court will usually dismiss the action because of the plaintiff's failure to exhaust administrative remedies. In the leading case, a company was served with an NLRB complaint alleging that it had engaged in unfair labor practices. The company took the position that it was not operating in interstate commerce and hence that the NLRB had no jurisdiction. Despite the company's claim that it would suffer irreparable harm if it were forced to participate in an unnecessary evidentiary hearing, its effort to obtain immediate judicial review was turned aside. Myers v. Bethlehem Shipbuilding Corp., 303 U.S. 41 (1938). The principle of exhaustion, which resembles the general rule against interlocutory appeal in the federal courts, has several purposes. It is designed to prevent regulated parties from delaying or obstructing the agency's ability to conduct an orderly proceeding. It also gives the court the benefit of the agency's factfinding capacity and expertise in analyzing the factual assertions that may underlie the plaintiff's complaint. Moreover, if a party has to postpone seeking judicial relief until the end of the proceeding, judicial involvement may not prove necessary at all—the agency might correct any initial errors at subsequent stages of the process, or the party might prevail on other grounds. Consequently, the exhaustion rule conserves judicial resources and reduces friction between the branches of government.

Many statutory review provisions authorize a party to seek judicial review of any "final order" of an agency, and the APA states that "final agency action" is subject to judicial review.   5 U.S.C.A. § 704.   For this reason, some cases speak of exhaustion problems as posing a question of whether the agency has taken "final action."   See, e.g., FTC v. Standard Oil Co. of California, 449 U.S. 232 (1980) (review of whether issuance of FTC complaint was politically motivated must await final adjudicatory order).

Courts do not always strictly enforce the requirement that the plaintiff exhaust administrative remedies before seeking judicial review.   The courts' application of the doctrine is highly discretionary, but a few generalizations can be made. Immediate judicial review is sometimes permitted when a litigant establishes that the agency is clearly exceeding its jurisdiction.   Leedom v. Kyne, 358 U.S. 184 (1958).   Indeed, there is some justification for relaxing the exhaustion rule when the plaintiff's challenge is purely legal in nature, because the court may be able to resolve the dispute without any need for the agency's factfinding abilities. Since a desire for the agency's perspective is not the only justification for postponing review, however, exhaustion is usually required if the alleged statutory or constitutional violation is not obvious. See, e.g., Rosenthal & Co. v. Bagley, 581 F.2d 1258 (7th Cir.1978).   Another line of authority maintains that one is not required to exhaust administrative remedies that are "inadequate."   Coit Indep. Joint Venture v. FSLIC, 109 S.Ct. 1361 (1989) (creditors of failed bank could sue FSLIC as receiver in state court without first seeking administrative relief from the agency, because FSLIC had adverse interests and might delay resolution of the claim while the state's limitations statute ran out). On the whole, however, courts have striven to avoid recognizing exceptions to the exhaustion requirement that would swallow the rule. For example, the expense and disruption of defending oneself against administrative charges—a burden that every respondent could allege—is not a basis for interlocutory appeal. *Standard Oil,* supra.

One recurring problem concerning the finality requirement is whether a plaintiff can obtain immediate judicial review when an agency grants or withholds *interim* relief during the pendency of proceedings looking towards *permanent* relief. In Environmental Defense Fund, Inc. v. Hardin, 428 F.2d 1093 (D.C.Cir.1970), environmental groups petitioned the Secretary of Agriculture, who then had the responsibility for licensing pesticides, to initiate a formal hearing for the purpose of revoking the certification for the pesticide DDT; they also requested that the Secretary use his power to suspend the marketing of DDT immediately as an "imminent hazard." The Secretary began work on the formal cancellation process, but he did not act on the request for suspension. His inaction on the latter request was held to be a "final" order. The court ruled that in the circumstances the agency's failure to act was "the equivalent of an order denying relief," and that this denial was ready for immediate review. Further administrative proceedings on the cancellation request could not cure any error the agency might have made in failing to suspend; nor would the courts ever have any other opportunity to review the agency's conclusion that the public should not be protected from DDT in the short run (a prospect that the plaintiffs alleged might cause "irreparable injury on a massive scale"). By the same reasoning, it would seem that an agency's *grant* of preliminary relief should also be reviewable immediately, although the cases are divided. Compare Nor–Am Agricultural Products, Inc. v. Hardin, 435 F.2d 1151 (7th Cir.1970) (en banc), cert. dismissed, 402 U.S. 935 (1971) (fungicide producers were denied review of administrator's decision suspending registration, because the action was not final and merely started the cancellation process), with Environmental Defense Fund, Inc. v. Ruckelshaus, 439 F.2d 584 (D.C.Cir.1971) (dicta rejecting *Nor–Am* 's reasoning).

Courts use a variant of the exhaustion doctrine in deciding whether a party in civil or criminal proceedings should be barred from litigating an issue that could have been raised earlier in an administrative forum. In McKart v. United States, 395 U.S. 185 (1969), a draft registrant had failed to appeal his Selective Service reclassification from an exempt category to one that made him eligible for induction. He was prosecuted for draft evasion, and the government argued that the court should not entertain his claim to be exempt because he had failed to exhaust his remedies within the Selective Service System. The Supreme Court, however, was reluctant to penalize a failure to exhaust when criminal sanctions were at issue, because the consequences of doing so could be severe: "The defendant is often stripped of his only defense; he must go to jail without having any judicial review of an assertedly invalid order." Moreover, the issues involved were straightforward questions of law that did not require the exercise of administrative expertise. Weighing these considerations, and the likelihood that few registrants would try to bypass the administrative process since they would risk criminal penalties by doing so, the Court held that the exhaustion doctrine did not bar the defendant from asserting the invalidity of his classification as a defense to the criminal prosecution. However, the Court distinguished *McKart* in McGee v. United States, 402 U.S. 479 (1971), another case involving prosecution of a draft resister who had bypassed remedies available from Selective Service authorities. McGee claimed to be a conscientious objector, a defense that turned on factual rather than legal issues. The Court invoked the exhaustion doctrine and held that he had lost his defense, because "[w]hen a claim to exemption depends ultimately on the careful gathering and analysis of relevant facts, the interest in full airing of the facts within the administrative system is prominent."

2. RIPENESS

The concept of ripeness overlaps that of exhaustion to a considerable degree, but it has a different focus and a different basis. The exhaustion doctrine emphasizes the position of the party seeking review; in essence, it asks whether she may be attempting to short-circuit the administrative process or whether she has been reasonably diligent in protecting her own interests. Ripeness, by contrast, is concerned primarily with the institutional relationships between courts and agencies, and the competence of the courts to resolve disputes without further administrative refinement of the issues. At the extreme, the ripeness doctrine serves to implement the policy behind Article III of the Constitution. Since the judicial power is limited to cases and controversies, federal courts cannot decide purely abstract or theoretical claims, or render advisory opinions. Usually, however, the ripeness defense reflects prudential considerations. The implications of an agency's action often become clearer as it is implemented. Its scope may be ambiguous (perhaps because the agency intended to leave some points unsettled), and its consequences difficult to predict. Consequently, a court may feel that it could render a more reliable decision on the validity of the action if it were to await further developments. The ripeness doctrine attempts to give effect to this concern, but also to reconcile it with the need of private parties for guidance as to their rights.

The leading case of Abbott Laboratories v. Gardner, 387 U.S. 136 (1967), defined the primary factors that determine whether a claim is ripe for review: the court must "evaluate both the fitness of the issues for judicial decision and the hardship to the parties of withholding court consideration." For example, a ripeness defense was rejected in *Abbott Labs* itself. The question was whether the FDA had authority to issue a rule regulating the labeling that drug manufacturers placed on their products. The parties agreed that this question turned entirely on congressional intent. Therefore, further factual development by the agency was not needed, and the issue was appropriate for judicial resolution. Moreover, withholding review would have been burdensome for the companies, because they were threatened with fines, seizures, adverse publicity and other penalties if they did not immediately change their labeling.

In contrast, the rule at issue in a companion case, Toilet Goods Ass'n v. Gardner, 387 U.S. 158 (1967), was held unripe for review. It required companies using color additives in cosmetics to give FDA inspectors "free access" to their plants, on pain of losing their certification to market their products. In this instance the Court believed that further development of the facts in the context of a specific enforcement proceeding might aid judicial review. Matters such as "an understanding of what types of enforcement problems are encountered by the FDA, the need for various sorts of supervision in order to effectuate the goals of the Act, and the safeguards devised to protect legitimate trade secrets" could all be more fully explored on the basis of an evidentiary record. At the same time, withholding immediate review would not injure the companies, because the burden of complying with the regulation was minimal. One should note, however, that *Toilet Goods* predated the decision in *Overton Park,* which ushered in the concept of judicial review on the record of an informal rulemaking proceeding. See pp. 105–09 supra. Thus, it is possible that a contemporary agency promulgating a rule like the one at issue in *Toilet Goods* would compile a rulemaking record that would answer most of the questions that the court was asking, and therefore even that rule might be ripe for review. Indeed, now that agencies routinely build extensive records during rulemaking proceedings, judicial review of rules occurs far more frequently in direct or "preenforcement" challenges than during enforcement actions.

A crucial factor in assessing whether an issue is "fit" for judicial review, according to *Abbott Labs,* is whether the agency's view is "final" in the sense that the agency has reached a definitive, rather than tentative, conclusion on the issue. This inquiry can be difficult when the challenged agency action is not a formally announced regulation, as in *Abbott Labs* or *Toilet Goods,* but an informal pronouncement such as an advice letter. In National Automatic Laundry & Cleaning Council v.

Shultz, 443 F.2d 689 (D.C.Cir.1971), the court said that such a letter, if signed by the agency head, should be presumed to be final, although the agency head could overcome this presumption by filing an affidavit stating that the matter was still unresolved. Of course, there is less basis for deeming an advice letter final if it indicates tentativeness on its face, see New York Stock Exchange, Inc. v. Bloom, 562 F.2d 736 (D.C.Cir.1977), or if it comes from the staff of the agency rather than its head. See Kixmiller v. SEC, 492 F.2d 641 (D.C.Cir.1974), discussed pp. 188–90 supra. The overall thrust of this line of cases is that the government should have ample leeway to work out its positions on key regulatory issues; eventually, however, the agency will have to speak unequivocally if it wishes to influence private conduct, and at that point it will be accountable in court for the legality and rationality of what it says.

E. PRIMARY JURISDICTION

Unlike the preceding topics examined in this chapter, the doctrine of primary jurisdiction is *not* a defense to judicial review of agency action. Indeed, it comes into play only in cases that fall within the original jurisdiction of the courts. However, it is often discussed in conjunction with exhaustion and ripeness because, like those doctrines, it is a tool by which courts seek to avoid interfering with an agency's ability to carry out its statutory functions in a coherent way. Briefly, primary jurisdiction questions arise when a court hearing a civil or criminal case encounters an issue that also falls within the distinctive competence of an administrative agency. If the court chooses to invoke the doctrine, it will suspend consideration of the disputed issue and refer the matter to the agency for an initial determination. Thus, the primary jurisdiction doctrine is somewhat analogous to the federal courts' practice of abstaining from deciding an issue of state law so that state courts may address the issue.

There are two principal reasons for requiring a private litigant to resort to the administrative process before pursuing court litigation. First, a referral to the agency may preserve needed uniformity in a regulatory program. Thus, in Texas & Pac. R.R. v. Abilene Cotton Oil Co., 204 U.S. 426 (1907), a shipper sued the railroad in state court, alleging that the railroad's rates, which had been approved by the Interstate Commerce Commission, were unreasonably high. The Court held that this question was within the primary jurisdiction of the ICC, because a major objective of the Interstate Commerce Act had been to achieve national uniformity of rates, and this goal would be frustrated if numerous courts across the country could enforce ad hoc judgments as to whether individual rates were excessive. Second, the litigation may involve issues that go beyond the conventional experience of judges, and on which the expertise of the agency could be helpful. In United States v.

Western Pacific R.R., 352 U.S. 59 (1956), a railroad shipped napalm in steel casings for the Army, charging its established rate for "incendiary bombs." The Army claimed that the (lower) rate for "gasoline in steel drums" applied, and the railroad sued for payment in the Court of Claims. On appeal, the Supreme Court again referred the question to the ICC: since that agency had approved the tariffs in which the two rates appeared, it was in the best position to know whether the purposes underlying the high rate for "incendiary bombs" were implicated in this situation.

On the other hand, if an issue raised in the court action falls outside the ambit of the agency's special expertise or unique authority, the claim will not be barred by the primary jurisdiction doctrine. An airline that had the bad luck or bad judgment to "bump" Ralph Nader from a flight on which he held a confirmed reservation learned this lesson in Nader v. Allegheny Airlines, Inc., 426 U.S. 290 (1976). Nader brought a damage action for fraudulent misrepresentation, claiming that the airline had deceptively failed to disclose that it might "overbook" its flights and deny boarding to passengers with confirmed reservations. One of the airline's defenses was that the question fell within the primary jurisdiction of the Civil Aeronautics Board, because that agency had power to issue cease and desist orders against regulated carriers that had engaged in "unfair or deceptive practices." The Supreme Court disagreed. The CAB's statutory power to abate deceptive practices was not synonymous with common law fraud and misrepresentation, and the Board had no power to immunize carriers from this kind of liability. More significantly, the issue was not one on which a decision "could be facilitated by an informed evaluation of the economics or technology of the regulated industry"; rather, the common law fraud standards "are within the conventional competence of the courts, and the judgment of a technically expert body is not likely to be helpful in the application of these standards to the facts of this case."

As these cases suggest, the basic justification for the doctrine of primary jurisdiction is to coordinate the work of agencies and courts. Their activities are most likely to come into conflict where the agency's regulation is pervasive, and where uniform interpretations are necessary to assure effective regulation. Therefore, the doctrine is most likely to be applied in cases concerning the intensively regulated industries—where agencies control entry, price, and nature and quality of service—than in cases concerning industries that are subject to less extensive controls. In the end, however, invocation of the doctrine is highly discretionary and seems to depend on whether the court actually feels out of its depth as it confronts the issues raised by the parties.

In any event, the doctrine does not transfer *exclusive* jurisdiction from court to agency; it only allocates jurisdictional priority. Once the agency renders its decision, recourse to the courts—through the normal mechanisms for judicial review of agency action—is still available. In Far East Conference v. United States, 342 U.S. 570 (1952), an association of steamship companies gave preferential rates to shippers who dealt exclusively with association members. The Justice Department challenged this dual-rate scheme under the antitrust laws, but the Court held that the matter fell within the Federal Maritime Board's primary jurisdiction. Subsequently, the FMB ruled that the dual-rate system was valid, but the Supreme Court reversed this ruling on direct appeal. FMB v. Isbrandtsen Co., 356 U.S. 481 (1958). Thus, the Court got the benefit of the agency's views, but also refused to overlook the possibility that the agency had been "captured" by the industry that it was created to regulate. This best-of-both-worlds outcome is somewhat unusual, however: in most cases, allowing the agency the first opportunity to decide an issue (or case) probably means giving it the dispositive voice as well.

F. DAMAGE ACTIONS AGAINST THE GOVERNMENT

Persons who are harmed by administrative action often seek to recover damages from the government to compensate them for their injuries. Such efforts always require a statutory basis, for otherwise they might founder on the ancient doctrine of sovereign immunity, i.e., the principle that the government may not be sued without its consent. (In the typical judicial review proceeding to compel or set aside an agency action, sovereign immunity is not an issue, because the APA waives this defense. 5 U.S.C.A. § 702. But the APA waiver does not extend to claims for "money damages," [3] and thus a litigant who hopes to recover damages from the United States must find a statutory waiver elsewhere.) For example, in the Tucker Act, 28 U.S.C.A. § 1491, the United States has consented to be sued for damages in the U.S. Claims Court for a breach of contract or a "taking" of property without just compensation. For tort claims, the proper avenue for redress is the Federal Tort Claims Act.

The FTCA generally renders the government liable in tort for any "negligent or wrongful act or omission . . . in the same manner and to the same extent as a private individual under like circumstances." 28 U.S.C.A. §§ 1346(b), 2674. However, the Act also lists a number of exceptions that effectively preserve much of the sovereign immunity doctrine. One of these exceptions denies tort liability for a wide variety of intentional torts, including defamation, misrepresentation, deceit, and interference with contract rights. Id.

---

3. Claims for equitable monetary relief, such as back pay or reimbursement of specific sums, are not considered claims for "money damages" and thus can be pursued through the normal APA review mechanisms. Bowen v. Massachusetts, 487 U.S. 879 (1988).

§ 2680(h). Originally the same provision also excluded liability for assault, battery, false arrest, and malicious prosecution; since 1974, however, these latter torts have been actionable if committed by law enforcement officers. Id.

The most sweeping of the FTCA exceptions bars suit if the responsible officials were exercising a "discretionary function," regardless of whether they abused their discretion. Id. § 2680(a). Two recent, unanimous Supreme Court decisions have shed light on the meaning of this vague exemption. In United States v. S.A. Empresa de Viacao Aerea Rio Grandense (Varig Airlines), 467 U.S. 797 (1984), a fire broke out in the lavatory of an airplane, killing most of the passengers and damaging the plane. The injured parties' FTCA suit alleged that the FAA had negligently used a "spot-check" system in inspecting designs for the plane, and thus had failed to notice that the manufacturer's plans did not conform to federal safety regulations. The Court ruled in favor of the government, explaining that Congress had intended the discretionary function exception "to prevent judicial 'second-guessing' of legislative and administrative decisions grounded in . . . policy through the medium of an action in tort." Thus § 2680(a) should be read "to encompass the discretionary acts of the Government acting in its role as a regulator of the conduct of private individuals." The FAA had been making policy, and thus exercising its discretion, when it had decided that a spot-check system would be the best way to promote safety given its limited enforcement resources. Similarly, the inspectors who implemented the spot-check system had made policy judgments in deciding where to concentrate their attention.

However, the Court limited *Varig Airlines* in Berkovitz v. United States, 486 U.S. 531 (1988). Berkovitz had contracted polio after ingesting a vaccine disseminated under federal supervision. Sustaining his FTCA complaint against a government motion to dismiss, the Court said that the discretionary function exception applies only to "the permissible exercise of policy judgment." This formula had two important implications. First, the defense could not apply to government conduct that violates a "statute, regulation, or policy [that] specifically prescribes a course of action for an employee to follow." In such a case, "there is no discretion in the [officer's] conduct for the discretionary function exception to protect." Thus, § 2680(a) would not prevent Berkovitz from recovering damages if he proved at trial that the NIH Division of Biologic Standards (DBS), in licensing the vaccine, had ignored regulations requiring it to obtain test data from the manufacturer; or if he proved that, despite a Bureau of Biologics policy that specifically required testing of all vaccine lots and suppression of lots that did not comply with safety standards, Bureau employees had knowingly released a noncomplying lot containing his dose. Second, the exception protected only judgments based on public policy considerations, not every exercise of judgment by a government employee. Thus, Berkovitz might prevail by proving that DBS had erred in finding that the vaccine met its safety standards, but only if this decision had called for purely scientific judgment and not policy judgment. The *Berkovitz* "permissible exercise of policy judgment" test may go far towards bringing coherence to an area of the law that has often been considered chaotic.

G. DAMAGE ACTIONS AGAINST OFFICERS

When a litigant seeks to recover damages from the pocket of a government official, sovereign immunity is not an obstacle, but a related doctrine, official immunity, may be. The longstanding rule has been that a federal employee is absolutely immune from common-law tort liability for any act performed "within the outer perimeter of [his] line of duty." Barr v. Matteo, 360 U.S. 564 (1959). The rationale for this strict rule is that officials should feel free to make decisions according to their concept of the public interest, without the threat that they might have to bear monetary loss if a member of the public is injured in the process. In 1988 the case law started to move away from the absolute rule of *Barr,* see Westfall v. Erwin, 484 U.S. 292 (1988), but Congress quickly acted to restore it in substance. The Federal Employees Liability Reform and Tort Compensation Act of 1988, 102 Stat.

4562, provides that, in any tort suit brought against a federal employee for actions he took within the scope of his employment, the United States will be substituted as the defendant and the plaintiff's rights will be determined in accordance with the FTCA. 28 U.S.C.A. § 2679(d). Tort recovery from the employee is specifically foreclosed. Id. § 2679(b).

However, when the basis for a damage claim is not the common law of tort but an officer's violation of the Constitution, the Act does not apply, and the parties' rights are determined by an entirely separate body of case law. This line of authority stems from Bivens v. Six Unknown Named Agents of the Federal Bureau of Narcotics, 403 U.S. 388 (1971), where the Court held that an individual could bring a suit under the Fourth Amendment to recover for injuries resulting from the actions of federal narcotics agents during an unlawful search of his apartment. The Court has extended the *Bivens* holding to violations of constitutional provisions generally, but it has also held that in some specific contexts the remedy is not available. These include situations in which Congress has already set up an elaborate remedial system, see Schweiker v. Chilicky, 487 U.S. 412 (1988) (Social Security disability claims); Bush v. Lucas, 462 U.S. 367 (1983) (grievances by federal civil servants), or where there are other "special factors counseling hesitation," such as in the military context. United States v. Stanley, 483 U.S. 669 (1987).

In a *Bivens* action, official immunity is again a factor, but usually in a modified form. In Butz v. Economou, 438 U.S. 478 (1978), the Court held that federal officers should have the same immunity defenses that the Court had been applying for some years in "constitutional tort" actions against state officials under the Civil Rights Act of 1871, 42 U.S. C.A. § 1983. Balancing the injustice of denying redress to an injured plaintiff against the injustice of imposing liability on an official who had exercised his discretion in good faith, and taking account of the risk that liability would make administrators overly cautious in reaching important decisions, the Court stated that the scope of official immunity depended upon the kind of function the official was performing. Executive officers exercising discretion were accorded only a "qualified" immunity: an official would be protected from liability only if he had a good faith belief that his conduct was lawful, and the belief was reasonable. In thus breaking from the strict principle of immunity represented by *Barr*, the Court did not seem to be motivated by any strong sense that an additional check on federal officers was needed, but rather by a belief that it would be incongruous to hold federal officers to a more lenient standard than state officers.

However, the Court went on to recognize that state judges and prosecutors have been accorded absolute immunity in § 1983 litigation. This led the Court to hold that their counterparts exercising judicial functions in the federal bureaucracy— such as ALJs and staff attorneys acting in a prosecutorial capacity—should also enjoy absolute immunity, even in constitutional tort cases. The Court felt that this complete immunity was necessary to assure that "judges, advocates, and witnesses can perform their respective functions without harassment or intimidation." At the same time, absolute immunity for officers exercising judicial functions would not be likely to cause many unredressed injuries, because the safeguards built into the formal adjudicatory process would provide substantial protection against possible constitutional violations.

A few years after *Economou*, the Court revised the standard for qualified immunity in *Bivens* actions. The test became whether the defendant "violate[d] clearly established statutory or constitutional rights of which a reasonable person would have known." Harlow v. Fitzgerald, 457 U.S. 800 (1982). The prior "good faith" standard, with its emphasis on motives, had led to burdensome discovery and had been difficult for courts to apply except by holding a trial; the *Harlow* test is purely objective and turns primarily on legal issues, so that groundless cases can often be terminated through summary judgment. Partly because of the stringency of the *Harlow* test, successful constitutional tort actions against federal officers have been extremely sparse, and probably will remain so. One can argue, however, that the real significance of the *Bivens* cause of action does not lie in its practical role as part of a compensation system, but in its symbolic reminder that executive decisionmaking must always remain subordinate to the dictates of the Constitution.

APPENDIX I

SELECTED CONSTITUTIONAL AND STATUTORY PROVISIONS

UNITED STATES CONSTITUTION

Article I

Section 1. All legislative Powers herein granted shall be vested in a Congress of the United States, which shall consist of a Senate and House of Representatives.

Section 7. [1] All Bills for raising Revenue shall originate in the House of Representatives; but the Senate may propose or concur with Amendments as on other Bills.

[2] Every Bill which shall have passed the House of Representatives and the Senate, shall, before it become a Law, be presented to the President of the United States; If he approve he shall sign it, but if not he shall return it, with his Objections to that House in which it shall have originated, who shall enter the Objections at large on their Journal, and proceed to reconsider it. If after such Reconsideration two thirds of that House shall agree to pass the Bill, it shall be sent, together with the Objections, to the other House, by which it shall likewise be reconsidered, and if approved by two thirds of that House, it shall

become a Law. But in all such Cases the Votes of both Houses shall be determined by yeas and Nays, and the Names of the Persons voting for and against the Bill shall be entered on the Journal of each House respectively. If any Bill shall not be returned by the President within ten Days (Sundays excepted) after it shall have been presented to him, the Same shall be a Law, in like Manner as if he had signed it, unless the Congress by their Adjournment prevent its Return, in which Case it shall not be a Law.

[3] Every Order, Resolution, or Vote to Which the Concurrence of the Senate and House of Representatives may be necessary (except on a question of Adjournment) shall be presented to the President of the United States; and before the Same shall take Effect, shall be approved by him, or being disapproved by him, shall be repassed by two thirds of the Senate and House of Representatives, according to the Rules and Limitations prescribed in the Case of a Bill.

Section 8. The Congress shall have Power . . .

[18] To make all Laws which shall be necessary and proper for carrying into Execution the foregoing Powers, and all other Powers vested by this Constitution in the Government of the United States, or in any Department or Officer thereof.

Article II

Section 1. [1] The executive Power shall be vested in a President of the United States of America. . . .

Section 2. [1] The President shall be Commander in Chief of the Army and Navy of the United States; . . . he may require the Opinion, in writing, of the principal Officer in each of the executive Departments, upon any Subject relating to the Duties of their respective Offices. . . .

[2] He shall have Power, by and with the Advice and Consent of the Senate, to make Treaties, provided two thirds of the Senators present concur; and he shall nominate, and by and with the Advice and Consent of the Senate, shall appoint Ambassadors, other public Ministers and Consuls, Judges of the supreme Court, and all other Officers of the United States, whose Appointments are not herein otherwise provided for, and which shall be established by Law; but the Congress may by Law vest the Appointment of such inferior Officers, as they think proper, in the President alone, in the Courts of Law, or in the Heads of Departments. . . .

Section 3. He shall from time to time give to the Congress Information of the State of the Union, and recommend to their Consideration such Measures as he shall judge necessary and expedient; . . . he shall take Care that the Laws be faithfully executed, and shall Commission all the Officers of the United States.

Section 4.   The President, Vice President and all civil Officers of the United States, shall be removed from Office on Impeachment for, and Conviction of, Treason, Bribery, or other high Crimes and Misdemeanors.

Article III

Section 1.   The judicial Power of the United States, shall be vested in one supreme Court, and in such inferior Courts as the Congress may from time to time ordain and establish. . . .

Section 2.   [1]   The judicial Power shall extend to all Cases, in Law and Equity, arising under this Constitution, the Laws of the United States, and Treaties made, or which shall be made, under their Authority;—to all Cases affecting Ambassadors, other public Ministers and Consuls;—to all Cases of admiralty and maritime Jurisdiction;—to Controversies to which the United States shall be a Party;—to Controversies between two or more States;—between a State and Citizens of another State;—between Citizens of different States;—between Citizens of the same State claiming Lands under the Grants of different States, and between a State, or the Citizens thereof, and foreign States, Citizens or Subjects.

Amendment I [1791]

Congress shall make no law respecting an establishment of religion, or prohibiting the free exercise thereof; or abridging the freedom of speech, or of the press; or the right of the people peaceably to assemble, and to petition the Government for a redress of grievances.

Amendment IV [1791]

The right of the people to be secure in their persons, houses, papers, and effects, against unreasonable searches and seizures, shall not be violated, and no Warrants shall issue, but upon probable cause, supported by Oath or affirmation, and particularly describing the place to be searched, and the persons or things to be seized.

Amendment V [1791]

No person shall be held to answer for a capital, or otherwise infamous crime, unless on a presentment or indictment of a Grand Jury, except in cases arising in the land or naval forces, or in the Militia, when in actual service in time of War or public danger; nor shall any person be subject for the same offence to be twice put in jeopardy of life or limb; nor shall be compelled in any criminal case to be a witness against himself, nor be deprived of life, liberty, or property, without due process of law; nor shall private property be taken for public use, without just compensation.

Amendment VI [1791]

In all criminal prosecutions, the accused shall enjoy the right to a speedy and public trial, by an impartial jury of the State and district wherein the crime shall have been committed, which district shall have been previously ascertained by law, and to be informed of the nature and cause of the accusation; to be confronted with the witnesses against him; to have compulsory process for obtaining witnesses in his favor, and to have the Assistance of Counsel for his defence.

Amendment XIV [1868]

Section 1. All persons born or naturalized in the United States, and subject to the jurisdiction thereof, are citizens of the United States and of the State wherein they reside. No State shall make or enforce any law which shall abridge the privileges or immunities of citizens of the United States; nor shall any State deprive any person of life, liberty, or property, without due process of law; nor deny to any person within its jurisdiction the equal protection of the laws.

ADMINISTRATIVE PROCEDURE ACT

NOTE ON THE STRUCTURE OF THE APA

Since its original enactment in 1946, the Administrative Procedure Act has been amended and recodified several times. Some legal materials, particularly the older judicial decisions, may cite to the sections of the bill originally enacted (sections 2 through 12), which have been substantially rearranged in the current codification. To convert these citations into the current sections of Title 5, consult the conversion table at the end of this Appendix.

UNITED STATES CODE, TITLE 5

CHAPTER 5—ADMINISTRATIVE PROCEDURE

§ 551. Definitions

For the purpose of this subchapter—

(1) "agency" means each authority of the Government of the United States, whether or not it is within or subject to review by another agency, but does not include—

(A) the Congress;

(B) the courts of the United States;

(C) the governments of the territories or possessions of the United States;

(D) the government of the District of Columbia;

or except as to the requirements of section 552 of this title—

(E) agencies composed of representatives of the parties or of representatives of organizations of the parties to the disputes determined by them;

(F) courts martial and military commissions;

(G) military authority exercised in the field in time of war or in occupied territory; or

(H) functions conferred by sections 1738, 1739, 1743, and 1744 of title 12; chapter 2 of title 41; or sections 1622, 1884, 1891–1902, and former section 1641(b)(2), of title 50, appendix;

(2) "person" includes an individual, partnership, corporation, association, or public or private organization other than an agency;

(3) "party" includes a person or agency named or admitted as a party, or properly seeking and entitled as of right to be admitted as a party, in an agency proceeding, and a person or agency admitted by an agency as a party for limited purposes;

(4) "rule" means the whole or a part of an agency statement of general or particular applicability and future effect designed to implement, interpret, or prescribe law or policy or describing the organization, procedure, or practice requirements of an agency and includes the approval or prescription for the future of rates, wages, corporate or financial structures or reorganizations thereof, prices, facilities, appliances, services or allowances therefor or of valuations, costs, or accounting, or practices bearing on any of the foregoing;

(5) "rule making" means agency process for formulating, amending, or repealing a rule;

(6) "order" means the whole or a part of a final disposition, whether affirmative, negative, injunctive, or declaratory in form, of an agency in a matter other than rule making but including licensing;

(7) "adjudication" means agency process for the formulation of an order;

(8) "license" includes the whole or a part of an agency permit, certificate, approval, registration, charter, membership, statutory exemption or other form of permission;

(9) "licensing" includes agency process respecting the grant, renewal, denial, revocation, suspension, annulment, withdrawal, limitation, amendment, modification, or conditioning of a license;

(10) "sanction" includes the whole or a part of an agency—

(A) prohibition, requirement, limitation, or other condition affecting the freedom of a person;

(B) withholding of relief;

(C) imposition of penalty or fine;

(D) destruction, taking, seizure, or withholding of property;

(E) assessment of damages, reimbursement, restitution, compensation, costs, charges, or fees;

(F) requirement, revocation, or suspension of a license; or

(G) taking other compulsory or restrictive action;

(11) "relief" includes the whole or a part of an agency—

(A) grant of money, assistance, license, authority, exemption, exception, privilege, or remedy;

(B) recognition of a claim, right, immunity, privilege, exemption, or exception; or

(C) taking of other action on the application or petition of, and beneficial to, a person;

(12) "agency proceeding" means an agency process as defined by paragraphs (5), (7), and (9) of this section;

(13) "agency action" includes the whole or a part of an agency rule, order, license, sanction, relief, or the equivalent or denial thereof, or failure to act; and

(14) "ex parte communication" means an oral or written communication not on the public record with respect to which reasonable prior notice to all parties is not given, but it shall not include requests for status reports on any matter or proceeding covered by this subchapter.

§ 552. Public information; agency rules, opinions, orders, records, and proceedings [Freedom of Information Act]

(a) Each agency shall make available to the public information as follows:

(1) Each agency shall separately state and currently publish in the Federal Register for the guidance of the public—

(A) descriptions of its central and field organization and the established places at which, the employees (and in the case of a uniformed service, the members) from whom, and the methods whereby, the public may obtain information, make submittals or requests, or obtain decisions;

(B) statements of the general course and method by which its functions are channeled and determined, including the nature and requirements of all formal and informal procedures available;

(C) rules of procedure, descriptions of forms available or the places at which forms may be obtained, and instructions as to the scope and contents of all papers, reports, or examinations;

(D) substantive rules of general applicability adopted as authorized by law, and statements of general policy or interpretations of general applicability formulated and adopted by the agency; and

(E) each amendment, revision, or repeal of the foregoing.

Except to the extent that a person has actual and timely notice of the terms thereof, a person may not in any manner be required to resort to, or be adversely affected by, a matter required to be published in the Federal Register and not so published. For the purpose of this paragraph, matter reasonably available to the class of persons affected thereby is deemed published in the Federal Register when incorporated by reference therein with the approval of the Director of the Federal Register.

(2) Each agency, in accordance with published rules, shall make available for public inspection and copying—

(A) final opinions, including concurring and dissenting opinions, as well as orders, made in the adjudication of cases;

(B) those statements of policy and interpretations which have been adopted by the agency and are not published in the Federal Register; and

(C) administrative staff manuals and instructions to staff that affect a member of the public;

unless the materials are promptly published and copies offered for sale. To the extent required to prevent a clearly unwarranted invasion of personal privacy, an agency may delete identifying details when it makes available or publishes an opinion, statement of policy, interpretation, or staff manual or instruction. However, in each case the justification for the deletion shall be explained fully in writing. Each agency shall also maintain and make available for public inspection and copying current indexes providing identifying information for the public as to any matter issued, adopted, or promulgated after July 4, 1967, and required by this paragraph to be made available or published. Each agency shall promptly publish, quarterly or more frequently, and distribute (by sale or otherwise) copies of each index or supplements thereto unless it determines by order published in the Federal Register that the publication would be unnecessary and impracticable, in which case the agency shall nonetheless provide copies of such index on request at a cost not to exceed the direct cost of duplication. A final order, opinion, statement of policy, interpretation, or staff manual or instruction that affects a member of the public may be relied on, used, or cited as precedent by an agency against a party other than an agency only if—

    (i) it has been indexed and either made available or published as provided by this paragraph; or

    (ii) the party has actual and timely notice of the terms thereof.

(3) Except with respect to the records made available under paragraphs (1) and (2) of this subsection, each agency, upon any request for records which (A) reasonably describes such records and (B) is made in accordance with published rules stating the time, place, fees (if any), and procedures to be followed, shall make the records promptly available to any person.

(4)(A)(i) In order to carry out the provisions of this section, each agency shall promulgate regulations, pursuant to notice and receipt of public comment, specifying the schedule of fees applicable to the processing of requests under this section and establishing procedures and guidelines for determining when such fees should be waived or reduced. Such schedule shall conform to the guidelines which shall be promulgated, pursuant to notice and receipt of public comment, by the Director of the Office of Management and Budget and which shall provide for a uniform schedule of fees for all agencies.

(ii) Such agency regulations shall provide that—

(I) fees shall be limited to reasonable standard charges for document search, duplication, and review, when records are requested for commercial use;

(II) fees shall be limited to reasonable standard charges for document duplication when records are not sought for commercial use and the request is made by an educational or noncommercial scientific institution, whose purpose is scholarly or scientific research; or a representative of the news media; and

(III) for any request not described in (I) or (II), fees shall be limited to reasonable standard charges for document search and duplication.

(iii) Documents shall be furnished without any charge or at a charge reduced below the fees established under clause (ii) if disclosure of the information is in the public interest because it is likely to contribute significantly to public understanding of the operations or activities of the government and is not primarily in the commercial interest of the requester.

(iv) Fee schedules shall provide for the recovery of only the direct costs of search, duplication, or review. Review costs shall include only the direct costs incurred during the initial examination of a document for the purposes of determining whether the documents must be disclosed under this section and for the purposes of withholding any portions exempt from disclosure under this section. Review costs may not include any costs incurred in resolving issues of law or policy that may be raised in the course of processing a request under this section. No fee may be charged by any agency under this section—

(I) if the costs of routine collection and processing of the fee are likely to equal or exceed the amount of the fee; or

(II) for any request described in clause (ii)(II) or (III) of this subparagraph for the first two hours of search time or for the first one hundred pages of duplication.

(v) No agency may require advance payment of any fee unless the requester has previously failed to pay fees in a timely fashion, or the agency has determined that the fee will exceed $250.

(vi) Nothing in this subparagraph shall supersede fees chargeable under a statute specifically providing for setting the level of fees for particular types of records.

(vii) In any action by a requester regarding the waiver of fees under this section, the court shall determine the matter de novo: *Provided,* That the court's review of the matter shall be limited to the record before the agency.

(B) On complaint, the district court of the United States in the district in which the complainant resides, or has his principal place of business, or in which the agency records are situated, or in the District of Columbia, has jurisdiction to enjoin the agency from withholding agency records and to order the production of any agency records improperly withheld from the complainant. In such a case the court shall determine the matter de novo, and may examine the contents of such agency records in camera to determine whether such records or any part thereof shall be withheld under any of the exemptions set forth in subsection (b) of this section, and the burden is on the agency to sustain its action.

(C) Notwithstanding any other provision of law, the defendant shall serve an answer or otherwise plead to any complaint made under this subsection within thirty days after service upon the defendant of the pleading in which such complaint is made, unless the court otherwise directs for good cause shown.

(D) [Repealed.]

(E) The court may assess against the United States reasonable attorney fees and other litigation costs reasonably incurred in any case under this section in which the complainant has substantially prevailed.

(F) Whenever the court orders the production of any agency records improperly withheld from the complainant and assesses against the United

States reasonable attorney fees and other litigation costs, and the court additionally issues a written finding that the circumstances surrounding the withholding raise questions whether agency personnel acted arbitrarily or capriciously with respect to the withholding, the Special Counsel shall promptly initiate a proceeding to determine whether disciplinary action is warranted against the officer or employee who was primarily responsible for the withholding. The Special Counsel, after investigation and consideration of the evidence submitted, shall submit his findings and recommendations to the administrative authority of the agency concerned and shall send copies of the findings and recommendations to the officer or employee or his representative. The administrative authority shall take the corrective action that the Special Counsel recommends.

(G) In the event of noncompliance with the order of the court, the district court may punish for contempt the responsible employee, and in the case of a uniformed service, the responsible member.

(5) Each agency having more than one member shall maintain and make available for public inspection a record of the final votes of each member in every agency proceeding.

(6)(A) Each agency, upon any request for records made under paragraph (1), (2), or (3) of this subsection, shall—

(i) determine within ten days (excepting Saturdays, Sundays, and legal public holidays) after the receipt of any such request whether to comply with such request and shall immediately notify the person making such request of such determination and the reasons therefor, and of the right of such person to appeal to the head of the agency any adverse determination; and

(ii) make a determination with respect to any appeal within twenty days (excepting Saturdays, Sundays, and legal public holidays) after the receipt of such appeal. If on appeal the denial of the request for records is in whole or in part upheld, the agency shall notify the person making such request of the provisions for judicial review of that determination under paragraph (4) of this subsection.

(B) In unusual circumstances as specified in this subparagraph, the time limits prescribed in either clause (i) or clause (ii) of subparagraph (A) may be extended by written notice to the person making such request setting forth the reasons for such extension and the date on which a determination is expected to be dispatched. No such notice shall specify a date that would result in an extension for more than ten working days. As used in this subparagraph, "unusual circumstances" means, but only to the extent reasonably necessary to the proper processing of the particular request—

(i) the need to search for and collect the requested records from field facilities or other establishments that are separate from the office processing the request;

(ii) the need to search for, collect, and appropriately examine a voluminous amount of separate and distinct records which are demanded in a single request; or

(iii) the need for consultation, which shall be conducted with all practicable speed, with another agency having a substantial interest in the determination of the request or among two or more components of the agency having substantial subject-matter interest therein.

(C) Any person making a request to any agency for records under paragraph (1), (2), or (3) of this subsection shall be deemed to have exhausted his administrative remedies with respect to such request if the agency fails to comply with the applicable time limit provisions of this paragraph. If the Government can show exceptional circumstances exist and that the agency is exercising due diligence in responding to the request, the court may retain jurisdiction and allow the agency additional time to complete its review of the records. Upon any determination by an agency to comply with a request for records, the records shall be made promptly available to such person making such request. Any notification of denial of any request for records under this subsection shall set forth the names and titles or positions of each person responsible for the denial of such request.

(b) This section does not apply to matters that are—

(1)(A) specifically authorized under criteria established by an Executive order to be kept secret in the interest of national defense or foreign policy and (B) are in fact properly classified pursuant to such Executive order;

(2) related solely to the internal personnel rules and practices of an agency;

(3) specifically exempted from disclosure by statute (other than section 552b of this title), provided that such statute (A) requires that the matters be withheld from the public in such a manner as to leave no discretion on the issue, or (B) establishes particular criteria for withholding or refers to particular types of matters to be withheld;

(4) trade secrets and commercial or financial information obtained from a person and privileged or confidential;

(5) inter-agency or intra-agency memorandums or letters which would not be available by law to a party other than an agency in litigation with the agency;

(6) personnel and medical files and similar files the disclosure of which would constitute a clearly unwarranted invasion of personal privacy;

(7) records or information compiled for law enforcement purposes, but only to the extent that the production of such law enforcement records or information (A) could reasonably be

expected to interfere with enforcement proceedings, (B) would deprive a person of a right to a fair trial or an impartial adjudication, (C) could reasonably be expected to constitute an unwarranted invasion of personal privacy, (D) could reasonably be expected to disclose the identity of a confidential source, including a State, local or foreign agency or authority or any private institution which furnished information on a confidential basis, and, in the case of a record or information compiled by criminal law enforcement authority in the course of a criminal investigation or by an agency conducting a lawful national security intelligence investigation, information furnished by a confidential source, (E) would disclose techniques and procedures for law enforcement investigations or prosecutions, or would disclose guidelines for law enforcement investigations or prosecutions if such disclosure could reasonably be expected to risk circumvention of the law, or (F) could reasonably be expected to endanger the life or physical safety of any individual;

(8) contained in or related to examination, operating, or condition reports prepared by, on behalf of, or for the use of an agency responsible for the regulation or supervision of financial institutions; or

(9) geological and geophysical information and data, including maps, concerning wells.

Any reasonably segregable portion of a record shall be provided to any person requesting such record after deletion of the portions which are exempt under this subsection.

(c)(1) Whenever a request is made which involves access to records described in subsection (b) (7)(A) and—

(A) the investigation or proceeding involves a possible violation of criminal law; and

(B) there is reason to believe that (i) the subject of the investigation or proceeding is not aware of its pendency, and (ii) disclosure of the existence of the records could reasonably be expected to interfere with enforcement proceedings,

the agency may, during only such time as that circumstance continues, treat the records as not subject to the requirements of this section.

(2) Whenever informant records maintained by a criminal law enforcement agency under an informant's name or personal identifier are requested by a third party according to the informant's name or personal identifier, the agency may treat the records as not subject to the requirements of this section unless the informant's status as an informant has been officially confirmed.

(3) Whenever a request is made which involves access to records maintained by the Federal Bureau of Investigation pertaining to foreign intelligence or counterintelligence, or international ter-

rorism, and the existence of the records is classified information as provided in subsection (b)(1), the Bureau may, as long as the existence of the records remains classified information, treat the records as not subject to the requirements of this section.

(d) This section does not authorize withholding of information or limit the availability of records to the public, except as specifically stated in this section. This section is not authority to withhold information from Congress.

(e) On or before March 1 of each calendar year, each agency shall submit a report covering the preceding calendar year to the Speaker of the House of Representatives and President of the Senate for referral to the appropriate committees of the Congress. The report shall include—

(1) the number of determinations made by such agency not to comply with requests for records made to such agency under subsection (a) and the reasons for each such determination;

(2) the number of appeals made by persons under subsection (a)(6), the result of such appeals, and the reason for the action upon each appeal that results in a denial of information;

(3) the names and titles or positions of each person responsible for the denial of records requested under this section, and the number of instances of participation for each;

(4) the results of each proceeding conducted pursuant to subsection (a)(4)(F), including a report of the disciplinary action taken against the officer or employee who was primarily responsible for improperly withholding records or an explanation of why disciplinary action was not taken;

(5) a copy of every rule made by such agency regarding this section;

(6) a copy of the fee schedule and the total amount of fees collected by the agency for making records available under this section; and

(7) such other information as indicates efforts to administer fully this section.

The Attorney General shall submit an annual report on or before March 1 of each calendar year which shall include for the prior calendar year a listing of the number of cases arising under this section, the exemption involved in each case, the disposition of such case, and the cost, fees, and penalties assessed under subsections (a)(4)(E), (F), and (G). Such report shall also include a description of the efforts undertaken by the Department of Justice to encourage agency compliance with this section.

(f) For purposes of this section, the term "agency" as defined in section 551(1) of this title includes any executive department, military department, Government corporation, Government controlled corporation, or other establishment in the executive branch of the Government (including the Executive Office of the President), or any independent regulatory agency.

§ 552a. Records maintained on individuals

[This section, known as the Privacy Act, is omitted.]

§ 552b. Open meetings

[This section, known as the Government in the Sunshine Act, is omitted.]

§ 553. Rule making

(a) This section applies, according to the provisions thereof, except to the extent that there is involved—

(1) a military or foreign affairs function of the United States; or

(2) a matter relating to agency management or personnel or to public property, loans, grants, benefits, or contracts.

(b) General notice of proposed rule making shall be published in the Federal Register, unless persons subject thereto are named and either personally served or otherwise have actual notice thereof in accordance with law. The notice shall include—

(1) a statement of the time, place, and nature of public rule making proceedings;

(2) reference to the legal authority under which the rule is proposed; and

(3) either the terms or substance of the proposed rule or a description of the subjects and issues involved.

Except when notice or hearing is required by statute, this subsection does not apply—

(A) to interpretative rules, general statements of policy, or rules of agency organization, procedure, or practice; or

(B) when the agency for good cause finds (and incorporates the finding and a brief statement of reasons therefor in the rules issued) that notice and public procedure thereon are impracticable, unnecessary, or contrary to the public interest.

(c) After notice required by this section, the agency shall give interested persons an opportunity to participate in the rule making through submission of written data, views, or arguments with or without opportunity for oral presentation. After consideration of the relevant matter presented, the agency shall incorporate in the rules adopted a concise general statement of their basis and purpose. When rules are required by statute to be made on the record after opportunity for an agency hearing, sections 556 and 557 of this title apply instead of this subsection.

(d) The required publication or service of a substantive rule shall be made not less than 30 days before its effective date, except—

(1) a substantive rule which grants or recognizes an exemption or relieves a restriction;

(2) interpretative rules and statements of policy; or

(3) as otherwise provided by the agency for good cause found and published with the rule.

(e) Each agency shall give an interested person the right to petition for the issuance, amendment, or repeal of a rule.

§ 554. Adjudications

(a) This section applies, according to the provisions thereof, in every case of adjudication required by statute to be determined on the record after opportunity for an agency hearing, except to the extent that there is involved—

(1) a matter subject to a subsequent trial of the law and the facts de novo in a court;

(2) the selection or tenure of an employee, except a[n] administrative law judge appointed under section 3105 of this title;

(3) proceedings in which decisions rest solely on inspections, tests, or elections;

(4) the conduct of military or foreign affairs functions;

(5) cases in which an agency is acting as an agent for a court; or

(6) the certification of worker representatives.

(b) Persons entitled to notice of an agency hearing shall be timely informed of—

(1) the time, place, and nature of the hearing;

(2) the legal authority and jurisdiction under which the hearing is to be held; and

(3) the matters of fact and law asserted.

When private persons are the moving parties, other parties to the proceeding shall give prompt notice of issues controverted in fact or law; and in other instances agencies may by rule require responsive pleading. In fixing the time and place for hearings, due regard shall be had for the convenience and necessity of the parties or their representatives.

(c) The agency shall give all interested parties opportunity for—

(1) the submission and consideration of facts, arguments, offers of settlement, or proposals of adjustment when time, the nature of the proceeding, and the public interest permit; and

(2) to the extent that the parties are unable so to determine a controversy by consent, hearing and decision on notice and in accordance with sections 556 and 557 of this title.

(d) The employee who presides at the reception of evidence pursuant to section 556 of this title shall make the recommended decision or initial decision required by section 557 of this title, unless he becomes unavailable to the agency. Except to the extent required for the disposition of ex parte matters as authorized by law, such an employee may not—

(1) consult a person or party on a fact in issue, unless on notice and opportunity for all parties to participate; or

(2) be responsible to or subject to the supervision or direction of an employee or agent engaged in the performance of investigative or prosecuting functions for an agency.

An employee or agent engaged in the performance of investigative or prosecuting functions for an agency in a case may not, in that or a factually related case, participate or advise in the decision, recommended decision, or agency review pursuant to section 557 of this title, except as witness or counsel in public proceedings. This subsection does not apply—

(A) in determining applications for initial licenses;

(B) to proceedings involving the validity or application of rates, facilities, or practices of public utilities or carriers; or

(C) to the agency or a member or members of the body comprising the agency.

(e) The agency, with like effect as in the case of other orders, and in its sound discretion, may issue a declaratory order to terminate a controversy or remove uncertainty.

§ 555. Ancillary matters

(a) This section applies, according to the provisions thereof, except as otherwise provided by this subchapter.

(b) A person compelled to appear in person before an agency or representative thereof is entitled to be accompanied, represented, and advised by counsel or, if permitted by the agency, by other qualified representative. A party is entitled to appear in person or by or with counsel or other duly qualified representative in an agency proceeding. So far as the orderly conduct of public business permits, an interested person may appear before an agency or its responsible employees for the presentation, adjustment, or determination of an issue, request, or controversy in a proceeding, whether interlocutory, summary, or otherwise, or in connection with an agency function. With due regard for the convenience and necessity of the parties or their representatives and within a reasonable time, each agency shall proceed to conclude a matter presented to it. This subsection does not grant or deny a person who is not a lawyer the right to appear for or represent others before an agency or in an agency proceeding.

(c) Process, requirement of a report, inspection, or other investigative act or demand may not be issued, made, or enforced except as authorized by law. A person compelled to submit data or evidence is entitled to retain or, on payment of lawfully prescribed costs, procure a copy or transcript thereof, except that in a non-public investigatory proceeding the witness may for good cause be limited to inspection of the official transcript of his testimony.

(d) Agency subpenas authorized by law shall be issued to a party on request and, when required by rules of procedure, on a statement or showing of general relevance and reasonable scope of the evidence sought. On contest, the court shall sustain the subpena or similar process or demand to the extent that it is found to be in accordance with law. In a proceeding for enforcement, the court shall issue an order requiring the appearance of the witness or the production of the evidence or data within a reasonable time under penalty of punishment for contempt in case of contumacious failure to comply.

(e) Prompt notice shall be given of the denial in whole or in part of a written application, petition, or other request of an interested person made in connection with any agency proceeding. Except in affirming a prior denial or when the denial is self-explanatory, the notice shall be accompanied by a brief statement of the grounds for denial.

§ 556. Hearings; presiding employees; powers and duties; burden of proof; evidence; record as basis of decision

(a) This section applies, according to the provisions thereof, to hearings required by section 553 or 554 of this title to be conducted in accordance with this section.

(b) There shall preside at the taking of evidence—

(1) the agency;

(2) one or more members of the body which comprises the agency; or

(3) one or more administrative law judges appointed under section 3105 of this title.

This subchapter does not supersede the conduct of specified classes of proceedings, in whole or in part, by or before boards or other employees specially provided for by or designated under statute. The functions of presiding employees and of employees participating in decisions in accordance with section 557 of this title shall be conducted in an impartial manner. A presiding or participating employee may at any time disqualify himself. On the filing in good faith of a timely and sufficient affidavit of personal bias or other disqualification of a presiding or participating employee, the agency shall determine the matter as a part of the record and decision in the case.

(c) Subject to published rules of the agency and within its powers, employees presiding at hearings may—

(1) administer oaths and affirmations;

(2) issue subpenas authorized by law;

(3) rule on offers of proof and receive relevant evidence;

(4) take depositions or have depositions taken when the ends of justice would be served;

(5) regulate the course of the hearing;

(6) hold conferences for the settlement or simplification of the issues by consent of the parties;

(7) dispose of procedural requests or similar matters;

(8) make or recommend decisions in accordance with section 557 of this title; and

(9) take other action authorized by agency rule consistent with this subchapter.

(d) Except as otherwise provided by statute, the proponent of a rule or order has the burden of proof. Any oral or documentary evidence may be received, but the agency as a matter of policy shall provide for the exclusion of irrelevant, immaterial, or unduly repetitious evidence. A sanction may not be imposed or rule or order issued except on consideration of the whole record or those parts thereof cited by a party and supported by and in accordance with the reliable, probative, and substantial evidence. The agency may, to the extent consistent with the interests of justice and the policy of the underlying statutes administered by the agency, consider a violation of section 557(d) of this title sufficient grounds for a decision adverse to a party who has knowingly committed such violation or knowingly caused such violation to occur. A party is entitled to present his case or defense by oral or documentary evidence, to submit rebuttal evidence, and to conduct such cross-examination as may be required for a full and true disclosure of the facts. In rule making or determining claims for money or benefits or applications for initial licenses an agency may, when a party will not be prejudiced thereby, adopt procedures for the submission of all or part of the evidence in written form.

(e) The transcript of testimony and exhibits, together with all papers and requests filed in the proceeding, constitutes the exclusive record for decision in accordance with section 557 of this title and, on payment of lawfully prescribed costs, shall be made available to the parties. When an agency decision rests on official notice of a material fact not appearing in the evidence in the record, a party is entitled, on timely request, to an opportunity to show the contrary.

§ 557. Initial decisions; conclusiveness; review by agency; submissions by parties; contents of decisions; record

(a) This section applies, according to the provisions thereof, when a hearing is required to be conducted in accordance with section 556 of this title.

(b) When the agency did not preside at the reception of the evidence, the presiding employee or, in cases not subject to section 554(d) of this title, an employee qualified to preside at hearings pursuant to section 556 of this title, shall initially decide the case unless the agency requires, either in specific cases or by general rule, the entire record to be certified to it for decision. When the presiding employee makes an initial decision, that decision then becomes the decision of the agency without further proceedings unless there is an appeal to, or review on motion of, the agency within time provided by rule. On appeal from or review of the initial decision, the agency has all the powers which it would have in making the initial decision except as it may limit the issues on notice or by rule. When the agency makes the decision without having presided at the reception of the evidence, the presiding employee or an employee qualified to preside at hearings pursuant to section 556 of this title shall first recommend a decision, except that in rule making or determining applications for initial licenses—

(1) instead thereof the agency may issue a tentative decision or one of its responsible employees may recommend a decision; or

(2) this procedure may be omitted in a case in which the agency finds on the record that due and timely execution of its functions imperatively and unavoidably so requires.

(c) Before a recommended, initial, or tentative decision, or a decision on agency review of the decision of subordinate employees, the parties are entitled to a reasonable opportunity to submit for the consideration of the employees participating in the decisions—

(1) proposed findings and conclusions; or

(2) exceptions to the decisions or recommended decisions of subordinate employees or to tentative agency decisions; and

(3) supporting reasons for the exceptions or proposed findings or conclusions.

The record shall show the ruling on each finding, conclusion, or exception presented. All decisions, including initial, recommended, and tentative decisions, are a part of the record and shall include a statement of—

(A) findings and conclusions, and the reasons or basis therefor, on all the material issues of fact, law, or discretion presented on the record; and

(B) the appropriate rule, order, sanction, relief, or denial thereof.

(d)(1) In any agency proceeding which is subject to subsection (a) of this section, except to the extent required for the disposition of ex parte matters as authorized by law—

(A) no interested person outside the agency shall make or knowingly cause to be made to any member of the body comprising the agency, administrative law judge, or other employee who is or may reasonably be expected to be involved in the decisional process of the proceeding, an ex parte communication relevant to the merits of the proceeding;

(B) no member of the body comprising the agency, administrative law judge, or other employee who is or may reasonably be expected to be involved in the decisional process of the proceeding, shall make or knowingly cause to be made to any interested person outside the agency an ex parte communication relevant to the merits of the proceeding;

(C) a member of the body comprising the agency, administrative law judge, or other employee who is or may reasonably be expected to be involved in the decisional process of such proceeding who receives, or who makes or knowingly causes to be made, a communication prohibited by this subsection shall place on the public record of the proceeding:

(i) all such written communications;

(ii) memoranda stating the substance of all such oral communications; and

(iii) all written responses, and memoranda stating the substance of all oral responses, to the materials described in clauses (i) and (ii) of this subparagraph;

(D) upon receipt of a communication knowingly made or knowingly caused to be made by a party in violation of this subsection, the agency, administrative law judge, or other employee presiding at the hearing may, to the extent consistent with the interests of justice and the policy of the underlying statutes, require the party to show cause why his claim or interest in the proceeding should not be dismissed, denied, disregarded, or otherwise adversely affected on account of such violation; and

(E) the prohibitions of this subsection shall apply beginning at such time as the agency may designate, but in no case shall they begin to apply later than the time at which a proceeding is noticed for hearing unless the person responsible for the communication has knowledge that it will be noticed, in which case the prohibitions shall apply beginning at the time of his acquisition of such knowledge.

(2) This subsection does not constitute authority to withhold information from Congress.

§ 558. Imposition of sanctions; determination of applications for licenses; suspension, revocation, and expiration of licenses

(a) This section applies, according to the provisions thereof, to the exercise of a power or authority.

(b) A sanction may not be imposed or a substantive rule or order issued except within jurisdiction delegated to the agency and as authorized by law.

(c) When application is made for a license required by law, the agency, with due regard for the rights and privileges of all the interested parties or adversely affected persons and within a reasonable time, shall set and complete proceedings required to be conducted in accordance with sections 556 and 557 of this title or other proceedings required by law and shall make its decision. Except in cases of willfulness or those in which public health, interest, or safety requires otherwise, the withdrawal, suspension, revocation, or annulment of a license is lawful only if, before the institution of agency proceedings therefor, the licensee has been given—

    (1) notice by the agency in writing of the facts or conduct which may warrant the action; and

    (2) opportunity to demonstrate or achieve compliance with all lawful requirements.

When the licensee has made timely and sufficient application for a renewal or a new license in accordance with agency rules, a license with reference to an activity of a continuing nature does not expire until the application has been finally determined by the agency.

§ 559. Effect on other laws; effect of subsequent statute

This subchapter, chapter 7, and sections 1305, 3105, 3344, 4301(2)(E), 5372, and 7521 of this title, and the provisions of section 5335(a)(B) of this title that relate to administrative law judges, do not limit or repeal additional requirements imposed by statute or otherwise recognized by law. Except as otherwise required by law, requirements or privileges relating to evidence or procedure apply equally to agencies and persons. Each agency is granted the authority necessary to comply with the requirements of this subchapter through the issuance of rules or otherwise. Subsequent statute may not be held to supersede or modify this subchapter, chapter 7, sections 1305, 3105, 3344, 4301(2)(E), 5372, or 7521 of this title, or the provisions of section 5335(a)(B) of this title that relate to administrative law judges, except to the extent that it does so expressly.

CHAPTER 6—THE ANALYSIS OF REGULATORY FUNCTIONS

[This chapter, known as the Regulatory Flexibility Act, is omitted.]

CHAPTER 7—JUDICIAL REVIEW

§ 701. Application; definitions

(a) This chapter applies, according to the provisions thereof, except to the extent that—

(1) statutes preclude judicial review; or

(2) agency action is committed to agency discretion by law.

(b) For the purpose of this chapter—

(1) "agency" means each authority of the Government of the United States, whether or not it is within or subject to review by another agency, but does not include—

(A) the Congress;

(B) the courts of the United States;

(C) the governments of the territories or possessions of the United States;

(D) the government of the District of Columbia;

(E) agencies composed of representatives of the parties or of representatives of organizations of the parties to the disputes determined by them;

(F) courts martial and military commissions;

(G) military authority exercised in the field in time of war or in occupied territory; or

(H) functions conferred by sections 1738, 1739, 1743, and 1744 of title 12; chapter 2 of title 41; or sections 1622, 1884, 1891–1902, and former section 1641(b)(2), of title 50, appendix; and

(2) "person", "rule", "order", "license", "sanction", "relief", and "agency action" have the meanings given them by section 551 of this title.

§ 702. Right of review

A person suffering legal wrong because of agency action, or adversely affected or aggrieved by agency action within the meaning of a relevant statute, is entitled to judicial review thereof. An action in a court of the United States seeking relief other than money damages and stating a claim that an agency or an officer or employee thereof acted or failed to act in an official capacity or under color of legal authority shall not be dismissed nor relief therein be denied on the ground that it is against the United States or that the United States is an indispensable party. The United States may be named as a defendant in any such action, and a judgment or decree may be entered against the United States: *Provided,* That any mandatory or injunctive decree shall specify the Federal officer or officers (by name or by title), and their successors in office, personally responsible for compliance. Nothing herein (1) affects other limitations on judicial review or the power or duty of the court to dismiss any action or deny relief on any other appropriate legal or equitable ground; or (2) confers authority to grant relief if any other statute that grants consent to suit expressly or impliedly forbids the relief which is sought.

§ 703. Form and venue of proceeding

The form of proceeding for judicial review is the special statutory review proceeding relevant to the subject matter in a court specified by statute or, in the absence or inadequacy thereof, any applicable form of legal action, including actions for declaratory judgments or writs of prohibitory or mandatory injunction or habeas corpus, in a court of competent jurisdiction. If no special statutory review proceeding is applicable, the action for judicial review may be brought against the United States, the agency by its official title, or the appropriate officer. Except to the extent that prior, adequate, and exclusive opportunity for judicial review is provided by law, agency action is subject to judicial review in civil or criminal proceedings for judicial enforcement.

§ 704. Actions reviewable

Agency action made reviewable by statute and final agency action for which there is no adequate remedy in a court are subject to judicial review. A preliminary, procedural, or intermediate agency action or ruling not directly reviewable is subject to review on the review of the final agency action. Except as otherwise expressly required by statute, agency action otherwise final is final for the purposes of this section whether or not there has been presented or determined an application for a declaratory order, for any form of reconsideration, or, unless the agency otherwise requires by rule and provides that the action meanwhile is inoperative, for an appeal to superior agency authority.

§ 705. Relief pending review

When an agency finds that justice so requires, it may postpone the effective date of action taken by it, pending judicial review. On such conditions as may be required and to the extent necessary to prevent irreparable injury, the reviewing court, including the court to which a case may be taken on appeal from or on application for certiorari or other writ to a reviewing court, may issue all necessary and appropriate process to postpone the effective date of an agency action or to preserve status or rights pending conclusion of the review proceedings.

§ 706. Scope of review

To the extent necessary to decision and when presented, the reviewing court shall decide all relevant questions of law, interpret constitutional and statutory provisions, and determine the meaning or applicability of the terms of an agency action. The reviewing court shall—

(1) compel agency action unlawfully withheld or unreasonably delayed; and

(2) hold unlawful and set aside agency action, findings, and conclusions found to be—

(A) arbitrary, capricious, an abuse of discretion, or otherwise not in accordance with law;

(B) contrary to constitutional right, power, privilege, or immunity;

(C) in excess of statutory jurisdiction, authority, or limitations, or short of statutory right;

(D) without observance of procedure required by law;

(E) unsupported by substantial evidence in a case subject to sections 556 and 557 of this title or otherwise reviewed on the record of an agency hearing provided by statute; or

(F) unwarranted by the facts to the extent that the facts are subject to trial de novo by the reviewing court.

In making the foregoing determinations, the court shall review the whole record or those parts of it cited by a party, and due account shall be taken of the rule of prejudicial error.

ADMINISTRATIVE LAW JUDGES

§ 3105. Appointment of administrative law judges

Each agency shall appoint as many administrative law judges as are necessary for proceedings required to be conducted in accordance with sections 556 and 557 of this title. Administrative law judges shall be assigned to cases in rotation so far as practicable, and may not perform duties inconsistent with their duties and responsibilities as administrative law judges.

§ 7521. Actions against administrative law judges

(a) An action may be taken against an administrative law judge appointed under section 3105 of this title by the agency in which the administrative law judge is employed only for good cause established and determined by the Merit Systems Protection Board on the record after opportunity for hearing before the Board. . . . [Actions covered include removal, suspension, and reduction in grade or pay.]

§ 5372. Administrative law judges

Administrative law judges appointed under section 3105 of this title are entitled to pay prescribed by the Office of Personnel Management independently of agency recommendations or ratings and in accordance with subchapter III of this chapter and chapter 51 of this title.

§ 3344. Details; administrative law judges

An agency as defined by section 551 of this title which occasionally or temporarily is insufficiently staffed with administrative law judges appointed under section 3105 of this title may use administrative law judges selected by the Office of Personnel Management from and with the consent of other agencies.

§ 1305. Administrative law judges

For the purpose of sections 3105, 3344, 4301(2) (D), and 5372 of this title and the provisions of section 5335(a)(B) of this title that relate to administrative law judges, the Office of Personnel Management may, and for the purpose of section 7521 of this title, the Merit Systems Protection Board may investigate, require reports by agencies, issue reports, including an annual report to Congress, prescribe regulations, appoint advisory committees as necessary, recommend legislation, subpena witnesses and records, and pay witness fees as established for the courts of the United States.

TABLE CORRELATING THE 1946 ADMINISTRATIVE PROCEDURE ACT WITH PARALLEL SECTIONS CODIFIED IN 5 U.S.C.A.

Parallel Section 1946 Administrative Procedure Act	5 U.S.C.A.
Sec. 2(a)	§ 551(1)
Sec. 2(b)	§ 551(2), (3)
Sec. 2(c)	§ 551(4), (5)
Sec. 2(d)	§ 551(6), (7)
Sec. 2(e)	§ 551(8), (9)
Sec. 2(f)	§ 551(10), (11)
Sec. 2(g)	§ 551(12), (13)
Sec. 3	§ 552(a)–(f)
Sec. 4	§ 553(a)
Sec. 4(a)	§ 553(b)
Sec. 4(b)	§ 553(c)
Sec. 4(c)	§ 553(d)
Sec. 4(d)	§ 553(e)
Sec. 5	§ 554(a)
Sec. 5(a)	§ 554(b)
Sec. 5(b)	§ 554(c)
Sec. 5(c)	§ 554(d)
Sec. 5(d)	§ 554(e)
Sec. 6	§ 555(a)
Sec. 6(a)	§ 555(b)
Sec. 6(b)	§ 555(c)
Sec. 6(c)	§ 555(d)
Sec. 6(d)	§ 555(e)

**Parallel Section
1946 Administrative
Procedure Act**   **5 U.S.C.A.**

Sec. 7	§ 556(a)
Sec. 7(a)	§ 556(b)
Sec. 7(b)	§ 556(c)
Sec. 7(c)	§ 556(d)
Sec. 7(d)	§ 556(e)
Sec. 8	§ 557(a)
Sec. 8(a)	§ 557(b)
Sec. 8(b)	§ 557(c)
Sec. 9	§ 558(a)
Sec. 9(a)	§ 558(b)
Sec. 9(b)	§ 558(c)
Sec. 12	§ 559
Sec. 10	§ 701(a)
Sec. 2(a)-(g)	§ 701(b)(1), (2)
Sec. 10(a)	§ 702
Sec. 10(b)	§ 703
Sec. 10(c)	§ 704
Sec. 10(d)	§ 705
Sec. 10(e)	§ 706(1), (2)
Sec. 11 (1st sentence)	§ 3105
Sec. 11 (2d sentence)	§ 7521
Sec. 11 (3d sentence)	§ 5372
Sec. 11 (4th sentence)	§ 3344
Sec. 11 (5th sentence)	§ 1305

APPENDIX II

THE FEDERAL ALPHABET SOUP: A GUIDE TO COMMON ABBREVIATIONS AND ACRONYMS

A common source of confusion is the tendency of courts, commentators and administrators themselves to refer to agencies by their initials. This Appendix provides a translation of some of these acronyms into their English equivalents. General information about the functions and organization of each federal agency can be found in the current edition of the Government Manual.

ACUS	Administrative Conference of the United States
AEC	Atomic Energy Commission (superseded; functions now divided between NRC and Department of Energy)
CAB	Civil Aeronautics Board (some functions terminated, others transferred to DOT)
CBO	Congressional Budget Office
CFTC	Commodity Futures Trading Commission
CIA	Central Intelligence Agency
CPSC	Consumer Product Safety Commission

CSC	Civil Service Commission (superseded; functions transferred to OPM, MSPB)
DOD	Department of Defense
DOE	Department of Education or Department of Energy
DOJ	Department of Justice
DOT	Department of Transportation
DVA	Department of Veterans' Affairs (formerly VA)
EEOC	Equal Employment Opportunity Commission
EPA	Environmental Protection Agency
FAA	Federal Aviation Administration
FBI	Federal Bureau of Investigation
FCC	Federal Communications Commission
FDA	Food and Drug Administration
FDIC	Federal Deposit Insurance Corporation
FERC	Federal Energy Regulatory Commission (formerly FPC)
FMB	Federal Maritime Board
FPC	Federal Power Commission (superseded by FERC)
FRB	Federal Reserve Board
FTC	Federal Trade Commission
FSLIC	Federal Savings and Loan Insurance Corporation (terminated; functions transferred to FDIC)
FHLBB	Federal Home Loan Bank Board (superseded by OTS)

GAO	General Accounting Office
HEW	Department of Health, Education, and Welfare (superseded; functions divided between HHS and Department of Education)
HHS	Department of Health and Human Services (formerly HEW)
HUD	Department of Housing and Urban Development
ICC	Interstate Commerce Commission
INS	Immigration and Naturalization Service
IRS	Internal Revenue Service
MSHA	Mine Safety and Health Administration
MSHRC	Mine Safety and Health Review Commission
MSPB	Merit Systems Protection Board (formerly part of CSC)
NHTSA	National Highway Traffic Safety Administration
NIRA	National Industrial Recovery Administration (terminated)
NLRB	National Labor Relations Board
NMB	National Mediation Board
NRC	Nuclear Regulatory Commission
NSC	National Security Council
OCC	Office of Comptroller of Currency
OIRA	Office of Information and Regulatory Affairs (part of OMB)
OMB	Office of Management and Budget

OPA	Office of Price Administration (terminated after World War II)
OPM	Office of Personnel Management (formerly part of CSC)
OSHA	Occupational Safety and Health Administration
OSHRC	Occupational Safety and Health Review Commission
OTA	Office of Technology Assessment
OTS	Office of Thrift Supervision
SEC	Securities Exchange Commission
SSA	Social Security Administration
TVA	Tennessee Valley Authority
USDA	Department of Agriculture
VA	Veterans' Administration (superseded by DVA)

*

INDEX

References are to Pages

†